Egoism

The First Two Volumes, 1890-1892

With additional materials.

Edited with an Introduction by

Kevin I. Slaughter

Stand Alone

Thank you to Trevor Blake for his feedback and assistance.

Special thanks to the Labadie Collection, part of the University of Michigan Library (Special Collections Library).

Egoism: The First Two Volumes, 1890-1892 constitutes *Stand Alone* SA1023, published in April, 2017.

ISBN: 978-1-943687-07-7

Published by the Union of Egoists
with assistance from Underworld Amusements.

For more information on Egoism:

www.UnionOfEgoists.com

The First American Egoist Journal

Georgia and Henry P. Replogle and James L. Walker Spread the Good News About Selfishness

Even in the rebel country, only a small number of Americans have taken the notion of the "rugged individualist" to both heart and head. Though an occasional nod will be made to an Emerson or Thoreau as being "quintessentially American," the majority of citizens cling to conformity and tradition for their own sake, and a religious framework that sprouted from the middle-east.

A pocket of America was ready for an articulation of "rugged individualism" into a worldview. The greatest articulations of that was from German philosopher Johan Capsar Schmitt, more commonly known as Max Stirner. His 1844 book *Der Einzige und sein Eigentum*,[1] is considered to be a sort of bible of Egoism, a philosophy of putting the self in the central concern, rather than gods, other man, "mankind" in the absract, or some other notion referred to by Stirner-influenced writers as "spooks."

Though relatively unknown compared to other flag-bearers of individualism like Friedrich Nietzsche, Robert Ingersoll, Ayn Rand and others, the impact of his book has had a critical place of influence on many writers and artists whose work would go on to make a great impact in Europe and America.

Stirner's great work, while having no direct connection to Anarchism, was explicitly championed early on by that milieu. First, in Germany by John Henry Mackay, who saved Stirner from the dustbins, to writers and radicals in Russia, France, Spain and England. Here in America, Egoism's champions were Georgia and Henry P. Replogle, and British born James L. Walker.

Georgia and Henry P. Replogle[2] were anarchists, free love advocates, and publishers. I have endeavored, here, to provide a short sketch of their movements and work. One thing about the Replogle's that is clear: there isn't much information available about them. I am confident that whatever is not relayed here is hidden away in the archives of Universities and Libraries and attics, waiting for funding, fervor and technology to collide and allow their names to be queried among the debris of time. What little modern research I have found has mostly been conveyed by Wendy McElroy and James J. Martin. I myself will be doing that as well, but am able to add a small amount of detail of my own discovery and to bring it together in one place for the only known biographical sketch of the couple.

Sometime before March 1881, Georgia and Henry moved to the experimental town of Liberal, Missouri. As the name would imply, it was founded in 1880 as an "atheist utopia," by George Walser, an anti-religionist, agnostic lawyer.

Henry was "well satisfied with his new abode," according to his now once removed hometown newspaper, the *Hagerstown Exponent* (Indiana). It says he had taken up work as a "section hand on the rail." It was on the front page of that issue that a letter from him was published, giving an accounting of his time there.[3] Three months later, in June, the *Exponent* reported Henry "met with an accident while running a hand-car." It states:

> His coat was caught on the handle while it was revolving and he was jerked around several times and severely bruised up. He is now engaged at work in the Liberal printing office.

For reasons not stated by the *Hagerstown Exponent's* June 17th, 1885 issue, the two "returned (to Indiana) and will remain for the summer."

The *Valley Falls New Era* (Valley Falls, Kansas) reports on March 25th , 1886, that "Henry Replogle and wife, of New Kiowa, have arrived and

1 First translated as *The Ego and His Own*, but a more literal interpretation would be *The Unique and Its Property*.

2 Of the dates of birth and death for the couple, only the date of death for Georgia is known: October 22nd, 1904.

3 The letter reprinted here in the front matter.

are now engaged in the *Lucifer* office." *Lucifer the Lightbearer*[1] was the individualist anarchist, "free love" and women's rights journal published by Moses Harman and others, and the first issue of *Egoism* coincides with one of Harman's many imprisonments under the Comstock Act.

It is unclear if, or for how long, they stayed in Kansas before returning to Liberal, why it says the were from "New Kiowa,"[2] or the reasons why they made any of these moves at all.

Once back in Liberal, the two began to publish a journal titled *Equity*,[3] and managed to cause a stir in a town ostensibly made exclusively for "liberals." *Equity's* prospectus read:

> "...emancipation from sex, wage, monopolistic and custom slavery, and state superstition."

The founding of Liberal was an international story, and a town of heretics and apostates was too great a temptation for Christians not to launch a missionary crusade against. They were so resolved to save the souls of liberal that eventually they established an entirely new town next to it when they failed an attempt to buy up the town properties.[4] The *Kansas City Star* reported that Walser actually posted guards at the Liberal train station to let Christians know they were not welcome in town.

One crusader, who made a name for himself as a dogged fundamentalist evangelizer Clark Braden, wrote a rather gossipy pamphlet about the town in 1886 titled: *A Dream and Its Fulfillment, an Expose of the Late Infidel Would-Be Paradise, Liberal, Barton County, Missouri.*

Without question, Braden was himself a divisive figure, drawn to the divisive town run by the divisive atheist like a moth to flame. George E. Macdonald, editor of the journal *The Truth Seeker*, gave its own clearly biased description of this meddling crusader in his book *Fifty Years of Freethough*:

> This man Braden, whose argument consisted in an attack on the good name of Freethinkers, usually did not return to serve the same Christian community twice. The religious people who employed Braden had a custom of meeting afterwards to pass resolutions repudiating him as too rank to be borne with. He professed to be a Campbellite, or "Disciple," and when the churches of that denomination could be worked no longer, he went to the Methodists.

So when an enemy writes of his foe, especially such a flamboyant one on a mission from their god as Braden was, I have to take what they write with skepticism. That said, his history of Liberal does discuss the Replogles, and even makes mention that a woman named Mollie Replogle, identified as Henry's sister, lived in the town with them. The tone of gossip parlayed by Braden is typified in the following passage:

> Mollie Replogle, one of the leading young females in Liberal, admitted to the *Globe-Democrat* reporter that she used to swear habitually, that her young female associates did, but said she had quit.

He does cite Replogle and his wife as being editors of the town paper named *Liberal*, but then goes into minute detail about who was supposedly co-habitating with whom and how they turned the depot into a whore house or type of love hotel.

According to Wendy McElroy, "the tiny sheet[5] was too brave. A mob forced the Replogles to leave town."[6] Many sources state unequivically that Georgia and Henry were run out of Liberal for their "free love" views.[7]

Complicating things was the fact that a second schism had emerged:

> During this year (1886) the difficulty of maintaining freedom of opinion in a small community became apparent in the experience which the town of Liberal, Missouri, was going through. The father of the town, G.H. Walser, had been converted to Spiritualism by a tricky "medi-

1 *Lucifer the Lightbearer* was published from 1883 to 1907 when the title was changed to *American Journal of Eugenics*.

2 The town changed to just "Kiowa" in 1887, and notably was where teetotaler Carrie Nation vandalized her first saloon in 1900.

3 *Equity* was published between 1886 and 1887.

4 *The Sikeston Herald* (Missouri), of December 1, 1938 reported: "In an effort to throw off the yoke of Walser, the Christians purchased an eighty-acre tract of land adjoining the town, called the place Pedro and moved their houses and places of business out of Liberal."

5 Referring here to *Equity*.

6 From *The Debates of Liberty: An Overview of Individualist Anarchism, 1881-1908* by Wendy McElroy (Lexington Books, 2003)

7 An article about their expulsion, written by Benjamin Tucker from his journal *Liberty*, is included in the frontmatter

> um" named Bouton,[1] and had displaced Henry Replogle, a Materialist, as editor of his paper, The Liberal. Mr. Replogle began to print a paper of his own called *Equity*, devoted to the principles of libertarianism. Mr. Walser objected to *Equity*, first, because he did not think the town needed two papers; second, because Equity was labor reform, while he was a capitalist.

The above, reported in Macdonald's *Fifty Years of Freethought*, certainly gives a compelling alternative or parralel hypothesis to the ejection of the Replogles. That he claims "a mob attacked Replogle's house, heaving rocks, firing guns, and sticking a dagger in his front door," certainly gives weight to the split.[2]

The *Chicago Tribune* of September 15th, 1887 notes the "resuscitation" of the journal *Alarm* by anarchist Dyer D. Lum, "the Chicago Red". The page two article mentions Georgia, "formerly of the Kansas[3] *Equity*," to be among the contributors. *Alarm* was indeed revived, and ran for two years. Listed among the contributers is George Schumm,[4] along with Joseph A. Labadie and others familiar to the individualist anarchism milieu. It is unclear what Georgia contributed.[5]

The couple moved to the Oakland, California area and founded a new journal titled *Egoism*.[6] The "1890" section of Macdonald's *Fifty Years...* conveys an interesting note on the transition:

> Henry Replogle shared our printing-office at 838 Howard Street and there resumed the publication of his paper called *Equity*, which was suspended when he left Liberal, Mo.

The "our" being Freethought Publishing Company, established in San Francisco to support the existing journal *Freethought*.

He also makes passing note that Replogle was printing *Egoism* on their "half-medium Universal," a specific type of printing press.

A few holes of history were filled in the "Prefatory Note" to the single volume edition of James L. Walker's *The Philosophy of Egoism*:

> The first chapters of this booklet appeared serially in *Egoism*, a little magazine published by Georgia and Henry Replogle, at Oakland, Calif., from 1890 to 1898. It was the intention to run the whole series in the magazine, then publish them in book form; but pressure upon the author's time interrupted his writing, and finally *Egoism* suspended publication before the articles were completed. Later, time was found to write the concluding chapters, and the Replogles put the whole in type and had matrices made from which to cast the plates, in 1900. But overtaken by adversity and sickness, the matter so lingered that in 1904, when the author, James L. Walker, died, the work had proceeded no further.
>
> A few months after Mr. Walker's death, Katharine Walker, his wife, desiring to have this magnificent monument to her adored husband's memory completed without further delay, undertook the task herself by providing the necessary money, leaving the details of the work to the care of the Replogles. However, the continued illness and final death of Georgia Replogle, and the prostrate condition of Henry Replogle which followed, further delayed the work to this date.
>
> It was one of the ambitions of the Replogles' lives to bring this booklet to the Progressive World with their own hands; especially was this true of Georgia, who, although lying on the bed from which she never arose, yielded with the greatest reluctance to publication of the inital edition by anyone else. In this connection, Mrs. Walker earnestly, but vainly, begged to furnish the means, and keep her own participation in the matter entirely private. But however kindly meant, this was not just the desired touch; hoping against conditions of palpable despair, Georgia Replogle still hoped in some undefined way to recover her health, and earn by her own hands credit for bringing before the world the first print of this Masterpiece of the Master Philosophy.
>
> The plates of this work are the property of

1 Liberal founder Walser not only became a fervent advocate of spiritualism, but eventually converted to Christianity, and writing a book titled *The Life and Teachings of Jesus*.

2 A great deal of reference material and research on Liberal, MO can be found on the website "Evermore": http://evermore.imagedjinn.com

3 I speculate this geographic misattribution comes from conflating Liberal, Missouri with Liberal, Kansas.

4 George Schumm was a friend of Benjamin R. Tucker, contributed to *Liberty* and assisted Steven T. Byington in translating *The Ego and His Own*.

5 Albert R. Parsons 1887 book *Anarchism: Its Philosophy and Scientific Basis as Defined by Some of its Apostles* has an advertisement for the journal *Alarm* that lists Georgia as being from California.

6 Though the journal had a new name, they retained the use of "Equity" for their publishing company.

the survivor of this now broken pair of veteran Radicals, and future possible editions will be entirely under his control, as was originally intended of all editions by both of them. So since the fondest hope has been denied by fate, the nearest approximation is maintained by kindlier human effort, in the spirit of Georgia Replogle's most loved passage from the *Rubaiyat of Omar Khayyam of Naishapur*:

> Ah Love! could you and I with him conspire
> To grasp this sorry Scheme of Things entire,
> Would not we shatter it to bits—and then
> Re-mould it nearer to the Heart's Desire!

The only other source for information during this time period is in your hands, scattered through the two dozen issues reproduced. In various notes and news items, the life and activities of the Replogles are somewhat illuminated.

Over the years Henry seemed to be willing and able to do various jobs of manual labor. In his 1881 letter to his hometown newspaper it noted working for a railroad laying tracks. Years later, in a footnote to his biographical sketch of James L. Walker, he details:

> This one has been written between rounds of oiling and inspection, while on duty in the engine-room of a steam plant, and without access to any data save those supplied by memory, possibly badly blurred by psychical prostration. The whole was then corrected to approximately the present shape by the kindly aid of some friends.

But Macdonald's *Fifty Years...* gives us a peek into a time when Henry wasn't engaged in such a rugged vocation:

> Henry had as his companion a sweet and lovely woman named Georgia. As she was the faster compositor[1] of the two, and hence had the greater earning capacity, she held a frame on an Oakland daily and he did the housework. Not being married, they were so absorbed in each other that when Georgia died, Henry nearly lost his reason through grief.

It is noted, in the *Oakland Tribune* (Oakland, California) of September 3rd, 1900, that a Georgia Replogle was an "Associate Member" of the Oakland Typographical Union, No. 36. Besides her work with the various journals and newspapers, there is no evidence of any other work.

The 1918 letter from Henry that is transcribed here is the latest known date for him to have been alive. In it, written well after Georgia's death, he details his struggle with blindness and his advocacy of "Maternalism" and "Excarnateism." As to what the latter even means, I have no idea, and a cursory search only confused the matter more.

This unprecedented collection of the first two volumes of *Egoism* brings lost information to light for scholars of American philosophy, the history of journalism and radical movements, and exponents of philosophical egoism. The Replogle's deserve recognition for their important role in introducing philosophical egoism to America and the English reading world.

This will be published on the first anniversary of the launch of UnionOfEgoists.com, a website I am editor-in-chief of. Union of Egoists is an essential resource for further study on philosophical egoism.

Furthermore, in 2012 I published a collection titled *A Bible Not Borrowed from the Neighbors.: Essays and Aphorisms on Egoism*. In contains James L. Walker's *The Philosophy of Egoism* and Henry Replogle's biographical sketch of Mr. Walker.

—Kevin I. Slaughter
Balto., MD, March, 2017

1 A compositor was a typesetter for a printer. Her job would be to build a page by placing letters and glyphs one at a time, line by line, into a frame.

"Letter from Missouri"

Letter from the March 30th, 1881 issue of Hagerstown Indiana Exponent *Journal.*

Editor *Exponent*:

As friends and others who are readers of the *Exponent* may wish to know what kind of a place Liberal is, I take this as a means to informa all. Liberal is located on a branch of the K., C., F., S. & G. Railroad, in Barton county; is surrounded by a beautiful prairie country, well adapted to the production of every kind of grain, and is also an excellent place for fruit growing. There is plenty of coal, which is being shipped away every day. Our town, though only six months old, contains about 150 inhabitants, two general stores, a drug store, a harness shop, an agricultural store, two hotels, a printing office, lumber yard, blacksmith shop, depot, telegraph office, etc. We expect to lay out a park and complete it, to have a place for amusement and recreation; we also expect, in a few years, to build a college, for the purpose of teaching the arts and sciences without sectarianism or creed. As our society is composed of the most intelligent Liberals, or Free-Thinkers, of the several States, we have neither church nor saloon, nor do we expect to tolerate them, but will substitute for the one a lecture hall, and for the other a public reading room, in which will be kept our public library, which has already attained a considerable size.

We have no revelation but that of science, no creed but that of liberty, no religion but of humanity and brotherly love. We wish to live for the happiness of this world only. We think more of the realities of to-day than the fancies of the barbaric ages. We are sure that no Bible or book is infallible but the book of nature, and that the author of the universe is the author of no other, and only by the light of science can we read it. If we have not that light, we wait until we can acquire it, rather than guess at it, and teach the guess work as infallible. We encourage progress in its every direction for the purpose of promoting happiness in this life, leaving the unknown future to take care of itself, as we did before the present existence. Wishing reason and common sense to be the test by which all things be tried, I remain, respectfully,

—H.P. Replogle

Liberal, Mo., March 21 (1881)

MONUMENT —AND— TOMB STONES. HATHAWAY & SON, HAGERSTOWN, - - INDIANA

FINEST ITALIAN MARBLE

HAGERSTOWN EXPONENT.

VOLUME 5. HAGERSTOWN, INDIANA, WEDNESDAY, MARCH 30, 1881. NO. 43.

INDIANA HOUSE.

Fifth Street, between Race and Elm CINCINNATI, O. OPEN DAY AND NIGHT.

LIVERY AND FEED STABLE, —at the— Old Stand of Baldridge & Mathews Hagerstown, Ind. Good Rigs at Low Rates.

BEYOND A DOUBT

You can save Time and Money by buying your Clothing and Gents' Furnishings at the

'WHEN' Clothing Store,

OWEN, PIXLEY & CO.,

Hittle Block, Richmond.

LINEN COLLARS, 12½ Cents.

Chromo Tobacco!

Miscellaneous.

THE INJURED HUSBAND.

Victims of the Infernal Scheme.

The Last of His Race.

Letter from Missouri.

Facsimile of first page of the issue of the newspaper that this letter apppears in.

Independent Slate-Writing Under Skeptic Conditions

Article by Henry Replogle from the April 30th 1885 issue of the Liberal.

We have been a few times invited to attend seances by our Spiritualistic friends, and have always reported them as we saw them, which was not always the most favorable to the purported phenomena. But we were true to ourselves by stating the facts as they appeared to us. Now that we have witnessed something that is more favorable to our friends' position, we are in honor, bound to acknowledge it, and again give the facts as we saw them, however much our senses may have deceived us. The accompanying circumstances are as follows:

A. Weems and his wife, Mrs. Lora Rosecrans Weems, our materialistic friends and neighbors who had been investigating the so-called phenomena of spiritualism at circles among the confirmed Spiritualists of our town, and had failed to find anything satisfactory, were visiting Dr. Bouton and wife of this place one evening, and they proposed in a jest that they try sitting at the table and see what the result would be. As they say, with no hope of any manifestation, Mrs. Weems and Dr. Bouton sat by a small stand or table, when in a few minutes the table began to tip and act as they are said to do at seances. After this our friends John G. Mayer and his wife, both confirmed Materialists, were invited to take part in the investigation of the phenomena, and after sitting regularly once a week for a few months, by means of a system of spelling by calling over the alphabet till the table tipped, when the letter was reached that the purported spirit desired to use in spelling out the sentence, several intellible [sic], and some strange communications were spelled out, and finally that the spirits would write on a slate if Dr. Bouton would hold it under the table. A slate was cleaned and examined to the satisfaction of those present, and held by one corner under the table by the Dr. The company watched him till the rapping announced that the writing was done, when the slate was laid on top of the table. On it were found the two words "That's all." So skeptical were they that each accused the other of writing it to have some fun in having the other believe it to be genuine; but good faith was restored and it was decided to try again another evening. So these skeptics met at the residence of Dr. Bouton on Saturday evening, and through the usual tapping learned that if they would put the slate in a closet or clothes press that was in the room, that the spirit of Mr. Mayer's father would write on it.

Mr. Mayer says up to this time he was as skeptical as ever, though he had asked for and received some marks upon the slate that he held under the table himself. He now cleaned his slate thoroughly making sure that no writing or marks were on it and put a bit of pencil on it, and the Dr. placed it on a shelf in the closet and closed the door, came away and sat down while the company sang. In a short time rapping was heard on the door and Dr. opened it and handed Mayer the slate, on which were the words: "My Dear Son I am not dead I Still live John G Mayer." Mayer declares this was written in a hand exactly like his father's. This was the test that completely upset his Materialism, as he and his father had agreed that whoever died first would make known to the other the fact of a future life if there was any, and it was possible to communicate. After this, under similar conditions, Mrs. Booth received the following: "Dear sister your hard days will soon end and you will hear good news. Lizzie Gearhart." Mr. Branson, the following: "Dear Father, I am often with you. Francis." This is a condensed history of the phenomena produced by this circle as gathered from them. We have lived by them and known them for several years and never had any reason to doubt their honesty or truthfulness. All this in our Materialistic associates and friends, aroused our curiosity to see for ourselves, and upon invitation went with a number of others to a seance at Dr. Bouton's residence, and the following is what we saw to the best of senses under what seem to us to be very fair conditions.

Arriving at the seance, we found Dr. Bouton, Mrs. Weems, Mr. and Mrs. Mayer seated around a small table which was answering questions by tipping and would tip until the legs on one side would be one foot from the floor. To touch it produced a very peculiar sensation when it was thus controlled. After a few minutes it was learned through this medium that a purported spirit friend of Dr. G. Thompson was present and would write on a slate if placed in the closet mentioned. As I was the hard-head of the occasion I took a lamp and examined the closet to my satisfaction, after which Dr. Thompson having his own slate handed it to us, when we cleaned it thoroughly, placed a small piece of pencil on it no larger than a wheat grain, and handed it to Dr. Bouton, who took it by the corner, holding it up to full view of the company and slowly placed it on the shelf in the closet, closed the door, and locked it, sat down beside the closet, placing one hand against it, while the rest sang a few minutes, when a faint tapping was heard from the closet.

All now ceased singing, and the Dr. arose, slowly opened the closet, and in full view of all took the slate by the corner from the shelf where it could be seen by us all, carried it to the table, and to our unutterable surprise there was in a full, bold hand three lines of writing as follows: "My son, I am glad to be able to say anything to you. Develop your wife, she will make a good medium. J. Thompson." It was tried again with other slates, but with no success. We were invited to attend another seance on Saturday evening, and wishing to satisfy ourselves better in regard to the closet, we went there and examined it as thoroughly as could be without taking it to pieces.

On Saturday evening we again went at the usual hour and found present, besides the four sitters, G. H. Walser, Mrs. Walser, and S. C. Thayer. It was but the work of a few minutes to get the table in full operation, from which it was learned that the spirit of Mary Rosecrans, sister-in-law of Mrs. Weems, was there and would write on a slate of placed in the closet. Mr. Walser being the "hardhead" on this occasion, as we had been at the previous seance, examined the closet to his satisfaction, and washed and dried the slate thoroughly. After he had satisfied himself that there was no writing on the slate, he carried it to Dr. Bouton, who, with one hand behind him, took it by the corner in the other and placed it on the shelf with Mr. Walser by his side in full light of the lamp, watching him closely. He then closed the door, fastened it, sat down in front of the closet with his back to it and his hands in front of him, while the others sang a few minutes, when rapping was heard on the door. The Dr. then arose and opened the door, and with Mr. Walser by his side took the slate from the shelf and handed it to Mr. Walser who brought it to the table and found to his unspeakable astonishment writing which read as follows, "Lora, I tried to show myself to you the other evening in my room, but it seems that you did not see me. I will try again soon. Mag."

After this the sitters arranged themselves at the table and soon found that a purported spirit friend of Mrs. Walser was there and would write. Mrs. Walser had brought her own slate and Mr. Walser washed this and dried it thoroughly. He then placed a small piece of pencil on it and carried it to the Dr. as before and saw it safely on the shelf. The Dr. then closed the door and seated himself as before. After singing ten or fifteen minutes old and familiar songs, and still no raps, it was concluded there was no writing or that we had failed to hear the rapping. So the Dr. said, "If you have written, please rap on the door," when three low but distinct, measured raps came; just while all were breathlessly listening. The door was then opened as before, and the slate carried by Mr. Walser to the table, and to the astonishment of all, contained the following: "Friend Walser. I am glad to have the opportunity to say to you that there is truth in spirit phenomena and a continued life. DMBennet," with the D. M. and B run together and the peculiar, crippled n's that characterize his signature. The signature was as perfect a facsimile of his signature whereever we have seen it, as could be on a slate. After interested inspection and commenting, and some more tipping of the table, the hour having come to adjourn all went to their homes. This is what we saw and as we saw it. Now it remains for some one to find out what we did not see; that is how the writing got on the slates, if no one present did it, and if they did do it, how they deceived our senses so completely that all failed to see the trick if such it was."[1]

---

1 Article as reprinted in the pamhlet *Two Years Among the Spirits in the Godless Town of Liberal: The Experience of the Famous Medium, Dr. J. B. Bouton, Liberal, Mo.* by Dr. J. B. Bouton (W.S.Allison, Liberal, Mo., 1888)

Fighting for Free Speech in Liberal

Article from the July 17th, 1886 issue of Benjamin Tuckers' Liberty *Journal.*

Equity is the name of a new fortnightly journal published in that misnamed town, Liberal, Missouri, by Henry P. and Georgia Replogle. It is a tiny sheet, but a brave one. Announcing its object as "emancipation from sex, wages, monopolistic, and custom slavery, and State superstition," its tone thus far seems pretty genuinely Anarchistic. One thing appears certain, —that it is waging a courageous battle for free speech in one of the most despotic and authoritarian communities in America. G. H. Walser, the founder of the town of Liberal, is evidently as thorough-going a tyrant as can be found anywhere. Beginning, as Owen proposes to begin at Sinaloa, by forbidding his fellow townsmen to establish churches or saloons, he has now reached the point where he is ready to supervise their morals in other respects. The name of the town has naturally attracted from time to time many really liberal people, most of whom have speedily gone away again. But there have always been enough of them on hand to constitute a thorn in the side of the tyrant Walser. The thorn just now seems to be Replogles. It appears that they and a few of their friends are out-and-out free lovers, and are damaging the reputation of Liberal for purity by advocating their doctrine in "Equity." Tyrant Walser thinks this will never do. So, with the aid of his hall devoted to "Universal Mental Liberty" and his paper also misnamed the "Liberal," he has begun a campaign to drive out the offenders. His first step was to import still another misnomer, a "freethought lecturer," whose other name is C. W. Stewart. The auxiliary delivered a lecture on morality at Liberal, which Walser reported as follows in the *Liberal*:

> The speaker handled that social evil called free love without gloves. He divested the hydra monster of its gaudy vestment, ripped open its rotten carcass, and exposed its foul hideousness in all its forms to public gaze that it might be seen as it really was.
>
> This lecture seemed to be called on the account of the frequent attempts of would-be reformers to subordinate the people of Liberal to polyandry (illegible), lust and debauchery, all under the sweet-scented name of free love.
>
> After the lecture was over, those of the audience who endorsed the sentiments uttered by Mr. Stewart were requested to rise to their feet. At once the vast audience with but few exceptions rose. The reverse side was then put, and those not agreeing with the sentiments of the speaker were a scene which was heartrending indeed. A brazen young man, whose aged mother was in the audience, and who has bright, pure, and intelligent sisters, who would naturally expect a brother's protection and a brother's defence of their honor, arose and placed himself among those whose lustful gratification was held paramount to the purity of mother, sister, wife or daughter. A shriek was wrung from that old mother's heart which evinced a sense of pain a thousand times worse than would be the fact should death strike the liveliest flower from the family. The scene was so painful that tears flowed from the strongest eyes in sympathy for the poor mother, with a corresponding feeling of disgust for the brazen wretch who stood unmoved, as dead to shame, before his mother's sinking, bleeding, broken heart.

This pathetic picture has another side. The following plain statement of facts taken from "Equity" forms a striking contrast to those mock heroics.

"On Sunday evening, June 27, C. W. Stewart gave a lecture in the Opera House of this place on sexual morality, in which he found occasion to recommend shot gun and boot logic for those who should attempt to teach his family other than that he had been preaching. G. H. Walser then arose, and, endorsing all of Stewart's mobocratic speech, added that this objectionable element referred to by Stewart should be led to the outskirts of the town and invited to leave, and other expressions in the same strain. He then called a rising vote of the assembly endorsing Stewart's speech. The most of the people arose. He then called for those who did not endorse it. Four only arose, — Owram, Thayer, Youmans, and myself, objecting each of us to some of his expressions. Numbers cried out against any of the four being heard, but finally all were. Walser ordered me to "shut up" repeatedly, though he was not chairman.

On Tuesday morning, about two a.m., as a result of Walser's violence-inciting speeches, a mob came to my door and demanded to see Mr. Youmans. When he asked what was wanted, they demanded an explanation of his conduct at the hall on Sunday evening. On being adversely answered, these midnight executors of Walser, Stewart & Co. gave Mr. Youmans twenty-four hours to leave, stoned the house, fired several shot into it, and left a long dirk at the gate of the yard.

These are the agents and agencies for spreading freethought and 'Universal Mental Liberty,' the motto inscribed on the hall. I would prefer that Walser, Stewart, & Co., lead their own reformatory schemes at midnight themselves."

Tyrant Walser, who fathered this outbreak of mob law, is violently opposed to Anarchy under the pretense that it means mob law in place of 'law and order.' He has not yet to learn that the difference between Archy and Anarchy is not entirely included in the distinction between mob and police. Mobs are often intensely Archistic, while the police of a voluntary association might be purely Anarchistic. The vital difference is to be looked for in the purposes for which either uses its strength. If the purpose is invasion, the force is Archistic; if the purpose is protection and defence, the force is Anarchistic. Walser and his mob are unquestionably invaders and Archists of a very offensive type.

I was considering the advisability of prodding my old friend, Jay Chaapel, who has lately been editing the "Liberal" for Walser, for aiding and abetting his master in such outrageous conduct; but I am relieved by the arrival of a later number of the paper, in which Mr. Chaapel severs his connection with it. Knowing his past record, I could not believe that he would stultify himself by allowing himself to be used for such purposes. I hope the Reploglеs will keep up their gallant fight, and that real Liberals and Anarchists will support them in it by subscribing for "Equity," which costs but fifty cents a year.

It is also to be noted that "Lucifer" is threatened with prosecution in consequence of its use of plain language in discussing sexual questions. There are evidently clearer instances of the denial of free speech than anything that has happened at Chicago, but I fail to hear a lisp about them from any of the men who are so excited because I am not as frantic as themselves concerning the fate of the men on trial in that city. In denouncing the ravings of the authorities and the press over the throwing of the bomb, I recently had occasion to say: "One would think that the throwing of this bomb was the first act of violence ever committed under the sun." It now seems appropriate to remark that there are some people who imagine that there are no offenders against free speech outside of the Chicago police force.

—Benjamin R. Tucker

Georgia Replogle

Memorial article from the Vol. 14, No 24, December 1904 issue of the journal Liberty.

It was on a day in this golden October, just past, that word came to me from Denver: "Georgia died this morning, at 4. End comparatively painless." Dated October 22. And my thoughts were carried back a year (just a year and two days) to another golden October day, when I first met Georgia Replogle. I had corresponded with this woman, off and on, for twenty years or so, and thought well of her indeed, but still I was not prepared for her as she really was. I found her on a bed of suffering, biting her lips with pain, emaciated and marked by an incurable disease. Nevertheless, what was left of her mode an impression on me not exceeded in vividness by any personality in the west.

I will not say she was beautiful, as men count beauty; for I really am not a critic of approved judgment on those matters. I find that men rave over women indifferent to me, and those I think beautiful they pass by. Therefore, I will only say that I found Georgia Replogle beautiful, not in flesh probably, but with that inner beauty which irradiates and shines through the physical as if it were a transparency.

I have seldom met a woman who seemed to me more disembodied, a creature more of flame and air. I had always known that she had an intellect like a man's, keen, logical, reason-controlled, as expressive in words as in her clear, graceful, firm, and uniform handwriting, but, and perhaps because of this, I was not prepared to find her no thoroughly and essentially womanly, intuitively sensitive, sympathetic, and refined. I had known her no long as brave and strong, enthused of nature and the wild, that I had never conceived of her as one who could be concerned, like any other daughter of Eve, with all little feminine touches of taste and adornment.

On October 22, the very day on which she was to die a year later, I visited her again, and, stricken as she was, she insisted on going with me to see various friends in Denver. And all that golden afternoon, as we went here and there in the balmy atmosphere, through the streets of the beautiful city, my constant thought was: "If she is like this now, what must she have been before!" Perfectly ladylike, even according to the most exacting conventional standards, there was still about her every gesture and motion an untamed, wild grace, remindful of the leopard, were it not so kind; of the antelope, were it not so brave. This proud courage and grace seemed the very expression of her personality. One felt she could dare anything, do anything, except lie or lessen herself. Yet equally insistent was the impression of her exquisite refinement, and of the instinctive, pathetic shrinking of her youthful, life-loving nerves from her awful and impending fate. I seemed ever to read in her eyes the dumb appeal of a stricken thing.

We visited Mrs. U. E. Hollister, who, her husband like myself being an enthusiast in Indian art, set before our envious eyes great store of Navajo blankets—precious "bayetas," old-time "squaw dresses," sacred symbols in native yarns and dyes and modern dreams in Germantown yarns. Then to a pleasant chat with Herrick at "Herrick's Bookstore." Then to sup at the home of Comrades John Sphis and Charles Greenhalgh, where Sphis, with honest pride, showed us his marvelous products in woodworking. Then home, in the trolley car, and a long evening of never-to-be-forgotten talk.

The Replogles lived in the skirts of Denver, but western cities are not often like our eastern ones, with a rotten edge of misery, and Denver seems to melt gently into the prairies round about, and the next morning, when we strolled out to my car, the weed-grown lot we crossed was like a country field, and in the western horizon were the snow-capped, azure-mantled peaks of the Rockies.

It was like a day of golden dreams, new-coined from the mints of Paradise, and how pathetically the heart rebelled to think that the stately, sensitive woman at my side, pacing with the long, free step, was as surely under sentence of death as if she were some doe of those mountains smitten with a poisoned barb.

And as I looked back from the car she was sitting, cloaked and sad, on the warm bank, courage on her face and shadowed pain in her eyes, waving me the farewell which was clearly in her thought forever.

—J. William Lloyd.
November 3, 1904

Liberty

NOT THE DAUGHTER BUT THE MOTHER OF ORDER — PROUDHON

Vol. XIV. No. 24. NEW YORK, N. Y., DECEMBER, 1904. Whole No. 386.

"For always in thine eyes, O Liberty!
Shines that high light whereby the world is saved;
And though thou slay us, we will trust in thee."
John Hay.

On Picket Duty.

The pope was dreadfully disturbed by the audacity of the freethinkers in holding their international convention across the street from him. Poor Joe! He imagines that all Rome still belongs to the vatican.

And so it seems that we have *lèse-majesté* even in this country. The report comes from Pomona, California, that a Canadian boy, who has been attending school there, refused, the other morning, to salute the American flag, when it was raised on the school building, and was expelled, the board of education subsequently approving the expulsion. The authorities consider it fortunate that he escaped lynching. Patriotism must be at flood on the Pacific coast.

Most of the readers of Liberty will remember Tak Kak as a contributor to these pages during a great many years of the existence of the paper, and many of them will regret to learn of his death, which occurred recently. His was a peculiarly clear and logical mind, and his articles on Egoism, to the philosophy of which he devoted a great deal of thought and attention, were cogently reasoned and exceptionally readable. He was a thinker of rare qualities, and much that he has written is worthy of being printed in a permanent form.

In October, says a newspaper report, "two hundred men at Bird Springs, Lincoln county, Nevada, notified the county clerk that they did not wish to cast their ballots at the coming election. They say that they are too busy, and desire that the precinct lately created in that district be discontinued." This is the most promising information that was published during the campaign. When the polling booths are deserted, the knell of plutocracy will be sounded.

boards) do not insist upon an educational qualification. In the second place, even if Tillman can read, he need have no qualms of conscience about reading that little injunction, since the alleged author of it, if certain extensively-credited reports be true, did not hesitate to violate that as well as other sections of the decalogue.

In the October number of the "Review of Reviews" Victor Yarros has an interesting article on "This Year's Strikes and the Industrial Situation." His summing up is as follows: "The industrial developments of the last few months have resulted in a distinct improvement. The period of active contention and strife is closed, the falling market and the number of unsuccessful strikes having doubtless hastened the change. At no time, however, did the labor movement bristle with more questions of moment and interest than now. This side of the subject requires separate treatment." This last statement is very true; but the chances are that Dr. Albert Shaw will not permit Mr. Yarros to treat it in the "Review of Reviews" as the latter gentleman *can* treat it.

One of the most amusing features of the recent campaign was the performance of a certain republican enthusiast of New York. He wrote a red-hot campaign pamphlet containing a lot of flamboyant charges against the democratic candidate for president, the chief purport of which was that the latter had favored the large gambling interests in the State. After the *brochure* was all printed and ready for distribution, the author found that there was a slight error in his statement. It was discovered that the republicans were responsible for the delinquencies charged against the democratic candidate. This was decided to be a sufficiently important mistake to render the document of doubtful value to the author's sponsors, so the

ment of criminals who can be proved to be at the mercy of their passions. He also urged that the State dispose of the incurably insane by putting them to an easy death. He advocated that the State prevent marriages of undesirable persons. Some of these propositions doubtless go beyond those of Dr. Chapple, and they did not fail to arouse the opposition of many other delegates to the meeting. The objections were mostly sentimental, but the discussion goes to show that, in this country as well as at its antipode, there is a tendency toward a more rational consideration of the problem involved.

In the "Truth Seeker" Mr. Steven T. Byington has recently been calling upon freethinkers to show that the children of irreligious parentage amount to anything—or some such proposition. His success has so far been rather indifferent, which, seeing that Mr. Byington takes the negative, is for him rather a matter for self-gratulation. Charles Darwin and Clarence Darrow, with a few other and lesser lights, are about the only famous men who can be pointed to as having had parents of the same ilk; while the rest of us, both famous and infamous, cannot plead heredity. A great many columns of the "Truth Seeker's" space has been devoted to this fruitless discussion without the gist of the matter having been reached. The fact is that most of us—in fact, all of us, except possibly a few theosophists—have had no choice in the matter of parentage. If we had had, the chances are that we should have chosen others than the politicians, preachers, and horse thieves who are responsible for the existence of some of us. Seriously, the whole question hinges on the matter of opportunity. When it is considered that the proportion of *rationally* irreligious parents to those of the opposite class is about as one to one hundred thousand, it will be seen that the chances for the great men to be the offspring of the former are very slim

Facsimile of first page of the issue of Liberty *that this article apppears in.*

From Georgia Replogle to "Dear Comrade"

An 1898 letter on The Eagle and The Serpent, *moving publishing to Denver.*

Facsimile of Georgia's letter to unknown recipient.

Dear Comrade:

Your $10 order rec'd. We will send the $6 on to the Eagle Pub. Co. with directions to have 10 copies of Eagle & Serpent sent to your address for one year, and a request that they send you 100 of the leaflets you desire. We are grateful for our share of the order and will apply it to the publishing fund as soon as we can renew publication, which time we shall make as short as possible. Allthough never asking for aid in publishing, we thoroughly appreciate it when it comes. <u>Egoism</u> will not come as far East as you place. Denver is the place where it expects next to launch. We have not yet rec'd The Eagle & Serpent. He expected to be out by the 15th inst, but it will be sometime coming.

George Replogle for Egoism

From Henry Replogle to Sarah C. Holmes

A 1918 letter about dealing with blindness, dream inventions, Maternalism, Excarnateism, etc.

Box 273 Arvada, Colo. June 15, 1918.
Sarah C. Holmes

Faithful Friend:

Your letter at hand. It was a total surprise, and as complete a gratification. I had been thinking about you lately, and wondering how your sight difficulty had terminated, and am glad to learn that you still retain some vision. I can think of no one that I would have blind, much less a good friend. I have heard from but few of the old Guard: Mr. Tucker and Henry Bool in Europe, and Henry Kuehn, C. V. Sprading, and C. L. Swartz of Los Angeles. The advertisement that appeared in the Truth Seeker, was placed without my knowledge, and I had it discontinued as soon as I heard of it. It was placed by a friend who had been many years a reader of our paper. We wanted to aid me by selling the Walker book, and while he asked my permission to insert the advertisement, he did not wait till he heard from me. I deeply regretted such as appeal. I do not own the edition, and while I am glad to have it distributed, its sale would not be of much financial aid to me. We raised the already high price, to get more commission for me. So I will send you two, hoping you can sell one, and get yours nearer the right price.

This town is practically a suburb, of Denver. I happened to be located there when I went blind, and it is necessary for me to remain here until lately. Now there is a possibility of a pension law for the destitute adult blind, and I will need to remain in the county to qualify, as the provision will, require two years residence in the county.

I will have been blind three years this November, and had my final eye removed last November. The first was taken a year and a half before. I suffered a great deal with each before giving them up. When they were about to drive me mad with pain I had to let them go.

The horror and despair of the first realization of my situation broke down an already weak digestion, and my strength has never been near normal since. However, some of this is due to lack of proper exercise, owing to the difficulty of moving about freely. While it is not reasonable to hope for much that is worth the while, I have not entirely given up to simply await the end. Meanwhile the State teacher for the adult blind has taught me to knit hammocks from seine twine, and I have made half a dozen or more. But the material is cotton product, and the war has made that so high that there is no pay for the work when the material is paid for. Besides, there is no demand now for that kind of goods. I have also learned the alphabet of New York Point, from the same teacher, and picked out the lessons of some twenty pages of the First Read er, but, like you, find it very nerve-racking. I also have a slate with which to write it, and can do that more readily than I can read it when it is written. I need it in writing, so that I can read and correct it before copying for others to read. So I shall try my best to master it. There is an opportunities school in Denver at which provision is made for the blind to learn typewriting free, and I shall try to take advantage of that when I get to Denver permanently once more. Having the realization of the torture to the adult blind of learning the Points system, I have been thinking of a typewriter for them that would raise plain capital letters on suitable paper which anybody could read, blind or seeing, This would put them in communication with all, whether they knew y blind systems or not. Such a machine would not be difficult to make, though it would need to be stronger in its parts than the ordinary typewriter, so that it could indent the letters into matrices. I have a writing board which we evolved, that anyone can learn to write on in a few minutes, and have some idea what they are doing, if attention is given to landmarks as the work proceeds. I had one of the instruments of torture with which the blind are provided, and after much heartrending effort, threw it aside and clamped a breadtoaster over the tablet and wrote between the wires, from which the one I am using was finally worked out. This one is a crude pattern of the finished idea, but it answers the purpose, and was the best that could be done with the means available to work with. It is an ordinary writing-board with a snap-clamp at the top end to hold the sheet. Then there is a frame with stiff wires across it where the lines are to be. The frame is then hinged onto the edge of the board in such a way that it has freedom to move from bottom end toward top end of the board, and has a spring set against it which normally holds it in its upper, or highest position. Then I write along the wire, following the wire and pencil-point with the first finger of the left hand, to space the letters and parts of letters, as well as the words against it with the pencil. The longer upward strokes are freely made up toward the above wire and the downward ones by pressing, the frame down against the spring, which instantly throws it to its upper or normal position, when the pressure is released. At the end of the wire above the one I am writing along I have a little ways in a tin marker hooked which projects down over the wire that I am writing along, and warns me that the end of the line is near. Then at the end of each wire there is a crease cut in the board into which I press a finger nail through the paper which indicates that that space is not yet written on and also whether I am on the first or on the second side, of the sheet, as if on the first side, there will be creases only in one edge of the paper, while if on the second side, they will be on both turn one upper corner in onto the written side, and this shows me which is the upper end, as well as the first side when putting it on the filing hooks. One could cut notches in the upper edge of the page to mark its number so that it could be determined if they fumbled in handling, if one would take the trouble to do it. And if entirely alone it might be well worth while. I have worked out the idea for several minor inventions, the best of which were suggested in dreams running from a washing machine to a steam turbine. The latter has long and tedious history connected with it running back perhaps five years or more during which I was an operating steam engineer by occupation when I worked still, and in a dream an engineer friend who was a Theosophist, and who had died, told me of a proposed engine, that he had seen it, and that it would work. Then I saw a chart and some changing diagrams, but never understood them fully until lately. There were then several other dreams along on the subject through the years, and lately some more, so that finally the whole and some thought-spoken suggestions have projected a combination so feasible-appearing that I am quite astonished as well as gratified at its effectiveness and simplicity. It should deliver twice the power from the same pressure that any engine does that I know of now, if it will do what I believe it will, and I can find a philanthropist to furnish the means to test and patent it in all the countries, I will devote it to propaganda for a federal pension for the destitute blind in each country. I would contract to release the patent in each as soon as such a law was in effective operation. This might interest the manufacturers to effort enough to secure the law in their respective countries for their personal benefit. In spite of the considerable run of super-normal suggestion, I almost failed to get this engine idea, and could not have come in a thousand miles if unaided by them in their various phases. I beat out half a dozen types of turbine, but all failed to embody the central idea over which I have battered since about 1886. As each one had failed to embody all the suggestions given, I was urged on, till I understood the idea on my own account, and finally, when they were all embodied, there was no more urge, and it seems perfect.

This pragmatic realization in mechanical projection, has caused me to give heed to some sociological suggestion which has gradually accumulated in championing the principle of Maternalism, the principle whose function it is to succor and protect the weak wherever found, and which has its reward in the pleasure of consciousness of relief accomplished. It cannot well violate liberty, and is operative for such success when liberty is not because of prejudice, and where it is not because of limitation. Liberty, computative is the final word for equity by force of compulsion, but there its scope ends. It can eradicate all artificial monopolies, but does not touch native favor in the individual. Maternalism can and will, for it is one of its peculiar attractions. The nature-neglected are weak, blamelessly weak, and equitably subjects of succor. To minister to this is the central function of Maternalism. A person may have even a monopoly-sized capacity to shiver(?), but not the manual or possibly mental capacity to cover it without any choice of his own, nature having failed in this obvious equity. Now it is little difference to the victim, whether ho suffers from an artificial, or from a natural equity, so long as he suffers. Therefore... even if liberty be in force, Maternalism must be his final salvation for equity. But if it actually relieves him, it will do so by covering the equity shortages of both artificial and natural delinquencies, and therefore necessary in the presence of liberty, is doubly so in the absence. Certainly its task must be the greater in the absence of liberty, but being prejudice free: it can also have resources that could be tapped by no other operating, be the best working expedient adoptable by libertarians, whether their ideal is ever realized or not. Suffering must be relieved while it is maintaining, if it is ever to be relieved end to do this the practicable means of that moment must be employed, and I believe it is more creditable for the discerning minority to help furnish quorum for such means, to get them into immediate action, than to wait even a definite tune here for their own terms while the relentless fangs tear ruthlessly away, to say nothing of an indefinite time which may be generations away. Just as the idealists are fighting or backing this war, although it is conducted by fraternalistic methods, and in the end must at last result in a doubtful ideal democracy in such plutocratic influence, if not even domination. But it must be done now, and must be done in such a way as the forces in hand will do it, or we will have a condition infinitely worse than even a rampant plutocracy, So I would labor to relieve what may be relieved now by such means as can be operated with the available forces at hand, never forgetting for a mo - (ment?) the ideal, and to bring as much conformity. to it as possible under the circumstances.

I do not specifically remember the quotation from Whitman, but I appreciate its spirit. However, I know of no avenue now that would welcome my message, should I speak as I take it Whitman means. Most Materialists are disposed to present a not overheated shoulder, on account of my acceptance of Excarnateism, and, I cannot blame them, since without my experience in matter of both their attitude and with the subject itself, I would feel the same way about it in another person. And the Spiritualists, while I have not mixed any with them in the dozen years that I have realized the central tenet of their philosophy, I am certain they would have little more use for my interpretation, as it does not assure all there is much that would be bliss to the manually weary and task-haunted... there is perhaps a decillion times a decillion years of periodical mental and emotional hardships of experience that will prove this life to have been realized every variation of every mortal's experience, and that of every native excarnate, both human and animal as well as that of every atom of which the universe is composed. Then we will be fitted to do the work and fill the purpose for which we were designed and built. We are said to be shiplets launched into concreted (?) area to gather experience from that environment to graft upon the myriads of thin-space creatures who could not, owing to their constitution, reach here, and finally are to return to the of individual faculties which launched us with our lading, and with it organize them into a great individual, which their environment had not permitted otherwise than through. this process. This is not all of the Geography of our department, so much of it only as covers such constitution as we combine; for there are still other faculties that we do, not possess which know that which we do not, just as we know what clams and oysters do not. Now all this would make even a Spiritualist tired, and is only a small part of the tea-picnic feature of their Christian heaven dream. For a year or two after initiation, I, like they, dealt with the next or mortal excarnates and their lore, and was content to remain there, but the faculty drifted on, and encountered sentients purporting to have dwelt on other planets, and still onto the native excarrates, or those who claimed to never have lived on any planet and on and on through all the years too long and tedious to describe in less than a volume, but with this disappeared the function of direct communication with the planet-born ones, and has not returned. But enough of this almost endless theme.

I agree with you concerning "stunting" by the blind. I know some who do most marvelous things, and do them every day, but everybody can no more do them than everybody can be any other marvelous character. The that I know of have been blind for years and devoted themselves to training, or were blind from childhood, and have grown their intuitive faculties into it. Some is actual mind reading, admitted by one that I lately heard of. The high-school girl variety of marvelmonger scoops in at a guess some feat that has cost months of heartbreaking effort to acquire, and conclude that the blind do so much that it is hardly a considerable misfortune to become blind, and act upon the conclusion ever after. I have said high-school girl marvelmonger, I meant the adult male who is like the highschool girl who find little, employing to prove it most endless expedients. I can make a complete hammock in a week to ten days, and at a glance much wonder is expressed, but the only wonder of those who watch me do it, is that I do not go stark mad. In spite of all precautions that I have provided against doing so on this board, every little while I fail to move down my marker correctly, owing either to absorption in my theme or difficulty in getting the marker off the wire on account of faulty construction, and thus. I write twice on the same line. Only the suffering of long repetition can line this measurably, and so it all is with my "stunting."

I would be glad to hear of the Schumms, W.C. Walker, J? Wm. Walker, George Macdonald and Grace, or any of the idealists.

Sincerely, Henry Replogle.

Copy.

Box 273 Arvada, Colo. June I5, I9I8.

Sarah C. Holmes

Faithful Friend:

Your letter at hand. It was a total surprise, and as complete a gratification. I had been thinking about you lately, and wondering how your sight difficulty had terminated, and am glad to learn that you still retain some vision. I can think of no one that I would have blind, much less a good friend. I have heard from but few of the old Guard: Mr. Tucker and Henry Bool in Europe, and Henry Kuehn, C. V. Sprading, and C. L. Swartz of Los Angeles. The advertisement that appeared in the Truth Seeker, was placed without my knowledge, and I had it discontinued as soon as I heard of it. It was placed by a friend who had been many years a reader of our paper. He wanted to aid me by selling the Walker book, and while he asked my permission to insert the advertisement, he did not wait till he heard from me. I deeply regretted such an appeal. I do not own the edition, and while I am glad to have it distributed, its sale would not be of much financial aid to me. He raised the already high price, to get more commission for me. So I will send you two, hoping you can sell one, and [illegible] nearer the right price.

Facsimile of first page of the letter transcribed on preceeding pages.

Egoism

Egoism

Vol. 1.—No. 1. SAN FRANCISCO, CAL., MAY, 1890. Price, Five Cents.

Pointers.

Duty is, and ever has been, the cross of human spontaneity.

Enlightenment makes selfishness useful, and this usefulness popular.

Men and women not having learned those things which others know, naturally think they know all that is known; and therefore persist in the inconsistencies which this knowledge would remove.

If men applaud your self-sacrifice, it is because that sacrifice benefits them, and so little is their interest in you that they will not give you even the kicking you desire when you realize your stupidity.

Improve every opportunity for pleasure. Even though that pleasure consists of the least pain, it is a bargain compared with anything worse, which is the only thing that could be except something better.

"The Reasons Why," on seventh page, by Victor Yarros, reprinted from "Liberty," is his contribution to this paper on that subject. It was placed so far back because of the lateness of advice regarding its printing. We gladly avail ourselves of its clear-cut and condensed exposition of Egoism.

Surprises continue not to cease! Here comes the Denver "Individualist,"—our first X— under the new management, a plumb-liner and an Egoist. It now has the clear ring, and challenges Egoism's deepest appreciation. To support it, will reflect great credit on the radicals of the country.

"Fair Play," of April 26th, in its hearty announcement of Egoism's coming, reaches the conclusion that its publishers could not produce the *ring* it discovered without outside help. If "Fair Play's" editors have detected any real ring in our announcement of the new paper it refers to, the facts are against their conclusion, for the announcement was written by its publishers.

"The Hour and the Need," on the third page, is the first of a series of articles which will appear in this paper from that able writer, Victor Yarros. Those who read attentively his exposure of authoritarian schemes of reform, will acquire that which will be of great service to them in the coming contest between the primitive impulse of authoritarianism and the evolved expediency of freedom.

We have been exceedingly fortunate in being favored with the promise of a series of articles on the central idea of this journal, the first of which appears on the fourth page, "The Egoistic Philosophy," by Tak Kak. All who wish to become acquainted with this universally misunderstood and all-important thought, will in this series get it from undoubtedly the ablest exponent of the subject on this continent, if not as able as any one who has ever written on it.

"The Economics of Anarchy; a Study of the Industrial Type," is Dyer D. Lum's latest work. This is a very valuable addition to industrial literature, being a complete and concise statement of the economics of Anarchy. Mr. Lum's attractive style of writing makes clear even the most abstruse subjects. It will greatly aid the progress of economic thought for this book to have a wide circulation, as it will help to overcome the prejudices against the treatment of economics from an anarchistic standpoint, and be of benefit to those who are studying in that line of thought. We will give it further notice in our next number, as it reached us late for this one. The pamphlet contains 59 pages, and considering the thought-matter is cheap at 25 cents. It can be obtained from Dyer D. Lum, 196 Washington street, Chicago, Ill.

The "Rag Picker of Paris," by Felix Pyat, translated from the French by Benjamin R. Tucker, will be concluded in the next number of "Liberty" (Boston). This novel is the most complete portrayal of human nature in every condition of life, that has been contributed to radical literature. Every line, every pause, has a fullness, a significance of thought, or a volcano of emotion seldom found anywhere singly, and not combined in the style of any other writer. It is probably the most vivid picture of the misery of poverty, the extravagance of wealth, the sympathy and forbearance of the poor and despised, the cruelty and aggressiveness of the aristocratic and respectable, the heartless greed of the middle class, the hollowness of charity, the cunning and hypocrisy of the priesthood, the corruption of constituted authority, the crushing power of privilege, and finally of the redeeming beauty of the idea of equality and liberty, that has ever been produced. If it is published in book form, as it should and probably will be, every radical can find great gratification in circulating it.

In its notice of "Monogamic Sex Relations," "Fair Play" claims that, while complex love relations are ably advocated by Ego, and monogamy earnestly defended by Marie Louise, the discussion is untimely and a misdirection of energy, because we cannot love in anyway without the consent of the State or Mother Grundy. Since monogamy is enforced by the State and Mother Grundy, and Ego, in giving the best of reasons why it should not exist at all, produces the strongest arguments against its being enforced by anything, it is difficult to see where the misdirection of energy comes in. Those who have extra good bargains in marriage can probably wait with more complacency while this generation fights to its grave for the overthrow of tyranny and invasive customs without misdirecting its energy in showing the evils of some of them, than can those who must choose between the ordinary monogamic tomb and no sex association at all. But Egoism inclines to encourage this side-show for the purpose of augmenting that from which "Fair Play" in its "cool" calculation thinks it would detract, while the latter circulates the "Law of Population," in face of the fact that this same invasive law which this generation must overthrow, does not permit the means of regulating the number of children.

The "Beacon," published at San Diego until its suspension a few months ago, is revived in this city, at 319 Fifth street, and will be published weekly at $1 per year. It will endeavor to weed out the superstition of government, and oppose majority rule, or rule of any kind, with such vehemence that if necessary it would insist on either using a majority of physical force to suppress it, or upon the expediency of being slain in a contest with a majority of such force. That the "Beacon" takes this position, Egoism is very sorry; not that it believes there is the least danger of bloodshed, but because the thought has a tendency to prevent that part of the community which constitutes its intellectual backbone, from investigating and becoming imbued with the principles of Anarchism, as must be before it can supplant political direction. Aside from the sentiment of being brave there could be no expediency in a physical contest; for when there is a majority it can successfully hold its rights by force of that circumstance, and until then a contest would be sheer madness on the part of the minority, and then, it would not be needed. Not only all this, but also the hatreds, prejudices, and peril of living among men whose bodies have been subdued, but minds not convinced, and on the ruins of whose power must be another authoritarian institution to hold them down. Egoism is not satisfied with a physical subjection, it must have its man safe by the full conviction of his self-interest. The editor of the "Beacon" is a sympathetic and warm-hearted man, who is impelled to take such an attitude only through his sympathy for the sufferings of victims of the privilege which they sanction through the superstition of "duty," loyalty, and ideas of fixed institutions. The impulse of all is to hurry when a principle is perceived, but haste is often most successfully made by deliberation.

EGOISM

Issued Monthly at Fifty Cents a Year

—BY—

EQUITY PUBLISHING COMPANY,

Post Office Box 1678, San Francisco, California.

The Name and Purpose of Egoism.

The word Egoism was chosen for the name of this paper because it expresses the conscious state of man as we find him and as he probably will always be found; because it is the last analysis of conscious action and all conduct comes from it and is accounted for by it. It thus furnishes the key to all human motives, and what comes from their normal exercise. Its philosophy so posits the mind that it is unawed by the fixed idea of any institution, belief, or custom. It holds nothing too sacred to be measured by its utility in attaining happiness, and to be dropped without regret, when found wanting. It acts on the impulse that if existence is not for man it is nothing to him; and that it may the more fully realize this ideal it no more allows itself to be deprived of the advantage of resignation to the inevitable, than of the self-hood whose calm scrutiny dispels the delusions of unanalytic conception. It seeks pleasure for man, and admits without offering an apology therefor, that it, the Ego, is the man. It adapts means to ends with all the advantage experience affords, but keeps an eye on the end while manipulating the means.

Egoism's purpose is the improvement of social existence from the standpoint of intelligent self-interest. To gain recognition of the fact, and popularize the idea, that self-pleasure can be the only motive of any act; that any attempt to ignore it must as necessarily be disastrous as an attempt to ignore any other part of the order of nature. Thus developing a principle for a basis of action, about which there can be no misunderstanding, and which will place every person squarely on the merit of his or her probable interests, divested of the opportunity to deceive through pretension, as under the dominance of altruistic ideas.

It finds that the delusion Altruism arises from taking the visible results of the giver's sympathy as an idex to the motive of the act, while its invisible, but real cause is a subjective one, an attempt to escape the mental torture caused oy a battle between the desire for placidity and the knowledge of the present suffering of others, stung by the memory of one's own past suffering.

It holds that, while wholly disinterested acts cannot be *intentionally* performed, they are continually being *un*intentionally so performed through the altruistic error of the duty of "duty"; resulting alike in the systematic robbery of its duped supporters and that of the more intelligent minority upon which it is forced. This "duty" fetich is the magical instrument of exploitation in every department of human association, from the general one of the religious and political delusion to the special one of lovers. It enables the manipulating cunning of the crafty to take advantage of the universal self-gratifying instinct by deceiving it with spiritual *credit* for "duty," in exchange for the material comforts and luxuries of life.

It will maintain that what is generally recognized as morality is nothing other than the expediency evolved from conflicting interests under competition. That it is a policy which, through the hereditary influence of ancestral experience, confirmed by personal experience, is found to pay better than any other known policy.

The belief that it is something other than a policy—a fixed and eternal obligation, outside of and superior to man, and may not be changed as utility indicates, makes it a superstition, in absurdity and effect like any other superstition. It causes its adherents to crystallize the forms of expediency for one period into positive regulations for another in which they have no utility, but become tyrannical laws and customs, in the name of which persecution is justified, as in the fanaticism of any fixed idea.

Egoism seeks to impress the fact that there are only selfs enough in the world to go once around among its inhabitants, and that attempting to shift any part of the responsibility of one's happiness upon another, can gain nothing per head in service. On the other hand, there is sure to be a great loss in efficiency, as one person cannot know, and is less likely to care, what another needs or wants to make him most happy. It, therefore, insists that each assume the responsibility of his or her own happiness, and thus all be secured against the exaction of "duty" and the uncertainty of dependence upon another. This does not deprive any of the opportunity for mutual exchange, and secures all against that which is not voluntary; thus leaving no excuse for invasion either by direct obtrusion or obligation.

From this basic principle it will defend the individual against every phase of invasion, whether it be the exactions of authority-protected privilege or the decrees of superstition-influenced custom. It will defend every act of uninvading self-pleasure and mutual exchange, from the products of industry between continents to the magnetism of the nerves between individuals. This is almost the opposite of existing conditions. The legal interference of political authority with free contract between individuals is a rule rather than an exception. Nothing is so private—so much one's own, that legal authority cannot assume the regulation and disposal thereof.

In industrial exchange its most disastrous prohibition is that of the making and use of free money, which would at one stroke abolish interest, and make it possible to capitalize all the unconsumed products of labor. Its next interference is its privileged paper titles in land, preventing the reasonable and just one of occupancy and use, that should prevail. Then follow its custom-house tribute and its patent privilege.

Quite as important, and more directly painful, is its tyrannical meddling and barbarous decrees in social affairs. There is its political disfranchisement of woman; its interference with the relations of the sexes; its property in wives; its mercenary alimony and breach-of-promise plundering; its heartless disposal of the children of divorced persons; its brutal policy of revenge, instead of restitution, in criminal offenses, and finally, its supreme power to violate the citizen, and its total irresponsibility for anything it does. It needs only to be understood to be boycotted to speedy death. To help get it so understood, and succeeded by protection in open market, for person and property, is part of the purpose of this journal.

The Hour and the Need.

Is progress a myth?

Is liberty a failure?

Is individuality hostile to equality and social order?

Is Egoism a vice and an infirmity?

These are questions which the people of this country have to consider and answer in these times that "try men's souls." Their civilization is threatened with destruction, their freedom with invasion, and to avert ruin prompt and intelligent action is necessary.

This country began its independent existence with reasoned adherence to the principle of individual liberty—the principle that the government which interferes least is best, that liberty is the mother of order, and that enlightened self-interest, refined and intelligent Egoism is the basis of true harmony and general happiness.

We are now asked to repudiate these principles, cast them aside as worthless, and—revive the blind worship of authority. The coming slavery casts its shadow before it, and we find our horizon obscured by "Nationalism" and "Christian Socialism," alias military despotism and the inquisition. We are brutally told that the majority has the right and the might to control the life of the individual citizen, and that the latter's labor and earnings should belong to the former. In the name of long exploded superstitions, detected shams, and exposed frauds, a system is being forced upon us which in point of absurdity eclipses the invention of the most ignorant tyrannical mind. "The will of God," the guidance of the "power behind evolution," the "demand of the social organism," the "interests of morality and religion,"—these and other phrases of equal value, are constantly on the lips of the new crusaders, who promise to cure society by annihilating the individual.

Of course these apostles of darkness and dull uniformity are not at all formidable: they vanish before the light of reason and thought as all other ghosts do before the light of day. But certain serious evils in society, certain diseases and maladjustments, the nature as well as the cause of which the masses of the people do not comprehend, but from which they suffer intensely, prepare these masses to lend an attentive ear to all quacks and humbugs who claim to have a cheap and sure remedy for the ills. And as the blind generally prefer to be led by the blind, as the ignorant are always predisposed to become the victims of the cunning (though, in a higher sense, ignorant) adventurers, there is danger that the partisans of majority-despotism will gather around them an army of miserable and discontented elements powerful enough to make successful war upon freedom and the results of progress.

But what, then should be done to check the advance of the coming slavery; to protect the liberties we enjoy and foster the progressive tendencies and aspirations of the healthiest portion of the people? It is necessary to disprove the assertions and affirmations of the authoritarians, and to show that our principal social evils are the product, not of individualism and personal liberty, but of denials of liberty, of violations of the principle of individualism. It is necessary to point out how the evils may be eradicated by a further extension of liberty, and that they can be eradicated *only* by a further extension of liberty. We must show that the struggle for existence is fierce and intense not because men are Egoistic, but because certain social institutions, traditions, and arrangements perpetuate inequalities and injustice. In a word, we must show that all the material, intellectual, and moral wealth and beauty which we possess are the direct results of liberty, while all the misery and poverty, in the lower as well as higher sense, that oppress us and darken our lives are the direct results of the lack of certain liberties.

Can we do all this? Are our contentions well-founded? We certainly think so; such is our conviction. We have carefully analyzed the nature of the disease; we have examined the proposals of our opponents; and we have come to the conclusion that liberty alone can solve our industrial, political, and social problems.

We hope to attract the attention and enlist the sympathy of critical readers, and we invite them to follow our arguments. VICTOR YARROS.

Business Announcement.

EGOISM will not be published oftener than once a month at the publishers' expense. If, however, it should retrograde so much as to become popular, and gather a large enough list of subscribers it will be proportionally enlarged in size and more frequently issued. Preparations for this are not among the publishers' plans at present. They will do what they can to defeat such an arrangement by making the paper approach as nearly as possible their ideal of advanced thought, which is not always popular.

Do not subscribe for it, unless you feel that you would rather read it a year than have the fifty cents required to pay for it. You are under no obligations to it. It assumes only its share of the world's "cause," and hopes for nothing, if not mutual advantage in exchanging its matter for your money.

MOSES HARMAN'S first trial is over, and he is convicted. It was found that E. C. Walker and George Harman were in no way responsible for the publication of the indicted articles, and they are free, which is as it should be. Through a web of unfortunate circumstances and some mismanagement, there was no defense of the liberty of the press made at the trial; and all the money contributed for that purpose is lost, so far as making an intelligent plea before the court for freedom in publishing is concerned. This is another object lesson in representation, and shows how well it pays to entrust any part of our work to others, even though they be partners and principals in it. A motion for a new trial was to be argued, from which nothing has been heard at this writing. Unless something comes of this, Mr. Harman, an old man and a cripple, will have to undergo the hardships and brutal treatment of a felon, with few chances to survive it all. Should he live through it he will be met at the prison door by the "protection" of the citizen's life and property and have it all to repeat. Yet he has neither injured nor attempted to injure any person living or dead. Thus the authority beast murders thousands, while its supporters writhe and worship at its feet.

The Egoistic Philosophy.

I.

We seek understanding of facts for guidance in action, for avoidance of mistake and suffering, and even for resignation to the inevitable. This statement may cover the chief aims of mankind in intellectual discussion, ignoring now that which is merely a scholastic exercise. I am not in favor of argument in the style of the debating school, merely to sharpen the wits. Sincerity is too precious to be tarnished by a practice which easily generates an evil habit, and there are, at least as yet, too many occasions in real life on which every person who loves to tell the truth and expose falsehood must consider time and circumstance lest he impale himself upon implacable prejudices. Consequently if duplicity have its uses there need be no fear that it will not be cultivated without concerted efforts thereto among those who are seeking intellectual light.

I have placed resignation last, though it may be first in importance for some individuals. I take it that the life forces are strong enough in most of my readers to exude in promptings to action which shall move things, in the liberal sympathy which would communicate to others any discoverable means to reach conditions of greater harmony.

Is it not a fact that there is a considerable amount of well wishing and at the same time an intricate series of reciprocal injuries practiced by mankind, such as is not discoverable in any other species on earth? Then, we may ask, what are the causes of evils in society, can they be generalized, and what is the nature or principle of an efficient remedy? If now the words *laissez faire* occur to the reader he will easily remember that all animals except man practice according to that principle. Do we hear of fanaticism among them, of fighting within the species except in defense of their persons and property or on a matter of rivalry between the males? But what do we read in the history of mankind except woes, wars, persecutions and catastrophes beggaring description, and all related in some way to the determination of mankind to interfere with each others' actions, thoughts and feelings for the purpose of making people think better and behave better as conceived?

The theological Liberal is never tired of affirming that the greatest cruelties have been perpetrated by bigots acting sincerely for religious right as they thought they understood it; yet among the theological Liberals may be found prohibitionists and taxationists manifesting a holy horror of a man or woman who simply wants to be let alone while he or she lets others alone, and who refuses to join in any scheme of coercion. They insist that he cannot enjoy such liberty without detriment to society, and their ire rises on thinking that he is insensible to a moral principle, as they view the matter. They are bigots unknowing.

But are there such people as I have alluded to, who practice the rule *laissez faire?* Certainly there are. (These words are French and mean "Let them do," or "Let other people alone as far as you can.") Properly understood and carried out in political science, as by Proudhon, a rational system of Anarchy is evolved from the motto. Anarchy in its strict and proper philosophical sense means "no tyranny,"—the regulation of business altogether by voluntary and mutual contract.

With some readers the perception of these relations as regards religious belief and political institutions and this comparison of human intolerance with the better habit of other species, to mind their own business, will have suggested the fundamental thought to which I am coming. We are digging now for bottom facts; not trying to invent any artificial rule, but to find the wholesome reality in nature if there be any good there for us, and to find the mainspring of normal animal action at all events, leaving for after discussion if advisable whether or not any artificial substitute be possible or commendable.

Now it is not my purpose to suggest that men should pattern after any other species of animal. We find the other animals acting naturally, seeking their own good, going each his own way and letting each other alone except under certain conditions which have caused a momentary conflict of individual interests. We find human life full of artificiality, perversion, and misery, much of which can be directly traced to interference, the worst of this interference having no chance of perpetuation except through a certain belief in its social necessity, which belief arises from or is interlaced with beliefs as to details of conduct, such for example as that the propagation of the human species would not occur in good form unless officially supervised, and so forth. Drawing such comparisons the conclusion appears that man needs to become natural, not in the sense of abandoning the arts and material comforts of life, but in the treatment of individuals of the species by others and in their collective action.

I may here anticipate an objection. Someone will ask whether I pretend that Egoism means the same as *laisser faire*. To this I say no, but the prevalence of Egoism will reduce interference, even by the ignorant, to the dimensions of their more undeniable interest in others' affairs, eliminating every motive of a fanatical character. Invasive developments of Egoism, no longer re-enforced by the strength of the multitude under a spell of personal magnetism, will probably not be very hard to deal with; then for want of success such developments will be attenuated or abandoned within the species. Thus Egoism is demonstrably the seed-bed of the policy and habit of general tolerance. And if vigilance be the price of liberty, who will deny that the tendency, within Egoistic limits, to some invasion is the sure creator and sustenance of vigilance? The vaporizing, non-Egoistic philosophers would place tolerance upon a cloud-bank foundation of sentiment and attempt to recompense with fine words of praise the men who can be persuaded to forego any advantage which they might take of others. Like the preachers who picture the pleasures of sin and urge people to refrain from it, their attempts are inevitably futile.

TAK KAK.

To the non-exercise of the political prerogative is due what liberty we have, rather than to the discretion with which it is used. If the real sentiment of the majority was crystallized into legal regulation as would be consistent with majority rule, the intelligent would nave nothing worth living for.

Selfishness versus Altruism.

The supreme desire of man is happiness. This is his motive to action. It is a delusion to talk of man doing this or that because of a sense of "duty" or because "morality" demands it, or because it is a "religious obligation." No matter how fervently men may speak of duty, morality, or religion, it is safe to say that they always act with reference to their own happiness. Mankind as invariably seeks pleasure as the needle points to the pole. It is true that the inexperienced seek it often where it cannot be found, but the fact remains that the desire to lessen the ills of life and to increase its joys is the permanent effort of humanity.

This struggle to escape pain and to secure the pleasures of life is *Egoism*. "Is it not selfish?" Yes; but so are all human motives. Christianity is a system of selfishness—its spirit of Egoism is unenlightened, as it rejects reason and relies upon fear and credulity. Enlightened Egoism is man's effort to attain the highest conditions, to possess those things that will make him most happy now; the Christian is also struggling selfishly to reach the highest position (heaven) and to rejoice in the unspeakable joys, but he is willing to wait for them until he reaches the sweet by and bye. His religion is all self-seeking. The motive that incites him is just as selfish as that of his more enlightened neighbor, the Egoist. Every incentive presented to man in the gospels is selfish. The importance of the human soul (?) is magnified to such an extent that the "believer" begins to reel under the hallucination that his soul is of more importance than the whole world. (So it would too, if he had one.) The command to lay up treasures in heaven is an appeal to man's selfishness. The sermon on the mount and the incentives spread before the eyes of the disciples have always cultivated in them gross selfishness, by such assurances as this: "For great is your reward in heaven." This yearning for happiness was so strong and so natural that it has never been suppressed. It has always asserted itself; but has done so ignorantly and blindly. Religion or mystery is the cheapest form of indemnifying man for the ills he suffers. Religion is the nepenthe that has soothed his troubled heart. We see, then, that the appeals made to man in the name of religion are selfish for the simple reason that man constantly demands to be assured of personal happiness, and that religion is nothing more than a blind explanation of how he may gain it.

Egoism is selfish, but it is in the very nature of human life to live for one's highest happiness. Living for others is ideal, not real, except in so far as living for others increases our own happiness. To love your neighbor as your self is impossible, and to talk about loving your enemies is foolishness.

"Whoever would be greatest among you, let him be your servant." This is sometimes quoted as teaching Altruism, but the motive here is not an unselfish one. The desire to be "greatest among you" is selfish.

Enlightened selfishness will not lead one to be indifferent to the welfare of others. He will find a large share of his wellbeing to consist in promoting the wellbeing of others. In the possession of his individual freedom he will not need to bestow charity upon his neighbors, for they too possessed of their liberty will not need charity; hence this matter of Altruism will not be in demand. Equal opportunities will be all that one can need to put him into the highest possible conditions. Heretofore the world has been moved by sentiment. The sympathetic side of human nature has been worked upon continually. It has taken many centuries of experience to develop in man sufficient intelligence to enable him to see that it is not so important for him to love his neighbor as it is to let him alone. The advice, to "mind your own business," would, if closely observed, do more for our neighbors and ourselves than the observance of any gospel that was ever written. It is objected to liberty when thus explained that it is not liberty, but license. This is a mistake. Liberty cannot be given man, as it is his by his nature. License is liberty to act by permission. Liberty implies responsibility, while license implies the right of others to assume the responsibility of the act for which license is granted. If liberty says to one, act as you please, it also says, remember, that you act at your own cost. Enlightened selfishness, or Egoism, is the best regulator, therefore, of human conduct.

W. S. Bell.

The Fiction of Natural Rights.

The very corner-stone of Anarchistic philosophy is often supposed to be a paraphrase of Herbert Spencer's "First Principle" of equal freedom, that: "Every person has a natural right to do what he wills, provided that in the doing thereof he infringes not the equal rights of any other person." Yet there lurks in the expression a fallacy that correct thought must repudiate, or we must carry with us a diagram explaining the meaning of the words we use.

What are "*natural* rights?" In the middle ages schoolmen believed that they had solved a problem in physics by asserting that "nature abhors a vacuum"; but a very little study sufficed to convince thinkers that "the web of events" we group as "nature" neither abhors nor likes. With the growth of the conception of law as a term descriptive of mode of being rather than a fiat imposed upon events, the term "natural" has lost much of its old teleological meaning. Still it is often used in that sense and too often implies it.

Blackstone defined "the law of nature" as "the will of man's maker." Mackintosh calls it "a supreme, invariable, and uncontrollable rule of conduct to all men." Sir Henry Maine also speaks of "a determinal law of nature" for the guidance of human conduct. Kent defines it as that "which the creator has prescribed to man." F. Q. Stuart, in his "Natural Rights," says expressly: "A natural right is a privilege vouchsafed by natural law to man to exercise his faculties," and his whole work teems with expressions implying the fixity of "real law."

The correct position is, I maintain, that what we term "natural rights" are *evolved*, not conferred, and if so they are not fixed and unalterable. Nature confers no more "privilege" upon us than upon dogs to exercise our faculties or functions. In fact, to my mind, the very assumption of "natural rights" is at war with evolution. Even if we no longer personalize nature as their giver, the term still carries with it the implication of rigidity, when, in fact, not even that mythical "right reason" with which we are supposed to be endowed can prove them historically so characterized. Every man is supposed to have a "natural right" to life. Is this co-eternal with man? Did it exist, though unrecognized, among our prognathous ancestors? If the savage transcended "natural right" in disposing at will of the life of a captive, where was it inscribed? It was not incarnated in the semi-brute. If the Roman law was based upon "a type of perfect law" in nature, was the recognition of the "natural right" of a father over the lives of his family contrary to the "right reason" of the time? And to this query convictions founded upon nineteenth century deductions are not pertinent.

Is woman's "natural right" as a "person" the same in all countries under polyandry, polygamy, and monogamy? or are those relations of the sexes, so important to "wellbeing and good conduct," ignored by beneficent nature? It has been conclusively shown by sociologists that human progress (and there is no other) consists in passing from the militant *regime* toward an industrial one. Yet the time was when the *lex talionis* sanctified revenge as the highest virtue. Time was when not a human being on the face of the earth differed from Aristotle's opinion of slavery as a natural condition. Where was this "privilege vouchsafed by natural law" then inscribed? The question whether society would not have been far more conducive to happiness if such right had been recognized, is as idle as whether eyes behind our heads would not have been equally so. If the "Principle" was not discoverable then, but has been now, are we to conclude that it is the final synthesis of "right reason"? or that its Incarnation is only now visible?

Having thus shown a few of the queries which arise to puzzle one who seeks for evidence of the immutability of "natural rights," let us examine closer into the nature of "rights" themselves. The human sphere is a province conquered from nature, and hence its relations cannot be termed "natural." It would be equally as permissible to call them moral or religious, for the qualifying adjectives being given to imply the highest validity, it would be so understood by all to whom either of these words conveyed such meaning. Equally permissible, but equally indefensible in evolutionary thought when implying fixity. But do there exist any such inherent predicates of *human* nature as "rights?" The same theological bias which characterized "rights" as "natural" also regards their assertion as positive. On the contrary, every assertion of a right purely human, paradoxical as it may seem, is negative. The assertion of a "right" is but a protest against iniquitous conditions. Social evolution ever tends to the equalization of the exercise of our faculties. That is, social intercourse has slowly evolved the Ideal that peace, happiness, and security are best obtained by equal freedom to each and all; consequently, I can lay no claim in equity to a privilege, for that which all alike may enjoy ceases to be privileged. The important deduction from social evolution is that as militancy has weakened and industrialism widened its boundaries, liberty has ever tended toward such equalization. Privilege finds no sanction in equity as right, because it violates the ideal of social progress—equality of opportunities.

Therefore it is that, as social relations have become more complex and integrated, the Ideal of "a more perfect form of liberty" rises in the form of protest against what only then are discernible as socially wrong, though ostensibly as assertions, such as "rights of women," "rights of labor," "rights" of children and sailors against flogging, the right to the soil, etc. They are fierce and burning assertions just so far as they emphasize a growing protest against inequitable conditions. In this sense they are Anarchistic, inasmuch as only by the extension, in other words, the abolition of restrictions, is the wrong righted. Our specific "rights" are thus dependent upon our ability to discern wrongs, or the violation of the ever-evolving industrial ideal—equality of opportunities, and exist but as protests. Abolish vested wrongs, and there will be no vested rights, natural or otherwise. Precisely as water flows to a level when obstructions are removed, just so will social relations flow to equitable conditions when restrictions are swept away. And precisely also as liberty comes in does the assertion of "rights" go out.—Dyer D. Lum in Pittsburg Truth.

Mrs. Grundy's Kingdom.

Kings may come and kings may go, princes may die and heirs apparent be born like meaner folk, dynasties may fall, and ministries may change; but one thing goes on forever and one person is the true Immortal—the power of Mrs. Grundy never fails and Mrs. Grundy herself never dies. Twin sister to Mrs. Partington, but of a sterner type, Mrs. Grundy is the tutelary deity of opposition and negation. She is the culminating point in the conservative element and denies all good in change of any kind. The world as it was when she first took its impress, is the world as it ought always to remain; and the moral forces which moulded her were the last expression of the truth of things. To go back beyond her time and into that of her mother's, would be to lose by restriction; to go forward with her daughter's, is to lose still more by the looseness of expansion. A fossil represents the long past; corruption is the doom of the near future. That moment of experience when life was young and Plancus was consul, was the only time of perfect development. Hence, all new thoughts, all new views of human duties, all further enlargement of political bases, all change in religious sentiment by philosophic application or scientific discoveries are strictly tabooed by her as the very superfluity of naughtiness, and false from start to finish.

In the same way she taboos all new fashions in dress, household management, social arrangements. Being new, they are therefore abhorrent. When time has through familiarity effaced the impression of strangeness, and she has become tardily reconciled to the things she so fiercely denounced in their inception, she repeats the process and falls foul of the next change as she fell foul of the last. She never learns by experience; and of all the lessons of life taught by experience, to that of the necessity for change Mrs. Grundy gives least heed.

Mrs. Grundy is the impersonation of the higher morality—the impersonation and the guardian. No cat scents a mouse with more keenness of detection, no truffle-hunter unearths underground fungus with more precision, than the keenness and precision with which she finds out the hidden sin where others see only futility, or at the broadest, folly. All life is to her as it were embroidered over with secret designs whereof she knows the occult meaning; and a kind of diabolical telepathy is ever at work between young people, more especially between the sexes. Mrs. Grundy does not believe in innocence. To her mind, more nuts have maggots in the kernel than are whole and wholesome. . . . . .

She puts her crooked old fingers into every person's pie, and offers to pick in concert the bones she has no business to touch at all. She is the universal Mrs. Putter-to-rights, and no man's dog must bark out of tune with the sol-fa she has intoned. She regulates, or seeks to regulate all science, all art, all literature. She is the measure of truth, the standard of proficiency. If discoveries are made which shake old faiths in their simple integrity and give a new gloss to ancient readings, Mrs. Grundy flourishes the *san benito* of the defunct Inquisition, and only regrets that she cannot clap it on the shoulders of the heretics, with the fire and faggot to follow. She does what she can in the service of vested faiths and consecrated ignorance. . . . . . In art she will have nothing that is not nice, pretty, tame, and commonplace. She discountenances all but the merest superficiality of intention, and understands only things with the most trite and trivial meaning. The nude is, as we know, her great *bete noire*, and she cannot understand the need of students drawing the human body from nature, or the obligation laid on women painters to know something about the bones, the muscles, or the outlines of the figures they represent. . . . In the larger things of life she has been of incalculable mischief. Like the toad which squatted by the ear of Eve, she was the viewless influence that whispered Galileo's condemnation to the sacred jury appointed to try him and pronounce on his innocence or guilt, on the truth or falsehood of his theory. She burnt Giordano Bruno. The early experimental philosphers she accused of the black art, and dealings with the Devil. She hanged innocent men and women in batches as sorcerers and witches, because those who doubted were too much afraid of her to advocate openly or ridicule freely. She still seeks to discredit all modern philosophers by branding them as Infidels! And when Darwin broke loose from her school and scoured the wide plain of nature on his own account, she beat her shrill alarm and called on her faithful followers to denounce the audacious insurgent who presumed to discover a law she had not endorsed.—Eliza Lynn Linton in the February Forum.

A NEW idea will look like a mistake to the man who is wedded to the old ones.—Sturdy Oak.

The Reasons Why.

I am an Egoist.

I recognize no authority save that of my own reason.

I regulate my life and my relations with the outside world in accordance with my understanding and natural instincts.

My sole object in life is to be happy,—I seek to avoid all pain and to gratify all my normal desires.

I cannot be happy unless I feel myself perfectly safe and secure in my possessions.

I can never be safe and free from fear of disturbance or injury until those around me are able to gratify all their normal desires, and they can never be completely happy without security.

Security can be only the result of perfect justice.

Justice consists in the recognition of equality and the rendering of equity.

Justice, thus defined, necessarily involves a condition of absolute liberty within its sphere.

Therefore, justice is *the* condition of my happiness as well as the happiness of all that are like me. That is to say, justice is the law of human society.

Thus I, an Egoist, recognizing no rights and no duties, become, solely and simply through prudence and a desire for security, a lover of equity, equality, and universal liberty.

But there is no credit due me for my policy. If I were strong, shrewd, and skillful enough to defy all danger; if my happiness could be achieved without the aid, co-operation, and respect of others,—I might have chosen to be a tyrant, and might have led a pleasant life, surrounded by two-legged beasts of burden. Not being superior to all creation, I involuntarily have to draw a line at men, and make terms with them.

Having wisely decided to be a modest member of society, I have by no means irrevocably surrendered my freedom. I stay in it because, all things considered, it is best for me to submit rather than rebel, but I can, at any time, reconsider my course and, risking the consequences, make war upon society. Who can say that I am under any obligation to be just? Obligation? To whom? to what?

The individual, once having entered the social compact, finds himself in the presence and under the influences of new impulses, new aspirations, new yearnings. He is changed, transformed, revolutionized. Social life becomes a necessity to him, not as a condition, but as an element, of happiness; not as a means, but as an appreciable and weighty constituent of the desired end. He learns to know new joys and pleasures; his wants multiply; his tastes change; and he comes to feel and realize that he would never, even if he could, isolate himself from his fellow-men or try to reduce them to slavery.

This process of adaptation, or socialization, of the individual, though largely unconscious, can, nevertheless, be theoretically and objectively conceived and analyzed. In thought man can separate his Ego from the mass of humanity and discuss the wants, interests, and advantages of his person apart from it. He may not be able to effect such a separation in reality, but the illusion is so thorough that it must be discussed as if it were real.

I *imagine* I can leave society; I *think* I am free; therefore I *am* free. I feel no obligations and no duties. I act for the sake of immediate or prospective personal benefits, and obey the voice of prudence.

Am I unreliable? Quite the contrary. There would have been no confusion in our modern social relations if all men possessed these ideas, just as an isolated community of desperadoes would present an example of peaceful and harmonious relations. The whole mischief arises from the fact that so many build their castles in the air. Once plant yourself on solid ground, grasp and admit these fundamental realities, and you will logically and intelligently develop a principle of conduct which will make it possible for you to pronounce judgment on all things without tracing them back to first and bottom truths.

As Danton loved peace, but not the peace of slavery, so I love justice, but not the justice of moralism and idealism. —V. Yarros in Liberty.

The Ethics of Property in Wives.

The following appeared in the Oakland Evening Tribune of April 4th:

> District Attorney Reed has issued a warrant for the arrest of Frank Olivera on a charge of an assault with a deadly weapon committed on the person of his wife at Pleasanton. The couple have seven children, and have resided at Pleasanton for a number of years. As soon as the husband learned that a warrant was out for his arrest, he left home, and has not been seen since.
>
> A short time ago Olivera became suspicious of his wife, and in order to punish her threw her upon the floor, tied her hands, gagged her and then cruelly assaulted her in a way that cannot be fully related, with a coupling pin, inflicting painful injuries.

This was placed near the bottom of a middle column with a heading no more conspicuous than one just above it announcing the catching of an unusually large fish at Benicia; thus indicating the tenor of the public conscience on such outrages, when committed within the bonds of matrimony. If she had been the property of another man, or not legally transferred by her parents to some man, the entire population would have been frantic with indignation, and out in arms until the "fiend dangled from a tree." But she was a "suspected" woman and, while it was regarded as rather rough treatment, it was also regarded as partly deserved. The punishment was too severe, that is the complaint; but that she should be punished is not questioned; and that it was proper for her husband to administer the punishment, as the old English laws provided for. Why not? It is the intention, the ethics of ownership, that man shall dispose of his possessions at will, without condition or interference, without regard to the volition of the object possessed. Once acknowledged to belong to him, and no further attention is paid to the manner in which he disposes of it. If he owns a bushel of wheat the ethics of property permits him to retain that wheat, let the result be what it may to his fellow men. Although a man die for need of the wheat the owner is defended in his right to keep it from him, even though the wheat rot instead of being utilized for the benefit of the owner. His horses, and other beasts of burden, work when he wishes. If they are rested and in a condition to serve him, well and good, but it is not the pleasure or welfare of the animals that is considered, but the desires and happiness of the owner. In the regulation of these possessions he is made secure by the fiat of the public mind.

The ethics of property in wives is identical with that of property in any other "live stock," so far as regards the freedom of action of the wives. It is the surface idea or claim that man and wife are partners. But in a business partnership a man never thinks of "punishing" his partner if he does contrary to his wishes, but the partnership is dissolved and that ends it. But on the other hand, where the partners are man and wife, as soon as society gives him a "deed" for her, it acknowledges his right to regulate her conduct and tacitly sanctions the punishment he may see fit to give her for a violation, or suspected violation, of the duties prescribed for her by it. For instance, in the case above quoted no heed is given to the woman's wishes in the matter, or whether she desired to be "faithful" to him. And if she had not been *his* woman, *his* property, the thought of punishing her would not have occurred to him. It was the ownership idea; it was because she *belonged to him* that he dared to "punish" her.

But the pulpit will ignore it, and the press will formally regret it—anything to keep the idea of property in wives intact.

G. R.

Egographs.

"It is not wickedness that does the most harm, it is stupidity."

Egoistic is whoever and whatever acts out the self.—Tak Kak.

"There is no blasphemy against nature comparable to the oath of fidelity earnestly taken."

"It is impossible to reason about love with one who does not treat it as an hypothesis."

"What distresses me is to see that human genius has limits and that human stupidity has none."

"The need of liberty is much less keenly felt than the need of authority. Convicts choose chiefs."

"The presentiment that man feels of eternity in another world arises from his despair at not being eternal in this."

"Men are so cowardly and servile that, if their tyrants should order them to love each other, they would adore each other."

"He who complains of the ingratitude of man is an imbecile; for it was necessary to be an imbecile in order to count on their gratitude."

The great difficulty is always to open people's eyes; to touch their feelings and break their hearts is easy; the difficulty is to break their heads.—Ruskin.

The tendencies of the times favor the idea of self-government, and leave the individual, for all code, to the rewards and penalties of his own constitution, which work with more energy than we believe, whilst we depend on artificial restraints.—Emerson.

Out of all this hodge-podge I really have retained but one thing,—namely, that morality consists in doing as one likes; that to do as one likes, one must be free; and that consequently the man who is not free, being unable to do as he likes, is necessarily immoral.—Eugene Mouton.

In the rapidly gathering gloom of the nineteenth century we must see, if not totally blind, the giant and ghastly form of Privilege in shadowy outline behind the millionaire. Privilege it is that robs labor of his pittance and gives it to the fortunate pets of the State.—Fair Play.

I have unbounded faith in what is called human selfishness. I know of no other foundation to build upon. When we cease quarrelling with this indestructible instinct of self-preservation and learn to use it as one of the greatest forces of nature, it will be found to work beneficently for all mankind, and "the stone which has been rejected by the builders will become the chief corner-stone."—E. D. Linton.

All upholders of government are blinded by the curious error which is at the foundation of so much social misery,—the error, namely, which establishes one moral code for the individual and another for the institution called government. Thus government, which is supposed to be necessary to repress theft, violence, and murder, finds no other way of maintaining itself but by the committal of like acts; and the State Socialists go a step farther, and after fuming against the iniquity of rent and interest when levied by private individuals, propose as a remedy that government should undertake to levy the same.—A. Tarn.

Those who cannot believe in themselves, unless they are believed in by others, have never known what truth is. Those who have found truth, know best how little it is their work, and how small the merit which they can claim for themselves. They were blind before, and now they can see. That is all.—Max Muller.

The instant formal government is abolished, society begins to act. A general association takes place, and the common interest at once produces common security. So far is it from being true, as has been pretended, that the abolition of any formal government is the dissolution of society, it acts by a contrary impulse, and brings the latter closer together.—Thomas Paine.

In modern society competition is far from occupying the sphere of its natural action. Our laws run counter to it; and when it is asked whether the inequality of conditions is owing to the presence or the absence of competition, it is sufficient to look at the men who make the greatest figure among us, and dazzle us by the display of their scandalous wealth, in order to assure ourselves that inequality, so far as it is artificial and unjust, has for foundation, conquests, monopolies, restrictions, privileged offices, functions, and places, ministerial trafficking, public borrowing,—all things with which competition has nothing to do. —Bastiat.

The genius performs his benefits for mankind because he is obliged to and cannot do otherwise. It is an instinct organically inherent in him which he is obeying. He would suffer if he did not obey its impulse. That the average masses will benefit by it does not decide the matter for him. Men of genius must find their sole reward in the fact that thinking, acting, originating, they live out their higher qualities, and thus become conscious of their originality, to the accompaniment of powerful sensations of pleasure. There is no other satisfaction for the most sublime genius, as well as the lowest living being swimming in its nourishing fluid, than the sensation, as intensive as possible, of its own Ego.—Max Nordau.

In proportion as morality is emotional,—*i. e.*, has affinity with art—it will exhibit itself in direct sympathetic feeling and action, and not as the recognition of a rule. Love does not say, "I ought to love"; it loves. Pity does not say, "It is right to be pitiful"; it pities. Justice does not say, "I am bound to be just"; it feels justly. It is only where moral emotion is comparatively weak that the contemplation of a rule or theory mingles with its action, and in accordance with this we think experience, both in literature and life, has shown that the minds which are pre-eminently didactic, which insist on a "lesson," and despise everything that will not convey a moral, are deficient in sympathetic emotion.—George Eliot.

The progressive nature of man causes spoliation to develop resistance, which paralyzes its force, and knowledge, which unveils its impostures. But spoliation does not confess herself conquered; she only becomes more crafty, and, developing herself in the forms of government, and in a system of checks and counterpoises, she gives birth to politics, long a prolific resource. We then see her usurping the liberty of citizens the better to get hold of their wealth, and draining away their wealth to possess herself more surely of their liberty. Private activity passes into the domain of public activity. Everything is transacted through functionaries and an unintelligent and meddling bureaucracy overspreads the land. The public treasury becomes a vast reservoir into which laborers pour their savings, to be immediately distributed among policemen. Transactions are no longer regulated by free bargaining and discussion, and the mutuality of services disappears. In this state of things the true notion of property is extinguished, and every one appeals to law to give his services a fictitious value.—Bastiat.

Egoism

Vol. I.—No. 2. SAN FRANCISCO, CAL., JUNE, 1890. Price, Five Cents.

Pointers.

Don't take life too seriously. Nothing depends on you but your own happiness, and you are not even obliged to be happy.

The article "Damp, that is the Enemy," on seventh page, is reprinted for the special benefit of our Pacific coast readers, as we believe the damp air to be the worst enemy of health in this climate.

For some reason unknown to us, the second of the series of articles on "The Hour and the Need" by Victor Yarros, has not reached us. These articles are to be put in pamphlet form when concluded.

The series of articles by Tak Kak running in this paper, will be published in pamphlet form when completed. This will be an able statement of the Egoistic philosophy, and a valuable leader in its propaganda.

The stage is said to be a great educator. If this be true, judging from the intelligence of the average theater goer, the "missing link" might be discovered by closing the theaters against that class for a generation or two.

In its characterization of the O'Neill letter as "reactionary, conservative, old-fogyish, and foul with the superstition that sex is inherently unclean," "Liberty" voices the sentiments of this paper, as it does also with regard to "natural" and "unnatural" practices.

Those who delight in seeing men of acknowledged brilliancy accepting the principles of philosophic Anarchism, can find gratification in reading in "Freethought" of May 31, the editor's conclusions on money, in commenting on the Stanford scheme, and in his criticism of Thomas Curtis's position regarding the State owning children.

The trouble with Wordsworth Donisthorpe seems to be that, like thousands of others, he is looking for a kind of eternal square by which to square social existence. In recognized self-interest under free competition, he might find a kind of tape-measure by which to measure it. It is hoped that the social square will go out of market altogether.

The latest news from Mr. Harman is that he has nearly recovered from the cold caused by the State's regulation shave, and is at work in the kitchen. It seems his treatment even by the sword of the State is in marked contrast with that of the vindictive cruelness of the civilian judge, who boasted of the power that he did not fail to abuse.

By a miscalculation of a few feet, in the operating of air-brakes, an engineer on the Oakland narrow gauge local train ran his engine and one coach into an open draw, drowning thirteen persons, but unfortunately escaping with his own life. The frenzied mob wanted to hang him on the spot, but the *revenge* "wisdom" of the State would now be satisfied to comfort the dead with imprisoning him for a number of years, if it could find him.

Husbands are queer creatures; they so criminally love their wives that they often kill another man for doing the same thing. They are outdone only by wives who will kill themselves rather than have their husbands loved by other women. They are both so interested in each other's happiness that the one is perfectly willing to allow the other to be in even the company of the other sex if they can only be sure that it is not pleasant to be there, but the greater that pleasure the less will it be tolerated.

In marked contrast is the comprehensive conception of the subject, clear-cut logic, and direct application to social and industrial evils of Benj. R. Tucker's "Why I am an Anarchist," in the "Twentieth Century" of May 29th, with that of the declamatory denunciation of Most; the evasion and generalizing of Gronlund, and the vicious personalities, and sky-scraping emotionalism of Haskell, each of whom have contributed articles to the "Twentieth Century" on their respective economic and political convictions.

If the average enthusiast were to realize that he and his great grand-children will die and his ideal still not have been generally realized, his enthusiasm would cool down to the point of pay in the pleasure of breaking the monotony of routine ideas instead of being stimulated by a dream of fame and influence. His efforts being thus better timed would be more effective, and better still he himself might be impelled to take some real pleasure as the days pass, even though sitting in the warm sunshine or cool shade be the best he can command.

The advocate of "duty" believes its performance to be the most creditable act conceivable, and his performance of it, the most unselfish. Yet so selfish is he that he will not allow another to do the laudable things, but wants to find *himself* being credited for doing them. If he is so thoroughly unselfish, why not let others have all the opportunities of gaining their fellows' good will. But even this would give him public credit if known by others, and subjective credit if he alone be conscious of it. Some way self-interest and consciousness are inseparable.

The Equity Publishing Company is not an old and well-known establishment in San Francisco, and the postoffice employees are not familiar with the persons of its members, therefore mail matter addressed to the editor of Egoism, or the Egoist Publishing Company, or some other name supposed to be in some way related to Equity Publishing Company, Box 1678, San Francisco, is likely not to reach us. It will be well before sending money for subscription or books to look on the second page of the paper, near the top of the first column, where will be found the address in bold relief.

The indifference with which the masses treat reform ideas would discourage most of those interested in progress were they to thoroughly realize it, but it is really their only protection; through it the beast, ignorance, is held at bay till an idea takes root where it is possible and leads it a little further on. If the prejudice-saturated majority realized what reformers really believe and are trying to inculcate, they would make short work of everything but the most popular crazes. We must watch for the opportunity, drop the seed, and be gone if we be wise.

Love seems to be a kind of subjective torture with which men torment themselves by thinking of women and women by thinking of men; parents by thinking of their children and the children of their parents; the living by thinking of the dead. It dies in the presence of its object or tortures still, being not satisfied. Its presence is not appreciable save by its gnawing torture, other times it does not exist. It can do nothing but sacrifice its possessor or demand sacrifice from its object. It is nothing but memory's phonographic vibrating needle running over the cylinder of personal and hereditary experience. Men heard it and thought it a voice, and have worshiped it as a god, like other phantoms.

Says Hugh O. Pentecost: "A moralist cannot advocate Socialism (or Nationalism)." "Pure morality has in it no place for compromise." "A moralist must be an extremist." In which "morality" is not different from any other form of bigotry, nor the Moralist from other fanatics, and he needs the power of authoritarian Collectivism to enforce what his "pure" and uncompromising code dictates and his enthusiasm would propagate. Otherwise morality is a matter of personal opinion and all are alike Moralists, which leaves it like God, a mere word-ghost. Verily, Hugh O thou worshipest still the nothing-gods. Come let us worship not gods at all, but see the relativity of things, lest whilst we be entangled in theological cobwebs progress pass us by and leave us dangling like flies on the wall.

EGOISM

Issued Monthly at Fifty Cents a Year

—BY—

EQUITY PUBLISHING COMPANY,

Post Office Box 1678, San Francisco, California.

Religion in Reform.

The constant factors of religion—aggressive enthusiasm, blind devotion, sacrifice, and cruelty indicate that its impelling force lies in its immediate relation to that most primitive faculty of conscious life, the sense of touch and repulison, the impulse of which as evolution added complexity and strength was to absorb or destroy everything with which it came in contact. The Ego having been made conscious of its being partly by the resistance of other objects, and through this consciousness feeling nothing but that being and such resistance, would by the nature of being endeavor to be all by annihilating all opposition. The life that during the ages has been sacrificed to this blind impulse while experience has been slowly impressing its uselessness is of course incomprehensible. Its spirit has prevailed in physical or mental strife in every age including the present. It is now becoming semi-physical. Men are inclined to use moral suasion first, resorting to physical force as a last expedient in carrying points. This is not due to a growing spirit of Altruism, but to the fact that as the more useless of the weaker elements gave away and the useful and those equal in strength confronted the Ego, it learned to conserve the energy of this root impulse by directing it along the line indicated by experience as productive of the longest pleasure, through preserving the useful and making terms with the strong.

The final basis of religion is nothing other than the crude expression of the sense of being, the blind impulse to be all, from which develops the enthusiasm, blind devotion, sacrifice, and cruelty required in persuing the ideal of becoming all. These elements enter every reform and systematically crucify its adherents in each succeeding crusade. The primitive propelling force expresses itself in the fixed idea of the reform, and from the enthusiasm of proselyting comes the "call" to "duty," the sacrifice to the "cause," the aggression of which aggravates conservatism to persecution—to making martyrs. This in its turn generates sympathy among the hitherto indifferent and secures their support while it adds in all the idea of reverence to those of duty and sacrifice. It now becomes the "holy cause," and intensifies the other elements of devotion to the point of fanaticism, which makes the demand for sacrifice severe and unrelenting. Self-sacrifice is the parent of the sacrifice of others. It says, "I must suffer, why not you." This sentiment combined with the reverence for a "holy cause," makes it easily possible for these reformers to as conscientiously persecute heretics as they themselves were persecuted. Thus animate existence bleeds through the ages while experience slowly grinds into it the expediency of moderation. It slowly but surely impresses the blind Ego that if existence is worth anything its value must consist in its benefit to such Ego; that in whatever degree sacrifice is imposed or risk incurred in that degree is the purpose of being defeated.

This religious fanaticism with its primitive impulse, is the mental state particularly of the physical force revolutionist. He preaches "duty," heroism; enjoins sacrifice, and consigns his comrades to the prison of the persecutor with the pious zeal of the early Christian martyrs while he exults over the benefit to the "holy cause." He refuses to attempt any steps toward their deliverance because it would deprive him of the opportunity of brandishing their impaled liberty before a partially indifferent public for the purpose of gaining the desired support for his violent revolution. So devoutly does he love his cause that he gladly sacrifices those to it whose suffering is the strongest reason for it. He derides as cowards and Christ-like turners of the "other cheek" those who direct their energies toward removing the errors that make oppressive institutions possible, while with exquisite fidelity to the seeming paradoxes of real life, we find that it is *religion* that posits *him* as we find him.

So slowly do we learn the variation of a consistent course in thought and conduct that some of our most radical papers are often found urging their constituents in a genuinely religious manner to forward contributions with which to propagate the cause—to prepare better conditions for posterity. This perpetuates the old tendency of religion, that of directing the attention of the Ego to some object or idea too far from himself. Humanity will probably always have a cause, and we can do nothing that will benefit posterity so much as to leave the example of self-defense against all exactions of "duty;" a policy of intelligent self-interest. We do not know what posterity may desire, but we may be reasonabiy sure that the prevalence of a custom enjoining each to attend to his own affairs will not be amiss, should we ourselves enjoy and leave such a custom. Since every oppressive institution that we now have is the fruit of somebody's solicitude for posterity or society, we may well abandon that idea. The living, suffering Ego of the now needs the fruit of his own efforts to provide his own pleasure while his flash of eternity lasts. Therefore any means for obtaining his support of reform that does not make it a pleasure as spontaneously entered as the other pleasures he persues is not defensible. If the matter be presented in a light of mutual benefit that inspires a spontaneous self-interest the pleasure of his flash of eternity is not invaded as by duty.

Another slight relic of the influence of theological dominance in the expression of thought is the use by some of our ablest radical writers of the terms "high," "noble," etc. in referring to conduct or complexity in development. Justification of their use in connection with evolution may be sought, but the relative nature of evolution even may soon confine it to being spelled with a little "e" so far as the merit or demerit of its various stages of complexity are concerned. These words are readily traced to the throne of God and the altar of self-sacrifice, and can mean little away from their respective homes.

H.

The "Duty" Fetich in Law.

The following pathetic description of legal outrage is clipped from the Daily Chronicle of this city:

A painful scene occurred in Judge Lawler's court yesterday, growing out of the removal of a child from its mother's custody.

On Saturday last a writ of habeas corpus was granted to David Reulein, commanding Mrs. Anna Clarke to produce her son, aged four years in court. The petition for the writ stated that Reulein and his wife, Kate, were the lawful guardians of the child, and that he had been forcibly removed from their custody by Mrs. Clarke and Rebecca Herringer, her mother. In a suit filed on the same day Mrs. Clark asserted that she had consented to the adoption of her son by the Reuleins some months ago, through fear of personal violence at the hands of her husband, James P. Clarke, a brother of Mrs. Reulein.

When the case was called, Attorney M. Cooney, representing the mother, asked for a continuance, basing his request on a physician's certificate, that his client was in such a delicate condition that it would be dangerous for her to leave home or to be subjected to any undue excitement. Judge Lawler, however, denied the request, and Mr. Cooney dispatched a messenger for his client and had her brought into court. Testimony was taken which showed that while the Reuleins had legally adopted the child fifteen months ago, he had ever since continued in the custody of his mother, and that she had provided for his support. An attempt was made by Mrs. Clarke's attorney to show that the adoption paper introduced in evidence was invalid. Reulein's attorney objected, and Judge Lawler sustained the objection. He further denied a motion to dismiss the writ, and despite the protest of Mr. Cooney, decided that the child should be returned to its guardians.

The bailiff of the court attempted to enforce this order, but the mother clung to her child with a strength born of desperation, and resisted every effort to take him from her. So heartrending were her cries that the bailiff at length desisted. Another deputy sheriff was sent for, and while the court waited, the mother strained the child to her heart and sobbed out in her grief such disconnected sentences as: "They shall not take him from me!" "I will go to jail first!" "He is my baby!" "I suffered for him and now they would steal him from me!"

The child also sobbed, and there were few dry eyes in the courtroom. When help arrived another vain attempt was made to wrench the boy from his mother's arms, and again the officers had to desist. Judge Lawler tried to induce Mrs. Clarke to give up the child peacably. She refused, however, and again the deputy sheriffs, obeying the judge's order, as he hastily left the courtroom, seized the distracted woman, and, while two of them held her tightly, a third person standing near seized the screaming boy and bore him from the courtroom. "My baby—oh, my baby!" shrieked Mrs. Clarke hysterically as she fell from the officer's arms to the floor. Again and again the heartrending cry was uttered, but it fell on ears that were deaf to her supplications. For fully ten minutes the poor mother refused to be pacified, but sobbed and moaned as though her heart was broken. Those about the courtroom withdrew and left her alone with her friends and her grief. She was finally sufficiently calmed to permit her parents to lead her from the courtroom and started toward home.

The fetich of "duty" to religion which caused all the sickening cruelties of persecution in the past, is paralleled only by the fetich of duty to law which characterizes the law-worshipers of our time. The crushing cruelness always comes from adherence to the letter of written law. The circumstances and equity of the case are not once thought of, everything must conform to mechanical routine or crude precedent. Despite the fact that the court knew that the mother had been forced through fear of violence to sign the adoption paper, the case was decided as though she had voluntarily signed it.

The incident is an exceedingly clear illustration of the psychology of the "duty" fetich in law. No movement in the whole proceeding was actuated by the least human spontaneity. Nothing but the force of the idea of duty to "law" could have forced these men to tear the child from its mother's arms. None of the officers really wanted the order executed; they saw its injustice, but the slavish psychology of a fixed idea drove them to it as the same superstition drives the religious fanatic to crucify his sympathies. The judge himself could not stand by his decision with the firmness that accompanies one's best judgment, but "hastily left the courtroom." He was not following his own desire or judgment, and could not witness the pain caused by following the letter of the statute.

Had the judge and officers made the same effort to adjust the case on its merits that they did to enforce a stereotyped law, how different would have been the result, for they realized that that law was not applicable to that case, but excused their act by the idea of doing their "duty." Duty to what? Duty to whom? Not to the father, for the child was not to go to him. Not to the guardians for they had no personal claim on the child, but only to a written law; an abstract idea; a thought, which has neither sensation nor sympathy, and cannot be pained or pleased by their actions. On the other hand they were dealing with a living, sensitive, human being, on whom they could see the immediate result of their actions; whom they had no reason to cause to suffer; toward whom they had no ill will; whose suffering even caused them pain, and yet two of them held her arms while a third party took her boy and fled. Physical strength, impelled by social superstition had triumphed, and the woman was left helpless without further consideration.

By forcing this separation these officers were carrying out the law, which is supposed to be the "will of the people," but that as much of the "people" as was present was as feelingly opposed to the enforcement of the law as were the officers, is evidenced by their tears. What a ridiculous spectacle: the people weeping because their "will" was being obeyed! Yet this is the logic of their position. In an age of science, philosophy, and invention bounded only by the imagination, we find a judge, officers, and people helplessly writhing at the feet of a superstition as palpable as ever terrified the most ignorant barbarian, and a public press manipulated by long-titled graduates from longer-titled colleges, which, while pathetically lamenting the fact, no more thinks of proposing a remedy than of proposing to stop the revolving of the earth.

Ye worshipers of "Duty" with a big "D," does it occur to you that it is in the nature of "duty" to be thus blind, or is this instance only an error in its administration, and if so, what but the abolition of the idea will prevent similar occurrences eternally? G.

Moses Harman.

Moses Harman is now in penitentiary, sentenced to five years, and to pay a fine of $300. There are only two things that can be done: one is not to attempt to do anything for him, the other, is to procure the signature of every adult who can be induced to petition the president for his release. EGOISM choses the latter, and desires its friends to procure each as many signatures to the petition as possible. Petition blanks and copies of a leaflet, containing for those canvassed, a statement of the case, will be furnished upon application to EGOISM, Box 1678, San Francisco, Cal. Attach blank sheets to the bottom of petition sheet until it is too long to handle conveniently, then return to us. Take none but adult men and women.

The Philosophy of Egoism.

II.

It is now time to meet the demand for a definition of Egoism. The dictionaries must be resorted to for explanations of the meanings of most words, but in any science, art, or philosophy there are some leading terms understood in a more precise manner than that general notion or mass of nearly related significations given in the dictionary under one term. The dictionary is like a map of the world, which shows where a country is with relation to all other countries. The definition of the dictionary is simply objective, not closely analytical. Its language is popular, as in the speaking of black and white as colors. All this is well enough. People need information which will be true to appearances, for practical purposes, and need so wide an extent of this in a moderate compass, that they are glad to get brief explanations or even hints at meanings, prepared by men skilled in classifying linguistic growths. Hence, however, they sometimes find the popular definitions as good but not better than to define cheese as condensed milk. The so-called synonyms have different shades of meaning, but disputants easily yield to the temptation to assume an identical import in two terms, sometimes for the purpose of blackening one by throwing upon it an evil connotation which adheres to the other: and conversely the hearer is usually able to understand immediately whether the speaker, if sincere, is friendly or hostile toward an object, merely by noting the terms chosen in alluding to its existence. We rarely find many sentences together without a moral judgment being conveyed. Such judgments, from an Egoistic point of view, could be illustrated by representing a beggar extolling charity.

The definition of the specialist, on the other hand, is like a map which shows the boundary between two countries, but does not attempt to show anything else. To the navigator land is that beneath his vessel which is not water. To the political economist a lake and a bed of coal are equally land. The two specialists are concerned with two different series of ideas, therefore with different aspects of the object.

The best that can be said of Webster's dictionary definitions of Egoism, is that a reader who already understands the term as it has been used in practical philosophy for more than forty years, may barely recognize the idea as one espies a diamond in a dustheap. "The habit of . . . . judging of everything by its relation to one's interests or importance," is Webster's nearest approach. In what sense can the individual and his interests be other than all-important to the individual? Only in the sense that, in order to reject Egoism, his interests are not to be understood as including his intellectual and sentimental interest in objects, including other persons. But the Egoist will take the liberty to inquire how any one can be engaged in judging of anything without having taken an interest in it. Let us assume that a new dictionary maker inserts in his work a paragraph like this:

Egoism, *n.* The principle of self; the doctrine of individuality; self-interest; selfishness.

Then I shall comment by saying that "the doctrine of individuality," is a happier expression than the single word individuality, for the latter is commonly used to convey the idea of distinctive, marked peculiarities of character. Self-interest is usually restricted to pecuniary interest and the like, ignoring what is reciprocal in the pleasures of companionship and what affords intellectual satisfaction. Selfishness is commonly used to indicate self-gratification in disregard of the feelings of others. All these words indicate Egoism, but they indicate it with special determinations. In the word selfish the termination arrests attention. It is generally disparaging; either connected with bad words or it gives them a contemptuous shade of meaning, as knavish, thievish, foolish, mawkish, bookish, monkish, popish. Hence when a man acts in certain ways causing disgust in other people they declare his action selfish,—not merely a manifestation of self, but one which they purpose castigating by adding the termination expressive of averision and contempt. The linguistic instinct appears correct to this extent, however incorrect may be the popular judgment regarding certain actions which are thus stigmatized. For want of this thought some writers have laid the whole popular judgment, expressed in the reproach of selfishness, to the account of opposition to the principle of self. There is certainly a great deal of that. It is selfism of course, which protests, and selfishness which protests most against the selfishness of others and against the principle of self in others. Selfishness argues that its pasture will be greener and richer in proportion as others yield in particular desires to the preaching of unselfishness and self-abnegation, which terms, the genius of selfishness cunningly declares to be synonymous whenever its ends are to be served by such a view. Self-abnegation, however, in its full sense, is evidently insanity, while unselfishness may be only selfism without any feature which can be calculated to arouse the antipathy of other individuals (that is, the un*ish*ness of the self). This is a new analysis and I do not pretend that users of the word unselfish are generally conscious of any force in the termination, to which the privative prefix may apply, but I refer to Webster's definitions of selfishness and self-love respectively for support as to the usage.

Tak Kak.

What is the use of putting our heads into the sand and dreaming of an impossible glory? Will it come by dreaming, by denying facts, by shutting our eyes to the enormous pain, and woe, and bitterness of things? Let us be brave and frank. Fling optimism to the winds, and recognize the burden of life, and bear it courageously. Recognize that this universe is for us a battle-ground, and if we don't fight we shall be borne under by advancing millions. Keep in mind that all the justice in the universe is human justice, and all love human love, and all wisdom human wisdom.—Samuel P. Putnam in "My Religious Experience."

The subjective origin of invasion in general is perhaps never better exemplified than in the well-meaning assurance with which a number of adults will obtrude their philoprogenitive impulses on a helpless babe.

The Science of Social Relations.

By the law of the Three Stages, so elaborately set forth by Auguste Comte, we are told that every science, each branch of knowledge, passes through three different theoretical conditions; the theological, or mythical; the metaphysical, or speculative; and the positive or scientific. "Hence," said Comte, "arises three philosophies, or general systems of conceptions on the aggregate of phenomena, each of which excludes the other. The first is the necessary point of departure of the human understanding; and the third is its fixed, or definite, state; the second is merely a state of transition."

This generalization is strikingly illustrated in the metaphysical character of current discussions of social problems, which are everywhere in the crucible of analysis. Every passage from one social system to another is accompanied by a transitional stage wherein scientific convictions are not yet reached and the old figments of the imaginative stage still survive to figure as metaphysical entities supposed in some way to control phenomena and determine events.

An illustration may be cited. The imaginative conception of the Nile and the Ganges as deities gave place later to more abstract conceptions. In the metaphysical stage this passed through a still further abstraction and became the Aqueous Principle. Thus in the middle age, the properties of water, such as being wet, were deemed fully accounted for by stating that its cause was the nature of Aquosity. Words were taken for events and endowed with generative causation. In the historical field this method has had full play, and to it we are indebted in no small degree for the incoherence distinguishing the political and social world.

The philosophy of history in its highest conception embraces not only the study of civilization and the underlying ideas which determine and interpret its course, but the search for its ultimate end, the true theory of order and progress, and a synthetic grouping of the phenomena of social life. Has human history any comprehensive significance? What is the law of progress? Is the evolution of social life interpretable by reason? In these great questions, it will at once be seen, exists the opportunity for the freest display of speculative inquiry. The first and most obvious interpretation of the phenomena of social life, was that of a direct guidance by divine providence in human affairs, watching over and determining all human actions; and even today the press groans beneath the works unceasingly turned out by

> "Those pseudo Privy-Councillors of God
> Who write down judgments with a pen hard-nibbed,"

by whom the workings of the almighty mind are as familiarly understood as the fluctuations on 'Change.

Later, we metaphysically personalized Nature and glibly talked of natural laws, natural rights, etc. Though the nasal accent had been dropped, the words had not even the significance of the old myth, for Nature remained but a word to represent the unceasing flux of events, without will or power save as human thought subjectively created it. They fail to realize that the correlations existing in logic are not necessarily real, objective, the subjective requirements of thought not carrying with them absolute existence outside of and beyond relations.

On the one hand science analyzes the feelings and sentiments, and subjects them to a microscopic study, submitting them to the law of averages, considering them as relations and reducing them to their phenomenal manifestations. On the other hand dogmatic theology and its progeny, metaphysics, searching after final causes turns its back on present needs of social existence. The one uses the microscope for increasing our knowledge of specialties; the other a speculative telescope for extra-mundane life. Science in freeing itself from the finite speculations of relative minds that law is an expression of will, rather than a generalization describing mode of action, in short, as an objective causative will acting in phenomena, instead of being merely an ideal conception of the phenomena themselves classified according to their resemblance to other phenomena, has been slow in extending its sway into the field of sociology.

The positive, or scientific method consists in three phases: first, observations of *facts;* second, their classification into generalizations, or *laws;* third, *verification.*

Turning from the historical to the social sphere, nowhere do we find greater the prevalence of incoherence than in political-economical questions. The same metaphysical conception of laws as an active force or creative energy in the renovation of society prevails today as in the time of the French economists of the last century. It forms but a part of the characteristic discord of the present regime, wherein the thousand and one quack remedies submitted for the redress of social ills attest the inability of prevalent methods to grapple with the problems.

The age is teeming with schemes, as before the French revolution, to secure the natural rights of those who feel their equal freedom abridged. Read the French economists, the debates in the parliaments, in the National Convention, and we find the remedy in—organizing liberty! By this mysterious and undefined principle, undefined save in metaphysical terms, all wrongs were to be righted, all ills redressed. Does the tenure of land cripple agricultural development? Does the industrial policy restrict manufactures? Does monopoly over capital limit exchange? In reply they set up abstract man, the isolated individual, without historical connection with the past or social ties with his fellows, and demanded for him metaphysical "natural rights."

The modern, or scientific method starting with facts explores the world for past and present social relations. From their collaboration we rise to the generalization that society is more equitable precisely as social relations are unhampered by interference. As generalization from facts constitutes scientific "law," we are led to posit the "law of equal freedom" as the true basis for social activity. Verification of this is unceasingly being developed, hence in sociology all rights are equal, all laws social; evolved, not conferred. To assert a "right" is but the negative form of stating that equal privilege is demanded because denied. In short equality of rights, of privilege, eliminates rights. The law of equal freedom being the product of social evolution, each age determines for itself its application. Regarded from the ethical standpoint truth is no longer spelled with a capital initial T, but becomes adaptation to environment; like all else, relative.

While we are social beings, the product of an evolved social environment, our moral sense the growing conception of an external self, still the basis of all social relations, rights, truth, ethics, becomes in the last analysis primarily the assertion of the individual within the lines of equal freedom, asserting for each equal right for unequal capacity, which necessarily carries with it respect for and the same assertion of the equal right of others. Mutual interests are thus seen to be not only based but furthered by self-interest, and both God and Nature relegated to the limbo of past personalizations, survivals of a more childish form of thought.

DYER D. LUM.

LIBERTY is essentially an organizing force. To insure equality between men and peace among nations, agriculture and industry, and the centers of education, business, and storage must be distributed according to the climate and the geographical position of the country, the nature of the products, the character and natural talents of the inhabitants, etc., in proportions so just, so wise, so harmonious, that in no place shall there ever be either an excess or a lack of population, consumption, and products. There commences the science of public and private right, the true political economy.—Proudhon.

Enlightened Selfishness.

The world justly condemns stupid selfishness, but when the world concludes that all sorts of selfishness are wrong and debasing, then the world itself is stupid. Enlightened selfishness leads a man not to wrong his neighbor or himself, while stupid or ignorant selfishness induces one to harm both himself and others. We have all been taught that to be selfish is to be base. We have learned to abhor the word selfishness, and it seems at first sight, that anyone who will try to make out that even enlightened selfishness is the real guiding power of human life, is attempting to corrupt us with error.

Most people cannot see how selfishness can take the place of morality, duty, and religion. In the first place a large part of the race does not rise high enough in the scale of intelligence to see that very many of the most familiar words are without meaning. They are worse than a mouldy chestnut; for even it has some sort of substance within, but the words God, heaven, morality, duty, are not words that have anything inside. They are absolutely empty, and void as a burst bubble, but the stupidly selfish are receiving them for face value. They are the bank paper of banks that never had anything more than an imaginary existence.

It is plain that blind selfishness seeks for immediate pleasure—it riots in overdoing the pleasure act, while intelligent selfishness takes a broad survey of life, and aims to secure the more elevating and lasting pleasures. Intelligent selfishness does not induce one to conform to justice and equal freedom from any sense of duty, but because it pays best to do so. There is no such thing as "duty." It is a figment of the brain, a fancy, a word-ghost. When the phantom-god is dissolved in the crucible of science, there are no grounds on which duty can rest. After the phantom-god has left the mind, man rationally turns to find his greatest happiness. Duty implies obligation, but to whom are you obliged? Echo answers "to whom?"

The Christian will say "you are in duty bound to tell the truth." But there is no duty at all in the matter. It is a question of expediency. The intelligent individual holds truth in high esteem because it contributes to human happiness. It does not pay to lie. The experience of mankind has established a concensus on truthfulness, but as a "virtue," or "duty," the concensus has fixed no definite standard respecting it. There is no standard of truth. You are responsible concerning truth, for yourself and only to yourself. You owe no obligation to any other human being, but your intelligent selfishness will lead you to pay due regard to the so-called cardinal virtues, as they lie close to the path that leads to the greatest happiness. The ray of light that falls on the path of every mortal is happiness

Some people drink so little from the cup of joy, that in their despair hope points them to another and better world beyond this life, where happiness is supreme and constant; there are others who are content with the consolations of this basement world. But all alike, saint and sinner, are moved by the selfish desire of happiness. The minister has a call from Georgetown with an increase of $500 in his salary. He leaves Jamestown, and goes to Georgetown. Like Moses, he has "respect unto the recompense of the reward." He still retains his title to mansions in the skies. Just a little selfish. Ministers and laymen are conscious of a genuine thrill of joy when you hold up before their possible grasp the "Almighty Dollar."

If one clearly comprehends the nature of intelligent selfishness he will not find it difficult to understand Anarchism, but until he can clearly see that the spur-wheel in the machinery of human life is selfishness, he has not yet learned the "a b c" of Anarchism. If he admits selfishness to be the constant motive, but decries it, he has yet to fix his attention upon the nature of selfishness seeking the highest happiness of the individual through the recognition of equal freedom.

W. S. Bell.

Gronlund's Time-serving Evasion.

Mr. Laurence Gronlund has contributed an article to the "Twentieth Century" entitled, "Why I am a Socialist." In it he makes a very curious and significant omission; he fails to use the word *State* throughout the whole article of over twelve hundred words. This word does not once occur. He very astutely confines himself to the word *Socialism*. Now Individualists know that Mr. Gronlund is a *State* Socialist. Mr. Bellamy, the father and founder of that new sentimental State Socialism disguised under the reputable name of Nationalism, is a student of Mr. Gronlund, and is heels over head in debt to him for all he knows or doesn't know of the science of State socialistic government. The omission of the compound word "State-Socialism," by Mr. Gronlund, is tacitly admitting that like "calomel and jalap" it is becoming a nauseous compound among men making a conscientious and intelligent study of economic freedom.

I am glad to see Mr. Gronlund's thoughtful admission of the unpopularity of the word "State," and this peculiar omission shows that the best way to ascertain what Mr. Gronlund knows about *State* Socialism is not to study what he says, but what he fails to say.

Mr. Gronlund cannot resist the temptation so prevalent among sentimental governmentalists to give the Individualists a back-handed slap. This is a custom that has been followed so long that not to do it would be to ignore the "customs of the country." See how gently and genteely he lays us out in the following sentences: "There are two temperments in the world: men of an individualist order of mind, who cannot bear to have their liberty in the least infringed upon, and who insist on the right not alone of using, but of *abusing* what is theirs, and men of the opposite spirit, the Socialist spirit [add the word "State" to catch Mr. Gronlund's true meaning]. The fact that I belong to the latter class is sufficient to explain my position. I further hold that it is perfectly useless to try to *convert* the *former* class (Individualists). Take for instance Henry George; he is from the crown of his head to the sole of his feet an Individualist; that means, that he, in my opinion, never will and considering his *maturity*, never can become a [State!] Socialist."

I wish I was as sure of Henry George's Individualism as I am of Mr. Gronlund's uninformed state of mind on that subject. Henry George undoubtedly has individualistic tendencies, and this fact alone places him a long step ahead of Mr. Gronlund's State Socialism. *If* Mr. George is an Individualist it is (as Mr. Gronlund unwittingly says) because of his *maturity—intellectual* maturity. It takes a somewhat *matured* mind to comprehend the full meaning of the word Individualism. If Mr. Gronlund understands this point he will know why he is not himself an Individualist. The self-complacency with which Mr. Gronlund treats the position of the Individualist, in the sentences quoted, shows his acquaintance with egotism to be greater than his knowledge of Egoism. If his idea of liberty consists in believing that twenty or more men know what the individual wants or needs better than he does himself, that it is something to be doled out to him from the Socialist *State* as soup is from a "soup-house" to a charity patient, then indeed would it be possible to "abuse our liberty" by demanding more liberty. But in case of refusal by Collectivists like Mr. Gronlund to allow us that which by equal freedom is really ours, we would be able to demonstrate to more comprehensive people our right to use or "abuse" our liberty providing in the abuse of our liberty we do not abuse the liberty of another individual, but confine ourselves to the abuse of our own. Surely Mr. Gronlund would not object to this unless he has turned Moralist and wishes to force men to do "right" in accordance with his theologically socialistic conception of what is right and wrong, by passing a *law* that would *prohibit* men from abusing their liberty. In that case the idea of liberty would undergo a transformation only equaled by the transformation scenes in the spectacular play of the "Black Crook."

Mr. Gronlund thinks it useless to try to convert the Individualists to Socialism. This is a gratuitous assertion on his part, and is an evidence that he himself is not a Socialist in its broad, true sense, or he would know that Individualists are already Socialists and need no conversion.

The trouble with Mr. Gronlund is that he, as he says, "believes in a *moral* ordering of this world." Now in order to enforce this conviction upon individuals you have got to have a State, a collective, centralized State, under the governorship of men with the same moral conceptions as Mr. Gronlund, therefore Mr. Gronlund is a State Socialist and should have so labeled himself in his article, "Why I am a Socialist." This would have prevented the confusion in the minds of beginners who do not thoroughly grasp the difference between Socialism pure and undefiled, and State Socialism. The first is Socialism *without* authority, moral or immoral, while the latter is Socialism *and authority*.

It is true that Individualists can never be converted to State Socialism, for the simple reason that they are subject in common to intellectual evolutionary growth (this being the only form of subjection that they will willingly submit to), and having once partaken of that, to them, social emetic called State Socialism, never return to swallow the rejected contents of a sick stomach. They prefer not to reverse the order of mental evolution for the same reason that an Agnostic never returns to the church, or that progress never walks backward like a crab. This is the reason that Individualists cannot accept State Socialism. "It is but a step from the sublime to the rediculous," and Individualists would be obliged to take that step backward in order to occupy the position that Mr. Gronlund does.

San Diego, Cal. F. B. Parse.

Damp, that is the Enemy.

Sir Edwin Chadwick, known in England as the "pioneer of sanitary science," opened the winter session of the London Sanitary Institute by reading a paper, in the Parkes Museum, Regent Street, on "The General History and Principles of Sanitation." He summed up his conclusions as follows:

I have desired to show that sanitation possesses a history as old as the oldest of religions, and may be looked upon, in itself, as a form, originally, of religious observance.

In the second place, turning from the first days of sanitation to some of the modern essentials of the art, I dwelt on the importance of the study of dampness of air as a cause of disease. I might, perhaps, have entered into a very wide field. I might have tried to indicate the manner in which damp affects the human body,—whether it acts as the bearer of morbific particles, living or dead, or whether it exerts its influence in a more direct manner by simple interference with vital activities essential to health. I must be content to state the main factor, damp, as the grand traitor, leaving it to others to find out and expound all the details. But, after all, they will not be able to convey to you more than one practical lesson that, if damp be kept out, disease will be kept out of the land, the town, and the dwelling-house. It is not invariably the new house that is rendered dangerous by being damp. There are in this country many old houses, picturesquely situated, which are not less dangerous. The stranger passing one of these residences is struck by its beauty. There is the ancient moat around it, or the lake in front, with the sailing boat and swans, the summer house and splendid trees down to the water's edge. The stranger may well enough be fascinated by the view; but let him inquire, and he will too often find a truly ghostly history of the place. He will be told, probably with some exaggeration of the truth, that the house is unlucky, that no one who has lived in it has reared a healthy child, and that a traditional malediction taints the place. If he enter the house, he finds a basement steaming with water vapor; walls constantly bedewed with moisture, cellars coated with fungus and mould, drawing-rooms and dining-rooms always, except in the very heat of summer, oppressive from moisture; bed-rooms, the windows of which are, in winter, often so frosted on their inner surface, from condensation of the water in the air of the room, that all day they are coated with ice. The malediction on the young nurtured in that mansion may not be so deep as is rumored, and it is much less obscure than is imagined; but it is there, and its name is damp.

In the third place, I have striven to urge the necessity of instant, continuous, and automatic self-cleansing of every house, town, and city. In primitive times, amongst nomadic people, the old Mosaic method was a good one, and under some conditions, this method, somewhat modified, is still, to a limited extent, applicable. The great principle, however, which I wish emphatically to fix in your minds is that of circulation versus stagnation: the only true and vital sanitary plan of drawing away at every moment, by an unceasing mechanical central engine power, all the dead human and other animal excreta of communities, and casting it upon the lands undecomposed, so that they may, through the intermediate work of plants, break out into life again, and give sustenance to man and animal. Let nothing move you from this lesson of sanitation. It is the foundation of the best sanitary work, beside of which all else of the kind is a mere compromise, and often nothing less than an aggravation of the mischiefs intended to be rectified.

In the fourth place, passing from the community to the individual, I tried to inculcate on modern scientific principles the force of the old motto, "Wash and be clean." It was my special desire in enforcing this lesson to make it applicable to the young, so that personal cleanliness may not only become a habit of life, but a habit that is felt as a necessity. Lastly, it was my wish to convey hope and confidence for the future by what we have learned of the past; and particularly to open up a vista of a new future for the wage classes of the population. I held out the modest expectation that under sanitation every family may, in a happier day, be provided with a dwelling well drained, well warmed, well ventilated, well lighted, well supplied with water, and well supplied with all comforts for preparation of food, and wholesome repose. I might have suggested more had I gone in for luxury; but my long experience has shown me so much cross danger from luxury that I am quite content to leave the recommendation I have offered where it is, convinced that that luxury will of itself follow comfort fast enough to be compatible with safety, without any urgent pressure from you or from me.—Transatlantic.

Could there be a greater, and apparently more dismal, paradox than the sight of the seer of democracy sitting serene under the total neglect of the democracy? If anything could bely the faith of the "Democratic Vistas," . . . it is the spectacle of the only great living American poet dependent in his old age upon the sympathy—and at one moment almost upon the maintenance—of foreign friends. And yet he keeps his faith in the faithless people unshaken, . . . if he is right in his robust belief, surely the solution of the paradox lies in the meaning of that much abused word the "people." The "people" in whom his confidence burns so unquenchably are not the rich people, not the millions of wire-pullers and place-hunters, not the spurious *elite* of culture, but the mass of the people, who know little of Whitman and his books, or of any books, who labor obscurely, manfully, and restlessly, who represent the vast sum-total of energy comparable to the energies of nature herself,—the mass of the people whose force and fertility are independent of all possible vicissitudes in institutions.—Oliver Elton, in the London Academy.

Egographs.

Original matter often sacrifices quality, and usually quantity, as the scissors are more prolific as well as select than the pen.

Anger and fury, though they add strength to the sinews of the body, yet are found to relax those of the mind, and to render all its efforts feeble and impotent.—Swift.

Out of a world of unwise, nothing but an unwisdom can be made. Arrange it, constitution-build it, sift it through ballot-boxes as thou wilt, it is and remains an unwisdom, the new prey of new quacks and unclean things, the latter end of it slightly better than the beginning. Who can bring a wise thing out of a man unwise? No one. —Carlyle.

There is inequality in nature, but it is a moderate, orderly inequality; excessive inequality, great poverty by the side of extreme wealth, is the work of the State. It is only in its shadow that, flying the flag of solidarity, the egoism of some fails to be checked by that of others. How, then, is it possible for the State to remedy this wrong? —Rouxel in the Journal des Economistes.

I found a wild flower one day, and, wondering at its beauty and perfection in every part, cried: "This lovely flower, then, and myriads of others, bloom unregarded, ofttimes unseen, by human eye." I seemed to hear the flower reply: "Thou fool! thinkest thou I bloom in order to be seen? I bloom for myself, not for others, because it pleases me. Therein, because I exist, is my joy and contentment."—Schopenhaur.

Government is a suction-pump, with its draught-pipe anchored in industry's pocket. It draws the valuables out of that pocket, and forces them into the pocket of idleness. This is the agent that makes the many poor, while it makes the few rich. The rich in turn loan the plunder to industry, at usury, acting as a blister on the wound made by government, intensifying the disease, till it becomes unendurable. The church then comes along and applies a poultice composed of two parts, one to "bear the burden for Christ's sake," the other a small sprinkle of charity—the mite it can spare from support of the priesthood. A small mite it is, too.—Selected.

I am told that it is for my good that I am governed; now, as I give my money for being governed, it follows that it is for my good that I give my money; which is possible, but calls nevertheless for verification. Moreover, in addition to the fact that no one can be more familiar than myself with the means of making myself happy, I also find it strange, incomprehensible, unnatural, and extra-human, that people should devote themselves to the happiness of those whom they do not know, and I declare that I have not the honor of being known to the men who govern me. Hence I am justified in saying that from my standpoint they are really too good and, in fact, somewhat indiscreet who concern themselves so much about my felicity, especially when it is not proven that I am incapable of pursuing its realization *myself*.—Bellegarigue.

Humanity in our century resembles a traveler who, on leaving the city which he is to see no more, lingers, has regrets, retraces his steps, has always forgotten something which he goes to find; and night overtakes him on the road, so that he has no shelter either in the city which he has left or in that at which he has not arrived, and must sleep in the beautiful starlight. We are very willing to go forward to liberty, but there is always something that we regret in authority. We return, we take what we can, we bring it along, we load ourselves down, and do not advance. And this simply from not understanding that liberty and authority are two different countries, which have nothing in common, that one cannot live in two places at the same time, and that we must stay where we are unless it is our formal intention to go somewhere else.—Henry Maret in Le Radical.

In all the attempts of moralists, I see this fatal error: a belief in the superior worth of some one state of mind in which we are supposed to have a true perception of reality. The aspect thus seized must be abided by, and our thoughts and actions subordinated accordingly. Whatever tends to question it must be thrown aside as frivolity, or stamped down as sin—not in ourselves alone, but also in others. That which at first was pure delight in us, a gift of grace, what have we made of it? A yoke for our own necks, and stocks for other men's feet. This is the misdeed of morality—that it takes the innocent pleasure we may have in our own ways, and replaces it by a duty that must rule when the pleasure which was the sign of life is gone; must rule at home and abroad. After which we look round, and marvel to find the world joyless and egotistical. And we try to warm in ourselves and in others the first day's enthusiasm; we expatiate on the sanctity of the law, in hopes that its defense in common will draw us nearer one to another. Not so. What we may thus stir up is a superficial emotion that creates in our imagination a bond of sympathy between us and our brothers, but leaves us as far apart as ever in our practical impulses. We fall into each other's arms while the sound of the church organ lasts, but as soon as it expires we are ready to condemn each other on appearances, and strictly by the letter of the law. The taint of egotism lies farther back—in our misconception of reality. The day we invested it with a character of permanence, and resolved to abide by it such as it appeared to us then, we were cut off from experience.—H. Brewester.

Egoism

Vol. I.—No. 3. SAN FRANCISCO, CAL., JULY, 1890. Price, Five Cents.

Pointers.

We fail to appreciate those evils which never come.

Persons in San Francisco who wish to subscribe for Egoism can pay their subscriptions at the office of "Freethought," 838 Howard street.

While Egoism contains adverse criticism of one of the "Individualist's" editorial writers, it is quite as anxious to commend the strong and sensible plea by "L," in the issue of June 16, for the enlightenment of the masses, as against preaching dynamite.

So much more valuable does William Holmes believe an active authoritarian to be than an indifferent citizen, that he "as an Anarchist" does what he can to stimulate such to active hostility by introducing Collectivist literature where he thinks that of Anarchism would not be acceptable.

Women's Rights have taken one step more. Women have stepped over the horse with one foot, and may now ride with a leg on each side. This is one step toward freedom, but it will not enable them to ride the political "hobby" there, for the reason that it does not travel in that direction.

It is with intense pleasure that we note the rapid strides to an impregnable position by the office editor of "Freethought," as evidenced by his article, "I Philosophize," reprinted in another column. Egoism has not existed in vain. Hugh O thou wilt yet be left in the rear with thy "duty" fetich and "moral" phantom!

But two persons have as yet applied to this branch for petition blanks to secure signatures for the release of Moses Harman. There is no positive assurance that a petition even numerously signed will effect such release, but as we have before stated, it is the only hope and it seems no one could afford to leave a stone unturned. A long list of petitioners would be a rebuke to the censor gang worth working for even though it failed to move the president to action. Has Egoism not some more friends who are acquainted with somebody that they could use in this way. Leaflets stating the case to those canvassed, will be furnished with blanks. Both petition blanks and leaflets are valueless lying here, but would at least do propaganda work if circulated.

The first number of "Free Life," Auberon Herbert's new paper, published in London, has reached us. That it is a formidable antagonist of political superstition will be seen by its salutatory, "One Fight More—the Best and the Last," reprinted on another page. It will be a strong standard bearer for Anarchism in England, and a rallying point for the firm individuality of the English character as it passes from native blustering to the unalterable dignity of the strength born of experience. Mr. Herbert's broad sweep and definite touch of details in handling the political dogmas all the more intensify the regret of the Egoist upon noting the shadow of the "morality" ghost floating about whenever ethical policy is approached. It is hoped that he will take the trouble to ferret out the "morality" delusion as completely as he has the political one. The paper contains four pages a little larger than those of this paper, is probably issued weekly, and at one penny. All orders are to be addressed to Auberon Herbert, Old House, Ringwood.

A friend, who has no controversial ax to grind, observes that the editors of this paper take the doctrine of Egoism for granted, and do not enlarge upon the idea looking to its establishment in a scientific sense. This is true, and two reasons are that, first, Tak Kak, whose long familiarity with the idea and scholarly ability enable him to treat it incomparably better than we possibly could, is developing its philosophy, and second, there are many who can better understand and appreciate a new departure in thought by assuming it and gathering the evidence by citations from their everyday experience, than by the more condensed method of abstract deduction. Thus with both methods employed, every variation between the two extremes of perceptive and reflective habit will be more fully met than otherwise. This explanation will probably be satisfactory to all save some pedantic controversialists, who will be considered when Tak Kak has finished his exposition of the subject, if they still think they can make the "moral" wart stick with evolution plaster. Tak Kak is laying a foundation for his argument so comprehensive and deep that jealous sophists will probably be silenced if they study his treatise in order to venture a criticism of it. We hope every reader will carefully read and digest these articles as they appear, so that at their completion each will find himself or herself master of a philosophy that is at the very foundation of all the happiness possible to conditioned beings. Close study is the lone condition of gaining knowledge, and can be facilitated only by advantage of a commanding view; this advantage an understanding of Egoism furnishes.

I Philosophize.

Every man should be able to give a reason for the hope that is in him, and should be prepared to explain his conduct when he does good as well as when he does evil. To do good for the sake of good, or to do right "because it is right," is not philosophical. Self-denial is unnatural, and therefore unwise unless some benefit results to the self-denier sufficient to pay for the inconvenience. Life, as far as I can see, has no object, but it may have its uses. Uses for what? To give the means of happiness to its possessor. One thing is not "higher" than another. A handful of mud from the bottom of the bay is as "high" as the brain of the philosopher. The latter is merely a more complex mass, and has attributes not belonging to mud. What we call intelligence, as I view it, is a result of complexity. Intelligence is not put into the brain, but is the recognizable manifestation of the working of the brain. There is no design in it, but a natural process. Therefore we are not required to indulge in sentimental admiration of genius. We need only to recognize it as a natural outcome of prior conditions.

Life having no object, and when rightly viewed no high aim or romance to the sane person, what shall he do with it? Spend it riotously? That will not pay, as witness the wrecks on the shores of dissipation. Shall we practice self-denial as regards the pleasures of the world? Yes, if it gives us happiness, in which case we have used life to its highest productivity, and in denying ourselves one pleasure we have achieved a greater. The monk in his cell, the anchorite in his cave, the priest among lepers, contemplates his reward and is happier, or thinks he is, than he would be elsewhere. Otherwise he would not be there. Life has no virtues and no duties as generally understood. To do that which we call virtuous is to do what experience has taught us brings most happiness, and therefore pays us in the end. It is no more praiseworthy than the act of paying our board in advance when we have no credit. To practice what goes under the name of virtue is simply to prepare conditions for selfish benefits. The duty idea is a superstition. If a person would be happy otherwise than in the performance of what he terms duty, he would not perform it. He has only followed his ruling inclination.

The question arises, What is life for? It is *for* nothing. We possess legs adapted to locomotion, and use them for that purpose. We have life adapted to the pursuit of happiness. Let us so employ it.

Gentle reader, do you ask me what I am giving you? I answer: If I understand the subject it is the doctrine of Egoism, the philosophical side of Anarchism. It appears to me to be a valuable line of thought for those who desire to get at the mainspring of human action, though at the end of the investigation they are likely to emerge from the same hole they went in at, and to find things the same as ever upon the surface.—George E. Macdonald in "Freethought," of June 28

EGOISM

Issued Monthly at Fifty Cents a Year

—BY—

EQUITY PUBLISHING COMPANY,

Post Office Box 1678, San Francisco, California.

Entered as Second Class Mail Matter.

The Courage Myth.

The word "courage," is another of the miracle words. Like the ideal of Altruism, it is impossible, and exists only in the misconceptions of loose analysis. Consistently defined, its ideal would consist in the virtue of placing the smallest value on the greatest considerations; of imperiling life and all that it means to the possessor for some one of its incidental matters. Indeed, the conception can be maintained only in the thought of jeopardizing the important and more desirable for the minor and indifferent. Otherwise, the thought of risk, and idea of "courage" disappears. It requires none of the ideal, "courage," where the thing imperiled is only equal to or a less consideration than the thing to be gained. Neither does any one really risk the greater for the smaller with a full sense of the fact. If one realize that life is worth more to him than the incident for which he is about to risk it, he simply does not take the risk. Who takes a real risk, must do it blindly and without consideration, which is foolish, and the lone condition under which a supposed courageous act takes place.

The strong man does not enter a physical combat with a sense of fear and an apprehension of probable defeat, but because he has an abundance of strength which assures him of a correspondingly less degree of danger than would present itself to a weaker man. The logician may be physically weak, but enters an intellectual controversy because he or she feels the position is correct; that facts sustain it and that the instances of proof can be satisfactorily cited. The champion of physical strength might shrink from a like contest with all the timidity that the other could manifest if urged into physical combat. Each would undoubtedly challenge the admiration of the other and win credit for great "courage," while really both are exercising only an economy of their forces to be in active capacity at all, and are not assuming what either regards as the great risk required to make it the "courageous" act for which each gives the other credit, else neither of them would be found there.

This brings us to the objective impressions with which we form the ridiculous conception known as "courage," to which so much worshipful deference is paid. We see others extravagantly using a function of which we have little ourselves, and could so exercise only at the peril of all that existence means to us. This objective impression subjectively appropriated without separating the fact of another's strength from our own weakness in that particular function, produces the idea of courage, or bravery for taking a great risk, because it would be a great risk to us. Subjectively, all acts follow what under the circumstances is to the Ego the line of the least resistance. All escape, if they can, from a hurricane or a sinking ship, where their ability for effective resistance is about equal. Any deviation from this line is an error in judging danger rather than a deliberate submission to it. Between the person who runs and the one who stands for fight, there is only a matter of difference in judgment, or of taste; one feels surest of safety and advantage in one course of conduct, the other in another; both wish to be safe. One prefers security and the other things of life to the fame of a given risk, while the other either feels sure of both, or forgets the one for the time being, which is so far insanity, and leaves the further results of that course of conduct mere accident so far as that person is concerned; a matter as far removed from his or her responsibility as the revolving of the planets.

Let whoever finds a "courageous" act analyze it before worshiping the actor and see if it is not either the accident of insanity, or the unimperiled feat of conscious strength. In either case the thought of risk, the imperiling of the greater for the less—the only condition that constitutes risk—has no influence, and an idea of courage without danger will be much like the hero—no more. Brave revolutionists, and brave defiers of greater powers, determine ye the difference between the brave, and the foolish.

H.

Moral Motives and Egoistic Methods.

That Moralists are only *blindly* selfish people, seems paradoxical to those who have not given the subject close enough attention to dispel the moral ghost. That physical force revolutionists are generally Moralists would seem equally so. But closer observation will show that they both come from a closely related mental indolence, and that those who have outgrown the force idea and claim the moral, do so more through not having scrutinized it as they have that of physical force, than to any consistency between moralism and educational methods. For it follows that if a thing is "right," as morality holds it is, there is no reason for not *making* people do it, as force advocates propose. On the other hand the upholder of force would not think of compelling a thing that was not "moral." Both are based on emotionalism, and consequently neither will take the trouble to trace conduct to its source and look for the remedy there, but slashes away at the surface without regard to cause and effect or consistency.

An all-around sample of this degree of mental penetration, is "T," of the "Individualist," who uses heavily of its editorial space and writes all its editorial nonsense. In the number of May 10, of that paper this writer in an article upholding force, is in a sense, an Egoist, and says:

> The public is nothing to me. I agree with Vanderbilt when he remarked "the public be damned." If they are on my side I will help them, if not, so much the worse for them. The person for whom I am fighting is myself...

Whether it is a policy for self-aggrandizement through pretended love for the welfare of others, or a real "change of heart," the reader may judge, but in the number of June 16, in evasively attacking the Egoistic position the same writer falls dead in love with the public, and says:

So the social question is not one of intelligence, primarily, but of morality. It is not as essential to teach men, as to mould their characters so that the sight of happiness in others gives them pleasure; so that they will be more careful not to infringe on the rights of others, than to be always on the lookout lest others curtail their liberty. Afterwards we must have intelligence to tell us *how* to accomplish these things. But only after morality has made us desire to do them.

It is not stated why Moralists, in strict accordance with this theory, do not take pleasure in the happiness of monopolists, nor why physical force is required, unless it be to do the moulding with, in absence of the intelligence which "need not apply" until men have had a dose of morality. The above remarkable conclusion was deduced from the premises that intelligence "gives us the power to do what we want to do," and that "if you give a man who lives off the labor of others more intelligence he can do so more effectually"; hence morality to cause him to use it for others. If intelligence will give us power to do what we want to or even tend to give such power, it has occurred to some persons that intelligence has a tendency to get around among other men as soon as the preaching of religion is abandoned, in which case it would not depend so much on the labor robber's desire to rob, even though he had no "morality," as it would on whether these laborers would permit him to do so. It is the peculiar doctrine of Egoism that as men are built, they are better adapted to understand and attend to their own desires than their neighbors are, and that self-defense can be more safely depended upon than generosity. It has occurred to Egoists that a very selfish person would naturally desire his neighbors to serve him before themselves, and that the sentiment is fathered by the *blindest* selfishness; *so* blind that it cannot see that this very sentiment gives it away.

Individual consciousness being somewhat subjective, has a tendency to forget the interests of other consciousnesses, which it can know or care little about. Separately organized beings must, from that very fact, consciously or unconsciously, act from and in reference to that separate organization, whether such action results in mutual interest or otherwise. It follows that under this absolute condition of being, equality of intelligence alone can bring equality of conditions. And the appealing to the native selfish instinct of the individual by causing his mind to dwell so intensely upon the idea that something is to be or should be done for him, that he forgets that this requires the same from him, and that nothing is thereby gained, prevents an approximate equality of intelligence, which permits the crafty to become robbers of labor, and makes these Moralists their most useful though unconscious tools. Hence Egoistic intelligence, against Moralism —religion. H.

An Example of Privilege's Pets.

Two more San Leandro vegetable men were arrested this morning for selling wares from their wagons. Officer Curtis made the arrests and accused the men with obstructing the streets. They deposited $20 bail each and were released. The arrests are being made at the instigation of the Eleventh street produce dealers, who assert that their business is greatly interfered with by these wagon peddlers, who go from house to house.—Tribune.

It is amusing to witness the assurance with which the municipal authorities pretend to do one thing while they are really doing another. This little incident above quoted is very thought-provoking, and clearly illustrates the falsity of the claim that protection of the weak is the function of government. The spirit and intention of the arrest of these men were to prevent them from selling fruit on the streets, while the charge of obstructing the streets was only a technical point to make the officers secure, as is shown by the following remarks of one of the privileged produce dealers of Oakland: "The question came up some time ago as to what could be done to rid ourselves of these peddlers, and the City Attorney and the Chief of Police said they could only arrest them for obstructing the streets. The nuisance had been carried so far that something had to be done to protect ourselves. That is why these arrests were made."

Now, mark you, these arrests were made at the instigation of the Eleventh street produce dealers, "whose business was greatly interfered with," and it was one of these men who said "something had to be done to protect ourselves." It was not the people of Oakland who desired protection, but those men whom the government had granted the privilege of monopolizing the produce trade. A more direct example is not needed to show that it is privilege that the law protects instead of the weak. Back of it all lies the monopoly in money, but more directly bearing upon this instance is the fact that by paying a high license these men buy the privilege of having the efforts of the police and other officers directed in their behalf. The government must protect them or it will not get the boodle. The San Leandro men were not even violating any of the city ordinances so as to attract the attention of the authorities; it was only those who were in the same business that were interfered with. If one of the peddlers had requested the authorities to arrest all of the other peddlers because they were "interfering with his business," they would probably have arrested him for a lunatic; and yet, if the real object of the police force is to look out for and protect the poorer and weaker portion of the people it would have been in place for them to have ascertained which was the poorest and weakest man in the crowd and given him their protection, but instead the strongest and richest men of all were the ones protected. The source of the injustice is easily traceable to the privilege granted by the licenses given to the produce dealers. If all unlicensed competition could not be prohibited the licenses would be of no avail; for where there is equal opportunity there is no privilege. If these produce men would cease to pay the tribute to the government they would at once cease to receive its protection, for it is by virtue of this tribute that it is given them. In open competition with opportunities equal the results of labor would of necessity distribute equally among the laborers in proportion to their capacity. But where government steps in and interferes with competition by granting privileges the results of labor as inevitably drift into the hands of those privileged as snow drifts into huge piles under a heavy wind, while other spots on the ground are bare. E. C. Walker said: "One must see, if not totally blind, the giant and ghastly form of Privilege in shadowy outline behind the millionaire. Privilege it is that robs labor of his pittance and gives it to the fortunate pets of the State." In this instance the outlines grew very distinct. G.

The Philosophy of Egoism.

III.

Egoism is (1) the theory of will as reaction of the self to a motive; (2) every such reaction in fact. This double definition is in accord with the usual latitude due to the imperfection of language, in consequence of which an identical term covers theory, individual fact, and mass of facts. I apprehend that in making this fundamental definition I shall have provoked the dissent of some readers well enough grounded in mental philosophy to perceive that on accepting the definition they must speedily consign any claim for an unegoistic philosophy to the realm of mental vagaries. They will accuse me of begging a question in the definition; but I cannot wish to lay down a definition less fundamental than that which will be found sufficiently comprehensive and exact in every relation of rational motive and resulting volition and action. When I shall have done justice to "Altruism" it will be seen that there is here no begging of any question. The alternatives which the "Altruists" propose may accord with such of their own conceptions as they wish to term "Egoism," with which, however, I have no complicity.

By "the self" I mean the living person or animal, as recognized by the senses and consciousness, and not by any mysterious, intangible entity or supposed entity,—"soul," "mind," or "spirit."

By "motive" I mean any influence,—sight, sound, pressure, thought or other energy,—operating upon the self, and thereby causing a change in the self, under which process it reacts to seize what contributes to its satisfaction or to repel or escape from what produces or threatens its discomfort or undesired destruction.

If my definition be imperfect, the gap is in omitting to mention reflex action together with will. I regard reflex action as probably connected with a species of will in the nerve centers (and in other plastic matter in the lowest animals). However this may be, reflex actions are not subject to serious dispute in any speculative moral aspect. The omission, therefore, if any, would concern the exhaustiveness of the definition, not its quality. But the merit of a definition is not in its exhaustiveness; it is in drawing the line at the right place. As I do not propose further defining "will," I will just say that reflex action being granted to be in effect self-regarding, all that remains to be done in order to universalize, according to these views, the recognition of the Egoistic theory, is to establish all determinations to voluntary activity as reactions, plus consciousness in the brain, like reflex actions without it. Any controversy against the Egoistic theory will rage along the line of voluntary action; hence that part of the line of Egoism is all that is essential to be put into a definition. But if I have omitted reflex action in (1) the theory, I have not ignored it in (2) "such reaction in fact," for "such" refers to the self.

Consulting convenience, I have written "the self" whether meaning apparently the whole co-ordinated energies of the self, or the attracting and repelling powers of any organ or member thereof. Probably never were the whole energies of any animal exerted at once under the stimulus of any motive or combination of motives; hence the common expression is an exaggeration.

A course of reading in history, philosophy, and science, especially standard literature on evolution, together with personal observation of animal, including human life, will gradually convince any intelligent person that all voluntary acts, including a certain class of acts popularly but erroneously called nonvoluntary, are caused by motives acting upon the feeling and reason of the Ego, and that the reaction of the Ego to a motive occurs as surely according to the Ego's composition and the motive as does any chemical reaction; that the only difficulty for our understanding is in the complexity of motive influences (motives) and composition of the subject acted upon. To avoid this conclusion the dogmatists have spoken of motive as if it were something self-originating in the thoughts. Plainly, motive is any influence which causes movement. There must be a cause for every thought as well as every sensation. That cause must affect the Ego, and the Ego cannot but react if affected,—therefore according to the character of the motive and the manner and degree in which the Ego is affected in any of its parts, otherwise there would be no nature, no continuity of phenomena. In short, man in everything is within the domain of nature; that is, the regular succession of apparently self-correlating phenomena.

A motive planted in the Ego (that is to say in the self) may be compared to a seed planted in the ground. Assuming that it germinates, the commonly observed effect is an upward growth of stalk and fruit, analogous to voluntary action; but I have defined Egoism by reference to the spring of such action rather than by reference to the action as phenomenon, for a reason which will be understood by following out the analogy. Beside the upward growth there is a formation of root. The stalk of some plants may be repeatedly cut off, but while the root is alive there is the probability of another upward growth. This is most generally the case with young plants. Though mental analysis should reduce will to a mere abstract term of convenience for an imaginary link between motive and act, and whether or not volition becomes differentiated to bear a more precise and active sense, it is necessary to have a conception correlating renewed activities with former ones, as perceived in repetition or in series, without the planting of new seed. This is found not in the simple and familiar illustration of seed lying without germinating for some time, but in the invisible growth beneath the surface, supplying energy and determination to forms which repeatedly appear and then take various directions accordingly as they encounter obstacles.

Tak Kak.

The proper work of policemen is to protect property and life against thieves and murderers and, perhaps, to answer questions for the information of persons who wish to get about town, and to assist women and children in crossing streets. This work they perform to a certain extent, and should have credit for it, but all the good they accomplish is greatly overbalanced by the harm they do in their illegitimate capacity of armed retainers of the ruling classes. —Hugh O. Pentecost.

Selfishness versus Unhappiness.

While it is true that we are always intent upon our own happiness, it is equally true that we are forced to devote much of our time and energy toward reducing our unhappiness. In our efforts to lessen our pains it seems sometimes as if our motives were altruistic. As for instance where one rushes into danger to save another from injury or death at the peril of his own life. But to be more specific, let us suppose a case: We shall imagine for instance a father and little daughter standing on the deck of a ship as it plows the ocean. By some accident the child loses its balance and falls overboard. The cry of the child pierces the father's heart and instantly renders him frantic, and he jumps overboard to save his precious child. But before the great ship can be stopped and boats lowered the father and child have been lost to the sight of the passengers. They have sunk beneath the waves, yet the boat's crew row back heroically to the place where they were supposed to be. But the search is in vain.

The act of the father in this case might be called unselfish or altruistic. Let us see. When his child fell into the ocean the father's heart was instantly filled with agony. His suffering was unendurable. He *must* do something. He is no longer self-possessed. He is driven by the storm of emotion to act, and the only thing to be done seems to him, is to plunge into the water after his child. His judgment and reason did not weigh and balance motives and the probabilities of success. It was uncontrollable feeling that moved him to act. He knew well enough that he could not swim a single stroke. One moment's thought would have told him that he was plunging into the jaws of death, as there was no prospect of his saving the child.

"Did he not love his child?" Yes. "Was it not because of his love of her that he sprang into the ocean after her?" No. The love of his child was the *occasion*, but not the *cause*. His unbounded affection produced agony and despair, and he could not control them; they controlled him. He could not live in such torture, and insane as was his act, it was the only one that promised *relief*. The imperative demand for less agony was the *cause* of his act. The love of his child was the cause of his agony, and the agony was the cause of his jumping into the water after her. The love of the child then was only an *indirect* cause, the *direct* cause was his *own* suffering. His action was obviously egoistic, and not altruistic. He could not endure the pain. He must have less pain, and in his momentary insanity no other thing seemed possible for him to do.

Now let us suppose another case. The father is an expert swimmer, and his child falls from a ship, the land is not far away, the water is smooth, and it is probable that the father may reach his child before it drowns and bear it safely to the shore. But in this case there is no more evidence of Altruism than there was in the other. It is not probable that a father takes into deliberate consideration his swimming abilities. In both cases the fathers acted from impulse. The love of the child caused the impulse in each case, but the direct demands of the Ego to lessen its pain were the direct cause. We love others, but never can love them better than we do ourselves.

We may die for a friend, but when we come to the last analysis we find Ego in front of *alter*. We shall find that the man who gives his life for a principle or a cause, as the martyrs are supposed to give theirs, generally gives it for himself. He gives it on his own account. He does not die for others, but dies for himself. He is built that way. And in most cases he would have but little hesitancy in making martyrs of others if he had his way. Those who have died as martyrs had the stuff in them for making others enjoy the same great blessing. Bruno did not die for others. He died because it was a fuller satisfaction to his nature to die than to live by denying the truth, by denying his manhood. He died in the enjoyment of a self-satisfaction which he could not have if he lived.

Living for others, and dying for others are fictions. Man lives chiefly for himself, and he tests all things by the amount and quality of happiness or unhappiness that he thinks they may bring to him. That he is benevolent, charitable, etc. at times there is no question, but these expressions of his good will are but safety-valves through which he puts himself on good terms with himself. He does the good things because it is a pleasure for him to do so, or because he thinks he will in some way derive pleasure in consequence of his act.

W. S. Bell.

"One Fight More--the Best and the Last."

[Auberon Herbert in his "Free Life."]

"Why have you come into existence, and what have you to say?" is the question which will be asked of us, and which it is our task to answer. We have come into existence to preach a great but simple truth, on which, as we hold, all real improvement of the human race depends. That truth is—as Mr. Herbert Spencer, above all other teachers, has taught—that a man's consent as regards his own actions is the only basis on which social relations can be happily and permanently founded; and that the struggle for power over each other, in which all classes are recklessly engaged, is a mere madness from which they have to be recalled. The gospel we preach is that force, when not carefully and exactly confined to one purpose, for which it may be used without positive wrong,—force to repel force—the force of self-defense—whenever it exists as an organized system, under which some men compel other men to accept their view of what is right or convenient, under which some men are the regulators and some the regulated, is a mere survival of barbarism, a mere perpetuation of slavery under a new name......

It is best at once to define what we mean by force. We mean the direct use of physical force, whether by tying a man's hands, or inflicting legal penalties upon him, to compel such a man to do certain things—whether good or bad things, we care little or nothing—without regard to his individual consent; and the task that we take upon ourselves is to show that all such force, outside the limits we have assigned to it, is unreasonable in its essence (that is, cannot be brought into conformity with reason or justified by an intellectual process); ......that it is opposed to the great laws under which all human improvement takes place; that it is opposed to the evolution of the race, and therefore destined in the end to involve in destruction those nations and societies who refuse to abandon the use of it; that it does not and cannot command any machinery by which it can be made a true servant of men; that tried by the test of an experience reaching over ages, it has always sooner or later, when confronted by reason ...—however great may have been the measure of the brutal license given to it—retired worsted from the field, in presence of those truer forces, whose evolutionary task it is, as knowledge grows and human nature improves, to place their heel upon its head. We know well that to emperors, popes, and cardinals, whose eyes turn fondly to an unreturning past; ......to bureaucrats built up from the stuff of pedantry; to politicians anxious to magnify their trade and calling; to those who run the great machine for their own glory and profit; to the half cunning and half self-deluded man who has never discriminated between his opinions and his interests; to the courtiers of every kind who crowd around the throne of the people; and, we will add, to many a good, worthy citizen who for want of careful thought uses the first weapon that is put into his hands, to fight evil,—to all these, force, or the idea of governing, shines in glittering colors, and seems the great prize worthy of the greatest efforts. We know all that, and we reckon with it at its true value. The army is great to look at, but it is poor and weak in itself. The emperors, the administrators, the bribers, and courtiers never have held the human mind in submission, and never will. Behind all these there are masses of men and women, misled, if you will, by many a human passion, by many a skillful appeal, by many an ingrained cause of error, yet through it all faithfully wishing to see and know the truth, and ready slowly and painfully to follow it, when sight and knowledge shall come to them. Were it not for this desire for truth, which neither passion, nor ignorance, ...can destroy, the world would be indeed in evil plight. We cannot deny that, since the days of Roman empire, never did governing force appear to hold all nations so closely in its grasp as today; and yet for all that, we believe, never were the days of its dominion so certainly numbered, never was the new reformation, which will break up the great governing machines of the world and give freedom to every individual to possess and direct his life in his own fashion, so distinctly within human view. "But will you take no account of that greatest of all forces, State Socialism?" may be the involuntary exclamation of our readers, as they hear us speak in such terms of the ultimate rejection of governing force. "The emperors, bureaucrats, politicians, may be passing from us, like pale ghosts overtaken by daylight, but the real enemy, State Socialism, is only now beginning to find and develop its immense powers." True, State Socialism is our real enemy, the real perfected outcome of governing force. For years and for years the kings and their governments and the classes have played with force; until at last, today, the grim image of a perfect force-system, perfect from its main lines down to the smallest detail, has been born in the minds of men and is greeted with enthusiasm by millions of those, who find in it their new hope. We can see—who cannot see?—the power that this new idea is exercising upon men. Swiftly and steadily over the whole world the shadow of the evil thing grows and deepens; and men rapturously pray to it to come speedily and fall upon them, just as in old days tribes smitten by their neighbors prayed to some great conqueror to come and take them for his own. Yet knowing all this, knowing that the advance of State Socialism may sweep with the violence of a hurricane through this country, and through other countries, knowing that for a time it may even overpower the resistance of sane men, we neither fear it nor shrink from it, but only welcome it. Why? Because State Socialism is the last great bribe of the worshippers of force; the last great stake which they have to place upon the world's table. Because the race has to live through this great final temptation, this great master-delusion, as it has lived through many other temptations and many other delusions. Because it is only after force has offered all it can offer those who live the hardest lives, and that offer has been contemptuously rejected, that force itself will sink down to those lower depths of impotence and slave's estate which wait for it...... The hour of our temptation is before us, and we must neither shrink from it nor fear it. We have broken the force of kings; we have broken the force of churches; we have yet to break the force that pretends to be of the people and speak in their name. To all men and to all nations it is reserved at some moment of their lives to climb the high mountain and see the fair things of the world spread out before them, and to know that such fair things may be their own, if they will only fall down and worship the false guide that stands at their side. On the peak of that mountain the peoples of the world now stand. Never was a seemingly richer show of fair things offered to those who would fain be at rest after toil and in safety after danger. Lands and cities, the workshops throbbing with energy, the palace with its dainty pleasures, sheltering all that the mind of man has planned and his hand executed,—all these shall be theirs, on the one condition that they shall fall down and sanctify power, sanctify the right of some to take from others, sanctify the right of some to regulate according to their passing will every faculty and every act of others; on the condition that they shall deny and tread under foot that right which is is inextinguishable and inalienable from manhood, the right of each to act and think for himself, the right to use his faculties for his own benefit and according to his own liking, the right to buy, to sell, to exchange the product of those faculties without let or hindrance, the right to live in a free world where each constructs happiness or unhappiness for himself, and in which none is the mere atom in the ordered and regulated crowd.

...... Until the love of liberty has grown strong enough and pure enough to reject the gifts of State Socialism it cannot be the guide and mistress of men.

Henrik Ibsen's Habits, Work, and Opinions.

Henrik Ibsen, as characterized by Walter Fren Lord, in the "Nineteenth Century," is a solitary man. For twenty-five years he has lived in self-imposed exile from his native country. No lands call him master; no household calls him its head. In his wanderings over Europe he goes in no society, and in his many temporary abodes he takes nothing with him that he calls his own, A friend charged with messages to him in Rome could only find him after much patient searching, and though well known by many by sight, he has no intimate friends.

> I live to myself (he says), without friends. Friends are a costly indulgence; they lay on us obligations of speech or silence, like parties in politics. I believe in no such obligations. I belong to no party and wish to belong to none. I will sacrifice my feelings to the claims of no organized mass, be it Party, Society, or State. From our early youth we are all brought up to be citizens instead of human beings; but we belong in reality to humanity rather than to the State. The expression of our own individuality is our first duty, not its subordination to the interests of the community. I, at least, have no talents as a citizen, the leader of a school, or a member of a party; and there must be thousands like me.

Concerning his manner of working, Ibsen says:

> When I am writing, I must be alone; if I have the eight characters of a drama to do with, I have society enough; they keep me busy: I must learn to know them. And this process of making their acquaintance is slow and painful. I make, as a rule, three casts of my dramas, which differ considerably from each other. I mean in characteristics, not in the course of the treatment. When I first settle down to work out my material, I feel as if I had got to know my characters on a railway journey; the first acquaintance is struck up, and we have chatted about this and that. When I write it down again, I already see everything much more clearly, and know the people as if I had stayed with them for a month at a watering place. I have grasped the leading points of their characters and their little peculiarities, but I might yet make a mistake in important points. At last, in the final cast, I have reached the limits of my acquaintances: I know my people from close and lasting intercourse; they are my trusted friends, who have no surprises in store for me; as I see them now, so shall I always see them.

Ibsen's fame rests largely on his social dramas, in which the revolutionary aspirations of the masses now agitating the world attain artistic expression. His position in relation to the burning question of the times may be gathered from a letter he wrote to Georg Brandes, in which he says:

> The State must be abolished. In a revolution that would bring about so desirable a consummation I should gladly take part. Undermine the idea of the commonwealth, set up spontaneity and spiritual kinship as the sole determining points in a union, and there will be attained the beginning of a freedom that is of some value. Changes in the form of government are nothing else than different degrees of trifling,—a little more or a little less absurd folly.

And from a speech to a club of workmen at Drontheim, in which he said:

> Mere democracy cannot solve the social question. An element of aristocracy must be introduced into our life. Of course I do not

mean the aristocracy of birth or of the purse, or even the aristocracy of intellect. I mean the aristocracy of character, of will, of mind. That only can free us. From two groups will this aristocracy I hope for come to our people,—from the women and our workmen. The revolution in the social condition now preparing in Europe is chiefly concerned with the future of the workers and women. In this I place all my hopes and expectations; for this I will work all my life and with all my strength.—Transatlantic.

A Technical Grievance Redressed.

New York, June 16, 1890.

EQUITY PUBLISHING COMPANY:—Your advertisement on last page of EGOISM for June concerning the pamphlet "Monogamic Sex Relations" discussed by "Ego" and "Marie Louise," impels me to send you expressions of disapproval for having brought that discussion before the public at large in a manner most damaging to myself and *my position.*

While you have carefully reprinted all of "Ego's" arguments on the subject, you have in a most unfair manner mutilated my own by striking out those which formed the solidest ground upholding my position.

As you describe in your advertisement, "Ego" has endeavored to charge monogamic sexual relations with all the terrible evils you describe, but I have proved, or attempted to prove that Monogamy is simply speculative, having no existence outside of our statute books, and that "Polygamy" and its inevitable correlative, "Polyandry," are the veritable conditions under which our race is propagated and the true parents of the evils of which "Ego" complains.

Comrades, why so cripple my position and damage the theory I have tried to uphold?

It is *incorrect* to advertise a discussion between "Ego" and "Marie Louise" when "Marie Louise" is but *partially* heard.

Are you then so afraid of the truth that you strangle it into silence? Your sincere comrade, MARIE LOUISE.

The "fear" and "strangling" of "truth" very readily occurs to those who find some part of their argument missing, but to intentionally attempt to suppress any real argument of such a hearty "kicker" as Marie Louise, would have been as unwise as it may prove to be for her to call public attention to bad argument unintentionally and partly through necessity omitted.

When the printing of "Monogamic Sex Relations" was commenced it was the design to publish from the "Alarm" the whole series of articles on the sex question by Ego, Marie Louise, C. L. James, and others, but when Ego's reply to Marie Louise was partly printed, sickness had so consumed the time allotted to the work that we could not complete it as at first intended. So we conceived the idea of making it a discussion between Ego and Marie Louise only, and accordingly ran hurriedly through her last article and selected such of those parts of the strongest paragraphs that referred directly to Ego and put them on the last page and a half of space that was left of the twenty-four. As will be seen, those paragraphs containing the argument the omission of which is complained of, named C. L. James directly, mentioning Ego only incidentally, and as it was awkward to have direct reference to another, in a discussion between Marie Louise and Ego, these paragraphs were left out of that discussion without duly considering their argumentative qualities. This is how she happened to be carelessly not maliciously suppressed.

As to the value of the argument it will be seen that no attempt was made to show how existing sexual relations produce the evils charged upon them in the grievance, while Ego did so show in citing the balanced electrical state of bodies in monogamic association, which is attested by medical writers in general in their advice to husbands and wives to sleep apart, as well as by the experience of thousands of those husbands and wives who have followed such advice. In view of the fact that these evils do exist, and of the reasonableness that the balanced electrical state of the body through partly perfect monogamic association does lead to many of them, it is hard to understand how a more perfect and therefore intense Monogamy would remove the evils arising from the nature of Monogamy.

By way of showing how far the tone of the grievance is justified we reprint the body of the argument omitted in the pamphlet, and will send it, along with this protest and explanation on a separate sheet, with all pamphlets sold in the future, which will rectify the matter as nearly as may be. —[PUBLISHERS.]

THE OMITTED ARGUMENT.

James says: "Whenever a nation advances to a certain point in civilization they grow feeble, and strict laws for the enforcement of Monogamy give place either to liberal laws about divorce as in America, or to disregard of marriage and its obligations as in Italy." The position of James is altogether indefensible. It is not the enfeeblement of the race which brings the necessity of liberal divorce laws or disregard of marriage obligations. It is the spirit of liberty with which progress inoculates the race. It is a phase when superstition and prejudices slacken their hold and the rights of the individual asserts itself. It is a revolution and does not prove enfeeblement more than did Luther and the reformation, or the destruction of the divine right of kings by Cromwell and Robespierre. It proves not an enfeeblement of the race, but a stronger intellectual development and a stronger insight into the science of life.

But I wish my readers to pause a moment and inquire whether our present civilization is monogamous—whether our present generation is the offspring of monogamous parents.

James says: "Our marriage laws equalize the tendencies by permitting men to be varietists while it requires women to be monogamists." Nordau says: "Out of a hundred thousand men, there would barely be one who could swear on his death-bed that he has never known but one single woman in his life." (Conventional Lies, p. 316.) Is this Monogamy? One half of the race acknowledged Polygamists, and as far as their male functions are concerned procreating polygamous children. But is this all? Must not the males have female co-respondents in their polygamous relations? I see James and Ego rush to the rescue and exclaim: "Prostitution is there." Yes—prostitution is there, appalling in its magnitude! Female prostitutes who sell themselves to male prostitutes, who buy them for the most debasing purpose. Loathsome mire into which men and women crawl while pharisaic society spreads a cloth over it and labels the very cloth itself as monogamous! But again is the acknowledged number of prostitutes adequate to meet the demands of the entire half of the male portion? We know that the number of males and females born is equal with a slight surplus of males. Here we are confronted with the hard fact that our generation is not only the offspring of polygamous fathers, making an equation of polygamous and monogamous heredity, but the monogamous section itself has to be divided into two parts pertaining to Monogamy and Polygamy (or Polyandry) respectively. Is this last division also an equation? If not, which side does overbalance the other? In short, how many women, say out of one hundred, does it require to meet one hundred polygamous men taking into consideration that we are not permitted to make eunuchs any more? It is useless to close our eyes to the terrible reality! Where shall we locate the monogamous children? How are they born? It would, indeed, be a blessing to be able to believe in spiritual incarnation as Christians do.

Monogamy in our civilization is a law, and nothing more, a dead letter by which one man having entrapped his neighbor's wife feels confident that his own wife knows the law and obeys it. Our marriage institution is anomalous in its principles. It does not unite two beings born free and equal. Man may dictate; woman must obey. Man may inflict pain; woman must forbear. Man may protect and respect, she must love. Respect a slave and love a master. What a paradox! Another demoralizing feature of our marriage institution is its indissolubility, and indissoluble it is, truly. Under our system of conventional morality no divorce can free a man, much less a woman. That fatal knot can never be untied. Powerful spider, it throws its webs and entwines our whole being. In vain do we try to burst the smothering envelope; it will not break. Under our pressure it may relax but never split open. Escape we never can; drag along the hateful burden, we ever must until worn out by the unequal struggle we sink down to die. Then death says to that legal murderer of soul and body: "Stop; thy power dares not profane the grave!" The union of the two sexes must be adjusted in accordance to the laws of nature. It is a question which is paramount to all others. From that union all good and evil flow. It is the principle of life; the first cause; the alpha of the universe. As long as it is not established on the ethics of the science of life, so long must our poor humanity groan under the chastising hand of nature...... Not until sexual union is properly adjusted can we hope for an amelioration in the race. To reform a man or woman is but a dream. External conditions may soften vulgar impulses and strengthen weak and vacillating tendencies. The moderating process, with propitious environments, will produce offsprings more and more assimilated with equitable conditions. But no perfect offspring can be produced under an iniquitous system of marriage relations. This problem is the greatest (because the highest in importance) which ever stood before the mind of humanity. But it is to be faced and grappled with cost what it may......

Conventional marriage and its laws having distorted our natural attributes, it is injudicious to judge of men and women as they are now. Give them unfettered freedom to act as their impulses bid and they will soon find the true road to happiness......

Egographs.

"Friendship ends where borrowing begins."

"We blame in others only the faults by which we do not profit."

Virtue, like piety, is a lack of experience; a pride in our ignorance.

A definition is a concise statement of how little we know about a subject.

"The wicked are preferable to the imbecile, because they sometimes rest."

The principle of conjugal happiness is a belief in nervous attacks.—Schopenhauer.

"The chain of marriage is so heavy that it takes two to carry it—sometimes three."

The easiest task is to render a service to one who may be useful to you.—Schopenh'r.

"Life is the last habit that we wish to lose, because it is the first one that we form."

"Honesty is of all things the most cunning, because it is the only thing the cunning do not foresee."

"Never discuss; you will convince nobody. Opinions are like nails; the harder you hit them the deeper they go."

The strength of Shakespere lay in the fact that he had no taste. He was not a man of letters.—Schopenhauer.

Man may love his fellow well enough to die for him; he does not love him well enough to work for him.—Proudhon.

"There are a number of people, especially in politics, who are like bottles; they have no value except that which is poured into them."

"Women who are absolutely beautiful have only that amount of modesty which is necessary to make the most of their beauty."

A reputation is a bell which no one is willing to be the first to pull. But let the wind cause it once to strike and there is a rush for the rope.—Schopenhauer.

What is due to the hearer of a clever saying is measured best by the sayer's appreciation of its appreciation. Yet he usually gives himself the whole credit.

An original maxim is cracking an old "chestnut" in phraseology so modern as to lead the thoughtless to believe it the first time it has occurred to any being.

"If the sentimental lent itself as readily as the material to chemical analysis, we should be frightened at the quantity of hatred and contempt that can be contained in the purest love."

Poetry is like a real cat catching imaginary elephants; the optical illusion of mental laziness. Yet where it produces pleasure it is as useful as existence, and a great saving of elephants as well as exertion of cat.

Evolution is the seine of experience dragging the sea of time, and the ever present generation the fish of the future ones. Fortunate will it be thus to be a fish and swim away to the north pole when the earth takes its "third motion" flop.

"What is a coquette? A woman who causes one, or several men to suffer without giving them anything. What is a man who can be made to suffer by a woman from whom he receives nothing? He is a simpleton. Why, then, despise coquettes, and where is the harm when a heartless woman destroys a headless man?"

There is always one person that you cannot hope to convince in discussion, that is the person with whom you are discussing. It is only the hearers, or better still, readers of such discussion who are susceptible to the logic of a position. If there is no third party to benefit by a discussion it is lost time so far as proselyting is concerned.

Sacrifice! I deny sacrifice: it is a mysticism. Talk to me of *debt* and *credit*, the only criterion in my eyes of the just and the unjust, of good and evil in society. To each according to his works, first; and if, on occasion, I am impelled to aid you, I will do it with a good grace; but I will not be constrained. To constrain me to sacrifice is to assassinate me.—Proudhon.

Indolent imagination combines known substances contrary to experience and sees a silver lake and golden sky, which pleases for a moment like another dream. Analytic imagination combines known substances contrary to known combination and produces an invention that pleases long and serves mankind throughout the ages. Both are different degrees of intensity of the same faculty. Which will you be content with.

To what uses may the laws of our country be put! Last Sunday the female members of two baseball clubs were arrested for playing ball at Danville, Ill., and charged with disturbing the peace. The women had advertised the game, and when it came off two thousand Danvillains were present to be disturbed. The arrest is a great outrage. Women have as good a right to play ball as men, on Sunday or any other day.—"Freethought," June 14.

Several men who within the past few weeks became murderers in order to vindicate their honor have been acquitted by San Francisco courts. As a natural result murders of the same kind grow more frequent. Last Monday Michael Conlin shot his wife because she drank liquor. Conlin is a drinker and was intoxicated when he did the shooting, yet he is more than half justified by the press of this city, and the "higher law" is likely to acquit him. All these tragedies spring from the mistake which men make that wives are their property and subject to their will and correction.—"Freethought," June 14.

Egoism

Vol. I.—No. 4. SAN FRANCISCO, CAL., AUGUST, 1890. Price, Five Cents.

Pointers.

The consolation of the ignorant is their ignorance of that ignorance.

Quite a number of dudes are wearing the Jenness-Miller skirtlet or divided skirt, or something very much like it on the streets of both this city and Oakland.

In the "Twentieth Century" of July 24, Mr. Pentecost asks to be joined in demanding the cessation of all restrictions against the issue of money. The effort made in that direction in this number of EGOISM should be gratifying to him as well as suggest a go and do likewise.

It is the fashion on this coast for women to wear dresses with the sleeve of the neck rolled far down. This does not indicate, however, that the same parties will likely roll up the sleeves of their arms for the purpose of doing their equal share of production. There is a wide difference in the function that follows the rolling of the different sleeves.

If you don't "fall" in love with anybody but yourself, and love wisely enough to do it well you have the advantage of the situation, for the object of your affection will never die or forsake you while you live, and when you die you will not miss it. There is a volume of philosophy in the idea, besides it dispenses with oppressive obligation, sacred duty, faithfulness, and a lot of such inconvenience unnecessary to social commerce.

Being under the impression that Auberon Herbert was an Anarchist, we predicted in the July number of this paper that his new journal, the "Free Life," would be a strong standard bearer for Anarchism in England. This was a little early. It turns out that "Free Life" is not an Anarchist paper, but only a kind of Spencerian half-breed. "Liberty" has taken it and that class in hand, and will bring them around if there is any such thing possible.

Comrade Parse, of San Diego, secured over a hundred signatures for the release of Moses Harman, among which were two men who were once Anthony Comstock's neighbors. Although one of them was a professing Christian, and loved Liberalism very little, he promptly signed the petition as a rebuke to Comstock, whom he characterized as "a contemptible puppy," without, as Comrade Parse remarks, intending to slander the puppy. Being acquainted with him, neither of the men have any use for Comstock.

A majority that rules without voting.—The silent majority of the graveyard. The dead past rules us with an iron hand. Its creeds, laws, monopolies customs tastes conceptions, ideals, and prejudices are the tyrants of our time, and they get there. It makes crime out of the most spontaneous and harmless acts; it has deeded the earth to individuals and their heirs forever, while the great mass of mankind are born without where to lay head or set foot; it bound us to contracts which enslave us as effectually and cruelly as a master's lash; it dictates the conditions on which the pleasures of love may be enjoyed, and what we may print, read, talk, and do; it makes us amenable to all these exactions in which we had no more voice than the dogs in the streets have in the cruel ordinance that blows out their brains for not wearing a tag which it is not in their power to procure or know of. We are the slaves of the ghost of dry bones and dust.

EGOISM's tardiness this month is due to running an edition of a pamphlet from the type of the article on money by Alfred B. Westrup, which occupies so much of the space of this number. It is, however, well worth the space, and it is earnestly hoped every reader will carefully read, and study its contents till thoroughly acquainted with the idea, for in a general appreciation of that principle lies the only possibility of industrial freedom, and its propagation depends on being understood and talked of. We can only reach our readers, they must enlist their acquaintances' interest, and these that of others till all are reached before it can be a power for relief. It is a matter that can be presented to all, regardless of religious or political bias, as it is written in a manner that appeals directly to the reason. For the purpose of spreading the light we will furnish the pamphlet to our subscribers at 60 cents per dozen. The retail price is 10 cents. It contains 21 pages printed on good paper from leaded Long Primer type, and will be ready to mail by the time orders from this notice reach us.

The most tyrannical monarchical government of the age, and the most democratic are at one in sex superstition; the former entirely suppressed Tolstoi's "Kreutzer Sonata," and the latter has excluded it from its mails, being as far as its present provisions will reach. But its fanatical chief executive has recommended such legislation as is necessary to compete with Russia. This should be an excellent object lesson for the believers in the "free institutions" of majority rule, on the nature of authority. There are yet two steps to be taken before a consistent level of majority prejudice is reached; one is to suppress all but popular religious publications and the republican and democratic newspapers, and the other is to prohibit the tell-tale inscriptions on tombstones. With this protection women could suffer and die to their hearts' content under the heel of forced maternity and monogamic depletion, and there would be no one to rebuke the holy murders of sacred institutions, nor record to show their extent. Benj. R. Tucker prophesied with mathematical accuracy when he said an unsuccessful effort to extend liberty of discussion would precipitate an onslaught along the entire line. Verily, the Dark Age of sexual superstition is upon us.

Frank M. Coburn, who in a letter to "Freethought" last week declared himself in fact a Nationalist, proposes some measures which I do not indorse. For instance, he says he would have all the churches converted into lecture halls, but he does not explain how that can be done. The churches belong to the people who built them, and however desirable it might be to have them converted, there is no way of effecting that end. I would propose as a substitute the conversion of the members, which can be done by inducing them to read "Freethought." Mr. Coburn would stop all immigration of laboring people. I would not. Foreigners do many kinds of work that I would not like to do. Some of them likewise surpass Americans in skill, and we can learn much of them. Besides, they might desire to live in America, and we should give to other human beings all the rights that we claim for ourselves. "I would have protection for those industries where there is competition of cheap labor in Europe," says Mr. Coburn. By which he means, I presume, that at every port he would station a number of licensed pirates, called custom house officials, with authority to forcibly seize and levy upon the property of passengers. Thus Mr. Coburn would exclude the poor entirely, and not admit those possessing goods until he had reduced them as nearly as practicable to the estate of those excluded. This seems to me to be a violation of the requirements of common courtesy. It is our duty to conduct ourselves like gentlemen toward those who have never injured or offended us. Argues Mr. Coburn: "It must be either right or wrong to sell liquor. If right, the license should be no more than any other business. If it is wrong, it should be stopped," presumably by law. I have come to the conclusion that we should be cautious about resisting by force anything that is not imposed by force. Under Mr. Coburn's rule somebody might remark that if the business of the Freethought Publishing Company is right it should be licensed; if not right, it should be suppressed. Only those having a physical majority on their side can afford to take Mr. Coburn's positions.—George Macdonald in "Freethought."

EGOISM

Issued Monthly at Fifty Cents a Year

—BY—

EQUITY PUBLISHING COMPANY,

Post Office Box. 1678, San Francisco, California.

Entered as Second Class Mail Matter.

The Orthodoxy and Tyranny of Moralism.

The spirit of Moralism is that of vicarious atonement. It demands that one shall suffer or be inconvenienced for another; that the duty of service to another is the debt of an occasion to render it, and the position of receiving it is in itself a receipt in full. It denies total depravity in affirming the possibility of moral conduct through conforming to prescribed rules, yet straightway affirms the depravity of mankind in its spontaneous, impenitent conduct, by requiring an abandoning of such conduct to follow the rules describing a "perfection" which the doctrine of total depravity contrasts with this conduct.

Like all other phases of orthodoxy it has an indefinable God; in this case it is the metaphysical personality of "society," in the name of which it enunciates its dogmas, and by the authority of which it appeals to the ostracism of popular ignorance as a hell with which all insubordination is threatened, and into the merciless fires of which rebellious subjects are cast. Like the agent of the universal God, if its agent is asked for a reason why, he appeals to the never-failing selfish instinct (which it is his duty to condemn), by pointing to the "necessity of serving others if you would yourself be served in turn." If this proposition as a general principle for universal application be analyzed, and it is shown that faithfully carried out there is no gain in such service, since there would only be servers enough to go once around, to say nothing of the disadvantage of one not knowing what another needs or wants as well as each knows his or her own wants, and from the standpoint of the alleged utility there is nothing in it, he can only reassert the duty of "duty" to others. When it is shown that like all conduct, "duty to others" is based entirely on self-regarding motives, and that his idea arises from taking the visible results of a giver's sympathy as an index to his motives, while the invisible, but real cause of his conduct is a subjective one, an attempt to escape the mental torture caused by the knowledge of suffering, which torture is in its turn caused by memory of personal suffering, when thus shown that his generally accepted theory is based on a misconception, he can, like his theological parents, only appeal to the "time-honored" prejudices of majorities and cry, "behold the blasphemer!" And when pressed for an intelligible idea of this social monster, he can of course no more define it or defend its claims on the grounds of equal freedom than can the agent of the theological God on a scientific basis. Yet they both flourish, and the most of the avowed enemies of the latter fondly embrace its moral offspring, while all parties are agreed upon its being just the sweetest thing out, though like other religious denominations they cannot in all respects agree as to what it is.

The absurdity of this theological ghost's tenets, however, would in itself be harmless, and call for no more than the notice of curiosity, but for the tyranny that it exercises over its victims and they over a progressive minority which, though rejecting the claims is dominated by their brute force. Teaching as it does, "duty to society," it is the justification of majority rule and all the tyranny that such rule exercises when it not only crushes the minority to the practice of the very tastes of an ignorant majority, but enables crafty manipulators in the name, and in that way through the support of the collective brute force, to enhance private interests by all the national and municipal robbery that now exists. Customhouse tax, licenses, public improvements, forced street paving, sidewalk making, and park improving, etc. are all a legal robbery of labor and the home maker for the benefit of contractors, land holders, money lenders, and official functionaries, which is the direct fruit of this moral fetich.

It is not only the basis of all this plundering machinery, but uses the force club to carry on its tyranny in social life. In sexual relations it meddlingly demands, in harmony with its doctrine of individual subordination to "society," a public announcement of the intention of lovers to exercise that function, and permits it only by the agreement of such lovers to accept monogamic association, with all its physiological depletion and mental stagnation. An open violation of this decree means confiscation of so much property and prison walls for one or both parties. Once in the solitary castle, the female is at the mercy of a master's long repressed passion and an enforced ignorance of its probable results. She must bear children until age or death relieves her. If the means of avoiding its necessity be imparted to her even, the cruel dogmas of Moralism, if not its influence on her master, forbid it; and lest in her anguish she be tempted to violate its infallible decrees, "society's" force club is invested with authority to fine and imprison any whose sympathies might tempt them to suggest a remedy. If she tires of the dragging misery and would escape, it is at the sacrifice of property, and possibly food and shelter at the start, with the uninviting prospect of poverty and this moral ostracism later, at which she usually despairs and under the iron rule of the "social good" sinks into a premature grave along with the myriads of ignorance's victims, and "decency" and "respectability" are preserved.

Not content with dominating political and social conduct, it must have a censorship over the intellectual function, lest some stronger and more analytic minds having detected its shams and absurdities, expose them and destroy its agents' mediocre prestige as Grundy priest, as well as their privilege lords' monopoly of industry's production, which this ignorance of the fundamental spring of conscious conduct keeps intact. Its more intense superstition consists in tabooing all the most important information regarding the most vital and delicate function bearing on the development of the human species. Its formal mock modesty prevents mothers generally, from instructing their children even in part, regarding the sexual function and its bearing on health, mental vigor, and the general happiness of each. And practically in no case is a full, free and exhaustive discussion of the subject permitted, but all are left to grow up under the abnormal conditions of repression and its destructive practices, with no sexual ideals save those emanating from prostitution to be wreaked on waxen figured victims in the iron cage of moral monogamy.

Thus boys grow to be men and for want of a knowledge of the delicate requirements of woman's constitution, which a free mother could impart accurately and impressively, reap ignorance's harvest of regret. Likewise girls grow into womanhood and under the powerful influence of its new impulse plunge into undreamed of responsibilities and exactions which the unreserved counsel of such a mother's experience could do much to avert and direct along the line of the longest pleasure and greatest happiness. But under the influence of prudish Moralism both gather little from sexual life save disappointed ideals, the loss of mental variety, and a false experience which usually serves only to intensify the error of a narrow creed.

The crushing grasp that it has on the minds of even theological Liberals holds starvation over the heads of their more radical publishers, while its sway over the public mind places the gaping door of the prison and the bloody club of the State in the hands of brutal prudes to silence those whose zeal causes them to face both poverty and ostracism to expose some of its more obtruding effects. It does not even wait for voluntary violation, but hires spies to decoy the sympathetic and unsuspecting into its savage clutches. H.

Hits at Heads and Hearts and Things.

Many persons are quite shocked when we say the basis of ethics is not the voice of God in the soul, not an innate moral sense, not anything of that sort, but just plain selfishness; or when we say that we have no duties to God or man, and should do nothing but seek our own happiness. But, nevertheless, any one who will carefully study the motives of his conduct will find that he does nothing that is not followed by regret except because the doing of it makes him happier than the not doing of it. People talk of their devotion to God or to their fellow-men, but there is no such thing. If men serve God or their fellowmen it is because it makes them happier to do so than not to do so.—Hugh O. Pentecost.

In the above, Mr. Pentecost shows evidence of having "caught on" again, and made close analysis of the basis of conduct, apparently loosing his grip entirely on the "innate moral sense" idea, and decides there is no such thing. But this morality fetich lurks in almost all phases of thought and is hard to shake off. In the very next number of his paper he exhibits signs of a relapse, and in the following note shows he has not given it up yet in every sense:

Under present industrial conditions it is very unwise—it is even immoral—for poor persons to have children. The children of the poor are simply products for the slave market. For poor people to have children is to bring into the world, without their consent, persons who must be slaves.

Now just how he makes it out "immoral" for poor people to have children, after he has declared there is no "moral sense or anything of the sort," I fail to see. I wonder if Mr. Pentecost considers it "immoral" for the poor overworked horse species to bring into the world colts, who must become slaves? If it is not as applicable to one animal as another it must in some way be connected with "duty" to man or God for poor people not to have children.

Of the family Mr. Pentecost says:

The husband and father should not be the head of the family. He should be simply one of the family. He and his wife should be equals in all particulars except as to their natural differences, in intellect, disposition, etc. He and his children should be friends. As for scoldings, or physical punishments, they should be unheard of in any family. And as for obedience —it should never be demanded nor practiced.

Mr. Pentecost speaks of the "family" with the same assurance that most persons use in referring to government; as though it was as indispensable as government is usually considered. He is concerned about its improvement just as governmentalists are about their institution. A real *husband*, according to Webster and common useage is a male head of a household; a manager of domestic concerns, while a wife is a *lawful* consort of a man. Mr. Pentecost as an Anarchist, cannot believe in law, but does believe, it seems, in *wives* and *husbands*, the creatures of law. And the family as such, is an authoritarian institution, a little monarchy, which Mr. Pentecost is willing to turn into a kind of voluntary association, providing it has a "husband and father" and a wife, and the father and his children are friends. But suppose the father was a friend of both mother and children but not a husband, or the mother owned the house and children and was not a wife, but an independent woman without a question about equals or fathers, would it not do just as well—better? This is a heresy, however, that Mr. Pentecost will do well not to assume publicly, if he "catches on."

Benj. R. Tucker, of "Liberty," has discovered that logic has gender, as witness his just criticism of Mrs. Stanton:

Elizabeth Cady Stanton, in an address at the annual meeting of the Personal Rights Association, held in London June 25, said: "I do not believe in compulsory education, but I do believe in free schools." That is to say, Mrs. Stanton does not believe in compelling people to educate their own children, but she does believe in compelling them to educate other people's children. This logic (pardon me, Mrs. Stanton) is truly feminine.

Eugene Macdonald holds and has published exactly the same idea regarding the school question; of what gender, then, is the logic in his case? certainly not masculine, for that would reflect unfavorably on the sex, as well as characterize Mr. Tucker's characterization.

When a person enjoys a bath; takes a drink of water; eats a palatable meal; sits in the sunshine; breathes fresh, invigorating air; inhales rich perfumes; or is relieved from a skull-splitting headache by the magnetic hand of a parent or other familiar relative, or in numerous other ways gratifies a desire or enjoys such pleasurable sensations of the nerves, it is taken in a matter-of-fact way, and no more thought of it than breathing, but when the same nervous system produces a similar pleasurable sensation through the magnetism of a less familiar person, of the opposite sex, it is "love!" with a two-line inital "l,"—an indefinable, mysterious, "high," "holy," "sacred," "serious" something, just like God. Yet, all are simple sensation, the result of a vibration. G.

The Philosophy of Egoism.

IV.

Beside individuals we encounter groups variously cemented together by controlling ideas; such groups are families, tribes, states, and churches. The more nearly a group approaches the condition of being held together by the interest of its members without constraint of one exercised over other members, the more nearly does the group approximate to the character of an Ego, in itself. Observation and reflection show that the group, or collectivity, never yet composed wholly of enlightened individuals joining and adhering in the group through individual accord, has always fallen short of the approximation which is conceivable for the group to the independent Egoistic character. The family, tribe, state, and church are all dominated physically or mentally by some individuals therein. These groups, such as they have been known in all history, never could have existed with the disproportionate powers and influence of their members but for prevailing beliefs reducible to ignorance, awe, and submission in the mass of the members.

With this explanation and corresponding allowance, the group may be spoken of as approximatively Egoistic in its character. Even when least swayed by individual members, the family, the nation, and the church are thoroughly selfy. These composite individualities, as it is the fancy of some writers to consider them, are appealed to in vain to furnish an exception to the Egoistic principle. When Jack imposes upon the ignorance of Jill or upon habits acquired during mutual aid, and Jill is too trusting to trace the transaction back to fundamental elements and calculations of mutual benefit, the matter is readily laid to Jack's selfishness, which of course lauds its victim's welcome compliance; but when the family demands a heavy sacrifice of each member, attention is mostly drawn by Moralists to the advantage of the family and the need of such sacrifices, never to the phenomenon of a ruthless form of Egoism in the family, imposing upon its members who have felt some of the advantages and then yielded to pretensions which will not bear analysis, or tracing back in an actual account of loss and gain. Thus it is said to the man that he needs a wife, to the woman that she needs a husband, and to the children that they needed parents and will need obedience from their own children by and by. On the strength of these views various sacrifices of the happiness of man, woman, and youth may be effected while they do not inquire precisely what they do need individually, and how they can get it at the least cost of unhappiness.

The family, attempting to become an Ego, treats its members as an Ego naturally treats available organic or inorganic matter. The supine become raw material. The person has the power to resign self-care and allow himself to be seized upon and worked up as material by any of the other real or would-be Egos that are in quest of nutriment and of leases of operations. The greater would-be Ego, the "social organism," reinforces the family demand with persuasion that hesitates at no fallacy, but first plies the individual with some general logic as to our need of each other, then with flattery, how it will repay him for inconvenience by praise, external and internal, all the while exerting a moral terrorism over every mind weak enough to allow it, and all to subjugate the real Ego to the complex would-be but impossible Ego. For not the good of the family, but of itself, is the object of the state and of the "social organism." The state prates of the sacredness of the family, but treats it with scant courtesy when its own interest conflicts with the family interest. The "social organism" reinforces the family against the individual and the state against the family, this already threatening the family, and obviously it will next threaten the state so far as this can be distinguished from the community; that is, the "social organism" will have no permanent use for separate nations.

But in speaking thus we should not forget that the group, or collectivity, reflects the will of some master minds, or at the widest the will of a large number under the influence of certain beliefs. Either one or two or three horses may draw a plow, and its motions will be different. The complexity of motion from three horses is certainly a phenomenon to be studied, but the way is not to disregard the elementary motive forces which form the result by their combination; and so it is with any society. Its phenomena will be according to conditions of information and to circumstances which determine the direction of personal desires. The certainty of desire and aversion as motives, founded in self-preservation, is found in the nature of organic as distinguished from inorganic existence. All desires and dislikes, acting and counteracting, make the so-called social will,—a more convenient than accurate abstraction. To make of it an entity is a metaphysical fancy. Unity of will is the sign of individuality. The semblance of a social self, apart from individuals, obviously arises from the general concurrence of wills. They could not do otherwise than run along parallel lines of least resistance, but the intellectual prism separates the blended social rays.

The church is an important group, under the theological belief. The primitive character of its dominant idea finds its complementary expression in the simple and transparent Egoism of its immediate motives. A personal ruler, judge and rewarder existing in belief, commands and threatens. The person sacrifices part of his pleasure to propitiate this master because he fears his power. Habits supervene and the investigating spirit is terrorized both by personal belief and the fear of other fear-struck believers, watchful and intolerant. The hope of heaven and fear of punishment are of the simplest Egoism. Morality on the same plane includes the fear of man and hope of benefit from man complicated with belief in reciprocal enforcement of ecclesiastical duties, and this as a duty. Becoming metaphysical it is doubtless more difficult of analysis, but this secondary or transition of mind is already disposed of as a whole by philosophy, so that the evolutionist predicts the passage of its phenomena and their replacement by positive ideas of processes. The metaphysical stage will pass away though its formulas be entirely neglected by the advancing opposition. In fact, spell-bound and mystified man is freed by courage to break off from the claim of phantasies which has succeeded to the chain of theological fear. In this progress example counts suggestively, and even demonstratively, and new habits of positive, specific inquiry give the intellect mastery of itself and of the emotions which had enslaved it.

To sum up this part of the subject, let those who preach anti-Egoistic doctrines in the name of deity, society, or collective humanity, tell us of a deity who is not an Egoistic autocrat, or who has worshipers who do not bow down to him because they think it wisest to submit; of a family which sacrifices itself to the individuals and not the individuals' hopes and wishes to itself; of a community or political or social state which departs from the rule of self-defense and self-aggrandizement; of any aggregation, pretending to permanence, that is not for itself and against every individuality that would subtract from its power and influence; of a collective humanity that is not for itself, the collectivity, though it were necessary to discourage and suppress any individual freedom which the collectivity did not think to be well disposed toward the collectivity or at least certain to operate to its ultimate benefit. Self is the thought and aim in all. Selfiness is their common characteristic. Without it they would be elemental matter, unresisting food for other growths. TAK KAK.

CITIZENS' MONEY.

[The following lecture was delivered by Alfred B. Westrup, in Chicago, and published in "Liberty," of Boston, in 1888, under the title, "The National Banking System," from which we change it to that of CITIZENS' MONEY, as better answering our purpose for propaganda work.—PUBS. EGOISM.]

Mr. George Easterly, of Whitewater, Wisconsin, has recently (1887) issued a pamphlet entitled, "Review of the National Bank System," as to how and why it should be continued.

In his preface he says: "This question of finance has received comparatively little consideration. Within the last few years the press and a few members of congress have attempted to discuss it to some extent, not always, however, with much skill. The business world, as a rule, have not given it much attention." It is strange that the experience that results in such an admission should not have prompted a more profound research than we find in his essay.

Mr. Easterly falls into the error common with most political reformers, in supposing that natural laws have nothing to do with the question; that human rights are created by and subject to constitutional provisions and legislative enactments, instead of constitutional provisions and statutes being subject to human rights.

The present or National Bank system is founded upon this idea,—that congress is authorized by the constitution to regulate the issue of paper money, and hence had the right to establish it, and that the individual must shape himself to the system thus provided.

I shall not discuss the question as to whether the constitution does or does not confer such power upon congress, for, if it can be shown that the operations of supply and demand will furnish a safer and a better money than the arbitrary system established by the State, it is but additional evidence that progress and institutions are ever at war, and that to attain the one we must sacrifice the other.

It would seem as though a "free people" would hardly have allowed such a mixture of "royal prerogative" and "infallibility" to be dressed up in a republican garb and imposed on them as "majority rule." How can a majority of the people be said to be intelligently in favor of the existing system, when as a matter of fact they are utterly ignorant of this, as well as all other systems, and do not even know the laws by which it is kept in force, much less the effect that it produces.

What right, I ask, has the State to regulate the supply of the medium of exchange we call money any more than it has to regulate the manufacture and supply of bricks, bread, cloth, or any other commodity, or how much a man may buy on credit? It was one of the "functions of royalty" when the people of this country threw off the yoke of British rule, and as the question of finance had received even less attention then than now, it was easy for the error to insinuate itself, and become a part of the constitution, that the State should supervise and regulate the coining of money; but does it necessarily follow that, because the constitution says so, therefore it is right? Suppose that after twenty years more of continued and increasing monopolies on the one hand, and poverty on the other, the people should realize that, after all, the State is powerless to effect a remedy, or that its interference is the direct cause of these evils. How shall we undo the wrong that has been done? How shall we make amends to the unfortunate victims? How shall we justify the stupidity that failed to question the dogma? What will be the anathemas of the next generation, with whom forbearance will cease to be a virtue? Let me remind my hearers that neither constitutions nor supreme benches, but JUSTICE, as voiced by the human conscience, is the court of final appeal.

The idea of the coining of money and the issue of currency by the State being borrowed from the despotism from which the people were emancipating themselves when they drove out the British tyrant; and since it is irreconcilable with the Declaration of Independence, which proclaims the right to freedom of exchange (liberty and the pursuit of happiness), how dare congress deny that right by restrictive and arbitrary legislation? If we are not to take the chances of this idea being wrong and of perpetuating the present evils in case they are caused by State interference, then we must fully investigate this question. If the business world, as a rule, has given this subject no attention now, it had given it less when the constitution was framed; hence, no one was prepared to question the wisdom of the clause in that document that relates to money; and, "as the business world as a rule has given it no attention," and "bankers are no exception to the rule," how do they know that the State should exercise this power? Mr. Easterly says: "I have talked on this subject with governors, judges, lawyers, members of congress, bankers, and business men, and almost universally, after a little conversation, hear them say, 'This is a subject to which I have not given much attention.'" How can men who have not given a subject much attention "legislate wisely" upon that subject? How does Mr. Easterly know that it is proper or that it is best for the State to control the currency?

On page 14 of his "Review" he says: "It is entirely safe to say that we have now the best currency in the world." This does not constitute an argument in favor of its continuance in view of the ignorance which he confesses is almost universal. To be the best that exists, and to be the best that can be devised, are two very different things. It can be the best that exists, and yet be very defective. Is this all the evidence he can produce to justify State control of money? How does he know that the operations of supply and demand, if allowed full scope, would not be an improvement on paternalism? The present system gives the banks control of the volume of money, "which," he says, "I admit should be obviated," but for which he gives no remedy. Before the present system came into operation, the cormorant corporation was unknown. On what, then, doth it feed that it hath grown so great, if not on the effects produced by the control of the volume of money?

In what does the best system of money consist? In the fact that its currency does not suffer discount in different parts of the country, and that it does not become worthless by failure of the bank that issued it? What other advantage has the present system? On the other hand, is not the question of the rate of interest as well as of the volume of currency vital in the consideration of a money system, and does not the present system give the rate of interest as well as the volume of currency to the control of the monopoly? Has it prevented banks from failing? May not monopoly and failure be associated in the relation of cause and effect? Of what consequence is it whether you lose a hundred or a thousand dollars by a depreciation in the purchasing power of the paper money you hold, or whether you deposit that much in the bottomless pit of a broken bank? If the State is a potent remedy, why do banks fail in spite of its supervision? The fact is that, whenever the State stops one leak, it causes two. If security to the holder of paper money and uniformity in its purchasing power are attained at the expense of low rates of interest and a sufficient quantity of the circulating medium, can we be said to have solved the problem of money and established the best system? Is there no other way of securing uniformity in the purchasing power of money than by State regulation? Can the question of security and moral obligation be settled by law? Does the State know how much money is needed? If so, how did it find it out? If it does not know, how does it presume to limit it? All these questions must be definitely settled before we can boast of having solved the problem and established the best system.

And is the intelligence that can erect these grand structures in our cities; that can annihilate time and distance by the telegraph and the telephone; penetrate yonder space and determine the size and composition of celestial bodies, their distance and their movements; that can photograph organisms that cannot be felt, or seen by the naked eye; aye, that can construct engines of war so destructive that they are afraid to use them,—is an intelligence, I say, so subtle, and a genius so profound, not capable of solving this problem. be it ever so complex? Let us boldly assume the task of contributing our best thought and earnest co-operation in so important a reform.

Mr. George Easterly believes we have now the best system of currency in the world. Mr. Britton A. Hill asserts that we must have an irredeemable money,—"absolute money,"—a money that shall depend for its acceptability upon the fiat of the State. Neither of these gentlemen seem to favor impartial investigation. On the contrary, they assert dogmatically, and then, like the attorney who has a bad case, construct an argument to justify their position. If paper money is amply secured, it needs no fiat; it will circulate on its merits. To force people to take currency that is not secured is as much a despotism as a forced loan, and is unjustifiable on any grounds whatever. In scientific analysis nothing is taken for granted. If we are to form an opinion as to any institution, we certainly must first know what is the method and object of such institution. Have we observed this course in choosing our money system?

It may be stated in general terms that the object of a money system is to furnish money; but here we are confronted with the question, "what is money? how is it defined?" We must also know what kind of money it proposes to furnish; of what material it is to be made; how it is to be issued; how it secures those who take it in exchange for commodities, and what is to be the cost to those who borrow it. First, then, as to the definition of money. The Encyclopedia Britannica gives Francis A. Walker's definition of money as follows: "That which passes freely from hand to hand throughout the community in final discharge of debt, and full payment for commodities, being accepted without reference to the character or credit of the person who offers it, and without the intention of the person who receives it to consume it or enjoy it or apply it to any other use than in turn to render it to others in discharge of debt or payment for commodities." This definition is applicable to coin as well as currency, and is acceptable so far as it goes, but it refers only to the office of money,—its function in facilitating the exchange of the products of labor or commodities.

In order to do this, money must have some qualities that are recognizable. For instance, coin may pass freely from hand to hand and purchase as much for a beggar as for an aristocrat, and so may currency, but the nature of coin is different from that of currency. It has market value at least to the extent of the quantity of metal it contains, while currency contains no market value whatever; hence its acceptability in exchange for commodities must be on other grounds than those on which coin is accepted.

Coin money is made of metal, which is a product of labor, and therefore has a market value. It is true, the natural limit to the metal and the fact that it is made a legal tender gives it an increased value artificially, but it is nevertheless market value. This is one quality. The fact that the stamp on it enables one to know how much of this market value it contains is another quality. The recognizable qualities of coin money then are, that it contains market or exchangeable value and that we are able to realize how much of this market value it contains by means of the stamp impressed upon it.

Paper money has no market value, or, to state it more correctly, the market value of the material contained in paper money is too inappreciable to be considered; but it is, or should be, a representative of market value, as is the case when it is issued in place of an equal amount of coin pledged to redeem it. I therefore define the nature of coin money to be wealth, and that of paper money to be a representative of wealth when wealth is pledged to secure those who take it. State paper money which rests solely on the promise to redeem in taxes may, I think, properly be defined as State scrip, but when, in addition to this promise, it is made a legal tender for private debts, fiat money would be a more proper definition.

Having arrived at a conclusion as to the correct definition of money, in regard to its nature as well as its office, I will now proceed with the main question,—in what does the best system of money consist?

The best system of money is the one that will furnish money made of the most suitable material; that will provide a sufficient quantity; that will afford the greatest security to those who take it; that will maintain the most unvarying uniformity in its purchasing power; that will furnish it at a just rate of interest and with the least partiality. It does not seem necessary to discuss these points, for there will hardly be any one who will dispute them. A money system that will come up to all these requirements would certainly be a most perfect one; but as to the questions, what is the most suitable material, how much is a sufficient quantity, what constitutes security, purchasing power, a just rate of interest, and impartiality in a money system, we must fully determine before we can judge of the merits of the present system or suggest a better, which is the special object of this essay.

First, then, as to the question of material. There are very few materials that are suitable for money, and, if we confine it to such products as are limited by nature, we thereby fix the limit to the amount of such product, and this, as we shall see when we come to the question of volume, is an objection. Paper, as already stated, is the material which, of all others, contains the smallest quantity of market value. It is the most convenient to carry. Its quantity is without limit. It offers greater protection against counterfeiting than any other material. It costs less than any other material to put it in the shape of money, and the wear and tear to paper money is far less in cost than that which results to coin. We have, then, in paper the best material for money that we know of.

Of the items that remain to be considered, it will be found upon reflection that volume, security, and purchasing power, are so intimately related that they must necessarily be considered collectively. To determine volume we must consider security, which is also the basis of its purchasing power. This, I think, can be readily demonstrated. What is it that makes a man's promissory note acceptable to those who sell on credit or have money to lone? Is it not the quantity of security he can furnish? Does the number of promissory notes that have already been issued in the same or other localities in itself have anything to do with the individual responsibility of each? Would not all the goods that are for sale on credit and all the money to loan be immediately disposed of if the price or rate of interest were agreed upon, without any halt in the proceedings on account of the large number of notes, and would not the only question be the same in each case,—namely, *ample security?* Now, if ample security makes the individual's promissory note good, why will not ample security make paper money good? If a certain amount of collateral, differing in quantity as it differs in kind, is good security for one paper dollar for a longer or shorter period, why would not a thousand or a million times that security be a good basis for the issue of a thousand or a million dollars in currency? Indeed, if this relative proportion of security to paper money be observed, why should there be any limit to the issue of currency? If some citizens can get money issued on collateral, why may not all citizens have the same advantage? If paper manufacturers and printers can furnish money for a certain class of security-holders, why can they not furnish money for all security-holders? If they can why is it prohibited? If they cannot, why can they not? Does the fact that some citizens borrow gold and silver certificates of other citizens on good security in any way diminish the risk of the holder of this kind of State money? Would the issue, direct to the borrower of additional similar currency, on the same security that these citizens are willing to loan their gold certificates on, in any way increase the risk to the holders of these certificates? Can this security be good collateral to loan on, and yet be poor collateral to issue on? Does the security furnished the national bank by its patrons have anything to do with securing the holders of its notes?

Let us summarize: we are considering the volume of paper money in relation to its purchasing power, and the question is: would its purchasing power be affected by the volume issued regardless of the *security that is pledged to redeem it*, or would ample security maintain its purchasing power regardless of the *volume issued?*

Let me consider for a moment what is meant by redemption, in order that the question of volume, security, and purchasing power may be fully understood. The term redemption, as it is generally applied, means the exchange of currency for coin. Specie basis means that provision is made for the exchange of currency for coin *on demand*. This is what it is said to be, but what is it in reality? In reality not more than one in five can obtain such a result; partly because there never is as much coin as there is currency, and partly because of the obstacles intentionally put in the way of accomplishing it. Nevertheless it is solemnly asserted that, unless we have specie basis, the purchasing power of paper money will not remain uniform. No wonder people do not understand the money question. It certainly takes a peculiar kind of intellect to comprehend that the stability of a currency depends upon false pretense!

But redemption of paper money, correctly speaking, means to retire it from circulation by rendering an equivalent for it; and can this not be done with any other product just as well as with gold and silver, if the money system is adapted to that end? The question to determine at this particular point of the discussion is whether redemption on demand is essential. We have seen that in practice it is a delusion, and I repeat that it is impossible; but it is well to go a step farther and inquire if it is at all necessary! Suppose that, instead of redeeming on demand, we redeem periodically. Here the question of security again comes to the surface. If, as I have already suggested, that collateral which is safe to loan money on for a certain period of time is safe to issue money on for the same length of time, and we devise a system that shall issue money direct to all borrowers who can pledge such collateral, we shall have periodical redemption instead of, possibly, no redemption at all; but which goes by the name of "redemption on demand." Gold certificates are receipts for so much gold that has been delivered to the State for "safe keeping." Would not currency issued on other products of labor which have been delivered for safe keeping, or pledged by mortgage to be redeemed at a specified time not to exceed one year, be practically receipts for other products, just as the gold certificate is a receipt for gold? And if the amount of paper money issued on any particular product did not exceed the amount that money-lenders would be willing to loan on such product in gold certificates, would not such currency be as good a circulating medium as are the gold certificates? The answer that a large number of people are likely to make to this reasoning is that gold does not fluctuate in market value as much as other products do. But such an answer shows a disposition, on the part of the individual who makes it, to avoid the trouble of thinking. Laziness is one of the contending forces of nature, and it seeks the line of least resistance. It is easier to raise an objection without thinking than it is to reflect long enough to know whether the objection is well taken; and if we wish to guard against being in the wrong, we should beware of its tendency. It is supposed that gold does not fluctuate in market value as much as other products; but even if this were true, it would only be an additional argument why currency should be issued on other products as well as gold. If the artificial advantage established by the legal tender act is withdrawn from gold, and all other products (always excepting those that are too perishable) may be made use of as well as gold as a basis for the issue of currency, there can be no fluctuation in market values, except such as is caused by the *uncontrolled* supply and the *natural* demand of each product; and with sufficient margin over the amount of paper money issued to allow for possible shrinkage in value, the fluctuations of any one product can have no effect whatever on either the purchasing power of such currency or the market value of other products, because the manipulation of market values by speculators will be impossible.

We have now considered the question of the volume of currency in relation to its purchasing power and security to those who take it. Its purchasing power is determined by the means of redemption: the borrower is compelled to get the amount he borrowed from the institution that issued it, from those who now hold it. He can do so only by selling something he has that they want, or by accepting it in payment of debt. He cannot depreciate this paper money and get it back on better terms, for that would be the same thing as selling his commodity for more than its market value, and this he is not able to do, if free trade prevails, because of competition; others will undersell him. Moreover, there is no more anxiety about this currency in the minds of those who hold it than there is with money-lenders about the mortgages they hold on good real estate on which they have loaned money only to the extent of one-third of its market value; hence, there will be no effort to get rid of this currency, except in the ordinary course of trade. We are, therefore, justified in concluding,—that in the issue of currency, on ample security actually pledged to redeem at a definite period, a provision is made whereby it can be redeemed by *compelling the borrower* to return an equivalent for it at the expiration of that period. Therefore, by such a system, the purchasing power of currency *can be maintained regardless of the volume issued.*

We now come to the question of interest. What is a just rate of interest? In order to answer this question intelligently, we must know something of the cost of issuing currency. We must also have a clear and a correct idea of the nature of the transaction that takes place when currency is issued directly to the borrower who pledges collateral. We will therefore first make some inquiries in this direction. There is the paper and the printing on the paper that is to be used as money; compensation for services to the clerks, officers, and directors of the institution; the rent, fuel, stationery, etc.; and the expense attendant upon taking care of the security. Colonel Greene, in his pamphlet called "Mutual Banking," gives it as his opinion that one-half of one per cent. per annum would cover all these items in the system he proposed. Of course it would depend on the amount issued. An institution that issued one hundred millions of dollars could cover its expenses with one-half of one per cent. better than an institution that issued only one million. In the former it would amount to five hundred thousand, in the latter it would be only five thousand dollars. According to information received from the comptroller's department at Washington, it has cost about one-fifth of one per cent. to make the paper money furnished the national banks for the last ten years.

This fact gives some idea of how far a half million of dollars would go toward paying the expenses of a bank of issue. From the information I have gathered and the calculations I have made, I am willing to risk the statement that a bank that issued fifty millions of dollars could pay all its expenses with less than one-half of one per cent. per annum; and when such institutions as Colonel Greene proposed become the source of currency instead of the State, they certainly will issue as much as that in all large cities, and in some many times that much. But the question under consideration not only involves the item of cost of issuing this currency, but also as to whether the borrower should be called upon to pay more than cost.

Let us analyze the transaction, to see what it is that actually takes place when an individual borrows paper money on good security of which he is the owner. Paper money we have defined to be a representative of wealth. Whose wealth does it represent? It represents the *wealth which has been pledged* to secure those who may take it until it is wanted again by the owner of the wealth in order that he may get his property (wealth) released from pledge by returning it to the institution that issued it. We may define the transaction, then, by saying that the borrower *makes use of his credit;* for he assumes an obligation and pledges his property as a guarantee that he will fulfill that obligation. He obtains printed pieces of paper (which might, not inappropriately, also be called certificates of credit) which are given him in exchange for his promise to pay back the same amount at a definite period, which promise he guarantees he will fulfill by pledging collateral in the form of some product, deposited, if movable, or mortgaged if immovable. Now, if the borrower pays the cost of the transaction, he in no way makes use of that which belongs to another; and as no one is entitled to compensation for that which he does not furnish, may we not conclude that a just rate of interest would be the actual cost of issuing paper money?

Finally, we come to the question of impartiality. What do I mean by the issue of paper money with the least partiality? A money system that proposed to issue currency on any product except gold and silver would certainly be regarded as very partial by the bullionists; but why is not the system equally partial which issues currency only on gold and silver? Obviously, impartiality in the issue of paper money means that any product of labor may be a basis for the issue of currency, which would not, from the nature of the product itself, involve a risk to the holder of the currency issued on such product.

Let us now review the various conclusions we have arrived at.

We have concluded that the definition of paper money is, a representative of wealth as regards its nature. That the best system of money is the one that will furnish money made of the most suitable material, that material being paper; that will provide a sufficient quantity, a sufficient quantity being such an amount as will afford a representative of wealth to all those who can pledge wealth as collateral; that will afford the greatest security, such security being only attainable by pledging actual wealth in sufficient quantity, deposited if movable, mortgaged if immovable; that will maintain the most unvarying uniformity in its purchasing power, the paper money that is best secured varying the least in its purchasing power; that will furnish it at a just rate of interest, a just rate of interest being cost; that will issue it with the least partiality, so that, to obtain it, one must pledge collateral in the form of wealth, not through favoritism or influence.

Now compare these conclusions with the present system. The present system, like all its predecessors, fails to provide the means whereby property owners may use their property for purposes of credit without submitting to the tax called interest, imposed by the monied class. A single illustration will demonstrate the truth of this assertion. An individual who has property, but no money, wishes to buy some commodities. If he buys them on credit, he has to pay more than if he buys for cash. If he borrows money giving a mortgage on his property, in order to buy for cash, he is confronted with interest. It is either interest on the merchandise or it is interest on the money; and this interest is enforced by prohibiting the issue of the currency directly on the property mortgaged to secure the money-lender instead of the money-holder.

And now let me point out to you the blunder at the door of which can be laid all the error that has confused the mind of every thinker, puzzled the brain of every financier, and defeated the efforts of every economist to solve the financial problem. It is the failure to recognize the difference between coin and currency. I have shown you that coin is wealth, and currency is but the representative of wealth. When the borrower borrows coin, some one is deprived for the time of that much wealth, and he is entitled to whatever compensation free competition will allow him when he consents to part with his property; but when the borrower obtains currency issued directly on his wealth, he is depriving no one of the use of his property. Therefore, no one is entitled to compensation. The human conscience was right, after all, in its repugnance to interest, for now we see its abolition realizable, not through philanthrophy, but through the effect of a principle; and this simple method of making use of one's credit, or obtaining money without depriving one of his wealth, changes the whole philosophy of political economy through the universal application of that element so obnoxious to our State Socialistic friends,—namely, *competition!*

Before summing up what has been accomplished, at least in theory, by a research deeper than most writers have made into this question; and lest I should be assailed for not providing, or for having overlooked, the supposed necessity for a "measure of value" or "standard of value," I will in a few words give it a passing notice.

If we never had used money and had no conception of what was a common denominator or unit of value, but which is improperly called "measure of

(Continued in Supplement.)

value" and "standard of value," such as the dollar in this country, the pound sterling in England, or the franc in France, etc.; if, I say, we had no generally accepted term by which we could convey the idea of a definite quantity of any commodity, it might be sometime before we could all agree and understand how much of any commodity was meant by a dollar's worth, if we should adopt that term, or how much was meant when we should mention whatever term was proposed or agreed upon. We might possibly, under such circumstances, even be compelled to coin pieces of gold and silver, although I am so rash as to think that perhaps some other way might be devised that would involve less labor. But such is not the case. The price of every commodity in this country that can be obtained with money is expressed in, and every individual who has anything to exchange for money uses, the term dollar and its subdivisions, and there is no misunderstanding or complaint as to what is meant. Yet, notwithstanding this, and the fact that for a period of about seventeen years in this country, and at other times for longer or shorter periods, and in England for a period of twenty-five years, and in the same and other countries for periods of many years at a time, in no place could coin be obtained on demand in exchange for currency at its face value, yet, I say, not withstanding these facts, it is solemnly asserted by the bullionists, as I previously stated, and also by many of the learned professors, that a stable currency cannot be had unless it is based on gold, or at least on gold and silver. What more need I say than what has been said as to the real object in limiting the circulating medium?

In summing up my criticism of the National Bank System, I ask your earnest consideration to the following points.

I commenced this essay by calling your attention to the extent of the ignorance that prevails in reference to the nature of money by quoting Mr. Easterly's statement of his experience, which corroborates my own for the last fifteen years, during which time I have given this subject constant, earnest, and careful study. The general idea is entertained that, since the ablest men in the world have been occupied with this subject, the present system must be the best that could be devised, and, therefore, to devote one's self to its study is a waste of time. This position is further strengthened by the very absurdity of prevailing notions; being so enshrouded in mystery, impossible of rational explanation, and irreconcilable with common sense, failure to comprehend is attributed to the profoundness of the subject rather than to its errors and inconsistencies. Thus we have been deprived of an intelligent popular verdict on this interesting and important subject. The very fact that there has never been any popular discussion of the idea of free trade in money,—which means the entire abolition of all State control,—or of the application of the mutual feature to the issue of paper money, is proof of how far we may yet be from a solution in the adoption of paternalism.

The inconsistency of our political constitution with the philosophy of liberty entertained by the founders of this republic is apparent in contrasting that document with the Declaration of Independence. The one declares the inalienable right to liberty and the pursuit of happiness; the other ignores that right by establishing a monied class that controls industry and commerce and denies the right of private property. How can such inconsistency be explained except on the ground of the ignorance that prevailed in reference to the necessity for State interference? It is a monarchical institution, and has no part or lot with a free people. The motive that prompts the thesis of State dictation is clearly *special interests*. The motive that prompts the antithesis is the interests of all. Whichever proves to be the best system of money, the people will voluntarily accept. The best and safest money is always competent to drive out inferior money, if there is enough of it.

I have shown you a glimpse of a system far superior to the present one; yet, lest it should be defective, I want *liberty*, that others may establish a better. This system would have been tried thirty years ago; but the monied power, ever alert to its own interests, ever able to command the best talent and the weightiest influence in its behalf, knew well how to secure for itself, through legislation, that which free, open, and fair competition will deprive it of, and succeeded in extending for itself a few more decades of supremacy. We profess to despise imperialism, yet we retain its essence,—the very diet on which it fattens and without which it must die a natural death.

When the State ceases to protect the banks in the control of the medium of exchange by prohibiting its issue except on certain commodities and by certain parties, and by "fixing" the value of those commodities by making them a legal tender for a definite amount, then the paper medium of exchange can be issued, as I have shown, directly to borrowers at the cost of the transaction through the mutual bank, just as you get fire and life insurance at cost from the mutual insurance company; then money lending as a speculation will cease, and with it will also cease the objectionable features of boards of trade and stock exchanges. Without you limit currency by an arbitrary money system, speculation is impossible! The right to use one's property for purposes of credit is as unquestionable as the right to sell it. The present system denies that right by compelling you to obtain the consent of a certain class of citizens who are provided by the State with certain pieces of paper which you are prohibited from obtaining directly through association at an average of one-tenth the cost.

With the greater part of the wealth in the country convertible into available capital for productive enterprise by the issue of paper money thereon, all monopolies would have to reduce profits and increase wages, because of the enormous amount of capital that would enter into competition with them, until at last the capitalist would be compelled to co-operate with labor for mutual good,—the natural result that must follow a surplus of capital instead of a surplus of labor, as now.

The prosperity that would result from the employment of all the people now idle, in addition to those already employed, at constantly increasing wages would terminate in each getting the exact proportion of what each produced. Poverty would thus be gradually eliminated and crime would cease, panics become unknown, and prisons and poorhouses no longer disgrace our civilization.

Egoism

Vol. I.—No. 5. SAN FRANCISCO, CAL., SEPTEMBER, 1890. Price, Five Cents.

Pointers.

Reverie is the exercise of mental indolence.

Moralism is the social expediency of our grandparents' prejudices.

Habits, with their inadaptation of means to ends may be laughed at, but what are we to say of the equally absurd institutions which the laughers themselves support.

Most women are kept so busy preserving a legal virtue and maintaining conventional lies that they get no time to think out better means for the attaining of greater freedom and pleasure, but torture themselves into the grave of the foolish.

We have consulted a map of San Francisco, and find that EGOISM exerts a wide, but not dense influence in this city. Its ten subscribers here are located in widely separated parts of the city, and nothing now remains to complete its influential success but the filling out of the intervening spaces.

"Fair Play" has removed from Valley Falls, Kansas, to Souix City, Iowa. All mail for it should be sent to Lock Box 353 at that place. It may be admitted that EGOISM would not object to "Fair Play's" abundant financial success in its new home; as to editorial success that it already has.

The article on another page, by F. B. Parse on "What will Society Do with the Thief under Freedom," is a synopsis of a lecture recently delivered by him before a progressive meeting of some kind in San Diego. There was a politician in the audience who tried to reply, but we are told that Comrade Parse "laid him out" in short order, and yearned for yet more victims.

In the "Individualist" of August 30, Editor "C" publishes section 3412 of the revised statutes of the United States 1878, and section 866 of the general statutes of Colorado 1883, showing in a nut-shell the source of privilege's greatest robbery today. The first of these and that of their respective states regarding the issue of currency, should be kept standing in reform papers.

A temporary break in his good health, prevents the appearance in this number of Tak Kak's usual contribution, but to the full-fledged Egoist his communication of the fact will be worth more than the earlier appearance of one of his excellent articles. It reads: "I have had a troublesome sore throat which makes exertion unpleasant this warm weather... Getting well. Not writing anything for your next issue... In again by October number. T. K."

EGOISM is later this time than before. This is partly due to the finishing of the pamphlet, "Citizens' Money" hanging over into this issue's time. This opens the way to say that not a solitary order for it has reached us, which indicates that there is a great scarcity of money, and a corresponding reason why the pamphlet should be circulated, or that the readers are not interested in that which instructs rather than amuses. If the money lender and profit taker share the fate of the pamphlet, we say Amen. If not, we know why they will not for a long time to come.

Faces that seemed beautiful to someone, have undoubtedly existed from far back in the unrecorded history of animal consciousness, and will probably exist to its end, but the waxen face of the present dude ideal, with its inexperience, absence of any traces of thought—an infant face on top of five or six feet of flesh and bones, would in some circles of association be the source of more mortification than the most angular visage cast from the mould of hereditary mental and physical slavery. Dude and dudine of today, prepare for the beauty of tomorrow by adding the line of a complex emotion to your sea of blank plateau countenance, or the light of an intelligent thought to your dollish eyes. Beauty, like virtue is the ideal of conception, which changes with the resulting complexity of experience.

California's admission day was celebrated the 9th of this month. The display of bunting was so ridiculously gorgeous that it put the efforts of the heathen Chinese' celebrations to shame. It was a Native Sons' affair throughout and the city was full of visitors. To take advantage of the fact that the most talented and brightest people will not march in parades or be labeled, and thus cast an unfavorable reflection upon the whole fraternity as lacking in preponderance of brain and character because labels may have been lacking to locate that which really existed, would be as ungenerous as is the alleged pledge of the Native Sons to boycott the Easterner because he was not born on this soil. At any rate, in this, as in all celebration war-dance exhibitions, there was little that is pleasurable to the more complex mind. It is to be hoped that the day of crowing will soon be past. Achievement is, as a contemporary has said of genius, the result of prior conditions, and the achiever the instrument of these as is the mediocre of the same in his unapplauded function.

The weary monotony of the Egoists' life among God and government worshiping people was pleasantly broken a few days ago by the arrival of "Lucifer," which announced the release of Moses Harman from prison, on a writ of error, procured by David Overmyer, Mr. Harman's present counsel. He will now have a new trial in November. It is to be hoped that his emotional friends will be judicious enough this time to give him as much advantage before the court as a criminal would have at least. This latter movement is another object lesson of the advantage of Egoistic methods of expediency over the storming of emotional fanaticism. These would have declaimed, and worshiped their hero, while they allowed him to remain during the five years if he could have survived the term. If the matter is left in his attorney's hands there is a fair probability of his acquittal. Mr. Tucker's successful blow at the censors will be a marked advantage, as will the public sentiment that has developed through the circulating of petitions during his imprisonment. The safest contribution that can now be made is dollars. These will be much needed.

To emphasize the conclusion of the comment in another column on Ida C. Craddock's appeal to the Anarchists to turn their efforts to the separation of church and State, we refer the reader to the production of a Bismarckian German criticising in "Freethought" of Sept. 13, George Macdonald's Observation on the marriage question, which among others will be found on another page of this paper. This typical Secularist seems to believe that people should be content with such sex association as can be maintained by the State's club, and fears if this guarantee be removed that helpless women with children would be deserted by a "husband and father who is a brute, for a younger and handsomer woman." Even this might be preferable to being landed in the grave before the younger and handsomer woman comes in as is now the case. At any rate it would be too bad to deprive a woman of the fostering care of a brutal husband. Then it is of course certain, that if legal ties were removed, "young and handsome" women would at once turn out and search for brutal men with helpless wives, just as Abolitionists were years ago supposed to want to marry their daughters to negroes because they wanted the negroes freed. But this is not the worst of this militant gentleman's fears. He thinks that if the State club did not keep a wife to her duty of bearing and caring for children she might desert her post and leave the husband to assume the incidental responsibility of his sensory pleasure himself, and that is the rub. Man has a hard enough time to get all the pleasure he wants, without women selfishly withdrawing their lives' efforts from him and directing them to the attainment of their own pleasure. Let whoever is content with the fidelity the sheriff can maintain for him, make the best of it now, for there is a growing taste for spontaneous affection which is sure to succeed forced servitude.

EGOISM

Issued Monthly at Fifty Cents a Year

—BY—

EQUITY PUBLISHING COMPANY,

Post Office Box 1678, San Francisco, California.

Entered as Second Class Mail Matter

Runners of The Editorial Gantlet.

Indiana White Caps are a geographical expression of the general doctrine of Moralism. They know what is "right," and noble martyrs that they are, risk even legal penalties in carrying it out. With an inclination, Moralists could get a pointer from this.

Recently a half dozen customs inspectors "shadowed" the Oakland jail for seventy-two hours to detect the exchange of some Chinamen who wanted to go to China passage free, for some Chinese prisoners that had been captured while attempting to cross the line near San Diego, and were to be sent back to China. They succeeded and survived the patriotic plaudits of the press, while Labor stood gleefully by and stupidly believed itself protected by the very agency that is employed to exact a robber's tribute from it for every protected article of food or clothing it consumes whether produced at home or abroad. With due consistency, it hopes to "vote itself free."

R. B. Westbrook, president of the American Secular Union, when last heard from was at the sea-side "weeding" a "book of morals" from the manuscripts of the contestants for a thousand dollar prize offered by himself and others for the best "moral guide." The product of this new theological venture we await with curiosity. It will undoubtedly be a great relief to the Moralists of the country to have a bible for authority, and have no longer to be taunted with the suggestive fact that morality like other religious creeds is only geograpical and without a standard "authority." Weak indeed is the mind that begs to have its pleasure prescribed to it; and who save orthodox fanatics pretend to live for anything else. Such superstition at such a place should be very encouraging to the church if she wishes to see her principal features preserved.

In the August number of the "Arena" is an otherwise excellent article on hypnotism or mesmerism, but has the usual law foolery at the end, for which purpose it was written by Emily Kempin with the LL. D. attachment, who is secretary of the New York Medico-Legal Society. It is argued that the State should have control or a monopoly of hypnotism. That "the practice of hypnotism should not only be forbidden to all but licensed physicians, but these even should not be allowed to use it without having authorized witnesses present." That is, the average citizen, who according to the writer's theory is too ignorant and criminally inclined to safely practice it is to be competent judge of the operations of the licensed physician, who was granted the privilege only by virtue of his acknowledged superior intelligence to the balance of the community that is now to be his judge. This is typical popular government logic.

The preponderance of chaffy matter that fills the popular magazines mirrors an almost hopeless stupidity on the part of the public that buys it, if not on that of the publishers who, knowing of the ability in depth of thought as well as artistic style of other writers, allow them to earn their livelihood by almost mechanical pursuits. That such writers' productions would be too radical cannot be consistently maintained, for in these magazines' purported function of presenting every phase of thought, lies before the public, ample justification for the appearance of every well-defined departure in thought. H.

Another crowd of women "made it up" and went to the "proper authorities" in Oakland recently to demand their names placed on the Great Register, which would entitle them to participate in the coming election. They of course failed in securing their unquestionable right to the exercise of tyranny equal with men. To those who consider the "right to vote" the ultimate of freedom this attempt is encouraging. But to those who have discovered it to be the ultimate of tyranny, to thus see the women attempting to enter the political swamp in which men have floundered and mired for generations, is only another indication of how far we are from even a desire for real freedom.

The ostensible object of the aforesaid crowd of Christian Temperance Women was their "right to vote," but their subjective and real idea was to obtain power to regulate the affairs of men who manufacture and those who drink intoxicants. The slave's ideal ever is to be master.

This "right to vote" is like other mirages of life, not what it appears to be. Not until one has studied the origin of "rights" and given up the idea of their existence otherwise than as the supposed expediency of each stage of social development, can they realize what the right to vote involves. Its central object is to gain the power to force the actions of others to conform to the ideas of those to whom power falls. What do they want to vote for? Is their mental world then, such a reflection of man's false ideals that they must struggle for the brute force that enlightenment is about to cause him to throw away in disgust? Can they not see one step farther, that of their social and industrial independence?

These women never having even dreamed of economic and social independence naturally attempt to avail themselves of the only means known to them by which women might possibly avoid the unpleasant invasions of drunken husbands. The fact is their trouble lies not in the manufacture, sale, or drinking of liquors, but in their industrial dependence on the men who drink them. In a condition of industrial independence it would matter but little to women whether the consumers of their products drank liquors or ate beefsteak. If such men were incongenial there would be nothing to do but decline to associate with them just as women do with unpleasant individuals of their own sex. Let them acquire the idea of individual freedom and responsibility; take their stand with the most enlightened men and women of the age and agitate for the opportunity to earn a livelihood, and for the removal of the monopolies that rob labor and the ignorance that consecrates social slavery. Let them do this kind of work, and every stroke will be toward equal *freedom* instead of toward *un*equal *slavery* as at present. Let them study out the fundamental relation of themselves to other things generally and learn the object of conscious existence, and cease to be mere apers of barbaric brutality. G.

So blind does the intensity of man's subjectivity make his selfishness that with any emotionalism it is next to impossible for him, even having traced conduct to its real basis, to always make applications in accordance with and reason from such irrefutable deductions.

Hugh O. Pentecost has already admitted that we have no duties as such to God or man, and that what we do is actuated by purely selfish motives, but not having digested this fullness of the principle of Individualism is found, unconsciously enough, invading Benj. R. Tucker by bringing upon his head a storm of ostracism and abuse from people who share Mr. Pentecost's superstitions, because Mr. Tucker's utilitarian principles failed to conform to these people's Moralistic creed. They no doubt believe him to be a bad man in refusing to be questioned regarding his private affairs, and perhaps imagine that he daily and without provocation cruelly beats his dog, allows his horses to suffer for food, and does not water his cow. Besides these things he may pi his forms of live type, tear his clothes, go without his dinner, work late at night, pay taxes or patronize the postoffice, buy protected articles of food or clothing, kiss a pretty woman, and do many other things of this kind, all of which are private affairs, which kind of affairs Mr. Pentecost believes subject to public criticism.

In the midst of all this ruin (?) stands Mr. Pentecost as innocently triumphant as a well-meaning but injudicious juvenile canine who has tugged cloth, dishes, victuals and all from the table down upon the floor. He does not seem to realize that what he regards as morality, justice, and goodness is nothing other than the order *equality*, which itself is relative, being absolute per head only as individual resistance makes it so, and therefore is only social expediency, varying in its expression with the intelligence of the social units. That the ideal social expediency is equality or equal conditions is due to the fact that men happen to be approximately equal in the possibilities of defensive capacity; that an Ego consists of a certain combination of desires the gratification of which makes up all existence means to him or her, and whatever opposes that gratification will meet with resistance from that Ego to the point of that opposition's removal or its equal resistance, by which is determined the limit of subjective gratification or private right, and not by some abstract rule deduced from the number of times a given number of noses are contained in a like number. Therefore when Mr. Tucker "did the wisest thing possible under the circumstances," if his fellowmen do not boycott him for it he did the most expedient thing possible under the circumstances, and Mr. Pentecost's ready rejoiner that every politician and privileged robber can offer the same excuse, will not hold in this case before even those of us who do not share equal benefit in privilege's expediency. For Mr. Tucker, in marked contrast with these, is doing everything in his power to *change* the *circumstances* which necessitate the use of such an expedient, thereby becoming a co-operator in the resistance which each of our Egos' desire for gratification offers against the common opposition of ignorance. If Mr. Tucker continues to get financial advantage through privilege, with which to fight our enemy, until public opinion be such that he or no one else can secure the benefit of privilege, we will not, so long as he is thus healing *us*, be stupid enough at any time to cry out, "Physician heal *thyself*." Consistency has yet another element, that of consistent consistency.

As Mr. Pentecost himself has shown in his ablest Sunday address, the spreading of knowledge is the effective factor of progress. It has a constant tendency to make social expediency become scientific, which induces conformity to our social ideal as rapidly as its general acceptance will admit of without sacrifice of one to the stupidity of the rest, the exaction of which would clearly be an invasion, and exactly what Mr. Pentecost's Moralism did exact from Mr. Tucker. Thus the difference between Moralism and Egoistic ethical policy, is the difference between superstitious slavery and enlightened spontaneity.

With the following, written by Mr. Pentecost sometime ago, I heartily concur:

> There are superstitious Roman Catholics, superstitious Presbyterians, superstitious Methodists, and superstitious *Freethinkers*. And when a Freethinker is superstitious he is, in that respect, exactly like any other superstitious person—it is very difficult to convince him that his superstition *is* a superstition.

In a politically composed appeal to the various divisions of the reformers of the Liberal element of the country, Ida C. Craddock, corresponding secretary of the American Secular Union, says this to the Anarchists:

> Anarchists! You who preach the gospel of Individualism, and who believe in co-operation only when it is voluntary! Do you not see that every refusal of yours to help your fellows in separating church and State results only in tightning the cord around your own necks? Are you not today, because of the exemption of church property from taxation, supporting the churches by compulsion? You are continually declaiming against having to pay taxes against your will. Help us to do away with the exemption of church property, and you at once lighten the burden of your own taxation. Moreover, you must remember that the Individualism which is your goal is not possible while the false standard of church authority is set up for the community to conform to. Ecclesiasticism in the State is your most deadly enemy—you know it well; and only when the church and State shall be forever separated, will you, or any of us, be quite free to work out an individual development without persecution.

Considering the absolute innocence of any understanding of the principles of Anarchism that the above paragraph displays, it is quite certain that a State run by people of that status would be little improvement over the present so far as the hopes of Anarchism are concerned. We may "declaim against having to pay taxes against our will," but are not so foolish as to direct our whole effort against our least grievance. And as for the "false standard of *churchly* authority," it is no more dangerous to Individualism than that *authority* which Miss

Craddock's language implies is not false; it is with authority as a justification for invading the individual at all, that we do battle, and one authority is no more *false* than another so long as it tyrannizes, as the State does and would without church domination.

This appeal is not for an expression of sentiment or a vote for the repeal of laws connecting church and State, for there is nothing like an approach to a majority in favor of it, which Anarchists could complete and carry by that means, and if there were the laws would be too dead to need repealing, to say nothing of the false impression thus created that voting is a justifiable method of disposing of any question. But the appeal means a contribution of money and time—dollars and labor, which, in the circumstances of the average Anarchist means food of a poorer quality if not less in quantity, poorer clothes, and a corresponding abandoning of his own agitation, the importance of which is incomparable both as regards plundering of property and restriction of personal liberty.

To the liberty-loving individual, who through money, land, "protection," and other artificially created monopolies is kept out of labor six days in the week, or obliged to labor for so small a proportion of his product that he cannot have both recreation and subsistence when unemployed; who must be taxed more on his home every time somebody moves into his neighborhood; who must pay for the education of other people's children; who must give a certain sum annually to the poll tax collector for existing; who must submit to the censorship of ignorant and unprincipled politicians the thoughts he publishes; who, if he desires the pleasure of the mutual caresses of love, must buy, with the condition of monotonous monogamy, the permission from parties disinterested in the matter, or be subjected to a long term of imprisonment—to such an individual thus oppressed, an appeal calling him from the fundamental uprooting of tyranny to give his means and efforts to the agitation for relief from the infinitesimally greater proportion of taxation arising from the exemption of church property, or from the restraint of Sunday recreation for which he would have no money to pay, is necessarily ridiculous. Between the superstition that supports all oppressions, and that which seeks only to throw off the latter, there is practically too little difference for the serious consideration of those who have been over the whole ground as Anarchists have. It is too much like a woman screaming to her neighbor for help to fish a hair-pin from the swill barrel, when his child has fallen into the well.

If Miss Craddock should by some circumstance be brought to take the time to study economics and individual freedom, she would not only learn that her cause is of comparatively small importance, but that such as it is, the Anarchists' agitation is the only step toward its effectual remedy. Over any save its willing subjects, with the superstition of political authority dispelled, the superstitions of the church are powerless. It is the State, the political State itself that furnishes the power to oppress and plunder both you and us, and would continue to do so in all the more important points after its separation from the church, as before. The lend lord would be as powerful in exacting interest by his monopoly; the land lord by his; the protected producer higher prices by his; the tax gatherer an increase when a neighbor moved into the community; the neighbor to make you educate his children; the poll tax collector to get his two dollars for letting you live if you can, and Mother Grundy's State club with which to meddle in your private affairs would be as potent as now, for the political superstition which fathers all these and kindred oppressions, the average Secularist holds in common with the church, and unwittingly looks to the cause of his oppression for relief. H.

An Important Point Cleared Up.

In his Oservations in "Freethought" of August 30, its office editor observes as follows:

> The editor of a San Francisco monthly paper of great typographical beauty, called "EGOISM," has many original thoughts. The doctrine of Egoism is what has been more or less known heretofore as "enlightened self-interest." I quote one of its editorial paragraphs. Be it understood that the editor of "Egoism" repudiates as a superstition the idea of sentimental love between the sexes. He says:
>
> If you don't "fall" in love with anybody but yourself, and love wisely enough to do it well, you have the advantage of the situation; for the object of your affection will never die or forsake you while you live, and when you die you will not miss it.
>
> There is one other consideration which the editor has neglected to call attention to, namely, that the person who falls in love with himself or herself, as a general rule, is not troubled with rivals.

The implication is, that to be without rivals in such self-love might be undesirable, but in these days of rampant paternalism much depends on whether such rival in one's pursuit of his welfare has in view the gratification of a mutual desire, or a subjective one which has no probability of becoming so. In the latter case the absence of a rival would be immeasurably desired, and it was to cover this point that the perhaps somewhat obscure clause, "love wisely enough to do it well," was introduced in the sentence quoted by the friendly critic, and which it is now the purpose to clear up.

Now the condition known as "love," is a subjective state of mind consisting of an intense desire to exercise upon and have exercised upon us, for our own gratification, various caresses and interest in our pleasure by a certain object desired to be in a similar state of mind. The object is usually determined by circumstances of proximity and favorable impressions on the semi-intellectual faculties by form or actions or both. The desired state of similar subjectivity on the part of the object of our subjective condition is, if at all, accomplished by suggesting to that object *our* subjective state so gradually and evasively that the object becomes reciprocally conscious of it without direct verbal communication of the fact, and is a process which admits of a skill the subtle delicacy of which taxes to despair the psychologic resources of the subjectively entranced lover. This incomplacent ordeal passed, the similarly subjective state between two such persons finds pleasant exercise in continually suggesting each to the other such state. The writer has sometimes witnessed this exercise between two in mixed company, and noted the entire absence of rivalry they enjoyed. The same is true in self-love. If the suggesting to self is marked, a corresponding absence of rivalry will accompany it, and the wisdom of thus loving depends upon judiciously making the *suggesting* conform to the desire for rivalry. This un-"fallen" in-love-with-another condition, leaves us ever free to sip the proffered sweets of the fair, as of the field, with the positive assurance of not paining our original lover with the ventures of the ever passing opportunities, one of which ordinarily is the occasion for the usual "fall" into—obligations of mutual slavery in which these sweets are seen only as the necessary bait to a trap that seldom opens save to take out the dead rats. It is an advantage, the taking of which relieves all from obligation.

What will Society Do with the Thief under Freedom.

That old bugaboo, "What will you do with the thieves and criminals under economic freedom, liberty,—Anarchy, with no government of force, no restraint, no control; would not the criminal be uncontrollable? would he not steal, murder, and destroy wholesale, the moment governmental restraint was lifted?" is a question that is continually confronting the advocate of self-government. Now this is a question that cannot be answered by the positive and negative of yes or no. We must first inquire into the nature and character of the thief, and criminal. If we analyze him, reduce him to the last analysis, we will find him to be the product of the present monopolistic state of society, divided into two classes, the legal and illegal thief or criminal, each having reflected in himself the spirit, character, and principles of the government and society under which he is born, and under which his character for aggressive acts is formed. The thief is thus what his predominating environment makes him; therefore society is responsible for its own devils, for there would be no devils if there were no hell. Conditions are always first, results follow. Man did not put in an appearance upon this earth until the climatic conditions were favorable to his advent. The devils (criminals) of society will not disappear until our present social atmosphere is purified by liberty—the liberty to *practice* self-government. Then the criminal will commence to disappear, for the simple reason that the socialistic climate under economic freedom will not be congenial for the production and growth of thieves of either class. Then the honest man will no longer be "crucified between two thieves"—the legal and the illegal thief. As society is now organized, the small thief, the committer of petit larceny, breaks the law while the legal, wholesale robber (speculator) both observes and respects the law; one is a law-breaker, the other oftentimes a lawmaker. Both obtain their desires by diametrically opposite methods, and yet, contradictory as it may appear, both are the products of the same authoritarian state of society, that of brute force—majority rule. One lives in virtue of the existence of the other, while the honest man lives not in virtue of either, but in *spite* of both. The small thief stimulated by the successes of his legal brother in crime makes feeble efforts to ape him in the magnitude of his stealings, but owing to his ignorance of legal and political methods, succeeds only in committing petit larceny; as a law-breaker he is a success, but as a thief he is a failure. Now in this monopolistic state of society nothing excites contempt like failure; the failure of the nickle thief to steal a "million" is the signal for society to "let slip the dogs" of law, and during the hubbub and excitement of the chase, trial, and punishment of the small thief, the legalized criminal escapes notice and conviction. All eyes are turned upon and attracted toward the liliputian thief, while the giant malefactor, the product of special privileges is elevated to a position of respectability, popularity, and authority, bearing upon his political coat of arms the monogram, "PPP"; Privilege, Power, and Pelf, or Pockets Picked Professionally. Over his place of business is the sign, "Rents Collected, Interest taken, and Poverty enforced according to Law." Here are the two classes of thieves, "look on this picture then on that." Both are chromos *given* away by society to the student of economic liberty; both painted by the same artist, one of the "old masters"—Monopoly. Of the two classes of thieves and criminals the Individualist and Anarchist fears the legalized offender a thousand fold more than the illegal outcast pariah of society, whose stealings and criminal acts sink to a ridiculous minimum in comparison with the legalized speculator and monopolist. Nothing but an intellectual rape committed upon the public mind by the superstitious god of political authority could blind "the people" to a clear conception of this important distinction between the two classes of criminals; a distinction and difference which the ignorance of, causes society to build jails and gibbets for one class, and Wall street castles and halls of congress for the other. If anyone who is enamored with brute force government—majority rule (whether he is a State Socialist or advocate of the present system), will analyze their lust for political authority they will find that they want it as the church wants eternal punishment, not for themselves, oh no! but always for that "other fellow," and that other fellow is the average voter whose attention is attracted to the small thief by the hue and cry raised against him while the legalized plunderer gets away with the interest, rent, and taxes.

It will be readily seen that the Individualist does not look upon the illegal criminal as being by any means the worst product of society, nor the most to be feared. Neither do we believe that the legalized speculator and monopolist is always conscious of his own criminality, for he has yet to learn that *equity* is a law superior to majority rule and special privilege; he is ignorant of the glorious truth that equity is the "principle of liberty applied to trade and commerce." If he were not thus ignorant, he would see that the word, "criminal" in the true sense would be more justly applied to himself than the ordinary law-breaker, and that the small thief will commence to disappear when the power of example set by the privileged plunderer is removed. This removal "so devoutly to be wished for" cannot be accomplished by threats, gunpowder, or dynamite; physical force will expensively and needlessly retard our objects and give the lie to our declaration that we are opposed to brute force.

For the sake of argument and truth we will suppose that the illegal criminal, all there is left of his peculiar species out of the present civilization, will be there when equal freedom is attained. Now, no thief, no murderer, no warrior ever risks his life or person in any aggressive act of violence unless he thinks there is a reasonable chance for success and his subsequent escape from the consequences of his invasive acts against his fellowman; it is only with the chances more in his favor than against him that he does commit them. In a free state of society—the absence of political authority—where mankind enjoyed the liberty to voluntarily associate for purposes of defense against criminal encroachments, the aggressor and invader would see that the chances for success were overwhelmingly against him owing to his numerical weakness, which is even now the fact in the present thief producing state of society; and the solidarity which an economically free people would thus present to his invasion, would convince him of the utter futility of attacking society at such a great disadvantage. He would then see that as a matter of self-preservation it were more expedient to gain a living, and even wealth by working for it than to steal it.

Soon as we can obtain freedom from governmental monopoly of land and money we will not only be in a position to practice self-government, but in a condition to convince men that it is easier to work than it is to steal. Then the criminal as well as the thief will in time become an honest man both from *choice* and *necessity*.

But before these favorable conditions prevail we have a certain amount of educational work to perform; we must teach men and women the art of *minding their own business*. This is one of the "lost arts," but its revival and restoration is not impossible, and it is an easy accomplishment for an Anarchist and Individualist, as they are not cursed with the governmental itch, nor a lust for control over their fellow beings. While we are teaching self-government let us *practice* self-control and self-reliance. We are striving for the liberty to practice what we teach, ours is an intellectual battle with political authority, and our battle ground is the public mind. We have no patent medicine, no governmental pill, plaster, or panacea to cure the social ills that now exist, we plead only for *conditions*, the condition of liberty—equal freedom; freedom from that old dogma that the collectivity rises higher than the individual; that society enjoys a monopoly over the stream of rising higher than its source. We look upon the present unequal and unhealthy condition of society as we would upon a sick patient to whom medicine will no longer do any good, and nothing but a complete change of climate and *conditions* will cure.

F. B. Parse.

The Right of Ownership.

To the Editor of Liberty:

Will you permit me to ask you for the definition, from an Anarchistic standpoint, of the "Right of Ownership"? What do you mean to convey when you say that a certain thing belongs to a certain person?

Before directing my attention to the study of the social question, I had a rather confused notion of the meaning of this term. Ownership appeared to me a kind of amalgamation of wealth with the individual. This conception could, of course, not be sustained in an analysis of the social question and the distribution of wealth. For sometime I could not obtain a clear notion as to what the term, as popularly used, really signifies, nor could I find a satisfactory definition in any of the books I had at command. The writers of dictionaries content themselves with quoting a number of synonyms which throw no light on the subject, and the writers on Political Economy seem not to bother themselves about such trifles. They need no solid foundations for their theories since they build their castles in the air. It is said that ownership is the "exclusive right of possession," but this explanation fails to meet the inquiry of him who can nowhere find a satisfactory explanation of the import of the term "right."

It is clear that a radical distinction exists between possession and ownership, though these concepts are in a measure related to each other. It seems reasonable, therefore, to expect to find a clue by examining the distinction that exists between the possessor and the owner of a thing. And this examination is not difficult. The owner of a thing which for some reason is in the possession of some one else, may demand its return, and, if it is not returned willingly, *the aid of the law can be invoked.* This leads to the conclusion that the right of ownership is that relation between a thing and a person created by the social promise to guarantee possession.

This is the only definition that appears satisfactory to me. But it implies the existence of a social organization, however crude it may be. It implies that a supreme power will enforce the command: "Thou shalt not steal." And in the measure in which this social organization gains stability and in which this social power gains a more universal supremacy, the right of ownership will assume a more definite existence.

Now I can perhaps repeat my question in a way to be better understood. Has Anarchism a different conception of the right of ownership, or is this right altogether repudiated, or is it assumed that out of the ruins of government another social organization, wielding a supreme power, will arise? I can at present see no other alternative.

Hugo Bilgram.

In discussing such a question as this, it is necessary at the start to put aside, as Mr. Bilgram doubtless does put aside, the intuitive idea of right, the conception of right as a standard which we are expected to observe from motives supposed to be superior to the consideration of our interests. When I speak of the "right of ownership," I do not use the word in that sense at all. In the thought that I take to be fundamental in Mr. Bilgram's argument—namely, that there is no right, from the standpoint of society, other than social expediency—I fully concur. But I am equally certain that the standard of social expediency—that is to say, the facts as to what really is socially expedient, and the generalizations from those facts which we may call the laws of social expediency—exists apart from the decree of any social power whatever. In accordance with this view, the Anarchistic definition of the right of ownership, while closely related to Mr. Bilgram's, is such a modification of his that it does not carry the implication which his carries and which he points out. From an Anarchistic standpoint, the right of ownership is that control of a thing by a person which will receive either social sanction, or else unanimous individual sanction, when the laws of social expediency shall have been finally discovered. (Of course I might go farther and explain that Anarchism considers the greatest amount of liberty compatible with equality of liberty the fundamental law of social expediency, and that nearly all Anarchists consider labor to be the only basis of the right of ownership in harmony with that law; but this is not essential to the definition, or the refutation of Mr. Bilgram's point against Anarchism.)

It will be seen that the Anarchistic definition just given does not imply necessarily the existence of an organized or instituted social power to enforce the right of ownership. It contemplates a time when social sanction shall be superseded by unanimous individual sanction, thus rendering enforcement needless. But in such an event, by Mr. Bilgram's definition, the right of ownership would cease to exist. In other words, he seems to think that, if all men were to agree upon a property standard and should voluntarily observe it, property would then have no existence simply because of the absence of any institution to protect it. Now, in the view of the Anarchists, property would then exist in its perfection.

So I would answer Mr. Bilgram's question, as put in his concluding paragraph, as follows: Anarchism does not repudiate the right of ownership, but it has a conception thereof sufficiently different from Mr. Bilgram's to include the possibility of an end of that social organization which will arise, not out of the ruins of government, but out of the transformation of government into voluntary associations for defense.—Benj. R. Tucker in "Liberty," Boston.

Press, Transportation, and Telegraph Censorship.

One feature of President Harrison's crusade against the lotteries may serve to illustrate the process by which encroachments on individual and local freedom are usually made. The postoffice was established without a moral censor to preside over it or any indication that it was intended to serve as a handle to control the speculations or private conduct of the people. But the growth of a considerable sentiment against lotteries enabled the moral coercionists and the government extensionists to make a combination of forces agreeable to both. The first contention was limited to this; that the United States mail should not be used to aid in carrying on the lottery business. That proposition was admitted to some extent by law of congress, but the line was drawn at any interference with newspaper advertisement, for this would involve the tremendous issue of a censorship of the press. Now, however, President Harrison proposes a distinct aggression upon the express companies and a curious supervision of the press. If his policy should be embodied in law the federal government will be committed to prohibition of any communication or transaction which congress disapproves on moral grounds and an instance will be offered in the application. Besides this he recommends action which would necessitate an official examination of all newspapers sent by mail or other conveyance. Then of course all telegrams must next be placed under a like censorship or the line of precaution will be ludicrously incomplete. Did many persons think of such a result when they assented to the proposition not to allow letters to be delivered to lottery companies? Probably not, but the progress being made in this agitation is as natural as in every other development of the policy of encroachment or the policy of exclusion. It is accompanied and hoped to be accomplished by loose and inaccurate description with an inflammatory tendency. Mr. Harrison must know that a bargain freely entered into, by which persons, whether rich or poor, pay a dollar knowing that 40 cents of it will be swallowed up in expenses and profits, is not robbery. But he viciously perverts language to arouse passion, pander to excited Moralism and intrusive benevolent paternalism and gain the consent of citizens and congress to an extension of federal authority such as must, if granted, have effects far overtopping all that directly concerns lotteries. There are other things which congress hereafter may be persuaded to control by prohibitions upon express companies and publications if congress can be induced to assume such control for any purpose which the majority thinks to be in the interest of good morals. With the masses, however, interest in the question will probably be confined to a narrow view. It is one of the singularities of militant legislative Moralists that they will seldom scruple to risk truth in bearing witness against a neighbor when that course is necessary to carry their point. Every objection to their plan will be assumed to be inspired by some lottery company. The moral reformers never credit any objectors with any moral and intellectual grounds of objection. Most newspapers and congressmen, if objecting honestly, nevertheless fear the scolding tongue of intolerance loaded with suspicions and ready to discharge a mess of virulent and blighting accusations. It is still safe and reputable for men in office to ask extravagant increase of powers for moral purposes, though a fair examination of their argument should convince any sane person that if they are correct the United States government was a mistake from the beginning and the country should have been organized as a theocracy.—Galveston News.

The Era of Egoism.

Will the world ever come, by progress and evolution to such a life? "But," says the thoughtless civilizee, "do you *want* such a life of selfishness as that would be?" It is not long since I fully realized what true Egoism means, and its possibilities and potencies. The true Egoist says to every other Ego, or combination of Egos, "hands off" from my individuality and personality. When all are developed up to that status, then, and not until then will there be entire freedom of mind and body for "man, woman and child."

Every growing, living plant, or animal strives and struggles to perpetuate itself, and one organism has the same or as much right to its Egoism or existence as another. When a man constructs a complex machine, he has the form and relation of the parts in his brain first. He is particular to give each part its individuality, that it may be joined to and co-operate with every other individualized part. He knows that if the parts are right, the whole machine will do its desired work easily and harmoniously. This to me, illustrates the only way in which it is possible to have a true order of life on earth. There has never (?) been a society, or government on earth, based upon, or that has acted upon that principle. The parts of the man-made machine, are *all* of equal importance to the whole; but the subjects of governments are mere passive instruments, and their Egoism is practically ignored. Happily for humanity, the arrangements, laws and, results of nature, in spite of man are in the direction of equality, justice, and humanity, so that when Egoism prevails, war, conquest, legal robbery, and anti-Egoistic governments and despotisms will cease, all wants will be supplied, and "peace on earth and good will to men" be realized. It seems to me that a true, practical Egoism will supply all human wants and give liberty to all as far as they can appreciate it. PROF. J. H. COOK.

An Observer Who Sees.

I registered at the City Hall the other day as a voter in the city and county of San Francisco, though what in the name of common sense I want to vote for is more than I know. City and State affairs are going along as well as ever, to all appearances; every vacant stool in all our public buildings seems to have an intelligent Milesian to hold it down and draw his salary; the present officials come around to collect some sort of a tax or license as often as I have money enough to pay it, and I see no reason to expect that a new set of stool-occupiers and tax and license gatherers would do any better. There is a youth at the City Hall who will take two dollars from me if I should ever desire to get married again or keep a dog, which I don't. Either of a hundred other clerks will take a tithe of my possessions once a year if I continue to stay in this office. Others will gather from me an annual poll tax of two dollars and allow me to live. Others will see that I pay them a license for handling merchandise, and still others will reach out their hands occasionally for the cigar license. Why not let these present incumbents stay there until they either die or get enough and retire? Better, saith the bard, to bear the ills we have than to fly to others we know not of.

I have often wondered what would happen if the president of the United States should seclude himself somewhere and be heard of no more forever and his office remain vacant; if our national and state legislatures should adjourn sine die; if our customs officials, our internal revenue gatherers, our supreme and superior court judges should go away and become gentlemen farmers; if our statute books should perish in the flames of our state houses and city halls; if our chaplains should all go to Africa as missionaries to the heathen; if, in fact, the greater part of our government machinery should become rusty and refuse to move, and election day should never come around—I have often wondered whether the people would miss anything except the expense. What would happen if every voter stayed away from the polls for ten years? Let him that is without sense among us cast the first vote.

If we find upon investigation that the most enlightened persons neither attend church nor political conventions; that the tendency of civilization is toward indifference or disgust with both religion and politics; that the men best fitted for teachers are not in the pulpits, and that the ablest political economists are not office-holders; and if on the contrary we find the church and State supported by the most unenlightened and unprincipled classes; the most enthusiasm among the most abandoned; the pulpits filled by men who are fit for nothing else, and public offices crowded with the dishonest, the fanatical, and the incompetent—what conclusions are to be logically drawn from these facts? I draw nothing except attention to things as they are in our centers of population.

I have been paying some attention to the doctrines of the newer lights of political and social economy, and these are the lessons I learn:

The shortest way to settle the Woman Suffrage question is to let the women vote. Mischief may follow; but mischief follows from marriage sometimes, and we do not therefore argue that only men should marry.

The shortest way to settle the liquor question is to remove license and tax from the traffic. This would make liquor so cheap that drinkers could get all they want for little expense and would have something left for other purposes.

The shortest way to settle the marriage question is to abolish legal ties. Then if people unhappily mated continue to live together in misery they would do so upon their own responsibility and have no one to blame but themselves.

The shortest way to settle the religious question is to withdraw legal privileges from the churches. Tax these as other property is taxed, protect their meetings only as other meetings are protected, pay no state money to religious institutions.

The shortest way to abolish land monopoly is to give monopolists no title whereby they can hold in possession more land than they use.

The shortest way to settle the financial question is to make coinage and currency free, so that every man may coin his own metal and issue his own paper money, and put his credit in competition with the credit of others.

The shortest way to settle all other questions is by the same simple methods, the only objection to which is that their adoption is a long way off.—Paragraphs from George Macdonald's "Observations" in "Freethought."

KEMMLER was put to an awful death but a few days before Charles Crumley, in a fit of jealousy, killed Robert McNeill, in this city. The killing, after careful premeditation, was done with great deliberation. Crumley knew he would risk suffering the horrors of the electrical chair, but that knowledge had no deterent effect on him. In spite of such demonstrative illustrations it requires an almost incredible time for most persons to learn that punishment has no tendency whatever to prevent crime. —Hugh O. Pentecost.

Egographs.

The selection of matter often expresses a taste for thought, though not fully defined, yet with its germs in the appreciator's mind.

The prudes of Detroit have dragooned the directors of the Detroit Museum of Art into putting drapery over the nude figures of a Venus and the Dying Gladiator. It will now be in order for these angelic beings to pray to their "God" to provide opaque coverings for all flowers and animals, for he, shameless old thing, neglected to do so "in the beginning" and the result is that the purists, his poor helpless children, can not step out of doors or into a greenhouse without having their dear modesty torn into little bits of pieces.—E. C. Walker, in "Fair Play."

A man and a woman were imprisoned last week in this city for attempting to kill themselves. Society is so ordered that people become so poor and miserable that they do not wish to live, but the State makes it a crime to try to die. The point is that the supply of poor people must be kept as large as possible in order to keep wages down. Hence, also, the church teaches that it is a duty to have children. With vacant land and money monopolized and the labor market crowded with helpless applicants for work, the capitalists have things all their own way. The more births and the fewer suicides there are the better it is for the land lords and the lend lords.—Hugh O. Pentecost.

"It is a matter of the simplest demonstration that no man can be really appreciated but by his equal or superior. His inferior may overestimate him in enthusiasm, or, as is more commonly the case, degrade him in ignorance; but he cannot form a grounded and just estimate." So says Ruskin; and herein we have the true explanation of the doubtless correct statement that "Liberty" is uninteresting to many, and "Fair Play" unreadable, and both worthless as missionary literature among certain classes. The old Greek philosopher was wise when he inferred from the fact that the crowd noisily cheered him that he had emitted some silly remark. "Liberty" expects to be abused, neglected, and misunderstood, for it is radical and philosophical and progressive. In the end, however, it and its real allies must obtain due recognition and triumph over all opposition. Let Ruskin explain this apparent paradox: "If it be true, and it can scarcely be disputed, that nothing has been for centuries consecrated by public admiration without possessing in a high degree some kind of sterling excellence, it is not because the average intellect and feeling of the majority of the public are competent in any way to distinguish what is really excellent, but because all erroneous opinion is inconsistent, and all ungrounded opinion transitory, so that, while the fancies and feelings which deny deserved honor, and award what is undue, have neither root nor strength to maintain consistent testimony for a length of time, the opinions formed on right grounds by those few who are in reality competent judges, being necessarily stable, communicate themselves gradually from mind to mind, descending lower as they extend wider, until they leaven the whole lump."—Liberty.

It appears that the censorship is already in operation. As noted in a press dispatch, an assistant attorney general is the censor, and one of Tolstoi's novels gets the free advertising. As the czar of Russia has not succeeded in preventing his subjects from getting the forbidden book, it remains to be seen whether the administrative machinery of the postoffice, supplemented by any that President Harrison's message may induce congress to provide for controlling express companies, will suffice to give the Russian government winning points in the matter. The czar has the advantage of controlling printing offices (or those above ground), also type foundries (known). Still nearly every Russian gets to read what he wants. Prohibition is perhaps the greatest appetizer known. Those who favor it are constantly confronted with the absurd inconclusiveness of the present measures. Whisky is made. After that it is sure to be sold. Novels are printed. After that they are sure to be read. If prohibition is to be anything evidently the United States must control the prohibited article. The Russian government has all that power, and yet the Russian people read manuscript books and import the works of republicans and socialists under false title pages and binding. They also get drunk on fluid contained in cologne water bottles. But our prohibitionists apparently think that they can succeed where Russian officialism fails. The experiment can be tried. It however involves delegating a good deal of arbitrary discretion to somebody. With a clear understanding of the condition American citizens may prepare for a show of hands on a test question. But if decided one way there will be no room for inconsequential complaints about the necessary means of enforcement by prevention, which is the only real prohibition, and there will not long be standing room for men occupying an illogical middle place.—Galveston News.

A case was tried in the police court the other day which the papers have not reported. It was the case of the People of the State of California against James Mehaffey, aged 9. The defendant, accompanied by his mother, sat in a chair with his feet dangling eight inches from the floor. The judge, the prosecuting attorney, all of the police officers, and a hundred spectators gazed sternly upon the culprit as the clerk, ordering him to stand up, read the indictment in a terrible voice. "Statecaliforny, ci 'n count' Sanfancis," yelled the clerk, and then rattled on: "Personally 'peared before me this steenth day of August, 1890, Peleg Yohansen, who on oath makes complaint, and deposes and says that on the blankety-blank day of August, annie domino, 1890, in the cit 'n count Sanfuncis, State of California, the crime of ROBBERY was committed, to wit, by James Mehaffey, who then and there did feloniously, and with force and arms make an assault upon Peleg Yohansen, and with violence to his person and against his will, did then and there feloniously and violently steal, take, and carry away by force from the person of the said Peleg Yohansen ONE POCKET KNIFE of the value of TWENTY-FIVE CENTS, good and lawful money of the 'Nited States, and of the personal property of said Peleg Yohansen. All of which is contrary to form, force and effect of the statute in such cases made and provided, and against the peace of the People of the State of California and their dignity." When the clerk got through with what "this complainant" alleged, said, deposed, and prayed, little Jimmie Mehaffey, who had violated the peace and offended the dignity of all California, was broken in spirit and ready to ask the state to forgive him. I did not stay to learn how the case terminated; but who ever heard of a two-bit offender going unwhipped of Justice?—George Macdonald in "Freethought."

Misfortunes will increase to one who deplores the selfishness of others.—The Sturdy Oak.

Egoism

Vol. I.—No. 6. SAN FRANCISCO, CAL., OCTOBER, 1890. Price, Five Cents.

Pointers.

Those who have not yet clearly distinguished between Egoism and *egotism* should read closely No. 5 of Tak Kak's series, which appears in this number.

The excellent sonnet in another column by J. Wm. Lloyd, is the first poetic fruit of EGOISM'S siring, and it is hoped it will not be the last. This was Anarchistic and not a case of forced maternity.

"Human Nature" is a new phrenological journal published in this city by Haddock & Fyfe, at 1008 Market street. It will introduce many new ideas to the conservative masses concerning the human animal.

Humor is an aggregation of misallied comparisons which are so clearly such as not to be taken earnestly, hence can do no harm. What a fund the doctrine of collectivism will furnish for a posterity complex enough to not regard it "scientific" as their ancestors did.

The mortifying typographical errors that sometimes creep into these pages are due to the fact that the proof-reader has an impression that the error looked for is farther down in the column, and in the rush to get to it, overlooks the point at which one is silently located.

A number of our readers have recently sent expressions of appreciation attesting the excellence of this paper, which is very gratifying, and we would not object to finding their friends becoming similarly affected. It is now six months old with no probability of bearing weaning soon.

Part of the purpose in publishing EGOISM was to fill the unexpired subscriptions of "Equity," suspended in Liberal, Mo., in 1886. A number of subscriptions to that paper will be filled with this issue, all of which will be marked at the top of this page with a blue pencil. Those who do not arrange at once to have it continued will be dropped from the list, as we desire to carry no deadheads except of our own selection.

In No. 168 of "Liberty," Victor Yarros, after quoting approvingly from EGOISM, says further that it "is an excellent Anarchistic paper, intelligent, keen and strong, although its editors do not always guard sufficiently against obscurity and vagueness." ... We fear this latter is too often true and shall try to profit by the kindly suggestion. But there is, however, one extenuating circumstance in the matter, and that is, if our readers were by some means to discover what we are driving at many of them might at once stop their paper.

"Sex Slavery," a lecture delivered by Voltairine de Cleyre before Unity congregation, Philadelphia, was jokingly sent by "Lucifer" to the "literary editor" of this paper. Unfortunately, it has no such editor, but one of its ordinary horse-sense editors thinks the lecture plain, strong, and well suited to the occasion, but too declamatory and emotional to please Egoists. All lovers of the "Twentieth Century" will like it. Price 5 cents. Send to "Lucifer," Valley Falls, Kansas, for the present. "Lucifer" will remove to Topeka, Kansas, the capital of the state, but its street address has not been published.

"Observations" by its editor, and "The Marriage Law," by G. A. F. de Lespinasse in a late number of "Freethought" go far toward supporting Victor Yarros's assertion that that paper "will furnish more instruction and delight than any organ published outside of Boston." Proud as EGOISM is of the editor of "Freethought," it will not indorse Mr. Yarros's statement without being qualified with, that Tak Kak's articles now running in this paper are as instructive as anything published either out, or in Boston. The publication of "Fair Play" being temporarily suspended, the columns of this paper are open to its editors to prove that their paper will not only be superior to "Freethought" and EGOISM, but the equal of "Liberty" itself.

Among the Egographs, on another page, will be found the announcement from "Freethought," of George Macdonald's desire to be considered an Anarchist so far as his qualifications will permit. These are happily so complete that he may be considered practically one of the handful of Egoistic Anarchists who teach industrial and social freedom as social expediency, and not as a religious duty. This is by far the most notable and valuable accession that Anarchism has received in a long time, and all the more delightful to EGOISM because it feels a kind of proprietorship in the prize. It believes that the frequent and quiet canvassing the subject has received during over two years of almost daily association of one of its publishers with Mr. Macdonald, as well as that of others of its immediate staff, has had much to do with bringing to that writer's attention the merits of Anarchistic socialism. Of course Mr. Macdonald's well-trained intellect was the principal factor, for all the people we associate with do not become Anarchists. However smoothly it may proceed, some efficient work may be looked for from him. In addition to the philosophic soundness that it has he will bring into Anarchistic writing a keen and witty ridicule of existing institutions that it has not hitherto enjoyed. No one should now be without "Freethought." We will furnish it with EGOISM for $2.25 a year.

Self.

To be sufficient unto self!—to me,
Who fain would stand on purest heights serene,
Where suns rise first, sink last, and all is clean,
This seems the acme of philosophy,
The one great need of whoso would be free:
Mine own sure friend, no matter how demean
My fellow selves, nor what may come between,
I know no lack of love, nor sympathy.
With reverence still before myself to stand,
To learn, to love, to honor all therein,
Knowing self-injury alone as sin,
And sin to others, sin at second-hand—
I deem a sane man's thought, and therefore grand,
The attitude of one whom truth helps win.

—J. WM. LLOYD.

THE enthusiasm of blind devotion to a fixed idea in reform always sacrifices the ever present to the never future; always sacrifices the pleasure of the hour on the altar, "duty to the cause," and finally places the crown of achievement on some assuming figurehead, as witness any movement which men and women suffer deprivation for.

MOSES HARMAN has been officially notified to appear before Judge Foster for trial on the 11th of this month answering to the indictment of last April on the O'Neill letter. Thus this more effective charge will be brought against him before the new trial granted on the writ of error can possibly take place, unless a continuance can in some way be obtained. In this way a man is harassed for years, plundered of his property, and finally murdered by inches for differing slightly from a few of his neighbors in certain opinions. Be it remembered the majority of his neighbors do not want him prosecuted. It is only a few, and these few by the fixity of law and through the natural indifference of a majority comprising the people of the whole United States can thus ruin and destroy a citizen for a technical violation, in spite of the efforts of all the friends that any but the most popular and influential men could possibly have. It is the inevitable majority indifference and disinterest that makes the tyranny of the few in the name of majority rule thus possible. It is that indifference which under Anarchism would become the individual's greatest protection against meddlers, for no one would be interested enough to leave his own affairs to help prosecute anything but violations of equal freedom. Prosecution would not be a great industry encroaching everywhere for material to feed its ravenous jaws. To send money is most effective now.

EGOISM

Issued Monthly at Fifty Cents a Year

—BY—

EQUITY PUBLISHING COMPANY,

Post Office Box 1678, San Francisco, California.

Entered as Second Class Mail Matter.

Hugh O. Pentecost's Shakerish Asceticism.

The sexual superstition is the darkest of the age, and I know of no person making pretensions to progress who is more deeply submerged in its murky depth than Mr. Pentecost. In his reply to my question in the August number of this paper regarding the family, he says:

> I have no private "heresies." Whatever I believe I am always ready "to assume publicly." When in the foregoing paragraph, I wrote of the "husband and father" and the "wife" I was writing of things as they are. All that I said applies to a man and woman and their children, whether the man and woman have been legally married or not. I do not regard the "family" as indispensable, or as having any necessary relation to government. Where a father and mother and child live together there is a family. What I have written in the foregoing paragraphs respecting the extract from the "Individualist" will, I hope, suffice for comment on the last portion of the quotation from "Egoism."

The last portion of the quotation from Egoism was this: "But suppose the father was a friend to both mother and children but not a husband, or the mother owned the house and children and was not a wife, but an independent woman without a question about equals or fathers, would it not be just as well—better?" The comment he hopes will suffice and with which he is content, is essentially the following:

> I believe that marriage laws result in more misery and lewdness than would obtain without them. But I do not believe in "free love" as that phrase is generally understood. Men and women should certainly be free to arrange their relationships to suit themselves. If they were thus free I think they would arrange those relationships better than they are at present managed by the politicians and clergymen. I think they would eventually learn the wisdom of establishing them on some other basis than that of sex. As the brain increases the sex nature decreases. As the "union of beings" grows, sexual love dies. The more we are men and women the less we are animals. Why advocate conduct of which all but beasts are ashamed? I commend to the editors of the "Individualist" and others these words from the "Kreutzer Sonata":
>
> "But," said I, with astonishment, "how would the human race continue?"
>
> "But what is the use of its continuing" he rejoined vehemently.
>
> "What! What is the use? But then we should not exist."
>
> "And why is it necessary that we should exist?"
>
> "Why, to live, to be sure."
>
> "And why live? . . . The object of man, as of humanity, is happiness, and, to attain it, humanity has a law which it must carry out. This law consists in the union of beings. This union is thwarted by the passions. And that is why, if the passions disappear, the union will be accomplished. Humanity then will have carried out the law, and have no further reason to exist."
>
> The reviewers do not understand the "Kreutzer Sonata." They call Posdnicheff a lunatic; but he is the only person who has ever spoken wisely and lucidly on the sex question. Clergymen, editors, and many "free lovers" alike reject his message. Is it because it is a call to personal purity? Take one other quotation from the same wonderful pages:
>
> The old foundation [legal marriage] is now shattered; we must build a new one, but we must not preach debauchery.
>
> Men and women should be free to regulate their conduct toward each other to suit themselves. The sooner they are thus free the sooner will they learn that they will be less miserable in the exact ratio in which they eliminate sexual passion from the "union of beings."

The expediency of "assuming publicly" or not any private heresy was the consideration in the suggestion. Whether it would probably cost Mr. Pentecost more to assume the position than to let it remain his private opinion can be the only question. For it is only a matter of being more or less foolish to express an opinion that places one in the power of any person or number of persons who can injure him or her by that knowledge. Nothing but the religious fervor of always being ready to acknowledge "Jesus" could consistently condemn a person for withholding any opinion at any time, or forever. But in this case Mr. Pentecost's conception of free love conforms so strikingly to that of the most ignorant and prejudiced that his publicly assuming his belief will bring him the hearty approval of the darkest sexual superstition of this or any preceding age.

It is precisely *because* all that Mr. Pentecost says of the legal family "applies to a man and a woman and their children whether they have been legally married or not," that I criticise the position. It is because in this case relief from legal meddling means nothing, that I remark the ridiculousness of his Anarchism in sexual relations. That position retains all the staidness and rigidity of the legal family idea and assumes that the fact of bearing the child or the relation that produces it is the process that marries; the very theory that all forced marriages and legal interferences are based upon. It implies that the pleasures of sexual relationship are for some reason to be adjusted by some other standard than the free contract by which other pleasures and all affairs in Anarchistic society would be carried on. Nothing other than sexual superstition is the basis of Mr. Pentecost's family idea.

From the tenor of his writings I felt certain that Mr. Pentecost was not familiar with the spirit of modern ideas on sexual matters, so to prevent the cry of "mad-dog!" from getting abroad in his brain, and to give him an opportunity to use the common sense that he uses on many other matters I placed the concrete fact before him in the example of a free and independent woman, to deal with as he must deal with his neighbors. The natural inference is that such an independent woman necessarily would be one who in her bringing up was freed from current superstitions and had acquired as much knowledge about the various functions of the human organization as might be known, as well as the skill of one or more industrial occupations, so that she might have secured not only a suitable home, but the means to carry her over the disabilities of motherhood if she chose to assume the financial responsibility in order to have full control of her children. But like a meddling and corpulent old woman of unpleasant memory, I couldn't fool Mr. Pentecost, he knew what I was getting at; it was "free love!" And he was perfectly willing to class the conduct of such a woman, who produced what she consumed and thus made herself as independent of men as men are of each other, as the "conduct of which all but beasts are ashamed." There is no escape from this conclusion, for he refers us directly to the paragraphs where free lovers are charged with advocating that kind of conduct. All this to justify a position which must finally seek refuge in a silly and fanatical ideal which proposes ages of suffering for the human race for the purpose of carrying out a "law!" What absurdity is not too gross for man to attempt to justify his prejudices by? it must be something the imagination has not yet formed!

Mr. Pentecost believes that men and women should regulate their relations to suit themselves, and believes they would arrange them better than the clergymen and politicians do. *Better!* Certainly. Why not; what could be better still than an arrangement that suited themselves? His language implies that there is; that mankind has some other duty than to please itself; that there is something superior to personal pleasure, like a theological duty. So it turns out. While the superstitious attitude of the legalist, in obedience to abstract society, makes sexual relations impure only outside of legal proscription, Mr. Pentecost, in obedience to an abstract ideal, would institute a social boycott more severe and illogical, by stigmatizing all sexual association as impure, and those who defend it among other pleasures, as beastly because they are not duly ashamed of it. It is only the dregs of the old idea that all pleasure is wrong and sinful. The idea of *establishing* a basis of relationship between men and women any more than between any other parts of nature, is a theological branch that has its root in the sexual superstition of Jewish theology. There is no more reason for such "basis of relationship" than for our relation to the sun, earth, or any other elements. If there is any enjoyment or benefit to be derived from anything, get it and let that settle it; or if there are any unpleasant or injurious results to avoid, avoid them and let that be the end of it. There is no reason why one pleasurable sensation should be more shameful than another. It would follow in such logic that the pressure of the hand, the lips, or any physical contact whatever is shameful. For if sexual prejudice be dispelled, one sensation to the brain is no less pure than another. The lessons of utility alone cover one relationship as they do another, and have no need for theological cant to impress their importance.

Mr. Pentecost says the more we are men and women the less we are animals. If this were qualified with the word "other," I could understand it. But to see a man or woman with all animal attributes extracted would be very interesting at least. Of course the more a tadpole is a frog the less it is a tadpole, but just why a tadpole should not wiggle in the water because a frog can jump on the ground I fail to see. The tadpole in the water is living out the fullness of his capacities which keep him there, but this does not justify depriving the frog of the enjoyment of the fullness of his being because it takes the tadpole environment to complete it. Since the human animal has a sexual faculty, and all the others that the less complex animals have, I see no reason for singling out this particular one for extinguishing the race. There are many others, among which the elimination of eating or breathing would be more benevolent, because more rapid. Aside from ascetic monkism I can see no reason for attempting to eliminate the sexual passion. The only thing necessary is to learn the requirements of its healthful exercise the same as another appetite. It is not the sexual passion that causes the misery in sex relations any more than it is the desire for food that causes dyspepsia, but the superstitious ignorance regarding that passion. Every animal has so many faculties which make up the fullness of its being, and all of which it spontaneously exercises, and whoever interferes with this rule in the life of the enlightened human animal will have to give a better reason than that of the soured old Posdnicheff.

And here we are before this gentleman's discovery—the philosopher's stone of humanity; that for which hogsheads of brain have been consumed to no purpose. And what is it? The "union of beings." What beings? Sexless men and women. Impossible! Yes; but yet, an unanalyzed conception of that kind could easily grow out of the lone experience of monogamic sexual relations. The balanced electrical or magnetic condition of monogamy, which destroys about all social pleasure except the harmony of intellectual exercise and the inhabitative propensity of association which people sometimes have for an old place or house, along with a heavy drain on the vital forces by mental confinement, and the invariable depletion of the exercise of the procreative function under these conditions, could easily lead the idealist to poetically conclude that sexual association is destructive of happiness. When the magnetic or sexual attraction thus dies or equalizes, as surely and probably the same as any neutralizing chemical action, then the sexual intensity does decrease in their case and further sexual association causes a sexual condition that causes them to imagine that they have grown or are growing "pure" and "holy," when they are really only electrically tired, and with other magnetic environment would be as carnal as before. The knowledge of facts has a wonderful influence in determining conclusions.

If Mr. Pentecost were to undertake to do nothing else until he proved his assertion that the imagination of the puggy old Christian on sexual relations is wiser and more lucid than the ample and profound exposition of the philosopher, Stephen Pearl Andrews, he would never have time to again assert the vague prognostications of his inexperience for an ideal for his leaders in thought to aspire to. G.

Editorial Vagaries.

"The Mannerless Sex," reprinted on another page from the "North American Review," for want of space is considerably "cut." Some paragraphs are omitted entirely, as are also some enumerating and commenting sentences indicated by the dots and dotted lines, but there is enough of it to awaken the minds of the majority to a fact they had hitherto not noticed. This is printed, not to indict woman because she is woman, but to show the result of repressing her activity and attempting to specialize her function to suit the supposed convenience of men. Influenced by the disabilities that a blind propagative instinct has through ignorance imposed upon woman, and his own convenience in developing the ideals of castle life, man now finds as he drifts into more variable environment that the instruments of the feudal ages do not suit him. The doll of the nursery or the drudge of the kitchen neither show off well in the role of responsible citizen. That subjective desire for reciprocity in his sexual faculty which fathers his gallantry, has through the convenience of slave service and resulting idleness of masters, produced an impudence in the dolls of others that is in decided contrast with the decorum of responsible equality, and practical man kicks. He loves inequality only in the castle, or hovel, where he is not the under dog, and if he could enforce equal responsibility in public under the guise of "manners," and retain unequal conditions at home in the name of "duty," he could again be at his ease for awhile. But woman has a firm hold on the gallantry snag, and lest she learn the idea of equal conditions from equal responsibility, exacting man had better let good enough alone, unless he is prepared for a fair contest in an open field.

Let those many women with "a watchfulness for the rights of others, and a gentleness in the assertion of their own, that deserves a respect little short of veneration," direct their superior comprehension to impressing all about them that equal opportunity would breed equal responsibility, and to convincing their weaker sisters that superstition is the tool with which the crafty few lash the herd into service, and that it may lurk everywhere except in the gratification of a desire, and they will thereby teach men that ill manners, instead of being the legitimate product of woman, is the result of a condition for which the ignorance of man is equally responsible with the inexperience of woman. Dudes, snobs, and many professional people are guilty of grossly invasive conduct in the presence of the toiler or others whom they believe less fortunate than themselves, while women of variable experience anticipate a need, or a point of equal liberty as readily as men of similar experience.

In the capitalistic press appears under the double heading, "Stimulating Home Industry. Immediate Result of the Passage of the Tariff Bill," the following safe presumption on popular ignorance:

> One result of the passage of the tariff bill, with its tin plate clause, will be the establishment of an immense tin plate factory at an early day, in Baltimore. A company of Eastern capitalists, principally from Baltimore and New York, have been quietly working on the scheme. The capital stock is $7,000,000, and the company will do business on an enormous scale. The concern will have its own tin mines and reducing plant in the West. About $5,000,000 will be put in the Baltimore plant itself. It will cover several acres and will be the largest tin plate concern on the globe. Foreign capitalists are to erect a tin plate mill at Duquesne, at a cost of $1,500,000, on the property of John A. Wood. About 600 men will receive employment.

Thus in order that a few hundred men may have work at wages that must compete with the men who must leave European works on account of the falling off of demand for their product that these new mills will cause, the whole people will buy tin at a price enough higher than that of a free market, to induce these capitalists to invest eight and a half millions of dollars that would have been employed in some other way than in levying a tax on the unprivileged industries of the country. It is said they have been quietly at work on the scheme. The quiet and principal part of the work presumably was to get the tin plate clause into the bill at the lowest cost possible. This is one of the ways by which business opportunities are made by law. Great indeed are the beauties of government, and stupid its patriotic asses.

Men subjectively under the influence of a certain limit of facts never could understand the actions of others who in possession of all these facts and others, deduced therefrom a different course of conduct as better adapted to wellbeing. Not appreciating they always persecute. H.

Some Managerial Experience.

When the company for the publication of Egoism was formed the honor of the entire management was conferred upon me, and I started in with the money furnished to get out the first number and a determination of my very own to prove myself worthy of the confidence that had been thus gratuitously placed in me. The money, as intended, was spent on the first issue, and my determination and the company's confidence evaporated as I approached the task of materializing the second without the necessary California eminence.

It was found that I could set the type and space it to perfection with Benton's Self-Spacing type, the best that an avaricious compositor ever drilled; that I could do the press-work on as good a press also as ever dispelled verdant ambition; that with a key I could get from our postoffice box the exchanges and abusive postal cards written us by old women of both sexes who have not the requisite quantity of blood and distribution of brain to make pleasant dispositions, or to maintain plumb-line positions; that owing to the fact that money of one-cent denomination will not be received here except by the postoffice, I could carry such change from one mailing of the paper to the next. In short, my management was found satisfactory in every way save in the one particular of obtaining any receipts from the business with which to conduct it. This function I had to resign into the hands of the rest of the company, since which I have worked no disappointment, yet have not been supremely happy with this very small niche in the otherwise smooth fullness of my responsibility.

But as the worst of things unable to grow worse sometimes change for the better, so changed this condition of things. A few days ago some of our more appreciative readers sent orders accompanied by postal notes and money orders for some of our extensive book list. Having long ago hoped for such an occurrence I had located in the notorious ruin temporarily used these twenty years as postoffice, the crevice from which shining metal is changed for Wanamaker's badly-printed money orders. Being posted from having read in the "North American Review" Adams's "Mannerless Sex," I took my place at the foot of the line of nervous men and inconfident women which reached ultimately to the cashier's window, and with the subjective air of a prosperous business man nudged resignedly along the rail on one elbow to that important point. Eventually arriving before the window I dextrously produced my notes and orders and with professional grace waited for the next act in my managerial role, when the complacent cashier inquired in a tone that sounded as if it might have said such things before, whose orders they were. In a confident manner and with audible distinctness I answered, Equity Publishing Company. He was not startled, but with more interest inquired if it was not a new company, what we published, and what relation I bore to to the corporation. I replied that the company, though reliable, was not old and well known, and that we published a monthly paper, pamphlets, and so forth, and I acted in the capacity of business manager. He said, "Sign your name on the money orders as manager for Equity Publishing Company." This I did in my not neat, but original handwriting while he scrutinized my dollar and a half flannel shirt and my three and a half years old blue flannel suit for which I paid ten dollars and fifty cents to M. Schwartz & Co., at Poughkeepsie, New York, and seemed to believe all I said. As he handed me the glitter he apologetically observed that his inquiries were due to my face not being a familiar scene at that window. To which I replied with illy-concealed emotion, that that fact had been the greatest obstacle in the discharge of my responsibilities. And I meant to explain to him how most of our subscribers are laboring people and inclose the postage stamps they send us with perspiring hands, which causes them to adhere so closely to the inside of the envelopes that we have to split them open and have them perforated and gummed in order to use them at all, but he mechanically motioned for the next man, and I politely retired with the consciousness of having made an impression and three dollars and thirty-five cents of cash in my hand. The Manager.

The Philosophy of Egoism.

V.

Can the Altruistic be included in the Egoistic? According to a standard definition, quoted and adopted in Webster's dictionary, from the Eclectic Review, the reply seems to be that it can. That definition reads as follows:

ALTRUISTIC, *a.* [from Lat. *alter*, other.] Regardful of others: proud of or devoted to others;—opposed to egotistic.

If Egoism were the same and as narrow in meaning as *egotistic*, of course the question would have to be differently answered. But egotism bears the same relation to Egoism as the term selfishness, used with purpose in the derogatory syllable, bears to my newly coined term, selfiness; hence we will set it down that some constructive use for the term Altruistic is not of necessity excluded from Egoistic philosophy. But let it be observed that claims made for Altruism, based upon an ignorant or capricious limitation of the meaning of Egoism, and a glorification of the doctrine of devotion to others, intended to produce a habit of self-surrender, are held in our mode of thought to be pernicious, and attributed, in conclusions from our analysis, to defective observations and reasoning, and to the subtle workings of selfishness. To be regardful of others within reason, is intelligent Egoism in the first place, but before we go far in this we draw a distinction between such others as are worth regarding and such others as present no title to regard unless a barren and superstitious form of respect obtrudes itself and makes a claim for "others" because they are "others,"—makes a virtue of sinking self before that which is external to the self. This is the principle of worship, mental slavery, superstition, anti-Egoistic thought. To be proud of others, of the right sort for us, is one form of Egoistic rejoicing. When reflection has done its work efficiently the habit of care for others, of the right sort for us, continues until checked by some counter experience; but let the habit become strong, let the avenues to esteem be unguarded and the sentiment of worship usurp the place of good sense, then the Ego is undone. He is like the mariner who has set sail and lashed his helm in a fixed position, fallen asleep and drifted into other currents under changing winds.

Some Altruistic writers remind me of the orthodox theologians. In face of the facts of physical science the theologian admits that everything in this world proceeds according to an invariable order, but he insists upon giving it a magical, ghostly origin. The Altruistic writers likewise admit that the immediate choice of action of each individual at each turn in his career is determined by causes with precision, but they plead for an Altruistic education, an Altruistic impulse now, so that hereafter the reaction of the individual to given causes may be this: that he will find his pleasure in the social welfare. I say that if he finds his pleasure in it, he Egoistically promotes it; and if those writers find their pleasure in planning a greater social welfare, their initial efforts in the matter are Egoistic. The reflecting person may perceive that there is room for mistake as to what is the social welfare. The doctrine which demands that a person shall forego some pleasure without having a deliberate conviction that by so doing he makes a wise individual choice, is responsible for a certain immediate lessening of welfare at one point. Beyond that it may be an illusion of ignorance.

The beliefs which prevail at one time regarding what is for the social welfare are widely different from those which succeed them. Once it was deemed injurious to society to teach a slave to read, and consequently injurious to tolerate in a slaveholding commonwealth the presence of a free person who ventured to follow his liberal inclination in this respect toward an intelligent slave of deserving character and conduct. Those who yielded to this social belief which they shared, rather than make an exception by following personal inclination, yielded to what has since been generally pronounced to be a malefic error. At the present day the beliefs prevail that conjugal rights of person over person are contributory to the social welfare; that children owe allegiance to their parents, and blood relations peculiar obligations to each other; that citizens need to feel other bonds than their own interested calculations and spontaneous benevolence; and so I might proceed with an array of phantom claimants exacting duties of the individual believer, prescribing what he shall and shall not do to be a worthy promoter of the social welfare; whereas on the whole there never has been any social welfare understood or realized, but meanwhile trumpery beliefs prevailing in the past and present have filled the world with individual miseries.

Some of the Altruists contend that their ideal man is wiser than to serve the beliefs of society. He works for his own ideal with his own reason for his guide. They fear that if he were to lose the urging sense of duty to the ideal he would cease to labor for a better condition of things. Now this is on their part, when stated, an insidious even if unconscious challenge to us Egoists to show them that Egoism is a better Altruism than Altruism itself. The matter presents itself thus, that the Altruist wants to inquire or discuss whether Egoism is "right," best for society, and so forth. Perhaps it will break up all the societies that now exist, and constitute new moral worlds, making new ideals possible; perhaps liberality of mind will prompt to all and more than the most intelligent and enlightened Altruist expects from the sentiment of duty; but however this may be, we Egoists are not arguing for the right of Egoism to be tried. We are trying to explain that Egoism is the chief fact of organic existence—its universal characteristic.

Let us analyze Altruism with reference to pursuits instead of confining all our attention to persons. A new acquaintance and a new thing are alike objects to the Ego. His aim is to make use of them. The Ego's mental caliber and his predilections, heredity, or habits with regard to association, distinguishing him as an individual, are exhibited in the appreciation which he shows for some objects which can be made use of as means to gain, or reduce to use, further objects. The less reflecting man finds grain and consumes it all, finds wood and uses all kinds alike for fuel. The more reasoning man saves some grain for seed, cultivates it and gets more, saves hard wood for durable uses, makes tools of metal, and studies his future welfare by planning means to ends instead of living from hand to mouth. In so far as he, in dealing with either persons or things, keeps in view the rational purpose of becoming better convenienced by any postponement or surrender of immediate pleasure, he is clearly acting with Egoistic judgment. Even when, having tested a series of phenomena, he establishes a rule and allows habits to supervene, saving himself the trouble of constant repetition of verifications, he is still the same Egoist; but if he lose the normal control of his exertions with reference to objects and ends which at first were to him means to other ends, he becomes an idealistic Altruist in the sense in which Altruism is distinguished from Egoism. In other words he becomes irrational, or insane. As some individuals have mind enough to be habitually regardful of others according to their merits, some artisans are habitually careful of their tools and more systematic and steady in their methods of work than others. Does this argue that they are less selfy or does it simply argue that they are more theoretical and, with excellent reason at the foundation, exemplify the law of character by which a process of reasoning having been settled the intermediate links in some chains of reasoning, become familiar, are passed over without self-consciousness? The selfiness of a farmer who goes out in the cold to save his stock, at the cost to him of some discomfort only, is not less in quantity, but is connected with more intelligence, than that of one who avoids the cold and lets his stock suffer. But a farmer may become so avaricious that he will get his limbs frozen in his craze to save a yearling for the sake of the few dollars it is worth to him. The love of money within reason is conspicuously an Egoistic manifestation, but when the passion gets the man, when money becomes his ideal, his god, we must classify him as an Altruist. There is the characteristic of "devotion to another," no matter that that other is neither a person nor the social welfare, nothing but the fascinating golden calf or a row of figures. We Egoists draw the line of distinction between the Egoist and the devotee. It is the same logically when a person becomes bewitched with another of the opposite sex so as to lose judgment and self-control, though this species of fascination is usually curable by experience, while the miser's insanity cannot be reached. The love-sick man or woman has the illusion dispelled by contact with the particular person that caused it; but in certain cases absence or death prevents the remedy from being applied, and in some of these instances the mental malady is lifelong. "Devotion to others," it will be observed, can be made a text for other sermons than those emanating from the amiable Moralists who pride themselves upon the alleged superiority of an unreservedly Altruistic habit of thought. T. K.

A Reaction, But When?

A thoughtful article in the "New York Commercial Bulletin" addressed to political leaders must have been read with great pleasure by such readers of Jeffersonian mind as are sufficiently hopeful to share the "Bulletin's" sanguine spirit. It is very admirable if regarded as a plea for the necessity of reaction against the paternalism of this growing generation. Its starting point is the declaration that "the great political want of the times is a policy that shall aim to expunge or reconstruct every vestige of federal legislation that has for its object the supersedure of free individual effort through the enforcement of artificial expedients." The "Bulletin" traces the growth of policies planted in loose seedbed of war times and exigencies, their indiscriminate tolerance and rapid extension, till congress has felt free to follow whatever course popular ignorance, class interests or party schemes may dictate in aggressions upon individual right and self-adjusting reciprocity of private business. The description of this dangerous progress is masterly and the warning is forcible that every interest in the country is beginning to feel insecure in the presence of a national communism armed with imperial powers. The "Bulletin," however, thinks that the reaction is coming. That paper takes a sanguine tone yet confesses that "the reaction has not yet reached the stage of distinct formulation in the popular mind." The "News" has not been inattentive to the trend of politics, and would qualify any hopeful statement with the most sober reflection. Indeed it is apparent that a sanguine view as regards the present popular mind is not justified by the evidence of current demands. The paternal spirit is active, aggressive, and growing. Perhaps one citizen in twenty is clearly cognizant of the danger which is amply illustrated to the discerning mind in the teeming schemes and proposals for relief from the effects of paternalism here and there by more paternalism. The "Bulletin" addresses political leaders. Now what is the function of the aspiring politician? Usually to ascertain and represent the will of the forces which make members of congress, senators, and presidents. The "great political want" of a small minority of sagacious men of Jeffersonian intelligence is surely not that which will decide the will of seekers after public place, honors, and emoluments. For these the choice lies between the conservatism of class interests, and the demagogic radicalism of a widening and intensifying retaliatory communism. The classes and the masses learn by experience rather than by theoretical reasoning. To reach the experimental demonstration of the evil of paternalism the country would have to push the experiment so far that the whole body politic, industral and social will have felt its exhausting effect. Then may come the reaction. A too optimistic view was well typified in the illustration of the ostrich hiding his head in the sand. The "Bulletin's" argument should be addressed to business men and people of philosophic mind. The politician is possibly capable of appreciating a reaction which will come after the lapse of years, but meanwhile the politicians will serve mammon or the multitude. It is obviously impossible to have practical politics on any other conditions.—The Galveston News.

The Mannerless Sex.

Perhaps it were best to say at once that woman is referred to under this title, that the reader may not remain one moment in doubt which sex is meant. The phrase, "the gentler sex," is, I consider, a most misleading one as applied to women, and I have been led to assume as a result of my personal observations that the title given to this paper is, on the whole, the most purely descriptive of woman.

. . . .

It is my purpose here to assert that, however great an influence may be exerted in behalf of the conservation of manners by exceptional women, the statement that woman in general is the refiner of manners is, in any large sense, an utterly false one. Furthermore, I have no hesitation in declaring that the code of manners followed in public by the average woman is disgracefully inconsiderate, superlatively selfish, and exasperatingly insolent; such a code, in fact, as would not remain in force among men in their intercourse with one another for one half-hour.

Regarding the rudeness of women in their intercourse with the world at large, I shall refer, in passing, to a few forms of it which have doubtless forced themselves upon the attention of very many persons who can readily furnish illustrations drawn from their own experience:

First—The indifference with which a woman will contemplate the fact that the convenience of others has been sacrificed to her caprice. Very observable in *young* women.

Second—The needless delay a woman often causes in

making her appearance when visitors have called upon her. Most commonly noticed among women who are no longer classed as girls.

Third—The unwillingness of a woman to wait for another to finish speaking before beginning to speak herself. Characteristic of nearly all women.

Fourth—Woman's failure to recognize the importance of an engagement. Most noticeable among women who have the fewest social duties.

The rudeness of women to men is, for reasons which will be sufficiently obvious to the discerning reader, less common than that of women to each other, but it is too frequent to be suffered to pass without comment in this place.

. . . .

We will suppose ourselves in a railway station in which a number of men are in line before the ticket window. A woman enters and, instead of taking her place at the foot of the line, goes to the front at once and informs the agent that she wants a ticket to Evercrech Junction by way of East Cato. Sometimes she adds that she is in a great hurry. She either cannot or will not understand why she is sent to the foot of the line, and when she arrives before the ticket window again, she becomes voluble over her grievance, and, after securing her ticket, remains to ask a number of questions, the answer to any of which she might learn from the railway time-table she holds in her hand, or from the porters at train doors. That any one is waiting behind her whose time is presumably as precious as her own is nothing to her, and if asked by the agent to make room for the next person, she is overwhelmed by what she terms his impertinence.

There is not a person who reads this who cannot recall similar scenes, I am very sure. At the postoffice or any other place where the invariable rule is "first come first served," woman endeavors to reverse this rule in her own favor, and, failing to secure this reversion at times, she sets down the fact to man's lack of gallantry.

Toward men of a rank which woman considers beneath her own she is often shamefully inconsiderate or shockingly impertinent. I have more than once in English railway stations seen porters, while staggering under the burden of heavy trunks, stopped by women who kept them standing several moments while they put to the unfortunate victims questions which would much better have been asked of the station master or of unemployed porters close at hand. But what of that? It is the duty of porters to be civil when questioned, no matter what Atlas-like load is crushing their shoulders. Then, too, I have witnessed American women browbeating persons whom they termed their "tradespeople" in a manner which would have resulted in their being knocked down had they been men...

It were useless to multiply instances in illustration for this part of my subject. To put it briefly, a very great number of women in their relations with men presume upon the privileges of their sex, the degree of presumption depending very often upon the rank of the persons with whom they are brought into contact.

. . . .

But it is when fair woman goes a-shopping that she becomes least admirable. Then her hand is raised against every woman who crosses her path. From the moment she pushes open the swinging doors of the first retail shop she enters, and lets them fly back into the face of the woman behind her, till she reaches her home again, she has laid herself open at every turn to the charge of bad manners. She has in her progress made tired clerks spend hours in taking down goods simply for her amusement, when she has not the smallest intention of purchasing from them. She has made audible comments upon "the stupidity and slowness of these shop girls."...... She has needlessly blocked the way when others wished to pass her... She has put up her glass and stared haughtily through it at the gown of the woman next to her at the bargain-counter... She, in short, has done very little that she should have done, and very, very much that she ought not to have done...

. . . .

I do not mean to declare in broad terms that man is mannerly while woman is not, for I observe with regret in many of my own sex an indifference to the rudimentary courtesies which is fatal to their reputation for good manners, and I recognize in many women a watchfulness for the rights of others, a gentleness in the assertion of their own, that deserve a respect little short of veneration. What I do insist upon, however, is this: that in public the average woman shows an inconsiderateness, a disregard for the ordinary courtesies of existence (which amounts sometimes to positive insolence), to a degree which is not anywhere nearly approached by the average man.

The reason for this difference in the behavior of men and women I do not propose here to discuss. I will not say, for instance, that man is altruistic and that woman is selfish, because I do not believe in any such putting of the case. But I leave for others the task of pointing out the causes of this difference... and indicating if they will, the remedy...—Oscar Fay Adams in "North American Review" for September.

An Egoistic Position.

The generous spirit that induces the sacrifice of self for others seems to be altogether admirable, yet a little reflection will show that this, like other good things, may be carried to such an extreme as to be a vice rather than a virtue. Sometimes the self-sacrifice defeats its own purpose by developing in others a degree of selfishness injurious to them and ultimately leading to their unhappiness. Take the case of a loving wife, who seeks to gratify every wish of her husband without regard to her own comfort or happiness; who forgives him all the wrongs he may do and continues to the end to worship an ideal existing only in her imagination. If he is selfish enough, to begin with, to allow such sacrifices in his behalf he will soon grow more selfish, and demand as a right those attentions and sacrifices accorded him through an excess of love. He will become arrogant, incapable of caring for himself, and except his wife is present to act as his hand-maid he will be made unhappy by having no one to pet and humor him in the way to which he has been accustomed. She thinks only of his happiness, anticipates his wishes, neglects her own desires that he may be gratified, and instead of promoting his ultimate good renders him unfit for the society of other more selfish companions. But it is mothers, and especially widowed mothers, who carry the spirit of sacrifice for others to the greatest extravagance, and often with disastrous results to themselves and those they love. Thinking only of the pleasures to be afforded their child, they humor him in every way, develop his selfish instincts, encourage him to dress and live beyond his true means, or at the sacrifice of home comforts, and find, when he has reached manhood, that he is utterly ungrateful, dissatisfied with his condition, perhaps made vicious by his idle habits and need for more money than he can command. Sacrifices that produce such results may have their origin in a kindly heart and in a loving and lovable disposition, but they are so little guided by reason and good sense that they are not to be commended.

Even in business and in the professions there are men who make sacrifices (through modesty or love of the arts and sciences) that are unjust to themselves and do injury to others by developing in the latter a degree of selfishness that could scarcely exist but for the presence of unselfish people to minister to its growth. A man devoted to science, taking no thought of himself or of the rewards to be won for his own support or gratification, makes a discovery which he gives freely to the world. Another of a more practical turn of mind takes up the discovery, turns it to good account, obtains a patent on the application and acquires a great fortune through a tax laid upon the real discoverer and others like him. The sacrifices made by modest men of ability out of devotion to some hobby of art or science or educational effort are often mischievous in two ways. They deprive the real worker of the rewards in reputation and money that are his due, and they give those rewards to some undeserving man whose self-assertion brings him to the front. The excuse usually made for such retiring modesty by the workers is that they care only for the advancement of humanity in some special line; that they are content to be unknown and have no selfish desire for money rewards.—Baltimore Sun.

Egographs.

Stupidity derives little benefit from experience.

We understand that the missionary societies are going to send some of the clothes, that were made for the heathen, to clothe the cold and naked statuary. Truly charity begins at home!—Individualist.

Government is the tool, to obtain which avarice and ambition strive; it is the sword with which now this, now that one strikes and hits, and calls it governing. We shall constantly be struck and wounded, let who will wield the sword, until we have destroyed the weapon itself.—Dr. S. Englander.

Competition, in fact, is the expression of collective activity; just as wages, considered in its highest acceptation, is the expression of the merit and demerit, in a word, the responsibility, of the laborer. It is vain to declaim and revolt against these two essential forms of liberty and discipline in labor. Without a theory of wages there is no distribution, no justice; without an organization of competition there is no social guarantee, consequently no solidarity.—Proudhon.

The family is not, if I may venture to so speak, the type, the organic molecule, of society. In the family, as M. de Bonald has very well observed, there exists but one moral being, one mind, one soul, I had almost said, with the Bible, one flesh. The family is the type and the cradle of monarchy and the patriciate: in it resides and is preserved the idea of authority and sovereignty...... It was on the model of the family that all the ancient and feudal societies were organized.—Proudhon.

Only a little while ago an article appeared in one of the magazines in which all women who did not dress according to the provincial prudery of the writer were denounced as impure. Millions of refined and virtuous wives and mothers [women] were described as dripping with pollution because they enjoyed dancing and were so well-formed that they were not obliged to cover their arms and throats to avoid the pity of their associates. And yet the article itself was far more indelicate than any dance or any dress, or even lack of dress. What a curious opinion dried apples have of fruit on the tree!—Ingersoll.

The time for asceticism is past. The futility and sterility of preaching and moral exhortation is patent to all. We do not denounce in the style of the religious censors, and do not mount the pedestal to be admired by the crowd. We reason with those who can think, and invite them to discuss with us the actualities and possibilities of life. It is purely and solely a question of intellectual agreement and harmony, this movement for social reform. Is this system of society one satisfactory to all concerned, or is it deeply objectionable? If so, lives there a man who can point out a better arrangement,—no matter who he is, what he does, or what his object,—and who can help us to solve our problem? This world is eager to hear from him. Come forward, one and all, express your opinions, and—let the wisest council prevail.—Victor Yarros, in "Liberty."

This is from "Liberty": "The editor of 'Freethought' says: 'I have come to the conclusion that we should be cautious about resisting by force anything that is not imposed by force.' In other words, Mr. George Macdonald has come to the conclusion that the wisest philosophy is the Anarchistic philosophy." I congratulate the Anarchists on having so good a philosophy, and I trust hereafter they will kindly regard me as one of them, at least so far as my qualifications will permit them to do so. I would not be willing to at once declare myself an Anarchist, with all that the name implies, but ask merely to be accepted on probation. Some people have a tendency to label themselves Anarchists, when they are really nothing of the sort, as Mr. Tucker has often pointed out. Indeed, it is Mr. Tucker's severity with these people that gives me pause. I know of progressive writers who have said one thing after another casually that pleased Comrade Tucker, and he quoted them in "Liberty." Emboldened by his approval they have declared themselves Anarchists and attempted to set forth the Anarchistic philosophy. Here was where they fell down, and Comrade Tucker cantered over them lengthways. When they were permitted to arise they apologized to the editor of "Liberty," and, expectorating on their palms, grappled again the great problems of political economy. I prefer to remain unlabeled, because if I were to mark myself an Anarchist, and at some future time Mr. Tucker should make it appear that I was something else, I should have to take the label off and store it away with the photographs I had taken when I wore whiskers, which are now no longer useful for purposes of identification. Meanwhile I shall continue to make observations of things as I see them, and shall not be disturbed if Anarchists or other good people discover that they agree with me.—George E. Macdonald in "Freethought" of Sept. 20.

The Robber's Shield.

Every National Banking Association, State Bank, or State Banking Association, shall pay a tax of ten per centum on the amount of notes of any person, or State Bank or State Banking Association, used for circulation and paid out by them. (Section 3412 Revised Statutes of the United States 1878.)

The legislature shall have no power to pass any act granting any charter for banking purposes, but corporations or associations may be formed for such purposes under general laws. No corporation, association, or individual, shall issue or put into circulation, as money, anything but the lawful money of the United States. (Article III. section 5, Constitution of California.)

We find but few who in their dealings do not seek to get "the best of the bargain."

The predatory instinct, or the disposition to rob and steal, is an almost universal trait of animal life.

The injunction, "Thou shalt not steal," was formulated, and has ever been enforced, in the interest of those who live by robbery.

The governing classes in all times and countries, have said to the producers, "You must not steal," and straightway have devised means by which they rob them (the workers), of the whole product of their toil, save only enough to keep life in their bodies.

J. W. Cooper.

Some Egoistic Catechising.

What causes marriage?—Law.

What causes divorce?—Marriage.

What causes marriage and divorce?—Law.

Who profits by marriage?—The priest.

Who profits by divorce?—The lawyer.

What is a marriage?—A mirage.

What is law?—The opinions of one set of men called the State, forced upon another set of men and women.

What would woman gain by neither marriage nor divorce?—Her freedom.

What would man lose?—A slave.

What is virtue?—Self-approval.

F. B. P.

Egoism

Vol. I.—No. 7. SAN FRANCISCO, CAL., NOVEMBER, 1890. Price, Five Cents.

Pointers.

We like the frankness of W. T. Minchen, of Carroll, Iowa. While he admits that ours is "no mean attempt of a paper," and pays his subscription several years ahead, he confesses to us that he is fairly "stuck" on the "Twentieth Century."

The "Mutual Bank Propaganda" on another page has been printed on a neat little 6-page leaflet, and will be sent out for distribution at 20 cents per hundred, which will about cover postage and the cost of paper. Interested parties will not forget that these should be out at work.

The latest accession to the ranks of Anarchism on the Pacific Coast is in the person of Eugene L. Macdonald, son of Grace Leland Macdonald, and of George E. Macdonald, editor of "Freethought." He declared on the 8th of this month. To the magnifying eye of the father the aforesaid ranks never looked so promising as now.

We wish to call our readers' attention to "Free Political Institutions" advertised in our book-list. No advocate of political freedom can afford to be without this and a thorough acquaintance with its contents. Nothing is so well calculated to answer the usual question, "How are you going to settle disputes under Anarchism?" We would like to see the pamphlet circulated by tens of thousands.

The Pacific Coast Laborers' Union of this city, recently adopted resolutions indorsing Senator Stanford for his action in regard to the land loan measure. This is an indication of an appreciation of a principle which lies at the bottom of industrial freedom. It is part of that political freedom which the union, following this principle to its logical conclusion, must indorse. We congratulate the P. C. L. U., and hope it will continue in the direction indicated. "Free Political Institutions," "Citizens' Money," "Mutual Bank Propaganda," and Egoism are matter that the members of this union will do well to read and circulate.

Women will probably not be out of something to render "duty" to yet awhile. They have been rendering it to God, to their husbands, to their children, to society, the church and the state, all of which are in a degree resisted by at least a few, but now comes a clincher for even these, in "duty" to biology. Ghostly gospels having failed, scientific theology is to try its hand at keeping them useful to the male. The new prophets are Patrick Geddes and J. Arthur Thompson, of England. They express strong aversion on biological grounds to the "recent attempts of some women to mould their sex into the fashion of men." Such women as are sufficiently bioplasmic will of course be regulated in their conduct by such an idea, but those with greater complexity of mind will know that their chief duty is to provide themselves with all the happiness possible, even though it becomes necessary to turn male. The "duty" racket with plenty of fools makes good business for drones.

One of Egoism's firmest home friends is W. S. Bell, and his presence often divides the air of the apartment from which this paper is issued. On one of these occasions he discoursed on the desirability of Webster's International Dictionary, just out. Having only a very old edition which our well-tried friend, Solon Thayer, presented us in 1886 at Liberal, Mo., we were soon puzzling our brains with the problem of getting one. The first thought was the one so common to the toiling millions, of plundering back and belly for the price of one, but investigation developed the probability of a funeral bill speedily following any shortening in that line. So we gave it up just as wiser people do, and with the hard facial lines of disappointment religiously a little sharper drawn and firmer set, turned and strode lengthwise of the wall of circumstances. When a few days later Mr. Bell laid a fine fresh-looking life-sized Webster's International Dictionary on the table and remarked, "There, don't say I never gave you anything," we didn't say that or anything else. What would have been the use; he is an Egoist and knew that we knew that he knew how much we appreciated it, and that his pleasure motive in giving and gratifying was mutually recognized. In Egoism there may be appreciation without oppressive obligation.

Life's Lover.

I love this little old queer precious life,
This floating isle the rumbling earthquakes shake,
This ship due somewhere, nowhere, 'mid the storms
And calms, this raft upon a heedless sea—
I swear I love it!—that is human too,
Loving I will praise it.
What do I care
That you remind me it is part a wreck,
Ill-built, about to break?—'tis not gone yet!
I know full well 'tis short from stem to stern,
And well I know 'tis thin athwart the beam,
I wist 'tis scant from keel to top—what then?—
Mark you!—it is the best I have, my all.

'Tis human that a man should love his own,
And my life's mine, my parents gift, my realm,
My native land and clime—patriot-like
I will defend it 'gainst your scurvy stroke.
Ay, life is worth the living tho' it be
Full one-half pain, joy is a sweet so sweet
'Tis worth a pinching price, and lifelessness
Contains no joy, and nothingness has naught.

Dost tell me of the wind and cold, the frost,
The noonday glare, the paralyzing calm,
The tempest's gloom, the gnashing hail, the rain,
The thunder's threat, the lightning's thrill, dim fogs,
Rocks, breakers, whirlwinds, maelstroms, waterspouts,
Pain, toil, thirst, hunger, fevers, sharks, corsairs,—
All the terrors of the voyage of life?
Ay I know them, and morbid tho' you deem,
And strange, in certain sort I love them too;
Evil is ill, I will not call it good,
And pain is pain, 'twere false to call it joy,
But ills, like beasts, may still be slain, like these
May yield us strength and pleasure in the chase,
Sweet flesh for food, soft furs, and trophies proud
Of horn and claw.
The world is wrong, but men
Are fitted to its faults, and still they love
Its battle's boast and blows and dangerous stir,
And glory in the perils of their paths.
So I!

There's honey in the hive tho' stings
Innumerable may cloud it round and warn
Hands off, Bruin stops not for that, nor I;
And there are roses 'mid the countless thorns;
And I love life because of honey comb
And roses plucked, and both in hand. Be sure
That stings do sting and thorns do scratch full sore,
But honey heals the hurt, and perfumes make
The mind forget,
And I know this full well
Things as they are (the universal course
Still being thus and so and nothing else,
Nor can be otherwise forevermore)
The good must ever lean upon the bad,
Without its aid and contrast standeth not;
Likewise the bad forever must the good
Support; its frosts start fires, its murders make
New men, its corpses feed new lives.
All years
And cycles hold a summer, so I deem
That as all things at least are one-half good,
I am indeed assured of half a loaf,—
* * * * * * * * *

Tell me, dull pessimist, eye full of gall,
Is not that better than no bread at all?

—J. Wm. Lloyd.

EGOISM

Issued Monthly at Fifty Cents a Year

—BY—

EQUITY PUBLISHING COMPANY,

Post Office Box 1678, San Francisco, California.

Entered as Second Class Mail Matter.

Egoizing Social Science.

One of the prominent obstacles to obtaining a general understanding and recognition of social science is the blind desire of many economic writers to have such science identified each with his person in the role of the original discoverer. The failure to take an Egoistic "tumble to himself" by analyzing this desire and guiding it to the completeness of a correct position, rather than to an ambition for originality, often makes him or her too willing to ignore any facts not enumerated among those sustaining the position assumed, and which would change it enough to impair its originality. The most disastrous feature of it is the confusion which the attempts to justify such positions creates in the minds of the unanalytic masses, who soon grow to regard each as a crank in pursuit of some metaphysical vagary. That all the real facts classified by one of these fit in with and are part of all that makes exact science, and are the only thing he really has, never occurs to him as he dodges about trying to keep his body between criticism and his unsustained position.

The most to be deplored case of this kind which has of late developed is that of Hugo Bilgram, who, according to so reliable a critic as Benj. R. Tucker, has in his book "Involuntary Idleness," produced a treatise on money and its relation to labor, which is second only to William B. Greene's "Mutual Banking," from the consistent course of which it departs by proposing that the government shall carry on the business of issuing money. Mr. Tucker has shown him that such a plan would be neither equitable nor economical. Since that time we have heard nothing from Mr. Bilgram on economic or social problems until recently when he asked "Liberty" for the Anarchistic definition of the Right of Ownership. Mr. Bilgram concludes that the right of ownership is "that relation between a thing and a person created by the social *promise* to guarantee possession," and that it "implies the existence of a social *organization* however crude it be" [all italics mine]. In his reply Mr. Tucker shows that while the Anarchistic definition of the right of ownership is closely related to Mr. Bilgram's idea of that right, it differs from his in that it rests on social sanction, or else unanimous individual sanction, based on the laws of social expediency as those laws are determined, and that it exists apart from the *decree* of any social power whatever—just as a valley does by the existence of two hills, or as two bodies cannot occupy a given space at the same time, decrees to the contrary.

Armed with a straw man to demolish, and a misconception of Mr. Tucker's answer, much out of keeping with the intelligence with which he asked the question, he proceeds in the "Twentieth Century" of October 2d to show the fallacy of Anarchism in a manner painfully much like an ordinary politician might be expected to do. The following is from that portion of his article:

> This brings us face to face with two important questions. First, who is to decide when an act constitutes a trespass upon somebody else's freedom? The opinions of different men will be found to diverge materially in numerous cases, and when disputes do arise for this reason, how should they be adjusted? Second, in what way and by what measure should the freedom of the trespasser be restricted? Should the one who is injured apply whatever measure he thinks proper? And if he is the weaker of the two, must he then calmly submit to any outrages of the other? Surely, the rational answer to all these questions can only be found in an organization of the people, who decree what constitutes an infringement of equal freedom, and who invest certain men with the duty of restraining trespassers by prescribed measures, those men having jurisdiction over all persons within the country in the event of their trespassing upon the equal freedom of others, whether the trespassers have or have not consented to bow down to this power. And such a "government" will always appear a tyrant to those not agreeing with its edicts, while it will be the defender of equity in the eyes of those whose opinions are in accord with its laws.

This is a remarkable statement, but scarcely for its originality, for I have always heard it from such sources alone as makes it remarkable that it should be repeated by the author of "Involuntary Idleness." The first sentence of Mr. Bilgram's article is this: "To those who have come to the conclusion that the present inequitable distribution of wealth has its source in the unwarranted interference of the government with the industrial and commercial freedom of men, the suggestion that the abolition of government is the only radical cure appears very plausable." It is just Mr. Bilgram's "rational" proxy representation that makes *unwarranted interference* of government possible, and the voluntary protection of social sanction impossible. By Mr. Bilgram's method, which is the prevailing one, the "restraining of trespassers by prescribed measures," becomes a great industry to which thousands of the strongest and brightest men of the country flock for employment, and which is continually extended and furnished with material by the "prescribing of measures" process, at the expense of a corresponding encroachment upon the liberty and products of the deluded "decreers" who "invest certain men" with this to these men industrial "duty." Now, industry is to human beings all right so long as they are not the material of the industrial exploiters. If the materials of other industries were conscious, or those which are conscious could resist, there might be a mighty revolt of even less equal freedom claiming material than the human life that Mr. Bilgram would so complacently devote to the jaws of a prescribing industry. So, intelligent human beings cannot afford to delegate their liberty to any institution the interest of whose members it is to convert the abridgment of that liberty into an industry. Industries can be successfully pushed only as unresisting material is available; and from this class of material Anarchism endeavors to rescue the human article by pointing out how it can escape.

The *people* happen to consist of numerous *individuals* with each no ultimate interest but his *own*, and as observation abundantly shows, this continues when one or more of them are "invested" with the duty of restraining trespassers by "prescribed measures." Then to avoid the abridgment of liberty which such industry necessitates, the people must keep the restraining prerogative in their own hands, to be applied by all the interested parties themselves in accordance with the facts and circumstances of each case, and beyond the possibility of any other motive. This is impossible by the proxy method, which in addition to unconscious negligence and the temptation of personal interests, labors under the disadvantage of applying a fixed prescription for every variation of disease; hence the inequities of technical evasion. The facts of progress are too closely knit with the every act of each day to be justly disposed of by prescriptive decrees enacted at widely separated periods, with even the best of intentions and talent on the part of legislators.

The method by which the people could keep the justice dispensing power in their own hands and as uncorrupted as the necessity for exact justice, is elaborately set forth in "Free Political Institutions," a rearrangement by Victor Yarros, of Lysander Spooner's "Trial by Jury." Suffice it to say here, however, that it consists of trial by a jury selected from the community by lot, and which shall be judge of both law and evidence, as well as what the cost shall be for prosecuting an unjust suit before it. This plan would cover every point of the sentiment of justice in human conscience, and avoid the inequities of statute fixity and technicalities, to say nothing of the displacement of the industrial inducement offered by the extension and privilege creating possibilities of Mr. Bilgram's "rational" prescribing method. Mr. Spooner's plan places each juror on his own responsibility, which of itself insures his greatest effort to render a just and equitable decision, for he must come from the performance of his function as a juror and live beside the man whose case he has disposed of as a neighbor and a fellow citizen. He cannot shift the responsibility off on a statute or a judge's instructions, nor can he afford to exercise tyranny on his own account, for he may in the future himself be tried before the same man he is trying, or before this man's friends. Neither will persons be likely to bring unimportant or meddling complaints, for they would be subject to paying the expense of a trial which served only to expose them.

It was hardly necessary for Mr. Bilgram to add in the concluding sentence of the paragraph quoted, that all save the beneficiaries of such a government would regard it as a tyranny. This may be seen all the way from Russia to the social "guarantee" of this country. If he will carefully read "Free Political Institutions," and study the nature of coercive government as thoroughly as he evidently has the relation of money to labor, he will see where his economics scientifically connect with the political freedom of Anarchism. And while it may deprive him of a temporary credit as inventor of a social panacea, it will also clear him of any suspicion of attempting through ignoring certain facts, to bring himself into notice by social quackery. This is a faculty far too primitive, and too common these times to be persisted in by those with sufficient breadth to follow where fact leads. What is needed, is not revered and mysterious originators of philosophies, but close observation, penetrating analysis, a sifting of theories, and generalization from the facts as a guide for combining a system of spontaneous order and security rather than momentary compliance by compulsion. This will leave out personal credit for philosophy making, but the field for combining facts into science or recognizing that which others have so combined, is yet very open. Let us have social convenience anyway, and get fame later if we can. H.

Editorial Slashes.

The generalizing vagueness with which men are usually content in applying a principle to their conduct, is aptly illustrated in the case of one of the "Twentieth Century's" correspondents, who acting on that journal's plan of religious crusade has sold his vacant land and put the money into business to clear his conscience of man-starving. The money he got for the land was undoubtedly somewhere in use bringing interest, and he must invest it so that it will bring interest for him or he will lose some of it in competition with those who get interest on their investment. Labor has to pay this interest out of its production just as it did before, while someone else will hold the land vacant, or using it, must in exchange tax labor with interest on the investment, or he might better have kept his money out of the land. So industrial emancipation will be left where it was, while the "Twentieth Century's" correspondent will be a man-starver by extortion instead of the same by exclusion, and have accomplished nothing more than the easing of his conscience through the performance of a kind of religious rite, just as more superstitious devotionalists do.

In No. 5 I noted that some customs inspectors had shadowed the Oakland jail for seventy-two hours to detect the exchange of some resident Chinamen who wanted to go to China passage free, for some Chinese prisoners who had been captured near San Diego while attempting to cross the line, and were to be returned to China. These inspectors succeeded, and the deputy sheriff was hopelessly involved so far as evidence was concerned, but Judge Hoffman of the United States district court was equal to the occasion. The deputy being indicted for releasing prisoners in his charge, and it being unquestionably evident that the Chinese were released, the judge held that they were *not* "prisoners in the meaning of the law," and the deputy is free. To this I have no objection for he had injured no one. But that he was released in spite of evidence, and the Chicago Socialists were hanged without the slightest evidence, is a fair sample of political protection to which I would call attention. These Chinese were arrested by an officer of the law for smuggling their persons into the United States, and lodged in the jail just like other prisoners, but the deputy had, according to this decision, a right to let such prisoners go. If they were not prisoners in the jail and could be released there, it is hard to understand why they were arrested at all, or why not released before the people had paid their fare from San Diego, if they might be released at all. A man out of work and without money has never been known to be thus set free when arrested for not being so well fixed as he would himself like. The languid-jawed citizen should "get on" the nature of the political god and compare its protection with that he gets from an insurance company for his house.

Trial by jury seems still to mean something in British Columbia, as the following from the daily press indicates:

> ...The prisoner was a woman. Continual brutalities on the part of Dugan, the man who was shot by the prisoner, were proved, and the defense set up that the shooting was purely accidental. Chief Justice Begbie charged strongly against the prisoner and asked for a verdict either of murder or manslaughter. The jury, however, found the woman not guilty.

Olive Washburn, the wife of a wealthy merchant of this city, is trying to establish a Nationalist colony on her seventeen hundred acre ranch near San Jose. Thus will *bourgeois* idealism be replaced by some useless experience, and more dreaming co-operators found looking for the "right persons" to co-operate with after having failed in this experiment. Some people have thought that with the privilege removed which would make labor cost the price of products, these products would be satisfactorily serviceable even if not produced by co-operatively religious co-operators. But to understandingly canvass an economic problem has not picnic element enough about it to attract the average idealistic Socialist. H.

We've Been to the Fair!

The Manager for this company was married some eight or ten years ago at an expense of six dollars and subsequent experience conferred principally upon his wife, and owing to the exorbitant prices sustained by government monopoly of divorces has established quite a "union of beings." It was this wife, a long-suffering victim of the marriage institution and the curse that all men do not sweat their noble brow for their "feed," who discovered by the picture on the posters of the Mechanics' Fair held annually in this city, that they had the very same man working for them that they had three years ago when we came here in the basement parlor of a coast steamer and a fit of reversed alimentation. She thought that people who treat their help considerately enough to keep it so long should be patronized. Besides she believed the society of these successful gentlemen might be beneficial to me by way of furnishing some useful pointers on my own activities. So having a dollar and a quarter which was not obtained from the profits of our publishing business she bought two four-bit tickets and one two-bit one from one of the Mechanics' wives at the pantry window. The two-bit ticket was for her little niece, whom we are bringing up on youthful ambition and compositors' pi, and whom I steered with difficulty past the numerous candy stands.

I dropped my ticket into the garbage schute at the gate with an air of reckless extravagance, and arriving inside the large barn in which the fair is held, I diffidently surveyed the ceiling, a precaution that I have noticed people invariably take upon entering a strange apartment, and a habit which is to me the strongest evidence of the correctness of the theory of the evolutionary ascent of man and the influence of heredity. I think the habit is due to the unpleasant experience of the ceiling coming down in rainy weather, when man dwelt in the caves of mountains instead of the caved fortune of his brother.

After having carefully scanned cans of the various brands of baking powder and from circulars furnished for the purpose ascertained their respective merits, we went into the conservatory. Here we found that the Mechanics had generously provided a large table covered with plates of every variety of California's finest grapes, intended we supposed for the refreshment of the visitors. But no one seemed to care for any, and as we were not so finely dressed as some of the other visitors my wife said we had better not take any first, as people might think we were too poor to buy a twenty pound box in the market for forty cents. There was nothing else in the conservatory but a tunnel which was not dark enough to kiss in and had no mountain to go through. Next we went to the other side of the barn floor and saw a good-natured Hungarian pumping with a gas engine the oppressive heat from some city water till it turned into real ice with which to keep some insignificant-looking fish from spoiling. This cooled our ardor for machinery, and we repaired to the Art Gallery. My wife is a lover of art, and I also love the art of lying—late in bed.

Out of consideration for the extreme sensitiveness of California's artists the gallery occupies one side of a large haymow where the light is very pure, being strained through the cracks and an occasional door in the partition. The paintings were generally in an unfinished condition, many of them having only a prime coat of miscellaneous paints carelessly spattered on. I failed to find a single one with the third coat and a marble-like finish such as may be seen on many houses without fee. But among these paintings were several pictures, and almost the first to attract my attention was a profile view of Jesus and the cross on night duty. The peculiarity of this one was that it had a full moon so located opposite and about one-third of it forward of Jesus's head as to make it look to devoted eyes like a halo. Of course to the critical eye of the Atheist it was simply "moonshine," but I noticed that its effect on the muscles which manipulate the corners of the mouth was not the same on all persons, therefore conclude that this particular view of the cross is distinctively the Christian view.

The next Bible scene was that of Samson and Delilah about three o'clock the next morning. It was an elegantly furnished room for those days that they occupied, and must have cost that dispenser of massage treatment at least fifteen dollars per month. Its more prominent equipments were Delilah and a luxurious sofa, modern fur robes, a wine-jug, and a large pudding dish of excellent California grapes and pears. This fruit had evidently been intended to facilitate the conventionalities of the earlier part of the evening, but owing to Samson's sanguine enthusiasm had been neglected. It must have been a hot night, for Samson had his shirt off and was bare-footed. He was not accustomed to staying up late at night and had fallen asleep sitting at Delilah's feet with his head pillowed on her knee in such an enviable attitude that she was about to awaken him with a hair cat-o-nine-tails to an appreciation of the rare occasion, when the police appeared at the door and thus getting the "drop" on him, pulled the verdant Nazarite. The public prejudice was so greatly against him in that neighborhood that the police judge was enabled to send him up for life. He suicided later by pulling down the center-pole of the mayor's house and mashing with the roof a whole company of half drunken aristocrats whom he was entertaining with a game of genuine blind-man's buff. In the gallery was one piece of draped statuary with an unattractive female bust placarded, "hands off," which forcibly reminded me, in that respect, of the bearing of the live prudes, outside of whose craniums no thought of touching them ever generated.

At one end of the barn floor in a large box was a Christmas tree in full bearing. Its precocious growth had probably been produced by the arts of the hothouse, as it was fully two months ahead of the season. I looked in vain for the young girls whom George Macdonald saw making baby-clothes. My theory was that my esteemed friend had been unduly influenced by usual experience in his inference that they were making these clothes for approaching personal convenience. I believed it was the timely assistance which these Mechanics' little daughters were able to render their mothers in the prospective event of additional heirs to the estate, but my idealism congealed into sober reflection, and I now believe what Mr. Macdonald's practical eye foresaw, that a number of human buds appear in these same clothes and have become the upper tier in this mundane vale.

Taking it all together I think the fair no mean accumulation for hard-working mechanics to save out of their earnings. I hope we may be able to show as much from our publishing business at the end of ten or a dozen years. Of course we would not object to showing it sooner if possible, and desire that no patronage be withheld under the misapprehension that we are anxious to wait so long before accumulating some. I have sometimes thought that driving a reform business to financial success is harder than to do the same in other business. There seems to be no constant and active demand to be reformed, and I find it hard to sell our literature to some folks even below cost; indeed, these are hard times!

Our patronizing the fair was a success so far as that went, but I did not meet any of the Mechanics and am short the hoped-for pointers, so am at the old disadvantage. THE MANAGER.

The Philosophy of Egoism.

VI.

The man who has fifty or a hundred suits of clothes made for his imagined use, the woman who keeps a colony of cats, the man who fills a private storehouse with all sorts of tools which he can never use, are equally illustrations of the subversion of reason and are to be classed as Altruists in the degree in which Altruism supplants a rational Egoism. Let us take up these cases and consider them in detail. To have more than one suit of clothes is mostly a wise provision for the future, hence the aim is Egoistic, but from the point at which the accumulator loses sight of the end for which his care and trouble are taken, and becomes a slave to the idea of clothes, he ceases to be intellectually his own master; he falls under the domination of a fixed idea and is in that respect like a fanatic. The difference between him and the fanatic is that his crotchet is merely a waste of time and means, whereas the fanatic's fixed idea is one impelling its slave to some sort of senseless interference with other people's conduct. The fanatic, too, is an idealistic Altruist. If his oppression of others were carried on in pursuance of a selfish calculation, he would not be a fanatic.

The woman who keeps an absurd number of cats embodies the exaggeration of the originally rational idea that it is a useful course to have one or two cats about a house to keep the mice down. Care for the useful domestic cat, without reasoning this matter over continually, is just as altruistic and no more so than fair treatment of good neighbors or of neighbors who would probably be dangerous if unfairly treated. The craze for cats is the same kind of Altruism as that which dictates entire self-sacrifice for the imagined good of other people.

One may need many appliances, but there is a rational limit to the accumulation of tools. It is quite clear that some men pass this limit and make collections of such things a hobby, not for exhibition and instruction, because they will eagerly accumulate a dozen or fifty articles of a kind, and not for commerce. This mild form of insanity cannot well be classed otherwise than as a degeneration from rational Egoism, through the altruistic process, to supernal Altruism.

I have dwelt upon these examples partly because it is sometimes assumed that professed Egoists should use neither foresight nor prudential self-denial. Critics who presume to argue in this way refer man to the improvident species of animals and forget even the squirrel. It is quite consistent with Egoistic philosophy and practice that foresight should be used and specific pleasures relinquished, and that habits of prudential self-denial should be formed, subject to searching review and ready self-control, especially as we are admonished on any change of surroundings.

And now, having traced the degeneration of the limited altruistic phase of Egoism (the rational postponement of immediate ends to means of no value in themselves but only to reach Egoistic ends), in other words having viewed Egoism as partly a pursuit of means, and—so a rational course, and Egoistically altruistic habits as a further rational economy of time, in place of endless minute examination and calculations of consequences,—having explained from the Egoistic point of view how, when the Ego has in some instance purposely dismissed the immediate gratification of self, he may and does sometimes fail to return to it for want of landmarks, memory and reflection, I would inquire whether there be any better explanation of the origin of the insanity of self-abnegation; I mean in the real, extreme unegoistic sense of the word; a sacrifice without expectation of compensation to the individual. The limited altruistic phase of Egoism is inevitable for a complex being. It involves the peril described. He runs the risk of going into supernal Altruism, much as the sailor, deliberately going out of sight of land to reach other land, runs whatever risk there may be of forgetting the object with which he undertook the voyage or of losing his compass and never getting back; or as an orator, entering upon the flowery path of illustration, may become captivated with the images of his fancy and utterly forget the logical conclusion which he intended only momentarily to postpone in order to reach it with greater effect.

As hobbies, miserly habits, and so forth, do not seem to admit of any other explanation than the one presented, and as fanaticism with its cruel deeds admittedly springs from concern for others, coupled with a belief that certain of their doctrines are errors, and is thus identified despite its deplorable characteristics, as being a pronounced Altruism, and yet in consequence of these characteristics it will not be defended by professed Altruists, but will be admitted by them to originate in unreason, I should not expect them to object to this way of accounting for all obviously evil forms of Altruism. But the obviously evil and the silly phases of Altruism are apparently as intense as those phases which are so much praised and expatiated upon by professed Altruists, and therefore presumably require an equal formative energy. Consequently until the contrary is shown, we shall be as thoroughly warranted by reason in assuming that if the one set have been accounted for by our theory of the development of the dominating power of ideas and sentiments, the other can be accounted for in the same way; precisely as we may say that if the physical development theory be admitted to account for the snake and the hawk, it will be taken to account for the sheep and the deer. And moreover, when a process of development is shown to hold good, the mute challenge of facts is not merely as to whether or not another and radically different sort of explanation can be supposed for correlative facts, but the presumption of a general unity of process is very strong. Let any considerable part of the foregoing reasoning be admitted and it is granted to us that the concrete good or seemingly good in Altruism is based in Egoism. Then it can safely be inferred that it must be subject to test by reference to the Egoistic reason of its existence; in each case of a development of altruistic motive the question will be: is it serviceable projection, an indirect means of Egoistic attainment, or is it an irrational movement, an aberration, to which we have seen there is a constant tendency?

Now, the reason why we need to speak with caution of the seeming good in Altruism is not founded in any doubt that rationally limited altruism is wise and a necessary part of human Egoism, but in the circumstance that Altruism appears to have been set up by some writers as a principle separate from and independent of Egoism, as if the latter were a preliminary ladder, passing from which they profess to reach their supernal structure, whereupon they would kick the ladder from beneath them. At this point we Egoists decide that such Altruism, considered as a principle, is not a thing of parts more or less good, but is posited as a rival or antagonistic claim, and therefore, from the Egoistic point of view, is wholly bad.

Here for illustration we may take the analogy of what is called government. If we say that each individual needs protection from violence and combinations for violence, that therefore the honest people should combine to secure such protection, this is well; but if upon this basis a governmental power is built which proves to be oppressive, we deny that such government is good, whatever good acts it may perform.

TAK KAK.

THE MUTUAL BANK PROPAGANDA:
Its Declaration of Principles and Object.

WM. TRINKAUS, - - - - - Recording Secretary.
ALFRED B. WESTRUP, - - - - - Corresponding Sec'y.
Room 325, 225 Dearborn street, Chicago, Ill.

At a series of meetings held to inquire into the cause of poverty and the general distress and unrest among wealth producers, it was conclusively shown that prevailing notions in regard to economics are erroneous; that interest, rent and dividends as compensation for the use of capital are inequitable and are perpetuated by arbitrary money systems which enforce this tribute from producers to non-producers by excluding the operations of supply and demand in furnishing the paper medium of exchange we call money, thus producing poverty and degradation among the masses, and abnormal accumulations of wealth on the part of a few; that this prohibition is accomplished by state and federal legislation, based upon the superstition that only authority can supply money, because of an alleged necessity for a "measure" or a "standard" of value, supposed to be established by the State coining some metal and making such coin a legal tender; that such notions have no foundation in fact, but have their origin in imperialism, which we have not entirely repudiated; that the "function of royalty" to supervise the money of this country, denied to George the Third by the triumph of American independence, but affirmed to be a function of the State as it exists here, was a transfer of an essential element of imperialism instead of its utter extirpation supposed to have been accomplished in the establishment of the republic.

To the end, therefore, that the medium of exchange may be freed from all arbitrary control, and that it be subject to the operations of supply and demand, we organize ourselves into an association to be known as the

MUTUAL BANK PROPAGANDA.

Object.

The object of this association is to lay before the public correct views on the subject of money; to show the fallacy of the idea that the State should regulate, or in any way interfere with its supply, and to aid in the establishment of similar associations in every city, with a view of organizing Mutual Banks of Issue whenever money is needed and there is collateral upon which to issue; thus putting an end to speculative interest by issuing money at cost.

Organization.

Any person may become a member of the Mutual Bank Propaganda by subscribing to its declaration of principles, and affirming his or her desire to aid in its object.

Contributions.

All contributions shall be voluntary.

Officers.

The officers of the association shall be a recording secretary, a corresponding secretary and a treasurer, who shall be elected each year.

Meetings.

The meetings shall be held once a week, and each meeting shall choose its presiding officer. For the transaction of business five members shall constitute a quorum.

The following preamble and resolutions were unanimously approved at the meeting of the Mutual Bank Propaganda, held April 18, 1889.

Whereas, This association, recognizing as its basic or fundamental principle, the inviolability of the person or property of the individual (provided it has not been forfeited by the commission of crime), and

Whereas, This association views with sorrow and alarm the increasing centralization of power in the State and the constant curtailing of the rights of the individual, therefore, be it

Resolved, That in assuming control of money and declaring what shall, and what shall not be money, the State prohibited competition in banking and established a monied aristocracy; that there is no valid reason nor is there any authority in the constitution for doing so; that the right to life, liberty and the pursuit of happiness, which is the ultimate expression of right we must appeal to, includes the right to private property, and the right to property must necessarily include the right to exchange that property, and the right to exchange it includes the right to determine what it shall be exchanged for, be it any article or commodity or a piece of paper with an inscription on it, be that inscription written or printed, and from whatsoever source; and therefore, that any restriction upon, or interference whatsoever with exchange, is a denial of the right to private property and should be resisted at any cost.

Resolved, That we affirm the following statements to be sound in theory, practicably applicable, and the most suitable to the needs of the people at this time. We therefore invite any opponent to make his statement and give us a chance to reply.

We affirm: that the application of the mutual principle to banking, including the issue of paper money and the issue of paper money on such products as bankers usually make advances or loan money on, would,

FIRST. Abolish speculative interest so far as money-lending is concerned, because the rate charged by the Mutual Bank would not exceed cost; thus a rise in wages would be possible, for there can be no increase in wages except by a corresponding decrease in "compensation to capital."

SECOND. All collateral used as a basis for the issue of paper money would then possess the advantages now confined exclusively to gold and silver by virtue of law; the owners of such products would be released from the grip of the speculator; such products could no longer be made the object of speculation; hence, the objectionable features of boards of trade will cease with the advent of the Mutual Bank.

THIRD. Increase the volume of money in proportion to the amount of collateral pledged instead of confining it to the quantity of gold and silver. Thus all ledger accounts would be closed up and the "balance due" would exist in the form of CASH ON HAND in paper money of the Mutual Bank. In other words, all credits would be obtained at the bank and all business transactions would be CASH.

PLAN FOR A MUTUAL BANK.

1. The inhabitants, or any portion of the inhabitants, of any town or city, may organize themselves into a Mutual Banking Company.

2. The officers of a Mutual Bank should be a board of directors, an appraiser, a manager, a cashier and a secretary.

3. Those who propose to become members, should elect the appraiser and the board of directors, who should hold their office for one year.

4. The board of directors should first elect the manager, cashier and secretary from among their number.

5. The manager, cashier, and secretary should hold office until they resign, or are removed by the board of directors, who should require each to give bonds. They should be subject to, and not members of the board, nor participate in its meetings, except when called upon to do so; and the same rule should govern the appraiser.

6. The appraiser and members of the board may be removed at a general meeting of the members of the bank, and others elected to fill their places, of which due notice should be given.

7. Membership ceases when a member pays his notes to the bank, and none but members should be directors.

8. The board of directors should employ a secretary of

its own, and a legal adviser, and fix the salary of the officers and employes.

9. The manager should manage the affairs of the bank, the cashier the usual duties, and the secretary should have charge of all documents, see that all mortgages are duly recorded before notes are discounted by the bank, and keep an account of the printing and issue of bills.

10. Any person may become a member of the Mutual Banking Company, of any particular town or city, by pledging UNINCUMBERED IMPROVED REAL ESTATE, NEVER VACANT LANDS, situated in that town or city, or in its immediate neighborhood, or other first-class collateral to the bank.

11. The Mutual Bank should print (or have printed) paper money, with which to discount the notes of its members, and should always furnish new bills for torn or soiled ones when requested, free of charge.

12. Every member, at the time his note is discounted by the bank, should bind himself and be bound in due legal form, to receive in payment of debts at par, and from all persons, the bills issued and to be issued by the bank.

13. Notes falling due may be renewed by the bank, subject to the modification which a new valuation may require, so that the note does not exceed two-thirds.

14. Any person may borrow the paper money of a Mutual Bank on his own note not extending beyond twelve months (without indorsement), to an amount not to exceed two-thirds of the value of the collateral pledged by him.

15. The charge which the Mutual Bank should make for the loans, should be determined by, and if possible, not exceed the expenses of the institution, pro rata.

16. No money should be loaned by the bank except on the above conditions.

17. Any member may have his property released from pledge and be himself released from all obligations to the Mutual Bank, and to the holders of its bills as such, by paying his note or notes to the said bank.

18. The Mutual Bank shall receive none other than its own money, or that of similar institutions, except such coin money as the board of directors may designate, and this should be discounted one-half of one per cent.

19. All Mutual Banks may enter into such arrangements with each other, as shall enable them to receive each other's bills.

20. The Mutual Bank should publish in one or more daily papers each day, a statement of its loans the day previous, describing the property pledged, giving the owner's name and its location, with the appraiser's value and the amount loaned on it. And also a statement of the notes paid, and mortgages cancelled during the same period, which statement should be signed by the manager, cashier and secretary.

The Entering Wedge Examined.

If the public free schools and the postoffice are to be made the entering wedges of Communism in the nation, a large interrogation mark will be required against statements laudatory of their advantages, for everything must be judged by what it entails as well as by what it primarily is. An argument for government ownership and operation of railroads premises the assertion that fares and freights can be made lower than private enterprise under the freest conditions will ever make them. The statement is put forward by a correspondent (Leber) as something incontestable, and is rested upon the example of the postoffice. Now, so far as the postoffice is concerned, the government charges upon letters a rate which for some years past the private carriers would have been very glad to obtain. They could make a profit out of it and could make the rate less. The government does some other postal business not only without profit but at a loss—made up from the profits of letter carriage and from taxation. The example is a weak mainstay for further communistic castle building. The government could of course make fares and freights as it makes postal charges, but if it runs any service below cost the people must pay the deficit another way. Let it be assumed, however, that the government will run all branches at their exact cost. Thus profit is eliminated. But if it is desired to have government conduct a business to avoid paying profits to capital that principle is broader than the business which may be taken hold of to illustrate it, and if a plan is a sound one the next demand will be that government take hold of other businesses successively as it is able; for the reason—a desire to eliminate profit—is the same and applicable in many directions. The relief to the people, if real, is the same. There is a circumstance to be considered yet. The government can not operate as a capitalist without drawing from the people capital for its use. If it devotes the capital to business without exacting profit it has first taken it from people where they were using it presumably at a profit. What really free competition can not do it is presumptuous for any man to affirm, for it has not been tried, but as a pointer it can be noted that the highest rate of profit goes with the most exclusive privilege and with accumulations and freedom capital visibly tends to lend itself for lower profits. It may reach zero under perfect freedom, its return being maintenance and protection from thieves and the process of decay. Therefore it is not at all demonstrated that government service at cost can economically surpass private enterprise, even assuming absolute purity of government. The trinity of profits, interest and rent in the abstract sense of the economists, meaning the offspring of privilege which curtails the industrial freedom of mankind, is the provocation to all state socialistic, greenback, and revindicating special tax schemes, and they find converts among the masses who accept the idea that the choice lies between a paternal solution of economic problems or a continuance of monopolistic privilege. But surely as the strife of interest grows more earnest—and honesty is not lacking on either side—there will be place for another alternative. With vast accumulations of labor's products in the form of capital; with a tendency to seek conservation for this at any rate, not so much thought for profit; with the idea of free barter making progress and other companion ideas therewith, though as yet greatly more misunderstood, may it not be perceived in time that capital can be made the faithful servant of all the people by the very simple process of letting it arise, grow and employ itself where it can, but without an iota of privilege, bounty or economic protection?—Galveston News.

MARRIAGE means *ownership*,—the exclusive right to use and abuse. If I *own* a woman and choose to keep her to myself—what! —may I not kill my rival for trespass, or kill her if she transfers my property, her person and affections, to him? I may do as I please with my own, and resist all invaders. If, on the contrary, I am grounded in the conviction that I do not own the woman I love, that all others possess the same rights in relation to her that I do myself, that any peculiar love she may have for me is a peculiar favor, unaccompanied by any obligation of extension or duration beyond the limits which she herself may freely set to it, it becomes plain that any jealousy I may feel will only manifest itself through the boycott, and even that, if I am wise, I will use only very gently lest I hang myself in my own halter. Briefly then, whether sexual relations are sensual or refined, the recognition of liberty means the abolition of jealousy. And liberty means vastly more than this. Liberty means that human beings will never associate on the sensual plane any longer than it is mutually pleasant; therefore all this resulting contempt, disgust, hatred, will cure itself by the simple method of mutual repulsion... In liberty no one will be a sensualist but whoso chooses, and as no one enjoys disgust, contempt, hatred, no one will choose to sensualize one moment after these symptoms develope, and, when and where these symptoms do not appear, ought we not to pause before we condemn any act as impure? Impurity is that which is mixed with evil, and evil is that which injures; where there is no injury, there is no evil, no impurity, hoary precepts to the contrary notwithstanding.—J. Wm. Lloyd.

EGOISM'S PRINCIPLES AND PURPOSE.

Egoism's purpose is the improvement of social existence through intelligent self-interest. It finds that whatever we have of equal conditions and mutual advantage is due to a prevalence of this principle corresponding with the degree and universality of individual resistance to encroachment upon the individual.

Reflection will satisfy all who are desirous of being guided in their conclusions by fact, that as organization itself is a process of absorbing, with no limit save that of outside resistance, every material useful to its purpose, so must the very fact of its being a separately organized entity make it impossible for it to act with ultimate reference to anything but itself. Observation will show that this holds good throughout the vegetable and animal kingdoms, and that whatever of equality exists among members of a species or between different species has its source and degree in the resisting capacity, of whatever kind, which such member or species can exert against the encroachment of other members or species. The human animal is no exception to this rule. True, its greater complexity has developed the expedient of sometimes performing acts with beneficial results to others, but this is at last analysis only resistance, because it is the only means of resisting the withholding by others from such actor's welfare that which is more desirable than that with which he parts. If, then, the self-projecting faculty of mankind is such that it will in addition to the direct resistance common to the less complex animals, diplomatically exercise present sacrifice to further extend self, and it being a fact that equality depends upon equal resistance, diplomatic or otherwise, what are its chances in an absence of enlightenment in which the individuals of the majority so far from *intelligently* using this resisting power in their own behalf, do not even believe that they should do so? The result of a general conception so chaotic, would naturally be what we find: the generalization from the practical expediency of certain consideration for others, crystallized through the impulse of blind selfishness into a mysterious and oppressive obligation, credit for the observance of which gratifies the self-projecting faculty of the simple, while the more shrewd evade its exactions, and at every step from the manipulation of the general delusions of religious and political authority to the association of sexes and children at play, project themselves by exchanging this mythical credit for the real comforts and luxuries of the occasion, which the others produce. Thus in addition to the natural disadvantage of unequal capacity, the weaker are deprived through a superstition, of the use of such capacity as they have, as may be seen in their groping blindness all about us.

To secure and maintain equal conditions then, requires a rational understanding of the real object of life as indicated by the facts of its expression. It is plain that the world of humanity is made up of individuals absolutely separate; that life is to this humanity nothing save as it is something to one of these; that one of these can be nothing to another except as he detracts from or adds to his happiness; that on this is based the idea of social expediency; that the resistance of each of these individuals would determine what is socially expedient; that approximately equal resistance makes it equality, and on such continued and a universal resistance depends equality. This can leave no room for any sane action toward others but that of the expediency most promoting the happiness of the acting Ego. Therefore Egoism insists that the attainment of equal freedom depends upon a course of conduct replacing the idea of "duty to others" with *expediency* toward others; upon a recognition of the fact that self-pleasure must be the final motive of any act: thus developing a principle for a basis of action about which there can be no misunderstanding, and which will place every person squarely on the merit of his or her probable interests, divested of the opportunity to deceive through pretension, as under the dominance of altruistic idealism. It will maintain that what is generally recognized as morality is nothing other than the expediency evolved from conflicting interests under competition; that it is a policy which, through the hereditary influence of ancestral experience, confirmed by personal experience, is found to pay better than any other known policy; that the belief that it is something other than a policy—a fixed and eternal obligation, outside of and superior to man's recognized interests, and may not be changed as utility indicates, makes it a superstition in effect like any other superstition which causes its adherents to crystallize the expediency adopted by one period into positive regulations for another in which it has no utility, but becomes tyrannical laws and customs, in the name of which persecution is justified, as in the fanaticism of any fixed idea.

Another part of its purpose is to help dispel the "Political Authority" superstition and develop a public sentiment which would replace State interference with the protection for person and property which the competition of protecting associations would afford. Then the State's fanatical tyranny and industry crushing privilege would torture the nerves of poverty-stricken old age or pinch tender youth no more. The most disastrous interference of this monster superstition is its prohibition of the issuing of exchange medium on the ample security of all kinds of property, which at once would abolish speculative interest and practically set all idle hands at productive labor at wages ever nearing the whole product until it should be reached. The next interference is by paper titles to vacant land instead of the just and reasonable one of occupancy and use, which with the employment that free money would give, would furnish all with comfortable homes in a short time, and even with luxuries thereafter from like exertion. Following this is its patent privilege, customs robbery, protective tariff, barbarous decrees in social and sexual affairs; its brutal policy of revenge, instead of restitution, in criminal offenses, and finally its supreme power to violate the individual, and its total irresponsibility.

Vol. I.---No. 8. SAN FRANCISCO, CAL., DECEMBER, 1890. Price, Five Cents.

Pointers.

J. Wm. Lloyd has "known Egoism," and **bears again and again. May he multiply and replenish the earth with Egoistic song. Some enthusiastic compliments for his poetry reach us.**

Owing to the exactions of more imperative work, Tak Kak has been unable to contribute his usual article. He hopes, however, to continue them soon. That they are the backbone of this paper need scarcely be mentioned when it appears without one.

Julia Huff, one of Egoism's Kansas subscribers, sat with a leg on each side of her race horse and rode it to victory at a fair in that state recently. To thus face the conventional tyrant would not have been slow even though the horse had been last in the race.

"My Uncle Benjamin," by Claude Tillier, is Benj. R. Tucker's latest translation from the French. It is a novel of humor, realism, satire, philosophy, which was brought to Mr. Tucker's notice by George Schumm. We have not seen it, but Mr. Tucker strongly recommends it to his readers in "Liberty," which is a sufficient guarantee for every radical to order one. It contains over 300 pages, and sells for $1.00 bound in cloth or 50 cents in paper cover. We will have it by the time this reaches our readers, and will furnish it at the above price.

As has been heretofore remarked, the person of W. S. Bell sometimes displaces some of the atmosphere of this large office, and from him we learn that "Fair Play" is to appear by January 1. Of this we are heartily glad. We had feared that those veterans were weary of getting out a first-class radical paper almost at their own expense, only to draw the denunciation of slush swilling gushers. But we are glad to have more good company in the attempt to pound sand into the world's rat hole of blind emotion. May support hover there and—here!

A friend who is in a position to know more of Hugo Bilgram's ideas than was gathered by Egoism from his article on the "Fallacy of Anarchism," in the "Twentieth Century" of Oct. 2, says we were a little unjust to Mr. Bilgram in our criticism of him in the November number of this paper. For this the critic is sorry because it places him in a disadvantageous position in the eyes of other people as well as Mr. Bilgram, when the injustice is known. The writer solicits Mr. Bilgram's sympathy by congratulating him on a forthcoming position that it is said will be sound.

We again call our readers' attention to "Free Political Institutions," advertised on the last page of this paper. So far a solitary order is the result of our advertising. If Anarchism succeeds it will be through its principles being embraced by all the intelligent men and women of the country. These can be reached more effectively by this pamphlet than by many times its cost in any literature that we have read. We desire to see the pamphlet circulated, and do not seek orders for their commercial value; if it is more convenient, order it from the publisher, Benj. R. Tucker, Box 3366 Boston, Mass. It may also be had from Fair Play Publishing Company, Lock Box 353 Sioux City, Iowa. Whoever is interested in spreading the light will be glad their attention was called to it if they read it.

A subscriber has kindly sent us a quotation from the address of President E. Benjamin Andrews, of Brown University, delivered before the Unitarian Ministers' Institute in Salem, Mass., Oct. 14, in which he says: "A thoroughly enlightened Egoism in ethics would not necessarily be a fatal basis for a social philosophy." When such an elite scholar and we horse-logic wage slaves agree on a principle so fundamental, there is hope for a better social adjustment even though there be no probability of mutual admiration. Benj. R. Tucker delivered a masterly address on the "Relation of the State to the Individual," before the same audience. It is not improbable that Mr. Andrews was stimulated to his declaration by Mr. Tucker's address, as the latter assumed the Egoistic basis of ethics. Mr. Tucker's address should be printed in leaflet form for distribution, but there is a limit to gratuitous labor even in radical propaganda.

In a two-sentence paragraph in the "Twentieth Century" of Dec. 4, Hugh O. Pentecost says: "It has been said that if Cleopatra's nose had been an inch longer, Antony would not have lost the Roman empire. In view of the situation in Ireland it is a pity that Mrs. O'Shea's nose is of the normal size." In view of the opportunities that Mr. Pentecost has had to learn better, if his sexual superstition had not been of an abnormal size, he would not have blamed Mrs. O'Shea for Ireland's making a fool of itself by poking its Grundy nose into her private affairs. Neither would he have in his address of Nov. 23, questioned the need of the church and State, but not of their creature, the wife; nor have assumed that there could be a "higher" or more desirable plane of social existence than the law of equal freedom is susceptible of. "A mutual waiving of rights" in association is an absurdity, and its attempt communistic slavery. It is justified on the "higher" hypothesis only by those so religiously indiscriminating as to regard their own invasions as generously-granted opportunities for others to gratefully sacrifice to them.

A Bon Voyage.

A Sonnet

Is't so? An it be so why leave it so.
Why war we with the inevitable?
Why seek to petrify the unstable?
We ever change, and change makes room to grow;
I float on deep-sea streams and with them flow—
You fair sail steers away inexorable—;
Come then sun, storms, loves, loss, facts or fable,
My sails are full of winds and I must go.
Why should I reck who pairs or parts with me,
I have no time her loss to brood upon,
Before me heaves the world-encircling sea,
She dips beneath the sun-set horizon—
Farewell!—I must be happy, wise, and free:
'Tis done!—I am *Myself*, and *I* sail on.

—J. Wm. Lloyd.

In a letter to the editors of this paper, G. A. F. de Lespinasse, says: "I never read anything with more pleasure than 'Mutual Banking,' by Greene. It convinced me that if it could be realized, a death-blow would be given the State. Take away the money monopoly and the direct and indirect profits therefrom arising, and it would put an end to the *raison d'etre* of politicians. Authority without power to enforce it is not a desirable position, and it is a generally accepted axiom that the one who rubs the purse rubs the people. And the money monopolists and their spawn, the politicians, understood that as well as we; therefore they passed an obstruction law levying ten per cent or more on all private issue banks, thereby making competition impossible. They understand that free money means free people. I think the Mutual Bank Propaganda should make it a special aim to expose the true inwardness of that law, and the reasons why it was passed at the time." This gives us an opportunity to call our readers' attention to the fact that we still have on hand a large number of "Citizens' Money," a lecture by Alfred B. Westrup, advertised on the eighth page of this paper. Some one or some number of people will have to be at the expense of distributing this kind of literature by tens of thousands before there will be a movement toward freedom inaugurated. **We have our work and the cost of material fastened up in the edition, and are offering it at less than cost, by the dozen. We cannot afford to do more than this until publishing becomes immensely more profitable than it now is, or until we are convinced that free money would be vastly more beneficial to us than to our comrades.**

EGOISM

Issued Monthly at Fifty Cents a Year

—BY—

EQUITY PUBLISHING COMPANY,

Post Office Box 1678, San Francisco, California.

Entered as Second Class Mail Matter.

Scientific, Against Religious Methods.

R. Henderson, of Trenton, Ontario, puts to me the following question:

By economy and self-denial I have saved $1,000. A young and industrious farmer in my neighborhood has been offered a farm at a price which will enable him to make money if he can secure $1,000 to complete the purchase, and he asks me to let him have my $1,000, for five years, at 7 per cent interest. Shall I take the risk and the interest, or say no to him, and leave him to grub along as a laborer for the rest of his days?

If you lend the one thousand dollars at seven per cent interest, at the end of five years you will have appropriated from among the young farmer's goods three hundred and fifty dollars that you will have done nothing to earn. Meantime he will have performed for you the useful service of taking care of your thousand dollars and returning it to you, for which you will pay him nothing. You run no risk and do not labor, yet he pays you three hundred and fifty dollars. He performs for you a considerable service, but you give him nothing. You ask me to tell you what you should do under the circumstances. Pardon me; you are the only person who should or can decide that question. You may lend the money and rob your neighbor of three hundred and fifty dollars; you may refuse to lend the money; you may lend the money and pay your neighbor for taking care of it for you; or you may lend it without either charging for its use or paying for its care. Either one of these things you may do. What you should do is to pursue the course that will make you happiest. Sit down with yourself and decide whether to rob your neighbor or to help him will make you happier. When you have decided, do what gives you the most happiness. This is what you should do, and what you will do.—Hugh O. Pentecost in "Twentieth Century."

Mr. Pentecost's answer to Mr. Henderson is very unsatisfactory. He tries to inculcate Altruism as a means of solving the money question, while at the same time he recommends Egoism and is considerable of an Egoist himself. It is the very essence of Egoism that if the ends sought by the Altruist are ever attained they will be reached through Egoism. Liberty may culminate in the supremacy of the Golden Rule, but it will not be through Altruism, and Mr. Pentecost should have answered the question from this point of view or invited some one else to do so. As it is, it would appear that unless money lenders are willing to forego interest it cannot be abolished.

Naturally he is not, but under the present money system, the borrower is at the mercy of the lender. To state the case in as few words as possible: the reason why borrowers who obtain loans from money lenders pay more than one-half of one per cent per annum (cost) interest, is because the money-power government has prohibited competition in the supply of money. When the borrowers are wise enough, they will repudiate the text books and the learned professors of political economy and establish Mutual Banks to issue money direct on their own collateral, thus abolishing the money lender. Interest will then cease, not because lenders will become Altruists, and refuse to take interest, but because they *can't get it*. The Egoism of the borrower will induce him to cease paying interest when he *don't have to.*

Those who are interested should co-operate to form an association to raise funds to pay the expenses of carrying the money question into the courts, affirming the right of associations to issue paper money. Let the association organize a Mutual Bank; issue money and it would immediately get into the state and federal courts. Then the association should protest and put in a plea that the State has no right to prohibit associative effort for mutual advantage. By this means the State is called upon to explain the object of such prohibition. As there is none except to sustain interest for money lenders, it will be an eye-opener for the people. The speeches against human slavery will appear tame compared with the efforts that can be launched against usury, for it is the basis of slavery. Even land monopoly is far less an evil than money monopoly.

Alfred B. Westrup.

The Religion of Emotionalism.

Christian devotees who change the ceremonial expression of their superstition by adopting the tenets of some other denomination, believe themselves prompted by different impulses and in the pursuit of new ideals. When the Agnostic finds them worshiping the same indefinable God, twisting their tenets from the same mythological authority, and sacrificing daily pleasure to the same abstractions, their mistake is obvious and he sees in them the same religious fanatics with no variation except the independence of attemping to choose for themselves. The same is true of the average Agnostic as viewed by the Egoist. He has studied little else than expositions of Bible absurdity, and is unconsciously so imbued with the ideals and impulses of church people that there is practically not difference enough between him and his Christian neighbor to constitute a well defined issue. He upholds the same political authority, has the same ideas on ethical policy, the same conception of sexual relations, and has like his neighbor, never even dreamed of economics.

Whether he is a Spiritualist, Materialist, spontaneous or contract lover, his movements are generally determined by his emotions only. Though he laughs at the martyr worship of the church, he must himself have a martyr to stir him to action. It must be a new and sweet-smelling one who is only theologically disreputable. Then with the help of old and respectable poems and the writings on issues now dead, he composes in prose or verse pathetic descriptions of the noble martyr in the dark and loathsome dungeon (too true, alas, for the ineffectual effort to prevent), and personal denunciations of the particular individuals then serving popular prejudice through the State, and reads them with delight even in the small type from which they are printed, while he gloats over the envy of his comrades who can not outdo him without actually appealing to God and the agonies of the cross for "soul" stirring language and comparisons in which to clothe a literary effort. This is an especially rich field for the exercise of the emotional nature which circumstances combine to make the limited gift of woman. It is better than Jesus, for he flourished a forgetable long time ago, and partaking of the God character, does not seem so realistic and familiar-like as the flesh and blood so very like our own of modern martyrs who may be geographically located and gazed upon. She can glorify her hero now and be heard not only by envious competitors but often by the appreciative hero himself, which adds personal appreciation to idealistic adoration. After the most has been made of this opportunity for emotionalism and the poor who have been wrought upon by its rhetoric have divided their means of subsistence while the rich contributed a little pin money and much advice to the holy cause, there is no important issue except church myths or the protection of American industries, until more martyr's blood flows.

When the industrial problem confronts the emotionalists they call meetings and read, with proper inflections and pauses, long essays and deliver, without proper inflections and pauses short speeches describing in technically true but highly tragical language the sufferings of the poor, along with a denunciation of monopolies in general and a recommendation of governmental monopoly of telegraph lines. Gould and the Vanderbilts receive due consideration, but the privilege granting institution that makes them, never. It requires slow, plodding, patient analyzing effort to get at causes, and is unaccompanied by the flourishing of palms and splitting the air with oratorical declamation for the amusement of emotional listeners and the gratification of the performer. It has no place for spasmodic notoriety, and its victories can receive little appreciation save from the achiever alone, for others cannot appreciate without doing the act themselves. This settles the pursuit of investigation upon its utility and its pleasure upon *realization* instead of upon the emotion-exercising *anticipation* which the church fosters in its heaven ideal, and some Agnostics unconsciously symbolize in the utopia of Nationalism. The faculty is characteristic of infancy, and is illustrated by the old story in which the child, impatient at waiting for seeds to grow into flowers, plucked some and stuck them into the prepared ground so as to have a flower garden at once. It was hard to find them wilting and have to plant seeds at last, but gardens are produced in no other way, as emotionalistic Socialists will find after the enthusiasm of epoch creating novels leaves the industrial problem to be solved by scientific methods, which might have been mastered while they were religiously exercising their emotions. They may boycott the "icy philosophic" and denounce his plumb-line policy, but for their pains will take their turn at the window of industrial solution so much later if at all.

The sexual question more than any other, is the field of Agnostic emotionalism. Here it is exercised either with orthodox rigidity or verbose fervency. The Agnostic is either a legal-contract-Bible-adultery-love-one-forever monogamist or he is a sacred-sentiment-high-holy-passion varietist *lover* who makes loving a specialty, that is, he is always industriously engaged soliciting sentiment and sympathy to the exclusion of many things obviously more useful.

The budding monogamist finds himself alone with his sexual faculty craving sympathy, and desires intensely to be loved by some one. The object and prize being located, the impulse is to possess it absolutely, forever, just as a starving man might feel without reasoning about it, that he should eat eternally when food could be procured. He does not think of enjoying the love of a lover as he would sunshine, scenery, or humor, but blindly desires to *have* it by owning the object from which it emanates; and about as reasonably as he might hope to retain all the scent from a perfume bag by *owning* the bag. Any contemplation of love must always produce this impulse, which will be followed by such reasoning as experience suggests. Usually, there is no definite experience until such an environment of circumstances is woven as makes it practically useless with the average mind. This gives us monogamy as the expression of an emotion circling in repetition instead of connecting with the utilitarian calculations of love pleasure characteristic of varietists. While monogamy is rigid and painfully staid, it is yet based on the blindest emotional impulse, like the desire for immortality, that of possessing forever the desire of the moment. It is the brother of the emotions experienced when contemplating inexaggerable space and its contents, or soaking in the glowing warmth of the sun; emotions which in one degree of mental complexity cause their subject to worship the sun, and in another to construct cosmogonies and theological systems of blatant worship, while in still another they prompt the poet to take the magnificence of the universe into partnership and celebrate.

The varietist emotionalist is a "nature"-theologian and a sexual devotionalist. He makes a religion of sexual love, and spends all his spare moments writing clothiers' wrap-perfuls of doughy love sentiments to absent female friends, while he is a constant menace to the peace of mind of local female acquaintances both in public and private. The most pronounced feature of his written declarations is his all-absorbing, soul-swallowing longing and undying devotion to the person addressed. When in her presence, the most noticeable thing is a continual affectional exacting and caterwauling, in sharp contrast with the conduct of the complacent Egoist who withdraws a half-impressed kiss from the lips of a companion to bring her a pillow or a drink of water which he finds her condition craves more.

When the average radical faces the real basis of ethics, if there is a particle of orthodoxy in his make-up it will show. It is then that he fondly embraces one superstition, if at no other time. He despises the selfishness of others as it effects his interests, and is unquestionably sure that the duty of "duty" to others is the foundation of social intercourse, justice, and fraternity. He feels this because in shaping the *policy* of his conduct toward others he considers their interests, but unconsciously only so far as he deems it necessary to insure no unfavorable reflection on him, otherwise he would become a slave to whoever should seize him first. It is too much trouble to analyze his theory applied. If he were to do so he would find that if it were possible to cause the rule to be universally observed, the result would be a universal service in each instance bestowed on those whose wants we could but imperfectly know, while our reward came from an equally disadvantageous source. All this while each would know exactly what he desired and be exerting the necessary energy to produce it, but owing to the insane idea of duty to others no one would be served. If the rule be not universally applied, some will render service without receiving any and in this degree become the slaves of others, destroying equality. We may perform service for which we do not desire anything except the gratitude of the object upon which it is bestowed, or the satisfaction of relieving our consciousness of the knowledge of suffering, which it would otherwise appropriate. But this is Egoistic projection or defense, just the opposite of the idea of absolute debt consistent with the *duty* of "duty" to others. If, then, universal "duty to others" results only in the misdirection and waste of energy, and that which is not universal, in a corresponding degree of slavery, and service beneficial to others which is performed spontaneously for the actor's pleasure is the opposite of the "duty" idea, there is but one other way in which we can rationally perform service for others, and that is in exchange. But this can in no way justify "duty" service, for if we may not exchange when and with whom we can and please, or if we may not at any time refuse to exchange, such exchange is slavery and equal freedom is denied. If exchange is voluntary the advantage is mutual, and is Egoistic projection. So all rational service for others is based in Egoism, and our emotional Altruist has a choice between slavery and insanity as a justification of his emotionalistic creed. But he has the multitude on his side and will assure himself by its approval and vehemently denounce the selfish sinner in genuinely religious style, while he will treat the argument of the Egoist with an abused air of silent contempt. He does not realize that the difference between his selfishness and that of the Egoist consists in the former's being so blind that he cannot tolerate the thought of selfishness in others for a moment, while the Egoist remembering his own can justify the same in others on the same grounds. The religion of emotionalism is the strongest foe to a scientific habit of thought. H.

Editorial Vagaries.

Each individual pursues the purpose of his desire with all the tenacity of his make-up, and finds the rest of mankind good or bad in proportion to the help or resistance it offers him in the pursuit of his pleasure; that is, in so far as others are in regard to themselves as we are in regard to ourselves, in that degree do we regard them as bad. The Egoist alone subjectively places himself in the objective and appreciates others' conduct both with the interest of their motives and its effect on his interests, enabling him to see in the seeming evil of resistance the only hope for equality.

The extracts on the sixth and seventh pages of this paper, from "The Ruthless Sex" by Oscar Fay Adams in the "North American Review" for November, are reprinted by us because of the statement of facts contained, and not in approval of the author's implied position that there is a difference, aside from a poor bargain, between the woman who sells her person for life, and the one who sells it on the "meals at all hours, day or night," plan. We hold with the above author that to woman's indifference is due any cruelty immediately connected with her actions, and that mental indolence is its cause. But we charge the temporary disability imposed upon her by childbearing as the cause of these, and find the mutual ignorance of man and woman responsible for the whole. As the world has gone, this disabled condition has imposed an inactivity upon woman which admitted of her doing such kinds of work only as could be done on the spot. It made protection by the male necessary under the circumstances, and generated a corresponding gratitude and sense of obligation on the part of the helpless female. These necessities, without an intelligent and determined resistance on the part of the disadvantaged female, easily led her to accept the routine of domestic drudgery and the resulting mental flaccidity complained of, while the increased responsibility of providing for her led the male to greater mental activity, and to a monopolizing of opportunities which tended to make independence still more difficult for woman even with physical ability and a determination to be independent.

Through time and invention came increased production, monopoly, and the resulting served and serving classes. This gave the females of the first, means and leisure, and without an industrial opportunity on which to exercise ambition, they easily adopted the "small profits and quick returns" activity of display in dress, which became a matter susceptible of sharp competition in gaining the favor of the males, upon whom they were dependent. This competition between themselves made them eager to take advantage of man's vanity to have some one "faithful to him," by making capital of the conduct of possible competitors who failed to pander to this exaction, and has finally led to all the ridiculous clatter about "virtuous," and "fallen" women. Now, religious reformers appeal to the custom-fostered vanity of the former by lauding their "stooping" to raise the "fallen," as charitable. The "raising," presumably, would consist of employing such women as kitchen drudges at lower wages than furnish the sexually inexperienced only a semi-barbaric grade of living, beside of which even some of the later stages of prostitution seem a luxury. In addition to this the women would be expected to serve as worshipful oral monuments to their saviors' magnanimity.

In the light of this position, industrial dependence is at the bottom of woman's shortcomings as a responsible citizen, and the securing of the means of independence becomes the real question. Here it grows relatively large, touching as it does the whole field of economic and political freedom, but in the immediate interest of woman, some pertinent suggestions can be made in a limited space. The disability of reproduction is the first thing that places her at a disadvantage with the male of her class in the present civilization. Let her learn the lesson of intelligent Egoism, and be rid of the superstition of "duty." Then let her see to it that her sex function shall not prevent her from competing with the male for an opportunity at every activity within her capacity. Let her shut right down on the reproductive industry until its reward shall in each case equal the expense, be it what it may. If those who would monopolize her industrial opportunity would not do an equal share, let the matter go until she could afford it as a luxury on her own account; she owes no sacrifice to the race, and can afford as well as man to let it stop. If reproduction cannot be maintained under equal conditions, let us have such conditions without it. But there is not the slightest danger of this; even men yield to resistance and make terms when it costs less to do so than otherwise. The possibilities of woman's self-projection in every sense, under that ownership of her capacities which her resistance alone can secure for her, are yet undreamed of. Let her learn to manipulate her at least one commodity intelligently, and it will place her in a position to carve out for herself all that man enjoys of material luxury and mental prestige, instead of the slavery and lashing criticism which her present course of launching it upon the sea of blind emotion and superstition brings her. Resistance may be expensive at first, but it cannot cost more than the slavish imbecility of submission.

GOVERNMENT.

BY W. S. BELL.

"We hold these truths to be self-evident: that all men are created equal; and are endowed by their creator with certain inalienable rights; that among these are life, liberty, and the pursuit of happiness. That to secure these rights governments are instituted among men, deriving their just powers from the consent of the governed."

These declarations are nothing more than flattering sophistries and glittering generalities. In the first place they are not "self-evident" truths, because they are not truths at all. Men are not created equal; they are not equal intellectually, physically, or socially. They were not created equal because they were not "created." They were not endowed by their creator, because they had no creator; they have no inalienable rights, because they have no natural rights whatever. Besides they have no rights that government does not destroy at any moment it wishes to do so; and as for government deriving its just powers from the consent of the governed, nothing could be farther from the truth.

One of our inherited delusions is that government protects us. Just how it does so, and from whom it protects us, is no particular concern of ours, as long as we have faith that it protects us. It is enough for the horny-handed sons of toil to pay their taxes and vote the straight ticket, without taxing their brains over such questions as "How does government protect?" His patriotic blood swells in his veins as the voter thinks of the never-to-be-overestimated vote he holds in his hands. Even the president of the United States has no more than one vote! A Gould, or Vanderbilt, has but one vote. What a great honor to be thus made the peer of these millionaires! Poor dupe does not see that Gould and Vanderbilt can sway the votes of thousands by their position, and thousands by the dollars they put out. The voter quite often prays to heaven for his daily bread, and yet he is well assured that if Vanderbilt should catch him voting the opposite ticket, heaven would be powerless to send him bread. He knows too well that heaven has less to do with the bread question than Vanderbilt has, yet he continues to pray for it while keeping one eye on Vanderbilt.

The saintly Wanamaker knew full well that heaven could not assist him in getting votes. Heaven does not care a fig which party is in office. In view of the fact, St. John went out to raise $400,000, not for Christ's sake, but for the Republican party's sake. This episode constitutes a fine illustration of the beauty of *democracy*—of the value of the elective franchise, and how governments instituted among men derive their just powers from the consent of the governed.

Let us cast about us to see how it is that government protects us in life, liberty, and our pursuit of happiness. We are painfully conscious that it does nothing of the kind. At any time we can be pressed into military service against our will, and sent out to kill men whom we have never seen—men who have never done us any harm nor wished to do us any. We are conscripted into service and sent out to kill or be killed,—by the government which derives its just powers from the consent of the governed. When did you give your consent to be drafted by the government? When did you concede to government the right to make war? How does the arbitrary and irrepressible power of confiscation of property and the impressment of the individual harmonize with the doctrine of inalienable rights of life, liberty, and the pursuit of happiness? Is coercing me to go to war to kill or be killed, and instance where governments derive their just powers from the "consent of the governed?" When did I consent to this arrangement?

Let us see how much protection the people have in the administration of justice in our courts. The workings of the police, the manipulation of the courts, jails, prisons, and other governmental institutions would never suggest to the most acute observer the existence of inalienable rights, except it suggest the inalienable right of the government officer. He certainly does not want to part with his office.

It is a well recognized principle of common law that there can be no crime without criminal intent. In all criminal cases of great importance, the motive of the accused is the thing that determines his guilt or innocence. In former times this principle was more fully recognized than it is now. The intention of the prisoner was the turning point in all criminal trials, great and small. The increasing arbitrary rulings of courts have changed this, so that now the question is not as to the intent of the actor, but only, did he violate the law.

"To accomplish this object they have in modern times held it to be unnecessary that indictments should charge, as by common law they were required to do, that an act was done 'wickedly,' 'feloniously,' 'with malice aforethought,' or in any other way that implied criminal intent, without which there can be no criminality; but that it is sufficient to charge simply that it was done, 'contrary to the form of the statute in such case made and provided.'" (Lysander Spooner, "Free Political Institutions," p. 36.)

It was too hard work for these public servants to be able to prove a malicious intent upon the part of the person arrested. The laws had become so numerous and artificial that it was impossible for judges and juries to get at the intention of the accused. Throwing a banana peel on the sidewalk is in some cities a criminal act; begging in the streets is a criminal act; having no business or no home is a criminal condition; sleeping in a stable, or in a hall-way, or in the public parks is criminal; working on Sunday is a criminal act in almost all states; allowing an automatic machine to be placed in front of your store, that will drop down a cigar after you drop in a nickle, if it works on Sunday, is a criminal act. This is almost as bad as the old Puritans who had such a holy horror of Sabbath breaking that according to Rev. Sam Peters:

> Upon the Sabbath they'll no physic take
> Lest it should work, and so the Sabbath breake.

But if automatic machines are a violation of the Sunday law because they take money for goods delivered, what shall we say about the organist and choir of a church, who work for pay. Also the preacher and policeman who work for pay. But I fancy someone shouting in my ear, "These are works of necessity and mercy!" And I imagine myself shouting back the inquiry, "Who is it calls preaching and running boys into the station house, deeds of mercy and works of necessity but the preacher and policeman." One stands for the state and the other the church, and these are the two legs that government stands on. They cheerfully exonerate themselves. The preacher gives us hell and the policeman shoves us into jail, and this is what they call the "protection" of government. Some minds, however, are so obtuse as to be unable to see how these procedures guarantee us inalienable rights.

In our large cities thousands of inoffensive young people are annually run into the lockups for some very trivial affair, as shouting, firing off pistols or some such thing. The young boys are commonly locked up in cells with older criminals. There is no care taken to keep the innocent away from the company of the vilest and most depraved. The injury done a boy by thus locking him up, even for only twenty-four hours with a hardened felon, is irreparable. It is just in this way that society makes its own criminals. Here is where government shows itself to be a beast. It makes laws to prevent crime, and then in the administration of these laws it makes criminals.

A very large part of those run into the lockups over night are discharged in the morning. They are guilty of no crime. The verdict then must be that they were unjustly arrested. But does this blunder of the policeman teach him not to arrest innocent people afterwards? Do these false arrests induce the magistrates to instruct the police to cease this sort of public protection? Not at all. The old brutal method of clubbing the tipsy, or old, or young, goes on now as it has heretofore. Suppose some man of large heart and still larger brain, and plead the case of an inexperienced person by saying, "There can be no crime without criminal intent," the parrot answer would be that, "Ignorance of the law excuses no one." This bald-headed fraud, has come down to us in the white livery of justice, from the black-hearted despotism of the past. "Ignorance of the law excuses no one." Why they have just told us that government is instituted for our protection, and if the innocent are not to be protected, who then is? "Ignorance of the law excuses no one." The claw sticks out from the velvet paw of the beast in this infinitely damnable clap-trap sentence. Some old lawyer in a tight place gobbled the legal maxim, "Ignorance of the law excuses no one," and since that thousands of young legal gobblers have gobbled the same infamous lie. When you see how the young, the poor, the orphan and helpless of all classes are mostly the victims of fines and punishment, is it not apparent that the great system of protective law is more like a spider's web than it is a shield and defense? "The court of justice," is a nice phrase, and looks harmless, nay seems beautiful to the unsophisticated mind. But so does a spider's web. How soon all this wonderful mechanism changes when mister fly gets caught in its meshes. In the twinkling of an eye a great big-bellied spider skips over his beautiful web and weaves his toils about the poor victim. Goodbye, fly!

Were you ever taken into a court of justice as a culprit? Then you remember how everything changed as soon as you were arraigned. Not always, but usually the judge comes out from the sanctity of his secret chamber to be the spider in your case. There seems to be but one prevailing sentiment in a courtroom, and that is, "How much can be got out of the case?" If he is rich, in nine cases out of ten he can escape punishment, but he has to be quite free in the use of his money. Sometimes when courts are greedy, they postpone the trial from term to term and from year to year, and this is another of the self-evident proofs of the inestimable value of government protection. How notorious is the fact that an honest man cannot go into court and get justice. Justice (?) is not an inalienable right, but a commodity to be sold to the highest bidder. See how difficult it is to drag a rich rogue into court and have him convicted. In criminal cases where the accused is rich or has rich friends he generally goes free; or if found guilty his sentence is remarkably light, and even then he goes into the hospital, where he has but nominal duties, and the chances are that he will be pardoned by the governor, or set free on a writ of error. The law that is professedly the safeguard of our liberties has become the mailed hand of tyranny. The custodians of our peace and safety have turned themselves into robbers. The poor people are slow to discover that our great criminals are not the multitude of offenders who break laws for the most part artificial, and that our law-makers are the real criminals of society, because they use the powers entrusted to them for personal aggrandizement and political preferment. Having gained wealth and power as members of our state and United States legislatures, they have nothing before their eyes but their own emolument. Congressmen constantly squabble over the spoils. Just think of it. Our jails and our prisons are filled with the poor and our United States senate is filled with millionaires; men who fatten on the weakness, ignorance, and toil of the third estate.

(To be continued.)

Egographs.

Thoughtlessness does more harm than selfishness; the "tribute of a thoughtless yes," is only equaled by a thoughtless No.

As the "brush of nature excels art," so does the man of principle excel the politician.

Morality and duty, like charity (to be voluntary and spontaneous), should not only "begin," but *end* "at home."

Virtue is self-approval. What we approve of in ourselves we are anxious to see others do; so great is our anxiety in this respect that those who believe in majority rule pass laws to *compel* the minority to sacrifice their Individuality to "virtue," "morality," and "duty."

It is a waste of energy to enforce an artificial law until the people are educated up to an intelligent understanding of the law, and then its enforcement is entirely unnecessary and superficial, as the free and full conception of a law by the people would place them above and beyond its power for either good or evil.

Self-appointed duties have the virtue of spontaneous voluntaryism; there never would have been an Ida Lewis known to the world had there been a *law* to compel her to the daring acts of heroism—the saving of human life at the risk of her own. The test of virtue in all our own actions is the voluntariness with which we perform the acts. It is the law alone which prevents the *free* exercise of self-appointed duties by stifling liberty. Not only are all our noblest acts the result of individual liberty, but also those of greatest utility. The *volunteer* fireman who rushes into a burning building and saves the life of woman or child, not only makes a heroic attempt but succeeds in virtue of the complete absence of a law or an obligation to compel his self-sacrifice and heroism. Had there been a law for the enforcement of such an act, the self-constituted life-preserver would have taken time for reflection, and hesitated before risking his life for others. In such an emergency "the man who hesitates is lost" with those he seeks to save, and the practical results with the hero are lost in the burning flames of authority.

Perfection causes carelessness. If a perfect government were possible, its effect would be to make people careless of their liberty, just as a perfect patent medicine to cure all diseases would tend to make people careless of their health, hence the utility of prevention in disease and the abolition and prevention of political authority in society. As prevention and abolition are insurance against diseases so is the abolition of authority a prevention of and an insurance against despotism.

What is economic liberty? A condition of society in which *nobody* gets something for nothing.

What is political sentimentalism? A politician delivering a Fourth of July Oration on Decoration Day, a ridiculous attempt to mix patriotism with the brotherhood of man.

What constitutes a leader? One who knows the rugged path of progress better than yourself, and none other should be followed.

What is love? An element in nature, which, like electricity, we know but little of except by its phenomena.

What is the phenomena of love? Under equal freedom in society, it is the attracting together of sympathetic and harmonious individuals. Under compulsion it is a beautiful, powerful, and pure stream of life dammed by law and abridged by authority, in which love is inverted, affection diverted, and harmony perverted.

What is hope? An attribute of the mind, which causes the "wish to be father to the thought"—thought and desire in preposession. Hope, when exercised without judgment, inclines the individual to be "carried away" by his feelings—optimism run riot and inclination rampant.

What is definition? A very precise and particular piece of business to engage in; one in which the definer or critic should never be above criticism, for this reason I do not make myself an exception.

F. B. Parse.

The Ruthless Sex.

If there is one more characteristic difference than another between man and woman, it lies, as has often been noted, in the manner in which any adverse criticism directed against either sex is regarded by the members of the particular sex supposed to be aspersed. If it happens to be the feminine sex upon which the remarks have been made, our sisters arise as one woman to defend themselves. And why? Simply because each woman feels that *she* is individually attacked, that *she* is at fault, that the writer or speaker is aiming directly at *her*. On the other hand, if it is the masculine sex which is criticised, man as a rule pays little or no attention to the matter. Generalities, he has found by experience, hurt no one in particular. No man's individual vanity is wounded by what may be said in disparagement of his sex as a whole.

Passing from the sex to the individual, we find a different state of affairs. If in the intercourse of social life some woman is harshly criticised, do her sisters at once rally to her defense? Very seldom, it must be confessed. Instead, the word of disparagement is echoed, very faintly by a few women, very distinctly by many more, and with a delicate ingenuity in the prolongation of the note of dispraise worthy of admiration from a purely artistic point of view. Let a man be disparaged or harshly spoken against, do we find as a rule his brother-men, those who know him well, uniting to swell the chorus of adverse speech? I think not. I think it is a well-established fact that men in their intercourse with one another display a chivalrous regard for their fellows to a degree almost unknown among women. The loyalty to individuals which flourishes so vigorously amongst men seldom finds its counterpart among their sisters...... There are men who delight in stoning him who is down, as, on the other hand, there are women whose spirit of charity at such times is little short of angelic; but the sexes in the order named are not largely made up of such members. In spite, then, of some exceptions either way, the broad, distinctive fact remains that as a rule men are loyal to their fellows, however carelessly they may view any attack upon their sex, while women are disloyal to their sisters individually considered, but quickly resentful of any slight, real or supposed, which may be placed upon their sex.

One result of the persistency with which women make personal application of general assertions is a perpetual air of being on the defensive, which manifests itself often in the adoption of a pitiless code of judgment passed mentally or otherwise upon those about them. This of itself would not establish the truth of the assertion that women are more cruel than men, but it certainly has some force as an argument upon that side of the question.

. . . .

Indifference, according to Ruskin, is the sin of which woman is most guilty—an indifference which arises from that narrow habit of mind which is exclusively occupied with the present moment, which refuses or is unwilling to grasp any other than the purely personal aspect of it. Her sympathies are quickly aroused to what is immediately before her eyes, to what no *mental effort* is required to perceive,—as, for instance, a horse savagely beaten by its driver, —but it goes no further.

Suppose that we are riding upon a street-car and the horses are straining every nerve to pull the heavily-loaded car up some sharp rise of ground. A street corner is reached and a woman standing there signals the driver to stop his car for her convenience. Unless he has received positive orders not to stop going up hill, he obeys her (with considerable inward grumbling), and the horses, which have stood their ground with considerable difficulty during the delay, are forced to redouble their exertions in order to overcome the inertia resulting from the stopping of the car. That she could have signaled the car from the foot of the hill or from the top never occurs to the woman, who, desiring to get on at that especial point, has no thought of anything further, the pain and even suffering which she has occasioned the horses being a matter of no moment to her. Or supposing the car is not ascending an up-grade, but is moving along upon a level stretch of road when signaled to stop at a street corner. A few steps further on a woman stands waiting for the car to come exactly opposite to her. It does not seem worth her while for her to walk those few paces and get on the car at the point where it has stopped for the convenience of others, and thus save the horses which draw it the strain and discomfort of an extra stoppage. Here is an instance of her indifference resulting in cruelty. Such occurrences as these cited are not exceptional, as any person who has occasion to travel on street cars knows, but are happening hourly on every horse-railway line. And the average woman never perceives that anything is wrong in her practice in this regard until some one else, usually a man, has told her of it. She acknowledges that she has never thought of it before, and forgets all about it by the next time she gets on a car.

I might instance other examples of cruelty resulting from woman's indifference, but those already named show the general character of those I have in mind. I pass on now to speak of a more flagrant kind of cruelty, springing from another cause. Miss Helen Gray Cone, in her poem, "The Tender Heart," describes a young man, who is devoted to hunting, so wrought upon by the pathetic pleading of a girl, who quotes at length from the poets against the sin of killing the fowls of the air and the beasts of the field, that

"At Emerson's 'Forbearance' he
Began to feel his will benumbed:
At Browning's 'Donald' utterly
His soul surrendered and succumbed.
'O gentlest of all gentle girls'
He thought, 'beneath the blessed sun!
He saw her lashes hung with pearls,
And swore to give away his gun.
She smiled to find her point was gained,
And went with happy parting words
(He subsequently ascertained),
To trim her hat with humming-birds."

It is not very long ago since the cry went up that certain species of birds were in danger of speedy extinction from wholesale warfare made upon them in the interest of the milliners and their customers. A few women, be it said, had always by voice and example protested against a fashion which demanded such a sacrifice of animal life for its gratification; but it was not until men had almost unanimously declared against it that any reform was accomplished. I fear there is very little reason to believe that, if fashion should again demand a sacrifice of birds, it would not be offered by a large majority of women till vigorous remonstrance on the part of the other sex induced the reform. But why should not women in general perceive the cruelty of such a fashion as quickly as men, and, not waiting to learn gentleness and mercy from the so-called rougher sex, exclaim against it immediately? Is it not because vanity supplemented indifference, in this case, with cruelty of the most unnecessary, indefensible kind as its consequence?

. . . .

The cruelty of man—for I am not asserting that man is not cruel—springs from a motive which in itself is not to be altogether contemned. Ambition to a certain extent is desirable...... It is the excess of ambition in its many forms which provokes man's cruelty.

Feminine cruelty is the outcome of less noble promptings, and, so it would seem, arises from indifference, vanity, or jealousy, according to its degree,—sometimes from a fusing of all three,—and it is seldom held in check by reason.

I wish that I might end here, for if this were all there were to urge, and I bring forward nothing that is new in this connection, the title of this paper might with some reason be termed unjust and its implied assumption declared too sweeping to be true; but. O you women who cry out upon the cruelty and selfishness of men; you who are defended from the storms of this world by the care of those rough men, and you who proudly defend yourselves without such aid; you who dwell as the daughters of kings, and you who fare as those to whom toil is no stranger; O you women who are virtuous and honest, how are your hearts steeled against those sisters of yours who stumbled on ways that seemed smooth enough to you, who fell where you have walked upright?

Have you defended that sister of yours whose good name has been assailed as earnestly as you have rushed to the defense of your sex when you fancied it was slandered? Have you refused to believe evil of her against whom some stone has been cast? Have you refused to record your sentence against one accused until her guilt was absolutely sure? Have you, when this last was proved, declared that guilt unpardonable and thrust the offender out from your life and from your thought forever? Have you stooped to help one of those who was weak where you were strong, who was tempted where you were not, or who fell because the way to her was rougher than you ever dreamed? Have you done all these things?

The judgments which man passes upon his fellows are tolerant where woman's are narrow, because, instead of the one aspect of the question which she perceives, he sees many; they are merciful where hers are cruel, because he recognizes more fully the stress of temptation and the complexity of motive which lead to transgression. There have been a few women who have helped their weaker sisters to rise when they had fallen, but they are indeed few. The majority of women have done what they could to keep those who are down still in that position. They have refused to believe in the possibility of reform; they have withdrawn from all contact with those who have once found temptation greater than they could bear; they have, by their inflexible attitude, made a return to virtue nearly impossible on the part of those who have once turned from it. Who should be tenderer toward a woman's sin than a virtuous woman, and who is harder? O you queens, who have with your virtuous hands thrust your weaker sisters still further in the mire; who have shown aversion where you might have shown mercy; who have hardened your hearts, that should have been soft with pity; who have turned coldly aside from those, your sisters, whom you might have saved, and gone your ways as though they were not; O you who have lifted from your heads the crown of gentleness and mercy that all your sex should wear, are you not "ruthless" indeed?—Oscar Fay Adams in the "North American Review" for December.

SOME GOOD BOOKS.

CITIZENS' MONEY. A lecture on the "National Banking System," by Alfred B. Westrup, delivered in Chicago and published in "Liberty," of Boston, in 1888. Mr. Westrup shows that every dollar's worth of property in the country may be converted into active capital, reducing interest to the cost of issuing money, and sending capital in search of labor instead of being the other way, as it is at present. It is short, popular in style, and well calculated for propaganda work. Whoever is interested in industrial emancipation can do no better work than procure and circulate this pamphlet by the dozen. It contains 21 pages, is printed on good paper in large type, and can be had for 60 cents per dozen, or 10 cents per single copy.

MONOGAMIC SEX RELATIONS Discussed by Ego and Marie Louise. This extraordinary pamphlet charges monogamic sexual relations with causing electrical poverty through balanced electrical conditions, which results in many common, and the most fatal diseases, and in mental deterioration, leading to narrow-mindedness, bigotry, tyranny, persecution, irritability, melancholy, drunkenness, suicide, and most of the vice and misery arising from the discontent of mankind. The every day experience of all close observers must corroborate many of its accusations with unmistakable accuracy. It is intensely radical, yet clothed in such language as will admit of loaning to your orthodox neighbor. It is printed on good paper, with new type, and contains 24 large pages. Price 10 cents.

FREE POLITICAL INSTITUTIONS: THEIR NATURE, ESSENCE, AND MAINTENANCE,—an abridgement and rearrangement of Lysander Spooner's "Trial by Jury," edited by Victor Yarros. It is treated in seven chapters under the following heads: I. Legitimate Government and Majority Rule. II. Trial by Jury as a Palladium of Liberty. III. Trial by Jury as Defined by Magna Charta. IV. Objections answered. V. The Criminal Intent. VI. Moral Considerations for Jurors. VII. Juries of the Present Day Illegal. Whoever desires to make plain to his conservative neighbor just how society may get on without tyranny and privilege fostering government, should have a copy of this pamphlet in his coat pocket and be prepared to not only defend his position but to take that of the opposition by storm. It is the much-needed propaganda material that should be circulated as fast as Anarchists can afford to devote money to the work. Price 25 cts.

THE RAG-PICKER OF PARIS, by Felix Pyat, translated from the French by Benj. R. Tucker. This novel is the most complete portrayal of the human nature of this century in every condition of life, that has been contributed to radical literature. Every line, every pause, has a fullness, a significance of thought, or a volcano of emotion seldom found anywhere singly, and not combined in the style of any other writer. It is probably the most vivid picture of the misery of poverty, the extravagance of wealth, the sympathy and forbearance of the poor and despised, the cruelty and aggressiveness of the aristocratic and respectable, the blind greed of the middle classes, the hollowness of charity, the cunning and hypocrisy of the priesthood, the tyranny and corruption of authority, the crushing power of privilege, and finally of the redeeming beauty of the ideal of liberty and equality, that the century has produced. Four thousand copies were sold the first week after its publication. Radicals can do much good work with it among the partly liberal-minded. It will, without arousing their prejudices, open a new field of thought for very orthodox people. Price in cloth binding $1; paper, 50 cents.

For any of the above address

EQUITY PUBLISHING COMPANY,

P. O. Box 1678. San Francisco, Calif.

EGOISM'S PRINCIPLES AND PURPOSE.

EGOISM's purpose is the improvement of social existence through intelligent self-interest. It finds that whatever we have of equal conditions and mutual advantage is due to a prevalence of this principle corresponding with the degree and universality of individual resistance to encroachment.

Reflection will satisfy all who are desirous of being guided in their conclusions by fact, that as organization itself is a process of absorbing every material useful to its purpose, with no limit save that of outside resistance, so must the very fact of its being a separately organized entity make it impossible for it to act with ultimate reference to anything but itself. Observation will show that this holds good throughout the vegetable and animal kingdoms, and that whatever of equality exists among members of a species or between different species has its source and degree in the resisting capacity, of whatever kind, which such member or species can exert against the encroachment of other members or species. The human animal is no exception to this rule. True, its greater complexity has developed the expedient of sometimes performing acts with beneficial results to others, but this is at last analysis only resistance, because it is the only means of resisting the withholding by others from such actor's welfare that which is more desirable than that with which he parts. If, then, the self-projecting faculty of mankind is such that it will in addition to the direct resistance common to the less complex animals, diplomatically exercise present sacrifice to further extend self, and it being a fact that equality depends upon equal resistance, diplomatic or otherwise, what are its chances in an absence of enlightenment in which the individuals of the majority so far from *intelligently* using this resisting power in their own behalf, do not even believe that they should do so? The result of a general conception so chaotic, would naturally be what we find: the generalization from the practical expediency of certain consideration for others, crystallized through the impulse of blind selfishness into a mysterious and oppressive obligation, credit for the observance of which gratifies the self-projecting faculty of the simple, while the more shrewd evade its exactions, and at every step from the manipulation of the general delusions of religious and political authority to the association of sexes and children at play, project themselves by exchanging this mythical credit for the real comforts and luxuries of the occasion, which the others produce. Thus in addition to the natural disadvantage of unequal capacity, the weaker are deprived through a superstition, of the use of such capacity as they have, as may be seen in their groping blindness all about us.

To secure and maintain equal conditions then, requires a rational understanding of the real object of life as indicated by the facts of its expression. It is plain that the world of humanity is made up of individuals absolutely separate; that life is to this humanity nothing save as it is something to one of these; that one of these can be nothing to another except as he detracts from or adds to his happiness; that on this is based the idea of social expediency; that the resistance of each of these individuals would determine what is socially expedient; that approximately equal resistance makes it equality, and on such continued and a universal resistance depends equality. This can leave no room for any sane action toward others but that of the policy promoting most the happiness of the acting Ego. Therefore EGOISM insists that the attainment of equal freedom depends upon a course of conduct replacing the idea of "duty to others" with *expediency* toward others; upon a recognition of the fact that self-pleasure must be the final motive of any act: thus developing a principle for a basis of action about which there can be no misunderstanding, and which will place every person squarely on the merit of his or her probable interests, divested of the opportunity to deceive through pretension, as under the dominance of altruistic idealism. It will maintain that what is generally recognized as morality is nothing other than the expediency deduced from conflicting interests under competition; that it is a policy which, through the hereditary influence of ancestral experience, confirmed by personal experience, is found to pay better than any other known policy; that the belief that it is something other than a policy—a fixed and eternal obligation, outside of and superior to man's recognized interests, and may not be changed as utility indicates, makes it a superstition in effect like any other superstition which causes its adherents to crystallize the expediency adopted by one period into positive regulations for another in which it has no utility, but becomes tyrannical laws and customs in the name of which persecution is justified, as in the fanaticism of any fixed idea.

Another part of its purpose is to help dispel the "Political Authority" superstition and develop a public sentiment which would replace State interference with the protection for person and property which the competition of protecting associations would afford. Then the State's fanatical tyranny and industry crushing privilege would torture the nerves of poverty-stricken old age or pinch tender youth no more. The most disastrous interference of this monster superstition is its prohibition of the issuing of exchange medium on the ample security of all kinds of property, which at once would abolish speculative interest and practically set all idle hands at productive labor at wages ever nearing the whole product until it should be reached. The next interference is by paper titles to vacant land instead of the just and reasonable one of occupancy and use, which with the employment that free money would give, would furnish all with comfortable homes in a short time, and thereafter even with luxuries from like exertion. Following this is its patent privilege, customs robbery, protective tariff, barbarous decrees in social and sexual affairs; its brutal policy of revenge, instead of restitution, in criminal offenses, and finally its supreme power to violate the individual, and its total irresponsibility.

Egoism

Vol. I.—No. 9. SAN FRANCISCO, CAL., JANUARY, 1891. Price, Five Cents.

Pointers.

Egoism's unusually late appearance this time is not due to financial shakiness, but to the reverse; its manager has been working for pay, and it is in high spirits.

In the "Twentieth Century" of January 1, Victor Yarros answers a Nationalist critic who undertakes to reason on the social problem. Having prepared himself with a false position for Individualists this Nationalist made the feat possible, and exposed himself to the blade of Mr. Yarros's logic.

We have received four numbers of the "Herald of Anarchy," published by A. Tarn, in London. It is the only Anarchist paper published in England, and is heavy and generalizing. It would be about right for Herbert Spencer to read. To us it is fully as interesting as the old Boston "Index" used to be. Those who wish to encourage it financially should address the editor at 27 St. John's Hill Grove, London, S. W.

Benj. R. Tucker published on the 10th of this month the first English translation of Count Tolstoi's latest work, "The Fruits of Culture." This book, like "The Kreutzer Sonata," has never been published in Russia. It is a twofold satire on "culture" and Spiritualism. The follies of the so-called "cultured" classes are exhibited in a humorous picture of their fashions, "fads," and mental freaks, and the story hinges upon the effect of Modern Spiritualism on an aristocratic family in Russia.

It sometimes occurs that we know things too soon. This was true in regard to Egoism claiming the siring of J. Wm. Lloyd's poems lately published in its columns. Mr. Lloyd hunts these out of a pile of them that have been written during years past, and before Egoism. The sentiment of the subjective mood of the two concluding stanzas of the present one is not in harmony with that of the publishers in the role of witnesses, but the rest we greatly admire and heartily indorse.

After several months' suspension "Fair Play" reaches us, transformed into a 24-page monthly, magazine form. One would not recognize it by its form, but the name, the same excellent motto, the "plumb-line penographs," and above all the editorial productions peculiar to the only E. C. Walker, constitute "Fair Play" with the exception of the name and piquant paragraphs of Lillian Harman, its other former editor. This we regret, as so few women are connected with Individualistic radical work, at which she succeeded so well. "Fair Play" is $1.00 per year, and published at 718 4th street, Sioux City, Iowa.

Love and Summer.

(Inspired by Solomon's Song.)

In the blaze of the morning,
In the sun and dew and bird song of the morning,
I walked forth in the meadow,
In the grove, and by the sweet singing brooklets of water.

Singing:

O Summer, Summer, Summer!
Glorious are thy heats and thy shadows,
Thy breezes and kisses,
Thy labors and languor,
Thy fruits, love, and thunder,—
O hot-blooded Summer!

There, under a liquid-amber,
By the side of the brooklets of water,
Having bathed in the pools of the water,
Saw I the form of the loved;
Her skin rich-tinted like cream,
Skin-tint of the meek Jersey heifer,
Yet rosy, like mist of the morning
When the sun rays pierce the warm vapors;
And her breasts, in their seeming, twin bubbles,
Foam bubbles afloat on a milk-field;
O sweet was the lilt of that brooklet, singing:

O Summer, Summer, Summer!
Glorious are thy heats and thy shadows,
Thy breezes and kisses,
Thy labors and languor,
Thy fruits, love, and thunder,—
O hot-blooded Summer!

Over the gleam of her sides and shoulders
Fell the rippling cloud of her wonder,
Her hair's glossy night and splendor;
Every hair a snare to her lover,
A lasso to capture and hold him;
And her soft orbs beamed in those tresses
Like a Texan-cow's eyes from a thicket.
Her limbs were rounded with glamour,
And flashed, in their whiteness, like silver,
While the rosy hands plied the soft towel.
O fair art thou, my beloved,
And tall like a queen among maidens!

Thus glimpsed I the bath of the loved one,
My fawn of the woods, and my chosen;
Then turned I, soft, and departed,
Not a dry stick snapt in the mosses,
Not a quail scared I in the bushes,
But I listed the lilt of the brooklet, singing:—

O Summer, Summer, Summer!
Glorious are thy heats and thy shadows,
Thy breezes and kisses,
Thy labors and languor,
Thy fruits, love, and thunder,—
O hot-blooded Summer!

Then filled was my soul with sweet music,
And forth came my voice in low singing:—

I will call thee my rest—
My love! my dove!
O roam not alone,
My love!

Come into my nest,
My love! my dove!
And call me thy own,
My love!

J. Wm. Lloyd.

W. S. Bell is going East next April, to be gone six months, lecturing in Utah, Colorado, Nebraska, Kansas, Illinois, Indiana, Ohio, New York, Pennsylvania, New Jersey, and probably Massachusetts. His address is Box 109, Oakland, California.

We have read "My Uncle Benjamin," Benjamin R. Tucker's latest translation from the French. It is a great book—too great we fear to sell as the "Rag Picker" did. It is the production of an intelligent victim of institution oppression who necessarily suffered more than he enjoyed. The splitting pangs of his intense pessimism are seasoned with ridiculing thrusts at the vanity of wealth. The characters are not made to "come out" in school girl ideal, but tumble along like real life, mostly at the mercy of other elements than human desire. The facts are not manufactured and put up in doses ready to take for building up a philosophy made to order, but are pointers which lead to unmistakable conclusions. The writer in his pessimistic or pathetic moods may exaggerate, but he does it in a way that implies the exaggeration, while it illuminates the point with electric intensity. Under the reign of a king, democracy is the writer's social ideal, and he often declares a blind devotion to abstract society, but his searching protrayal of the Egoistic motive, which so clearly demonstrates the fetich of his duty idea, and the age that he wrote in makes one readily forgive this unanalyzed supplication. He dissects conduct and illustrates the charlatanism on one part and the superstition and stupidity on the other that create fame with quite diagramatic plainness. Living in an age when our grandfathers were too prejudice-ridden to wear boots, buttons, and suspenders, we find him in his philosophy dashing off almost our most radical concepts with a lucidness scarcely equaled by the descriptions of the most commonplace affairs of our time. His wit is like springing a dark-lantern in a sub-cellar, while his humor penetrates your anatomy to the marrow without allowing you to roar with laughter, so skilfully is it woven in with philosophy, pathos, or tragedy. To read it is the only satisfactory way to learn about it. We keep it; price in cloth $1.00; paper cover 50 cents.

EGOISM

Issued Monthly at Fifty Cents a Year

—BY—

EQUITY PUBLISHING COMPANY,

Post Office Box 1678, San Francisco, California.

Entered as Second Class Mail Matter.

Is Faith Alone, Enough.

Anarchism is either a practicable principle that if generally understood could be applied to our social relations today, or it is a pleasant because unanalyzed dream to be indulged in, like poetry, for mental recreation. The reverie in which Anarachists generally move about would indicate their conviction that the latter is true. They take the Anarchistic papers and read the excellent articles with applause often bordering on adoration, while the writers sift and analyze under the critical eyes of all every proposition with geometrical nicety, but who thinks of trying to convince his influential neighbor Practiceworthy that these incontrovertible principles should be taken advantage of for mutual projection. No one. If that is our purpose there is little to indicate it. It would seem that our purpose is to congratulate ourselves on being Anarchists by admiring the ability of our leaders in thought. If we lack the advantage of long practice, intensity or persistence in following an idea to produce such well qualified and accurate expositions of the subject as a Tucker, Yarros, Tak Kak and the others, we sit down and refuse to do anything. We cannot get the premium at the fair, therefore will raise no potatoes at all. If the premium for literary and logical excellence, and not the potatoes of industrial and social freedom is the object, our course is consistent. But if on the other hand, we want the potatoes of free money and resulting reward for labor, and wish also to escape statute regulation and the tax collector, our conduct presents the spectacle of some impractical visionaries who are so busy dreaming of luxury that they allow themselves to starve. If it is this freedom that we desire we have to get about it and remove the popular ignorance that prevents its inauguration.

This brings up at once the question of how to go at it. We have a flaccid-minded and prejudice-steeped herd, and a privilege-fortified autocracy to deal with and to overcome by no other weapon than our logic appealing to the interest of each. The herd being without mental tenacity, it is almost impossible to make an idea stick, and if we succeed, it is very easy for privilege to neutralize its effect by an appeal to some popular prejudice. This makes it next to impossible to gain the adjustment of economic science through an overwhelming public sentiment generated from the sufferers themselves. The opposition has the advantage of a hold on the public ear through the well-trained sophistry of both press and pulpit, and to cope with these, even with the facts on their side, requires an understanding of Anarchism in its every bearing so thorough as will enable its advocates to point out the fallacies and sophistries of the opposition at every turn. This will gain the interest and confidence of that portion of the public which when stimulated by the consciousness of an impregnable position and the opposition of fraud, will control the swaying herd and its manipulators, to which it is ordinarily more or less indifferent.

To this end then, I would suggest that all we faith Anarchists, who comprise probably nine-tenths of the readers of Anarchistic papers, set about it and acquaint ourselves thoroughly with the basic literature of the philosophy, and especially with its *significance*, so that we will be impelled to apply it as above described. That the percentage of listless readers is so great as I have indicated may be denied by the more sanguine, but according to my experience it is even understated; in fact very few see what the writers think they have abundantly illustrated. We may skim over the pages and get a glance of the general idea sufficient to base a change of heart upon, but we must have a change of head—a change so complete as to enable us to change other heads. Each reader will of course *know* that this does not apply to his case, but do not be too sure. Perhaps I am little more indolent than the rest, and often as I have been exasperated with myself for mental laxity and careless reading, I was again forcibly reminded of the continuance of the habit upon reading the discussion on copyright between Benj. R. Tucker and Victor Yarros in a late number of "Liberty." I had read Mr. Tucker's editorial of 1888, which he quotes in reply to Mr. Yarros's criticism and in conclusive refutation of the claims of copyright, but as it exposed Henry George's jugglery in dealing with that subject, and I was more interested in his being exposed than in the question, I allowed the point to escape me as completely as though it had not been printed. This I believe is true of the majority of readers of Anarchistic papers, in regard to almost every important question discussed. They do not master the principle sufficiently to state it in a manner that will attract the attention of people not hostile to new ideas, nor do they appropriate the arguments so as to be able to use them readily and effectually against opposition. They simply believe them and are satisfied with themselves. If they say anything at all to anybody about the subject it is likely to be no more than a declaration of faith. This would not do even though there were no multitude to convince, for in that case these principles would have to be applied, and of course understood. But when practically the whole population remains to be converted, what must we say of the prospect in face of such facts.

Before us to be reached, are the people just as they grew up, and the task will be none too small, take such advantage as we may. After having ourselves mastered the subject to a handling degree, we should select with the greatest care the material operated upon. This should consist of persons esteemed in the community for their practicality and general good judgment, so that they in their turn become effective workers. If these can be interested at even a cost of many times the labor required to convince people of smaller working capacity, they will still be the cheapest. In getting these first there is also the advantage of evading the useless, but more weighty resistance that they would naturally offer to a new idea which they were not first to champion in their vicinity. It is also important that the subject be presented in such doses only as will interest without boring the partially indifferent. Too much discretion cannot be used in this particular. Then care should be taken also that the most pressing question be kept uppermost, and minor ones not allowed to uselessly call prejudice against it; that is, it will probably be found expedient not to preach sexual freedom to a conservative who is not searching for information on the subject, and whom you are anxious to convert into an active advocate of free money.

Every Anarchist lives in a community and has it in his power to lead that community if he will abandon his contentment with faith alone, and prepare himself to defend and extend his idea against both ignorance and sophistry. There is in print already all the necessary argument, besides that which everyday observation connected with study will add to each in the extent of his capacity to perceive and classify.

That free money is the first step toward economic emancipation is settled among Anarchists; and happily it is one which they can work most successfully if they go at it with sagacity and determination. Country people can get it into the country newspapers where all the readers are likely to become interested. They can discuss it with their neighbors, always being on the lookout for some real transaction that it would facilitate or some desired one possible that is now impossible. City people can better still illustrate its advantages, and contrive also to get it effectually presented if not thoroughly discussed in the daily papers. Nothing will come so near interesting everybody, if it can only be presented in such a way as to reach their understanding.

On this question, "Citizens' Money," being a short, popular, and comprehensive exposition is the best thing to begin with, and should be followed with "Mutual Banking," especially by those who intend to do something at illustrating the idea in detail. As literature for principals to distribute, "Citizens' Money" will, owing to its popular style and cheapness be found the most satisfactory.

Among the literature setting forth and sustaining the principles of Anarchism, none is perhaps better for even old readers of Anarchistic papers to brighten up on than "Free Political Institutions," and it is indispensable in introducing to the raw Philistine the idea of protection for person and property and the settling of differences between individuals without voting or collecting taxes. Then treating society and economics in a general way comes "The Science of Society," by Stephen Pearl Andrews. On the relation of the sexes, no one can prevail against the comprehensive, exhaustive, and unequaled arguments of the same author in his "Love, Marriage, and Divorce." And finally most profound and searching of all is "Economical Contradictions," by Proudhon. Besides these principal works there are numerous excellent pamphlets advertised in the Anarchistic papers.

If those who have these books and have read them only as novels are usually read, would study them, and those who have not got them would procure and also study them, and each would go to work in his own community, the present rush to State interference would not only be blocked, but a reaction toward economical and social freedom would be marked within five years. A very few of the great daily papers manifest an inclination in that direction, which if supplemented by the intelligent fraction of public sentiment which all Anarchists in simultaneous and determined action could create, would be followed by that canvassing of the social problem which must come before it is started toward final settlement. These papers are published for money first, and principle only incidentally, but we could use them in this way. Of course we don't have to if the ways of unresisting clay suit us better. H.

Editorial Slashes.

It must be very satisfactory to capitalism intelligent enough to realize what its privilege rests upon to see, as voiced by the labor press, the inexpressibly murky depth of ignorant prejudice from which labor has to extricate itself before it can comprehend a solution of its bondage. The following is from the San Francisco "Star," the most popular labor paper of the city:

> Daniel Sewell, just elected a member of the board of education, has been charged by Secretary Bennett, of the Society for the Suppression of Vice, with photographing, circulating and selling indecent pictures. His case was postponed, when called, until Tuesday next, by Police Judge Lawler. We have seen just one of these photographs, and we blush to think that the education of our youth should, in any degree, be entrusted to a wretch so base as it proves Sewell to be. We congratulate Mr. Bennett, and hope that his expose may result in placing Sewell behind prison bars; and that public indignation will be so pronounced as to prevent his ever taking the position which he would not only disgrace, but in which he could do much harm. No woman in the department should be humiliated by his association, and no child should be under his baneful influence.

This Bennett whom the bashful and blushing editor so fondly embraces, is the man who could get no prosecuting attorney to conduct his case against a victim because, the officials held, Bennett could not be believed under oath.

Mr. Sewell has since been released from custody, and even the moss-spined society for which Bennett is scavenger was forced under the ridicule of the daily press to acknowledge that the pictures were not indecent and that he was hasty. The photograph is that of a vigorous potato of the "peerless" variety, and bears a striking resemblance to a form of human organism in a state of psychologically-induced congestion. It was raised south of this city, by a journalist, and is a great curiosity. I have been exposed to a copy of the photograph. Its effect was to set me at once to cogitating upon what unseen forces cause the shape of things, and to thinking how fortunate it would have been for the community if these forces had so combined as to have formed into garbage carts the material from which the vice society is made, and thus have gratified it with enough real filth to prevent its agent getting stuck on the "shape" of a potato. This would have been an adaptation of means to an end worthy of inspiring a belief in an intelligent designer, and would have placed these people in a position to serve humanity in creditable contrast with their present efforts.

George Macdonald thinks that if our institutions are to be preserved there must be some legislation regulating the growing of vegetables in lascivious and indecent form. To suppress the rising spud I would suggest that a secret circular appealing to the esthetic temperment of declining years be sent to the head of every potato growing family requesting him to plant none but strictly modest potatoes, in the most weary sign of the moon, and that he take the precaution to employ old men who have developed large families and a pain in the back to occasionally visit his field early in the morning while the cocks are crowing and before the women are up, and grapple such tubers as show an aspiring tendency. I regard this as a better method than the other in that it discourages the practice of State interference and continues to direct the minds of parents to that end which has ever intensely monopolized the combined solicitude of the whole race.

The New York "Truth Seeker" of Jan. 3 contains a letter from the secretary of an auxiliary Secular Union, who has discovered that there are some reforms more pressing than the securing of taxation for church property, a change of form in oath before courts, the saving of the salaries of chaplains, the discontinuance of the State proclaiming Thanksgiving, and the abolishing of a particular interference prohibiting Sunday work, and he would work for physical liberty. To this the editor seriously objects and shows how it kills Liberal Leagues by the introduction of discussion, thus depriving humanity of the benefit from the mental freedom which the American Secular Union could bestow by the restriction of such discussion. Concerning its effect on the American Secular Union, the editor is right; no organization can maintain itself as such if issues more live than those it supports are countenanced. The church would be ruined in six months by such a policy. It, however, is not a champion of mental liberty, and is not inconsistent in decrying discussion other than that sanctioned by its creeds. But if people persist in becoming convinced that it is more important that they should pay no taxes at all, than that they pay a little less than now; that any form of oath before a court is ridiculous; that the abolition of the salaries of the thousands of other equally useless and more harmful State officials is more urgent than that of the comparatively few chaplains; that the abolition of the laws which rob labor of all but the barest subsistence during six days in the week, is a more crying need than to be permitted only to fish on the seventh; if they thus persist, it falls upon the editor to point out their error. But this he cannot do. Not that he is less able than others; but because it would be a miracle. A position without facts is too hard for any one to sustain. But it has the advantage of being sanguinely popular.

H.

The Philosophy of Egoism.

VII.

All the appetites and passions afford subjects for observation and study of the process traced in several of the preceding paragraphs, but it is not my purpose to give an exhaustive review of the various fixed ideas and facinations, or forms of mental slavery. I would suggest, as a useful exercise to the student of this philosophy of the actual, that other forms of subserviency to fixed ideas be analyzed as instances present themselves.

Sometimes it will be necessary to look beyond the individual experience of the subject. Indeed it is certain that heredity plays an important part in predisposing the individual to one or other craze, so that he falls into it when the inciting cause arises, or else in organizing him with well-balanced powers so that he happens to be happily proof against their influence. For example it may be interesting to the reader to take up for himself the passion of revenge, study its origin in the facts of warring species, families, and individuals, self-defense and precaution, habits of thought becoming fixed, the destructive propensity developed perhaps beyond the need of the individual in actual circumstances, while the sense of relation between means and ends is blunted or lost; consequently when some hurt is experienced or apprehended,—or it may be an insult to his "honor" or a bundle of altruistic beliefs,—the person seeking self-protection or vindication will act as if what has been destroyed were still to be preserved by annihilating the destroyer, or on a menace he will act with the energy of concentrated race experiences, and in sympathy with his family, nation, or race will generalize an injury to someone as being precisely the same as an injury to another or to himself, though in the case it may be really otherwise, as a cool judgment might determine. Thus what is primarily self-defense leads, under the influence of this passion, and perhaps quite as often or oftener than philanthrophy, to the sacrifice of his own life by the subject. Such action has the mark of that supernal Altruism already abundantly illustrated and clearly distinguished from a rational Altruism consonant with the reign of self-interest.

We have now dealt with Altruism as fact, but we have yet to consider it as a preachment of duty. Before entering upon a consideration of the claims of the preachers of "moral duty" and showing what their alleged obligatory Altruism is,—putting it to the test, whereupon I apprehend that it will be found to be easier for a man to pass through a needle's eye than to enter into the moral kingdom of heaven,—I wish to anticipate an objection or criticism which some reader may have raised in his own mind while we were discussing the illustrations of fixed ideas. The miser took pleasure in hoarding gold, but because he was under a fixed idea I classified him as in the bad sense altruistic; yet for an individual to act under the rule of pleasure is Egoistic. This is the seeming difficulty. It is resolved, of course, by disregarding verbal quibbles. The mesmerized subject seems to act as an individual but he is under a foreign control. The miser seems likewise to act as an individual but he is intoxicated or mesmerized by the force of the idea which has obtained an ascendency incompatible with the reign of individual reason.

A further remark seems appropriate here, and I have brought this case up partly to explain how far the philosophy of Egoism differs from the logomachy of the moralists, who, not content with dividing men into sheep and goats, would be glad to divide ideas of facts in the same way and on the lines of their own prejudices. With them the facts must be opposites, absolute opposites all the way through, if there be opposition in them in some relation. They have right and wrong, good and evil, Altruism and Egoism in their brains as opposites. Though nothing in fact is simpler to sound reason than the conformity of the crazy man's conduct to the order of the sane man's conduct, barring the substitution of an abnormal motive which practically supplants individual reason, the genuine moralistic theorist does not want an analysis of the facts. He is on the lookout for some peg whereon to hang a charge of inconsistency in argument. Verbiage is his stronghold for such occasions. He may be painfully surprised to learn that we Egoists profess to find the altruistic subject manifesting Egoistic modes of operation as nearly as the nature of the craze will allow, and that we find in this an expected corroboration of the central fact of organized, sensitive existence. A little shock or whirl of this kind will prepare the less fossilized among my moralistic readers for the greater astonishment which they must undergo when they for the first time read of right and wrong as they will be treated in these pages, as conceptions having each a separate and independent origin and not logically requiring the usual forced moralistic treatment as if they were necessary and invariable opposites. Just at this point, however, I need only say that modest Altruism confesses its foundation and haughty Altruism is self-betrayed, as surely as there is method in madness. Altruism is conspicuously selfish to make gains for Altruism. Method is a prime characteristic of sanity. There may be such madness as shows no method, but it is rare. The Altruism that contains no Egoistic alloy is still more rare if it exists at all. We have yet to look about and see whether it can be found and to examine whether or not it appears to be a vain profession of self-deluded men who have never contemplated the sacrifices which it would involve if consistently and diligently carried into action. TAK KAK.

GOVERNMENT.

BY W. S. BELL.

What a farce is government! No it is something worse, government is the parental crime, the pandora box whence comes all social evils. It pleases the people, who are intellectually but children, to put plausible and flattering sentences in their mouths, as for instance—"a government of the people, by the people and for the people." It is rather a government of politicians, run by bribe takers and bribe givers, and sustained by hordes of professional office seekers.

Whether you go to congress, to court, or to church the only constant factor in the administration of law and gospel is money. On which side is the larger pile? On that side you will find law and gospel. On that side you will find the new gospel of, "Damn the public." Go to law with your neighbor or enemy and you will soon find yourself playing with loaded dice. Go to the almshouse, house of correction, jail, or penitentiary and you will find that the superintendents of either and all these institutions are exerting their best energies in trying to make the largest possible amount of money out of their positions. Why? Because they had to buy votes, or buy men who would buy votes for them. It costs a man a small fortune to get an office that has rich stealings connected with it. Elections are political jobbery. Every species of cunning, of treachery, lying, malicious libel are unscrupulously used to defeat an opposing candidate. Not unfrequently the greatest liar and biggest thief is elected to an office where it is expected he will devote his whole mind and soul toward protecting the interests of the people.

I need not emphasize the fact that all government institutions are manipulated by force and brutality. It is obvious that it could not be otherwise since all governments are founded and perpetuated by violence. The only protection worthy the name that government affords, is the *protection of government.* If it occasionally does some good by way of timely legislation or proper execution of laws, it is not because of any love it has for the people, but it is done out of the prudential consideration of self-interest,—self-preservation.

How do policemen protect us from the invasions of criminals? The policeman is anxious to excel. He would like to have a good reputation with his superior officers. How can it be done? If he makes but few arrests he will be suspected of shirking, hence the policeman has to have to his credit a good number of arrests. It is no agreeable task to arrest strong men, gamblers, and toughs. But tipsy men, and young people who are innocent of all intention to do any crime are easily handled, and as he follows the line of the least resistance, it is more to his mind to gather this class in. Here is a premium put on unnecessary arrests. "Probably not less than ten per cent of all confined in this class of prisons (lockups) for the first and trifling offense, or for no punishable offense at all; and the aggregate number every night shut up in them, throughout the entire country, can hardly be less than ten to fifteen thousand. Think of it! Not less than a thousand every night in the year locked up for the first time for a small offense, or for no offense. Not a few of them children—boys and girls under fifteen years of age, whose chief fault is that they have never known a parent's love, never enjoyed the blessing of home." (Altgeld's "Live Industry," p. 173.)

It is not an uncommon sight to see a drunken policeman clubbing some one whom he has provoked a row with; for if you say anything at all in reply to a policeman that he can construe into a defy, he is likely to collar you and drag you into the lockup, and charge you with resisting an officer. There are multitudes of cases in every large city, where drunken policemen have clubbed unoffending men, and many witnesses ready to testify to the fact, but the corruption of the political ring protects them. There are many cases where policemen have clubbed men to death, men who were conscious of having done no wrong. And nothing is done with these men. Some of them are put through the form of a hearing, but in ninety-nine cases out of a hundred they are not convicted. If they are punished at all, it is such a light punishment as to show the trial to be nothing more than a farce.

There is no redress to be had against an officer of the law, whether he be a policeman or a judge. They bar your way to justice—they themselves have taken possession of the temple of justice and converted it into a den of thieves. Still the temple remains,—her dome glitters in the sunlight, her walls are massive and grand—her archives contain the ancient law, the statue of justice from above the door-way looks down upon you, holding in her right hand the sword, and the scales in the left. But this temple is like the whitened sepulchers of old, fair to look upon but filled with corruption inside. And the deluded people think that somehow the courts are all right, until one of them is caught in the meshes of the law, and comes out singed or fleeced. Then he curses Judge Jones and the jury. He does not dream that judge and jury are not the primary cause of his misfortunes. He does not dream that government, no matter what kind of government it may be, is the cancer in society that poisons the whole body politic. He never suspects that all the institutions about him from congress down to a policeman and police court are pregnant with invasion.

Another way in which government perpetuates crime is by the brutality of its officers. It matters not what kind of government you take whether it be civil or military, home or school government, the supposed efficiency depends upon coercion, and coercion in the last resort means brute force. Prisoners heretofore have been treated as if they had no rights. And just here is where prison management, sustained by public sentiment, has made something worse than a blunder. The public has itself been guilty of committing greater crimes than those it vainly attempts to repress. But the criminal public is irresponsible, and so too is govenment.

It was supposed that the best way to preserve good order and complete control over the soldier, sailor, prisoner, child, and scholar, was to crush out the first and least symptoms of individuality. But the "crushing out" method has not been a success, and although prison government is vastly better than it heretofore has been, yet it is barbarous. The atmosphere of courts and prisons is still tainted with the spirit of revenge.

Formerly the prisoner was tortured. Torture was supposed to be the administration of justice. The beasts who inflicted torment were made cruel by the system of religion and government under which they lived. They supposed that torture would reform the criminal. The more he was made to suffer the more purified he would become. Millions of people believe the same thing today. The reformers have pointed out the insanity of such methods,—and although small reforms are effected—still prisoners are almost everywhere robbed of their rights and treated brutally. It is evident that cruel treatment is not reformative, but on the contrary, demoralizing. The prisoner who is abused cherishes savage and revengeful feelings. He thinks of escaping from prison, of shirking by feigning sickness, etc.

We have scarcely emerged from the time when flogging was a panacea for all delinquencies. The sailors were tied up to the mast and lashed. School children were flogged. In fact it was the pride and boast of the teacher to report a large number of his scholars that he had whipt. In the house of correction brutal whippings were common. And even in the almshouses and insane asylums the rawhide or club was used upon the refractory. Today the practice of painful physical punishments in schools is rapidly passing away, but it does not pass away so rapidly from our prisons. Not only because prisoners are more difficult to manage, and that superintendents of government institutions are less humane than teachers, but because government in every form is essentially cruel and brutal. It is government itself, arbitrary and irresponsible, that inspires officers with cruel and brutal feeling toward those under their control.

As we take away from the teacher the arbitrary power of punishment, he and his scholars make progress together. But so long as government remains it will be despotic, arbitrary, and cruel. Policeman, judge, and congressman get their places by "ways that are dark and by tricks that are vain." The corruption of politics brings to the surface some of the worst men, and they become our rulers. Instead of government being made for the people, it is the people who are made for the government. Let us suppose a case of a man suspected and thrown into prison. After six months' detention, he has a hearing and is proved innocent. He has lost six months' time; he has suffered the dishonor of being cast into jail; his family has endured privations, and perhaps his health is impaired. After undergoing all this what does government do to right the wrong it has done? Does it attempt to compensate him for the loss of time? Does it do anything toward indemnifying him? Nothing. He is to consider himself happy that he escaped so lightly. He may not even complain too bitterly, for the "majesty of the law" might become incensed, and in that case the great American voter would be rearrested for "contempt of court," and flung into prison again with an emphasis. He could then muse at his leisure how government moves in a mysterious way its wonders to perform, while it is protecting the loyal and patriotic citizen in the peaceful enjoyment of all his inalienable rights. No matter where we touch government, we find that it exists for the benefit of its officers, and not for the people. Whether we look at the legislatures, both state and national, at the courts or custom houses, or elsewhere, we find everywhere the persistent fact, that there is no good in government because its laws are mostly bad, and executed with a vengeance by bad men.

As a government institution, the postoffice is often cited to show what the government can do. And we see that one reason why the postoffice is a superior institution is because it is a purely business institution. Its officers are not exposed to such constant temptations of bribes as are the police, judges, congressmen, and custom house officials. But government, like cancer, spreads and poisons all it touches. Hence the postoffice was too good, the people had some liberty that was the pure article; accordingly, government enacts its Comstock bill, and now the postoffice and the United States courts are joined. The postoffice can interfere with and destroy the liberties of the people.

The district attorney shares with all other government officials in the desire to uphold government. To uphold the government is to keep the people down.

He has a case to prosecute. His success and popularity depend largely upon the number of cases he wins—upon the number of persons found guilty. In his case as in the case of the police judge and the policeman, the very animus of his office leads him to disregard justice. It is the perpetuity of government that most concerns him, and he is the government, or that part of it whose official existence he is most anxious to prolong. How obvious is it that man needs protection, and the protection he needs most is to be protected from the crime, cruelty, and barbarisms of government.

That our courts do not administer justice, we have only to take a case or two: a man steals a watch, and is sentenced to three years in the penitentiary, while another who steals a watch is sentenced by some other court to six months or a year's imprisonment, and the third one who steals a watch gets clear.

One man knocks another down, and is sentenced to two years in prison; another kills his wife, and gets two years. And thus I might go on citing cases that happen every day, showing that our administration of law and justice is nothing of the kind.

Government is something we think we need, but when man advances to the point of individuality where he is willing to take the responsibility of his own life, the need of government will fade away. That day is distant, but that should not excuse us from assuming our own personal responsibility now.

Managerial Experience.

With a pang as large as a two-inch sea-grass rope boring beneath my left shoulder, I spring to my feet and frantically apologize to our readers for not appearing last month. I was so exhausted by overmanagement that I couldn't write a line. My wife is a strong-minded woman and insists on the privileges of a regularly appointed male husband, by working out at a salary and being served at home for its absorption. This leaves me in addition to having the children—of my neighbors educated, the management of my hope for future remuneration in our business; the management of my wife's little niece and that of the other housework. I have to prepare my wife's breakfast in the yawning and gaping hours of the morning, and manipulate our washtub and bathe the kitchen floor weekly.

For breakfast I lay a steak on a plate and with the end of a sharp caseknife jab it spasmodically both ways till I'm just out of breath. Then I melt in a spider some of the tallow which the butcher considerately leaves clinging to the steak at fifteen cents a pound. When all is popping hot I slap the punctured steak in, and interestedly try to claw the hot grease out, that splashes into my eyes at every frying. In a minute all is ready, then I authoritatively brawl out for my legal companion to come and surround it before it gets cold, a remark with which many of my male readers are doubtless familiar. After she finally starts on the steak I set the clock on the table before her, showing fifteen or less minutes till her train comes. I then hunt from under the bed, behind the door, in the coal box, and from among piles of papers on the secretary, her purse, gloves, handkerchief, coat, umbrella, and rubbers, and prance nervously about assuring her all the while that she will miss the train. In all this, she being of a placid temperment, remains painfully tranquil usually late into the next morning. The train stops before our door, and at the last moment, with a triumphant smile and both hands she grasps the hand-rails of a car as the train moves away and draws herself aboard and myself a sigh of relief. I then dash either at the washtub, EGOISM's cases, or go to the office of "Freethought" where I unravel and erect columns of type at so much per thousand ems and found—often eating the editor's lunch. All these things combined, kept me out of the paper and caused me to long for an income so large as to enable us to hire a housekeeper or to eat at a good restaurant, to have a change of sheets for the beds, a new suit of clothes every spring, and to afford fire on both sides of the stove at once. As it is, I save fifty per cent on the coal bill by occupying one end of the grate with some fire-bricks; and by washing and drying the sheets between morning and night save a similar per cent in investment of capital, while I buy a ten dollar suit of clothes only every four years and a pair of shoes every spring. This is a system of economics which EGOISM desires to disestablish as quickly as possible, as it is unsatisfactory at home and knocks our neighbors out of income by shortening the demand for their product. Herein lies the cause of all the misery of our country.

The hornet-poking editorial on emotionalism in last month's paper was another thing that occupied my time; it was so long that I could hardly get it in type before my birthday, which came off the thirteenth. I well remember twenty years ago when my father was thirty-three, and a young fellow only twenty-four unwisely attempted to hold him down. I wrote to father on my birthday to remind him that I was then as old as he once was, and that he is still stronger than I am. This will please him, and he may give me his gold watch when he is run down. We are not agreed in our ideas of existence. He does not subscribe for Egoism, which is due to the carelessness of my grandmother, who was old-fashioned and kept no novels about the house except those by Moses, Paul, and others, all bound in one volume. These she allowed my father to read when he was quite young without telling him that the stories were fictitious, and he believes to this day that all the incidents therein related actually occurred, including even the sexual relations of Mary and the ghost. We are bringing up my wife's little niece quite differently; we teach her that about everything is a lie except poverty, which latter proposition we demonstrate by daily examples.

My wife says I shouldn't refer to myself and personal matters so frequently as I sometimes do in these communications, because, she says, other folks are not interested in my affairs. This is not, on her part, a well-verified statement, for my experience is that others are interested in my affairs, especially if that affair be gold or silver, an event, I must admit, now almost obsolete. But there are many other facts in my favor, prominent among which is Ireland and Hugh O. Pentecost's interest in Mrs. O'Shea's affairs. We have experienced even a more enthusiastic interest in our affairs; one in which it was necessary to repose on shotguns and revolvers to repel the sanguine solicitude showered upon us. These arguments I pressed in our discussion in a low, earnest tone, while I made a loud noise with some tin pans I was washing, and by this means carried my position uncontradicted. Those of our readers who wish to establish a "union of beings," should try this method, for I am sure it would be more of a success in developing such a union than the union itself would be. We are willing to give our patrons advantage of such useful experience as we may possess.

This brings me at once to the purpose of this article, which is to call attention to some of Egoism's advantages. Being published monthly you will not be bored so often by it as with one which comes every week. If you wish to hobnob with your orthodox neighbors and assure them that although you are not clear on the certainty of their God, you are with them in their ideas concerning sexual relations, morality, and majority rule, it will rebuke you only monthly. If you wish to be compromisingly non-committal and seem very wise by eclectically assuming that the solution of the industrial problem is to be found halfway between all opposing theories just because they do oppose, it will show you where such a position lies, only twelve times per year. If you wish to settle philosophical propositions by your emotions alone, it cannot laugh at you so often as other radical papers now published. If you wish to grope indifferently along while the collectivistic press miseducates, the capitalistic press diverts public attention from the real issue and monopoly tightens its grasp on your neck, this paper won't exact your co-operation in spreading economic knowledge as a duty, but it may show you that self-preservation depends on your enlightening those around you. It will not beg you to save yourself, but will tell you that you are a fool if you don't. Then it has another advantage. If you have it on your desk or table, and your conservative neighbor drops in and reads it, your sympathies will not be exposed thereby, for he will not understand a single sentence, and will regard you as a great thinker and student, which indeed you must be to read the paper at all, as witness the testimony of one of our San Francisco subscribers:

855-861 Bryant st., San Francisco.

Gentlemen Equity Publishing Company:—With the approaching new year, I desire you to discontinue sending Egoism to my address. I approve of the paper, but have no time to read the same or better study it, as "Liberty" and the "Twentieth Century" give me sufficient food for reflection. Very truly, H. Royer.
December 23, 1890.

That no careful reader can peruse "Liberty" long without finding something to reflect upon is clear to me, but what a person who has understandingly read "Liberty" for years finds to reflect upon in the "Twentieth Century" is not so clear unless, like myself, he tries to determine whether Hugh O. Pentecost will come out of his emotionalism and sexual prejudice, or start a church embracing them. He could certainly find thousands of followers in this particular stage of emotional disturbance (I cannot say intellectual agitation). Mr. Royer is no slave to the duty idea. Although the paper is a home enterprise and struggling in its infancy, he does not for the sake of the "cause" fool away four bits a year for a paper from which he has no time to disentangle the ideas. I defend him. He is in his equal right in so doing. His four bits are his own, and we have no claim on them whatever. He is not responsible for the paper being started here to be patronized. Besides he is already, as I judge from his address, doing business from several doors, and the industrial freedom which is our ideal, even realized, would scarcely improve his financial condition. As a matter of social self-projection I question the policy. If health and opportunity to exchange labor for money permit, the publishers of this paper may in a few years have enlisted the interest of many intelligent people who will exert an influence, a partnership in which might insure a social appreciation more satisfactory than several dollars. For every lover of liberty cannot help appreciating whoever does something to forward such lover's ideal, as witness yourself appreciating:

Burlington, Iowa, Dec. 20, 1890.

———Dear Friend:—I enclose express order for five dollars. Four of these dollars I wish to invest in Mr. Westrup's lecture, "Citizens' Money," and the other dollar put to my credit for Egoism. I will scatter this lecture around in this neighborhood, and possibly may do some good. Not very enthusiastic over the prospect however. Am very much pleased with your paper, or rather the Equity Publishing Company's paper. San Francisco alone ought to support a paper like Egoism. Not so strange though as the city of New York not supporting the "Twentieth Century." Man is a slow-moving animal. I wish you good health and unfailing courage. Cordially, C. Boecklin.

Socially, the self-projecting effect of this is in sharp contrast with that of the first letter, although both are self-projecting within the law of equal freedom. Every Anarchist who reads both will involuntarily applaud the latter and feel an impulse to reward the act in some way; something having been done for his cause he appropriates it as a personal favor. Besides, these seven dozen pamphlets distributed in that neighborhood will be read by as many or more persons, and undoubtedly by some who will appreciate the ideas and especially esteem those who maintain the same, to say nothing of gratitude to the person who brought them to their notice. And as all prefer to bestow material benefits upon their friends rather than upon strangers, these five dollars and more may be returned to the giver by such benefits, which otherwise would not have been directed that way. Thus does Cornelia Boecklin not only project herself in the satisfaction of extending her ideas, but wins friends and admirers abroad as well as at home, and stands a chance of receiving again even the value parted with in the first place. This is why I question the self-projecting policy of the writer of the first letter. If, however, he would not appreciate such consideration, and is as well satisfied without the particular benefits and pleasures which the course of the latter brings as he would be with them, then, barring the effect of enhancing industrial freedom, he is as well off as one could be in an opposite choice, and has so much more for a rainy day which is doubtless already well provided for. But most people enjoy esteem and need industrial freedom. For these there is but one paying course.

Although Mrs. Boecklin liberally patronizes, far from her home, an enterprise espousing her cause, and Mr. Royer declines to patronize at home an enterprise similarly related to him, she is no more dominated by the "duty" idea than he is. She avows that man is a slow-moving animal, and that she is not enthusiastic over the prospect, but she well knows that even the slow move will not be made unless something is done to cause it. The many are moved only as they are acted upon by the more intelligent few, and when the intelligent are fastened in the social mire with which the ignorant flood them, it may pay to act vigorously. This Mrs. Boecklin perceives, and running the risk of accomplishing nothing tries the experiment for her own satisfaction at least. It is only a question of self-projection, and surely such projection is most complete when we exchange that which is less pleasant for that which is more so. Therefore when we have more goods than we need it is wiser to generate good will with the surplus than not to utilize it at all. And young people who spend money to circulate economic literature, if they distribute it wisely, are likely to be making a profitable invesment; profitable, not by exploitation of others, but in changing conditions to prevent exploitation by others. So ardently do we desire to see the light spreading go on that in addition to spending all our savings on it we feel like a whole country full of appreciators when occasionally some one gives the cart a boost.

The type has about run out or I would go ahead and show our readers just how five thousand picked ones could spend five dollars each in Egoism and its book list, and be five hundred dollars better off in ten years than they will be if some one does not. Those who do not believe that such readers would be "picked" can make a number of people deliciously happy.

New Year's came and was unusually severe here this time, as the minute it struck us it set the semi-barbarians among whom we live to whooping, shooting, and blowing horns and steam whistles in such a manner as would put a Chinese eclipse demonstration to shame. We are truly a great people. The Manager.

EGOISM'S PRINCIPLES AND PURPOSE.

Egoism's purpose is the improvement of social existence through intelligent self-interest. It finds that whatever we have of equal conditions and mutual advantage is due to a prevalence of this principle corresponding with the degree and universality of individual resistance to encroachment.

Reflection will satisfy all who are desirous of being guided in their conclusions by fact, that as organization itself is a process of absorbing every material useful to its purpose, with no limit save that of outside resistance, so must the very fact of its being a separately organized entity make it impossible for it to act with ultimate reference to anything but itself. Observation will show that this holds good throughout the vegetable and animal kingdoms, and that whatever of equality exists among members of a species or between different species has its source and degree in the resisting capacity, of whatever kind, which such member or species can exert against the encroachment of other members or species. The human animal is no exception to this rule. True, its greater complexity has developed the expedient of sometimes performing acts with beneficial results to others, but this is at last analysis only resistance, because it is the only means of resisting the withholding by others from such actor's welfare that which is more desirable than that with which he parts. If, then, the self-projecting faculty of mankind is such that it will in addition to the direct resistance common to the less complex animals, diplomatically exercise present sacrifice to further extend self, and it being a fact that equality depends upon equal resistance, diplomatic or otherwise, what are its chances in an absence of enlightenment in which the individuals of the majority so far from *intelligently* using this resisting power in their own behalf, do not even believe that they should do so? The result of a general conception so chaotic, would naturally be what we find: the generalization from the practical expediency of certain consideration for others, crystallized through the impulse of blind selfishness into a mysterious and oppressive obligation, credit for the observance of which gratifies the self-projecting faculty of the simple, while the more shrewd evade its exactions, and at every step from the manipulation of the general delusions of religious and political authority to the association of sexes and children at play, project themselves by exchanging this mythical credit for the real comforts and luxuries of the occasion, which the others produce. Thus in addition to the natural disadvantage of unequal capacity, the weaker are deprived through a superstition, of the use of such capacity as they have, as may be seen in their groping blindness all about us.

To secure and maintain equal conditions then, requires a rational understanding of the real object of life as indicated by the facts of its expression. It is plain that the world of humanity is made up of individuals absolutely separate; that life is to this humanity nothing save as it is something to one of these; that one of these can be nothing to another except as he detracts from or adds to his happiness; that on this is based the idea of social expediency; that the resistance of each of these individuals would determine what is socially expedient; that approximately equal resistance makes it equality, and on such continued and a universal resistance depends equality. This can leave no room for any sane action toward others but that of the policy promoting most the happiness of the acting Ego. Therefore Egoism insists that the attainment of equal freedom depends upon a course of conduct replacing the idea of "duty to others" with *expediency* toward others; upon a recognition of the fact that self-pleasure must be the final motive of any act: thus developing a principle for a basis of action about which there can be no misunderstanding, and which will place every person squarely on the merit of his or her probable interests, divested of the opportunity to deceive through pretension, as under the dominance of altruistic idealism. It will maintain that what is generally recognized as morality is nothing other than the expediency deduced from conflicting interests under competition; that it is a policy which, through the hereditary influence of ancestral experience, confirmed by personal experience, is found to pay better than any other known policy; that the belief that it is something other than a policy—a fixed and eternal obligation, outside of and superior to man's recognized interests, and may not be changed as utility indicates, makes it a superstition in effect like any other superstition which causes its adherents to crystallize the expediency adopted by one period into positive regulations for another in which it has no utility, but becomes tyrannical laws and customs in the name of which persecution is justified, as in the fanaticism of any fixed idea.

Another part of its purpose is to help dispel the "Political Authority" superstition and develop a public sentiment which would replace State interference with the protection for person and property which the competition of protecting associations would afford. Then the State's fanatical tyranny and industry crushing privilege would torture the nerves of poverty-stricken old age or pinch tender youth no more. The most disastrous interference of this monster superstition is its prohibition of the issuing of exchange medium on the ample security of all kinds of property, which at once would abolish speculative interest and practically set all idle hands at productive labor at wages ever nearing the whole product until it should be reached. The next interference is by paper titles to vacant land instead of the just and reasonable one of occupancy and use, which with the employment that free money would give, would furnish all with comfortable homes in a short time, and thereafter even with luxuries from like exertion. Following this is its patent privilege, customs robbery, protective tariff, barbarous decrees in social and sexual affairs; its brutal policy of revenge, instead of restitution, in criminal offenses, and finally its supreme power to violate the individual, and its total irresponsibility.

Egoism

Vol. I.--No. 10. SAN FRANCISCO, CAL., FEBRUARY, 1891. Price, Five Cents.

Pointers.

A few months ago we printed an edition of the Chicago "Mutual Bank Propaganda" in leaflets and offered to send them out for distribution at a price that little more than covered postage. Alfred B. Westrup took one-third of the edition, and a man in Oakland ordered a hundred, which was the extent of their sale until Mr. F. A. Matthews, of London, ordered the rest. As indicated by this, our native brethren are a lively set.

George Macdonald's Uncle Benj. R. Tucker, published on January 28, "Church and State," a new volume of essays on social problems, by Count Leo Tolstoi. "Church and State" is translated directly from Tolstoi's manuscript. It was written several years ago, but it being the author's boldest work, severely denunciatory of the powers that be, he has thus far kept it in manuscript in consequence of the arbitrary *regime* existing in Russia. Now, however, it is published in the United States. It is an assault upon both Church and State from the standpoint of Christ's teachings.

Moses Harman has been sentenced by Judge Philips to one year's imprisonment on the O'Neill letter, and the writ of error trial is yet to be heard from. Steps for an appeal to the United States circuit court on writ of error were taken by Mr. Harman's attorney, pending which the prisoner is at liberty on his own recognizance. Thus a man so upright and honorable that the courts and State officers allow him his liberty at their own risk, is permitted by the social guarantee of protection to life and property, to be dragged about and persecuted at the instance of a few semi-barbarians who have just intelligence enough to touch the button and set the law mill grinding for personal revenge.

Having in previous issues published extracts from Oscar Fay Adams's articles in in the "North American Review" on the "Mannerless Sex" and the "Ruthless Sex," we publish in this number his article from the same journal on the "Brutal Sex." As in the case of the others, while not indorsing his ideas of implied conventional virtue, we regard the general tenor of the production as excellent. The brutality of the male sex is undoubtedly due to a race experience of physical combat in assuming the additional subduing responsibility in the struggle for existence which woman has incidentally been forced to leave to man with her liberty owing to the disabilities imposed upon her by the breeding function.

"Fruits of Culture," by Tolstoi, the publication of which by Benj. R. Tucker, was announced in our last issue, has been received and read. It is a drama and therefore a little tedious to read, but well worth the pains. It vividly reproduces our experience at spiritualistic seances, and we advise Ex-Medium Dr. Bouton of Liberal, Mo., to get a copy. The spiritualistic part of it could be more thoroughly appreciated by him than any one we know of. This is not its only merit though. It presents fine illustrations of the vague idealism and often indulgent disposition of idle aristocracy as well as its weakness and cruelty, and sets forth in bold relief the rakish character that underlies the transparent veneer of its young men, along with the contemptible frivolity of its feminine dronery. The ingenuity of servants and the simplicity of peasants each come in for a goodly touch of the eccentric author's pen. It contains 185 pages and sells in cloth for 50 cents; paper, 25 cents. Address Benj. R. Tucker, Box 3366, Boston, Mass.

Egoism announces with delight that Alfred B. Westrup has secured funds with which to push the Mutual Bank propaganda vigorously. An office will be opened in Chicago and printed matter distributed in every direction. Now is the time for the friends of this, the most important economic, factor, to lend a hand and work this opportunity for all there is in it. If every reader of Egoism will put himself in communication with Mr. Westrup and co-operate with him by doing that which is impossible for Mr. Westrup to do; that is, see to it that the literature is distributed to every person in his neighborhood, and likewise distributed by his friends in other communities, such an impression can be made on the public mind as will date the beginning of a movement ending in a not hopelessly distant victory. This will be the opportunity; wisdom enough on the part of reformers to "catch on" is the only other requisite. Let us be wide awake upon his further announcements!

The members of the old National Liberal League had always been so accustomed to a spontaneous conducting of their work, and also to regard their constitution as a kind of literary production without binding force, that they were easily led by their conservative and puritanical president, Judge Westbrook, into amendments to it which they cannot indorse as he interprets them. But with the parliamentarian's brutal cunning he attempts to bulldoze them into keeping their contract when they protest against pandering to the champions of a superstition they believe themselves organized to oppose. The thing is sustained by voluntary taxation however, and they can let the legal light run it at his own expense if they wish, while they re-organize to suit themselves. Now if he could compel them to pay in their money or give up their lives and money both, they would have a sample of what Anarchists are continually subjected to by the State, with the Secularists' full consent. The Anarchists dare not withdraw their support from the State and proceed to secure protection from adequate sources and at competitive rates, but must submit to taxation, plundering by State-created privilege and regulation more tyrannical than the church would impose upon the Freethinkers, who indorse and defend all its social and moral codes. If they were half as anxious to learn from this a lesson of liberty as they are to teach one to the church, they would soon be found trying to wrest the sword from the beast instead of importuning it not to strike in their direction.

The religiously respectable president of the sexually respectable American Secular Union is evidently an old, weary, and correspondingly virtuous man, and seeks to protect the Secularists against their wives and daughters by sending among them a field secretary whose weariness their charms cannot tempt into unconventional familiarities. He evidently believes Charles Watts to be perhaps the only Freethought lecturer of this kind. In this he may be correct, as Mr. Watts has also lived probably a half century, and if we mistake not, legally experienced in this latter part of it a companion much younger than himself, which in removing curiosity concerning such youthful favors would be an additional safe-guard. This prospect the Secular husbands and fathers would hail with joy. They could rest assured on the one hand that they would not be murdered by the field secretary in order that he might rape any chaste wives and daughters, while on the other they would know that however ungovernable these women's passions might be, and whatever seductive wiles they might exercise, they could not tempt from the president's chosen an adulterous response, for he will be a man who can be "trusted in our families." This might be true of any Freethought lecturer were it not for this lewdness which President Westbrook's imputation implies on the part of the women. For are we not safe in assuming that not one out of a dozen such lecturers would kill their patrons in order to assault their wives and daughters. And if they would not there could be no danger without the willing co-operation of the women. One thing is certain, Mr. Westbrook cannot remain popular among female Secularists, for if his solicitude is well-grounded they will feel cruelly deprived, and if it is not so grounded it is a slander they will not be slow to resent when they realize its logical import.

EGOISM

Issued Monthly at Fifty Cents a Year

—BY—

EQUITY PUBLISHING COMPANY,

Post Office Box 1678, San Francisco, California.

Entered as Second Class Mail Matter.

Money Lending at Present.

Reading the article by Mr. Westrup on "Scientific, Against Religious Methods" I agree with him that Mr. Pentecost's treatment of the interest question is unsatisfactory. It is so not only because a sentimental consideration predominates in Mr. Pentecost's presentation of the case, but also because that presentation is very incomplete.

The man who by economy and self-denial has saved $1 000 has probably done much more than $1 000 worth of work in exchange for that sum. His labor products are somewhere in the mass of wealth and not his possession. While he has the money there exists a suspense account between him and capitalistic society. Let us assume that it has $1 500 of his product. If now necessity compels him to spend his $1 000 for immediate support, he has lost $500 worth of his labor. But say this man is not compelled to spend his $1 000. So much the better for him. He has been underpaid in amount, but paid in a privileged money. The possession of it affords him a prospect or chance of ultimately getting $1 500 worth of products,—or what he has earned. We can leave out of account the unscientific nature of the arrangement, which may give him more or less, while we are analyzing a pretense that the man is not entitled to more than $1 000 worth of products. The persons who paid him in money could not pay him in full, because money was with them a scarce thing. They paid him a sum with a potentiality of recovering from society the balance due him if he can wait. This is one point which Mr. Pentecost has not considered.

If now he lends his money at interest he is told that he will be appropriating from among the borrower's goods a sum that he will have done nothing to earn. Has the borrower no judgment about that? The lender who saved "by economy and self-denial" has already earned more than he lends if he lends without interest, for he has earned $1 000 worth of scarce, interest-commanding money, which is a very different thing from earning $1 000 in a free currency that would represent only labor value and that value fully paid up at the time. But the principal point to which I now wish to direct further attention is in this question: from whose goods is the interest taken? Mr. Pentecost says from the borrower, and he means it strictly, of course, for he suggests a loan without interest; a loan, mark, of this very monopoly money which one has worked disadvantageously to get. But the fact that the borrower pays the interest and has more left than he would have if the loan had been refused, may be deemed proof that the interest does not come out of the borower's goods. It comes out of the general stock of wealth through the borrower.

One must smile when one hears the assertion that the borrower under the present regimen performs for the lender a service for no equivalent. The borrower who could get money without interest would compete with others who have to pay interest and would put so much more profit in his pocket.

To view this subject the better let us suppose that the owner of the $1 000 locks it up instead of lending it. Mr. Pentecost has aroused the man's conscientious scruples or his pride and he will not take interest, but he does not feel in duty bound to lend, neither willing to allow another to perform a gratuitous service for him, and after all he is not such a ninny as to pay the borrower for taking his precious monopoly money and exploiting society with it. So he does nothing. Now society has provided little currency and has not calculated upon men's refusing interest, what will be the effect of locking the money up? That the would-be borrower may seek elsewhere, with a tendency to higher interest; that some labor seeking employment will come to a stand; and that while the owner of the money will not draw from the general store any products in excess of $1 000 valuation the interruption of labor caused by his withdrawal from circulation of $1 000 in money under present circumstances will arrest production so as to leave the total stock smaller than it would have been if he had accepted interest and let the money go into circulation. These points also Mr. Pentecost does not touch upon, yet they concern one taking any comprehensive view of the subject.

There is one expression used by Mr. Westrup which is perhaps questionable. He says: "It is the very essence of Egoism that if the ends sought by Altruists are ever attained they will be reached through Egoism." I think that nothing which is contingent or doubtful can be logically of the essence of Egoism. But I will take it that Mr. Westrup means: the essence of Egoism is such that an inference may be drawn to the effect mentioned. With this understanding Egoism is logically as independent of any process of negation or deliverance from altruistic dogmas as Freethought is independent of any negation or deliverance from the dogmas of Christian or other theology. The transition stage, however, presents certain phenomena in modes of expression and in eagerness by the individual to vindicate his new tenets with special comparisons. A general unconcern about any sort of Altruism that does not seem to interfere with the enjoyment of life will be found to characterize the mature Egoistic mind. With Mr. Pentecost Egoism is probably as yet a theory rather than a condition—a theory which he perhaps understands well enough and which he would have applied better if he had looked carefully into the complicated question of money as it is. TAK KAK.

"There's Plenty of Money in the Country!"

So far as I have been able to discover, there has been no attempt to reconcile the recent financial phenomena with the teachings of the professors of political economy. The popular journalists are all lord Dundrearys. To them the ways of finance are like those of an "Inscrutable Providence"—"something that a fellow never can find out." Listen to the wisdom of one of the great lights of this city. Under the subdivision "Financial" in an article headed "The Commerce of 1890," today's "Tribune" says:

The year 1890 was full of financial anomalies. The rules regarding the course of the money market which experience had more or less clearly established were turned upside down. Events played havoc with the predictions of the most experienced financiers.

This is what one might call giving themselves away. It is in fact quite refreshing to thus have them confess their own stupidity. Indeed it would be difficult, if not impossible for the opponents of the present money system to write in as few words a more withering sarcasm than these utterances from one of its avowed champions. If the "Tribune's" statements mean anything, they mean that the popular theory about money is not worth the paper it is written on, and that its most experienced experts are entirely unreliable. But not withstanding all this the sleepy old thing does not know that it is exposing the very worst features of the system all through the article. Boasting of the ability of the bankers to maintain high rates of interest, as though scarcity of money and high rates were not an incalculable detriment to the general welfare of the country, it says:

> In January the rate for call money was held firmly up to 6 per cent and the discount rate kept steadily at 6 to 7 per cent. Easier rates were confidently looked for as the season progressed, but the increasing demands of borrowers held down the surplus and bankers found no difficulty in keeping 6 per cent the minimum rate...... ...... The half year closed with all business in a whirl of unprecidented activity, and with the resultant demand for funds that began to bring out the opinion that there was not money enough to comfortably do the business of the country when business was pitched at such an extreme rate of activity...... Borrowers found themselves closely questioned regarding the use to which they intended to put the money they asked for...... And it mattered little what security he proposed to offer. In August came the first really startling deviation from the usual course of the market. Instead of the moderately easy money that generally comes with midsummer the New York money market got into a state of stringency that carried it to the verge of a panic and the local situation was sympathetically affected though in a much less degree. It was less the result of financial laws than it was of financial fears.

Here we have a paper, sustained by the general public, whose interests it utterly ignores. It complacently relates that bankers can maintain high rates of interest and can even refuse to allow you to go into business if it does not suit their purpose; "borrowers found themselves closely questioned regarding the use to which they intended to put the money they asked for, and it mattered little what security was offered." It would seem pertinent here to inquire: if borrowers put up satisfactory security what business is it of the lenders what they do with the money they borrow? How does it come about that bankers are in a position to dictate to borrowers? That they are is made very evident by the "Tribune's" statements if such evidence were necessary. Imagine a pawnbroker demanding of a customer: "providing I lend you the sum of money you wish to borrow on your watch, what are you going to do with the money?" Has this generation lost that independent manhood that revolts at such invasions of personal liberty, that should rise up and interpose resistance, even, to such intermeddling with what belongs to another? What constitutes the right of private property? What has become of the spirit that a few years ago was so loud in its anathemas against the Paris Commune?

"There's plenty of money in the country!" we are often told. But to those who care to use their reason, we ask: of what use is it, even admitting it to be true, which we do not, if rates are too high to make it profitable to borrow, or if a certain class of citizens have it in their power to determine whether you shall be allowed to borrow or not? Industry, husbandry, and commerce are being strangled to death by the cords that the money power has wound around them by means of the superstition that State control of money is essential. The explanation to all this is that the people as well as the journalists are most woefully ignorant on the subject.

An editor of a daily paper once said to me while discussing this question of money with him: "but you are mistaken in supposing that we are reformers; we are Bohemians; we are here to make money." "Yes," I said, "that is what I supposed, the only difference between us is that I don't believe you are following the course that will make the most money." ALFRED B. WESTRUP.

Chicago, Jan. 1, 1891.

A Daily Paper's Socialism.

The "Chronicle" of Jan. 25, contains an editorial on the "Growth of Socialism," and defends in a non-committal way the idea of social equality. This will be encouraging to the State Socialistic agitators of this coast. To Anarchists it is simply a landmark; it indicates that the agitation so long ago begun, has been so constantly justified by the encroachment of privilege-instituted monopoly that it is being indorsed by a per cent of the population great enough to make a commercial consideration which can no longer be ignored by the money-getting daily press. But whether this influential agency becomes a help or a hindrance to early industrial freedom, depends upon how clear the publishers are in their ideas of economics and the fundamental basis of liberty. If they were clear on the economic question, they could, with a little concerted action on the part of the great ones, turn the tide toward the final adjustment of social freedom. The dread among the wealthy and among the intelligent in the middle classes, of Communism, is such that a clear statement of the inevitable result of the principle of political interference, would insure their vigorous support of Anarchistic measures and of the papers proposing and defending such. While a similar exposition of the effect of economic freedom on labor, would finally win the indorsement of the voting herd, when the struggle for social equality would be practically at an end. But the probability is that a majority of these publishers do *not* understand the question well enough to see that this course would be an incomparably better policy for them in the long run than any other. And such as do, or are willing to trust to a staff so understanding it, cannot stem the tide in competition with contemporaries who pander to popular prejudice and secure the support of the great industry of politics. Therefore Anarchists may safely regard this new agitating spoon in the social soup, as advantageous only in so far as it hurries on the lesson of political folly and the resulting reaction to freedom, which is the only hope in the absence of sufficient intelligence in high places to turn the tide now.

The "Chronicle," while fully justifying the discontent of the impoverished, studiously avoids giving any clue to its idea of a remedy, if it has such an idea. It says Socialism "is not a question of State policy," which would indicate anti-State Socialistic measures, but it also admits that for the strong to help the weak and the wise to care for the foolish is a *duty*, which betrays the old paternal beast at least as much as its other thought suggests the economic idea. Another evidence against its advocacy of the economic theory, is in an editorial of recent date vigorously condemning Stanford's land loan bill on the grounds that a mortgage held by the federal government would prevent any State collecting taxes on such lands if the owners so chose. This is true, but a matter too easily remedied for an intelligent economist to base a rejection of the scheme upon without suggesting a remedy, either in an amendment or by substituting the mutual banking principle.

It admits that the growth of Socialism may not be wholly unselfish and that the favored in their foresight probably see the expediency of concession over unconditional surrender, and it further affirms that it is not worth while to inquire too closely into motives so long as the desired result is obtained. This annuls the *duty* idea, and carried to its logical conclusion must end in Anarchistic Socialism. I think also that the "Chronicle" has on its force men who can treat the subject from an impregnable position. What it will do remains to be seen. While I shall watch it with interest I shall be more surprised at a favorable than an unfavorable result. Ignorance and immediate dollar interests are generally constant factors, and may be even in a ten-story building. H.

Nicholas Brokovitch.

This man suicided at Kansas City on January the 10th. I met and became acquainted with him at Liberal, Mo., seven or eight years ago. There he was known as Nicholas Brook, having shortened his name upon coming to America from Russia, where he was an officer in the czar's army. He was an impressive person; very tall, erect in his bearing, and as tender and sensitive as a sympathetic woman. He had a fine intelligent face, and a high forehead with all the marks of mental cultivation, and was especially marked in the phrenologically indicated region of ideality. His was a dreamy disposition, and his worst misfortune one of those sympathy-craving natures with which association becomes a kind of oppressive obligation. This I believe it was that deprived him of the social appreciation that would have afforded him at least the opportunity to provide the necessaries of life, for want of which he ended the hopless struggle. His ideas he formed rapidly, but English seemed to stick near the end of his tongue, which made conversation with him tedious to those not especially interested in these ideas. In spite of these things his susceptibility and appreciative manner attracted my interest and I learned to like him more than others did, but much less than would now be the case should I meet another.

He soon became weary of this freethinking community which was contented with clubbing an obviously non-existent God, and left the place, after which I never saw nor heard of him until I received a copy of the Kansas City "Times" with a two-column account of his suicide and the poverty-stricken condition that led to it.

According to the "Times," he has lived in Kansas City for six years, and formerly worked in a cabinet shop, but for the last few months eked out a bare subsistence by repairing furniture, stoves, and cobbling shoes. From a letter written to a paper two months before, it seems he had tried to get into some of the communistic colonies, but could not because he had no money. All this it seems drove him to that final degree of despair in which he made the most deliberate preparations for the last act without leaving a solitary word to anybody. He sold his stove and bed the day before, with which he probably raised the means to buy the revolver that did the final work. In his room were only his books, covering a wide range in economic and socialistic matter, his trunk, a kit of stove repairing tools, and an upholstered arm-chair in which he was found with a 44-caliber bullet-hole in the middle of his forehead and a bulldog revolver in his lap. His pockets contained one dollar and eighty-three cents and a cheap silver watch. The books were piled carefully up in one corner and surmounted by the group picture of the Chicago martyrs. He was buried by the Kansas City Socialists who, as is usually the case found themselves more inclined to do a useless act to a dead man than a useful one for the same in life.

His chair was the only piece of furniture left, and this, in which he spent his last night, seems to have been retained on purpose for his last service. His room was in a building tenanted by a class of poor and illiterate Poles and Russians and his surroundings generally most miserable, but the old upholstered arm-chair and the books in the midst of this squalor, were at once an index to and a pitiful expression of the love of refinement within that battled so unsuccessfully with the poverty fiend while beastly and besotted wealth rolled in the luxury to which went the lion's share of what he could get the opportunity to produce.

It is no wonder he took advantage of the possibility of death to escape the torture of a plundered life. I honor his good sense. He had tried it long enough. To look in helpless old age for opportunities that youth and strength could not secure, is the fancy of a weakening mind of which he was not a victim. A remedy was in his hands which he could apply and he did not fail to use it. If I fail to secure a better condition for myself at that age, I aspire to no more praiseworthy disposition of my case. He is in my eyes a model hero; he died for the only person worth his dying for—himself. The inharmony between his make-up and the world he must live in making his life to him a failure, he made death his success, while he set a towering example to other victims hopelessly crushed. H.

The Secular Bubble Punctured.

It has been some time since I last read the constitution of the United States clear through, but I remember there are some things in it to which many Freethinkers would object. Supposing a citizen is a Freetrader, he cannot give his full consent to the section of the constitution that says congress shall have power to lay and collect duties and imposts. That class of people called Individualists might oppose the greater part of the instrument. So far as I am concerned, therefore, the constitution is not in it. I would argue against a union of church and State, and the enforcement of the dogmas of both, first, because the State as we have it is essentially a tyranny, and second, because the church is a fraud. I can maintain these propositions without appealing to a document from any of whose provisions I dissent. I would as strongly object to being held by the constitution as by the Presbyterian Confession of Faith. The constitution may be sound from clew to earring, but I claim the right to question it. Likewise the Confession may be composed of eternal verities, but I doubt it. The question is arising in these days whether a State creed is really any more binding than a church creed upon people who have not subscribed to it. If I should say I objected to church and State union because the constitution forbade it, and somebody arose and inquired whether I should support such a union if the constitution enjoined it, I should hardly know what reply to make. On the whole, therefore, I prefer to take the ground that the dogmas of religion are false, and that we have as loud a call to show their falsity when taught from the pulpit as we have to question their unconstitutionality when incorporated in the laws of the land. Religion in the constitution is a political question, and when we oppose it on purely constitutional grounds we are giving the church the choice of weapons; but when we declare that we object to ecclesiasticism in the State for the reason that ecclesiasticism is an imposture we take a position that is perfectly impregnable.—Geo. E. Macdonald in "Freethought."

In still other words, the State is a tyrant and the church a fraud seeking to impose itself through the former's brute force. Both are superstitions. Education alone can remove them. Let the State tyrant be removed, and the church fraud will be powerless. But the latter delusion dispelled, the State tyrant remains. The American Secular Union's function is educational or it is nothing. In the face of majority rule its hedging for political influence is simply madness. If it could succeed it would only have carried the fire tongs out of the burning building. The human-devouring State with all its privilege granting and barbarous custom-perpetuating powers would remain, wearing even the laurels that the Secularists would have won; for if the politicians, such as they pray to for a recognition of their principles, are not the State these Secularists can make themselves the center of no mean interest by satisfactorily establishing such a fact. These things, as above indicated, the brains of the Freethought ranks realize, and if the Freethinkers wish to retain the co-operation of such men as well as the prestige their old guard won in the reform world, they had better wake up and look about them. The church may yet deride them for their orthodoxy on live issues. H.

The Brutal Sex.

When Mrs. Poyser, in the course of her memorial arguments with Mr. Craig on "the woman question," wound up by admitting that, though women might be foolish, "God Almighty made 'em to match the men," she supplied a statement of the seemingly unanswerable variety which her sex have not been slow to make use of in discussions regarding the respective merits or failings of the sexes. As *Malvolio*, however, when questioned concerning Pythagoras's assertion that the soul of our grandam might haply inhabit a bird, replied that he thought nobly of the soul and in no way approved of the opinion, so I must declare that I think too nobly of woman to approve altogether of Mrs. Poyser's theory and assent to its proposition that women were made to match the men. If it were true, then the human race were in a most parlous state. If it were true, then the masculine would not be *the brutal sex*.

To be cruel is not necessarily to be brutal, in the ordinary acceptation of those terms, however lexicographers may decide the matter for themselves. A person may be both brutal and cruel, or only cruel, or, again, only brutal. In ordinary speech we distinguish between the two words by applying the term "cruel" to merciless acts which seem to imply a definite amount of deliberate thought preparatory to their execution, and "brutal" to similar acts committed without such thought and on the impulse of the moment. So it is that we speak of "refined cruelty," but not of "refined brutality." I have elsewhere intimated that women are often cruel; I should be sorry to believe that they could be brutal.

Cruelty is a defensive attribute of weakness; brutality the vice of strength. The exhibition of these two traits manifests itself early in our human nature. Let any one observe groups of boys and girls at their separate games, and he will see among the former the brute nature asserting its presence with more or less vehemence, according to circumstances, in a free interchange of kicks and blows, while among the girls he will observe actions that are cruel rather than brutal, and which involve mental rather than physical distress. But it is the brutal rather than the cruel side that comes into boldest relief. And among men and women the same degree of difference exists. The stronger sex is still the brutal one.

With brutality is often blended a vein of reckless generosity, a doubtful virtue, the exercise of which often serves to moderate or even dissipate in the public mind the effect of the brutality. But this is somewhat aside from the main theme. It is not needful to go back to the past to sustain the assertion that the masculine sex, taken in its entirety, is a brutal one. We can find proofs enough of it close at hand in our own time. Nor need we take exaggerated instances of it, such as now and then shock us in Whitechapel atrocities or the acts of Stanley's rear-guard in darkest Africa, or in the practices of semi-barbarous peoples. We have but to look at existing states of things in the most enlightened nations of the globe.

Among the rougher elements that form part of the social structure, we find most inhuman practices to be of common occurrence. Men think little of beating their beasts of burden most savagely, and nearly as often and as savagely, their unfortunate wives. The impulse to either act is in no way restrained by reason, and is simply the result of an outbreak of brute nature.

If the brutality of modern life touched no greater extremes than these and was confined to the lower strata of society, we might look for its elimination in time, for the progress of intelligence would supplement the workings of law. But brutality is deep-rooted in man's nature; its motives are not the accidents of the moment in their source when its most baleful consequences are concerned, but among the fundamental passions of man.

Think for a moment what is implied in the single fact that in no part of the world is it deemed safe for a woman to go alone after dark, nor, in many localities, by day even. It is not enough to reply that woman must have a trustworthy masculine escort because she is timid. Why should she be timid? Under similar circumstances a man may fear the personal violence of an enemy or the loss of his money and valuables. A woman has to dread man's "wildness and the chances of the dark." In plain words, she fears that, if unattended, some man will seek to rob her of her honor. And is not this fear of hers an arraignment of civilization itself? How much better does civilized man show above his savage brother in relation to this matter?

It may be urged that it is unfair to hold all men responsible for the lawlessness of a minority; but what is this but to confess that the majority are powerless to restrain the minority, or to say that improvement in this regard is impossible? If in the vicinity of every large town in the United States there lurked a dozen or more fierce wolves that, after nightfall, went into the town and banqueted on such of the citizens as they could secure, we may without much doubt assert that such a state of things, when once found to exist, would come to a speedy termination; for every man would feel that the common safety of all demanded the exertion of his strength in the contest with the wild beasts. But let it be understood that the honor of every woman is endangered when she goes from place to place alone at night, and we accept the fact as no reproach on our common manhood, but merely fancy that all requirements of duty are satisfied if we provide defenceless woman with a responsible male escort.

But woman's timidity is an inheritance, says some one. That is true enough; but is there no active present reason for its continued existence? Let any newspaper with its numberless accounts of brutal assaults upon women make answer to this. That the perpetrators of such crimes often meet with swift retributive justice at the hands of an enraged mob has little influence in the creation of a public opinion strong enough to make crimes of this kind eventually unknown, simply because public opinion, when it thus becomes the instrument of justice, is not worked upon by the nobler aspects of the case.

Crimes against property are always looked upon by the average man as more heinous than any others, and it is useless to deny that the average man regards his wife as his property. She is

"Something better than his dog, a little dearer than his horse,"

it is true, but his property nevertheless. The indignation which he feels on hearing of some assault upon a woman differs in degree, scarcely in kind, from the horror with which certain frontier communities regard the crime of horse-stealing. In each case the sin is committed against property. In the frontier town every man feels that his own property is in danger while the horse-thief is still at large; and similarly the average man argues with respect to his own wife while the ravisher goes unwhipt of justice. Hence his speedy resort to the swiftest punishment possible in each case.

But suppose the idea of personal ownership is not involved in any way, as it is, refine it how we may, in all instances of the kind first cited, or in all accusations of adultery brought by the husband against his wife. Suppose we consider simply one prominent attitude in which the majority of men stand toward womankind. And what is that attitude? Briefly and plainly it is that man's physical welfare requires for his maintenance the moral ruin of unnumbered thousands of women.

It is prudery to be shocked at such a putting of the matter, when we know that the practice of the average man is in fullest accord with the statement just made. Our age is easily shocked in certain directions, but our superior virtue is not incontestably proved by the fact that we are less plain spoken than our ancestors. What should most concern us is to see whether or no such a statement be true or false.

That it is a false or misleading presentiment I leave for others to maintain; that it is a true condensation of the theory held by the majority of men I do not hesitate to assert.

The tolerant attitude taken by many men of blameless lives towards sexual sins is often urged against them as a reproach by women. In this women are partly right and partly wrong. They are in the wrong because they are prone to magnify the guilt of sins of this kind so far above that of other violations of the rule of right living as thereby practically to ignore at times the existence of other sins. They thus exhibit a distorted sense of proportion in morals, and so weaken the influence they might otherwise exert upon the practice of men in this direction. But they are in the right to a certain extent in urging their reproach because the easy judgment passed upon sexual sins, even by men who have no notion of committing them, helps in its way to make the commission of those offences more readily possible.

Masculine society tacitly assumes that the overwhelming majority of men will not remain virtuous. It also assumes that a vast number of women must lead unchaste lives in order that the sexual appetite of the before-mentioned men may be gratified. Now see how differently the two sets of individuals involved in these assumptions are regarded by the world at large. The first-named are seeking the gratification of a natural instinct, we say. If the men are young and unmarried, we say "boys will be boys," and if married, we are not very much inclined to severer judgment so long as there is no outraging of conventionalities. But if young women indulge in practices of this kind, we do not good naturedly excuse them by saying "girls will be girls," or extend to them the same leniency of judgment passed upon their brothers; what is natural in the one sex appears to be most perverse and unnatural in the other. We forgive the one class readily enough, or even deny the need of the exercise of forgiveness: the other class we refuse to respect, if we be men, or if we be women, we refuse to forgive.

To tacitly admit that incontinence is, if not commendable, at least a very venial transgression for the male sex, but something quite opposite for the female sex, carries with it the practical confession that right thinking as well as right acting in relation to so important a matter is for the present unattainable. It is to admit, moreover, that man has made but very little progress from the animal to the spiritual in this respect in all the ages that have gone before up to the present, and it seemingly involves the denial of the possibility of such advance in the future.

. . . .

It matters little what advancement is made in any or all departments of human knowledge, or what increase or refinement marks our progress through the centuries, if men are to remain at the end of it all as essentially brutal in the satisfaction of sexual desire as the savage in his wilderness countless æons ago. So long as the average man, refined or otherwise, persists in acting upon his belief that the physical well-being of his sex inexorably calls for the separation from the ranks of virtuous women of hundreds of thousands of their sisters, and the consequent moral ruin of these ministers to his pleasure; so long as he contentedly suffers this perpetual sacrifice to be offered up in his behalf, so long may ours be truthfully as well as sadly called the brutal sex!—Oscar Fay Adams, in the "North American Review" for January.

A Word of Mending and Defending.

How now, good Egoism, wherein have my erotic stanzas offended? The "two concluding" you impeach, the implication whereof is that they are not "straight dox" with the Egoistic ism. I do not think the reproach is deserved. I understand that it is the idea of ownership in those we love, that you think you discover in "my love," "call me thy own," etc., but the possessive "my" does not necessarily imply actual property ownership. Observe: There is not far from here a curious old-fashioned house, which perhaps saw Washington in the days when he dwelt in Jersey and dined, as tradition saith, with one of his generals in Westfield. In that house I was born, and I call it *my* birthplace. But I *own* it not, never did own it, nor any of my family; my father rented it, merely, at the date of my advent. America is my native land, but I do not own it. You are my friend, but not therefore my chattel. My neighbor is truly mine, yet not to buy or sell or control. Is it enough?

Did you know that in the stanzas you "heartily endorse," occur "my beloved," and—

"My fawn of the woods, and my chosen"?

Surely not.

By the way, you mar one line:

"Saw I the form of the loved one,"

by omitting the word "one" after "loved."

You were not so wrong, after all, in what you knew so soon. If the poems I sent you were not of Egoism's "siring" at least they, and many others, were of egoism's siring; so what matters the lack of a big E where the big I is not forgotten. I—

J. Wm. Lloyd.

Against our supposed position the argument would be overwhelming. But our objection was less serious. We enjoy with the discoverer the beauty of his picture and share the spirit of his desire to possess, but the subjective mood that induces him repeatedly to call her "love," and such poultry as "dove," is the point at which we want suddenly to go down town, or out to the orchard for apples—anywhere—we are not in it then, that is all.—[Eds.]

The great lesson for the world to learn is that human beings do not need to be taken care of. What they do need is such conditions of justice and freedom and friendly co-operation that they can take care of themselves. Provided for by another, and subject to his will as the return tribute, they pine, and sicken, and die. This is true equally of women as of men; as true of wives as it is of vassals or serfs. Our whole existing marital system is the house of bondage and the slaughter-house of the female sex. Whether its evils are inherent or incidental, whether they belong to the essence or the administration of the institution, whether they are remediable without or only by means of revolution, are the questions that have now to be discussed.—Stephen Pearl Andrews.

Managerial Experiences.

We live in Oakland over a German cigar store and Tutonic debate combined. The Tutonic debate is a joy and a thing forever, as it seems to me. As conducted it has many advantages over the method in vogue among English-speaking people. It saves fifty per cent of the time consumed in the ordinary method. It is also conducive to economy of argumentative material. To obtain these results both disputants talk as rapidly as they can and at the same time, thus accomplishing the task in one generation. The saving of material results from the fact that neither pays the slightest attention to what the other says, and thus can bring forward with confidence at the next meeting the same argument, which otherwise might have been exploded. This unconsciousness of any damaging evidence is also a protection against the humiliation and envy of defeat. I noticed the advantage in this particular when I was growing up. My mother's parents were native Germans and strangely enough retained many of their former proclivities when stepping on American real estate. These their children absorbed more or less by one means or another. When my mother was married she embraced in addition to his person my father's selection of religious prejudices, which were supposed to differ materially from those entertained by her father and brother. These variations of the master superstition were frequently discussed in the above described manner, and always ended in mutual and joyous victory to all parties until finally some written argument, which they were obliged to consider, passed between them, whereupon the umbilical temperature immediately fell to a pleasant absence of any religious solicitude at least.

Returning to the underlying debate of my present environment I do not complain of it bitterly; it disturbs me no more than anything else of equal capacity would. In volume and constancy it is like Niagara Falls, and being suspended over it at a high rent, it is as good as the Niagara suspension bridge, suspense, toll, and all. In this monopoly of location where is the unearned increment.

Not long since I found that I was standing before a case of type in the office of "Freethought," environed by twilight and Mr. F. L. Browne, the foreman of that office, who sat patiently upon a stool by my side and affably threw together a notice of the Paine celebration since held in the city. My eyes rested upon an intelligible but unkempt page of manuscript from which I communicated to a composing stick the information that Ex-Governor Waterman had sued for slander a man who stated before witnesses that the governor had received in remuneration for the toil of pardoning prisoners, a contributed commission besides his regular salary. It was easy to see that if this gentleman had gone to a railroad station to meet a belated night train, or to some other place devoid of witnesses and made the statement, no further trouble would have followed. I therefore resolved to evade witnesses when I should have uncertain remarks to make about any one. I have since tried the experiment upon my wife and other acquaintances, and find it a smiling success.

In an after-dinner speech at the Manhattan Athletic Club not long ago Colonel Ingersoll said among some other good things that millions of people go from the cradle to the coffin without knowing what it is to live; they simply defer dying. Yet he preaches a policy of State interference with exchange which caused us to have my wife's little niece take the pair of six-years-old three-dollar blankets we possess and disperse to the edges the large hole in the middle by sewing the more sound former edges together and ripping from the hole of the former center to each end. My wife sprung this upon us, and it makes a pair of much narrower but far less etherial blankets than in their previous condition. It also illustrates the beauties of a protective tariff and furnishes at the same time a recipe for retaliation upon privileged mutton covering. If Ingersoll's wife's little niece had thus to combat the effects of protection he might see the inexpediency of taxing one laborer to "educate" another in how capital takes the legal plunder from both, while he shivered in the attempt to warm an unreciprocal cotton sheet to the responsive glow of an unprotected new woolen blanket. There is a difference in view from the point at which I stand before a case or washtub, and the one at which he sits before a well-loaded table, or in a revolving chair. He has a way of seeing too exclusively in directions.

Rose Terry Cooke, an authoress about whom I know as little as about any other department of literature, says: "I would not advise a girl, even with the strongest taste that way, to attempt literature as a means of living. It is the hardest work for the poorest pay a woman can do." My experience, though oppositely sexed, corroborates hers exactly in this particular. It is remarkable that persons with so much in common should be no better acquainted.

I have recently experienced two pictures strikingly alike in that neither looked much like what it claimed to represent. One was the photograph of a potato, and the other a woodcut in the San Francisco "Chronicle" purporting to be a likeness of my friend W. S. Bell reading the resolutions for the California State Liberal Union, which held its third annual convention in this city on the 29th of January. Here I was impressed with the immeasurable blessing of letters. But for the fact that his name was announced beneath the illustration in emphatic italic type, I should have passed to the potter's field without connecting it in any way with a daily associate. To be sure the pose from which the resolutions may have been read was at least duly abdominal, but the trouser-legs were too short. I have never seen them shrink from his well-polished shoes in that abnormally modest way. Neither have I seen his face thus unrecognizably convulsed. There were also some other pictures alleging to represent other participants with whom I am not familiar enough to judge as regards a faithful resemblance to the originals. But in the case of Mr. Bell the reporter's camera was leveled at an unfortunate moment for those friends who have none of his photographs from an authorized edition taken during normal mental action. I know no kinder-hearted man than George Macdonald, who wrote the resolutions which Mr. Bell read, and I am sure that if he had realized that the propositions were so subtly qualified as to cause in grasping them, a contortion of Mr. Bell's face that would draw the bottoms of his trouser-legs up to his ankles and cause him to be published to the world in that way, he would have had the resolutions promptly tabled. It was misplaced confidence on Mr. Macdonald's part to prepare such abstruse resolutions for a convention of merely anti-Bible Freethinkers. And since it has resulted in an irreparable public misapprehension of my colleague's face and feet I am inconsolable, and could endure to witness a similar illustration of Mr. Macdonald evicting from "Freethought" office the man who accorded to the editor an erroneous genealogy.

THE MANAGER.

EGOISM'S PRINCIPLES AND PURPOSE.

EGOISM'S purpose is the improvement of social existence through intelligent self-interest. It finds that whatever we have of equal conditions and mutual advantage is due to a prevalence of this principle corresponding with the degree and universality of individual resistance to encroachment.

Reflection will satisfy all who are desirous of being guided in their conclusions by fact, that as organization itself is a process of absorbing every material useful to its purpose, with no limit save that of outside resistance, so must the very fact of its being a separately organized entity make it impossible for it to act with ultimate reference to anything but itself. Observation will show that this holds good throughout the vegetable and animal kingdoms, and that whatever of equality exists among members of a species or between different species has its source and degree in the resisting capacity, of whatever kind, which such member or species can exert against the encroachment of other members or species. The human animal is no exception to this rule. True, its greater complexity has developed the expedient of sometimes performing acts with beneficial results to others, but this is at last analysis only resistance, because it is the only means of resisting the withholding by others from such actor's welfare that which is more desirable than that with which he parts. If, then, the self-projecting faculty of mankind is such that it will in addition to the direct resistance common to the less complex animals, diplomatically exercise present sacrifice to further extend self, and it being a fact that equality depends upon equal resistance, diplomatic or otherwise, what are its chances in an absence of enlightenment in which the individuals of the majority so far from *intelligently* using this resisting power in their own behalf, do not even believe that they should do so? The result of a general conception so chaotic, would naturally be what we find: the generalization from the practical expediency of certain consideration for others, crystallized through the impulse of blind selfishness into a mysterious and oppressive obligation, credit for the observance of which gratifies the self-projecting faculty of the simple, while the more shrewd evade its exactions, and at every step from the manipulation of the general delusions of religious and political authority to the association of sexes and children at play, project themselves by exchanging this mythical credit for the real comforts and luxuries of the occasion, which the others produce. Thus in addition to the natural disadvantage of unequal capacity, the weaker are deprived through a superstition, of the use of such capacity as they have, as may be seen in their groping blindness all about us.

To secure and maintain equal conditions then, requires a rational understanding of the real object of life as indicated by the facts of its expression. It is plain that the world of humanity is made up of individuals absolutely separate; that life is to this humanity nothing save as it is something to one of these; that one of these can be nothing to another except as he detracts from or adds to his happiness; that on this is based the idea of social expediency; that the resistance of each of these individuals would determine what is socially expedient; that approximately equal resistance makes it equality, and on such continued and a universal resistance depends equality. This can leave no room for any sane action toward others but that of the policy promoting most the happiness of the acting Ego. Therefore EGOISM insists that the attainment of equal freedom depends upon a course of conduct replacing the idea of "duty to others" with *exped ency* toward others; upon a recognition of the fact that self-pleasure must be the final motive of any act; thus developing a principle for a basis of action about which there can be no misunderstanding, and which will place every person squarely on the merit of his or her probable interests, divested of the opportunity to deceive through pretension, as under the dominance of altruistic idealism. It will maintain that what is generally recognized as morality is nothing other than the expediency deduced from conflicting interests under competition; that it is a policy which, through the hereditary influence of ancestral experience, confirmed by personal experience, is found to pay better than any other known policy; that the belief that it is something other than a policy—a fixed and eternal obligation, outside of and superior to man's recognized interests, and may not be changed as utility indicates, makes it a superstition in effect like any other superstition which causes its adherents to crystallize the expediency adopted by one period into positive regulations for another in which it has no utility, but becomes tyrannical laws and customs in the name of which persecution is justified, as in the fanaticism of any fixed idea.

Another part of its purpose is to help dispel the "Political Authority" superstition and develop a public sentiment which would replace State interference with the protection for person and property which the competition of protecting associations would afford. Then the State's fanatical tyranny and industry crushing privilege would torture the nerves of poverty-stricken old age or pinch tender youth no more. The most disastrous interference of this monster superstition is its prohibition of the issuing of exchange medium on the ample security of all kinds of property, which at once would abolish speculative interest and practically set all idle hands at productive labor at wages ever nearing the whole product until it should be reached. The next interference is by paper titles to vacant land instead of the just and reasonable one of occupancy and use, which with the employment that free money would give, would furnish all with comfortable homes in a short time, and thereafter even with luxuries from like exertion. Following this is its patent privilege, customs robbery, protective tariff, barbarous decrees in social and sexual affairs; its brutal policy of revenge, instead of restitution, in criminal offenses, and finally its supreme power to violate the individual, and its total irresponsibility.

Egoism

Vol. I.---No. 11. SAN FRANCISCO, CAL., MARCH, 1891. Price, Five Cents.

Pointers.

Do not fail to read J. Wm. Lloyd's poem to Walt Whitman, on the fifth and sixth pages of this number. Its mingled tribute, criticism, and philosophy is delugingly gratifying.

Tak Kak asks for questions from careful readers of his series running in this paper. If there are any persons who do not understand clearly all that he has written, we hope they will put their questions in clear, pointed sentences and send them to our address.

W. S. Bell will start for the East on a lecturing tour about the 10th of April, and desires engagements. Mr. Bell is the broadest, most radical, and thorough-going thinker now devoting time to anti-theological lecturing, and if any of our readers have money for that cause they can do no better than engage him for a course. They will besides benefiting themselves be patronizing a good Egoist and supporter of the most advanced ideas of the age.

The editor of the New York "Truth Seeker" quotes "Liberty" as follows: "F. Q. Stuart, who is editor of the Individualist department of 'Living Issues' regards municipalization as in perfect line with Individualism. But who regards Stuart as authority on Individualism?" The editor then adds: "Exactly. But who regards Mr. Tucker as authority on authorities?" But again, who regards the authoritarian editor of the "Truth Seeker" as authority on the libertarian editor of "Liberty."

J. W. Cooper, one of our stanchest supporters when publishing Equity, in Liberal, Mo., died of pneumonia on the 15th of last December, which we had not learned in time to report before. He contributed fifty dollars to the defense fund of the Chicago martyrs, which is the key to an impulsive generosity that left his wife without means to pay his funeral expenses. In this she seeks aid from his old comrades. We have sent our mite and will acknowledge in the paper and forward to her any donations sent to our address.

We are, in common with all newspapers, exchanging advertising for the "Scientific American," but on our own account we advise our readers who cannot have access to it, to contrive some way to raise three dollars a year to pay the subscription price, and keep it continually. It is a 16-page weekly, and keeps you posted on all scientific facts and fads, mechanical inventions, discoveries astronomical and chemical, architectural accomplishments, and everything new in art and science. Especially is it useful in families of inquiring children. Address Munn & Co. 361 Broadway New York. N. Y.

On the sixth and seventh pages we have reprinted from "Liberty" "A Gambler," by George Forrest. We have not heard of the man who buys poll-tax receipts under that name, but that does not prove that there is no such person. The hero's position is the nearest our ideal that we have ever seen in a story. His broad, searching sympathy combined with his cool, utilitarian philosophy, and the camera-like descriptive completeness of the story point to Tak Kak as the author. If he is not then we congratulate George Forrest.

The Toledo (Ohio) "Evening Bee" of Feb. 12, says: "The meeting of the Toledo Society of Economic Inquiry last evening was unusually interesting. The speaker of the evening was Alfred B. Westrup, of Chicago, well known as one of the leaders in that school of economic thought which is properly classified as 'philosophic Anarchism.' The speaker's subject was 'Mutual Banks,' in the establishment of which, he thinks, lies the only solution of the money question, which underlies all other questions of reform, and overtops them, too... Mr. Westrup expects to aid in establishing a bank of this kind in Chicago in the near future, and as it will clearly be illegal under the laws of Illinois, he expects the concern will be cited before the courts where, in his own words, 'the government can do the fighting.'" The same paper of Feb. 20, says: "There was a larger attendance than usual at the special meeting of the Economic society in Walbridge Hall last evening. Mr. Alfred B. Westrup, of Chicago, an Anarchist of the philosophical school, further defined and defended the mutual banking theory. His subject was 'Citizens' Money: Analysis of Free Trade in Banking,' and the paper offered was a very able one indeed. As its underlying principle is mutual contract, and the ignoring of governmental authority, the theory cannot be accepted by any who believe the government's fiat is necessary to establish a currency." It is to be hoped that the readers of this paper will "catch on," and assist when Mr. Westrup is ready to distribute literature. A lecture club should then be formed through which interested parties could co-operate to do pioneer work in sending Mr. Westrup and others to the field to lecture, where they could gather sufficient recruits to prosecute the propaganda to a successful termination. A few hundred dollars to start the ball rolling would do it if properly manipulated. There are men in our ranks who could easily start it if they can see the point as clearly as we think we do.

George E. Macdonald has written some very laughable and interesting things about Judge Westbrook's paternal efforts to secure a field secretary for the American Secular Union with benumbed propagative instinct, and this paper has also given some more sober reflections regarding it, with all of which I am in sympathy; but they both leave the judge in the serio-comic dilemma in which they found him. I would help him out, and offer a physiological solution of the problem which will relieve him from the consciousness of being instrumental in placing the families of the Liberal public in danger. What puzzles his brain is to find a "man who is safe to send into our families." My suggestion is, that he appoint one of the female Liberal lecturers. This would secure the mothers and daughters against temptation. And further, the men can also be secured against the assaults of such a secretary by having her vote at regular State polls before she starts, which Cardinal Gibbons says unsexes women. Thus the entire family would be safe, and the secretary untortured with evil impulses.

At the Woman's Convention at Washington recently Frances Willard had this to say anent the Parnell case: "The woman question has had no triumph so signal. It was not many years since any man of splendid public achievements was, as a man in his relation to women an entirely different personality with whom the public had nothing to do no matter how basely he might conduct himself. This was because the estimate of woman was so much beneath that which is now held." This woman is either very shallow or has implicit faith in public stupidity, for the case had no direct bearing on the woman question at all. If Mrs. O'Shea had claimed injury, that she had been deceived, that Parnell in his greater experience had taken advantage of her amorous propensity and inexperience and then left her in an undesirable position, and an indignant public had rebuked him with political defeat, it might well be considered that it was due to a higher estimate of woman than has hitherto been evinced. But this was not the case. Mrs. O'Shea nor anyone else has ever claimed that she was wronged in the matter. Indeed it was quite the opposite in popular conception; a man, Mr. O'Shea, was looked upon as the injured party. This leaves nothing for woman's influence to claim unless it be the tyrannical meddling in private affairs with which one politician was able to defeat another, and in this there is nothing except something to be ashamed of under the certain condemnation of an enlightened future. This it would be well for Miss Willard to learn if she really desires to help in freeing woman; but if it is political notoriety that she seeks, she is going just right, she could do no better. G.

EGOISM

Issued Monthly at Fifty Cents a Year

—BY—

EQUITY PUBLISHING COMPANY,

Post Office Box 1678, San Francisco, California.

Entered as Second Class Mail Matter.

The Practicability of the Mutual Bank and Absurdity of the Idea of a "Measure" or "Standard" of Value.

Let us suppose a community where there is only one bank and that each individual in that community secures an account current by depositing collateral to a greater or less extent with the bank. Is it not clear that in such a system of payments money would not be needed, every individual would pay by checks, the account being adjusted by offsetting on the books of the bank; the monetary unit we call "dollar" answering the purpose of a conventional denominator or denominant.

We will suppose also that this bank is conducted on the mutual plan, and therefore, charges are made to cover cost only. Gold and silver bullion, like any suitable commodity, could be used as collateral, but no coin would be necessary and none would be used. It would therefore seem to be sufficiently clear that a unit to act as a measure or standard of value is but a fiction, a fetich.

It is admitted that the proposed bank, for various reasons would be an impracticable method of effecting exchanges, but the absence of a coin unit-measure-standard would not be one of them. Not everyone can have a bank account; the inconvenience of paying small amounts by checks as well as the uncertainty, in many instances, as to the acceptability of checks at the bank are insurmountable difficulties, but one can hardly contemplate the foregoing and yet conceive how the advocates of a coin basis to paper money would defend their theory of its necessity. It is not difficult to comprehend the nature of the error they have fallen into. A monetary unit (a conventional denominator or denominant) to facilitate the expressing of amounts in the realm of value is apparently so similar in its function to that of the units employed in physics such as the inch, the pound, etc., especially as certain coin is made legal tender that the notion has become well nigh universal that this monetary unit must be a definite quantity of some commodity just as the inch is a definite and unvarying length or the pound is a definite and unvarying weight; but this notion is utterly devoid of reason. As there is nothing definite or permanent in value, a unit of value is a physical impossibility. The monetary unit is as near a unit or measure of value as the "x" in an algebraic equation is a known quantity. You can ascertain the exchangeable value of a gold dollar in any commodity by inquiring the price of that commodity; so also you can find the quantity "x" by ciphering out the equation.

The value of the gold dollar varies with every change in market price, just as the quantity "x" differs with every change in the equation. The gold dollar is a certain quantity of gold. It is not the gold however, but the value of the gold that is supposed to do the measuring, and it is the value of the gold that is the uncertain quantity. How can an uncertain quantity be a unit or measure? And if it is not a measure, what is the object of a coin basis? If it is answered that it is not a measure, but a "standard" of value if by "standard" is meant denominant, then the use of the term "standard" is equivocal and therefore sophistical or dishonest. If it is claimed that it is more than a denominant there is no escaping the dilemma that confronts the paragram "measure." If paper money is issued as proposed by the Mutual Bank Propaganda with ample security but not legal tender nor redeemable in any special commodity, the monetary unit dollar, will simply be a denominant. Its purchasing power could not be affected by a rise or fall in the price of any commodity any more than an order for a pound of butter would command more than a pound at one time and less at another. The Mutual Bank paper dollar will buy more butter at one time than another, but this will take place in consequence of the operation of supply and demand in regard to the butter; and so with regard to all other commodities; the Mutual Bank paper money will have no more effect on the price of commodities than the order for the butter will affect the priec of butter; whereas when the monetary unit is a legal tender commodity dollar, variations in the price of any commodity are affected not only by supply and demand in that particular commodity, but also "supply and demand" in the arbitrarily limited legal tender commodity dollar, which limit enables a class to own and control it, the scarcity or abundance of which (dependent upon combinations among this class) must affect the price of all other commodities. Under any system therefore, which recognizes any special commodity as a legal tender basis for its paper money, especially as that commodity must necessarily be one that is limited by nature, fluctuations in prices become complicated by compound causes resulting from the limitations to credit through this control of money. No such effect can occur under the Mutual system, the volume of money being unlimited except by the quantity of collateral offered, and the rate of interest being the same to all borrowers.

Of course it is not contemplated that this system shall remain as it must necessarily start—each bank independent of all the others, although any bank may remain so as long as it considers it to its interest to do so—but as the Mutual Bank is not a speculative institution, but rather an institution to defeat speculation, the system can best subserve this end by the banks becoming a general co-operative institution throughout the entire country, establishing headquarters and clearing house at some central point.

The association of the Mutual Banks thus guaranteeing each individual bank, their bills would circulate as free from discount as do those of the National Banks. What objection then could a mutual bank have to joining the national organization, since its purpose is to carry out generally what each mutual bank is established to accomplish locally; namely, the supply of an abundance of reliable exchange media.

The capitalists form trusts and combinations and seek protection in law. Repeal the law and their protection ceases. It is liberty, therefore, that affords protection to the people. Both are prompted by selfish motives, but if liberty prevails no monopolies can be possible, while at the same time there is opportunity to discover by experiment the best and most economical methods, a result not obtainable where systems are established by law.

ALFRED B. WESTRUP.

The Philosophy of Egoism.

VIII.

To plead before a tribunal is generally understood to be an acknowledgment of its jurisdiction. The intelligent Egoist does not seek to justify his views or conduct according to rules or principles of Moralism which works by awe, aping theology and religion, of which this Moralism is the ghost. Such words as morals, morality, right and wrong, duty and obligation have not lost their limited Egoistic meanings. The theoretical Egoist may be termed a moralist in so far as he thinks out a course of conduct in conformity with his observation and reason. If in a genial way he soars above business calculations then he "sings as the bird sings." To him duties imply persons who have wants and make the non-satisfaction of those wants a source of discomfort to him. But supernal Moralism with its absolute Duty he apprehends as a claim of an essentially religious character fettering with ghostly terror or enthralment all who yield to the mystic spell.

Persons who have been reared in a religious belief find themselves years after they have become disbelievers in the doctrines taught them in childhood still so far under the influence of religious sentiment that light remarks on the subject give them a shock, and apparently in the same way a generation that does not know God or ecclesiastical authority, a generation that does not know the sacred political State and the sacred authoritative family of its fathers, still retains some portion of the conscience that would fain subjugate Egoistic reason. For thousands of years preachers in the service of rulers have been preaching Duty, humility, submission, piety to the people, and Egoism has been their unspeakable horror. In our day the results of criticism applied to religious belief are apparent in general scepticism regarding the foundation of their authority, of their dogmas. Still the heredity of preaching, exhorting and warning must find its outlet, to say nothing of calculations made by men whose wealth is insured by the system of belief and submission preached, and to say nothing of calculations by ex-preachers of theology whose prospect of an income seems limited to finding something on which to preach and by which to obtain contributions, and thus the relations of man with man, philanthrophy for equity, sentiment for science, serve to continue the comedy-tragedy of preaching and servility.

If Shylock does not go to church he takes a magazine and enables the publisher to pay a few dollars a page for essays on ethics, the purport of which is that Morality, Conscience, Duty reign where God formerly reigned and with much the same restraining effect; that all honorable men will agree that these forces are indispensable, ineradicable and necessary for the conservation of property, the family, government and social order, hence a proof of Moral Being in man, while self-interest as a principle would be subversive of Moral sentiment and ruinous to society; wherein it is assumed that society is about as it is desirable to keep it. By such process Shylock makes 5000 per cent on his investment in Moralistic literature simply in the economic sphere, as he is protected by the State. He accepts any incidental assistance toward keeping women in a receptive and docile condition of mind as being so much clear profit, though really if the enterprise had to be sustained for this purpose alone he must be a miser only or else a free lover and not a "proper family man," if he did not see the advisability of paying out the few dollars even with this sole end in view.

All reformers who are not intelligent Egoists or endowed with the genius of Egoism continually render themselves ridiculous by complaining of monopolists and tyrants. Thereby they proclaim their Moralistic superstition. Their method is abortive. It can at the best lead people from one form of trustful dependence to another. At the worst and often it causes people to commit acts of ill considered hostility and to indulge in sentimental declarations which enable cool and intelligent masters to incite stronger forces against the reformers. Reform, indeed, is a word for conservative mediocrity. Egoism when understood by the many means nothing less than a complete revolution in the relations of mankind, for it is the exercise of the powers of individuals at their pleasure, and not a plea for their "rights."

The Moralists, or Altruists, come with a tale of Duty, or moral obligation. They say that I ought to love my neighbor as myself and to put aside my selfy pleasure. It is horrifying to them that I act on consciousness of satisfaction, on genial impulse, on calculation of gain, and not in submission to the Moralistic judgment of "conscience." I understand very well that it is their ignorant fear of an independent person which is at the bottom of their pleading. They are accustomed to think of a man as a dangerous animal unless controlled by "conscience." Few of them have met one who does not profess to defer to such a "spiritual guide." I however regard their "conscience," as identical with the superstition which impels Hindoos to throw themselves beneath the wheels of the sacred car and to allow sacred animals and sacred men to devour their substance.

Are the Altruists, the Moralists willing to examine the logic of their principle and carry it out to its consequences? Will they follow where it leads? Then we need not insist upon the prominence of the oppressive idea of Duty and its degradation of the individual, but we may take their own favorite idea of pure, disinterested love expelling self-interest wherever the two conflict. Of course the intelligent Egoist will perceive that I am trying to accommodate the Altruists, to get as near their position as possible, but that nevertheless there is something of falsehood, of contradiction, in the idea that love can be other than a personal interest in the object when love overcomes other interests without a sentiment of sacrifice arising; and that if the consciousness of sacrifice be present the motive is Duty, not love. However, I am discussing an alleged possibility,—a life of Altruistic devotion,—and I do not expect in the statement of the question to succeed better than the Moralists themselves in making the fanciful scheme appear wholly real.

Apart from theology with its gross dogmatism about "souls" in men and the animals as "soulless" machines of flesh and blood, the dogma of Moralism, the duty of love to others, obviously bears a direct and essential relation to the capacity of others to enjoy and to suffer, and no radical distinction can be made between a human subject and any other animal. The anti-vivisection Moralists stand up to the logic of their principle in one particular when they insist that pain ought not to be inflicted upon the inferior animals for the advancement of science intended for the benefit of mankind and not of the species or individual animals operated upon.

The consistent Moralist will now see what his principle requires of him. Though the animal, by reason of its inferior intelligence and want of speech and hands, cannot fully express its complaints, assert its "rights," and maintain its liberty, he will neither use his superior ability to enslave it nor permit others to do such wrong if it be within his power to prevent them. The animal's inability to participate as an equal in social affairs is ground for certain exclusions, but not for usurpation, detention, subjugation, castration, enforced labor, shearing off the natural coat, robbery of the mother's milk, and driving to the slaughter house. By what right does the Moralist shoot deer or crows, cut off the heads of chickens and turkeys, and cast his line or his net for fish? If by the authority of God, I reply that God is the archetype of personal despotism,—Egoism without the balancing force of approximately equal powers in different individuals; and that there is no such authority. The philosophical Altruist has left that ground. I refuse to recognize the plea. I look to the Altruistic Moralist for a less barbarian answer. And let him remember the incapable of his species,—the idiot, the maniac. Does he exploit them with a good conscience, as he tames and rides a horse? Does he refrain from fattening and killing them only because he thinks they are not good eating? Where and what is his conscience, then as to other animals?

Permit me to suggest that a man is safe in reflecting that he will never be a buffalo or a rat,—unless he believes in transmigration, whereupon his unconfessed Egoism crops out keenly self-regardful. Hence buffaloes and rats have no rights that a man even though a professed Moralist need respect, except the right of exemption from torture. (Torture is a bad example. It can be inflicted upon men as well as upon other animals and it does not minister to any demand of enlightened self-interest.) But what man may not be accused of feeble-mindedness or suffer some accident which will impair his mental powers? How then can self-concern be silent when one of his species is ill treated? The other animals—indeed he is never to be one of them: what does it matter to him how you use them so that you do not cultivate cruelty in yourself? (The cruel man is dangerous to us and ours.)

I call upon the Moralist to vindicate his doctrine by applying it consistently to the treatment of all animals. Confining it to our own species is too Egoistic to be deemed pure Moralism. I shall be very much surprised if any such practical response comes as to disprove my new version of scripture, which says that the Moral kingdom of heaven is inaccessible to men of ordinary sanity. Who will rejoice to see the grasshopper getting his fill, and keep sacrilegious hands out of the hen's nest? Who will feed the lambs and neither feed upon lamb nor wrap in woolen blankets, for conscience sake? One Moralist has one hobby and another has another hobby, but if there be one who proposes to live a life of self-denial for the happiness of all other sentient beings as far as they are capable of experiencing pleasure, to respect their liberty and embryonic offspring as conscientiously as any Moralist does those of his own species, I shall regard his appearance upon this scene as the exception which will very strikingly illustrate the rule in individual conduct, and I shall be glad to have an opportunity of learning how he manages to live. TAK KAK.

[Before this series is finished I should be glad to receive questions from any attentive reader. T. K.]

Managerial Experience.

My most soaking experience this month was the resignation by George E. Macdonald of the editorship and management of "Freethought." For three years he has maintained an unquestioned credit with such business men in this city as his responsibilities brought him in contact with. But even so mild an innovation as anti-theological Liberalism, has so little support that more than a thousand dollars a year had to be raised by contributions to meet expenses. This uncertainty Mr. Macdonald carried on the sympathetic nerve of his anatomy until his nerves were shattered, when, having enough, he promptly unloaded, the irreligion of which act commands my admiration.

He no longer writes without apology large blue suggestions on the margins of my proof-sheets, but is himself the frontispiece of a rack and case in the same office, and seems light-hearted and happy. He stands by the side of the handsomest girl in the composing room, and when I climb upon the cross-brace of my rack to reassure my mind concerning the expression of the girl's neck and backhead, I can also see him. As he stands there selecting thoughts from the case he seems to my admiring gaze a "safe man to send into our families," and I think he should be appointed field secretary for the American Secular Union now that he has left the editorial pen, in which, thrust into a poetic warning to "keep out," is a large dirk, and on one of the walls of which hangs a twenty-pound sash-weight labeled "The Editor's Companion." Traveling and two thousand dollars a year would be a much needed change which he admits he has not carried in his private purse since he assumed the bill paying for "Freethought."

For two years I have waited for the Freethought Society of this city, to discuss a question in which I should be interested. This threatened on the evening of February 22d, whe 1 the Stanford Land Loan bill among other subjects was to be touched. This event also furnished the occasion for the debut of a new pair of pants of which I am happily the possessor. My four-years-old blue flannel ones have tasseled out at the bottoms of the legs like corn in August; the pockets hang languidly open like an extremely monogamic deacon's mouth; they have taken on an intermittent polish, and acquired a compound odor of their own. All these things my wife observed and smelt, and believing it an unfavorable reflection upon her as head of the family, gave me two dollars and four-bits with which I purchased a pair that were not flashy but yet conspicuous. Concealed in these to the waist, I dashed up the broad stairs of Union Square Hall with assurance and a faded umbrella. The hall had a vacant look and lighted gas. In the ante-room was a discussion under Teutonic rules on which I am not stuck, so instead of taking the responsibility to turn out the gas as George Macdonald did on a similar occasion, I took my spraddling umbrella and an oath to fool no more time away in that manner, and stumbled off through the darkness to the Oakland ferry wondering whether men will ever try half as hard to learn facts as to enforce emotional bias.

I sometimes furnish myself with considerable of more or less unsatisfactory amusement when I contemplate the conduct of the human beast in general and my own in particular. I have only about vitality enough to comfortably exist if I could be well fed, clothed, and lodged with so little labor as would constitute moderate exercise for the average biped. My legal companion is no better off, and yet she pulls away about sixty hours a week at a case on an evening paper, while I kick myself out of bed early every morning and after a yellow-jacket-fighting day's work drag myself back late at night. Half the time I work for wages and the rest I spend at home in the kitchen, at the case, or trying to write profound articles. At the latter I spend some of my most wakeful moments. When I get a galleyful of this matter set and corrected and carefully wrapped in a newspaper (that won't fold without breaking) I take it on one arm and an umbrella and some parcels under the other, and wriggle away to the train straining and puffing as though the continuance of all animate existence depended upon my getting the matter into print. At the ferry gate, with the help of my teeth, I get my ticket in shape to be punched, and upon a time arrive at the office of "Freethought." Here I labor with professional deliberation and bulldog persistence at hair-line adjustments on the press, after which I make a run. When all this is repeated from four to seven times, my wife helps me on Sunday to get the paper ready for mailing, while her little niece purports to take care of the house by wading through mud on the streets and plastering it on the floor with her feet. The next day I could be discovered at the rickety old postoffice weighing in a short strapful of papers at a cent a pound after explaining to the clerk that Egoism is entered at pound rates, a fact so unimportant to him that he forgets it by the next issue. Thus like the Salvation Army, Holiness Band, or the idealistic Communist, we with deprivation and a printing plant publish a paper from which we hear little and for which we receive less. But this daunts not. Why do we persist in work apparently so fruitless? Why do any maggots wiggle. We must wiggle, and we want to do it with a little variation from the general custom of the human larva. But we bump uncomfortably against the rest when they don't know the motion, so we try to teach it to them. It is interesting to reflect upon the trouble the human grub has taken to vary the wiggles of its history, but not so lively as to attempt a vary. The Manager.

To Walt.

I know you Walt Whitman, and I love you.
Great soul, you are the brother of all free men.
And I know your poetry; it is Hebraic.
I understand and appreciate you.
I am not as broad as you think you are, but I think I am as deep and high as you are.
You celebrate yourself, and I celebrate myself, (you are the Kosmos, and I am a part of the Kosmos, the Mikrokosmos Man), that is the style.
Every man should celebrate himself, and every woman herself, and every thing itself.
I have always noticed that the man who celebrated himself was a good fellow to his equals.
It is the O-I-am-modest sort of chap who has to be watched.
He is not honest, he will get you under if he can.
You are "a Kosmos," you integrate yourself with the universe, you march with all armies, you wag all tongues, you blow hot and cold with the same breath?
It's no use talking Walt, you don't do it! you are not so big as you think you are.
You think you include all, you spout bravely about being the poet of wickedness as much as the poet of goodness;
You would like to fool us into the notion that there is no such thing as evil.
But I reckon that we are not so green after all.
We don't believe it, and you don't believe it, and I will show you that you don't believe it.
Let me ask you one question, Walt,—are you as much the poet of tyranny as the poet of liberty?
Aha!—I have you, and you know I have you.
Old boy!—I dusted the back of your jacket for you that time!
You haven't a page that celebrates tyranny, and you haven't a page but what celebrates liberty.
It is easy for you to say a *laissez faire* word for vice, for that is looking toward liberty.
And it is easy for you to say a good word for prostitutes and convicts and lunatics, staggering sots and gamblers, because you really don't think they are as evil as they are supposed to be.
You somehow suspect that they have not had a fair show.
They are like animals, and you are in sympathy with animals.
They are not respectable, and you like them the better for that.
You have found out that the biggest hearts are apt to beat under the dirtiest shirts.
You are a big fellow, you have a big hug, you include a good deal; but can you include chants authoritarian with chants democratic, sneaks and tyrants with free individuals, lawyers and liars with the scorners of lies; prohibitionists with rumbloats, the shriveled prude simpering scandal with the pimpled prostitute, the heart-broken widow nursing her dying babe with the landlord who turns both into the street?
When you chant the merry little girl, red-cheeked, happy-hearted, chasing butterflies into the wood, do you chant just as merrily of the hell-faced ruffian who rapes her to death in that wood?
You have songs for the anguished slave, have you a song for the sleek master who holds him in the dust with his dainty heel, and nonchalantly strips the blood from the lashes of his cat with his white fingers?
Are you as much the poet of laws, theories, conventions, as of the opposite?
You celebrate yourself, you celebrate egoism, you celebrate free individuals, democracy, liberty, equality, the citizen the center toward which all things tend.
Do you celebrate taxation, protection, regulation, legislation, proscription, conscription, confiscation, repression, permission, prohibitions, inquisitions, censorship?
Bribes, privileges, classes, castes, titles, sinecures, whitewashings, machines, rings, centralization, monopolies, trusts—the privileged man and the office-holder the center toward which all things tend?
I tell you, Walt, you are not big enough! there's not room enough inside the bag of your shirt or the waist-band of your breeches to hold them all.
You are like all the Christs—full of charity till you get a lick at the money changers.
Some things Jesus Christ himself couldn't stand.
Come, I will challenge you! You are the poet of wickedness. Of all wicked things there is nothing so wicked as tyranny—the invasion of free individuals—nothing else so damnably, monumentally bad as that. It includes about all the evil worth fussing about. Are you the poet of tyranny? I dare you to be the poet of tyranny.
If you are not the poet of tyrants, you are not the poet of evil.
You celebrate heroes, you celebrate Washington—do you celebrate vampires and sneaks? Do you celebrate Caligula, Loyola, Calvin, Judge Jeffries, Judge Gary, Anthony Comstock?
But you feel the point; I don't need to stick it into you.
You are one of the apologists and explainers away of evil—I know the breed.
They all blow thro' the same horn; they are all blind in the same eye.
They all sing the same song: "Whatever is is right!"
But pretty soon something sticks in their throats, and then they gag and sputter just like common folks.
They all have to acknowledge something evil, even if it is only your refusal to acknowledge everything good.
No use to tell me everything is good in its place.
Who said it wasn't?
And if it isn't in its place—what is it then?
I am like you, Walt, I like all the despised and homely things—elder and mullen and pokeweed, skulls, cobweb, scabs on the worm fence, cacti, toads, brush-piles, rots, puddles, sex, gutteral tones, oaths, slang, aroma of arm-pits, rags, awkwardness, jackasses, dust, snakes, stable manure, skunk cabbage—but none of these things are evil.
Nor are whips evil, nor fetters, nor prussic acid, nor claws, nor stings, fangs, lightning, bullets, daggers, malaria, parasites.
Evil is not any object, or person, or piece of matter, any thought or sound, or act—it is a position, an attitude, a relation.
Stand here, good: stand there, bad. Turn it this way, right; turn it that way, wrong. Today, excellent; tomorrow, outrageous.
The tyrant is not an individual but an attitude; change the attitude and he is no tyrant.
Liberty is a position.
Justice is a relation.
Equality and fraternity are of the same.
You are all right!—you are the universe, and you talk just like the universe. If I were the universe I should talk just as you do. But I am not the universe, and you are not the universe.
(From the standpoint of the Kosmos nothing is evil; from our standpoint anything may become evil.)
I am where I am, and you are with me, and I with you.
I know that evil is necessary, and that we are adapted to it, and

that without it there would be no good—no matter that doesn't make it good.

Is it evil?—turn it the right way and it will be good. But it has to be turned and it is our business to turn it. Turn the cock to the right, stop—to the left, open. Which is evil?—neither, and yet always one.

Evil is *the turn you don't want!*—it is the relation of the turn to you at that moment which makes it either good or evil.

Knowledge is the great good, and ignorance the great evil.

But knowledge is a relation, and ignorance is a relation, a relation of the intellect to facts.

And sometimes it is evil to know, and sometimes it is good to be ignorant, but that is because of previous misrelation.

I am not against all evil, but against that evil which is evil to me, and against that which is evil to me thro' being evil to others who are good to me.

And yet I am against all evil, because the evil which is not evil to me is not evil at all but good.

Between man and man it is good for us to be free, but between man and the not-man it is good for us to be tyrants—to do evil.

The more completely I am the equal of that which is man, and the more completely I am the master of that which is not man, the better for me.

Evil is a shifting, visible, invisible, omnipresent fact, but it is a fact, and it were better for a man that he had no brains than that he should butt his head against a fact.

Everything is in motion; and evil is here, there, nowhere?—but it is always somewhere, and we must be on guard, always, to maintain our liberties, and maintain our tyrannies.

No, Walt, you celebrate yourself, and you are a man; there's no use in your trying to celebrate something else.

You are "Walt Whitman one of the roughs," a free socialist; you will never be counted one of the smooths, or the superfines; one above or against men.

But no matter if you do applaud evil; you do *not* applaud it and everybody knows it.

It is strange!—no matter what we say, those who listen to us long enough understand us.

Tho' we speak in paradoxes, or borrow unknown tongues.

Tho' we contradict our souls.

There is something in the belly and the back of the head, and in the knots of the nerves, that teaches them, and they see thro' the clothes.

We shall all be sorted right.

Men will say, Lloyd the Anarchist (or what I mean by that), and they will say, Whitman the big-heart, egoist, radical, free man, free-lover.

They will never say, Whitman the big-bug politician, conservative, dandy, priest, mealy-mouth. I know you Walt Whitman!—you stand for free-men, free-society.

We are comrades.

So long!

—J. Wm. Lloyd.

A Gambler.

FROM "LIBERTY," BY GEORGE FORREST.

He was leaning back comfortably in the large wicker rocking chair, the soft red light from the shaded lamp of brass just barely illuminating his features and the broad expanse of his white shirt front, rescuing them from the darkness of the room. He yawned and glanced at his watch, the reflections of the gold case sending sprays of light shivering around the room, drowning themselves finally in the cool depths of the mirrors and the wall. The glittering watch amused him; and it was so pleasant to be amused. Amusement, pleasure, before all things, thought he; but *ennui* was dreadful. When he first suffered *ennui*, he rather enjoyed it,—so novel, you know; quite a sensation. Again he yawned; his watch had ceased to amuse him; and he picked up a book, but that cursed, fashionable light forbade his reading—really he was *ennuye*. But a knock at the door, and a voice calling, drove away the weary expression from his face.

"My dear boy," he was saying to a blonde young man who stood in the door-way. "My dear boy, I'm deuced glad to see you. I heard you were coming; and really, I've been waiting nearly an hour."

He held the newcomer by the hand, and rested the other on his shoulder. In the dim light they looked very much like each other: the same clear-cut features, the same cold eyes; the delicate, quivering nostril, alike in both. As they walked into the better light and seated themselves near the lamp, the newcomer's features showed the younger and more sanguine cast. He was smiling, and saying:

"Not more glad than I am to see you, George; it's like meeting an old sweetheart. We liked each other some in old college days, you know."

His voice was soft and musical, and his mobile face reflected the tenderness of his tones. The soft light from the lamp seemed to exercise a silent effect on the room, so that, when they spoke, it felt as though an everlasting stillness had just been broken.

"Like each other!" exclaimed George, "ah, it was nearer love—that friendship of ours. But we've grown cold since then; I am a man of the world, who cares for no one, for nothing,—you a brilliant young physician, caring only for your profession; perhaps with great ambitions, which I have not, nor wish for; yet to me, that old friendship is as real today as ever, the sweetest thing of my life."

He became quite earnest as he spoke, and his voice had that beautiful modulation, cold, yet tender, which is common to those who are without an emotion, yet have felt all: in their voice lingers the memory of what their life has been.

"And you, Harry," he continued, "I suppose you sometimes think of those old days; of our plans to reform the world, of your devotion to your profession and the great good you were to do, and of my devotion to everything—nothing. You remember it all, do you not?"

There was something of irony in his voice as he referred to their youthful ambitions, and he smiled in his usual sarcastic manner. Even his smile was slightly grave, and his sarcasm was of that soft, delicate kind which never gives pain.

Harry laughed; there was yet a boyish ring in the laugh, young and fresh.

"Yes," he answered, "I remember well, and when I received your letter yesterday, stating that you had just returned from one of your long tours, all the old memories became revived. But they're not so old either, it's scarcely five years since we left college. I wondered if you were just as independent as ever, if you had reached your ideal and become the 'perfect man,' you used to preach so much about. Are you that self-sufficient, unemotional personage yet, or have you changed your views?"

Harry spoke laughingly at first, but his tone changed as he noticed the sad gravity of his friend's features. He knew how well George had loved that ideal, and himself had, almost unconsciously, endeavored to attain it also.

"My views have not changed," answered George, enunciating every word gravely and clearly, "except to become more thorough. And you," he said, his gaze becoming clear and penetrating," have you attained the ideal?"

"I have married," stammered Harry, and his sanguine face clouded a little.

"And you are beginning to think you have made a mistake."

"No, no; you do not understand me. My wife is a most excellent woman, and we loved each other," interrupted Harry.

"I do understand you, my boy," said George, slowly. You fell in love and married; but you are not in love now. True, you do not seem to be very unhappy. You have settled down to make the best of it, but you no longer have an ideal; home, duty, and family have taken its place. I see you understand me. You have done what I expected you would do; it was very natural. What matter if we prove that love can very seldom last a lifetime; people will still agree to love a lifetime—but love is not made by agreement. You may think that I am criticising you. I am not, I am merely stating general truths. You know we used to discuss the question of love and marriage years ago; my views have changed but little since then, but yours have, or you would not have married."

He paused and toyed with his watch-chain. Harry looked up as his friend ceased speaking and said:

"I remember your ideas about love and my own were almost the same; we thought that true love for life was exceeding rare. Three years ago I changed my mind; it was then I first met my wife. But I will be frank with you, as we have always been with each other. Well, I fell in love with her and we were married, and for a year we were very happy: our views were the same on everything, our natures were parallel; but soon our individuality began to creep back on us and we grew apart. I no longer love; my wife no longer loves; yet we agree very well together; a staid friendship has taken the place of love. I am not unhappy, yet I confess to you that I would be happier if I had not married."

George listened attentively, and he stretched forth his hand in sympathy and clasped Harry's as he spoke.

"I know it all," he said; "it is always the same story. I early found love to be a very unstable thing, which changes as we change. That which I loved ten years ago I care nothing for now, and that which I care for now I may detest next year. When I was a boy I was religious; I vowed to love Christ above all things, as long as I should live."

He smiled softly, and slowly said: "Poor little fool—poor little fool." He sighed, and then continued:

"I broke my vow, as you know, for I now love myself above all things; yet I was as much in earnest then as I am now. My agreement to love amounted to nothing, and love and belief were shattered at the same time."

"But even you have not reached the ideal that you had in view," said Harry. "Have you done better than I, or worse?"

"I, ah, I have lived, that is all—sometimes ill, sometimes well, but I have not reached the ideal. The ideal, the perfect man is an impossibility in an imperfect environment. The greater our culture, the greater must be the pain of our vulgar surroundings. Of course I found it difficult to live up to my ideas, but—ideas are flexible things, so I modified some of them. I have not made a martyr of myself; I have enjoyed life; and, in the words of Gustave Fallot, 'I suffer, I labor, I dream, I enjoy, I think; and, in a word, when my last hour strikes, I shall have lived.' How well I remember that sentence! You know, when we used to read Proudhon, Fallot's letter impressed me very much."

He remained for some time silent, the memories of the past drifting through his mind.

"Well," he resumed, "I haven't read Proudhon in a long time. I spend most of my time drifting about the world, seeing men, places, and such, and doing a great many foolish things. When I read, it is generally George Moore or some other author that the world thinks I should not read. Of late Ibsen has attracted me; in fact, he almost aroused me from my lethargy, and I felt like preaching the old ideal again; but I have subsided, for I know the uselessness of my efforts. Yet the old thoughts were not downed—I was still the cool idealist, though my life seemed to contradict it. While drinking in the *cafe*, smoking on the boulevard, or card-playing, the old thoughts would come before my mind. I wondered how many days' labor the workmen had to give to supply the young fools with the money I fleeced from them at poker; and I saw the parallel clearly; the workingmen were fleeced by the fools, and the fools were fleeced by me; and I thought it very, very strange. Then I'd take a brandy and soda and think over it."

"Why, George," interrupted Harry, "I never thought you would gamble. I'm afraid there's very little of the old ideal you care for."

George smiled, as though he enjoyed his friend's perplexity. He stroked his moustache lazily and seemed in no hurry to relieve the anxiety regarding his morals. At last he spoke, still stroking his moustache, and uttering his words with a pronounced drawl:

"I see you are startled: you think me immoral. I am not. True, I have gambled; in fact, lived by gambling. You undoubtedly think that wrong; but you are mistaken. To obtain money by winning it is no more immoral than receiving it as a gift. Most people think it is; but then"—

He paused abruptly, evidently for effect, and then finished the sentence quietly:

"Most people are fools."

Again he resumed stroking his moustache. He was evidently waiting for Harry to speak. The silence became embarrassing. Finally Harry spoke.

"I hardly thought that of you, George," he said seriously. "I never supposed you would become a professional gambler, much less endeavor to justify it. You were always so high-minded, so conscientious, that it seems impossible."

"It is because I am conscientious that I am a gambler," he replied. "Startling, isn't it?—I know how it appears to you, impregnated with conventionality as you are,—liberal conventionality though it be. To you my actions appear immoral because you do not understand them. I remember in old days, when we used to chum together, I frequently startled you, and, liberal though you were, there were many truths which so conflicted with general belief that you would never accept them."

He became quite in earnest; the train of thought seemed to please him, and he continued fluently:

"General belief is no measure of truth; while it has been the passport of all the great falsehoods of the ages. That the world was flat was general belief; general belief was responsible for the horned devil; that the sun moved, that Christ rose from the dead, that the king could do no wrong, that the voice of the people was the voice of a vague, indefinitely-defined, eternal being—all were general beliefs; some of them are still believed in. The list of general beliefs of today which are lies is a long one: the sacredness of marriage, the life-lasting of love, that this is a free country, and, to approach what we were talking of that gambling is a vice. I repeat, I am a gambler, because I am conscientious and cannot earn a living by fraudulent means."

He stopped speaking and lazily leaned back in his chair. He had become so much in earnest that he had spoken rapidly, forgetting his assumed drawl; but he now again assumed it.

"Really," he said, "it requires too much energy to talk on these subjects. It is always the same: one talks and argues, and writes and occasionally thinks; but it doesn't amount to anything: the energy is wasted. The vast majority still insist on not thinking."

"Ah!" said Harry, sadly, "I'm afraid you've changed much since we were boys together. There is no longer the same affinity between us,—we have grown apart"—

"As lovers do," said George, finishing the sentence. "Well, what matters!" he continued. "It nearly always happens so."

Then as Harry arose to go, he arose also, and put on his coat and hat to accompany him, saying as they walked out:

"Well, there is one thing upon which we can agree."

"What?"

"To take a brandy and soda together."

SOME GOOD BOOKS.

CITIZENS' MONEY. A lecture on the "National Banking System," by Alfred B. Westrup, delivered in Chicago and published in "Liberty," of Boston, in 1888. Mr. Westrup shows that every dollar's worth of property in the country may be converted into active capital, reducing interest to the cost of issuing money, and sending capital in search of labor instead of being the other way, as it is at present. It is short, popular in style, and well calculated for propaganda work. Whoever is interested in industrial emancipation can do no better work than procure and circulate this pamphlet by the dozen. It contains 21 pages, is printed on good paper in large type, and can be had for 60 cents per dozen, or 10 cents per single copy.

MONOGAMIC SEX RELATIONS Discussed by Ego and Marie Louise. This extraordinary pamphlet charges monogamic sexual relations with causing electrical poverty through balanced electrical conditions, which results in many common, and the most fatal diseases, and in mental deterioration, leading to narrow-mindedness, bigotry, tyranny, persecution, irritability, melancholy, drunkenness, suicide, and most of the vice and misery arising from the discontent of mankind. The every day experience of all close observers must corroborate many of its accusations with unmistakable accuracy. It is intensely radical, yet clothed in such language as will admit of loaning to your orthodox neighbor. It is printed on good paper, with new type, and contains 24 large pages. Price 10 cents.

FREE POLITICAL INSTITUTIONS: Their Nature, Essence, and Maintenance,—an abridgement and rearrangement of Lysander Spooner's "Trial by Jury," edited by Victor Yarros. It is treated in seven chapters under the following heads: I. Legitimate Government and Majority Rule. II. Trial by Jury as a Palladium of Liberty. III. Trial by Jury as Defined by Magna Charta. IV. Objections answered. V. The Criminal Intent. VI. Moral Considerations for Jurors. VII. Juries of the Present Day Illegal. Whoever desires to make plain to his conservative neighbor just how society may get on without tyranny and privilege fostering government, should have a copy of this pamphlet in his coat pocket and be prepared to not only defend his position but to take that of the opposition by storm. It is the much-needed propaganda material that should be circulated as fast as Anarchists can afford to devote money to the work. Price 25 cts.

THE RAG-PICKER OF PARIS, by Felix Pyat, translated from the French by Benj. R. Tucker. This novel is the most complete portrayal of the human nature of this century in every condition of life, that has been contributed to radical literature. Every line, every pause, has a fullness, a significance of thought, or a volcano of emotion seldom found anywhere singly, and not combined in the style of any other writer. It is probably the most vivid picture of the misery of poverty, the extravagance of wealth, the sympathy and forbearance of the poor and despised, the cruelty and aggressiveness of the aristocratic and respectable, the blind greed of the middle classes, the hollowness of charity, the cunning and hypocrisy of the priesthood, the tyranny and corruption of authority, the crushing power of privilege, and finally of the redeeming beauty of the ideal of liberty and equality, that the century has produced. Four thousand copies were sold the first week after its publication. Radicals can do much good work with it among the partly liberal-minded. It will, without arousing their prejudices, open a new field of thought for very orthodox people. Price in cloth binding $1; paper, 50 cents.

For any of the above address

EQUITY PUBLISHING COMPANY,

P. O. Box 1678. San Francisco, Calif.

EGOISM'S PRINCIPLES AND PURPOSE.

Egoism's purpose is the improvement of social existence through intelligent self-interest. It finds that whatever we have of equal conditions and mutual advantage is due to a prevalence of this principle corresponding with the degree and universality of individual resistance to encroachment.

Reflection will satisfy all who are desirous of being guided in their conclusions by fact, that as organization itself is a process of absorbing every material useful to its purpose, with no limit save that of outside resistance, so must the very fact of its being a separately organized entity make it impossible for it to act with ultimate reference to anything but itself. Observation will show that this holds good throughout the vegetable and animal kingdoms, and that whatever of equality exists among members of a species or between different species has its source and degree in the resisting capacity, of whatever kind, which such member or species can exert against the encroachment of other members or species. The human animal is no exception to this rule. True, its greater complexity has developed the expedient of sometimes performing acts with beneficial results to others, but this is at last analysis only resistance, because it is the only means of resisting the withholding by others from such actor's welfare that which is more desirable than that with which he parts. If, then, the self-projecting faculty of mankind is such that it will in addition to the direct resistance common to the less complex animals, diplomatically exercise present sacrifice to further extend self, and it being a fact that equality depends upon equal resistance, diplomatic or otherwise, what are its chances in an absence of enlightenment in which the individuals of the majority so far from *intelligently* using this resisting power in their own behalf, do not even believe that they should do so? The result of a general conception so chaotic, would naturally be what we find: the generalization from the practical expediency of certain consideration for others, crystallized through the impulse of blind selfishness into a mysterious and oppressive obligation, credit for the observance of which gratifies the self-projecting faculty of the simple, while the more shrewd evade its exactions, and at every step from the manipulation of the general delusions of religious and political authority to the association of sexes and children at play, project themselves by exchanging this mythical credit for the real comforts and luxuries of the occasion, which the others produce. Thus in addition to the natural disadvantage of unequal capacity, the weaker are deprived through a superstition, of the use of such capacity as they have, as may be seen in their groping blindness all about us.

To secure and maintain equal conditions then, requires a rational understanding of the real object of life as indicated by the facts of its expression. It is plain that the world of humanity is made up of individuals absolutely separate; that life is to this humanity nothing save as it is something to one of these; that one of these can be nothing to another except as he detracts from or adds to his happiness; that on this is based the idea of social expediency; that the resistance of each of these individuals would determine what is socially expedient; that approximately equal resistance makes it equality, and on such continued and a universal resistance depends equality. This can leave no room for any sane action toward others but that of the policy promoting most the happiness of the acting Ego. Therefore Egoism insists that the attainment of equal freedom depends upon a course of conduct replacing the idea of "duty to others" with *expediency* toward others; upon a recognition of the fact that self-pleasure must be the final motive of any act; thus developing a principle for a basis of action about which there can be no misunderstanding, and which will place every person squarely on the merit of his or her probable interests, divested of the opportunity to deceive through pretension, as under the dominance of altruistic idealism. It will maintain that what is generally recognized as morality is nothing other than the expediency deduced from conflicting interests under competition; that it is a policy which, through the hereditary influence of ancestral experience, confirmed by personal experience, is found to pay better than any other known policy; that the belief that it is something other than a policy—a fixed and eternal obligation, outside of and superior to man's recognized interests, and may not be changed as utility indicates, makes it a superstition in effect like any other superstition which causes its adherents to crystallize the expediency adopted by one period into positive regulations for another in which it has no utility, but becomes tyrannical laws and customs in the name of which persecution is justified, as in the fanaticism of any fixed idea.

Another part of its purpose is to help dispel the "Political Authority" superstition and develop a public sentiment which would replace State interference with the protection for person and property which the competition of protecting associations would afford. Then the State's fanatical tyranny and industry crushing privilege would torture the nerves of poverty-stricken old age or pinch tender youth no more. The most disastrous interference of this monster superstition is its prohibition of the issuing of exchange medium on the ample security of all kinds of property, which at once would abolish speculative interest and practically set all idle hands at productive labor at wages ever nearing the whole product until it should be reached. The next interference is by paper titles to vacant land instead of the just and reasonable one of occupancy and use, which with the employment that free money would give, would furnish all with comfortable homes in a short time, and thereafter even with luxuries from like exertion. Following this is its patent privilege, customs robbery, protective tariff, barbarous decrees in social and sexual affairs; its brutal policy of revenge, instead of restitution, in criminal offenses, and finally its supreme power to violate the individual, and its total irresponsibility.

Egoism

Vol. I.---No. 12. SAN FRANCISCO, CAL., APRIL, 1891. Price, Five Cents.

Pointers.

Although EGOISM was properly due on the first of each month it has seldom been out before the middle. The coming year it will not be due until the fifteenth.

We acknowledge the receipt of 50 cents from Prof. J. H. Cook for the funeral fund of J. W. Cooper, mentioned in the preceding number of this paper. This is the only response to that appeal. Surely the poor are the lone friends of the poor.

In "Liberty" of April 4, Victor Yarros in correcting Bellamy, favors its readers with an imaginary conversation between a Nationalist and an Evolutionist which subtly exposes in easily comprehended language the vague generalizing and erroneous conclusions of these socialistic amateurs. Nationalists should read the article, and permit themselves no longer to be exposed to the ridicule of more patient thinkers.

Alfred B. Westrup has published a new edition of "Citizens' Money" with an appendix consisting of the "Mutual Bank Propaganda: Its Declaration of Principles and Object." This makes it more desirable than our edition. It is neat and well-printed, contains 27 large pages and sells for 10 cents. We hope this edition of the excellent pamphlet will not be left on Mr. Westrup's hands, as much of our edition has on ours. Pamphlets can do no work so long as they remain on the publisher's shelves. Address The Mutual Bank Propaganda, 343 Michigan Ave. Chicago, Ills., or this paper.

The advertisement of "Fair Play" on the seventh page of this number is dead. That paper has suspended publication. Its publishers state that it has never received more than fifty per cent of the amount required to publish it. Aside from all considerations of sympathy for its publishers as friends having to abandon it, we are very sorry to see "Fair Play" stop. Being partly devoted to anti-theological propaganda and circulating among that class of innovators, it was enabled to carry Anarchistic ideas into places where exclusively Anarchistic papers never go. Its unexpired subscriptions will be filled by "Liberty," of Boston. Its editor has also joined that paper's staff and takes the field in the West as traveling salesman for it and Mr. Tucker's other publications.

The uncle of his nephew George Macdonald, has just translated and published Zola's latest novel, "Money," and says concerning it: "So boundless is my admiration for Zola and his works that I cannot bring myself to write soberly on the subject. For this reason I have asked Mr. Yarros, who is not yet as crazy as I am in this direction, to write an article for the next number on Zola's latest novel, "Money," which I have just translated and published. Meantime I congratulate myself upon my self-control in confining myself to the moderate remark that "Money" is perhaps the greatest novel yet written by the greatest novelist that has yet lived." We are reading it and do not wonder at the enthusiasm of a person even so cool as Mr. Tucker usually is. When we have finished it more of our impressions will be given the habitually indifferent reader. Those who have faith in Mr. Tucker's judgment, and a dollar, will immediately send the latter to his address, Box 3366, Boston, and get a copy in cloth, or 50 cents of it for one in paper cover.

The case of the New Orleans massacre furnishes another illustration of the weakness and indifference of government in protecting life and securing justice. In the first place it allowed the prisoners, unarmed and defenseless, to be butchered by a crazy mob, and now dares not or cares not to bring it to trial as it would a helpless individual, if indeed it does so at all. The "investigation" will be a covering up and an apologizing expedition for the community instead of an attempt to find and dispose of the invaders and repair as far as possible the loss of the sufferers from this cyclone of Grundy rage. If the victims had been the subjects of some of the stronger powers it would have been different too. The treasury would have been plunged into with large scoops, and the leaders of the mob put through a trial of some kind at least. But in this case there is no danger of punishment, and no refusal to render boodle to the State, so why should the political priests trouble themselves. Let New Orleans refuse to pay taxes or to obey any plunder gathering law, and if the standing army and the militia were not sufficient to bring her to time every laborer in the United States would be put into service for that purpose. But a few Italians shot and hanged without trial by "leading citizens" calls of course only for a formal investigation.

We have so often adversely criticised Hugh O. Pentecost that we are very glad for an opportunity to commend some of his utterances. These composed the principal part of his address on "Selfishness," delivered on Sunday March 29. This is in our estimation his ablest and most important effort. It was so radical and strong that J. W. S., whom we understand is his partner, deemed it necessary to apologize to the readers of the "Twentieth Century" by assuring them that Mr. Pentecost is not so bad as he would be willing for others to be if they liked. This apologist also attempts to refute Mr. Pentecost's position. He deduces from the fact that man can adapt means to ends more successfully than dogs can, the basis of a "right law" which embraces monogamy, the family, the State, morality, immortality, and God. And we deduce from such drivel, that J. W. S. is an old granny. That government, monogamy, morality, immortality, and God are all off the same cloth is obvious, but they are in no way supported by the fact that superior intelligence adapts means to pleasurable ends more successfully than inferior intelligence. This metaphysical acrobat confesses that arguing on this subject is not his forte, a statement which W. S. Bell declared to be the only correct one in the whole article. All this reveals acres of reactionary environment for Mr. Pentecost, and goes far toward accounting for the incoherence of his position taken as a whole.

In the face of equal resistance our civilization boasts of its refinement, but to the discriminating eye it betrays its barbarous brutality at every turn in which it is not met by such resistance. Right under our noses, while Americans hording gold in China and rich Chinese hording it here are protected, it is no uncommon thing to see a score of our citizens who assume heavily on their refinement, witnessing without rebuke, a dozen hoodlums or children pelting an inoffensive Chinese laborer with stones or mud as he passes along under a heavy load. He is helpless; successfully competing with the native slaves of a privilege-granting government, he is hated by them; and being only laboring material in the hands of either rich Chinamen or well-to-do Americans, they have no interest so long as he is not disabled and hard to replace; and being ignorant of how to proceed for redress before the courts and too poor to pay for it even if he knew how, he escapes each time as best he can. The same brutal indifference to invasive cruelty may be observed wherever helplessness is met by collective strength shielded by custom, as with the helpless minority, disfranchised woman, impoverished labor, a "fallen" woman, the lone heretic, and dumb beasts. It would seem that a continual array of such facts would attest the legitimacy of the claim that intelligent resistance and not preaching of "duty" and sacrifice is the remedy, but the subjective shell of the emotional clam closes too quickly to be affected by an object lesson. When race experience shall have added to his sense of touch or feeling, that of sight with deliberate comparison, facts will have a leading part in determining conduct. Until he reaches that stage the mental mollusk must gap and close at each disturbance till he is sufficiently accustomed to them to remain open for an impression.

EGOISM

Issued Monthly at Fifty Cents a Year

—BY—

EQUITY PUBLISHING COMPANY,

Post Office Box 1678, San Francisco, California.

Entered as Second Class Mail Matter.

One Year Old.

EGOISM reaches with this number its first anniversary. Its influence has been greater than its publishers expected, though its management and editorial work fell very short of their ideal. It has usually been edited on the jump, writing and correcting against time. Even the first number had to be gotten out hastily, and appeared without a comprehensive and concise statement of its purpose. And its work is not yet as well systemized as it should have been at the start, but we mean to catch up with it sometime.

So far, such matters as happened to be thrust upon our notice were treated, while in the absence of systematic canvassing others of more importance have been overlooked. Henceforth we hope to remedy this.

During the past year we have promulgated the principle in a general way, but at the suggestion of Cornelia Boecklin, of Burlington, Iowa, we have concluded to apply it editorially more to local and Pacific coast affairs. This idea had occurred to us before, but was only superficially canvassed in that we rejected it on the grounds that such a course would destroy general interest and having no local support would be suicidal. But when Mrs. Boecklin described such a paper as the one she was looking for, it began to grow upon us how everybody is living in and necessarily connected with the doings of a community, and daily confronted with just such questions as such a paper would have to treat, so would be interested in it all the more for handling local subjects even though they were those of another place. Therefore we have decided to try that policy the coming year. We shall of course have to depend upon the daily press for notes, and as such news is likely to be doctored or the depredations of privilege not reported at all, it will be uphill work. If all our local friends would keep a little on the lookout for State invasions reports of which do not appear in the papers or are trimmed if they do, and send us a correct account of the facts they could thereby render the paper valuable service at little cost. In this way an efficient corps could be organized, resulting in great benefit both to its members and EGOISM's readers. Nothing could be better calculated than this to excite both local and general interest.

The contributed matter will necessarily and properly continue as in the past to apply the idea in a general way. The philosophy of Egoism, the principles of Anarchism, the discussion of the money question, of the sex question and kindred subjects will occupy their usual space. The paper will not, like some others, be a free-for-all horn on any or no particular subject. Our purpose is to propagate the Egoistic idea as the eliminater of every kind of superstition and as the basis of equal freedom, and Anarchism as the scientific and only method of reaching such freedom. And such contributions as do not relate immediately to these questions either in extending or intelligently criticising them, cannot occupy space that costs us so much save as they are chosen from other considerations than keeping open house. Poems, stories, and relative selections such as we have been publishing, will be welcome and will receive as fast as practicable more and more space. We like poetry with thought and beauty combined, and fiction that teaches pleasure and provokes mirth or with utilitarian philosophy reduces bigotry to despair and chases, like a lizard into a rock pile, gushing emotionalism into its religious crevice in the theological ruin.

Be on the lookout, EGOISM will be commencing soon to be two-years old cattle, and when on sunny days the wormil of the Egoistic gadfly begins to come through its skin it may kick very high and dash recklessly across coventionality's mossy lawn.

Co-operative Schemes.

Friends in writing to the publishers of this paper often refer to co-operation. Some with the unquestioning assurance common in speaking of happiness, liberty, or equality. Others noting the constant failures of co-operative attempts have plans by which they believe it can be "made to work." These plans deviate from those of co-operative experiments, in an endeavor to secure individual freedom with combined industrial effort. They seem to realize to a certain extent that the question hinges on liberty, but persist in remaining on the wrong track to secure it. Liberty and communism mix only as oil and water mixes—each by itself. Liberty is a gratification, the imperative demand of a separate consciousness for unhampered action, while communism is an economical manipulation of material, a utility. Rock and mortar arranged in a wall is a success in combining materials. A thousand human bodies ground with lime would be an equal success in fertilizing land. But the thousand object; it makes a difference whether they be material for something else or something else for them. Conscious beings will not become material when they realize it. They do so without knowing it, but only for that reason. Indeed, the great effort of life it seems is to invent schemes to get people without knowing it to become material for the manipulators. It is the game of the church, the State, and of Moralism.

Consciousness chooses and choice implies purpose, a proposer and his pleasure. The idea of pleasure to be consistent with the function of choosing implies the greatest pleasure. If our intelligence were great enough to determine acts ideally consistent with the prerogative of choosing, there would be no suspensive breaks at all in pleasurable sensation. In the degree that our conduct is inconsistent with imperative choice, in that degree we become material for something else, some element, combination, or person. If we absolutely refuse to become material for fertilizing land, because it deprives us forever of pleasure, then it is consistent to refuse as far as possible the role of material for a month or a moment because we are deprived of pleasure for that length of time. Limited intelligence struggling with environment for existence is of course obliged to break the most pleasurable sensation for various lengths of time; we cannot always gratify the imperative demand for unhampered action, but the rule of the least break holds good just the same.

We wish to avoid these breaks as much as possible, and co-operative schemes expose us to them the most that with equals is possible. It is their very nature to do so. Your impulse to be unhampered is necessarily opposed at every turn. You are not only as at present exposed to State plunder, and majority rule in some private and all public affairs, but in addition, this spinal monument of animal evolution thrusts its impudent nose into your *every* private affair. It is the basic law of collectivism to do so. Your labor, food, clothes, reading matter, conversation, recreation, and even sexual pleasures are regulated by its irresistible gore. In the work your cog must be there when the rest of the wheel revolves or there will be a jar with a social reaction. You cannot do less labor and live more frugally or use more of one thing and make up for it in less of another at your own expense as in individual effort, for the whole unwieldly machine would be affected by such a move. You must eat such food as the majority, manipulated by ambitious officers, decides is in the interest of the institution's success. Your clothes, reading matter, and recreation are subject to the same control for a similar reason. You must be careful what you say, for the institution holds your stored labor in a way that makes it hard to separate, and the officers can make it unpleasant for you if you displease them. And above all does the moral standing of a great institution require conformity to popular ideals in the expression of sex love. There is no privacy for kindred convictions on this subject there. The majority "knows what is right" and enforces it. It will not share labor with a "moral leper." It is like Ireland's Irish; any amount of oppression, but no unconventional departures in sexual association. Starvation, suffering and death are as nothing beside the horror of sexual caresses without the consent of the collective beast. In short, you have become material in the hands of ambitious chiefs. You are the fertilizer of an institution instead of the earth, and are in addition, at the disadvantage of being conscious of it, whereas in the former case you could perform the function with the indifference of oblivion. If your choosing faculty would not allow the role of fertilizer in oblivion, it must much less allow it in consciousness.

Besides protoplasmic ignorance and reptily meanness, there is a divergence of taste and capacities that is fatal to close association. One is fond of a kind of food the smell of which sickens another. One is boisterous, another loves quiet. One likes to declaim, sing, whistle, dance, and cat it in general about the house of evenings, while another desires to read or write matter of an intricate nature. Each should be allowed to enjoy himself undisturbed, but both cannot go on very near each other. One is careful of material and tools, and turns out good work; the other wastes material, wears out or breaks tools, and turns out work which if it passes at all lowers the grade of the goods in the market. The latter shares the benefit of the former's care while the first must help bear the effects of the other's incapacity. No official inspection and regulation costing a sum equal to or less than the difference between the respective products could adjust this. It requires an open market and free competition to give each his due. There is no dispute about quality when a free customer chooses between the two articles by paying cash for one and leaving the other.

I am well aware of how after having dragged wearily through a day's drudgery and the first ox tiredness has worn away a little we long for congenial companionship as we sit alone or among the chattering apes of religious and political superstition. I know well how the thoughts run to our ideal of the characters of the radical literature we read, and how it seems we must flash our avoirdupois across thousands of miles of deeded earth to warm our lonely consciousness in the soaking glow of their intellectual radiance, or feed our famishing nerves on their thrilling magnetism. I am acquainted not only with the lot of the single radical hermit, but with that of those others, the monogamy-environed pairs of social hermits who in a similar mood sit and gaze despairingly into each other's eyes conscious of their impotency to generate the faintest thrill on their magnetic dead sea. I am familiar with their disgust and bitter pessimism as they jostle amid multitudes of burstingly-charged batteries of custom-insulated magnetism and note their cattish will and won't writhings. And it is not surprising that such hermits realizing that life is but once to live would speculate on gathering together kindred spirits and gladly abandoning the orthodox zoological garden. Furthermore the impulse is not erroneous, but usually misdirected. There is something in it, as I know by experience. Persons of similar ideas can make life not only more bearable but immeasurably happier by living in easy reach of each other, but not in that contempt breeding nearness necessary to co-operative schemes. It is not necessary in order to enjoy a charming woman's company to help her do her cooking and washing, nor for her to help a man dig ditches or build houses to appreciate his social qualities. This indeed, would go far toward destroying such pleasure, for the very surroundings of vexation and weariness unconsciously become to our impressions a part of the unpleasantness.

When we come to analyze it we find it is the society under the most favorable circumstances, and not the physical labor of congenial people that we desire to share. The real ideal of the co-operation enthusiast is congenial companionship, a picnic attraction which he hopes to continue all the week, by working as well as playing together. But work is a matter of everyday compulsion, while picnicking is rare and voluntary at that. If we were compelled to associate in pleasure seeking as we should be in co-operative production we might not feel so slabberingly agreeable as we now imagine when in our isolation we dream fancies and forget facts.

So far as they can without sacrificing bread getting opportunities, it will pay radicals to seek social proximity, but if they leave material advantages which they cannot in a fair degree replace, in order to be in the company of other radicals they will soon have a job of kicking themselves to engage the leisure hours that are breeding starvation for them.

The superficial reasoning with which people usually content themselves in replying in their own minds to all these objections, is that the capitalistic system (which they term "competition") robs us of everything but the barest existence and that we cannot be sure of this much even; that co-operative effort is the only escape from this, and that we must get along with somebody and it might as well be those who hold at least some general principle in common with us. And it is true that we must get along with someone at labor, but it makes all the difference in the world in that getting along that we need not be responsible for their mismanagement; that we know that so far as they are concerned we can consume what little we get as we please. They cannot dictate what we shall eat, drink, and wear, nor *all* the pleasures of our recreation. And freed in production from the toll of privilege, these liberties which co-operationists are so willing to abandon, constitute much of the conditions necessary to the greatest happiness. But it is not true that co-operative effort in any sense different from that which would exist with free money added to present methods of production is necessary to escape the plundering of the capitalistic system. Free money would remove speculative interest, with which all capitalists would immediately seek to make their money help make a living by engaging in production, which in its turn making a greater demand for labor would raise wages. And then the competition between these capitalists in disposing of their products would lower the price to the laboring consumer. So between capital's bid for labor to employ it and its competition in selling its product to labor, the tendency would be ever nearing the point where labor would get the whole of its product, leaving capital merely intact and desirable only as a means to furnish its owner labor for his own hands first. Capital under free competition would be cheaper than in co-operation even, because it would drift toward the most skillful hands, the hands which could offer labor the greatest inducements.

There then we are delivered not only from the brutal slavery of capitalism, and the ignorant tyranny of communism, but the ineconomical unwieldliness of machine co-operation. This is a method of attaining industrial freedom, at once so simple, and a prospect so magnificent as must monopolize all the effort in that direction, of whoever will take the trouble to understand it, H.

The Philosophy of Egoism.

IX.

If self-renunciation be a virtue, surely it is the purer when the sacrifice is made for individuals of another and widely different species. In caring for our own species we may obtain a return, and we can cherish the imagination thereof if it seems improbable; and so it is in caring for one of any other species between which and ourselves there is some communication of mutual intelligence and mutual sympathy; but if a man wants to show pure disinterestedness let him sacrifice his pleasure his comfort and his life for other species that will neither understand nor return the manifestation of benevolence. Such a supernal Altruist will reject cleanliness as a sin, if convinced, as he must be by ordinary observation, that parasites thrive best on the human body when there is an entire avoidance of soap and water. Such a self-denying Moralist will not dress a wound or purify his blood, for these practices mean death to animalcules. Here I am reminded of the story of the devout Hindoo who was horrified on looking at a drop of water through a powerful microscope. He found to his consternation that he could not drink without destroying life.

Supernal Moralism should be viewed sometimes from the point of view of universal animal motives and conduct, excluding the idea of selflessness. If the survival of the fittest be not an empty phrase, supernal Moralism is an excessively silly insanity. The "sacredness" of the germs of human is impressed upon the mind of the devotee of Moralism, and in some cases the result is that a child is born as the offspring of rape. The simple, pious people may wonder that "God" can assist in giving effect to crime. The supernal Moralist who prides himself on scientific acquirements may well feel confused when a hybrid form appears as a practical commentary upon the alleged "sacredness."

Spiritual terror, the strangest, most melancholy phenomenon in human motive, is essentially the same influence, while it lasts, in the man or woman claiming to be emancipated from theological dogmas, as in the believer in those dogmas. It usually remains after its generally supposed root is destroyed, in the Agnostic, like an air-plant. This indicates that its foundation is not precisely where some anti-theological writers suppose. Mere disbelief in Jehovah may leave the agnostic mind subject to fixed ideas of a most irrational character. The belief in Jehovah in the first place occupied an ignorant mind and when that belief is expelled neither ignorance nor fear is altogether banished. There is some improvement in the prospect for positive Egoistic thought and sentiment to occupy its own. There remain, however, numerous fixed ideas of Duty to Society, Duty to the State, Duty to Humanity and such rubbish, which are fertile of intoxicating and paralyzing influences, and our talking Freethinkers in general still shudder to contemplate a person uncontrolled by such "restraining influences." They imagine, after all, that he will go to the devil or run amuck without moral "restraint." The triumph of sanity, then, lies not in the expulsion of any one form of insanity, but in the acquisition of an Egoistic consciousness and self-control. TAK KAK.

Wakemanized Science.

Under the heading, "Some Essentials that Mr. Pentecost Overlooks," Mr. Wakeman made a criticism upon his teachings and upon Anarchism in general. It is presumed that this subject was not taken at random, or without forethought, by Mr. Wakeman for the grounds of his address before the Liberal Club of New York. As he selected his own theme it is to be supposed that he had given it some attention. Many of his statements would imply that he thought so, but very little can be found in them to confirm the supposition.

It did not seem at all important to go into details in the discussion of this subject, as it was more to his mind and method to make affirmations and call them scientific. Some of his statements were known before science was such a common commodity. He accuses Mr. Pentecost of harboring unconcealed hunks of unwisdom, and to wake him up to a lively sense of his sinful and lost condition he opens a broadside upon him by informing him confidently that society is an "organism," and that if he had "but the slightest smattering of the science of sociology he would know that society is an organism, and human life an organic action, therefore subject to laws greater than the will of the individual." The reader who has not read Mr. Yarros's reply in "Liberty," and Tak Kak's in "Fair Play," to Mr. Wakeman, has missed a treat. These two writers have made it painfully evident that Mr. Wakeman's acquaintance with sociology is only the "slightest smattering." For there are somethings regarding sociology with which Mr. Wakeman cannot be said to be strictly familiar. (1) He did not know that Spencer does not maintain that society is an organism in the sense that an animal is an organism, and that he says that society has peculiarities which agree with individual organism, and that it has "on the other hand" "differences." (2) Mr. Wakeman's "smattering of the science of sociology" is so slight and diaphanous that he does not seem to know but that society and government are one and the same thing. I will notice this at length presently.

Mr. Wakeman asks, "What has Mr. Pentecost done? During the later years nothing but harm. He has placed himself outside of society and made war upon society." The confusion in Mr. Wakeman's mind arises from his obtuseness in not distinguishing between society and government. Mr. Pentecost has not gone outside of society. He could not do so if he wanted to unless he plunged into some immense forest, and there resolved to live and die. On the contrary, he lives in the very heart of civilization. He does not violate the laws of the land. Besides and above all he advocates the law of equal freedom.

This does not look like declaring war upon society. It is true he objects to brute force in government. He admits that under present conditions government is a necessary evil, but that by free and intelligent discussion the time will come when the people will discover that government is a despotism, a fetich, a superstition, and then it will be an unnecessary evil. Mr. Spencer says a propos,—"It is a mistake to assume that government must last forever." Again, he teaches that government is "essentially immoral"—that it is the individual's right to "ignore the State." And further he says, "Thus as civilization advances does government decay." From the London "Times" he approvingly quotes: "The social changes of our progress are determined rather by the spontaneous workings of society, connected as they are with the progress of art and science, the operations of nature, and other unpolitical causes, than by the proposition of a bill, the passing of an act, or any other event of politics or of State."

Thomas Paine was a manufacturer of governments, and his opinion on the subject is of great weight. He says: "A great part of that order which reigns among mankind is not the effect of government. It had its origin in the principles of society, and the natural constitution of man. It existed prior to government" (Spencer says the same thing), "and would exist if the formality of government was abolished. The mutual dependence and reciprocal interest which man has in man, and all the parts of civilized community upon each other, create that great chain of connection which holds it together. The landholder, the farmer, the manufacturer, the merchant, the tradesman, and every occupation prospers by the aid which each receives from the other, and from the whole. Common interest regulates their concerns, and forms their laws; and the laws which common usage ordains, have a greater influence than the laws of government. In fine, society performs for itself almost everything which is ascribed to government." (Rights of Man, Part 2. chap. 1.)

How clear in the mind of Thomas Paine was the distinction between society and government, and besides he made no pretensions to "the slightest smattering of sociology." Hear this government maker still further: "Government is no further necessary than to supply the few cases to which society and civilization are not conveniently competent; and instances are not wanting to show that *everything* which government can *usefully* add thereto has been performed by the common consent of society *without* government."

"For upwards of two years from the commencement of the American war, and a longer period in several of the American states there were no established forms of government."

"The instant formal government is abolished, society begins to act. A general association takes place, and common interest produces common security." (Ibid.)

"Socialism and Nationalism," says Mr. Wakeman, "which are in the line of evolution" (so are cobwebs), "have a future before them. They aim at emancipation from nature and monopoly; they are scientific." It does not seem important to Mr. Wakeman to support his scientific statements with anything like proofs. He gives us his solemn word for it, and that he seems to think ought to be enough.

He says Mr. Pentecost has done nothing but harm, yet he does not show us any harm done.

"To him (Pentecost) there is but one factor the *ego*." What evidence is offered in support of this libelous assertion? Is not Mr. Pentecost as greatly interested in the dissemination of truth as Mr. Wakeman? Because Mr. Pentecost advocates equal freedom for all, Mr. Wakeman cries out, "It is high treason against the organic life of society." "Organic life"! chestnuts. "Society cannot exist without co-operation. It is like a great machine." Here again he confounds society and government. Government is the machine for collecting taxes and doing a thousand despotic things. Mr. Spencer points out the way this machine works in legislation: "The history of one scheme is the history of all. First comes enactment, then probation, then failure; and after many alternate tinkerings and abortive trials, arrives at length repeal, followed by the substitution of some fresh plan, doomed to run the same course, and share a like fate."

Another writer whose name I cannot recall, says of legislative enactments: "They are bills which have been placed in the hands of their legislators to give some one man or body of men some advantage over his or their fellows, or through the instrumentality of the law to exonorate some man or body of men from some burden and pressure of general law, or to give some locality the right or privilege to do or refrain from doing something which either the law forbids or requires to be done."

Mr. Spencer informs us that governments are the product of violence. That they are a necessary evil, for the present, and that it is "a mistake to assume that government must necessarily last forever." And yet "Socialism and Nationalism, which are in the line of evolution, have a future before them." They promise to lead the people out of the wilderness by giving them more government, more taxes, more oppression, more political corruption. By this means society will be emancipated from monopoly! And this is what is called the scientific method of getting out of the woods! More government but less monopoly! Remember this is scientific and if you have "the slightest smattering of sociology" you will see it.

Hear him again: "Government of some kind or other is a necessity, and although I admit that in the current sense of the word it is in most instances nothing but tyranny, it was not so in the past, and will not be so in the future." This is another section of science. Why did not our sociologist point out the governments that have not been tyrannous in the past? To go into details did not come within the scope of the master sociologist's mind. Common people have to take his word for it, as they do much else of his oracular wisdom.

"The Anarchists were (are) but overgrown children; they needed a guardian, and he proposed to be one himself." His confidence in assuming this role is riper than his capacity. He appealed to (Cæsar) Spencer and was turned out of court. Even his mother goose melody.

Each for All,
All for each;
From each his highest deed,
To each as he may need,

finds no resting-place in Spencer, who affirms that "The society exists for the benefit of its members; not the members for the benefit of society." Exit humpty dumpty sociologist. W. S. BELL.

Will it be Only a Change of Superstitions.

Judge Westbrook's prize for the Manual of Morals goes to Boston. I am not in it. In fact, realizing my incompetency, I did not compete and cannot have any of the sympathy that the committee sends out to the unsuccessful moral essayists.......

The Liberal public has a long time between now and the first of September to speculate on what the new manual will contain, and to hope that when it appears it will not be open to the charge of teaching religion in the form of emotional morality. Freethinkers are religious to a certain extent, their religion having mainly to do with their relations toward one another and the balance of mankind. This is what is called morality when viewed emotionally. Scientifically it is economics; but the emotional view is so generally taken that I am afraid the Christian world will claim that in seeking to introduce this manual into the schools Secularists are merely trying to oust one sort of religion in order to substitute another which suits them better.

There is one thing on the subject of which the world is more bigoted, intolerant, and hypocritical than on the subject of theology, and that is the question of morality. It is rather worse to be a heretic in morals, like Heywood, than unorthodox in religion, like the rest of us. I have known quite a number of unpopular persons who repudiated the ethical standards set up by general and ignorant assent, and the one feature that distinguished them from the crowd was their remarkably circumspect conduct in precisely the direction in which they claimed the liberty to be otherwise. Perhaps they were afraid to tread the path they pointed out to others, or perhaps they had tried it and found it rough.—George E. Macdonald in "Freethought."

Mr. Pentecost Strikes Bottom.

Regarding a case of legal tyrannizing in sexual relations, Hugh O. Pentecost says:

Harry Gordon promised to marry Maggie Murphy, both of New York city. Then Maggie enjoyed with Harry that form of pleasure known as carnal knowledge. Then Harry refused to marry Maggie. Then Maggie had Harry arrested, and he is now in jail. It will be seen that Maggie trusted Harry and on the strength of her trust voluntarily enjoyed herself with him. Is it not fair to ask why the politicians should punish Harry for lying to Maggie? Did she not have the history of the ages to guide her in her conduct? If, in the light of all past experience in similar cases, Maggie chose to trust Harry, should she not be allowed to suffer the consequences of her own willing deeds? How else are women to learn how to take care of themselves?

On the Duty idea, in replying to a letter from Joseph Anthony, Mr. Pentecost makes the following sound utterances, with which all his others are not consistent:

......I would not seriously object to sweeping the streets or cleaning a sewer for an hour or so; and if it were something that I liked to do I could enjoy five or six hours' work a day; but drudgery, slavery, I hate, and ease and joy I like. And what keeps me in a constant state of rage is that men and women have to drudge till they drop into the grave, for food, clothes, and shelter, and mighty little of them, because monopolists, backed by the government, which in turn, is upheld by the toilers' senseless superstitions, rob them, and intelligent men like you preach the gospel of "work" and "ought" to them, and would have them believe that "ease and joy," the only things worth living for, are things to turn one's back on. You say I would be glad to do as I wish and not as I "ought." Pray whence comes this "ought"? It is not "man-made," you say, "but natural and inevitable." I deny the existence of any such ought. People should do as they please, and the only reason why we are not all wealthy and happy is because our rulers and our superstitions do not allow us to live so.

I know something of you through your writings for this and other publications, and I judge you to be the kind of man I like. The foregoing letter to me increased my liking for you; but if I understand your position, your whole philosophy of life, in my opinion, is wrong. You do not believe in any of the gods and you do not like the church, but you cling to the old priestly idea that it is wrong to take one's ease and have uninterrupted joy; and you seem to think that we should always be sacrificing our own desires for the good of other people—a "spirit of brotherhood" I presume you would call it. This doctrine of self-denial I hate; I regard it as one of the most injurious doctrines men have ever believed. I believe men will never become wealthy and happy until they become entirely [consistently] selfish, never sacrificing anything unless they can increase their wealth and happiness by so doing. The only reason, I think, why men should abandon their vacant land and cease their other monopolies is because they would thereby increase their own happiness by removing the poverty, ignorance, and crime [and anti-frigid influence of the dispossessed] which make it impossible for any one to be happy. I believe even Jay Gould would be happier if there were no poor people in the world.

I am not a humanitarian, not a philanthropist. The only reason why I work for the cessation of poverty, cruelty, and arbitrary restrictions is because they bear directly on me, hindering me from doing what I wish to do, and because the sight and the knowledge of so much misery and slavery depresses and pains me so that I am constantly debating whether it is better to live and endure it or die and escape it. I know how happy life would be if men and women were free from poverty and rulers, and I am working in the hopes of enjoying a little of that happiness. And in spite of all the exceptions which may be taken to this philosophy of selfishness, I am entirely sure that everybody lives by it as necessarily as that they breathe. I believe that no one ever voluntarily does anything except because he thinks it will promote his own happiness.

Managerial Experience.

This number closes the most eventful year of EGOISM's existence. It has been a year full of surprises and fleas as well as some pleasant disappointments for the publishers. They have had the satisfaction of seeing some of the most popular disturbers of bioplasmic habit indorse the central principle of their publication, while still others propagated it as original with themselves. They have heard from able editors the inquiry, "What is it printed for?" The comprehensible answer to such is, "Fifty cents a year." The publishers have seen Altruists become subjectively exultant over its unanswerable defense of selfy motives, and then turn purple with anger when shown the unavoidable equal freedom that such universally distributed resistance must result in without giving to any one credit for being gratuitously good. Another surprise lying truthfully concealed in the folds of impending experience was found in that almost all the support received came from persons they had never before heard of. Comparatively few of the readers of their former publication, "Equity," took appreciatingly to the new idea. The most of them so far have been indifferent and allowed the expiration of their respective credits on "Equity" to end their relations with EGOISM, thus demonstrating that a little gushing emotionalism and sentimental protest constitutes the length of their mental lariat. It is obvious that the majority of innovators are a little too umbilically religious to appreciate a consistent generalization from protruding facts, and too impulsive to conform to the conventionalities of the theological domination whose ideals they adore.

While most of our radical contemporaries have shown unmistakable evidence of constantly reading the paper, some of them have failed to publicly acknowledge its existence. "Fair Play" on receipt of the prospectus heartily announced its coming, and afterward copied from and complimented it, which in addition to sentimental satisfaction has put clear cash into our five-cent sheepskin purse.

"Freethought" announced its appearance with a lavish compliment by describing it as being like "Liberty," and later copied from it. To George Macdonald, former editor and manager of that paper, we owe obligations for constant favors. He has helped us by every turn in his reach, and is the Egoistic prize of which our staff is proudest.

"Liberty" noted along with that of others, EGOISM's arrival, and then waited patiently for five months for something it could approve. Finally Victor Yarros discovered some sentences and parts of sentences which in Mr. Tucker's absence he quoted, and upon which he based a strong two-line indorsement followed by seven lines of much needed advice. Thus "Liberty," EGOISM's reluctant and unenthusiastic parent, has not lost its reputation for impartial judgment by philoprogenitive gushing over the accident of an unguarded moment, but has thereby retained the brat's confidence with no loss save a clam's smile from a pulpy hopeful.

The Denver "Individualist," "Lucifer," "Farm View," and the Hastings (Mich.) "Plaindealer" have all quoted from these columns, and the "Plaindealer" has advised its patrons to try the experiment of sending us four-bits for a year's subscription. If its publisher's influence with his readers is no greater than ours is with our patrons, we shall have to credit him only with a safely-exercised good will.

Although the editor of the "Twentieth Century" noted in eulogistic words the reappearance of "Fair Play," and has occasionally, though inconsistently and smatteringly appropriated the Egoistic idea, he failed to more than incidently refer to Egoism. He possibly did not think about it, for he has no opinion that he does not confide to the public. This he must accomplish by doing the clergyman's act of drawing the blind when a gleaming argument forecasts an undesired conclusion. Popular Mr. Pentecost, he plants his garden with plucked violets, which will wither under the glow of growing analysis.

We have witnessed that some of our friends who have voluntarily declared our journal to be the most consistent and refreshing one published, contribute ten times as much to conservative and prosperous papers, while a man who admitted his preference for another journal made us the only present we have received. We have also experienced our own mother and mother-in-law combined, as a diligent canvasser for the "Twentieth Century" while she has not even complimented our efforts. I believe this to be due to her being a reformer such as described by Tak Kak in the preceding number of Egoism. I congratulate her, however, on manifesting no other trait characteristic of mothers-in-law. She evidently does not appreciate the qualifying generalizations that differentiate this paper from the "Twentieth Century." A reputable Anarchist living in its own city refuses to renew his subscription for our paper, while others who do take it seem indifferent, and from sample copies sent to the rest not a response comes. Alleged radicals and reformers swarm all about it and are not hostile, but evidently feel no need of a paper whose manager wears a blue flannel shirt and a lean expression. There is practically no support for the paper on the Pacific coast. Nearly all orders come from east of the Rockies.

"Fair Play" announces that its publication now costs two dollars against only one received, and that its list must be doubled in the following thirty days if its subscribers want it to continue. Its condition, however, is a bonanza compared with that of Egoism. Each subscriber gets for fifty cents what costs us just four dollars and a half to furnish, counting no time for editing, mailing, and necessary correspondence. No other paper in the country offers such inducement to a greedy public. This must be stopped in some way or every speculator in the United States will be into it. It beats government bonds, gold mines, and California real estate for plunder. It could be remedied by our friends rustling up six or seven hundred more subscribers for us or by those we now have, paying in the other four dollars. Otherwise we would have to put the subscription price up to five dollars to prevent the property of the country from drifting through this speculation into the hands of the few—who subscribe for Egoism.

We have tried very hard to make the paper worth what it costs us. We have teased all our philosophical friends for articles, and have ourselves written editorials so deeply philosophical that we could not understand them after they were printed. We have emphasized in the most pointed language at our command the crushing evil of monopolies and the superstitious fanaticism of sacrifice, only to find in the end that we have ourselves been both maintaining a sacrifice and creating such an opportunity for speculation as has not before existed. But we are not disheartened; the paper has escaped for a whole year any scorching criticism from "Liberty," and besides has been congratulated by nearly all the high privates in the Anarchistic skirmish line, as well as by many of the growing reserve force. People are telling their friends of it and it is constantly picking up new subscribers in the East and North. If this is kept up and the old ones promptly renew, we will be on a paying basis in less than five years, which is saying a great deal for a journal that panders so little.

It is great fun to run a paper about a year. Everyone should try it. It quickens the faculties and enlivens the bowels. It also puts you in close sympathy with those who can remain quiet with such great difficulty that they find it easier to labor hard and spend all they make in saying their say. If you can control your crowing and cackling instinct readily enough, it will be a saving of money to print a small pamphlet or make an almanac every year containing your opinions upon the pages usually occupied by other "chestnuts." You might procure patent medicine and novelty advertisements to help pay the printing expenses. The calendar at least will be useful to your friends, to whom you must of course send it prepaid. You need not necessarily have second-class postal rates, as that necessitates issuing at least four times a year, and it is a great deal of trouble to rearrange the same old ideas in a new form so often; it will be cheaper to pay third-class rates and spend the remainder of the time thus saved from writing and printing, in reading your exchange almanacs and pamphlets. Nothing else could be so productive of satisfaction and pamphlets. The comparison of your this year's ideas with last year's thought and its presentation will impel you surprisingly toward consistency and starvation. But I wander—what this has to do with the actual experience I meant to relate. THE MANAGER.

EGOISM'S PRINCIPLES AND PURPOSE.

EGOISM'S purpose is the improvement of social existence through intelligent self-interest. It finds that whatever we have of equal conditions and mutual advantage is due to a prevalence of this principle corresponding with the degree and universality of individual resistance to encroachment.

Reflection will satisfy all who are desirous of being guided in their conclusions by fact, that as organization itself is a process of absorbing every material useful to its purpose, with no limit save that of outside resistance, so must the very fact of its being a separately organized entity make it impossible for it to act with ultimate reference to anything but itself. Observation will show that this holds good throughout the vegetable and animal kingdoms, and that whatever of equality exists among members of a species or between different species has its source and degree in the resisting capacity, of whatever kind, which such member or species can exert against the encroachment of other members or species. The human animal is no exception to this rule. True, its greater complexity has developed the expedient of sometimes performing acts with beneficial results to others, but this is at last analysis only resistance, because it is the only means of resisting the withholding by others from such actor's welfare that which is more desirable than that with which he parts. If, then, the self-projecting faculty of mankind is such that it will in addition to the direct resistance common to the less complex animals, diplomatically exercise present sacrifice to further extend self, and it being a fact that equality depends upon equal resistance, diplomatic or otherwise, what are its chances in an absence of enlightenment in which the individuals of the majority so far from *intelligently* using this resisting power in their own behalf, do not even believe that they should do so? The result of a general conception so chaotic, would naturally be what we find: the generalization from the practical expediency of certain consideration for others, crystallized through the impulse of blind selfishness into a mysterious and oppressive obligation, credit for the observance of which gratifies the self-projecting faculty of the simple, while the more shrewd evade its exactions, and at every step from the manipulation of the general delusions of religious and political authority to the association of sexes and children at play, project themselves by exchanging this mythical credit for the real comforts and luxuries of the occasion, which the others produce. Thus in addition to the natural disadvantage of unequal capacity, the weaker are deprived through a superstition, of the use of such capacity as they have, as may be seen in their groping blindness all about us.

To secure and maintain equal conditions then, requires a rational understanding of the real object of life as indicated by the facts of its expression. It is plain that the world of humanity is made up of individuals absolutely separate; that life is to this humanity nothing save as it is something to one of these; that one of these can be nothing to another except as he detracts from or adds to his happiness; that on this is based the idea of social expediency; that the resistance of each of these individuals would determine what is socially expedient; that approximately equal resistance makes it equality, and on such continued and a universal resistance depends equality. This can leave no room for any sane action toward others but that of the policy promoting most the happiness of the acting Ego. Therefore EGOISM insists that the attainment of equal freedom depends upon a course of conduct replacing the idea of "duty to others" with *exped ency* toward others; upon a recognition of the fact that self-pleasure must be the final motive of any act: thus developing a principle for a basis of action about which there can be no misunderstanding, and which will place every person squarely on the merit of his or her probable interests, divested of the opportunity to deceive through pretension, as under the dominance of altruistic idealism. It will maintain that what is generally recognized as morality is nothing other than the expediency deduced from conflicting interests under competition; that it is a policy which, through the hereditary influence of ancestral experience, confirmed by personal experience, is found to pay better than any other known policy; that the belief that it is something other than a policy—a fixed and eternal obligation, outside of and superior to man's recognized interests, and may not be changed as utility indicates, makes it a superstition in effect like any other superstition which causes its adherents to crystallize the expediency adopted by one period into positive regulations for another in which it has no utility, but becomes tyrannical laws and customs in the name of which persecution is justified, as in the fanaticism of any fixed idea.

Another part of its purpose is to help dispel the "Political Authority" superstition and develop a public sentiment which would replace State interference with the protection for person and property which the competition of protecting associations would afford. Then the State's fanatical tyranny and industry crushing privilege would torture the nerves of poverty-stricken old age or pinch tender youth no more. The most disastrous interference of this monster superstition is its prohibition of the issuing of exchange medium on the ample security of all kinds of property, which at once would abolish speculative interest and practically set all idle hands at productive labor at wages ever nearing the whole product until it should be reached. The next interference is by paper titles to vacant land instead of the just and reasonable one of occupancy and use, which with the employment that free money would give, would furnish all with comfortable homes in a short time, and thereafter even with luxuries from like exertion. Following this is its patent privilege, customs robbery, protective tariff, barbarous decrees in social and sexual affairs; its brutal policy of revenge, instead of restitution, in criminal offenses, and finally its supreme power to violate the individual, and its total irresponsibility.

Egoism

Vol. II.---No. 1. SAN FRANCISCO, CAL., MAY, 1891. Price, Five Cents.

Pointers.

This number begins the second volume of EGOISM.

The tenth chapter of the "Philosophy of Egoism" has not reached us.

We have been too busy to give Zola's "Money" a second reading as we desire before attempting to recommend it with the limited language at our command.

From a communication by Lillian Harman we learn that C. H. Swartz, who published "Lucifer" while Moses Harman was imprisoned, is now confined in the Topeka (Kan.) jail awaiting trial for selling the Kansas City "Sun" to newsboys. So frightful was the crime that his bail was set at $4000. Thus fanaticism crucifies its victims with almost no opposition.

Although EGOISM has on another page criticised an article of the editor of "Freethought," it must heartily congratulate that paper's home editorial writers on their work in the issue of May 16, especially the editorial "Herbert Spencer on Nationalism." George Macdonald continues his irresistible hits in "Observations," and will at no distant day be one of the most popular exponents of Anarchism.

We must apologize to our readers for putting so long an article in such small type as in the case of F. K. Blue's criticism of "Citizens' Money" printed on other pages. We had asked him to question in an article not exceeding a given space, such points in the pamphlet as were not clear to him. This he did except that his manuscript was almost twice as long as specified, and was with his permission cut down to its present length. His manner, and perversion of Mr. Westrup's position has probably led the latter to dismiss him with so condensed a reply. The subject now being up will likely be continued by other members of EGOISM's staff.

A Prostitute.

A prostitute you brand her, and because
That she hath sold her body's use for coin?
Wherefore you leer, because a woman she?
Wherefore you jeer, betrayed by woman's trust?
In lecher's lust and perjured troth?
Wherefore you sneer,—O pitiless, bloodless, false,
I hate you!

A prostitute you brand her!
And is it not a loving woman's part
To give her person to the man she loves
Freely? Does love delight in prudery,
And cold reserves, and shams of modesty,
Pursed lips, and words precise, and feet tucked in,
And finger tips at meeting, and kisses
Small and proper at the stiff good bye?
Prudes!
Hypocrites!—cold in heart and foul in soul,
Nature herself, and Love are never pure
Enough for you; the Holiest of holies,
To your smeared thought, is but a voiding place
Of filth.

I say it is a woman's part,
When that she loves, to wholly yield herself
To him, the man she mates, in nakedness
Of form and soul, to strip off every mask
And vail that treachery of man to man,
And foulness of human thought bids wear;
pure,
Warm, sweet, in Eden innocence and faith,
She keeps no secret, no reserve, no bar,
But nestles close. 'Twould seem a very fiend,
So trusted must be true.

I say it is
No shame to any maid, her misplaced gift
Of confidence in some man's faith. Nay, it
But proves her womanhood, innocence, trust
(For never yet deceit knew aught but doubt,
While innocence is trustful as a fawn),
Her warmth and ardency of loveliness,
Her everything but knowledge intimate
Of sin.

O fools and false!—O hypocrites!—
Soul-seared by ancient lies, a maid betrayed,
I tell you is the purest of her sex,
Most womanly, most sweet; her "bastard" babe
Is a living seal by Nature set
To her fair proof of mother-perfectness.
Love only makes a babe legitimate,
And every "love-child" is a little Christ,
Conceived immaculate, the son of Man,
Redeeming us, rejected of his own,
And every virgin mother stands a saint,
Revealing holiness, demanding praise.

And when this pure one with her helpless babe,
In agony of ruined love, and pain,
Unfathomable, of trust evanished,
And deeper agony of public scorn,
Shamed, crushed, blinded, heart-broken, and out flung
Like some stale remnant of a feast upon
The street, down-trodden under heedless feet,
Caressed of dogs, without a hope or help—
When she, yielding to fate and all-compelled,
Barters her beauty to your lust for coin
That she may live, then, then, you scorn her—
Ah!—
If she be foul, who fetched the filth that smirched?
Who flung it? Who yielded beauty captive
To the beast? Who sacrificed this lamb
A tortured victim on the altar bed
Of lust?
You! Everyone holding statute's
Holier law than Nature's, who proclaim
Marriage mightier for purity
Than trusting love and artless innocence.

A prostitute! She is no prostitute
Touched by the test of truth; a victim she
Of rape most foul, and torturous murder
(And *you* her murderers!), a man compelled
To steal is not a thief, voluntary
Sin alone can stain, and free she was not.
A prostitute!—O lying-lipped and blind!—
These are your prostitutes—the priest, sleek-faced,
With gilded perch 'bove dusty, sleepy pews,
Exerting all his learning, eloquence,
To hypnotize men's minds with sounds and forms,
To turn their thoughts from asking Nature's truth,
Be it or that or this, and still to prove,
Or feign to prove, an ancient precept wise,
A hideous fear well-based, a dreamy hope
Assured:—the cunning lawyer, sophist like,
Perverting all his intellect and wit
To make injustice seem but just, and weave
A legal labyrinth of tangled paths
To foil all feet that seek the central right:—
The doctor crying—"And if it please ye, sin!
For verily ye shall not surely die,
My philters shall force Nature to forgive":—
The soldier, prostituting courage, strength,
To murderous madness and the trade of hate:—
The editor, his ink made black by lies,
Controlled like some ghost medium by spooks
Of party policy, fermenting all
He hears and thinks into rotton a beer
To swill the public pigs:—and last, and least,
A woman who from sex-diseased, and taint
Inherited from parents marred in love,
From itch of lust, and greed, makes sex her trade.

These are your prostitutes, and them, the last
Except, ye praise, and let them drain your wealth;
For they are strong, and they are not deceived,
And they love not, nor trust in anyone;
But she, true woman, this babe-blessed mother—
Is she not weak?—did she not love and trust,
And add life to Life without consent
Obtained from these whores of Church and State?
Then fling her back and tread her down, yea, lift,
O virtue, lift thy dainty skirts, without
A carnal taint, at least a lust unblessed,
And tread her 'neath thy shapely booted heels!
O cold, cruel, pitiless, false and foul,
Contemptible and desolate with shams,
Forever drunk with guiltless blood and wine
Of honeyed lies, hypocrites, I hate you!

—J. WM. LLOYD.

Editorial Slashes.

A law intended to prevent children being sent to groceries or saloons for beer was part of the work of our late legislature. But it is "law," and the stupid inhabitants cannot see that it characterizes them as not having sense enough to bring up their children without police supervision. These people believed themselves responsible sovereigns on election day, but their selected masters think not.

The height of all the ridiculousness regarding the New Orleans mobbing was hopelessly outstripped on the 8th of this month at Boston by the calling of a mass-meeting to form a society for teaching "poor and ignorant" Italians respect for and obedience to the laws of this country! When a crazy mob of "respectable citizens" massacred the helpless prisoners as a mad bull might gore babes the outrage was almost imponderable; and when the moss-backed and truckling press brutally justified it and the caricature papers all crowed over it, disgust would have been ecstatic beside my state of feeling, but when culture steps in and gravely proposes to teach the rest of the victimized class respect for the great fuzzy-cheeked brute, cynical wrinkles corrugate the length of my nose and I sit me down to reflect a bitter reflection upon the human grub in general.

San Francisco's twin societies for meddling in people's private affairs—the Society for the Prevention of Cruelty to Children, and the Pacific coast branch of Anthony Comstock's infamous vice society are now endeavoring to force Police Judge Rix to resign because he refuses to lend his power to help them persecute their victims. These officious meddlers are too tough for even the law mills, which depend on prosecutions for existence. They have been repeatedly rebuked by prosecuting attorneys, the press, and their cases dismissed by the courts, but the agents are anxious for notoriety and are backed by a horde of Grundys loaded with current sexual superstition and ambition to impose their prejudices by the tyranny of political authority now everywhere so rampant.

The secretary of the former says the object of his society is to force parents who can do so to provide for their children, and where they are unable to do so, to put these away from vicious and contaminating influences. Further statement shows that the society has elephants' ears for all the petty revenges of neighborhood brawling and domestic turbulence. With all its willingness, out of 72 "complaints" and 60 investigations it found but 14 prosecutable cases, six of which are pending. An example cited, proved to be what might be expected of collective tyrants, a case of a man's refusal to support his wife, on grounds of real or imagined infidelity, in either case forcing an individual to spend his earnings to suit the society instead of himself, if indeed he was fortunate enough to have work at all. It is further stated that in some instances the father promises to provide and the case is dismissed, but that they keep track of it just the same. Just what is to be gained in the way of support for his family by arresting and fining a man is hard to understand, or if he is neither fined nor imprisoned where the efficacious terror of prosecution comes in. It can gratify a brutal revenge on the part of the prosecutors, and generate a life of immeasurable hatred between the parents thus living together by the forging of the policeman's club, as well as create a hell for children about whom the society pretends to be so solicitous, but it can do nothing better. Charity is humiliating enough, but to force it from the hand of hatred is burning humiliation in with the flame of horror. But all these things and forcing its opinions of what is contaminating upon helpless parents, is faithfully representative of a religio-legalistic institution. The way to really help in such cases would be to provide in addition to immediate sustenance, work at good wages and freedom from legal bondage to these fathers, so that the mother's efforts and person might be under her own control thereafter. But independence and divorce are not conventional.

Ira P. Rankin, president of the Comstockian vice society assured an "Examiner" reporter that if it were not for the society's work the "city would be flooded with the most obscene kind of literature!" Horrors! How awful it would be to read some of our own thoughts in grammatical sentences, or cultivate the imagination with imagery more poetical than we can invent. Suppose the population should see on paper what it performs daily in person, and should thereby lose its feverish curiosity about such things what could these meddlers then have to make them conspicuous. They have succeeded so well in heightening curiosity concerning sexual imagery that the society's president unwittingly declared that an "indecent" book will bring $2 where a "moral" one can't command 20 cents. When the society gets the price up to $4 some of its enterprising members can reprint them at a big profit and help out its treasury. Before these societies were established in the country such books could command no more than 25 or 50 cents each.

These societies prey on the universal sexual superstition as the church does on the first cause superstition. Their influence is much greater, however, for in addition to the whole church their tyrannous meddling commands the approval and sympathy of the theologically sceptical world, so dense is public prejudice. Thus they are enabled to suppress the publication of any scientific facts or ideas supporting theories contrary to those accepted by the societies' officers. This they have not failed to do as is amply illustrated in their restrictions on Dr. E. B. Foote's "Plain Home Talk," Dr. Kinget's "Medical Good Sense," "Cupid's Yokes," "Lucifer," and the "Word." Thus in addition to its primitive ignorance society organizes itself against knowledge until it is forced upon it by its favorite method, the blood of martyrs.

If the world could once learn to have faith in liberty, about which it continually prates, everything would soon reach a normal state. But the reactionary, restrictive idea is everywhere rampant. Restriction of money, commerce, labor, publication, divorce, and even knowledge by parents is the prominent feature of this country. If parents who are so afraid sexual vice will reach their children, which it always does, should once get the competitive idea into their heads and attend to their children's "obscene" education themselves or have it done under their supervision, sexual knowledge would soon be only a matter of hygiene like eating, bathing, exercise, and the rest. Parents are sure that the widest knowledge is best for themselves, but for their children, never. If they would open up existence to their children as it is known to them witholding no thought, fact, or possible experience, "obscene" literature might be piled up in every house with about as much danger as so many cook-books. So long as cerebellums grow, so long will sexual impulses exist, and the best safeguard against injury from excess is the greatest possible knowledge emphasized by suggestions from experience. Let a fully exercised power to comprehend be the only difference between yours and your children's knowledge, and you have the "obscenity" spook down. Continue to fear liberty and you continue the prey of politicians, preachers, and vice societies who will take care that you do not obtain the knowledge which alone can save you and must destroy their monopoly for praise and plunder.

The barbarities of the sexual superstition continue to bloom. Near Ducktown, Tenn., an elderly man was recently married two weeks after his former wife's death to a girl seventeen years old. Six weeks later some of the women of the neighborhood mobbed the girl and whipped her with a hundred lashes, resulting in her death a few days later. These fanatical brutes were formally put under arrest, but their male friends declare they shall not go to jail, and a fight between these and the officers was in prospect when last heard from. Three men have already been killed in this meddling.

At Abingdon, Va., a doctor and another man's wife gave way to the spontaneous desire for magnetic change under the infatuation of which to remove conventional barriers they were induced to poison their respective legal companions. The doctor's wife was thus murdered, and the woman's husband escaped by accident.

Not long since a girl from the country, who had become pregnant, sought medical assistance in this city to evade social ostracism and perhaps banishment from her home. On the way back she died, and the doctor has been arrested and charged with murder.

The first instance is that species of insanity known as "respect for the dead" because they are dead. When the man's first wife was living these groveling fanatics were perfectly willing that he should hold her in a bear's embrace of depleting monogamy to death, no matter what her torture be, but the moment she could suffer no longer from any imposition whatever, of "duty" she became an object of respect for which they demanded that the survivor suffer as much and long as possible. But he would not be tortured long enough to suit them. Having as the necessary result of years of magnetic starvation developed an ungovernable craving for change, he probably used its overwhelming power on the yearning inexperience of the young girl and rushed legally on to the gratification of a legitimate desire without so far, invading any one. This was so new and inexcusable to the magnetically disinterested that, obeying the impulse of cattle and turkeys when a new wagon is driven into the barnyard, they proceeded to dispose of it according to the dictates of their muddled emotions. In the minds of the men such an old man's exploitation of such a morsel created perhaps an unconscious but real envy, while the women were, unconsciously, outraged at seeing their chief stock in trade squandered at so low a price. If she had been an old woman or he a young man things would have been different, and could have been so for no other reasons than the ones named. The old man probably escaped because they could not blame him for taking so good a bargain, while the girl received double condemnation because it was supposed that her sex passion, so desirable to men and detestable to women, led her to accept so poor a one. To women there is nothing so unspeakably hateful as another woman's sex faculty, and to men nothing so much so as to be left out of its consideration. And in this case their mutual gratification demanded a most ferocious murdering of an innocent girl.

Thus while the first instance was murder by society for not conforming gratification to its ideas, the second was murder by the individual in trying to conform gratification to its ideas, and the third accidental death in attempting to escape its ostracism after gratifying without its permission. This last will probably result in great cost if not imprisonment or death for the doctor for doing a kindly turn earnestly solicited by a helpless victim of Grundy tyranny.

At the bottom of all these lies the idea of "duty to others"—the implacable foe of all freedom—the fetich of political authority. But for the idea of "duty" to something other than one's own uninvading pleasure, the girl would not have been more fiendishly murdered than savages do it. And but for the same idea prescribing marriage as the only passport to full sex association, the doctor and the other man's wife would no more have thought of poisoning anybody in order to associate more freely, than they had hitherto in order that either might eat a meal or sit in the cool shade. And in the third case the girl would not need to have risked and lost her life and exposed a doctor to imprisonment or death for performing a solicited service, for none but Altruists would have dreamed that it was any of their business to meddle in her private affairs, even the exposing or taking her own life. Only think of the horrors of a state of society in which an old man and a young girl could marry as often or at any time they pleased without either of them being murdered; or in which any man and woman might sleep together to their hearts' content without the need of poisoning any one; or in which a girl could be pregnant without social ostracism. Only think of a society in which all these sexual acts might have taken place unaccompanied by murder or imprisonment. Yet the Egoistic basis of ethics is the only one on which such a non-invasive society can logically exist. Why then should the philosophy of "selfishness" be a greater horror than these murders.

In "Freethought" of April 25, its editor, Samuel P. Putnam, gives his readers a lesson on practical reform through the "Eclectic Philosophy." Proudhon long ago exploded the idea of making science by the practice of long division upon a conglomeration of facts and fancies. But Mr. Putnam proposes to select the good from all theories, and we might infer from this that he is a scientist from the stump, intending to gather facts regardless of schools and classify them into a scientific method bringing up on ground with which Anarchists are well acquainted. But his summing up disposes of this optimistic hope:

> Anarchy means personal liberty. We select that and stand by it. Socialism means fraternal co-operation. We select that and stand by it. Nationalism means the rights and dignity of labor. We select that. Communism means a commonwealth. We select that. Free trade means reciprocity. We select that. Protection means industrial advancement. We select that. But at the same time that we select, we also reject. We must combine the methods, even though they seem to be contradictory. As we must combine

the supremacy of the nation with the doctrine of State rights, so we must combine free trade with protection and individual freedom with associated action.

Oh! the echo of Proudhon's satire rings like a scientific maxim. He must have based his generalization on a long list of verifications. For behold, despite his proposition to select, Mr. Putnam rushes into the "long division" method of solution as spontaneously as a duckling into water. We are to combine tyranny with freedom as we combine the supremacy of the nation with the doctrine of State rights. Sure enough. How well that word *doctrine* fits the place in which it is used. In the "combination" it is only a doctrine —an empty phrase. Where supremacy exists rights are gone. The federal power does not meet the individual State as an equal to compromise and agree upon points of difference, and State rights are of course a myth. We combine the *doctrine* of State rights with national supremacy by submitting—by having no State rights on that occasion. We "combine" as the slave combines with the master. And in this way we are to "combine" individual freedom with associated action and free trade with protection. We are free to trade wherever we are not suppressed by protection, and may enjoy individual freedom until we are oppressed by "associated action." This is not exactly new. We have been thus "combining" freedom with tyranny for more than a century. It is just this restriction of competition in some directions that furnishes the privilege from which our devouring monopolies spring. It is this "combining"—this free trade in buying labor and protection in furnishing credit, that impoverishes the workers and enriches the drones. It is this "associated action" spook which enables monopolists and politicians to pool their interests and control not only the production and commerce of the country but the education as well. Freedom in theory, protection for capital, and free trade in the sale of labor is a "combination" of which we are chock full. We do not care to combine with tyranny any longer. We shall be content to stand by personal liberty alone, and let Mr. Putnam justify this combining while his baggage is rummaged on the wharf and he goes about all day on Sunday longing for a cigar in obedience to associated action.

In the light of this eclectic discovery we should look for Mr. Putnam to stop his crusade against Sunday laws and other Secular points, and "combine" them with personal liberty as we do protection and other State interferences. But consistency is not a part of his program; if it were the two first sentences quoted would make him an Anarchist—an all-around defender of equal freedom, to whom the evils opposed by Secularists would be but incidental to an authoritarian regime responsible for both political and industrial slavery. He would then not be found apologizing for oppression, even if he was not in a position to fight it openly. Reciprocity would then mean what it is—free trade in such instances as will not through an unfavorable balance of trade carry our masters' legal gold-lash out of the country, forcing the adoption of an abundant and economical medium of exchange which would launch us on industrial freedom. And protection would also mean what *it* is, the taxing of one industry for the profit of another. Both would be seen as they are, machines for creating and perpetuating monopoly through political authority—the most effective superstition of the age.

This criticism assumes that Mr. Putnam's article was intended as a presentation of social science, and not an eclectic sop slinging. H.

Agrarian Paternalism.

A correspondent who views some subjects with a fair degree of sagacity, perhaps goes wrong as to the supposed inherent danger of allowing possessors of land to contract debts upon such property as they have in, upon and inseparably mingled with the land, and at their pleasure to sell such products—elliptically expressed by speaking of the sale or incumbrance of the land. How in the world is an owner to sell his improvements, such as can not be removed, without quitting possession in favor of the buyer? It is not an ideal of freedom that the man shall be enslaved to a particular spot of land because he has put improvements there. In a former discussion there was no question of disturbing the homestead law; there was no question of the unwisdom of many borrowers; but there was a square challenge to choose freedom or paternalism and stick to what is chosen. It seems to "The News" that dolorous descriptions of the progress of the farmer to poverty under mortgages would be very much more to the point if the writers were illustrating the consuming power of usury than they are when thrown up against any plan the prominent feature of which would be to afford currency at something like what it should cost to manufacture and securely control such a necessary and important aid to exchange of products. Instead of declaring that the owner of land has control of finance, every day's experience shows that the control of finance throws the real ownership of land to the financier on the present scarcity and usurious basis. One arbitrary restriction to cure another is an old way, but not a way that "The News" can indorse. Every product of a man's labor that he may sell he may borrow money upon, save only the product of his labor in land, says the new gospeler of agrarianism. But such a law would at once put a disability upon farm and garden labor. More, the new reformer would not allow land to be sold. Who then could buy a peach orchard? Dig up the trees? Impossible. Labor would be deterred from expending itself in the soil. That will not do. If land could not be sold there would be notice to men that they need not put their labor in land unless they were content to relinquish the common right to sell some of the products of their labor. Some reformers go daft about land, as if it were not more abundant than products, and as if it were not in final analysis a mere condition. To say, then, that one may sell his labor product but not his land is, as to some products, like saying that the author may sell his writings but not the paper upon which his writings are expressed.—Galveston Daily News.

What is Interest?

The questions that immediately arise in my mind upon reading Alfred B. Westrup's lecture on "Citizens' Money," which I would like to have him answer are: why should one of his mutual banking notes be required to be redeemed periodically, as suggested on page 14, if the borrower could according to practice immediately borrow it again? How will he define what he means by the value of a dollar, an ounce of gold, or a bushel of wheat? Why is it that ordinarily Smith can borrow a hundred bushels of wheat of Jones only on the condition that he will pay him back perhaps a hundred and ten bushels in a year's time? In a currency without any unit of value, what will prevent the nominal price of wheat and shoes which is now $1 a bushel and $3 a pair, from changing in a year to $2 a bushel and $6 a pair, to the loss of those who have contracted debts in terms of such currency; that is, what will prevent the nominal price of all property from changing while its relative rate of exchange, perhaps may remain the same? Now I will not dispute to a certain extent his idea of what constitutes the best kind of money, but he certainly makes a very unwarranted comparison when he compares paper to coin as money as if their economic relations were of a similar nature. The choice between paper and coin is not at all a question of the relative quantity in existence, but is primarily a question of whether a certain quantity of property itself, or a right or ability to obtain a certain property shall be circulated as currency, that a promise of property when sufficiently secure, is generally regarded as more convenient and economical to use in commerce has been abundantly proved in England, where it is estimated that in commercial transactions only one per cent of the exchanges of property are effected by the use of coin. That security good for a promissory note is good to issue money on is amply illustrated by the Scotch system of banking. And I would also ask all mutual bankers to explain why interest was not abolished in Scotland if it depends on the prohibition of the issue of currency directly on the property mortgaged as stated on page 17?

I can agree that ample security would maintain the purchasing power of paper currency regardless of the volume issued, but only on the condition that it be redeemable in property on demand. When so issued the quantity can never exceed what is economical for the community to retain in circulation, but just as soon as it is made redeemable in property at some future time, it will only circulate in excess of such economical amount at a discount corresponding to the time before which it is likely to be redeemed in property. The amount of currency that is economical to be kept in circulation in a community is determined by the amount of property each one finds of greater utility to them to devote to the use of facilitating their exchanges rather than enjoy its utility when put to any other uses. In banking business redemption is performed with other property as well as gold and silver, whenever a customer of the bank settles up his account with the bank by returning banknotes to pay his indebtedness. The amount of gold that the notes are expressed in is no more actually used to effect the exchange than the standard yardstick at Washington is actually used to measure every yard of cloth in the country. It is simply when a debt is contracted by the issue of a banknote, it is expressed in terms of the value of gold in exchange at that time, to be redeemed at an equal equivalent, to the value of gold when it is paid. That the actual property borrowed shall equal the actual amount returned depends upon whether the relative value of gold to the property bought with the banknotes when they are borrowed and sold for them when they are returned, remains the same at one time as the other, and this depends ultimately on the relative amount of effort required to produce the other property.

To analyze Mr. Westrup's criticism of the present system, no one need deny the assertion that "the present system like all its predecessors, fails to provide the means whereby property owners may use their property for purposes of credit"; that is, get property in the present for a promise to pay property in the future "without submitting to the tax called interest"; that is, without paying the economic difference between the value of present and future property "imposed by the monied classes"; that is, required by every one who furnishes present property or a right to present property in exchange for a promise of property to be paid in the future. And no system can do otherwise than fail to provide such a thing, until perhaps some people become so generous as to be willing to allow others instead of themselves to enjoy the advantages of the use of their property for a time without asking any compensation for such use, a state of society the Socialists seem to be trying to induce. "An individual who has property, but no money, wishes to buy some commodities. If he buys them on credit, he has to pay more than if he buys for cash." That is, if he receives the property of another now, he has to pay more of his property at a future time (credit) than if he pays him property now (cash in gold received for property just sold to Jones, a promissory note on demand on Jones, taken instead of gold, or an accepted bill of exchange on demand, in favor of himself, or a banknote which is a promise of property on demand at the bank.) So when a person gets property from another, he must either pay out his property in exchange at the time of such exchange, or pay more of his property at some future time. "If he borrows money, giving a mortgage on his property, in order to buy for cash, he is confronted with interest." That is, if he gets property in the present for tho same paid in the future, he will have to pay more of it in the future when he pays for his borrowed cash than he would have if he had paid property at the time he received the cash.......

If the borrower can receive currency to the same amount, at the same time he redeemed what he borrowed the year before, why ever compel him to redeem what he has borrowed? But does Mr. Westrup suppose that interest is paid for the cost of "making" money? does he imagine that when a farmer mortgages his farm for a thousand dollars worth of this currency redeemable in one year, and buys tools with it that he really pays for these tools and can thus have the use of them for one year for the cost of making his promise to pay currency! I think if such a proposition should be made, every one would mortgage their property to the fullest amount in order to be able to enjoy the use of so much more property for a year for merely the cost of making a promise to return it. But what would really be the result of such a method, certainly if any one wished to buy anything he would prefer to pay his own "promise to pay" rather than that of some one else for which he would part with some of his property.

Our farmer wishes tools and our merchant wishes grain. Both have their whole credit to offer in currency at a year's time to exchange for property. Now suppose the farmer sells his grain to the merchant, receiving "currency" in exchange. Immediately the farmer wants tools, he goes to the merchant and offers this "currency" in exchange for them, but we can imagine the following dialogue to take place:

Farmer—Here is $1 000 in your promises-to-pay, for the tools I have just ordered.

Merchant—Yes. But I don't care to pay my own debt till one year from now, since it stands practically without interest, and if I accept your "currency" at one year's redemption, I will have no right to demand property of you in exchange for my tools until one year from now, unless you choose to pay your debt sooner which you certainly will not do if you value the use of $1 000 worth of property for one year's time. Besides I think I can sell my tools to Farmer Jones for $1 000 worth of property on demand; however you may have the tools for $1050 of your notes at one year without interest, and I don't think Merchant Smith will be willing to furnish you tools on any better terms. If you had sold your grain to me for a note on demand, of course I would have been obliged to give you the value of such notes in property at once. But of course I could not afford to offer you in property on demand more than 95 per cent of the amount that I would not be obliged to pay until one year from the time I received your grain.

I think my dear farmer, when you anticipated the possibility of "borrowing money without interest"; that is, a real property on demand which would enable you to buy tools at one time and pay for them in one year when you redeemed your currency, that you unknowingly failed to understand the very important if not under all circumstances very perspicuous distinction between a paper entitling its holder to a certain property on demand, and one obliging the payment of property at some future time, hence you thought by mutual agreement to circulate future property on the same terms as present, but economic relations transcend even mutual agreement. The fiat of the Roman church could not suppress interest, and even mutual agreement cannot make a thousand bushels of wheat promised to you in a year from now, worth as much as a thousand bushels given to you now. Hence you cannot buy as much with currency redeemable in one year as in currency on demand, or if you choose to make one year notes a legal tender; that is, to estimate all rates of exchange in property at one year's time, as you would by Mutual Banking with one year currency, then notes obliging the payment of property on demand would circulate at a premium equal to the economic difference in the value of property at a year's time. So you find yourself after all no better off than you would be to borrow currency redeemable on demand, paying the economic rate of interest for it as by the Scotch banking system. For $1 000 in such notes I could give you $1 000 worth of tools at once for I can take them to the bank immediately and pay my indebtedness for money borrowed, or my debt to Farmer Jones for grain, which he had sold to the bank and was charged to my account, or if I have no debts to pay I will have $1 000 balance at the bank to my credit which will enable me to purchase more capital.

"And now let me point out to you the blunder at the door of which can be laid all the error that has confused the mind of" Alfred B. Westrup, "puzzled the brain of" every mutual banker and "defeated the efforts of" every one of that school "to solve the problem of" borrowing money without interest; that is, of borrowing a right to present property with a promise to pay in the future, without paying the economic difference in the value of present and future property. It is just "the failure to recognize the difference between coin" which constitutes a real exchange of present property "and currency" which may be representative of property in the present or in the future according to its nature.

So far Mr. Westrup has stated in this paragraph what no economist would pretend to deny, but when he finishes by saying that "this interest is enforced by prohibiting the issue of the currency directly on the property mortgaged to secure the money-lender instead of the money-holder" he can have but a very inadequate idea of the nature of property, for as we have seen, it is not for the cost of "making" banknotes that interest is paid for, but for the assumption of the bank by its notes of the responsibility of paying property on demand in exchange for the borrower's obligation to pay property at a future time, and neither will the issue of money on his own promise to pay on demand allow him to use property on his credit without paying interest, for, since on the average he must have as many notes in his possession all the time as he has in circulation, he would always be loaning out as much property as he borrowed, and he cannot customarily alter the balance in his favor without paying interest or discount.

It cannot be denied that gold currency costs more than credit currency. That a mutual banking currency would cost only its cost of making, and that if all exchanges were made on demand, on the average no one would pay or receive interest, because what they paid when each was in debt would come back when he was in credit. But what does this difference amount to? Not by any means as Mr. Westrup seems to suppose; the interest that is paid on all the debts existing in the community, but simply the interest on all the property currency in the community. Suppose the quantity of gold in circulation in a country amounts to $10 per capita. This at 5 per cent interest would be 50 cents a year for each person that gold would cost more than credit currency, or suppose the reserve to be one-fiftieth as in Scotch banking, this would be one-tenth of all currency borrowed at 5 per cent interest, or suppose the reserve to be one-fifteenth as in National banking, the difference would be ½ per cent on all currency borrowed at 7½ per cent interest.

Perhaps the principal source of misconception among mutual bankers and others who have thought to avoid interest in such a manner, has arisen from the idea that the banks by being able to get interest on their notes seem to be the only ones that make a clear gain to that extent on all the notes they are enabled to keep in circulation on account of the greater economy of credit currency, even if gold currency of sufficient amount were always available. The fact is that by lending such banknotes the rate of interest is lowered from the rate on gold or rent on property, to the extent that money is useful in facilitating exchange; that is, to the extent that the utility of a certain amount of money in a person's possession is greater than its equivalent value in property in other uses. To the extent that the community is willing to keep banknotes in their possession without receiving interest, instead of presenting them for redemption in property, all debtors may profit by a slightly lower rate of interest.

But though debtors may so profit by the use of credit money, the holders of banknotes are no better off than the holders of coin, so it is becoming more and more a modern custom for merchants to avoid this loss by making their money when they want it; that is, by accepting a bill of exchange at the time they receive a certain property, instead of losing interest on coin or banknotes for perhaps a week or two, that they would otherwise have to keep in their possession to make such payment at the proper time.

This may in a measure account for the decrease in the amount of the National Banking circulation in the United States. People do not want money that they will lose interest on while it is in their possession when they can do business by credit that can be made just at the time of every transaction.

I do not suppose what any one can say will make much difference with those who have so dogmatically accepted the mutual banking fallacy that they regard all arguments to the contrary as unnecessary to be considered, but those who will go over the subject carefully and critically, I am sure will see where they have been led into error, and I can better understand their position since I at one time sincerely held such views myself, but upon a clearer understanding of the nature of economic relations I have come to realize how I was in error. F. K. BLUE.

San Francisco.

In answer to Mr. F. K. Blue's attempt at criticism of "Citizen's Money" I would say that a more careful reading of what he finds fault with, and a more effectual effort to digest the ideas he has but so recently come in contact with, would result in greater credit to himself. Nothing is said on page 14 of that pamphlet about "Mutual Bank notes being required to be redeemed periodically." If he will read Article 13 of the "Plan for a Mutual Bank," as he should have done before risking exposure of his unfamiliarity with the subject, he will see that his objection is not well taken. There is no such statement in my pamphlet as "the value of a dollar, an ounce of gold, or a bushel of wheat." I do not have to give definitions to sentences formulated by other people. It is evident he has been studying the text-books and regards them as authority, and so got himself all tangled up trying to make the dogmas of political economists apply to economic science. He should not trust to the learned professors, but rely upon his own judgment. They are very profuse with the use of the terms "measure of value" and "standard of value," yet it is just as absurd as to write, "the curvature of a straight line," or "the right angle of a circle." Value is not a fixed or permanent quality, hence, there can be no measure, standard or unit of value. The dollar is a monetary unit or conventional denominant, and when there is no commodity dollar,—nothing but a paper dollar that is amply secured and therefore no risk in taking it in exchange for commodities, its purchasing power (not its value) will be unchangeable; and when it is available to all borrowers (with first-class security) upon a strictly equal footing, and at the same rate—cost, all speculation will come to an end, for speculation has its origin, not in natural, but in artificial opportunities created by law; hence we favor free (from government control) money. Mr. Blue should now be able to see why Smith can borrow of Jones only on usurious conditions.

Mr. Blue will find on page 10 of "Citizens' Money" that I have been very explicit in showing the difference between the nature of coin and the nature of paper money.

The reason why speculative interest has not been abolished in Scotland is the same as that which exists here and everywhere else,—because it has not occurred to them to establish Mutual Banks in place of Joint Stock Banks. The former would do the business on the co-operative plan *at cost*. The latter, in addition to cost charge a profit (speculation) which goes to the stockholders.

Mr. Blue must become more familiar with this subject, especially our views, and not attribute to us the antithesis of what we affirm. It is we and not our opponents who recognize the fact that "economic relations transcend," not only "mutual agreements," but legislative enactments.

I cannot further follow his labyrinth of confused idea; and if he does not see his way clear through liberty to a solution of the economic question I shall have to leave him to his fate. ALFRED B. WESTRUP.

343 Michigan Ave., Chicago.

Managerial Experience.

This is May. I was always stuck on May whether of the feminine or neuter gender. I have been most familiar with the latter. The other never gets near enough to do more than stick in the quagmire of social conventionality. Sour grapes! I dismiss her and prate about the neuter, the one that keeps open house and bars with no price of either gold or respectability. This May that tosses a green velvety curtain over the rugged hills with its shades of open light and mystic dark under the slanting rays of the morning sun; and which spreads a rich carpet over the fields and slopes, along the sides of dusty roads, and tacks narrow strips between ditches and fresh-plowed ground, with scraps neatly fitted in lonesome nooks and unvisited fence-corners. This May which dots this sea of green with intricately patterned flowers of yellow, blue, red, and mixed shades formed with exquisite delicacy and by systematic process only to be ruthlessly plucked at the whim of a plucker. This May which makes the muscles under eyes quiver and causes wrinkles to gather on the bridge of the nose; which fills the air with undefined prospects and the perfume of blossoms; May with its poets and leaves thin and tender, its barefoot boys and their chapped feet; its hatching hens in empty salt-barrels lying on their sides south of sheds and coops; its old potatoes and chirping young chickens, its wooly ducklings and mellow-looking gozzlings, its bunting calves and their pails of skimmed milk, its clean young pigs and high-priced corn, its corn planting and chorus of frogs, its abundance of bacon and scarcity of eggs, its hungry plow-horses and their musty chopfeed, its stale strawstacks and mangy colts, its bragging bulls and philoprogenitive cows, its basking dogs and lazy cats, its vain gobblers strutting alone behind barns; its half-hatched broods fumed over by frowzy and wrinkled women with thoughts of hungry and smirking ministers; its sharp plowshares and cloven ground-worms, its useless shade and back-breaking spade, its labor-kicked languor and unharrowed fields; its white dresses cruelly masking shapely limbs or generously concealing bones bound in raw-hide; its broad hats covering acres of prejudice and imbecility, its buggy-rides and their insatiable hugging, its bouyant hope mingled with a touch of uncertainty, and its beautiful and cozy homes with their Egoistic contentment. I like to stand mornings at the south-east corner of the house in the sunshine with squinting eyes and wrinkled nose while I bleach my teeth and ponder over all these things, even if my pants-legs are too short and there *is* a seedy-looking hole in my cheap derby. May is my first of the year ending the next spring just before the grass begins to crowd the sunshine back. I influenced the launching of EGOISM at that season of the year, and with a large and enthusiastic list of subscribers could hail its return many times with a full purse and delight. May I! ....?

I regret having indirectly in my previous "Experience" prodded at my mother-in-law for soliciting subscriptions for the "Twentieth Century" while she left EGOISM to its fate. I find the solicitous mother had through philoprogenitive impulse tried to raise a club for the strange duckling she had hatched from what she thought a genuine hen's egg, but the poultry she circulated among declared it a gull and that they were not gullible enough to part with four-bits for that kind of fowl. So thereafter she tried for the "Twentieth Century" with more success. It still sometimes chases God and the old Jewish novel, and this they like vehemently.

Now, when I subjectively appropriate the anguish on such an occasion of a person more inflated with good will than Egoistic philosophy, I feel much more uncomfortable than when I poked fun at a serious person. To prevent the recurrence of a similar break in my pleasurable complacency I shall not repeat it. Now if I were so unselfish as to be incapable of having my *own* consciousness pained with a knowledge of this anguish I might continue to joke as innocently as an Altruist applauds a bestowal of gifts in accordance with *his* desires. But I am so intensely *selfy* that a knowledge of suffering diverts my pleasure-seeking faculty so much as to cause me to refrain from acts producing pain which I will appropriate through such knowledge. Hence outside of her own resistance and that of the equal freedom interest of the community she has a protection against me through my selfiness in not desiring to suffer by such appropriating of pain. Sympathy then, is the subjective appropriating of a condition through a knowledge of its effects, and sympathetic acts, attempts to escape that knowledge.

The most conspicuous thing now about our abode is the absence of W. S. Bell, with whom we have for two years pooled house-rent and a desire for fortune. These evenings after having dragged myself by lagging strength and a dusty hand-rail up our stairs I do not meet the smiling countenance of a fat man who fills a thirty-two inch doorway like a new sausage does its skin. My wife prepared for disappointment, looks an inquiry for the mail, but no cheerful voice rings out: "What's new, how's George?" and upon being assured that George is all right and that things are the usual "chestnut," exclaims: "What, a man been to the city and knows nothing new? why we know that much and have scarcely been out of the house." When I want kindling I cannot reach behind the stove and find it prepared for lighting. When our beans and soap are consumed I have to carry more home myself. If there are repairs needed on the house I find myself having to face the landlord. If, as sometimes happens, I get a postal note I must go to the postoffice to cash it. When I want the mail and am too busy to cross the bay I cannot get it by generously offering Mr. Bell the ride, for which he is not spoiling, but have to wait till *I* can go. If I want to know how to spell a word I have to go to the dictionary, a thing I do not always do. When "Liberty" comes we no longer hold a convention and declaim upon its merits. I read it on the boats and trains, and at home rush inarticulately over its sharpest drives for my wife's benefit, who is obliged to economize eye-sight for other purposes. Upon the arrival of "Freethought," we do not now read and shout by turns while devouring "Observations." I, having previously shaken my ribs loose with laughter, read the paragraphs with matter-of-fact familiarity to my wife who, hitherto kicking and screaming upon such occasions now threatens only an accommodating smile. Verily, our home is filled with a large gone and a few dry bones.

EGOISM is now printed with an 8x12 Columbian lever press and great care. In operation, this press winks at you, grasps the sheet of paper, doubles itself up like a small boy actuated by a green apple, then straightens out and presents you with a sprained arm and a lightly-pressed page. But with plenty of ink and patience it does much better than no press at all. It has, however, a history as well as an appreciator. Its first service was to print in a sod-house region of Kansas the "Thomas Cat." (How gladly I would devote it to pressing the Thomases who dispute in our backyard at night!) Then it fought for us a perilous battle at Liberal, Mo. A year or two later it did similar service at the same place for other dissenters. Now it is about to kill me in my attempt to make it do work equal to that of a Colt's Armory. It does not rush heedlessly through its work. At the deliberate rate now operated it would require twenty days to run an edition of one thousand of EGOISM. On press days I am grateful to a generous public for not running our subscription list up to such a hopeless number. When we get fifty dollars with which to buy the necessary material we will have it printed by steam on a cylinder press at three dollars a thousand. We will then use the Columbian for a relic. I am certain that it will be much pleasanter for me to operate it in this way than as I now do it.

Not long since the report reached us that Eugene L. Macdonald the young Pacific coast Anarchist would bring his mother and visit the publishers of his favorite journal, EGOISM. As this promised to be an unusual occasion I immediately corralled my wife's little niece and set about enlarging our apartments by excavating the dirt and grease from the window and door casings and sweeping the delicate but dusty cobweb frescoing from the ceiling and corners. We also harrowed and bathed the kitchen floor, spreading its valuable California real estate with unvarying evenness of color. With the skill that I have acquired in operating my jaw and hands simultaneously since the arrival of my wife's little niece I believed the work could be rapidly executed, but my calculation miscarried conspicuously. I found that with the utmost guinea-hen persistence of my masticatory organ I could induce the kid to put only about as much pressure and speed to the brush as would be required in dressing boils. It was in vain that I elaborated on the idea that the woodwork wasn't sore and could be safely scrubbed to the limit of her strength. But the woodwork of the occasion was principally on the wall, not with her, for she wouldn't. Finally this part of the task was completed, minus its result. Youngster Macdonald and his mother didn't come, and I found myself plunged into the most frenzied gyrations of a war-dance all the next week attempting to keep things up to this standard of glitter. Complacency was, as usual, found in defeat.

Mrs. Macdonald has since sent the photograph of their budding innovator to my wife, and we have it exposed with that of Tak Kak and other philosophic celebrities. This brings me to the long-threatened canvassing of a report in "Freethought" several months ago in which it was stated that the subject of this "Experience" attempted to disturb the meeting while W. S. Bell was delivering his address on "Government" before the last convention of the California Liberal Union. It was said that his mother had to carry the young fellow out and that he hurled defiance at the meeting as she disappeared with him. It was also implied that his purpose was archistic; that it was an impulse to invade. It is this version that I combat with a more probable theory and one consistent with his principles. Mr. Bell has no equal in delivering radical lectures before conservative audiences without being mobbed, and this ability lies in his skill in introducing glittering generalities at the point where an eruption on the part of his listeners is scented. On this occasion he had just reached such a point sweeping the young listener's enthusiasm with him like a pennant in the breeze, when it became necessary to throw in something like "liberty struck to the ground crushed and bleeding." This meaning nothing in particular, was of course too much for the patience of the youth, who echoed an involuntary protest. His imprecations at the door were undoubtedly directed against the clamishness of a people who pretend to follow rationalism to its logical conclusion, yet make such tactics necessary on the part of their instructors.

I'll bet on one thing however, and that is when he grows to be two yards long and a yard wide like his father, no little woman however winsome will take him out of a meeting when he has remarks to make.

It has been inadvertently remarked and advertently reproduced, that history repeats itself. It is a phenomenon that I have myself experienced. My parents were born and, later, a similar accident occurred to me. To those things I have finally become somewhat accustomed, but when my youthful associates fall into the antedeluvian habit of breeding it disturbs me like a railroad disaster. It is not a fact that I have been trying to bring about nor a thing that I have lost, but there it is, life size, just the same. It was not there before and now that it is there I have no use for it. I cannot get it out of my memory and yet I do not need it there. The knowledge of how to deposit money in a bank would be no more useless. The latest demonstration of the aforesaid kind among my friends took place recently in the apartments of F. K. Blue, of this city. There, in the immediate presence of Mrs. Gertie Blue, Mr. Blue's wife, —— Blue, their first son, blew his whistle and started off on his run as a separate consciousness. He appropriated from his former environment a large strong body and an equally strong social bond with all of which it is believed he will prosper.

I am somewhat embarrassed at having thus to brandish the news of a matter so delicate, but in common with George Macdonald I find myself oppressed by a prejudiced public which will not allow itself to be prepared beforehand for such announcements by indicating their probability. I could have done it just as well as not. These friends visited us but a short time before this occurred, and as such an "event always casts its shadow before" rather more than in any other direction, I was reasonably certain that some such thing would happen.

We once had some woolen blankets about which some remarks were made in these columns. These were so narrow when last referred to that they could be used by but one person at a time. My wife being the most important member of the family and best adapted to their width they were reserved for her use. But they became still more bigoted and narrow; so much so in fact that to make them last till spring we had to wind them on her at night like thread on a spool or silk on a cocoon. She spun no silk however, only yarns of approaching desolation. Thus an ignorant majority with wool protectively drawn over its *eyes* fancies its *body* covered, while we, to sleep, must wind ourselves into balls of carpet-rags.

Benjamin Harrison, now chief knob of the United States privilege pull, has been on exhibition in our city lately. I should have been delighted if it had been George Macdonald's Uncle Benjamin Tucker, but he has to pay his own expenses when he travels, and I shall probably never see him. The president and myself are natives of a similar state. He did not call on me, but I saw him hanging around the post-office entrance one day when I went after the mail. He wore a committee-pecked expression and a white shirt. He made no remark to me save a request that I pull down my vest. But I blandly explained to him that the stretched-looking gap in my raiment was not due to aspiration of the vest but to the shortness of my trousers which, in order to reach my shoes had to be swung considerably below the vest.

EGOISM'S PRINCIPLES AND PURPOSE.

Egoism's purpose is the improvement of social existence through intelligent self-interest. It finds that whatever we have of equal conditions and mutual advantage is due to a prevalence of this principle corresponding with the degree and universality of individual resistance to encroachment.

Reflection will satisfy all who are desirous of being guided in their conclusions by fact, that as organization itself is a process of absorbing every material useful to its purpose, with no limit save that of outside resistance, so must the very fact of its being a separately organized entity make it impossible for it to act with ultimate reference to anything but itself. Observation will show that this holds good throughout the vegetable and animal kingdoms, and that whatever of equality exists among members of a species or between different species has its source and degree in the resisting capacity, of whatever kind, which such member or species can exert against the encroachment of other members or species. The human animal is no exception to this rule. True, its greater complexity has developed the expedient of sometimes performing acts with beneficial results to others, but this is at last analysis only resistance, because it is the only means of resisting the withholding by others from such actor's welfare that which is more desirable than that with which he parts. If, then, the self-projecting faculty of mankind is such that it will in addition to the direct resistance common to the less complex animals, diplomatically exercise present sacrifice to further extend self, and it being a fact that equality depends upon equal resistance, diplomatic or otherwise, what are its chances in an absence of enlightenment in which the individuals of the majority so far from *intelligently* using this resisting power in their own behalf, do not even believe that they should do so? The result of a general conception so chaotic, would naturally be what we find: the generalization from the practical expediency of certain consideration for others, crystallized through the impulse of blind selfishness into a mysterious and oppressive obligation, credit for the observance of which gratifies the self-projecting faculty of the simple, while the more shrewd evade its exactions, and at every step from the manipulation of the general delusions of religious and political authority to the association of sexes and children at play, project themselves by exchanging this mythical credit for the real comforts and luxuries of the occasion, which the others produce. Thus in addition to the natural disadvantage of unequal capacity, the weaker are deprived through a superstition, of the use of such capacity as they have, as may be seen in their groping blindness all about us.

To secure and maintain equal conditions then, requires a rational understanding of the real object of life as indicated by the facts of its expression. It is plain that the world of humanity is made up of individuals absolutely separate; that life is to this humanity nothing save as it is something to one of these; that one of these can be nothing to another except as he detracts from or adds to his happiness; that on this is based the idea of social expediency; that the resistance of each of these individuals would determine what is socially expedient; that approximately equal resistance makes it equality, and on such continued and a universal resistance depends equality. This can leave no room for any sane action toward others but that of the policy promoting most the happiness of the acting Ego. Therefore Egoism insists that the attainment of equal freedom depends upon a course of conduct replacing the idea of "duty to others" with *expediency* toward others; upon a recognition of the fact that self-pleasure must be the final motive of any act; thus developing a principle for a basis of action about which there can be no misunderstanding, and which will place every person squarely on the merit of his or her probable interests, divested of the opportunity to deceive through pretension, as under the dominance of altruistic idealism. It will maintain that what is generally recognized as morality is nothing other than the expediency deduced from conflicting interests under competition; that it is a policy which, through the hereditary influence of ancestral experience, confirmed by personal experience, is found to pay better than any other known policy; that the belief that it is something other than a policy—a fixed and eternal obligation, outside of and superior to man's recognized interests, and may not be changed as utility indicates, makes it a superstition in effect like any other superstition which causes its adherents to crystallize the expediency adopted by one period into positive regulations for another in which it has no utility, but becomes tyrannical laws and customs in the name of which persecution is justified, as in the fanaticism of any fixed idea.

Another part of its purpose is to help dispel the "Political Authority" superstition and develop a public sentiment which would replace State interference with the protection for person and property which the competition of protecting associations would afford. Then the State's fanatical tyranny and industry crushing privilege would torture the nerves of poverty-stricken old age or pinch tender youth no more. The most disastrous interference of this monster superstition is its prohibition of the issuing of exchange medium on the ample security of all kinds of property, which at once would abolish speculative interest and practically set all idle hands at productive labor at wages ever nearing the whole product until it should be reached. The next interference is by paper titles to vacant land instead of the just and reasonable one of occupancy and use, which with the employment that free money would give, would furnish all with comfortable homes in a short time, and thereafter even with luxuries from like exertion. Following this is its patent privilege, customs robbery, protective tariff, barbarous decrees in social and sexual affairs; its brutal policy of revenge, instead of restitution, in criminal offenses, and finally its supreme power to violate the individual, and its total irresponsibility.

Egoism

Vol. II.--No. 2. SAN FRANCISCO, CAL., JUNE, 1891. Price, Five Cents.

Pointers.

W. S. Bell's address for the summer is 654 Monroe st., Brooklyn, N. Y. All personal matter should be addressed to him at that place. Orders for his handbook should be sent to Box 1678, San Francisco, Calif.

Benj. R. Tucker's next publications will be "What's Bred in the Bone," by Grant Allen, and "The Rights of Women and the Sexual Relations," by Karl Heinzen. The latter is translated from the German. These titles bespeak interesting works the appearance of which we anxiously await. The price of each is 50 cents in paper cover, and $1.00 in cloth binding. Address Mr. Tucker at Box 3366, Boston, Mass.

Dr. Hall, referred to in the May number, who was arrested for the murder of a girl who died from the effects of abortion, is still in prison. So appalling is the cloud of prejudice, and prostrate the apparition worshiping community that the $50,000 bail has not been secured. He simply failed in a patient's case, as thousands of doctor's are doing in their treatment of other kinds of cases against the failure of which there happens to be no law.

Ambrose Bierce has written lately some of the best matter that we have seen in a daily paper outside of the "Galveston News." He is not satisfied with the republican form of government, derides monarchies, and says Anarchists are the humorists of politics. We would read with interest Mr. Bierce's proposition for the best order of society, and if it is one which he does not care to offer to the popular press, would gladly publish it in these columns, subject to the criticism of Egoism's staff. Remuneration for any contribution is of course out of the question with this paper.

At Galena, Ill., on the 1st of this month a wealthy farmer's daughter and his farm hand suicided because the girl's parents opposed the marriage deemed necessary for the satisfying of the sympathetic and magnetic craving which unassuaged terminated in their foolish act. Mercenary and sex prejudiced parents and inexperienced youth done the work. Wiser parents, not having previously guarded against such a contingency by furnishing the girl with the necessary approximative experience, and not desiring her to marry, would have protected her as well as possible against undesirable results and secretly allowed her marriage experience without its bonds until she learned that her love was an ungratified appetite that could be satisfied without death or marital slavery. Instead of a dead body and a life-long regret they would now at worst have no more than a young mother and a bright grandchild, and at best a grateful, experienced and happy daughter. They might not have been so respectable, but if they could not in spite of this have been happier we do not begrudge them their grief.

In Oakland a youngish man succeeded in convincing an older woman that he was the Messiah, and she was willing to board and lodge him for his distinguished company. But the sex bugaboo got into their neighbors' bonnets, and the man was arrested on the all-purpose charge of vagrancy and thrown into prison by the sweet-scented virtue of majority brutality. Fraud that he is, he is a shining example beside the crude and barbaric meddlers who believe that it is refined to mix in matters that one deems indecent. Cats, dogs, roosters, bulls, and mediocre human animals meddle in others' sexual affairs when they get a chance.

Although the "Examiner," of this city, is a ranting prohibitionist on personal affairs like gambling, it has recently published the best satire on that other species of legal meddling, protection, that we have read in a long time. This State offers $5 for each coyote scalp that can be captured, and an editorial writer takes this for his text and appropriates the usual protectionist argument, showing how coyote ranches will spring up on hitherto barren and unused lands, how the money paid the huntsmen will be spent for arms and ammunition, creating a demand for labor in their manufacture which will patronize the merchants and farmers, so that industry will be stimulated throughout the whole community, establishing through this tax prosperity and life where poverty and stagnation had reigned.

A sewing woman in this city finding that she could no longer support her sick mother and two children with her needle, and being offered a position in the country at $25 a month with board, accepted it after arranging with a friend to care for her mother at $10 a month. She could not take her children with her, but thought it would be an easy matter to get them into some of the many homes for children in the city. This proved no small task. She went to nine places without receiving the slightest encouragement. Finally, exhausted and despairing, she went to the last on her list, the Nursery for Homeless Children on California street. Here she received kind treatment and help regardless of religion or social connections. At each of the others in this city and Oakland they were either full, objected to her religion, would take no children whose parents were not one or both dead, or must have the children's clothes furnished and $5 to $8 a month for caring for them. Everyone had endless red-tape and regulations to be complied with before children could be put in them at all. It was plain that the principal effort was how to keep children out rather than to relieve the distressed. It is the only business in the city in which each house cheerfully recommends and advises customers to go the other. The sex ogre too reigned at most of them, as the children of deserted women would not be received. At each place this woman was treated with indifference or contempt until she reached the Nursery for Homeless Children, where her condition was immediately appreciated and the spirit of her case entered into. She was counseled to provide for the sick mother first and do what she could for the children later, but to send them right along anyway. The matron as spontaneously manifested interest and sympathy as an own sister could have done.

It appears that Egoism has seemed to be putting its number ten foot in it clear to the neck by editorially assuming Alfred B. Westrup's argument on a "standard of value," which argument has been interpreted as implying that currency is proposed that does not express a known quantity. That is, that these notes would not call for such an amount of product as would exchange for a definite quantity of some known article. This would of course not work. No one could afford to give such a quantity of products as would exchange for twenty grains of gold for a note without knowing the note would be redeemed with such a quantity of products as would then exchange for twenty grains of gold. We say gold because it is supposed under present circumstances to be the most practicable measure in which to express an order for products; any commodity costing about as much labor and maintaining about the same demand at one time as another would do as well, so long as the redeeming products were estimated by the same standard as were those given for the note. We can hardly think even now that Mr. Westrup intended to controvert this, though a re-reading of his argument in the light of the aforesaid interpretation strongly impresses that implication. Tak Kak's article on "Mutual Banking," in reply to F. K. Blue touches on this point, and "Valuation for Security," copied from the "Galveston News," treats it similarly only at greater length. Regarding the relative nature of value Mr. Westrup, Tak Kak, and the "News" agree, but the deduction of the latter is apparently widely different and to us satisfactory. We had been regarding Mr. Westrup's article as directed against that position which adopting gold as a standard of value implies that it is necessarily the only basis for currency. These articles will probably bring a reply from Mr. Westrup stating his position unmistakably clear to all.

Mutual Banking.

The first thing one wants to know of any writer on the money question is whether or not he is in favor of our having liberty to try and solve the problem of reducing interest. When they say that free banking will not work out in such a way as we think, I feel like replying: What is the use of saying so while liberty to make the demonstration or to fail in making it is denied? The monopoly State virtually admits that interest can be reduced or abolished. Its prohibition on free banking,—its refusal to formulate conditions with which we might be able to comply to guarantee that our experiments are to be at our own cost and not to deceive the unwary,—are sufficient confession that the monopoly money power fears we should succeed. If F. K. Blue be a libertarian why does he not put in his protest against the financial monopoly gag law? We cannot practically prove the beneficence of free banking without having liberty to try it. For the present therefore we have to be content with proving or claiming it theoretically.

Several of Mr. Blue's queries and criticisms show that he has not sufficiently reflected upon the subject. He asks why should a note be redeemed periodically if the borrower can according to practice immediately borrow it again? I would ask him what is a loan without term? Obviously the security will deteriorate with time and a revaluation will be necessary to show whether the loan can properly be renewed in the same amount. This is a principle governing established business.

He says that gold is merely a standard like the yard-stick at Washington. Now there is no prohibition on making yard measures of wood, tape, or other material; hence there is no scarcity-toll on the use of yard measures, but there is always a scarcity-toll on the use of money. At this time the drain of $50,000,000 of gold to Europe is credited with a general reduction of prices amounting to three cents on the dollar.

He asks: Why can Smith borrow 100 bushels of wheat of Jones only on condition of paying him back say 110 bushels next year? I answer, because Jones can sell the wheat for money and loan the money for 10 per cent.

The distinction between extension as a quality of one object and value as a result of objects in relation, but not inherent in gold or any other object, does not alter the necessity, in my view, for estimating by some agreed, definite mode of comparison the value of property on which a loan is made. Gold is a fair elective standard article. If I have a house and you a steamboat and both are valued by comparison with gold, both will fare alike. If a 40 per cent margin be allowed for possible variation and the variation be 20 per cent in one instance and 25 in the other both loans will still be safe. The valuation is just as empirical as the reward of labor by sale of labor products in the market, but good enough.

Mr. Blue seems to have overlooked the mutual acceptance feature in Mutual Banking, by which each note is provided to be redeemed in products and services, and he signally fails to appreciate the effect upon relative spot and future values which would follow a greater facilitating of employment, hence production. Every product tends to decay. Increase activity in production and the securing of a market for accumulating products begins to weigh as a reason why one's interest may be in selling rather than in holding. If houses are abundant and I own two I shall be glad to sell a house now for the cash which will pay for as good a house at a future time. Capital under liberty will be content with replacement. It is by maiming and laming production and exchange that the money monopoly in connection with land monopoly has kept the balance uneven.

Mr. Blue speaks of borrowing money as borrowing property. Mutual Banking is proposed so that we may borrow evidences of property and make these answer the same purpose as the literal circulation of that rare kind of property —coin—which is most convenient for division, preservation and delivery,—and which therefore under the regime of prohibition on currency has of course obtained an oppressive power for its owners. Tak Kak.

Editorial Slashes.

The most prominent thing in approaching this sort of diversion is the overgrown inadequacy of the space that the whole of such a paper could furnish in which to properly "slash" a month's conduct of a muddled community.

The California State board of health deprecates heart failure as a cause of death and has resolved that it, along with "fever, dropsy, childbirth, and cold shall not hereafter be recognized as a satisfactory cause of death when returned in physicians' certificates." That is, who hereafter dies from such ailments is not legally dead and the attending physician is forced to lie about the cause of death or be liable to prosecution for allowing the body to be buried alive. Yet men of alleged intelligence vote, and prate of the wisdom and dignity of the State without laughing in each other's faces. What a humorless race of animate mummies!

Oakland's Society for the Prevention of Cruelty to Animals and Children, has petitioned the board of supervisors for a monthly allowance from the people's pocket. Not satisfied with the glory purchasable with the voluntary contributions of those who profit by privilege, the society asks for the use of the policeman's club to plunder the disinterested citizen for amunition as well as beat its victims into court. The society, preying upon popular prejudice has acquired numbers, to these the politicians must pander, and finally the once voluntary charitable institution is squarely loaded on the producers' backs, an exacting tyrant firmly riveted to the popular superstition, political authority. It is then safe and the whole serving community must help pay for the glory harvested by a few officials.

When reading in a late "Lucifer" the contradictory and weak aspersion of E. H. Heywood on Benj. R. Tucker and his work I thought Mr. Heywood's confinement was deranging his mind, but when I found the matter had been published without apology or comment from "Lucifer's" editor, and that he believes it advantageous to go from St. Louis to New York by way of the West Indies, I realized that when the mental cup is encrusted with ossified religion, more subtile fluid will simply overflow when poured in, and that the slandering was induced by incapacity to understand mingled with a desire for revenge, so sweet to fanatical Altruists. Mr. Tucker has several times in discussion vanquished these thirteenth century zealots, and they cannot get over it. Besides, he has with material profit instead of sacrifice accomplished more work in their line than they probably ever will. The reason in such instances faintly recognizes the expedient method, but the preponderant and habituated emotions cannot accustom themselves to the new arrangement and resentment bubbles up whenever its work comes to the notice of the mistaken.

San Francisco has 20,000 citizens who seriously need $75,000 worth of sewer at one point as an outlet. They have paid for it in taxes many times, but Communism always has too much "general good" to dispose of to be just, and the money all went for that. Now the finance committee can contrive no way to raise the means, and those of delicate health must beat the cemetery if they can, with the odds greatly against them. But for the tax plunderer these people could have used their money in their own neighborhood and long ago had an outlet for sewage. It would be better for them even now to raise the money by subscription and put the sewer in at their own expense than wait on the government machine to spin red-tape until it is too late to do the work this season. And it will surely be forgotten by the authorities next year if allowed to run over. Nationalists could get another hint here of how a net-work of officialism could appropriate every stroke of labor for the "general good" consisting of official architectural hobbies and ambitions, while the individual would be left not only without a sewer, but with little to exercise one upon.

Few things are better calculated to disgust a person matter-of-fact enough to get from under a falling tree, than the British and American cant about gambling, generated by the baccarat scandal. Everybody with sense enough to distinguish dry from wet knows that gambling is carried on by every class of people with a stake and leisure. It is also well known that no one is forced to gamble, and that they do so with a full knowledge of the probabilities. It is not likely that anybody could believe that the Prince of Wales, having spent thirty or forty years in dissipating pleasure-seeking, did not gamble as freely as he indulged his sexual instincts. Yet each fully conscious that the other knew, howls as if the royal gamblers had been disemboweling and roasting children and mothers for their amusement. When the prince, through a political superstition, plunders his mother's subjects of clothes-basketfuls of money and squanders it for his own pleasure it is bearable for the Britisher, but when he enters a game on a fair and equal footing both the British subjects and "democratic" Americans bite the dust before a time-honored prejudice. Even the "Examiner," usually more or less rational on such subjects, refers to the mayor of Oakland as choosing the side of decency in vetoing a poolroom ordinance. As if there were anything sticky or stinking about gambling. Or as if it in any way invaded equal freedom. It may be foolish for some people to gamble, but when all fools are to be suppressed gamblers will be found to constitute an indiscernible minority in comparison with the rest of the globe's "virtuous" inhabitants.

It is seldom that one can glance through a daily paper without finding several accounts of the ravages of the sex superstition. At Sacramento about the first of this month a man named Zwald, in a fit of religious frenzy, confessed to having murdered two wives. The disposal of the first victim was the legitmate fruit of monogamic monotony and its magnetic starvation. He met a woman nearly enough in his own condition and of proper temperment to spontaneously glide into the consummation of a mutual desire. But it was instinct alone and not a comprehension of the principle of freedom that dictated their conduct, and being dominated by the marriage idea and under the infatuation of new magnetism their natural impulse was to get rid of Zwald's wife, which they did by poisoning. Their nerve fluids, however, became neutralized before the anticipated union and they went their respective ways properly satisfied, but at the useless and fearful cost of another's life. If they had all understood the Egoistic nature of motive and individual rights, as well as something of sexual science, they would have known that the attraction would probably abate, or if it did not that there was no reason for anyone interfering and consequently none for getting rid of such an one. But "mysterious" love, "sacred" marriage, Mother Grundy and murder are a homogeneous lot and usually get to the surface where there is inherent energy enough for a demonstration. Now desperate, Zwald married for convenience a woman who proved to be a fiend at the pipe, negligent, and abusive and he strangled her to death one night while they were fighting and strung her to a beam in an outhouse, raising an alarm of suicide which passed. Thus dominated by the marriage custom he could think of pleasure with a second woman only by the death of the first, and instead of leaving the second wife he remained and was finally provoked into killing her. A rational conception of equal freedom would have allowed the two women to dispose of their own lives, and saved his without a loss of any pleasure enjoyed and a saving of all the pain endured. But mediocrity prefers respectability and murder to equal freedom.

Clara Luster, a young Jewess, for a promise of the respectable and customary price that he would support her for life by marriage, delivered the first installment of her sexual favors to Martin Quinlan, a police court lawyer of this city, and when he refused to come to time tried to shoot him. She raves about being ruined and by this unconscious pandering to Grundy has enlisted some useful sympathy. She was a working girl and with Jewish commercial instinct was undoubtedly quite willing to advance favors with the hope of catching a lawyer for a supporter. This is evident from the fact that having been fooled into a dive to work she left it as soon as she saw what was required, but when the higher price of a lawyer's wife nibbled she was not so virtuous as in face of the dive fee. He is likely to get the worst of it in this case, as another lawyer for some reason, perhaps professional enmity, tendered the girl his services in her defense against a charge of assault to murder, and will prosecute Quinlan for seduction under promise of marriage. The girl, with the sympathy generated by the notoriety, will probably fare as well or better than before, and the lawyer will not be so free with the marriage pension which most working girls are so anxious to bite at if only a sure catch can be made. Neither have my sympathy, but the case illustrates the commercial phase of the superstition both in the sympathy she has gathered by her wailings and the lawyer she attempted to gather with her favors. Were it not such a superstition she would not have been pregnant unless she so desired, and so desiring, ruin and the shooting would not have been thought of. Neither would it be necessary for men to offer a life pension and mutual slavery for favors that should end with the act.

At Wheatland on the night of the 12th a "respectable" mob tarred and feathered a man whose stepdaughter, on her dying bed, charged him with her ruin, which led to her suicide. Though the man's torture was better than death the outrage of the "respectables" was just as marked. It was they and not the stepfather who supplemented the "ruin." Had they withheld ostracism and given patronage she would have been all right. But the superstition they propagate drove her to suicide and in her absence they torture the man they unconsciously envy.

The carnivorous daily press proclaims that Sir William Gordon-Cumming's brand new wife has an income of $60,000 a year in her own "right." That is, somewhere in our "free" America the equivalent of an army of 360 men are rendered slaves by having to turn to her use all the savings of constant toil, counting that the average laborer gets $500 per year and can house, clothe, and feed himself on two-thirds of it. She probably does not dream that so many human lives are sacrificed to furnish her silly whim with a title and parade her as perhaps forty-second fiddle to a crumbling monarchy. No doubt the dollars seem to her as legitimately hers as the berries one gathers from his own garden. Such is the fruit of privilege; human beings toiling in ox weariness and possessing ambitions and desires that mean everything to their existence that desires can mean to consciousness, are crushed into the function of soil for others of their species and are exploited with as little thought of invasion as the farmer feels in raising a crop from real soil. This woman's case is only one among the millions of those whose luxury and show enslaves the toilers of earth under the burning sun and in stifling shops, wallowing in the mud of mines or sweltering before furnaces. Those semi-conscious drones and these ghost-worshiping slaves move along in frog-like innocence of the ethereal web that keeps each where they are and as they are. H.

The Philosophy of Egoism.

X.

Under the head of Religion Webster's dictionary says: "As distinguished from morality, religion denotes the influences and motives to human duty which are found in the character and will of God, while morality describes the duties to man, to which true religion always influences." Granted belief in a personal ruler, submission to his will is prudence, and prudence is Egoistic. With this conception the duty spoken of is not mysterious: it is service by a subject,—the slave's submission to the power which he fears. He believes that the sovereign ruler has laid upon him special commands favoring his species and therefore he must treat men better than other animals. If this belief be an error, still there is no line to be drawn between the alleged duty and his interest. There is no disinterestedness or generosity in religious duty or moral duty,—or say rather in duty to God or man, for both are ultimately duty to the supposed heavenly master.

But Moralists, having gained some rational ideas of mutual relations, while unhappily ignoring the fact that these ideas are the proper foundation of willingly assumed mutual duties, fancy that they have discovered the justice of the alleged divine command or will, which is nothing but a reflection of their own thoughts, and thenceforth they fall under the hallucination of mystic Duty, independent of either calculation or pleasure. It is one task of Egoistic philosophy to analyze this notion of theirs as a confusion of ideas. They go so far in some instances as to dismiss belief in a moral lawgiver of the universe and yet remain under the same fascination to Duty as if they had him, and his will were equitable, and their servility were swallowed up in admiration of his justice. What they lack is the insight to perceive that conduct which makes for the good of the species is naturally agreeable to the feeling of each well developed individual, hence that the conception of Duty is skepticism as to spontaneity. The fixed idea of Duty unrelated to interest and not reducible to calculation, arises by abstraction and fascination like other aberrations reviewed in preceding papers. It reaches clear insanity in self-sacrifice if this occur in unreasoning ecstacy.

Of course an self-inflicted pain of some particular kind or even death is sometimes chosen in order to terminate anguish which none but the subject can appreciate. In such cases the action is Egoistic, though it may be of a terribly ignorant sort, as for example, when the cause of the pain is an imaginary object or such a real relation as is humiliating to the person's feeling only because of irrational notions about it.

If morality be regarded from the point of view of the social utilitarian, as that course of conduct which promotes the welfare of the species, it is only necessary to repeat that the species acts as Egoistically as it can. It cheerfully sacrifices individuals to its own welfare. It has a subtle economy of means in planting Altruistic conceits in those that are willing to entertain them. When intelligence comes to recognize mutual interest this instinctive trickery of social influence will vanish, no longer seeming to be needed.

As for the virtues, such as benevolence, every observing person knows that we seek to get rid of painful impressions. Such, usually, are those of suffering in others. Many writers have pointed out how pity is stirred by the sight of wasted bodies and hearing the cry of pain, and how much weaker it is when only an ordinary description is given of the occasion; also how much more ready the poor are to help other poor people than the rich are. What has perhaps not been so generally observed is the reason for this, viz., that the rich do not feel that they are likely to need alms, while the poor are on the edge of such need. There is quite enough in the difference of circumstances to make it instructive, although at the same time, personal character varying in susceptibility, it is doubtless true also that those most inclined to benevolence are most likely to be poor in a society like ours, where money is supposed to grow by lending and profits are consolidated from the results of unpaid labor.

TAK KAK.

Valuation for Security.

It will occur that in emphasizing one argument there is such need of passing others by with seeming unconcern, that to some minds other truths seem slighted—truths which also need emphasizing perhaps in an equal, or it may be, for useful practical reasons, in a superior degree. The "News" aims at illustrating one thing at a time, but it is both receptive and grateful to those correspondents who intelligently extend its work and indicate useful subjects for discussion, giving their best thoughts thereon. A Boston reader speaking of the standard of value, states an undeniable truth to the effect that without a thing or things of value to which paper money can be referred and which can ultimately be got for it, such money would be untrustworthy or worthless. The "News" in a past article was discussing primary commerce and the transition to indirect exchange. No agreed standard for valuation is needed while mere barter is the rule; but it is indispensable as soon as circulating notes are issued. The vice of the greenback theory is that the notes do not call for anything in particular and so if their volume be doubled their purchasing power must apparently decline one-half. A note properly based on gold, silver, wheat, cotton or other commodity has a tangible security behind it. The one thing may be better than the other, but the principle is there in all. It is, however, a notable truth that the standard for valuation can be nothing better than an empirical one. Like mathematical quantities, value has no independent existence, but unlike mathematical quantities, value has not even existence as a quality of one object. It can not be compared to a measure of length, which possesses the quality of extension in itself. Gold is assumed to vary little in relation to other things and they to vary much in relation to gold. Nobody can know how much gold does vary in the relation. The notable steadiness is in the amount of labor which will produce a given quantity and the length of time which it will last. The basis of the assumed steadiness of gold is thus found. But if the standard for use in making valuations be confessedly empirical and value an elusive quality not of things separately but of things in relation, there is a countervailing difference between a standard of length and a standard of value, which results in disposing of the objection that the standard is empirical. Why would it be a serious objection to a yardstick if it were longer or shorter from day to day? Because thus the customer would get more or less cloth than was intended. But why is that? Because the function of the yardstick is to measure for delivery as great a length of cloth as its own length. But now let us visit a bank or insurance office. We want a loan of circulating notes or a policy of insurance. The property offered as security is valued. Assume that gold is taken as the standard and that the loan or the policy is for $600 on a valuation of $1 000. It is no matter in these cases if the standard varies, provided it does not vary to exceed the margin between the valuation and the obligation. The property pledged is merely security for the loan, or in the case of insurance the premium paid is a per cent of the amount insured. The amount between the valuation and the loan is established to make the loan abundantly safe. The policy is safely written through the same expedient. The empirical standard of value has a needful compensation about it which the yardstick or other measure neither has nor needs, viz., the valuing of goods does not deliver them. It is provisional. In case of default in paying back the loan the goods are sold and the same money borrowed is paid back, but the residue goes to the borrower. It is therefore an efficient compensation for the lack of an invariable standard of value, that the actual standard in any case is simply used as a means of estimating limits within which loans are safe. All danger is avoided by giving the borrower the familiar right in case of foreclosure. It is sometimes a fine thing to discover distinctions, but it is frequently a finer thing to discover whether or not the distinctions affect the question.—Galveston News.

Race Troubles.

According to the statements of Mr. A. Van Deusen in the "Twentieth Century," conditions down South seem to be getting rather unpleasant to the white masters of the soil. It appears that the poor ignorant and loftily despised negro is working his way up steadily, and by saving and thrift is gaining a foothold as proprietor. Taking the statements of the author for true, it seems in fact probable that the ex-slave race will in the course of the next twenty-five years virtually own the soil of the South.

If handicapped by surrounding difficulties the race has made use of the personal freedom granted it, to take firm and steady root, and plant itself as owners on the soil it formerly tilled as serfs, it shows its capabilities. And if its growing influence in the political struggle for superiority begins to be a menace to the supremacy of its quondam masters and now race enemies, it only shows that nothing but freedom was necessary to bring it in due course of time to the same level with its white co-citizens.

If starting poor and intellectually inferior, with the soil in the hands of their opponents, they succeed in gaining footroom for themselves and slowly but surely oust their opponents from possession, it would seem to indicate that for the locality in question, the negroes are not the inferior race.

And has not in all ages possession of the soil given the right to govern (if indeed such a right can exist)? Why then should it be denied to the blacks? Why should not a black politician have as much right to rule as a white one? Why, if a negro pays his taxes should he not have a vote in the spending of them as well as the white man? The drift of this feeling in the white population is easily explained, this feeling that wants the negro disfranchised. If citizenship and equality were denied, it would stamp the black an inferior and prevent his rising in the social scale to a higher place than that of taxpayer to the masters who rule him. There is never any objection made to the negro's taxpaying.

To me the black race seems to be a very valuable kind of yeomanry, because according to the writer's statements, it keeps its holdings free and unincumbered, which does not seem to be the case with the *superior* white rulers.

I claim that if a negro behaves himself and pays his own way he has as much right to be here, to be a citizen, and to vote as any other human being. How he will live, spend, or save is entirely his own concern. Where does the title of the mighty Anglo-Saxon come from, that he presumes to keep a black man off the soil.

And if in a community, where the majority rule is an acknowledged and revered fact (however nonsensical and unjust it may be) the majority are black voters, and owners of the soil in the bargain, why should they not rule the roost? Or is according to Anglo-Saxon ruling the majority only a majority when composed of Anglo-Saxons and not when of "niggers"?

The whole difficulty lies in this fact: Who shall rule? If no ruling was attempted there would be no trouble. White and black could live peaceably together if each would follow his own way and not try to apply arbitrary regulations to the other.

Continues the author: "If things were as they should be the African race should be in Africa and the Chinese race in Asia." The same logic would return the Anglo-Saxon to Europe, and if the negroes are so thrifty as represented, they should follow the writer's advice, buy the Anglo-Saxons out and ship them back to their native land, bag and baggage.

If the Chinese on the same principle act the same on the Pacific coast, the outlook for an Anglo-Saxon exodus toward England will become exceedingly bright. The remnant now East, which according to the same writer is slowly being ousted from business by the superior skill of the Jews, will have to follow suit, for the Latin race from the North is raising community after community of prolific Canadian French on the soil of Puritan New England, and soon the land will know the Anglo-Saxon no more.

And if by superior business skill and thrift these four so-called inferior races can drive the Anglo-Saxon out, the only way left open to him is to amalgamate with them and by intermarriage regain the stamina lost in the course of time.

But here "decency" comes in. O howling Jehoshaphat! An Anglo-Saxon might possibly marry a Jewess, particularly if she possesses shekels, but a negress it would be shocking, and a Chinese would be positively "indecent." And why is it more indecent to love a black than a white woman, a Chinese than a Jew male? What can there be indecent in the performance of a personal right? What right has your decency to drive my black love from my arms or banish my Chinese lover? Why is it that three hundred years ago intermarriage between Jews and gentiles was forbidden as indecent, while no penalty is attached to the act now?

As soon as people will cease ruling each other; refrain from meddling with things that do not concern them; not despise one another for belonging to different clans; not defraud each other from the soil that each has a right to; not interfere with each other in the making of an honest living; not fight with each other any more about who shall pay and who shall spend the taxes wrung by power out of labor's earnings, the time will have come that negro, Jew and gentile can live together in the same land without reviling each other for the color of their skin or the length of their queues.

As long as government lasts there will be strife between races and between individuals for power. De Lespinasse.

Managerial Experience.

If my Experience is less philosophical this month than usual, there is ample reason for it. I have recently sprained my mind a little and dare not turn on a full head until the swelling is reduced and the soreness leaves it. It was a sort of accident. C. P. Huntington, president of the Southern Pacific Railroad Company, visited Oakland, my place of residence, and found the boys so contemptuously jumping his local trains while in motion, that it made him mad and he threatened to build a depressed track with sharp iron pickets on both sides to keep them away.

Now my contempt-breeding familiarity with depression makes me bitterly opposed to it, and after reading the president's intention I determined to defeat it by inventing an elevated track and train that will be cheaper than his depressed one, and will attain four times the speed. (I like elevated things; wages for instance.) This cost me one night, several hours of study so intense that the next morning a goodly number of gray hairs were found in my hitherto brown and silken rim locks. This must not be repeated or my appearance will no longer belie my condition and I will be regarded as an old man before my childhood vanishes. This would be disastrous socially; for when I found the girl who became my wife I had boiling youth and her extravagant inexperience in my favor. There are now multiplying reasons why so strong-minded and able a woman should shake me, and with physical defects piling up and my passion for women abating not a jot, I find myself wrapped about some unpleasant forebodings. If, however, this mental economy in writing develops the popularity common to thought-barren productions I shall have money, and the things that it will not procure can be made at home by hand. Thus hope standing at the crack of its own brain gazes expectantly into the future waiting for a great city to rise from the sand. The "grate" at least always comes.

As stated in another paragraph, I manage to impair my digestion and beat myself out of a good deal of sleep by trying to invent things. In this I succeed to my own glowing satisfaction till a critic as much interested in making my ideas look small as I am in magnifying them, pours in some fundamental objections. I then revise, finding as a usual thing that he is only partly right. But I have a problem now that knocks the most arrogant of them silly. It is the reversing of my sight. I find that I have a powerful and penetrating hindsight, which if reversed into such a foresight would make me complete master of the situation. It would cause me to succeed upon the very occasions that I now fail, and these are so numerous that I am relentlessly impressed with the importance of solving the question at the earliest date.

If I could have seen the point twenty years ago as clearly as I now do, instead of learning to run a stationary steam engine, or later, something of the tactics of drilling type, I should have learned the millionaire trade. It is now clear to me that there is a marked advantage in being a millionaire over that of being an engineer or compositor. It is a fact that the millionaire has to be on duty just the same, but the vocation is susceptible of conforming its duties more to the variations of desire than is true of those into which I was pumped. If I had seen when growing up what I now see I should not have been so religiously virtuous as I was, and would now be considerably stronger than I am. I should also not have sold out an opportunity to do business for the purpose of going to school and left school to brake on a railroad. But I should have left, as I did, the railroad to keep from breaking my neck. Later I should not have been so fanatically devoted to progressive ideas as to beat myself out of their advantages. Then every day I should not be doing things that I do, and should do many things that I fail to do. A little reflection will convince the reader of the existence-wringing importance of the question, "How Shall We Reverse Our Sight."

I have lately experienced an instance of character-photography. It was in the case of a Missouri acquaintance, J. G. Petgen. Mr. Petgen is a hard-sense German, who lives on a square mile of farm near Liberal, Mo. He is too practical to heartily share current prejudices and not quite idealistic enough to do battle for radicalism. When my mother-in-law solicited him to subscribe for EGOISM he said, "The paper is too far in advance, I cannot understand and get interested in it." Then he illustrated: "When I go into the field or near my cattle they will follow me as long as they can see me, but when I get over the hill out of their sight they lose all interest in me and begin to browse. That is the way with the people concerning EGOISM; it gets out of their sight and they don't care anything about it." This illustration is so characteristic of Petgen that it impresses his personality more forcibly upon me than his photograph could. One could hardly converse with him for five minutes without hearing some such comparison.

When mossy-spined Liberal made its first Grundy charge upon Freelovers, the Lyons were the principal victims. They had in their possession some beautiful specimens of the nude in art. Among the charges brought against them was that of "corrupting youth" by allowing visiting girls to look at these pictures. The rustic howl made the air purple, but when Mr. Petgen heard about it he said, "If my girls find anything at Lyons' house that they don't like, let them stay away from there." He took no further interest in the matter, and went about his own affairs as usual. Thus he lives his life on the very borders of that combination of thought and taste which would make the cramped ideas of his superstitious associates positively repugnant to him. He does not understand the ramifications and qualifying influence of Egoistic thought, yet is negatively an Egoist. His realistic comparisons extended a little further and applied to every topic would soon land him in a field with an infinitely larger life than is possible to glean from the institution worshiping mediocrity comprising his present environment. And this is true of thousands of more or less bold thinkers, who will live and die in a half-hatched condition for want of a little stirring up to the idea of getting the *most* possible from their flash of eternity.

This Experience is intended for "women only." Men may sleep under it however, if they don't kick on its complexion. It is a bedchamber secret which I wish to convey to my feminine readers. It borders not on the "obscene," but on the bedstead. It is a bed-sheet—a *colored* sheet; not that agonizing color between that of a smoked ham and a snowdrift which we of the female function succeed in boiling and bleaching out only when the sheets have evaporated, but a genuine oil painting color, such as girls and women have kitchen aprons and factory dresses made in. Such sheets can be washed so clean as not to generate cholera, without rubbing the skin off the knuckles and choking one's self in sudsy steam when lifting them from a boiler with the bald end of a broomhandle. A year or two of this experience generated in my invent tank the idea which I now put in practice and print. My wife bought me part of a bolt of gingham painted in blue for a background and striped with white. The bolt was not an old and rusty one. To be sure, the head and nut were gone, but it had good thread and was twenty-two yards long. This she measured into sheet lengths by holding one end to her nose and reaching as far out toward the other as she could with her hand. She was built with a standard yard stick, and can measure a bolt of cloth without losing a thread. I tried it, but lost just one sheet out of four. She says my nose is too long. But upon consulting the brevity of my flannel shirt-sleeves I conclude that it is my arms that prevent my being an automatic dry goods clerk.

One Sunday, when this material had been smelled into the proper lengths, I sat me down and buoyantly began to sew the strips together in pairs and to hem them across the ends with white thread and a long time. It was with delight that I matched the stripes at the beginning of the seam and despair that I found them missing each other and traveling toward me at the end. I had always yearningly desired such spontaneous intimacy on their part, having noticed them mostly about plump female flesh, but now when they really approached me I was stung with shegrin, or a knowing smile of my wife's which she conferred upon the wall and I absorbed from a mirror. After I had spent five hours in this way on two of the sheets, and was growing a little impatient at the procrastinating tendency the task was assuming, she laughed right out at me a great deal and tried a very little to teach me a sweeping wiggle of the hands by which she feeds the cloth on a needle-point as one does sheaves into a threshing machine. But I frankly admit that I can't make a strip of cloth lie still on the air while I stick and tug at it as is required in sewing. Neither have I a needle and thimble so trained that I can grasp them in my hand with some cloth like a bunch of grass, and the thimble will push the needle through the cloth in stitches of geometrical evenness and with railroad speed. And I told her that if she expected to make a hemmer, tucker, and feller out of me all at once, she was getting ahead of the band-wagon. She then turned feller herself, falling into sarcasm by rejoining that if I were a Tucker my talents wouldn't allow me to do either of the others and might even induce a change in her condition of servitude. I felt the force of this observation and a pang penetrate the thorax, landing amid my small intestines, and I looked doggedly out of the window at the local train while she gaped and seemed to realize that the truth is not on all occasions in demand. But colored sheets will save a great deal of labor and muslin.

Yours sillily, THE MANAGER.

Our George Stands On Them.

The readers of this journal have learned from an editorial paragraph printed last week that I am responsible for the contribution appearing in the preceding issue under the head of "Herbert Spencer on Nationalism"; that the ideas expressed are repugnant to "Freethought," which holds to Nationalism as the forlorn hope of industrial progress; and that Mr. W. N. Slocum has clearly pointed out the absurdities of Mr. Spencer's position. The paragraph is in the nature of an apology, made necessary by the inadvertent admission into these columns of Mr. Spencer's views with apparent editorial sanction. I did not write or inspire the apology. It is Browne's.

Mr. Slocum affirms that Spencer wilfully or ignorantly refuses to know what Nationalism is, and that he persistently misrepresents it as what it is not. Now I have read Socialistic books and papers, listened to Socialistic orators, and conversed with professors of Socialism more or less for the past fifteen years, and it does not appear to me that Spencer has misrepresented them as to their proposed form of reconstructed society. Of course he does not agree with them about the working of the system. The central idea of Socialism is an industrial army so officered and directed as to produce the greatest results with the least amount of labor. It strikes me that such an army without officers having absolute authority would be very much like a mob. It is quite easy to draw, on the walls of the imagination, a picture of a perfect society, with men and women that have no life and consequently no volition of their own. It requires only a slight exercise of the organs of speech to say that members, actuated both by interest and pleasure, will volunteer their service; that then not to labor will be a disgrace; that under the inspiration of Nationalism emulation will take the place of competition; that labor will be wholly voluntary; that all will follow useful occupations; that fitness will determine position; that officers will be constantly changing; that the children of the highest will begin on the same round of the ladder with the lowest; and that such a thing as classes will be not only unknown but impossible. For this picture Mr. Slocum has a distinguished original to copy from; it was drawn a hundred years ago by Thomas Paine, who had as much faith in democracy as Mr. Slocum and Editor Browne have in Nationalism.

Describing America, Paine said: "There the poor are not oppressed, the rich are not privileged." The exact opposite of this is true today. Paine goes on: "Industry is not mortified by the splendid extravagance of a court rioting at its expense." Is that so? Who paid the expenses of the presidential junketers who recently exhibited themsevles from Washington to San Francisco? If industry was not mortified by the "splendid extravagance" of special trains and seventy-five dollar dinners, it is due to the fact that industry was not represented on the reception committees. "Their taxes," proceeds Paine, meaning the American people, "are few because their government is just; and there is nothing to render them wretched, there is nothing to engender riots and tumults." At the time Paine wrote taxes were few, the billion dollar congress had not met; when he said the government was just, Bennett and Heywood and Harman had not been imprisoned: the Chicago men had not been hanged. He was attacking the English monarchy, and endeavoring to show by contrast how much better it would be to have a republic. If somebody had told him that in a hundred years riots would be as frequent in America as they are in England; that Congress would be more corrupt than Parliament; that Americans would be called upon to submit to oppressions and impositions that Englishmen have thrown off; that the monarchy would hold the lead in literature, science, education, and general progress, as well as in the larger industries; that, in fact, the government which he aided in establishing would soon get to be rather worse than the one he attacked—if somebody had hinted these things to Paine, I have no doubt he would have been as indignant as Nationalists are when told by Spencer that their system is more potent for evil than either democracy or monarchy.

Paine was the foremost political writer of his day. He was more popular than Herbert Spencer, and not open to the charge of pessimism or of hatching things in the quiet of his library. He was much in the common walks of life, and in a position to judge the signs of the times. Still he could not forecast, with the slightest degree of accuracy, the future of the republic under democracy. He never guessed how soon public office was to become a private enterprise, nor at what an early period statesmanship would be lost in politics and degraded into an unlearned profession.

It is in the line of this investigation to inquire: If the simple form of government inaugurated by Paine and his contemporaries was capable of developing the evils of the present day, what might a hundred years of so complex a system as State Socalism be expected to produce?

The battle of Freethinkers is against the privileges granted to the church by government, and this battle they are now fighting with a ray of hope to encourage them. That ray, in my poor opinion, will not be any brighter when Nationalism has multiplied the functions of the State and given us a swarm of officials to hold the balance of power.—George E. Macdonald in "Freethought" of May 30.

It is a remarkable example of the conservative character of men that the reformers of our day, who as a class have given up the belief in the revealed word of God, who claim to believe in evolution, in the struggle for existence and in the survival of the fittest, cling yet almost to a man, to the idea of duty of man toward man, and make it the basis of all their schemes of improvement, and are loud in their condemnation of selfishness, which is really the basis of all improvement.—Albert Chavannes.

The Omaha young man who flung a chair through the canvas of Bouguereau's famous picture of the nude, "The Return of Spring," was defended on his trial on his plea "I did it for the protection of woman's virtue." The connection was so obvious to the Omaha mind that they just naturally acquitted him, ignoring the unfortunate implication that the Omaha woman's virtue needs that kind of protection.—Oakland Tribune.

PROSPECTUS

EGOISM is published Monthly

at 50 cents a year.

It is promptly discontinued when subscription expires, and no bills are sent out. It is run by the publishers, and admits only such contributions as they believe extend, or intelligently criticise its position.

[*Entered as Second Class Mail Matter.*]

EQUITY PUBLISHING COMPANY,

P. O. Box 1678. San Francisco, Calif

MUTUAL BANKING: SHOWING THE RADICAL DEFICIENCY OF THE PRESENT CIRCULATING MEDIUM, AND THE ADVANTAGES OF A FREE CURRENCY. It is a 52-page pamphlet by William B. Greene, and to the advocate of free money is indispensable, as it discusses the subject in detail and at length. Price 25 cents.

LOVE, MARRIAGE, AND DIVORCE, AND THE SOVEREIGNTY OF THE INDIVIDUAL, is a pamphlet of 121 pages composed of a discussion of marriage by Henry James, Horace Greeley, and Stephen Pearl Andrews. What Proudhon's works are to Anarchism is this to freedom in love between the sexes. It is the most comprehensive, searching, and exhaustive work ever written on the subject. No advocate of sexual freedom can afford to be without a full acquaintance with its contents. Price 35 cents.

MY UNCLE BENJAMIN: a novel by Claude Tillier, an intelligent victim of institution oppression, who necessarily suffered more than he enjoyed. The splitting pangs of his intense pessimism are seasoned with such ridiculing thrusts at the vanity of wealth as to almost hide the exaggeration. The characters are not made to "come out" in school girl ideal, but tumble along like real life, mostly at the mercy of other elements than the reader's desire. The facts are not manufactured and put up in doses ready to take for building up a philosophy made to order. He dissects conduct and illustrates the charlatanism on one part and the superstition and stupidity on the other that creates fame, with diagramatic plainness. Living in an age when some of our grandfathers were too prejudice-ridden to wear boots, buttons, or suspenders we find him in his philosophy dashing off almost our deepest concepts with a lucidness equal to the description of the most common affairs of our time. His wit is like springing a dark-lantern in a sub-cellar, while his humor penetrates your anatomy to the marrow without allowing you to roar with laughter so skillfully is it woven in with philosophy, pathos, or tragedy. We heartily recommend it to our full-grown readers. Price in cloth $1.00; paper 50 cents.

For any of the above address

EQUITY PUBLISHING COMPANY,

P. O. Box 1678. San Francisco, Calif

EGOISM'S PRINCIPLES AND PURPOSE.

EGOISM'S purpose is the improvement of social existence through intelligent self-interest. It finds that whatever we have of equal conditions and mutual advantage is due to a prevalence of this principle corresponding with the degree and universality of individual resistance to encroachment.

Reflection will satisfy all who are desirous of being guided in their conclusions by fact, that as organization itself is a process of absorbing every material useful to its purpose, with no limit save that of outside resistance, so must the very fact of its being a separately organized entity make it impossible for it to act with ultimate reference to anything but itself. Observation will show that this holds good throughout the vegetable and animal kingdoms, and that whatever of equality exists among members of a species or between different species has its source and degree in the resisting capacity, of whatever kind, which such member or species can exert against the encroachment of other members or species. The human animal is no exception to this rule. True, its greater complexity has developed the expedient of sometimes performing acts with beneficial results to others, but this is at last analysis only resistance, because it is the only means of resisting the withholding by others from such other's welfare that which is more desirable than that with which he parts. If, then, the self-projecting faculty of mankind is such that it will in addition to the direct resistance common to the less complex animals, diplomatically exercise present sacrifice to further extend self, and it being a fact that equality depends upon equal resistance, diplomatic or otherwise, what are its chances in an absence of enlightenment in which the individuals of the majority so far from *intelligently* using this resisting power in their own behalf, do not even believe that they should do so? The result of a general conception so chaotic, would naturally be what we find: the generalization from the practical expediency of certain consideration for others, crystallized through the impulse of blind selfishness into a mysterious and oppressive obligation, credit for the observance of which gratifies the self-projecting faculty of the simple, while the more shrewd evade its exactions, and at every step from the manipulation of the general delusions of religious and political authority to the association of sexes and children at play, project themselves by exchanging this mythical credit for the real comforts and luxuries of the occasion, which the others produce. Thus in addition to the natural disadvantage of unequal capacity, the weaker are deprived through a superstition, of the use of such capacity as they have, as may be seen in their groping blindness all about us.

To secure and maintain equal conditions then, requires a rational understanding of the real object of life as indicated by the facts of its expression. It is plain that the world of humanity is made up of individuals absolutely separate; that life is to this humanity nothing save as it is something to one of these; that one of these can be nothing to another except as he detracts from or adds to his happiness; that on this is based the idea of social expediency; that the resistance of each of these individuals would determine what is socially expedient; that approximately equal resistance makes it equality, and on such continued and a universal resistance depends equality. This can leave no room for any sane action toward others but that of the policy promoting most the happiness of the acting Ego. Therefore EGOISM insists that the attainment of equal freedom depends upon a course of conduct replacing the idea of "duty to others" with *expediency* toward others; upon a recognition of the fact that self-pleasure must be the final motive of any act; thus developing a principle for a basis of action about which there can be no misunderstanding, and which will place every person squarely on the merit of his or her probable interests, divested of the opportunity to deceive through pretension, as under the dominance of altruistic idealism. It will maintain that what is generally recognized as morality is nothing other than the expediency deduced from conflicting interests under competition; that it is a policy which, through the hereditary influence of ancestral experience, confirmed by personal experience, is found to pay better than any other known policy; that the belief that it is something other than a policy—a fixed and eternal obligation, outside of and superior to man's recognized interests, and may not be changed as utility indicates, makes it a superstition in effect like any other superstition which causes its adherents to crystallize the expediency adopted by one period into positive regulations for another in which it has no utility, but becomes tyrannical laws and customs in the name of which persecution is justified, as in the fanaticism of any fixed idea.

Another part of its purpose is to help dispel the "Political Authority" superstition and develop a public sentiment which would replace State interference with the protection for person and property which the competition of protecting associations would afford. Then the State's fanatical tyranny and industry crushing privilege would torture the nerves of poverty-stricken old age or pinch tender youth no more. The most disastrous interference of this monster superstition is its prohibition of the issuing of exchange medium on the ample security of all kinds of property, which at once would abolish speculative interest and practically set all idle hands at productive labor at wages ever nearing the whole product until it should be reached. The next interference is by paper titles to vacant land instead of the just and reasonable one of occupancy and use, which with the employment that free money would give, would furnish all with comfortable homes in a short time, and thereafter even with luxuries from like exertion. Following this is its patent privilege, customs robbery, protective tariff, barbarous decrees in social and sexual affairs; its brutal policy of revenge, instead of restitution, in criminal offenses, and finally its supreme power to violate the individual, and its total irresponsibility.

Egoism

Vol. II.---No. 3. SAN FRANCISCO, CAL., JULY, 1891. Price, Five Cents.

Pointers.

George E. Macdonald, former editor of "Freethought," has severed his connection with that paper altogether, and gone to Snohomish, Wash., to take charge of a tri-weekly paper. His brilliancy besides winning him an enviable reputation in the Liberal world has secured for him a lucrative position in bohemian newspaperdom. He took passage with his wife and baby and everybody's good will, on the 5th of July.

Last month we noted that the Society for the Prevention of Cruelty to Children and Animals had petitioned the board of supervisors for a monthly allowance from the people's pocket, and we stated that appealing to popular prejudice gave it numbers, to which politicians must pander, and finally the society would be loaded squarely upon the people's back. All of this has not happened yet, but since that time an Oakland judge has decided that the society shall have all the fines collected from cases prosecuted by it, which besides the glory of charitable conquest, puts a financial premium upon the tyrannical meddling that characterizes this Christian police philanthrophy. The victims are unpopular and with this incentive will be hunted down like wild beasts by this "humane" society.

Comrade Westrup's suggestion to the Farmers' Alliance embodied in the appeal printed on another page is in part anticipated by a few weeks in Kansas, where the farmers are organizing the subtreasury scheme by means of private capital. The plan is to organize banks with warehouses at which farmers may deposit their grain or any imperishable product and receive in the bank's paper 80 per cent of the market price of the product, which is to be sold when the farmer orders it. This is a good start toward the Mutual Bank, as the banks' paper may come in conflict with the law that imposes a tax of 10 per cent on all unprivileged money. If they engage and overcome this point the Farmers' Alliance will not have existed in vain, and the road to free money will be well opened. The notes are redeemable in gold at any of the Alliance banks any time. This dependence on gold could put them to a great deal of trouble, as only 10 per cent is deposited with which to take up notes, and if their enemies should buy up the notes and present them before the farmers ordered the grain sold, a nice little premium could be exacted by the furnishers of the gold. The Mutual Bank, which proposes to redeem with products—the only things anybody has any use for save a jeweler, would not be subjected to this danger, nor be limited in its issue to the amount that can be redeemed with gold. But as the Alliance's present proposition is not encumbered by legal regulation, this feature can be changed as soon as the public calf is strong enough to be weaned from the golden confidence. We would not be surprised, however, to find that this is a scheme of Alliance politicians to illustrate the workings of the system in order to more easily drive the legal spike. The only hope is that they may be brought to see that the illustration is more desirable than the legal scheme they wish to inaugurate through it. The illustration is in the direction of freedom; it will allow any addition, or striking from the list of products deposited, that the convenience or safety of the interested parties may require, while under legal regulation a bad security must continue until congress meets and is convinced, or a new and good one may be deprived of credit in the same way. Besides these unavoidable evils there is the looseness of official favoritism in loaning government credit on insufficient security, or requiring more than a sufficient amount from a political opponent, and also a fixed rate of interest which if above cost cannot be reduced by competition, or if below cost must be made up from the pockets of those who have practically no voice in the management.

Zola's "Money," hitherto mentioned in these columns has been read, sketched, and much pondered over, but it is hard to give a comprehensive description of it in any ordinary space. It is at once a camera and chemist of human conduct and motive. Zola not only describes the carnivora, from the den it inhabits to the changing reflections of its glossy coat, but he tells what it is thinking about and will do. He realizes that the human animal is a none too much evoluted wild beast on the front of whose skull the experience of ages has worn only a bright spot, and he exposes all the greed, ferocious brutality, tyranny, cunning, hypocrisy, ostentation, truckling servility, idealism, and stupidity embodied in the kings, manipulators, and victims of a modern speculative world. The cruel and the generous, the detestable and the admirable traits of each character are delineated with an analytical nicety and a realistic accuracy that make the reader live the life of each and absorb the apology for their shortcomings without for a moment losing sight of the expedient course that should have replaced undesirable conduct. With an eloquently-implied regret he rebukes the horrors and cruelties of financial conquest without the wearisome moralizing or the narrow hatred common to the critics of social outrages. He is not a world builder nor a hero worshiper. Even Caroline, the lover of life, intelligent, educated, experienced, unprejudiced, and the heroine of the most trying ordeals of the story, was in his critical eyes full of weaknesses between which she was, inconsistently with her ideal of life, constantly vacillating. At world building he strikes State Socialism one of his efficient implied blows but sensate to the difficulties of wide innovation, he offers no remedy for industrial troubles, contenting himself with painting in bold relief and sharp contrast the almost fabulous extravagance of the rich and the horrifying wretchedness of the poor, along with emphasis on the fraud, sham, and wholesale manipulating of the unsuspecting, practiced by speculators. Yet he describes with effective force the spirit of rivalry, the entrancing pleasures, the magnificent enterprises, and even humanitarian dreams that prompt men to speculate even by the most gigantic fraud. And it is this, along with his realistic repletion that makes Zola such an admirable and to us unequaled novelist. His plot embraces almost every shade of character constituting modern civilization, and he depicts the virtues and weaknesses of each with a disinterest as faithful as his realism is striking. Even his reference to Egoism, a subject that impulsive French blood might readily balk on, is characterized by this faithfulness to the spirit of the subject in hand. His Egoist, though not the expansive utilitarian of our ideal, is nevertheless intrinsically Egoistic and approvably utilitarian in a comprehensive view of the subject. Although the story, true to life, contains a full complement of unsanctioned sexual alliances, the only woman rich or poor that gold could not influence was a little Freelover who contracted such association with desirable men just once through curiosity for pleasure alone. Saccard, his chief character, is a financial poet, a speculative madman who dreams only of money—millions, power, conquest, supremacy, the prostration at his feet of "all great, cowardly, truckling Paris." Ambitious, active, unscrupulous, assuming, an appropriator of other men's ideas—of everything that came in his reach, he wove from his own and borrowed imagination such alluring prospects as placed at his service the means beginning a career of speculation and spoilation the incidents and characters of which in Zola's masterly hands constitute the most startling expose of the power and tyranny of privileged money, the blind recklessness of stock gambling, and the ravenous greed of human avarice that we have read. We regard it as the ablest in our list, although no one can afford to be without the intensification of thought and feeling generated by all of them. The price of "Money" in cloth binding is $1; paper cover 50 cents. It may be ordered from us, but judging from the past, we think it doubtful.

Moralism Necessarily Criminal.

Such generally acceded principles of civilization as this age sustains are based on the law of equal freedom and maintain their solidity through the spontaneous support that the approximatively equal mental and physical strength of individuals involuntarily accords to the idea. So irrepressible is this rule that institutions organized to impede its operations affecting some parts of society, are immediately compelled to recognize it among their own members in order to hold together, illustrating that it is the fundamental principle of social existence. And if it is the fundamental principle of social existence, a violation of it is the fundamental social crime, and the first and in fact only one calling for restraint; for where equal freedom is not infringed there can be no rational complaint since the existence of an object enforces its occupancy of space.

It follows then that whoever does not violate the equal freedom of another is in no way amenable to another, and his actions are no more subject to restriction so far as the other is concerned than if neither actions nor that other existed. So to interfere with any one who is thus acting within the bounds of equal freedom and make him do what he does not wish to do, is to invade his equal freedom. And as people do not need to be forced to do what they like, it follows that there is nothing left for Moralism to do but to force people to do what they do not like, and thereby violate their equal freedom. And it is this fact that makes Moralism necessarily criminal, however popular it may be. Some may claim that enforcing equal freedom by restraining invasion is the Moralistic function, but that would leave the Moralists without a name for the major part of their action, which is not based on equal freedom, but is an obvious violation of it. It would also have to drive the term "equal freedom" out of use for want of an idea to represent, while it left the invasions of Moralistic practice as undefended as before.

The plausibility of the theory that Moralism is necessarily invasive because there is nothing else left for it to be, is fully substantiated by the facts of its practices. Take the instance of the State's love of others' welfare in securing for "society" a "sound" exchange medium. It intrenched interest, and placed the control of trade in the hands of privileged property owners by depriving all except one kind from being represented in exchange by certificates, thereby violating the equal freedom of almost the whole community to the extent of the whole deprivation and misery of idle, and of underpaid labor. But for this piece of Moralistic authoritarianism there would be no labor question today. Simple, spontaneous, equal freedom would have made a garden of what is now desert, and feasting and vigor would reign where starvation and lingering death hold sway in the midst of unparalleled production. All is due to that popular and overweaning solicitude for others' welfare which hesitates not at violating their equal freedom even to the extent of taking their lives for their own good. A recognized enemy is readily repulsed, but palavering Moralism with its scoop-shaped sympathy for abstract society and its contempt for the individual, is not suspected. In the name of the "general good" it can systematically violate equal freedom with its coercing of the variability of genius into the deep-trodden trails of majority mediocrity.

Take for instance its invading proclivity in sexual relations. It will persecute to the grave participants in the most spontaneous and voluntary sex association imaginable, while it defends and perpetuates a sexual institution productive of and practicing the most outrageous of invasions. One which forces women into almost continuous maternity through the best years of life, sapping their strength, monopolizing their time for intellectual improvement, and leaving them either in the grave or impulseless and uninteresting machines living only to envy pleasure and disperse joy. And men with splendid social natures and fine intellects capable of spreading pleasure and enlightenment in the most effective manner, are harnessed to jealous frames, hedged in by commonplace ideals, and driven from the enrichment of social life to money gathering drudgery and "family duty." It also countenances the forcing by strong men of weakly wives into nothing less than actual rape. But if men and women of equal strength and willingness seek pleasure without the slavery attachment, it imprisons and persecutes them until their lives are unbearable.

A conspicuous local instance of Moralistic meddling is the case of the Oakland pool-rooms. Here certain men have arranged conveniences for gambling, and certain other men stake their own money on races at odds great or small, winning or losing as the case may be. They are not compelled to gamble and if they failed to go to the rooms at all, the pool-sellers would not capture and carry them there. Those who go can stop at any time. Everything is voluntary and no one is invaded in any way.

How different the conduct of the Moralists. Instead of going about the pursuit of gaining independent livelihood and pleasure, as equal freedom requires, they were found appealing to the State club to drive the uninvading pool-sellers out of the town. Failing in this they at once set about defaming the city council and creating antagonism and bad blood where peace and at most disinterest had hitherto prevailed. This proving fruitless they sought to injure the patrons of the rooms by publishing their names for the purpose of injuring them in business and social advantage through the prejudice against gambling. And all this in a matter that was none of their business whatever, since it violated no one's equal freedom, while they did everything in their power to do so by trying to have the pool-room men removed by force.

It is admitted that the pool-rooms are no more advantage to the city than the churches, preachers, and politicians, but the Moralists have said nothing about driving out the latter because of their uselessness. The pool-sellers in particular are harmless beside the politicians who force the unwilling to patronize them. Yet the Moralists defend the latter. They defend the terms of privilege which constitute the State a great pool institution through which a few win while the great mass loses—a game in which all must stake or die. There is no freedom to let it alone as with the pool-rooms. It compels you to stake when you are sure to lose. And it is this flagrant violation of equal freedom that makes it criminal, where at worst the pool-sellers' game is only foolish for those who lose. And in confirmation of the theory advanced, it is the criminal game that the Moralists defend, because their function is not needed to make people do what they like by following their interests. H.

Editorial Slashes.

The Young Men's Christian Association clubs are now giving stereopticon exhibitions of the Johnstown flood. Thus God, besides killing a lot of human fowl, kills two other birds with the same stone by exhibiting his divine wrath and filling his treasury at the same time. This suggests his Jewish heredity.

California has modestly secured only one-fourth of the space allotted to state exhibits at the World's Fair. This will be plenty of room in which to exhibit its massive pumpkins, energetic fleas, and marvelous beets, but I fear that sufficient provision has not been made for its principal production—real estate boom. The beets referred to do not include the beats of the real estate transactions. Like our big trees, the latter would have to be transported in sections. A sufficient number can be produced right at the exhibition, while you wait.

The mayor of Oakland recently appointed a homeopathic doctor to fill a vacancy on the board of health. The appearance of a strange fowl in the allopathic barnyard caused a regular stampede and all the old force threatened to resign—but they didn't. The newspapers took up the cry and made much sport over some misspelled words in a death certificate made out by this man of "little pills" who aspired to sit in council with doctors whose prejudices are as strong as their medicines. It strikes me that these allopathy doctors have as much to learn about the rational treatment of diseases—of course prevention is no part of their business—as the homeopathic doctor has to learn about orthography. The difference in the number of death certificates the two schools have to issue would be one solution for the difference in spelling.

About six months ago a young man well stocked with flattery and gall canvassed the aristocratic residences of Oakland and succeeded in selling to a great many women books in sets of four each, at $36 per set, by representing that the amount would be collected in installments at the rate of five cents a day. He had them sign what purported to be two receipts, one for himself and another for the company. One of these proved to be a promissory note for the full amount, which was presented recently by a collection agency for the women to pay. In reporting the affair the Oakland "Tribune" said:

> The cause of woman's suffrage has received another setback, and the superiority of man has again been demonstrated. A red-headed book agent has swindled nearly all the lady leaders of Oakland society.

This is remarkable! But when farmers, for the purpose of ridding their locality of troublesome birds or insects, sign purported contracts which they afterward discover to be promissory notes, their verdancy is attributed to inexperience, not having been rendered cautious by business competition and commercial trickery. But when women who have had no business experience are caught in the same net it is due to their sex and inferiority. No one ever heard that the farmers were unfitted for suffrage on account of being victimized, nor is there anything to indicate that they are, since they have failed to show themselves bigger fools than their city brethren at throwing away liberty. But how women could do worse than either would be an interesting piece of illustration. G.

As evinced by his attitude on the "obscenity" cases of Elmina D. Slenker and Moses Harman, and later the persecution of C. L. Swartz, at Topeka, Kansas, the editor of the New York "Truth Seeker" appears to be considerably afflicted with sex superstition. This has caused him to say some things of Mr. Swartz that he will be less proud of as time passes. A "western correspondent" whom the editor seems particularly anxious to believe has in an assertive and prejudice-smacking paragraph informed him that the Kansas City Sunday "Sun," for the selling of which Mr. Swartz is under arrest, is a blackmailing and libelous sheet which thrives by circulating social scandal, gathered by "backdoor sneaks." Thereupon the editor rushes to the front to say that Mr. Swartz "ought to be buried a mile deep under libel suits, and whether he is held in bail in four or forty thousand dollars he gets nothing more than he deserves." Mr. Swartz is not under arrest for circulating libelous matter, but that of "immoral literature," just as a vender of the "Truth Seeker" might be charged if the church had at its command a blasphemy law. Blasphemy and immorality are alike real and alike criminal; the "Truth Seeker," a step ahead of the church, has dropped one superstition and not the other, which is the only difference. Neither is it probable that the "Sun's" reports are not as true as those of the daily press, a matter which venders can know nothing about. If the matter was generally true Mr. Swartz is not only innocent of invasion, but indirectly a social benefactor as legitimately as any one who circulates the "Truth Seeker" or any other paper that exposes a hypocritical and tyrannous institution. If the "Truth Seeker" does not know that society's pretension to chastity and its cruel attempts to enforce it are as unreasonable, hypocritical, tyrannous, and subversive of equal freedom and general happiness as are the claims and the practices of the church, it is because it closes its eyes and ears to ever present evidence just as the church does. The "Sun's" scandal necessarily consists of accounts of non-conformity to the senseless demands of popular error regarding sexual relations, and thus negatively attests the inadequacy of present institutions to fill the requirements of general advancement just as newspaper accounts of theological heresy attest the same of church dogmas. Before church people the latter is scandal, but it helps expose tyrannical church domination and anti-theological Liberals do not complain of the scandal the victims are subjected to among church people, because such scandal is irrational and logically a credit to the slandered person. The same is true of sexual innovators, their conduct rationally considered is correct; they have not violated equal freedom and are in no wise logically subject to reproach, but on the contrary have inaugurated a course of conduct better adapting means to pleasurable ends, winning the approval of all rational people and the gratitude of those desiring the benefits of such a better way, just as in the case of theological heretics. The unsociable acts are all committed by those who boycott rational conduct because it is not conventional, and not by those who circulate accounts of it, showing the old way is no longer satisfactory. Of the boycotters the "Truth Seeker" is evidently one, for it regards such conduct as scandalous just as the church does that of its heretics, because it is not the old way. As present sexual ethics give away to more freedom the "Truth Seeker" will be less and less proud of its attitude against their exposure.

Last month Arthur McCartney, of this city, had an experience with the effect of the sex superstition in the shape of a howling Missouri mob at Kansas City. He probably nurses this superstition as devotedly as the mob did without realizing it, illustrating how members of the race may for ages writhe from being impaled on the spear of a superstition and not be conscious that each is treating his neighbor to the useless torture that he himself endures. Mr. McCartney, when escorting his two daughters from a carriage to a train, was mistaken for Schweinfurth, a female captivating modern Messiah, and the mossy roosters believing that he was taking two of Kansas City's women away, attempted to mob him. Fortunately he carried a revolver, with which he held at bay their frenzied virtue until he had time to explain that he was not the Messiah, whereupon the pelvic despots sheepishly retired.

They had rushed upon him shouting: "Kill him, he's no Christ! He cannot take our women to Rockford. Say, you had better confess before we give you a coat of tar and feathers." Pitiable plight of helpless brutality. There they were publicly acknowledging their inferiority in not being able to compel the admiration of their women by physical symmetry or mental subtlety. Their wives confined to the dull monotony of monogamic life make an epoch of a thrill of new magnetism, and their daughters, suppressed beyond even the miserable advantages of this depleting palliative, are likely to lose their heads altogether and follow off a wagon, if exposed. Cognizant of these facts without knowing their cause, and too blindly selfish to allow the remedy if they knew it, these primitive barbarians were ready to resort to the methods of wild beasts by destroying competitors instead of outshining them, or better still, leaning as little on others as others do on them. What a satisfaction it must be to men with "faithfulness" as their ideal, to be caressed in arms so willing to receive another that the other is absent only by virtue of a ready club or bullet! How proud these women should be to be heralded as choiceless spawners who, if not herded, would follow off anything male! H.

A Varying Standard of Value and a Neutralizer.

As contrasted with a standard of value it appears correct to say that a measure of length possesses length in itself, for whereas the variations in value of other things exchanged affect the value of the object taken as a standard, on the other hand the variations in length of things measured do not cause changes in the length of the yardstick. Its variation, if any (ifintesimal and therefore left out of account), depends upon its physical qualities, which without entering upon metaphysics is a way of saying that it possesses extension in itself to the apprehension of the human mind. Having noted the comparatively serious theoretical difference as to a standard of value, the "News" had thought to show a countervailing difference touching such standard. If not all that could be desired, still it is claimed as countervailing to a large extent referring to valuation for security. But the Boston "Liberty" while holding to the necessity for a standard of value, thinks that the best must remain very imperfect, and presents the following illustration:

> In the supposed case of a bank loan secured by mortgage, the margin between the valuation and the obligation practically secures the note holder against loss in decline of the value of the security, but it does not secure him against loss from a decline in the value of the standard. Suppose that a farmer, having a farm worth $5000 in gold, mortgages it to a bank as security for a loan of $2500 in notes newly issued by the bank against this farm. With these notes he purchases implements from a manufacturer. When the mortgage expires a year later he fails to lift it. Meanwhile gold has declined in value. The farm is sold under the hammer and brings instead of $5000 in gold, $6000 in gold. Of this sum $2500 is used to meet the notes held by the manufacturer who took them a year before in payment for the implements sold to the farmer. Now, can the manufacturer buy back his implements for $2500 in gold? Manifestly not, for by the hypothesis gold has gone down. Why, then, is not this manufacturer a sufferer from the variation in the standard of value precisely as the man who buys cloth with a short yardstick and sells it with a long one is a sufferer from the variation in the standard of length?

But it sagely concludes that such evils, so far as they arise from natural causes, must be borne. The statement of this difficulty is an interesting contribution to the study of the money question. In reply to the direct question it might be answered: the manufacturer is suffering from the variation in the value of gold as a means of payment. But it is strange if the manufacturer has held these bank notes a year in his safe. He might have paid them away and received them again several times, spreading the loss by the decline in the value of gold over the mass of traders. It can be said that one and the same yardstick does not vary, hence part of the illustration goes to reaffirm the distinction made between a standard for valuation and a measure of length. The chief interest, however, of this very suggestive criticism is that it leads one to reflect both upon the necessity for capital to be active in order to be conserved, and upon the possibility of having bank notes secured not merely upon an ample basis such as a double amount of valuation in gold, but otherwise as to substitute payments. The notes themselves would not necessarily share the decline of gold were the mortgage not to be released on optional payment of a fixed sum in gold. Some provision must always be made for settlement when notes are lost; but for example, it might be agreed that the alternative settlement should be as much gold as would buy 20 per cent of the present value in each of five specified articles of general necessity.—Galveston News.

A Proposition to Extend Mutual Bank Propaganda.

To the Friends of Liberty:

A new and equitable monetary system is essential to save the people from impending ruin and ultimate revolution by violence.

The first and all-sufficient objection which Greenbackers and Nationalists have not duly considered before advocating an exclusive government money system, is the principle of liberty which is involved. The Mutual Bank Propaganda affirms that no government has the right to interfere with the production and exchange of commodities; that authority in the Constitution, if there is any, is no valid reason for doing so. The question is not whether it is constitutional, but whether it is right. This is fundamental and unavoidable. To say that an act is right because it is constitutional is to affirm the dogma of infallibility and put and end to progress. That the Constitution has been amended several times proves its imperfection, and we regard human welfare of such paramount importance that we seek the shorter method of creating public sentiment in favor of liberty, realizing how futile are appeals to the class that make and unmake the laws.

These are sufficient reasons for opposing the Greenback or Nationalist idea, although they are not the only ones, as will be seen by our literature.

What are the Greenbackers' and what are the Nationalists' reasons for opposing us? If they really want a money that will supply money at cost to all borrowers who can furnish good security, issuing the money direct on the collateral, why do they prefer the government to the mutual system? In all my experience of sixteen years' study of this question I have never met a Greenbacker or a Nationalist or Socialist who had any more than a vague idea of our aims and methods, while those who are reading our literature are deserting the ranks of the paternalists and now help the party of freedom. On the other hand, who ever heard of a Mutual Banker becoming a paternalist? Some day you will all be Mutual Bankers. You are not so already, because you do not understand our system. With the numbers, and the influence and means at the command of the Alliances, a movement could be inaugurated that would result in complete victory in less than a year. Is such assurance not worth investigating? We affirm that our plan is the *only* means by which the money power can be defeated. Let me earnestly ask our brothers in the cause of justice: Look squarely at the difficulties staring you in the face and tell me frankly, what hope is there for establishing your system in one year—ten years—ever? You are clamoring for law! You do not need law; in this case it is your worst enemy.

For thirty millions of workers to endure unspeakable sufferings and wait year after year, begging of a few thousand of their fellow men the privilege (?) of becoming prosperous, is a spectacle that staggers the intellect and faith in manhood! Money controls legislation, and you ask money to legistate against itself. Money creates its own privilege and derives its power, not as a medium of exchange, but that of *monopoly*, from the laws which it had no right to enact, and instead of contesting such laws you bow with superstitious reverence, continue to suffer and meekly ask money to release its grip. Our method is quite different. We declare that it is not law, but good security that makes paper perform the functions of money purely as a medium of exchange. Therefore we call upon all who want a system that will furnish such an instrument of exchange at cost to all borrowers to join the Mutual Bank Propaganda and help raise ten thousand dollars to establish a Mutual Bank, issue money and fight the money power in the courts. By this means we bring the question before the people in double quick time by compelling the daily papers to grapple with instead of ignoring it as they do now. The issue must be fought on its merits—the right of citizens to associate and provide a medium of exchange for their own use and to relieve themselves from the oppression of usurers and promote prosperity. This right cannot be denied—take it! You are the majority! This method of settling the money question is new to most people. It is a phase of the question that the people generally are totally ignorant of, it never having been a subject of general public discussion; but when it shall have been thoroughly discussed by the whole people, a mighty wave of indignation will go forth and will wipe out forever the only stronghold of tyranny—*the monopoly of money*.

There is no advantage claimed for the Greenback, or any other system that is not transcended in the Mutual system as is clearly set forth in our literature. We have spent thousands of dollars in time and money advancing these ideas although we do not expect to reap any advantage that will not result alike to all our fellows, except, perhaps, a little fame for having advocated it so persistently; but in addition to this we will put up one thousand dollars in cash and we have been promised another thousand as soon as an additional sum of eight thousand dollars is subscribed; thus making an expense fund of ten thousand dollars to establish a Mutual Bank and defend our right in the courts.

Those who have not read carefully our literature on this, the gravest of all questions, should procure our pamphlets and post themselves on the *mutual* feature applied to banks of issue.

Of those who are with us we ask all the encouragement you can give. It is your fight as well as ours, and it will not commence until those who know they have rights, dare maintain them. Remember our object is to make a test case in the courts. This course [...] will stimulate thought and discussion, creating public sentiment on the side of right, until we shall have overcome all opposition, from whatever source.

Let us hear from you. ALFRED B. WESTRUP,
Corresponding Secretary.
343 Michigan Ave., Chicago, Ill.

Managerial Experience.

I have many even marked experiences that are not noted in these columns, but I have just masticated one that has not escaped my memory, one which I had for some time looked forward to as one might to undesired death; without longing, yet under heavy suspense. It was the extraction from this city and my companionship of George E. Macdonald. It has seldom been my privilege to be an intimate of ever refreshing genius, and it was with reluctance and ocular tide that I gave it up. His temperment and manner are much like those of my father, and this semi-conscious biological attachment supplemented by sentimental congeniality, his searching sympathetic nature, and the kaleidoscopic variability of genius brought him as close the quick of my appreciation as a male is likely to get. In these years of almost continual association the time never came when he passed in and out of my optical range leaving the sense of wearying monotony that so many people impart in common with dreary scenery and lazily buzzing flies on a sultry August morning. His presence was always marked with an undivined word or act. If he failed to do a new thing he did not fail to do the old one in a new way.

Evenings and Sundays when everybody else was gone it was his custom to bring a chair and his pipe to the composing-room, after which my case accumulated little type during the hours that followed in which we held mental stereopticon exhibitions, canvassing every thought and experience with that abandon mostly confined to the walls of a single cranium. We propounded every suggestion of a question and left many of them unanswered without apology. We determined, however, that consciousness is all that is experienced of life and, free from pain, independence is its greatest pleasure. Therefore when the body is provided for, instead of pandering to hoary prejudice to better gather surplus wealth, we will prop our hands upon our hips and denounce oppression, after which we will join our friends in an informal picnic in the sunshine or in the shade, and at night the body will have been comfortable, the mind independent, and pleasure not broken by the drawn faces or bleaching bones of plundered victims. We found that the nature of consciousness being such that it can act only in ultimate reference to self, fraternity is a mirage arising from a failure to recognize the advantages of social intercourse as advantages of social commerce instead of charitable generosity; that its existence would displace equal freedom, without which there could be no conception of justice or standard of conduct; and that sacrifice and invasion are synonymous terms not differing in their effect upon the general welfare. Therefore the rational business of life is personal pleasure, to which all social principles are subservient expedients or subversive superstitions. Thereupon we put on our hats and coats and went home because it seemed more pleasant than to sit in the office the rest of the night.

Mr. Macdonald and his wife and their son, the Young Pacific Coast Anarchist of radical fame, spent part of what Mr. Macdonald termed their last Sunday on earth, visiting EGOISM's aristocratic publishers. The father carried the youngster up our stairway, from the ceiling of which I had carefully swept the cobwebs for the first time in the two years that we have lived here. When our guests had crept in, my wife and her little niece promptly took charge of torturing the baby, and it being one of the three famous hot days of the season, Mr. Macdonald when urged to make himself as comfortable as possible by removing his coat, like a true philosopher did so, while I allowed the brisk breeze of my conversation to blow coolingly upon Mrs. Macdonald. We all diluted ourselves freely with iced lemonade and with ice-water straight, and drifted about the flat for a cool place like flies between meal hours. Mr. Macdonald and I explored in his absence W. S. Bell's den, and later EGOISM's 7x9 printing office. There is not room enough in it to hold two persons at one time, so Mr. Macdonald stood in the doorway while I showed him through, then we went into the kitchen and turned around and he went in the office first and sat him upon the pile of dampened paper from which this issue is printed, while I seated on my heels reclined on the veals of my shanks and we communed as we are wont in a composing-room. As with a dull butcher knife he found near by he whittled a piece of box-wood quoin and seriously discoursed on the heaviest and most radical issues of the day, few of his thousands of admiring readers would have suspected him of being the renowned Freethought humorist whose productions have so relentlessly exhausted their diaphragms.

At the table he discovered that we keep house about as they do and expressed himself as feeling very much at home in such environment. However this may be it is nevertheless a fact that he enjoys the hospitality of those who condense in the fare of one person at a single meal the price of several days of such board as we were corralling. But this did not prevent his accommodating himself with Grace and the baby to the proletaires' victuals, and we lingered pleasantly amid the cherry pits and remnants of ice-water. After we had played eat, I showed Mr. Macdonald the model of my new elevated railroad the intricacies of which caused him to reflect so deeply that he fell asleep while I was explaining its workings to him but upon waking agreed with me that it was a great thing, which was to me a joyful surprise as I sat on my hock joints puzzling how to gracefully emerge from this inflicting of so intense a theme upon my esteemed guest.

I of course do not *know* just what will happen in the hence, but the drift of things indicates that the contact intimacy that I have enjoyed with my friend is forever past, and this bitter thought has driven me to seek what comfort I can in writing this obituary with an unreserve that might in some respects displease him under other circumstances unless he were inanimately dead.

San Francisco has a society known as the Koreshan society. Among other intellectual acrobatics its members have to perform the feat of believing that the earth is a hollow globe and that we live inside of it. This I think is not difficult for many of them to do as they have not been biased by other astronomical theories of any sort. The charter members were, I am informed, generally old women of both sexes who being to diffident to encourage the sexual faculty of others into the more sanguine exercise of the function, gave themselves up to the cultivation of theosophical asceticism and are now celibates, at least for awhile. Celibacy is very bearable to very weary people. I have been one sometimes, and often against my will.

But proposed crucifixion of the flesh in modern times is no good, it always invents some alternative. These celibates hold that by some method which I do not understand, they can turn back to the condition of that more primitive stage in evolution when the individual animal could impregnate itself. This would be eminently more respectable, and does not involve that democratic, if not even communistic mixing up with others now practiced in reproducing the human animal. If it works it will also be convenient and economical, as no marriage license will be required and mothers will not have to worry themselves with match-making. It will also dispense with bastardy suits and divorce, as well as prove "Marriage a Failure." It is an improvement on Elmina D. Slenker's inferiority-of-the-male-sex theory, for it dispenses with the use of that sex altogether, while she would have it around for impregnating purposes and perhaps to do other chores when not thus engaged. I do not know whether the whole human race can hope to unravel back to this ante-vertebrate degree or not, but I feel certain that people with these ideas have a biological incomplexity of structure that gives them a long start of the average coarse and unesthetic mortal in this race of crawfishing.

There are so many advertisements on the backs of country newspapers, offering treatment for the ravages of unsuccessful attempts at this kind of celibacy that I advise these people to wait at least until all traces of the spinal column have disappeared before they attempt reproduction in this newfangled way. Meanwhile, to help tide them over inherited tendencies, I would prescribe for their use pulverized alum. It should be taken internally in such quantities as prove effective. The effect can be intensified by baths in a strong solution of the mineral. I know of nothing more productive of virtue, and I earnestly hope they will heed this solicitude on my part, and not palm off on an unsuspecting community offspring purporting to be the result of the new self-impregnating process, which are really the old make. The fact might be concealed for awhile, but when these helpless victims of ascetic suppression grow up the inherited and intensified longings of their parents will cause them to assault men and women at sight as spontaneously as they breathe. Popular suppression, with its laws to protect rape under certain contracts gives us enough of this tendency. Let us not be afflicted then with its intensification through a fraudulent celibacy. I have to be on the streets of this city a great deal and am not strong enough to be exposed to such an attack. Breeding will not be necessary anyway, for as long as the feeble-minded old bourgeoisie can maintain free board and lodging they will, under present economic conditions, have an abundance of disciples. I admonish them therefore to use the alum and give the world a lesson in the science of chemical morality.

The preceding remarks break the ice for a few suggestions to the vice society of San Francisco. If, instead of attempting to suppress pictures of voluptuous beauty and thereby heightening curiosity concerning it, the vice society would employ means to make the population indifferent to "obscene" literature and pictures, it might hope to succeed in spreading ascetic principles. If the secretary would arrange with all the bakers, brewers, and butchers to salt their goods well with pulverized alum, the most vigorous attitude of the most exquisitely chiseled muscle, feature, and form would no more produce licentious thoughts in the citizens' minds than gazing upon the monster of a Chinese banner. Prostitution would cease, and the secretary could not then hire its members to dance before him in nude attire that he might arrest them. I think, however, a great saving of alum and happiness for the community could be effected by the society *only* taking copious and continuous doses of it. This would cause the society to lose interest in the subject, and as no one else is visibly disturbed by the fact that growing intelligence loves beauty of form and develops sexual poetry, life would move along in that variable fullness that makes it nearer worth living.

Besides death, nothing is so virtuous as alum, and it is ardently desired that until these people can secure virtue in its most rigid and ideal form they will not spare the drug.

Although the "Beacon" and Egoism are at swords points regarding methods in the great social revolution which is past and which will be coming as long as energy concentrates in consciousness, we nevertheless maintain cordial social relations, and after much arranging and appointing between us Egoism was favored on a recent Sunday with a visit from some members of the "Beacon's" staff accompanied by a friend. It wouldn't do to show a weak hand in the commissary department in entertaining competitors, so I bought two-bits worth of green peas which were too ripe, a hunk of calf thigh, box of cherries, and a new brick of butter. "Brick" does not indicate the solidity of the butter at this time in the year but describes it in the sense in which a man is said to be a "brick" or hard case. When all these raw and rare luxuries were piled high in the pantry I did not pry off the lid of the cherry-box, for that would probably have resulted in a chemical combination of my wife's little niece and the cherries which might have exploded.

In order to have things out of the way and the house nicely cooled off by the time our guests should arrive, I arose in the youthful and fuzzy hours of the morning, and with excruciating diligence and a short-handled shovel cleaned about three pecks of soot and ashes from under and around the oven of our cook stove. After I got the soot off the floor except what little went into the ash-pan at which I aimed it all, I built a fire and took a wash and hearty swear at stove-cleaning in general. Then I walloped the calf limb and the front of my iron-gray pants in flour, and when the other calf's anatomy was secured in the oven I poked the fire and in my attempt to keep the infant bovine comfortable roasted my countenance to a finish. I found that heat goes upward mostly, and am much surprised that stovemakers in their apparent anxiety to keep the oven cool never struck the idea of locating it in the cellar in an ice-chest instead of just back of and below the fire. It seems to me that a person with even half sense should know that meat kept so near the fire a little while will spoil. In this case it produced quite a fever in the veal which I soothed as best I could by dipping gravy on its "parched lips." I am a tender nurse—more tender than this roast proved. This dipping is called "basting," and is better than the method now in vogue among dressmakers, as the threads do not show in fitting the roast to the form.

About six o'clock, a few hours after I had things moving, my wife vacated the posterior part of the secretary in which she sleeps and helped hull the peas and pick the sound cherries from among the mouldy and rotten ones, so that by the time our visitors came everything was placid.

In entertaining I tried to be very affable and pleasant, but am so out of practice and looked so agonized that my wife thought I had stolen and eaten too many cherries. I saw that she seemed provoked at my hilarious sallies, and thought that she was jealous of my superior entertaining capacity. Having eaten a fill of rotten ones, I had not stolen any of the good cherries, and in my innocence did not suspect the real nature of my wife's uneasiness until going to the glass to adjust the silken garter I had that morning borrowed and was using for a tie, I witnessed one of my smiles congealing. It strongly resembled the facial exercise of cholera morbus mingled with that of a bruised shinbone. I immediately retired to the kitchen to reflect upon the vanity of life and cook the peas. I could notice that the company grew easier when left to the spontaneous grace of my unostentatious wife.

That they might attend a meeting at San Francisco at 2 p.m. our guests had to take the 1 o'clock train, and at 12:30 the peas were scarcely done, but I franticly tumbled them along with the butter, cherries, and other luxuries upon the table, and after the guests were seated and I had inflicted upon them the joke I studied up the week before, I glode triumphantly from the pantry with the roast, only to find that after all my anguish our guests, except one, were vegetarians and I a damfool. Of the latter I was still more certain when fifteen minutes later they had to leave a half-finished meal to catch the train. If we ever succeed in getting anybody else to visit us I shall neither roast meat, smile exaggeratingly, nor get them so late to the table.

I have read in the "Beacon," from the pen of Mr. Sigismund Danielewicz, one of the guests, some physical resistance matter that might easily frighten a policeman with a diamond-set finger ring and a complacent gait, but he is not a dangerous-acting man at all. On the contrary he is a very mild-mannered man, almost pathetic in disposition. Even I do not feel afraid of him. I do not think it consistent however, for people to be so reckless of human life as physical revolutionists propose to be, and at the same time refuse to eat flesh on the ethical ground of thereby discouraging the taking of animal life, a position which at least part of the "Beacon's" staff assumes. I once heard a good man say he would rather eat a dead man than kill a live one, if he had to do one or the other. I want my human flesh alive but it must not be that of a man, nor will I eat it, although some that I have witnessed looked sweet enough to make me feel as though I would like at least to bite it caressingly.

Gems, and Straws in the Breeze.

OPPORTUNISTS are misled by number. They believe in working for any reform which is "a step in the right direction," provided they can thereby influence a large number. Frequently the "reform" contains about one per cent of truth, the other ninety-nine per cent being made up of sentimental bosh and lies. The opportunists waste energy in fighting for all sorts of foolish measures simply because they happen to contain a little truth. One hundred persons influenced for a little one per cent reform, arithmetically speaking, would be equal to one person influenced for thorough reform. Opportunists should not, therefore, be misled by number, but should remember that one person, where ideas are concerned, is frequently an "effective majority" over hundreds. Convince that one person that your ideas are right and you have effected more perhaps, than if you had turned an entire party "in the right direction."—George Forest.

WERE free banking added to the repeal of duty on lead and the repeal of all government certificate privileges in the interest of any private owners, whether of silver or gold, the country would be better supplied with better currency and this excessive silver mining would become quite unnecessary. It does not seem too much to say that labor might be better employed in cultivating the ground or sinking artesian wells than in feverish attempts to add to a stock of metal to be kept in bars. But under the present scarcity system of currency basis the prompting given to individual interest can be only what it actually is. Public policy shapes private conduct in this as in so many other matters where the law has stepped in to supersede natural inducements with its own paternally contrived ameliorations of the distresses inflicted by its repressions.—Galveston News.

THIS feeling, which has been called Sympathy, has usually been considered as feeling *for* others. I believe it to be a mistake and that we actually feel *with* others. The difference is immense. For if we feel for others, whatever we do for them is of no benefit to us, while if we feel with others, in helping them we are at the same time helping our own happiness, and this duty to self includes the welfare of others, and selfishness can be truly taken for our guide, for the care of self includes the care of others.—Albert Chavannes.

THE teachings of Christ had more in view the suppression of selfishness than the salvation of souls, and his followers have faithfully preached the duty of taking care of others at the expense of care of self. From these teachings has bloomed out the ethical idea of our day, the *duty* of taking care of others, an idea that permeates all the reform movements of our times, but which being false in its inception and false in its deduction, can never be made the basis of a successful progressive movement.—Albert Chavannes.

THE cadets at West Point each have from thirty-five to fifty pairs of white duck trousers. At least three pairs are worn each day. They and the laundry bills are paid out of the products of the toilers by compulsory taxation. But then, the toilers, as a rule, are well pleased to have it so. When a man is under the influence of the government superstition, he is willing to and finds pleasure in wearing ragged trousers in order to have the cadets extravagantly dressed. —Hugh O. Pentecost.

THE "Times" tells a pretty story of a married couple who were unhappy and who went to Ohio and procured a divorce. The divorce was not complete, however, until the papers were filed in a certain official's office. After getting the papers and before filing them, the couple talked matters over and agreed not to file them for awhile. They have been living happily together ever since —for ten years. The papers may be filed at any time, the "Times" says, and the divorce be consummated, but since each can be free from the other neither wishes to be. The lesson is plain whether the story is true or not. Freedom is necessary to a happy marriage, as it is to happiness in all the relations in life.—Hugh O. Pentecost.

MY countrymen, I am proud of you; your interest in these people [the noble baccarat party] shows that you are incontestibly superior to the incurious hog and indolent cat. To "begin to take notice" has ever been considered in the young of our species, a symptom of dawning intelligence. As with the individual, so with the race of which he is but the concrete expression. As a tribe we Americans are young; we are but a child —a kid—a dambrat. We lie in the cradle of Fate, earnestly gumming away at our precious thumb, with almost human voracity, and—we "begin to take notice!" We observe a king, a prince, a nobleman, a baronet, even a knight. Attesting their conspicuousness in the main and general sum of things, we knock off work upon the edible thumb and stare with both our beady eyes. O, we're a sweet young thing, and it has wisely been pointed out by one of our most illustrious wet-nurses that our future is all before us. It looks at present as if our national career might be as striking and picturesque as that of the Gadarene swine.— Ambrose Bierce in the "Examiner."

MR. C. R. BENNETT, who is secretary of a society for the suppression of vice in others, announces his intention to head a mob to lynch the Oakland pool-sellers if they do not leave town and their supporters in the city council if they do not resign. Mr. Bennett is a gallant man, but when the mob convenes and takes up the line of march he will not head the procession: he will move along on a parallel line, a little to the rear, strenuously deflating his lung of formidable whoops. It is pleasant, all the same, to observe that this child of light is not so austere a stickler for observance of law as he has been thought to be. While he has not as yet shown any symptoms of abated zeal in the prosecution of such giant criminals as those who favor the co-existence of the sexes, there is a reasonable hope that in assassinating objectionable public characters we shall enjoy henceforth a reasonable immunity from his molesting hand. The hope represents a distinct advance in the pursuit of happiness. Whenever we are permitted to hang our neighbors according to the dictates of our conscience, the most trivial circumstance may become a minister of pleasure and a herald of good by suggesting the hanging of Mr. Bennett.—Bierce in "Exa'r."

EGOISM'S PRINCIPLES AND PURPOSE.

Egoism's purpose is the improvement of social existence through intelligent self-interest. It finds that whatever we have of equal conditions and mutual advantage is due to a prevalence of this principle corresponding with the degree and universality of individual resistance to encroachment.

Reflection will satisfy all who are desirous of being guided in their conclusions by fact, that as organization itself is a process of absorbing every material useful to its purpose, with no limit save that of outside resistance, so must the very fact of its being a separately organized entity make it impossible for it to act with ultimate reference to anything but itself. Observation will show that this holds good throughout the vegetable and animal kingdoms, and that whatever of equality exists among members of a species or between different species has its source and degree in the resisting capacity, of whatever kind, which such member or species can exert against the encroachment of other members or species. The human animal is no exception to this rule. True, its greater complexity has developed the expedient of sometimes performing acts with beneficial results to others, but this is at last analysis only resistance, because it is the only means of resisting the withholding by others from such actor's welfare that which is more desirable than that with which he parts. If, then, the self-projecting faculty of mankind is such that it will in addition to the direct resistance common to the less complex animals, diplomatically exercise present sacrifice to further extend self, and it being a fact that equality depends upon equal resistance, diplomatic or otherwise, what are its chances in an absence of enlightenment in which the individuals of the majority so far from *intelligently* using this resisting power in their own behalf, do not even believe that they should do so? The result of a general conception so chaotic, would naturally be what we find: the generalization from the practical expediency of certain consideration for others, crystallized through the impulse of blind selfishness into a mysterious and oppressive obligation, credit for the observance of which gratifies the self-projecting faculty of the simple, while the more shrewd evade its exactions, and at every step from the manipulation of the general delusions of religious and political authority to the association of sexes and children at play, project themselves by exchanging this mythical credit for the real comforts and luxuries of the occasion, which the others produce. Thus in addition to the natural disadvantage of unequal capacity, the weaker are deprived through a superstition, of the use of such capacity as they have, as may be seen in their groping blindness all about us.

To secure and maintain equal conditions then, requires a rational understanding of the real object of life as indicated by the facts of its expression. It is plain that the world of humanity is made up of individuals absolutely separate; that life is to this humanity nothing save as it is something to one of these; that one of these can be nothing to another except as he detracts from or adds to his happiness; that on this is based the idea of social expediency; that the resistance of each of these individuals would determine what is socially expedient; that approximately equal resistance makes it equality, and on such continued and a universal resistance depends equality. This can leave no room for any sane action toward others but that of the policy promoting most the happiness of the acting Ego. Therefore Egoism insists that the attainment of equal freedom depends upon a course of conduct replacing the idea of "duty to others" with *expediency* toward others; upon a recognition of the fact that self-pleasure must be the final motive of any act; thus developing a principle for a basis of action about which there can be no misunderstanding, and which will place every person squarely on the merit of his or her probable interests, divested of the opportunity to deceive through pretension, as under the dominance of altruistic idealism. It will maintain that what is generally recognized as morality is nothing other than the expediency deduced from conflicting interests under competition; that it is a policy which, through the hereditary influence of ancestral experience, confirmed by personal experience, is found to pay better than any other known policy; that the belief that it is something other than a policy—a fixed and eternal obligation, outside of and superior to man's recognized interests, and may not be changed as utility indicates, makes it a superstition in effect like any other superstition which causes its adherents to crystallize the expediency adopted by one period into positive regulations for another in which it has no utility, but becomes tyrannical laws and customs in the name of which persecution is justified, as in the fanaticism of any fixed idea.

Another part of its purpose is to help dispel the "Political Authority" superstition and develop a public sentiment which would replace State interference with the protection for person and property which the competition of protecting associations would afford. Then the State's fanatical tyranny and industry crushing privilege would torture the nerves of poverty-stricken old age or pinch tender youth no more. The most disastrous interference of this monster superstition is its prohibition of the issuing of exchange medium on the ample security of all kinds of property, which at once would abolish speculative interest and practically set all idle hands at productive labor at wages ever nearing the whole product until it should be reached. The next interference is by paper titles to vacant land instead of the just and reasonable one of occupancy and use, which with the employment that free money would give, would furnish all with comfortable homes in a short time, and thereafter even with luxuries from like exertion. Following this is its patent privilege, customs robbery, protective tariff, barbarous decrees in social and sexual affairs; its brutal policy of revenge, instead of restitution, in criminal offenses, and finally its supreme power to violate the individual, and its total irresponsibility.

PROSPECTUS

EGOISM is published Monthly

at 50 cents a year.

It is promptly discontinued when subscription expires, and no bills are sent out. It is run by the publishers, and admits only such contributions as they believe extend, or intelligently criticise its position.

[*Entered as Second Class Mail Matter.*]

EQUITY PUBLISHING COMPANY,

P. O. Box 1678. San Francisco, Calif

Egoism

Vol. II.---No. 4. SAN FRANCISCO, CAL., AUGUST, 1891. Price, Five Cents.

Pointers.

Egoism is now printed on a steam press, and is getting up in the world.

"Liberty," of Boston, is changed from an 8-page fortnightly to a 4-page weekly. This is very desirable.

Colonel Ingersoll says one man in the right will finally get to be a majority. In this case the degree of right and that of finality will exactly correspond. If a man is very right the finality will impress him quite as seriously as the majority realization.

Lillian Harman, one of the publishers of former Fair Play, has gone to Boston to manipulate the leaden alphabet in Benj. R. Tucker's publishing house. E. C. Walker will probably also be employed in some department of the business.

The English Anarchists have formed a Free Trade Extension League and issued a circular with a program of 12 items of governmental prohibition for the abolishment of which they will agitate. A list of subjects and lecturers will soon be issued and the work begun.

The last book published by Benj. R Tucker is "Russian Traits and Terrors," and promises to be a critical and able analysis of that people's characteristics as well as an authentic and startling description of the atrocities practiced by the Russian government. We have received, but not read it yet. It contains 288 pages and sells at $1.00 in cloth binding, and at 35 cents in paper cover. Address the publisher at Box 3366, Boston.

"The Rights of Women and the Sexual Relations," by Karl Heinzen, announced in the June number, has arrived and been read. To have been written in 1852, it is remarkable for the breadth of its position as well as plainness of analysis and force of conclusion, which makes it excellent matter for propaganda work among the idealistic conservative portion of the community. But a number of monogamy-derived ideals and empirical deductions occurring like interpolations in his magnificent argument are very provoking to the radical reader who finding the author in the very jaws of a bold and consistent conclusion sees him suddenly wheel about and justify by a monogamic prejudice. Those of our readers who only tolerate the paper will be delighted with the book and should circulate it among their conservative friends. It contains 173 pages and sells in cloth for $1.00; paper cover 50 cents. Benj. R. Tucker, Box 3366, Boston, Mass.

Egoism is glad to note the change of the Chicago "Liberal," formerly an anti-theological paper, into the "Auditor," a paper devoted to free money and industrial emancipation. It is edited by Alfred B. Westrup, with S. V. Westrup business manager. Mrs. Freeman, who was publisher of the "Liberal" has severed connection with it except as a contributor. It is a 16-page monthly, printed on excellent paper with large clear type, at $1.00 a year. But for one, and a fatal error, it would be a sound and powerful propagator of Mutual Banking. This error consists in the proposition to issue currency without being denominated in some standard of value; that is, without it being understood that a note of a given denomination will be redeemed in such a quantity of products as would exchange for a definite quantity of some commodity. It is equal, as we understand it, to giving a promissory note without stating the amount to be paid. Of course Mr. Westrup will not admit this, and declares that the Mutual Bank dollar taken in lieu of current money would express how much product the note calls for. So it would, but only because the Mutual Bank dollar is measured by the current dollar and the current dollar represents a definite quantity of gold or silver. It is easy to print a note but impossible to tell what to give for it without knowing its denomination and impossible to denominate it without doing so in some definite amount of something, and the moment a definite amount of something is named it shows how much to give for the note and becomes a standard of value, a measure of valuation in exchange. This is so self-evident, and has been so clearly set forth by others, and Mr. Westrup so persistent in ignoring that he uses a standard while he denies one, that we are grieved to be unable to see any other reason for such a course than that of an overmastering desire for originality and a distinctive leadership based thereon. Among thinking people it is such a well-verified fact that a thought may be original in a number of minds at the same time or at different times and therefore no one of the number be *the* originator, that it seems a desire for credit for originality should not tempt a mature thinker to base such credit on so preposterous a proposition. The leadership in the movement for free money will be hard to locate and will probably be credited to the farmers, and yet not one in a thousand will know who originated the idea nor even realize but that they always had it in an undefined sort of way. (This refers to their private scheme.) Warning our readers of the error propagated on this point by the "Auditor," we would be only too glad to return in part the many favors Mr. Westrup has bestowed upon Egoism, by inducing them to subscribe for his paper and otherwise help him agitate for freedom to issue currency. Address the business manager at 343 Michigan Avenue, Chicago, Ill.

Epicurean.

Ah!—sing glad heart, sing
Thy pean;—
There is but one wisdom, even joy
And kindly wishing!
Well saith the Epicurean:—
Today be happy, for tomorrow die
Thou must.
Therefore today is glad perfectness of life,
Breath,
Innocence, and happy-hearted laughter,
With manly earnestness of strife;
Tomorrow cometh sweet Death,
The blending with the dear brown dust,
And—how think you?—nothing after.

J. Wm. Lloyd.

An Oakland stenographer fell in love with a teacher in one of the public schools; that is, as most men are, he was impressed with the qualities in a woman desirable for the combination instrument known as wife. But the teacher had a job and was not enthusiastic. And in seeing him come out of a saloon she found an excuse for a final jilt. His desire to possess her did not cease and he allowed it to seep out in devotional verse through a paper he published. Of this he claimed she made stock to ridicule him among his and her friends, which stung him so that he annoyed her in print with trifling thrusts and editorials paralleling their differences, and finally looked up the record of her family to further retaliate. He then sought an interview but she refused. Finally an interview between him and the girl's father was arranged by a mutual friend and they met in the stenographer's office to talk the whole affair over and drop it. But it was scarcely begun when the men became irritated and the girl's father emptied a five-barreled revolver into the defenseless stenographer's body, from the effects of which he died five days later. And the herd, those sovereign rulers whose ignorance and brute force make public ethics and political science, justify the killing and it is likely the slayer will in the future go unrestrained in his methods of defending such honor as such men have. And the doctors found that the stenographer under the circumstances, died from a failure of the heart. This made the victim criminal, for such death is illegal, as the State board of health long ago so declared and will not allow physicians to return it in certificates as a cause of death. For his conduct toward the young woman the stenographer should have been subjected to some sharp derision and a severe social boycotting, but was a shining light beside the fanatical vertebrate who took such advantage to riddle him with bullets. Killing the murderer would help no one, but at his own expense he should be kept from ever repeating such an act.

Editorial Slashes.

Mrs. Potter, the actress, has not seen her little girl for three years, and cannot be her guardian because American law does not think an actress a proper person to rear even her own children. Mrs. Potter desires to bring up her child in her profession and make an intelligent an accomplished woman of her, but the tyrant fetich, political authority, declares that the millions of mere vertebrates who are mothers as clams are by force of their exposure, are eminently fitted to train children, while an experienced woman and intelligent artist must be fenced out like a duck with a brood of chickens from a pond. This idea of duty to society is a delightful thing when a lot of anatomical specimens want to force some one to trot their own affairs in the trail of barbaric zoography.

Those authority worshipers who manage without laughing to point to the government postal service as an illustration of their schemes of officialism, could get some pointers from the "Examiner" of August 11, and 12. It shows that under and owing to official irresponsibility it takes mail as long to reach points only 200 miles from San Francisco as is required to land it in New York city; that in other cases it takes six days to get mail from point to point only 60 miles apart, and eight days to reach another 108 miles away. In Tulare county its two principal towns are 12 miles apart and are connected by a railroad with three trains a day each way, but the mail is carried by a roundabout route that it consumes three days to cover, requiring a week to get an answer from a letter when it could easily be had in one day by carrying the mail over the direct route. In another case mail with daily papers is delayed 23 hours by forcing the stage to leave a railroad station one hour before this mail arrives, and in many other places mail is uselessly held from 12 to 18 hours. The department at Washington was long ago notified of all these facts and furnished with suggestions showing how they could be remedied. In one case the carrier was willing to put on faster service at his own expense, and even this was not allowed for some time till some big names protested. Sometimes protests were retaliated by depriving the communities of half the service they then enjoyed. The whole affair shows that a study for the worst management could scarcely outdo that of the present. No attention at all is paid to complaints not made in regular red tape form, and to these the saintly John retorts: "*If the people of the Pacific Coast don't like the way I do business let them take the business and run it to suit themselves!*" A better suggestion could not well be made if they dared to do any such thing, but he well knows they dare not, and further that their groveling worship of political authority in general and a political party in particular, will insure his position, so he sneeringly taunts them. And what is true in this case is true of political authority in general; local interest, from a community to an individual, can care for its own affairs better than is possible by centralized management even if it were interested, to say nothing of the cases wherein such management's interest is at variance with that of a locality or individual that cannot retaliate. Political authority aside, if a thing does not pay the payers it can be abandoned, and if a community desires a particular kind of service it can have it by paying the cost. As it is the pay is in part or all collected and the service is unsatisfactory, yet however willing the community to pay for a better, no one dares compete. And why they should not is no more asked than why rain does not always fall to the best advantage of the crops. The people do without rain when it does not come, and with the same unquestioning resignation do without whatever government chooses to withhold. Indeed individuals will cause rain and regulate temperature at will before the masses give up the superstition of political authority—that inconceivable proposition that the government and people are one, and yet these people helplessly chew their own necks off.

Toes Unwittingly Trodden.

The wisdom of government crops out amazingly in the mayorial Oakland board of health appointment. It is the tendency of governments to shower favors on sycophants. A homeopathic physician, who could not spell, certainly owes his success to anything but his learning.

Notwithstanding Egoism's left hand undercut at the allopathic members, it may be inferred from its not stating to the contrary, that they know how to *spell*. It is a blessing to humanity that the non-speller took the infinitesimal route in conducting mankind's steps heavenward. If he had stumbled onto the allopathic way of doing business, his success instead of a place on the board of health, by favor of an ignorant politician, might have been a prison cell for unintentional manslaughter.

Advocating alum in one column and homeopathy in the other is an inconsistency of which I did not dream Egoism capable. Or has alum only the described results when administered in homeopathic doses? It seems not, for it is expressly stated not to use the drug (rather say mineral) sparingly.

Alum being an emetic and at the same time an adstringent, will lessen the sexual appetite. Just imagine a person thinking of the sexual act with a puking dose of alum inside and an adstringent bath outside. But if the contracting agency of the mineral acts beneficial on the sexual parts of man, as far as his propensity to commit rape is concerned, conjoinedly with the nauseating effects it has on his stomach, how will it act on the power of his brain where the contracting and nauseating effects are working in the same way? We know that a full blood supply is necessary for correct thinking.

Before the editor continues to advocate homeopathy in one column and alum in the other, I advise him to dismiss the use of alum, not because its effect on his sexual system interests me any, but because it seems to interfere materially with the use of his brain, with which I am much concerned. Respectfully, De Lespinasse.

I wrote the note on which the above is a criticism, to rebuke the prejudice of the allopathic board of health mentioned, and with no intention of attacking the entire school, for I supposed the prejudice confined to this particular board, perhaps. In the start I frankly confess that I know almost less than nothing about the technical difference between the two theories. The assertions only reflected my experience with and observation of their practices. It is not a prejudiced opinion that I have for, as in this case, allopathic doctors have always happened to be my friends, but in spite of this I years ago lost faith in customary doctoring. I have noticed, however, that homeopathic doctors lost almost no cases in fevers and seemed successful in treating nervous diseases, while allopathics lost many patients from fevers and succeeded but indifferently with nervous afflictions. I accounted for the difference on the grounds that both medicines were practically useless, and that the homeopathic did not kill so quickly because a weakened system could resist it more easily. This may be a little sweeping, but is a rashness that I heartily choose as a rule in life. My single personal experience with homeopathic remedies, was once when I was suffering with neuralgia, and a friend gave me some little white pills that the very thought of taking made me smile in face of the pain. However, I was soon asleep and the next morning all trace of pain was gone and there was no noticeable reaction from the medicine, and I have never been troubled with neuralgia since. In several instances before that I had been very sick with other ailments and was attended by allopathics who, I have reason to believe, did all in their power, but not until they gave up and quit dosing did I grow better. And this causes me to agree with Dr. De Lespinasse when he says that if this homeopathic doctor had stumbled onto the allopathic way of doing business he might be in a prison cell for unintentional man-slaughter, for I believe it takes a very smart man to administer allopathic treatment without killing the patient.

Now no one is more ready to find fault with government than myself, but if the homeopathic doctor got the place because he was a sycophant, how shall we account for the monoplization of former appointments by allopathics?

EGOISM was not inconsistent in advocating alum and homeopathy in the same number. It was unmistakably implied that the alum was to destroy the surplus life that seemed to be giving the purists so much trouble, and not a health-restoring prescription at all. And besides the two notes were written by different persons; the homeopathy by myself, "G.," and the alum prescription by the "Manager." As there are two editorial writers, we use the initials, "H." and "G.," and are not "one" and the same person, as the doctor seems to conclude, although we once went through a legal performance that is supposed to make two "one."

It does not follow that the "Manager" had experimented with the alum upon his own person because he prescribed it. I venture that Dr. De Lespinasse does not use all his prescriptions on his own system, but goes by a theory and observation largely.

It may be said that the "Manager's" "Experience" is not always to be taken too seriously, although he often regards some of it decidedly so. G.

Majority Taste Brutality.

On the 17th of last month the society for meddling in others' affairs crushed two more victims in this city. A girl 17 years of age ran away from her mother in Oakland and came here, where she lived with her aunt for a time, but took to leading an "irregular life." Complaint was lodged with the Society for the Prevention of Cruelty to Children and Animals, and its secretary, Holbrook, immediately proceeded to help the girl's mother treat her worse than animals are treated, by forcing her to marry a bartender whom she hated or go a year to the Magdalen Asylum. Her mother went to the bartender and threatened him with imprisonment unless he should "right" the wrong *he* had done the girl, and he consented to marry her. The following from the "Examiner" gives a fair idea of the barbarous and ritualistic ethics with which the community's censors are content:

They had a hard time with Lena, who objected strongly to the marriage. In the women's room of the prison hospital her mother and a friend, with the matron of the prison, argued and pleaded with the girl.

"But I don't want to get married," she whimpered in reply, "and especially to him. I don't like him."

"Still, you cannot hope to marry any other man, and marry you must," argued the mother.

"Why must I marry?"

"Because, if you do not they will send you to prison for a year."

At the word "prison" Lena gave up, and in another minute her consent had been gained.

......She wept bitterly as she placed herself at the side of the groom, who scowled and edged away from her, while Lena's mother observing his action looked fiercely at him.

Justice Low read the marriage ceremony sharply as if to impress what he said on his odd audience. Everybody looked uncomfortable.

"Do you take this woman to be your lawful wedded wife?"

Druhm muttered something that sounded more like an imprecation than "I do."

Lena murmured her response in a scarcely audible tone, and Justice Low hurried the ceremony to a finish.

Holbrook led the way out of the prison, Druhm shuffled after him, the bride and her mother brought up the rear, and that was all.

And this is the work of the Humane Society and of a mother and the "wisdom" of the age. This machine ethics—this military drill—this violation of every principle of spontaneity and free will is sanctioned by society, by the people we must live among and to whose barbaric instincts we are exposed in living the only share of conscious existence we shall enjoy. If we would escape the impersonal and irresponsible majority beast, we must make our tastes, or at least our habits conform to its dictation, whatever be the torture.

When it had decreed here the bartender returned to his work with the consciousness that a garnishee hangs over every dollar he can earn and that his efforts henceforth must go to benefit a person he hates. He cannot escape this slavery if he remains in the country, for it is the acknowledged business of the society that enslaved him to arrest and fine him if he fails to provide for the woman it has forced upon him. Whatever may be his ambition in maturer years, he is chained affectionally to a corpse. If he finds a congenial companion he might as well be a Hottentot for all the good it will do him. To appreciate his position more thoroughly one has only to imagine himself bound to some of the women he hates and then remember the desirability of those he is most attracted to. And it cannot be maintained that this man is only completing responsibility that he had assumed, for there was no such an arrangement either contracted or implied; the girl asked him for nothing. She was as unwilling to be imposed upon him as he was to have her. Neither party demanded anything; they were mutually done when a mutual appetite was gratified. To force them to marry was a piece of brutality as invasive as it would have been to force them to wade through fire.

The girl returned from that prison to the air and sunshine practically a slave. If she went to apartments her now husband may have had, her lot living with a person who hates her and whom she as cordially hates in return, can well be imagined by those who find monogamic life under the most favorable conditions only bearable. If she went with her mother who subdued her by the brute force of the State, to live from the hand of a hating man her case is still little better, for whoever her unengaged affection may attach itself to, she must smother it and live without hope or she will be regarded as a prostitute and her child taken from her by her husband or by the society which enslaved her. Other women find it hard enough to accomplish a satisfactory destiny with full freedom of choice in directing it, but this one has had hers fixed against her will and must bear it. Great, ruthless, brutal society that lives life as a matter of pleasure, has set hers as a matter to be borne, and rushes heedlessly on, having enforced its taste in sex arrangement.

The mother, though the victor of so grim a triumph, is better off; she is formally acquitted by her neighbors, her opportunity for accomplishment has not been impaired, and she believes she is a benefactor in securing a part of the bartender's earnings for her child. Yet she was an active invader, selling her daughter's liberty for the possibility of a support and to please the girl's worst enemies.

The justice of the peace certainly got a fee, and the "humane" society came out with the greatest slice in the glory of a "rescue" the expense of which it was enabled to saddle off on others, besides it has a possibility for more should the bartender neglect to turn over sufficient cash to the wife. And it is with this society's officers that the active tyranny rests. The members of society at large are too much concerned with their own affairs to have made this aggression, and the position and the pay of State officers does not depend upon the number of such cases they can manufacture. But let this society's officers fail to report a glorifying amount of business and its members will shortly leave them to earn a living and fame by the ordinary method, and so all available material is worked for all there is in it. I say available, because its work as reported by the press plainly indicates that motive, for it is at one time, generous and at another tyrannous, without discrimination. It seems the only question is what will go, and on the go all the stress is laid. If a case is to be tried before a jury every resource is exhausted to secure one favorable to the prosecution. For instance, a woman was to be tried for inducing a minor into prostitution, and the society wanting the prejudices of married men as against the idea of the desirability of prostitution probably felt by unmarried men, managed to get away with a list of eighty men before it secured a jury before which it would risk its case. Success for the society and not redress for the wronged is plainly its motive. The community is taxed to pay civil officers high salaries to attend to criminal prosecution, then allows a few meddlers to make an industry from their implied neglect, but really from enforcing majority taste upon unpopular and defenseless individuals.

This is accomplishable by the principle of majority rule. The majority feels no need to seek a social science by which to square its conduct. It is all powerful and has but to exercise its will, no matter whether equal freedom be invaded or not; it cannot be brought to account for any crime so long as it is the majority. It is also impersonal and never learns anything from experience as a majority. Therefore sycophants have but to learn and pander to its taste and they can perpetrate any tyranny they choose regardless of a well-verified application of the law of equal freedom which is at the time operative in other matters behind each variation of which there is sufficient force to make violation inconvenient. This then, makes popular taste instead of equal freedom the active standard of conduct, and no matter how correct the conduct of individuals may be when tested by science and equal freedom, it must conform to the error of majority taste if there be any persons who can afford to spend their time to bring such innovations to majority notice. And this is the function of these meddling societies. The officers are paid by the members of the society and the members find their reward in enforcing their tastes which they mistake for a standard edition of perfect conduct. Society at large having the same tastes is not cognizant of the equal freedom invading character of this meddling, and will not be until an element of equal strength to that of the active persecutors exposes their violation of the same law operating in other affairs. When a fair sprinkling of intelligent and active individuals in each community can be brought to recognize the law of equal freedom and the importance of deducing from it the rule for every social adjustment, the work of making it the one law of social life will move rapidly, and with that will disappear majority rule as *ruling*. It will not then cost all life is worth to discover and practice in one's private affairs a new variation two days before everybody else adopts it.

But before this the very men who are now content with a certain amount of recognition in trade, a severely earned respectability, and the semi-compulsory fawning of wife and family dependents, will have to learn that a well-defined extension of the compromise in occupying space is the intensest virtue of social ethics, and not that of the habits of dead men. H.

The Philosophy of Egoism.

XI.

The suggestion has been heard that if all acts are Egoistic this term has no distinctive meaning. The same thing has often been said as to "matter" when the Materialist has affirmed that there is no "spirit," —no opposite of matter. Matter then becomes synonymous simply with existence. The Materialist replies that he is content with the conclusion that there is no alleged existence unrelated to other and known existence; none exempt from manifestation according to a regular order or subject to the inherent law of its being, to speak according to appearances. There is a regular order of succession of phenomena. The Spiritual theory asserts a break in what is popularly called "the reign of natural law," Materialism denies such assertion and exists as a distinctive *ism* to deny and disprove it. This statement will indicate in part what is the proper reply when it is charged that Egoism is almost meaningless if it embrace all acts. It was believed that men acted disinterestedly. Closer examination finds the motive and the form of their interest. Thus a parallel to the progress made from the time when men believed in miracles to the time when they have learned enough of natural law to expel the former belief.

By referring to the definition already given of Egoism it will be seen that it covers a theory as well as facts. If every act of every animal were perfectly Egoistic, nevertheless the demands of intelligence would not be satisfied without understanding the phenomena, which are explained according to natural law as reactions of individual will to motives presented in circumstances. To act Egoistically is universal, but to be in part ignorant of the fact seems to be also nearly universal. The theory of Egoism has its opposite in the theory of Altruism, evidently joined to Spiritualism by ignoring and denying the necessary sequence in phenomena. (I make no allusion to modern Spiritualism, which professes to be Materialistic.)

But beyond this it can be firmly said that until the Egoistic theory is understood and has had its full influence upon character, those irrational actions will continue which are the fruit of error, illusion, fascination, fixed ideas, rendering the individual practically not an Ego,—not in the possession of his faculties,—hence there will be as there are, actions not properly Egoistic, but insane, though not generally so understood. Thus the Egoistic theory has a practical purpose. The half insane,—that is to say all worshipers, religious, political, or personal,—are to come to consciousness of their individuality and become wholly sane.

As to submissive actions performed simply under fear or hope their Egoistic character is quite clear.

TAK KAK.

Emotional Gush Not In It.

Mr. Polk, the Alliance president, has remarked that he does not blame great financiers for making out of the people what the laws and the circumstances of the age allow, or words to that effect. Hereupon several papers assailed Mr. Polk, crying shame and that he is confessedly wicked enough to do what he does not condemn in others; that he would gouge the people if he were rich and controlled a bank or a railroad. Now all this outcry is ignorant or dishonest. What would the organs have said if Polk had denounced capitalists for making as much as the law and circumstances allow? It is safe to say that they would have sneered: "Does this man say that he would not have done the same? Why denounce individuals? Mankind average the same under given circumstances." They would, in short, have charged Polk with being a vain pretender, ignorant of himself, lacking opportunity to take advantage of others and discover his own character, or else a hypocritical demagogue, ready to do what he denounced in others more luckily situated than himself. Mr. Polk is correct in viewing individual conduct in civil relations in the philosophical manner announced by him. It would be useless to expect a correction of industrial evils by appealing to the individual generosity of capitalists. For example, it would be absurd to continue the high tariff on cotton ties and appeal to manufacturers not to charge what the market, as thus protected for their benefit, will bear; that is, what they can make out of the necessity of the planters. And so it is with questions of trade and profit. The exceptionally harsh landlord or grasping usurer is indeed placed under the ban of social disapprobation, but theories and policies of reform in government, bearing upon economic relations, contemplate a general condition the result of average conduct under certain laws and inducements. The task of the reformer is to show that some laws give unfair advantage or that such advantage is usurped and that law is needed to restrain the usurpers. Mr. Polk claims that there is in money, as now known, a power to oppress. Whether or not he individually would waive such power had he much money is not a pertinent question. Rich or poor, he is but one in millions. The law of self-interest will operate with general regularity. The men who are too scrupulous to accept 10 per cent and foreclose mortgages will not be "in it," but others will. This is as sure as the fact that one man's nervous susceptibility does not in the least prevent a more robust man from following the trade of a butcher. Such criticisms as those referring to Mr. Polk's personal inclination or philanthrophy in connection with a sociological question are indicative of pitiable ignorance or worse—a sycophantic desire to enlist in the service of monopoly. The tender is made by hastening to ridicule and snarl at the honest men who avow themselves opposed to unjust privileges.—Galveston News.

Managerial Experience.

One Sunday evening in July as I shuffled undulatingly over the uneven and careworn plank walks from the post-office to the ferry I was for once a flutteringly happy mammal. The corners of my mouth were hooked back over my ears and a silly smile twinkled behind them; I could hear my eyes glow and see my cheek bones crowd up for a warm; my hair flapped gaily in the breeze and my slim mustache swung sweepingly over my shoulders like a Texas steer's horns. Even the stoop in my shoulders pushed itself down into my chest against the back side of that joy which was smashing my windpipe and chucking my Adam's apple up against my chin. I was oblivious to small affairs and even forgot to feel, as is my habit, whether a tuft of hair was protruding from the hole in my derby. Neither did I nervously tug at my vest in a time-tried attempt to make it cover the intermitting stature between it and my low-necked pants. The bay, hitherto an endless stretch of waste time in the absence of a tractable waist, now seemed a small affair and the enormous gang plank creaked threateningly as I strode ponderously over it from the boat to solid ground. My illy-suppressed joy attracted the attention of the passengers and they seemed to think me drunk on cereal exhilaration, but my artificial stone walk and gastric breath did not tally with that generalization. I felt like a citizen and as if I was no longer the under dog of privilege oppression, propping out my ribs with philosophic wickers instead of excellent dinners and deep inhalations of champagne breeze. At home I did not, as usual, wait for the train to stop, but sprang lightly to the ground and walked broadly up our stairs just like a proprietor. With a drew-in-the-lottery expression upon my face I dashed before my wife's mingled gaze a piece of speckled pink paper with figures and dollar signs punched in it. It was a check, a real, live check—a check on Columbian lever-press-work and a New York bank. It ordered either an old or New Yorker to fork over to my body in hard cash $50, and was, as I found the next day at the typefounder's, a remarkably potent kind of paper and I heartily wished for a whole ream of it. In spite of my rather incoherent appearance, it caused the gentleman in charge to manifest an almost motherly solicitude for the furnishing of our office, and gave him a confidence in me worth years of ordinary unchecked acquaintance. He talked with affectionate familiarity and even offered to sell me more things than I asked for. This joy-spouting paper was purchased by G. A. F. De Lespinasse, of Orange City, Iowa, for the purpose of putting EGOISM on a steam press, and was accompanied by a subtle apology to the effect that we need feel under no personal obligation to him, as he desired to push this paper's general line of thought on his own account, and had seized this opportunity which had been recently suggested by a paragraph of my experience with our little Columbian lever press.

This voluntary act of Mr. De Lespinasse's fairly opens for the first time in EGOISM's case, the question of co-operation in propaganda work. The problem for every innovating publication is how to secure a good circulation and the accompanying influence. Those who need such a paper can hardly be induced to read it, and will not buy it. Someone must always furnish it free at least until the new reader becomes interested. This is usually done partly at the publisher's expense and partly at that of the adherents of the reform, for there is no other known way to do it. In this, "duty to the cause" plays a conspicuous and successful part, since men's selfish proclivity is much more effectually appealed to by a big thing like a "holy cause," than by ordinary, calculated self-interest which will not admit the possibility of another motive for conduct. The purpose of this publication being to dispel the idea of "duty" for duty's sake, we are deprived of that most popular expedient, and as the comprehensive adherents of the philosophy are few and a little from each does not amount to much, we have had to confine the propaganda work to our own financial resources. And, indeed it must be so unless some of the few, like Mr. De Lespinasse, feel disposed to do a great deal such work at their own expense for the pleasure of spreading their ideas. Five such propagandists spending $50 a year would so cover the core of EGOISM's publishing expenses that with the labor we now put into it and the income that would follow, it would in five years gather readers enough to be read in as many thousand families. Such an achievement would afford any Egoist who is already well fed and clothed infinitely more pleasure than would the consciousness of $250 more of property for his heirs to quarrel over when his pleasure capacity is no more.

When Dr. De Lespinasse sits with his feet on a window sill of his office reflecting, or reviews life as he rides in the cool of the evening, he can now be conscious that he has away out in lovely California $50 worth of tools constantly transmitting the ideas that he is anxious to have afloat. And I dare say it will be as satisfactory as would the thoughts of many other radicals if they realized that they are investing their money in a legacy to be left by the "old man" or "old woman" whose ideas and companionship were limited to a narrower circle by a desire for figures of a little higher denomination on the credit side of their bank account, the only real use that an unused dollar can be to its owner. This is, of course, exclusive of such reasonable reserve as might be necessary for support in declining age. Memory chiseled in living, reciprocating brain fiber is much more desirable than in piles of marble as irresponsive as the dead they represent. We want our monument while we are here to enjoy it, and are confident others will like the idea as well when they think it over. It is for this reason that we have against some reluctance on Mr. De Lespinasse's part used his name in acknowledging his co-operation in pushing the paper. And for this reason we propose to go still farther and keep standing in our prospectus the amounts and names of as many propagandists as help push the work we are interested in the most. This is just, and eminently proper, for it shows who are standing the pressure of propaganda and how much of it; a fact that every friend of the innovation will like to know, and the means of an appreciation that every propagandist will be proud of.

As is understood by Egoists, and as is manifest in another column, this co-operation takes none of the independence from the paper, nor prevents us combatting any opinions from which we differ. We propose to run the paper as nearly to suit ourselves as our ideas of safety will permit, and if that way pleases any one so well that they are willing to risk money on it, the kite takes another leap. But such persons must always consider the possibility of being displeased with the very next issue. No one has criticised the paper so much as Mr. De Lespinasse, and no one has done one-fourth as much to push it. One woman of journalistic experience is so well pleased with it that she regularly remits a dollar upon the receipt of each number, but the $50 that puts Egoism on a steam press is an effectual lift that must be followed by many favorable results. We shall keep standing a full list of the propaganda fund for each volume even if it becomes so large that we have to print sixteen pages to accommodate it.

When Egoism was to be printed on a steam press we deemed it incumbent upon us to seek a slice of pleasure. I like pleasure and think it great stuff to have. So we decided to go to the seabank one Sunday, which costs two and a half individuals two and seven-eighths fares, amounting to one dollar and twenty cents a trip. On Saturday night my wife bought two-bits worth of decrepit nuts and I got fifteen cents worth of granite-ware apples and some tender steak. The next morning without a sensation of the pleasure on which I was bent, I rolled out at 4 a.m. and the front side of the bed. After finding in the dry goods box on which I hang a case, two socks that mated not in color but in having the holes on the little-toe side, I dressed and amputated my beard with a diffident razor and fervid soliloquy. Then I dislodged my wife and her relative from bed, and they dislodged the breakfast while I prepared the lunch. We then ran down the 7:30 train rolling lively for the ferry, and were soon on the boat and well at bay. I wanted to do something becoming the occasion so I reflectively probed my ear and silently contrasted the many gliding palaces with the scene several hundred years before, when the tide hugged Goat Island in broad daylight without danger of scandal. But I noticed that my reverie caused no disturbance outside of my own rind, and my wife nudged me and said that my sock was turned down over my shoetop. I pulled it up and realized that the grandest of thoughts are very subjective in their influence. And the sun poured upon my corns. At the landing we took our lunch basket and a Howard street cable car to the beach road. Howard street is a long strip of paved sand with two iron slits near the middle over which these cars chassa between two rows of weary-countenanced houses. As we neared the Lick baths the conductor observed: "Transfert'tenth?" and I nodded with my head, whereafter he gave me three pieces of cardboard containing a statement that "drifted snow flour is the best," and after changing cars we arrived at the depot of the beach road. It is not hard to get on its cars; all you have to do is to buy a ticket, go through a door and fall over a post, then walk through the dining hall to the back porch and throw your ticket into a vacant aquarium and a man pumps it with a handle into the waste basket and you can step right on. These are funny little cars without weatherboarding, which as they hackle the drifting sand with one's nose put him in mind of the tail end of a threshing machine. It was here that I discovered the significance of the remark on the cardboards that "drifted snow flour is the best,"—better than drifting sand. When we arrived at the beach I lay me on the dry sand and gazed comely upon the mysterious deep and fell into speculation on physical geography and infirmity without losing by the decline. All ill-starred people should thus gambol on sand. I like to sit on my elbows and let myself hear the brine roar and the seals sing with leathery voice and refrain from chorus.

My wife allowed her little niece to wade in the wet surf, having made her wash he feet for the purpose the night before. It looks bad and is exposing part of the skeleton outside of the closet, to take off one's stockings before a crowd when one's shanks are all streaked and scaly with a season's accumulation. Anybody can wade if they are not ashamed.

The beach seems to affect the human insect like the order of equal freedom; everybody rushes up to it and not much farther. The mighty element awes the gobbler faculty into basic democracy like a great fire or battle, before which all are about equal. This is what would happen if government privilege were removed; all would stand an equal show at the beach of opportunity, and fine airs would take a drop—not of champagne. The whole country would then be as the beach now is. Here no policeman paces nor trots, and all do as they please without displeasing. Squabby women squat about like gobs of stray dough on the kitchen floor; fat men step touchily on the soft sand as though they were walking in a half trough of eggs; waspish girls walk mechanically by the surf and display such calves as would not have won the heart of Podsnap in George Macdonald's "Sweitzer Tomato;" ladley lovers crouch spaniel-like about their awkwardly-seated sweethearts; for the moment gallant husbands, ostensibly show off to their disinterested wives the swimming qualities of psychologized dogs who seldom get knee-deep into the water; vain men strut along with fishing tackle in hand, and carry strings of fish they have bought of fishermen; splendid teams with well-fortuned drivers of democratic mien dash along the surf-made track; waxen-faced girls who ride like bags of wool, make their horses flounder through soft sand with the solid track not two rods away; counterfeit cowboys with more stirrup-guard and hair than brains ride coyotishly through the crowd and long—so long for notoriety; bourgeois families bring large basketfuls of the finest victuals and noisily devour them; middle-aged men and knowing young women throw sand at each other with expressions suggestive of larger gravel; monogamy-languored couples with diagonal affection drive to the beach for a change of air, but other heirs soon give them a breeze that starts them with dark complexioned looks for their legal sepulcher, which is white on the outside only; diffident, but tortured girls in subjective mood court each other with the pitiable inefficiency I have observed among other stock of one sex only; the waffle man bakes waffles between crimping irons; the vender with peanuts and disappointment wades through the sand from group to group widely separated, and has plenty of peanuts left. Amid all these scenes my accumulating appetite suggests that I mix it with the lunch, and my wife and her little niece are hungry too, and at eating we are happy.

After mingling freely with her lunch my wife slept bareheaded upon the sand, and a squinty old man and his second edition daughter passing us eyed her curiously while I sat near by watching some girls chew drifting sand as they tried to read gossip. We had an umbrella along but I was so stupid that I sat like a bag of flour at a murdering and allowed the sun to cook one side of my wife's face like a Kansas tomato in a hot wind as she lay dreaming that she was helping Olive Schreiner dream her "Three Dreams in a Desert." And the sand blew through my mustache and I said: "It's time to hump ourselves." "And slowly the creature staggered on to its knees," and I stood "close to her, and looked into" the depot and saw the train pulling out, but another was coming and soon we "came to the bank of" the bay, "and on it an old man met us, who had a long, white beard, and a" ticket punch "was in his hand, and" he let us on a boat and soon we were in Oakland, where my wife doped her face all the evening, and I reflected upon the amplitude of the room for success in the business of life—pleasure getting. Cloverly, The Manager.

Straws in the Breeze.

England mourns because six of her sailors were killed by the bursting of a gun while they were practicing the art of killing other men with it. It is sad, no doubt, but let us be thankful that Providence has been thoughtful enough so to order matters that when guns burst the disadvantages fall mostly to gunners.—Ambrose Bierce.

"Our country, right or wrong" is becoming a popular war cry.—Morning Call.

It was always a popular war cry. From the earliest invention of the political boundary that rascally sentiment or its moral equivalent has been in the mouth of every anthropoid idiot sufficiently enlightened to observe that he lived in one place instead of another.—Ambrose Bierce.

A dead coyote is worth $11 in Mendocino county and they (the live coyotes) are increasing so fast that the sheep owners have called a convention to decide what is to be done. If a similar convention of the gentlemen who are raising coyotes could be called the two bodies might agree to divide the territory, or the sheepmen might sell their flocks and unanimously go to raising coyotes.—Oakland Evening Tribune.

San Jose is not at all proud of one of her citizens, who had a little girl arrested for carrying away two or three blocks of wood which, having been sawed off a new fence, had fallen on the sidewalk. Fortunately the child was brought before a justice who took a humane view of the affair in dismissing the case, and a sensible view in making the complainant pay the costs. We do not know whether this was law or not, but it was a pretty fair article of justice.—Exchange.

No woman with any self-respect will continue to live with a man after she has ceased to care for him and yet her so doing is applauded by the conservative sisterhood, who live on traditions and never think for themselves, whereas if she had the courage to leave her husband and live with the man of her maturer choice—the divorce courts not being open to her—she would be indiscriminately classed with "bad women"; people who have not been taught to think are like the color-blind, to whom scarlet, cardinal, pink, cherry, and claret are all the same shade of red.—Gertrude Atherton.

The monitor Monadnock was launched at Mare island so long ago that most people have forgotten their surprise at the fact that she would float right side up. It is now estimated that at the present rate of progress of the work on the vessel she will be ready for war in about ten years—when she will be more than that much behind the times. Since the Monadnock went into the water the Union Iron Works has launched three great war ships, two of which are now in commission. There is a lesson in this. The government could save much time and money by wiping its navy yards from the face of the earth and having all the work on its navy done by private contract.—Oakland Evening Tribune.

OUR BOOK LIST.

LOVE, MARRIAGE, AND DIVORCE, and the Sovereignty of the Individual, is a pamphlet of 121 pages composed of a discussion of marriage by Henry James, Horace Greeley, and Stephen Pearl Andrews. What Proudhon's works are to Anarchism is this to freedom in love between the sexes. It is the most comprehensive, searching, and exhaustive work ever written on the subject. No advocate of sexual freedom can afford to be without a full acquaintance with its contents. Price 35 cents.

FREE POLITICAL INSTITUTIONS: Their Nature, Essence, and Maintenance,—an abridgement and rearrangement of Lysander Spooner's "Trial by Jury," edited by Victor Yarros. It is treated in seven chapters under the following heads: I. Legitimate Government and Majority Rule. II. Trial by Jury as a Palladium of Liberty. III. Trial by Jury as Defined by Magna Charta. IV. Objections answered. V. The Criminal Intent. VI. Moral Considerations for Jurors. VII. Juries of the Present Day Illegal. Whoever desires to make plain to his conservative neighbor just how society may get on without tyranny and privilege fostering government, should have a copy of this pamphlet in his coat pocket and be prepared to not only defend his position but to take that of the opposition by storm. It is the much-needed propaganda material that should be circulated as fast as Anarchists can afford to devote money to the work. Price 25 cts.

THE RAG-PICKER OF PARIS, by Felix Pyat, translated from the French by Benj. R. Tucker. This novel is the most complete portrayal of the human nature of this century in every condition of life, that has been contributed to radical literature. Every line, every pause, has a fullness, a significance of thought, or a volcano of emotion seldom found anywhere singly, and not combined in the style of any other writer. It is probably the most vivid picture of the misery of poverty, the extravagance of wealth, the sympathy and forbearance of the poor and despised, the cruelty and aggressiveness of the aristocratic and respectable, the blind greed of the middle classes, the hollowness of charity, the cunning and hypocrisy of the priesthood, the tyranny and corruption of authority, the crushing power of privilege, and finally of the redeeming beauty of the ideal of liberty and equality, that the century has produced. Four thousand copies were sold the first week after its publication. Radicals can do much good work with it among the partly liberal-minded. It will, without arousing their prejudices, open a new field of thought for very orthodox people. Price in cloth binding $1; paper, 50 cents.

MY UNCLE BENJAMIN: a novel by Claude Tillier, an intelligent victim of institution oppression, who necessarily suffered more than he enjoyed. The splitting pangs of his intense pessimism are seasoned with such ridiculing thrusts at the vanity of wealth as to almost hide the exaggeration. The characters are not made to "come out" in school girl ideal, but tumble along like real life, mostly at the mercy of other elements than the reader's desire. The facts are not manufactured and put up in doses ready to take for building up a philosophy made to order. He dissects conduct and illustrates the charlatanism on one part and the superstition and stupidity on the other that creates fame, with diagramatic plainness. Living in an age when some of our grandfathers were too prejudice-ridden to wear boots, buttons, or suspenders we find him in his philosophy dashing off almost our deepest concepts with a lucidness equal to the description of the most commonplace affairs of our time. His wit is like springing a dark-lantern in a sub-cellar, while his humor penetrates your anatomy to the marrow without allowing you to roar with laughter so skillfully is it woven in with philosophy, pathos, or tragedy. We heartily recommend it to our full-grown readers. Price in cloth $1.00; paper 50 cents.

MOMEY is at once a camera and chemist of human conduct and motive. Zola not only describes the carnivora, from the den it inhabits to the changing reflections of its glossy coat, but he tells what it is thinking about and will do. He realizes that the human animal is a none too much evoluted wild beast on the front of whose skull the experience of ages has worn only a bright spot, and he exposes all the greed, ferocious brutality, tyranny, cunning, hypocrisy, ostentation, truckling servility, idealism, and stupidity embodied in the kings, manipulators, and victims of a modern speculative world. The cruel and the generous, the detestable and the admirable traits of each character are delineated with an analytical nicety and a realistic accuracy that make the reader live the life of each and absorb the apology for their shortcomings without for a moment losing sight of the expedient course that should have replaced undesirable conduct. With an eloquently-implied regret he rebukes the horrors and cruelties of financial conquest without the wearisome moralizing or the narrow hatred common to the critics of social outrages. He is not a world builder nor a hero worshiper. Even Caroline, the lover of life, intelligent, educated, experienced, unprejudiced, and the heroine of the most trying ordeals of the story, was in his critical eyes full of weaknesses between which she was, inconsistently with her ideal of life, constantly vacillating. On world building he strikes State Socialism one of his efficient implied blows, but sensate to the difficulties of wide innovation, he offers no remedy for industrial troubles, contenting himself with painting in bold relief and sharp contrast the almost fabulous extravagance of the rich and the horrifying wretchedness of the poor, along with emphasis on the fraud, sham, and wholesale manipulating practiced by speculators upon the unsuspecting. Yet he describes with effective force the spirit of rivalry, the entrancing pleasures, the magnificent enterprises, and even humanitarian dreams that prompt men to speculate even by the most gigantic fraud. And it is this, along with his realistic repletion that makes Zola such an admirable and to us unequaled novelist. His plot embraces almost every shade of character constituting modern civilization, and he depicts the virtues and weaknesses of each with a disinterest as faithful as his realism is striking. Even his reference to Egoism, a subject that impulsive French blood might readily balk on, is characterized by this faithfulness to the spirit of the subject in hand. His Egoist, though not the expansive utilitarian of our ideal, is nevertheless intrinsically Egoistic and approvably utilitarian in a comprehensive view of the subject. Although the story, true to life, contains a full complement of unsanctioned sexual alliances, the only woman rich or poor that gold could not influence was a little Freelover who contracted such association with desirable men just once through curiosity for pleasure alone. Saccard, his chief character, is a financial poet, a speculative madman who dreams only of money—millions, power, conquest, supremacy, the prostration at his feet of "all great, cowardly, truckling Paris." Ambitious, active, unscrupulous, assuming, an appropriator of other men's ideas—of everything that came in his reach, he wove from his own and borrowed imagination, such alluring prospects as placed at his service the means beginning a career of speculation and spoilation the incidents and characters of which in Zola's masterly hands constitute the most startling expose of the power and tyranny of privileged money, the blind recklessness of stock gambling, and the ravenous greed of human avarice that we have read. We regard it as the ablest in our list, although no one can afford to be without the intensification of thought and feeling generated by all of them. The price of "Money" in cloth binding is $1; paper cover 50 cents.

For any of the above address
EQUITY PUBLISHING COMPANY,
P. O. Box 1678. San Francisco, Calif.

EGOISM'S PRINCIPLES AND PURPOSE.

EGOISM's purpose is the improvement of social existence through intelligent self-interest. It finds that whatever we have of equal conditions and mutual advantage is due to a prevalence of this principle corresponding with the degree and universality of individual resistance to encroachment.

Reflection will satisfy all who are desirous of being guided in their conclusions by fact, that as organization itself is a process of absorbing every material useful to its purpose, with no limit save that of outside resistance, so must the very fact of its being a separately organized entity make it impossible for it to act with ultimate reference to anything but itself. Observation will show that this holds good throughout the vegetable and animal kingdoms, and that whatever of equality exists among members of a species or between different species has its source and degree in the resisting capacity, of whatever kind, which such member or species can exert against the encroachment of other members or species. The human animal is no exception to this rule. True, its greater complexity has developed the expedient of sometimes performing acts with beneficial results to others, but this is at last analysis only resistance, because it is the only means of resisting the withholding by others from such actor's welfare that which is more desirable than that with which he parts. If, then, the self-projecting faculty of mankind is such that it will in addition to the direct resistance common to the less complex animals, diplomatically exercise present sacrifice to further extend self, and it being a fact that equality depends upon equal resistance, diplomatic or otherwise, what are its chances in an absence of enlightenment in which the individuals of the majority so far from *intelligently* using this resisting power in their own behalf, do not even believe that they should do so? The result of a general conception so chaotic, would naturally be what we find: the generalization from the practical expediency of certain consideration for others, crystallized through the impulse of blind selfishness into a mysterious and oppressive obligation, credit for the observance of which gratifies the self-projecting faculty of the simple, while the more shrewd evade its exactions, and at every step from the manipulation of the general delusions of religious and political authority to the association of sexes and children at play, project themselves by exchanging this mythical credit for the real comforts and luxuries of the occasion, which the others produce. Thus in addition to the natural disadvantage of unequal capacity, the weaker are deprived through a superstition, of the use of such capacity as they have, as may be seen in their groping blindness all about us.

To secure and maintain equal conditions then, requires a rational understanding of the real object of life as indicated by the facts of its expression. It is plain that the world of humanity is made up of individuals absolutely separate; that life is to this humanity nothing save as it is something to one of these; that one of these can be nothing to another except as he detracts from or adds to his happiness; that on this is based the idea of social expediency; that the resistance of each of these individuals would determine what is socially expedient; that approximately equal resistance makes it equality, and on such continued and a universal resistance depends equality. This can leave no room for any sane action toward others but that of the policy promoting most the happiness of the acting Ego. Therefore EGOISM insists that the attainment of equal freedom depends upon a course of conduct replacing the idea of "duty to others" with *expedency* toward others; upon a recognition of the fact that self-pleasure must be the final motive of any act; thus developing a principle for a basis of action about which there can be no misunderstanding, and which will place every person squarely on the merit of his or her probable interests, divested of the opportunity to deceive through pretension, as under the dominance of altruistic idealism. It will maintain that what is generally recognized as morality is nothing other than the expediency deduced from conflicting interests under competition; that it is a policy which, through the hereditary influence of ancestral experience, confirmed by personal experience, is found to pay better than any other known policy; that the belief that it is something other than a policy—a fixed and eternal obligation, outside of and superior to man's recognized interests, and may not be changed as utility indicates, makes it a superstition in effect like any other superstition which causes its adherents to crystallize the expediency adopted by one period into positive regulations for another in which it has no utility, but becomes tyrannical laws and customs in the name of which persecution is justified, as in the fanaticism of any fixed idea.

Another part of its purpose is to help dispel the "Political Authority" superstition and develop a public sentiment which would replace State interference with the protection for person and property which the competition of protecting associations would afford. Then the State's fanatical tyranny and industry crushing privilege would torture the nerves of poverty-stricken old age or pinch tender youth no more. The most disastrous interference of this monster superstition is its prohibition of the issuing of exchange medium on the ample security of all kinds of property, which at once would abolish speculative interest and practically set all idle hands at productive labor at wages ever nearing the whole product until it should be reached. The next interference is by paper titles to vacant land instead of the just and reasonable one of occupancy and use, which with the employment that free money would give, would furnish all with comfortable homes in a short time, and thereafter even with luxuries from like exertion. Following this is its patent privilege, customs robbery, protective tariff, barbarous decrees in social and sexual affairs; its brutal policy of revenge, instead of restitution, in criminal offenses, and finally its supreme power to violate the individual, and its total irresponsibility.

PROSPECTUS

EGOISM is published Monthly at 50 cents a year.

[*Entered as Second Class Mail Matter.*]

It is promptly discontinued when subscription expires, and no bills are sent out. It is run by the publishers, and admits only such contributions as they believe extend, or intelligently criticise its position.

The following are the names and amounts contributed by propagandists who wish to spread this line of thought and in that degree are its "Continental Congress," pledging so much "life and fortune" toward the establishing of their ideals and making their personalities felt in the world they live in.

PROPAGANDISTS FOR VOL. II.:

G. A. F. De Lespinasse, - - -	$50.00
A Friend, - - - - - - - -	5.00

EQUITY PUBLISHING COMPANY,

P. O. Box 1678. San Francisco, Calif

MONOGAMIC SEX RELATIONS Discussed by Ego and Marie Louise. This extraordinary pamphlet charges monogamic sexual relations with causing electrical poverty through balanced electrical conditions, which results in many common, and the most fatal diseases, and in mental deterioration, leading to narrow-mindedness, bigotry, tyranny, persecution, irritability, melancholy, drunkenness, suicide, and most of the vice and misery arising from the discontent of mankind. The every day experience of all close observers must corroborate many of its accusations with unmistakable accuracy It is intensely radical, yet clothed in such language as will admit of loaning to your orthodox neighbor. It is printed on good paper, with new type, and contains 24 large pages. Price 10 cents.

CITIZENS' MONEY. A lecture on the "National Banking System," by Alfred B. Westrup, delivered in Chicago and published in "Liberty," of Boston, in 1888. Mr. Westrup shows that every dollar's worth of property in the country may be converted into active capital, reducing interest to the cost of issuing money, and sending capital in search of labor instead of being the other way, as it is at present. It is short, popular in style, and well calculated for propaganda work. Whoever is interested in industrial emancipation can do no better work than procure and circulate this pamphlet by the dozen. It contains 21 pages, is printed on good paper in large type, and can be had for 60 cents per dozen, or 10 cents per single copy.

For any of the above address

EQUITY PUBLISHING COMPANY,

P. O. Box 1678. San Francisco, Calif.

Egoism

Vol. II.---No. 5. SAN FRANCISCO, CAL., SEPTEMBER, 1891. Price, Five Cents.

Pointers.

The article, "A Few Good Books," by George Forrest, which appears on another page was originally written for "Fair Play" and forwarded to us after that magazine ceased publication.

Paternalistic Russia's censorial interest in its subjects is well known but now when hundreds of thousands of them are starving the State does not know of them. But of course when they have nothing to be plundered of it has no function to exercise in connection with them.

The "Beacon," of this city, hitherto published by Sigismund Danielewicz, announces Mr. Danielewicz's retirement and its continuance by its former assistant editor, Clara Dixon Davidson, and by H. C. B. Cowell. The new management is evolutionistic in sentiment and the paper will no longer be an advocate of physical force revolution. While we esteem Mr. Danielewicz as a friend we welcome the change and his successors.

What the press tries to conceal in its lines it usually exposes between them. "Life" is a paper devoted to caricaturing the living habit and exposing its frivolities and vanity. The striking feature is that it illustrates none but bourgeoisie life; all other animate function being realistically regarded as commodity—horses, cows, sheep, fowls, and the laboring biped. The existence of these is not legitimate "life," only the blank lottery tickets that make drawing numbers be what they are.

A Socialist paper in London has been suppressed for attacking the emperor and chancellor of Germany. The wealthiest families of this country are making it their chief accomplishment to marry their daughters to extra copies of the nobility. This collusion of the powers against kickers, and this social engrafting of the wealthy with members of the powers should impress even the dullest that government as a principle is the enemy of equality; the science of brigandage—absolute plundering prerogative combined with full social benefits and public honors.

Quebec furnishes an example of the efficiency of municipal supervision. A fire recently broke out there which turned seventy-five families in the streets. The firemen could do nothing because the pipe of the water supply was too small to furnish sufficient water. Insurance companies maintaining private fire forces would never be caught in such a stupidity, for they would have money at stake. But the collectivity having only political obligation at stake without competition, soon reaches the impossible and lets God, the next authority, fill the subscription list.

San Francisco "Freethought" is no more. It has consolidated with the New York "Truth Seeker," and Samuel P. Putnam's "News and Notes" are published in that paper and a branch office with its books and pamphlets is kept at the old stand in this city. As usual, insufficient support was the cause of this change. Egoism is now one of the only two radical papers on the Coast, and has just nine paid up subscribers in California. No other state is so near home, so the prophet is much greater in many others. While support is yearningly desirable, the regular appearance of the paper does not absolutely depend upon it. It has a habit of materializing anyway.

An employers' union to be extended over the entire state has been organized in this city to resist trades unions. This will bring organization against organization. The proprietor backed by the government will be pitted against the sentiment-bolstered laborer. It will expose the ineffectiveness of unionism to solve the labor question when it comes to the final test and tend to cause labor to look deeper than the surface for the cause of its helplessness and a solution. But it will not swell the ranks of the economic solvers yet. Political demagogy must have a good long pull on labor before it will listen to a more profound canvassing of the subject. It is so easy to drop a little piece of paper in a slot and get a brand new legislator who will square things right up (gradually). Nearly all the leaders of the unions are State Socialists at heart, and as their proposition is only a consistent extension of present methods it will not be hard to get numbers, and we may look for a crop of that ism at no distant day. Ambitious political aspirants are as plenty and ravenous as fleas, and they use the same methods to a dot that are employed by the old party manipulators. The same glittering generalities, barrenness of logic, and appeal to gushing sentiment characterize their public efforts. There are probably not many of them aware that they will not effect any remedy, but their methods of propaganda are precisely as if they were so aware. They go straight for popularity and power and do not attempt to inculcate a solitary tenet of economic science. New men will get into office, some restrictions will be set, stagnation will follow, and the ox-eyed toiler will gaze in astonishment at the vacancy from which the phantom of alleged relief has vanished. If by that time the giants of fortune and men with superior natural endowments have paternal regulation enough, the handful of rationalists may secure a hearing for economic science, and the final start toward equal opportunity and the spontaneities of equal freedom will be made.

A Face Serene.

An Egoistic Ideal.

I would my face were as a god's in mien,
Not proud, or pitiless, or taint with scorn,
But calm, illuminate with joy i[illegible];
The face of one whose eyes to smile are seen
As deep, still fountains, crystal-clear and clean,
Hold visions sweet of blue-sky peace 'mid thorn
And crag of rudest wilderness, uptorn;
"Self-peace!—To others peace!" from depths serene.

Ah, beautiful are lips that restful move,
And strong, smooth brows that fairly, calmly think,
And gentle eyes whose courage is to death;
The fair, strong features whoso sees must love,
The firm, strong hands that with yours truly link,
The pleasant mouth whence cometh Truth's sweet breath.

J. Wm. Lloyd.

The English clergy recently asked the prayers of the people that the increased freedom in education of a new educational act might not have an injurious effect on religion. They know their danger and expose the weakness of their cause fully as well as those people who deem it necessary to teach patriotism in the public schools, since there is no inducement to spontaneously harbor such a sentiment.

The "American Non Conformist" has removed from Kansas to Indianapolis, Ind., without missing the regular weekly issue. It is now published by the Vincent Bros. Pub. Co., and has acquired among other new members to the firm, Watson Heston, the famous Freethought cartoonist. When Egoism's publishers were still political authoritarians one of them was slightly acquainted with the junior Vincent and found him a democratically good fellow, which makes it seem good to note the brothers' influencive and financial success. Then comes that other thought, not to throw an ordinary wet blanket but a whole water-soaked show tent upon our ardor, by the consciousness that that success marks the ripening for an extension and intensification of State interference, the only enemy of freedom and prosperity. Not that these men love or desire the exercise of tyranny and reaction, but because a political effort which does not work for repeal alone, necessitates such tyranny and reaction. This will be clearer when the excitement of political contest leaves the mind to calmly review the work in the light of its ineffective effect.

Editorial Slashes.

The "Examiner" of this city has published some cuts of a Chinese woman at the beginning and at the end of four years of marital bliss with a certain *Chinaman*. As the first picture is the embodiment of vigor and fleshy plumpness, so is the latter that of lassitude and bony angularity. But let the press publish a representative number of representative cases of American monogamic marriage at its beginning and four years after, and it will illustrate that the barbarism consists chiefly in the institution, and that our alleged civilization in this respect is yet as far removed from the really civil as the same barbarity of the stationary race. The beastly crudity of meddling by word or deed with others' sexual relations must become more unpopular than it now is before we can afford to criticise the results of other barbarians' domestic habits.

Oakland has been having one of the most provoking divorce cases that I have ever noticed. The husband was the chief employee of an insurance company and was much away from home. The president of the company became sensitive to the wife's physical charms. Her isolation evidently accumulated such a surplus of vitality as made her susceptible to his advances, and they indulged in mutual orgies which prostrated her. Weakened, regretful, and the slave of the duty superstition, she confessed the cause of her prostration to her husband. He became dramatic and went to his employer's office and fired a few bullets into him. Then fearing the gallows he pathetically begged his wife for a confession of her intimacy with the wounded man with which to save the shooter's life at the trial, promising her a home and protection. Finally, with the understanding that she was to burn it after use, she dictated and signed a confession. It cleared him. He refused to destroy it and used it to secure a divorce from her and try to drive her to the gutter, which he swears he will do. Language fails to fittingly describe such a wretch.

The claim that government regardless of form is an autocratic institution for suppression received another confirmation in the attitude of the United States toward Chile's insurgents. The insurgents naturally expected sympathy and at least not interference from the great republic for the like of which they were fighting, but the stiffest monarchies prompted by commercial interests were more ready to favor them. Innocent people! when they have been blessed with majority tyranny and minority royal prerogative for a hundred years as we have, some of them may discover that plunder and privilege is the real purpose of political authority under whatsoever name, and then the cause of American indifference to the principle sentiment in the matter will be clearer. They were fighting privilege authoritarians there and appealed to the same class here, and it is not surprising that they should be disregarded. Intelligent sentiments on the idea of equal freedom occasion more surprise and opposition on the part of the average American than perhaps any other nationality. He has no idea of such a thing and prides himself on the fact that his government is as severe as any other. His conscience and ethics are legally constituted, and the breadth of thought which underlies revolution and new social regimes has no more place in his mind than in that of the simplest peasant.

About the first of this month a woman who was in Paris received a dispatch that her husband in New York was dangerously ill, and she at once started for Liverpool but was unable to secure passage for two days. After losing so much time she finally arrived at Boston in the night and tried to get off the vessel, but was refused permission to land until the health officers had been aboard. This kept her the rest of the night and when red tape finally allowed her to go to a train she had been thus uselessly detained too long and arrived at her husband's bedside just a half hour too late. This is another of the beauties of the machine regulation which impulsive and shortsighted collectivists wish to extend to every department of industrial activity and social intercourse. Nobody was to blame; the captain could not afford to be fined for landing passengers illegally; the officers could not know of the case and be ready to land the single passenger, and yet she was uselessly and outrageously detained. Personally, neither captain, officers, nor the people objected, but the unwieldliness of a representative regulative system was the cause. The captain could not get at the officers to permit the landing, nor the officers could not get at their constituents to explain a failure to perform contracted duty had they failed to arraign the captain. And if even a judge had allowed him to go free, there was the loss of time as well as risk of not so escaping a fear of which caused just what occurred. Had restraint from invasion instead of paternal regulation been the executive force of the country, this outrage would not have been perpetrated. No person would have risked coming before a local jury with so groundless a charge, and if they had there would not have been the slightest danger of a penalty for the captain. On the other hand to land contagious disease among the people would be followed by punishment so swiftly and adequate that no one could any more afford to do such a thing under such a regime than under the present. What would be true of freedom's administration in such a case would be as true of all other kinds of more important cases in social compromise.

When we read the history of bygone ages as seen by modern commentators, the active brutality in high places is prominent and constant, but the phenomena of course disappears just as our self-sufficient age or country is approached. Any one similarly exposing similar infractions of equal liberty in this age can become just such a victim by just such powers under just such subterfuges as those we read of, and few indeed see the least resemblance. The daily press in its chase for sensation recently discovered that Martinez of this state has become a Mecca for release from matrimonial bondage by divorce. Upon this discovery the preachers of the country, with the brutal ferocity characteristic of those men of alleged sympathy with suffering, raised a coyote chorus that set their monogamy-smashed she eagle-beaks popping like so many screech owls. Not the least shadow of an argument was offered against divorce—nothing but hysterical shrieks of, "a crying shame," "it's a disgrace," a "burning shame," and other such stereotyped and senseless guinea clatter. And the discovery that called out this shower of five thousand years-old Asiatic stone-'em-to-death sentiment is, that certain people who have a vague idea that pleasure is the legitimate purpose of life, are freeing themselves from what they believe to be their greatest impediment to greater happiness. And more happiness, especially if it is not of the theological brand, is a thing that God's good people cannot witness with composure. The idea of enjoying refreshing new magnetism more than once in a lifetime is too wildly extravagant. This crude mental infusoria cropped out in the recommendation of a "humane" reverend who would allow divorce only for infidelity and not allow the guilty party to marry again. This conformity to a barbaric concept,—this slavery to an idea—a mere word ghost, is the Christian and the popular conception of ethics. No matter how unpleasant or even wretched one might care to make the life of another by cruelty, neglect, or the most outrageous invasions, there would be no escape for him or her. But if one did an act in no way really injuring the other, that other might drive her from her home and her property or if it be a man he might be driven away and his labor ever afterward plundered with alimony. In either case the one who risks everything for even momentary gratification, is to be deprived of not only everything else, but as nearly as possible from further such gratification. The sensitive, suffering, animate, must always be sacrificed to the abstract. It would never do to let people in domestic turbulence and wretchedness enjoy complacency and after a time perhaps intensify the rest by the pleasures of a new conquest. Such breaks in the humdrum of institution monotony tend to divert the mind from a hereafter in which it hopes for relief from the miseries born of popular superstition, therefore these echoes of Jewish barbarism must do everything in their power to maintain a demand for their stock of futures. This is easily accomplished with the theological bivalve by a mad dog cry at innovation. It must have been an interesting sight to see the laity knock its geniuses down when the quadruped human species begun to develop ambition to rise and walk on its hind legs. It could not appear so absurd, however, as the efforts of the more evoluted biped to prevent individuals from improving at their own expense their conditions for happiness. H.

The Philosophy of Egoism.

XII.

The word *right* has the same fundamental meaning as *straight*. When no obstacle stands or lies between an animal and the object of its desire, the shortest way, which is a straight line, is the way the animal takes to reach the object; but when approach by a right line is impracticable the nearest known path is chosen, all considerations such as safety being weighed according to intelligence. This is then the line of least resistance,—the one most approximating in convenience to a right line. The right hand is so named because usually the stronger and more serviceable. A man's right is his straight way to the satisfaction of his desires, and he takes no other way except under adverse circumstances or hallucination.

It will be objected by Moralists that such an exposition of right reduces it to nothing but might. In this inference they are correct, but their objection does not disturb Egoistic philosophy, which regards their alleged supernal, sacred Right as a superstition. I have a right to what I can take and openly keep, and another has a right to take it from me if he can. Those, however, who believe that a superior authority has laid down a rule to which they must conform, will take up that rule or law as they understand it, and their idea of right will be that of conformity to the command of the authority. The Moralist is under an impression that instead of pursuing his own pleasure he has to fulfill a purpose which may be at variance with his pleasure. His conception of Right is not an Egoistic conception. He has surrendered himself, and with himself his own right, and has begun to serve an abstraction. He is in the way to commit great folly and wrong to himself. To the Moralist Right and Wrong are two fixed ideas, forever in opposition in all senses. To the intelligent Egoist they are two words generally perverted from their meaning and used as scarecrows. There is a frequent clash between the right of one and the right of another, and they fight it out. It is settled by the triumph of one and the defeat of the other. Max Stirner in his matchless book, Der Einzige und Sein Eigenthum, (the Individual and his Property) says: *Ist es mir recht, so ist es recht.* (If it be right to me, it is right). The Moralist would say: if it be right *for* me, thus implying that he is under some mysterious authority. The Egoist would not use the latter prepsition except when recognizing some law or definite arrangement which prescribes certain rights. When I say: "if it be right for me—," I admit an authority. Now in fact I must often admit one,—that is a power, —but I admit it simply as a power, not at all as the Moralist admits it. I do not bow down to it in my thought or regard it as anything but an enemy to my freedom, and if it cease to assert its power and compel me by penalty or the prospect of penalty, I assert my full power to do my own pleasure and nothing but my own pleasure. The Moralist consents to serve as his own jailer; not so the Egoist. Assert your right, your power, your pleasure, I claim none of that, I assert my own. I appeal to no Moral law of the world. I recognize none. We shall find our interests coincide or we shall give each other battle or we shall steer clear of each other, according to circumstances.

In words you can assert my right, but when you attempt to do so in deeds you succeed only in asserting your own right. I alone can prove my right by deeds.

The Moralist pretends to be under an obligation to respect the rights of others and never do them any wrong; but he defines their rights and does not allow them all their rights. He abdicates his own and cripples theirs and then flatters himself that the mutilation and effacement constitute superior Right. He protests against Egoism because it wrongs his system. At times he imagines that the Egoist must talk in the language of Moralism and must mean that in acting with Egoistic right the Egoist would pretend not to do wrong to another; wherein the Moralist becomes absurd, for the Egoist does not pretend that he can always exercise his right without wrong to another. It is a matter of expediency with the Egoist what wrong to another he shall do.

"Right wrongs no man," exclaims the landlord, and drives the tenant out of a house. The inclement weather beats upon the unsheltered, and their nerves are wrung. The landlord exercises his right, but lies moralistically.

The word *wrong* is a variation upon the past participle of the verb *to wring*, to twist. Victor and Vanquished are two, and the Moralist simply looks away from the facts of life when he preaches a universal natural Right and ignores individuals with their various wants and powers and the probability that what is good to one may entail some ill upon another.

But the species? The Moralist, driven from the former position of a divinity ordering all things in harmony in the world, or at least the conceit that his own species is favored at the expense of all below it, and this not by its intelligence but by a divine decree, arbitrarily making the spoilation of the world and rule over inferior animals Right, takes refuge in a belief that the welfare of the species may give Moral law to the individual. Hence the dogma that the individual dies for the species. Were it so, the individual might insist upon existing at any cost, assuming that he is what he knows best of the species, and that his stubborn will might probably be a provision for the species. That is Right, says the Moralist, which best serves the species. And what best serves the species? The Moralist will generally reply: "that which is Right," thus completing a little circle in dogmatism. Nature, however, seems to say that species survive by the survival of their individuals. The Egoist will find in himself certain loves and aversions, and he may think that the species is taking care of itself just in proportion as he is following those paths which give him satisfaction.

The Moralist, becoming more philosophical, suggests that the war of interests will cease as men understand their similar needs and the possibility of mutual benefit, hence wrongs in the species may become fewer or cease. With all our heart say the Egoists, only you are not to begin by sacrificing us. If the later Moralism be merely a prophetic dream of a harmony of interests through wisdom, we are not without hope that at last the dreamers will recognize individuality as the condition precedent to the fulfillment of their hopes. The fellow feeling in the species is a certain fact. Let us take it for what we find it to be and not attempt to place it in antagonism toward our individualities. As these are developed the necessity will appear for each one to recognize somewhat the individuals of his species, and thus the "claims of the species" will be recognized. TAK KAK.

SEPARATED from nature by monopoly, cut off from humanity by poverty, the mother of crime and its punishment, what refuge remains for the plebeian whom labor cannot support, and who is not strong enough to take? To conduct this offensive and defensive war against the proletariat a public force was indispensable: the executive power grew out of the necessities of civil legislation, administration, and justice. And there again the most beautful hopes have changed into bitter disappointments. As legislator, as burgomaster, and as judge, the prince has set himself up as a representative of divine authority. A defender of the poor, the widow, and the orphan, he has promised to cause liberty and equality to prevail around the throne, to come to the aid of labor, and to listen to the voice of the people. And the people have thrown themselves lovingly into the arms of power; and, when experience has made them feel that power was against them, instead of blaming the institution, they have fallen to accusing the prince, even unwilling to understand that, the prince being by nature and destination the chief of non-producers and greatest of monopolists, it was impossible for him, in spite of himself, to take up the cause of the people. All criticism, whether of the form or the acts of goverment, ends in this essential contradiction. And when the self-styled theorists of the sovereignty of the people pretend that the remedy for the tyranny of power consists in causing it to emanate from popular suffrage, they simply turn, like the squirrel, in their cage. For, from the moment that the essential conditions of power—that is, authority, property, hierarchy—are preserved, the suffrage of the people is nothing but the consent of the people to their oppression,—which is the silliest charlatanism.—Proudhon.

A Few Good Books.

BY GEORGE FORREST.

Among the number of scientific works, novels, and dramas pertaining to modern social questions, which have appeared of late years, there are some of great value; yet it must be confessed the major portion are merely passing contributions of no lasting worth. Of least value are the novels, which, while they may treat of social questions in a radical manner, are written by persons who are unscientific, incompetent, and who write on the spur of the moment, simply because they know there is a demand for the radical novel. Very frequently these novels become popular, the authors are set up as great teachers, and that which was written in an empirical manner is declared to be infallible. People are ever ready to set up a hero and worship him, frequently for qualities which he does not possess, and thus every new prophet in the social movement has a number of followers, who swear by whatever he writes. Sentiment carries them away,—they are going to reform the world—what use have they for facts. Thus there are constantly arising hosts of these heroes, and they all attract worshipers.

But among these books there are some which are not of the "plan-of-campaign" character. They do not give directions in instantaneous world-reform—they give facts; just simple facts. They do not seek popularity by catering to the sentimental foolishness of the people—for the majority of the people are fools—therefore they never become really popular. It is of late years, as I have said, that so much time has been devoted by scientists, novelists and dramatists to the social question. Yet there are some works which are not of late years, but which were so far in advance of their time that it is only lately they have begun to be read.

Of novels which are of artistic value, and whose subject-matter is of the highest order, are Tchernychewsky's "What's To Be Done?" and Olive Schreiner's "Story of an African Farm." These two are probably the only ones in the long list of radical novels which will live. They are both philosophical and both concern the woman question. "What's To Be Done?" is perhaps the more artistic as a whole, though some critics have called it crude. The egoistic arguments between Kirsanoff and Lopoukhoff, the two young medical students are delightful. It is one of those books that you like to have within reach after you have read it, for no matter where you open it there is nearly always food for reflection in what you read. "The Story of an African Farm," has also attraction for you after you have read it—there is so much written between the lines. It is loved best by young people who are just beginning to understand that religion is not always what it is painted. It is the story of the evolution of a young man, or boy, rather, from belief to disbelief. Those who may read it when they and orthodoxy are parting company, will feel a deep sympathy with the ideas in the book, and its philosophy will help them. These novels should not be confounded with even the better class of radical novels; they are of superior merit, their authors taking rank among the leading novelists of the world.

There are a few scientific works which every person who desires to understand the basic principles of modern thought should read. Spencer's "Social Statics," for instance, is one of the best of books to "give you a center around which to hang your ideas," as Olive Schreiner would say. "Social Statics," "First Principles," "Data of Ethics," and "The Man Versus the State" will give you a fair idea of Spencer's worth.

Proudhon's "What Is Property?" contains the economics of Anarchy, and it is brilliantly written. The different phases of the land question about which there has been so much discussion, and which is one of the principal points of difference between Individualists and Anarchists, is well considered. Proudhon was undoubtedly the first to see this question in the proper light, and to show the great injustice caused by property in land. Proudhon, as a writer, was masterly: brilliant, sarcastic, kindly, bold, almost reckless; he wrote what he thought and cared not what the world said—so the world treated him shamefully. But "against the enemy revendication is eternal," and thousands are now demanding what he demanded—Liberty.

Then there is John Stuart Mill's "Liberty." The very name is attractive. State Socialists, who believe in regulating other people's morals, health, pleasure, business, misery and life ought to read it, and then try minding their own business for a day or two. "Liberty" is an excellent little work, protesting strongly against the assumption of infallibility by any person in regard to another's affairs. Mill's "Subjugation of Women" is also an excellent work.

Until the past few years there has been no dramatic writer of any ability in the field of Individualism. One has, however, arisen, who has astonished the world. Henrik Ibsen is now the most widely read dramatist living, and this, too, in spite of the extreme radicalism of his writings. His war is against the State; he wishes to abolish it, mere changes in the form of government he regards as "more or less degrees of trifling." All of his dramas are well worth reading for their literary value alone, but his social dramas are of most interest to Anarchists and Individualists on account of their subject-matter. The influence exerted by Ibsen has undoubtedly done more to spread Individualistic doctrines than that of any other writer of late years. Ibsen is a thorough Egoist, and therefore an Anarchist. This is clearly shown by his dramas and letters. Of course the great fashionable world—those who attend Ibsen readings—would never think of him as an Anarchist. They read Ibsen because Ibsen is the fad—they haven't the slightest idea what his theories are, but simply know that he is fashionable. When they discover what it is they have been reading they will be horrified, and—get a new fad.

A LIBERTY which anybody else in the universe has a right to define is *no* liberty for me. A pursuit of happiness which some despot, or some oligarchy, or some tyrannical *majority*, has the power to prescribe and shape for me, is not the pursuit of *my* happiness. Statesmen, politicians, religious dissenters, and reformers, who have hitherto sanctioned the principle of freedom, have not seen its full reach and expansion; hence they become reactionists, conservatives, and "old fogies," when the whole truth is revealed to them. They find themselves getting more than they bargained for. Nevertheless, the principle, which already imbues the popular mind instinctively, though not as yet intellectually, will not wait their bidding. Hence all middle men, far more than the conservatives, are destined in this age to be very unhappy.—Stephen Pearl Andrews in "Love, Marriage, and Divorce."

Managerial Experience.

I experienced last month an impulse of evolutionary propulsion, and have some idea how that intellectual pride is acquired which permits its victim to make a fool of himself several times before he will acknowledge his error once. Last May I predicted that with the necessary material to print EGOISM on a steam press I could operate the little Columbian as a relic with great ease, and it has turned out just so. This causes me to feel like a budding philosopher, and gives me a touch of the inductive spur that has tickled the racial flank from the state of the complacent-minded snail to that of the tasseling vertebrate with his remarkable logic that a universal desire for service from others justifies its exaction, instead of provision against it. Having carefully realized this generalization, it was with great felicity and both eyes that I watched a genial pressman and Hoe press cultivate EGOISMS as rapidly as hickory nuts fall after a heavy frost from a bumped tree. When all is deliberately made ready the pressman prods the machine in the ribs, and a great cast stove drum starts to roll, pops its bill, and from the top of the pile grabs a sheet which races down among rollers and over strings like a lizard through a rock pile and is slapped upon a table with four printed pages quicker than I can give a thought. It is interesting to see the form chasing about under the press like a mouse under benches, and to hear the rollers smack their lips every time they get a fresh bite of ink, and thereafter to observe them mixing up with each other like smooth and reciprocal nether limbs. This press not only snaps and lizards and prints fast, but has four boards on a table which stand on their edges and joyfully dance a quadrille around the newly-coined thought on EGOISM's pages. All this is in delightful contrast with the centenarian duration and parturitive agony of the Columbian lever act. But though without gray, it has its drawbacks. The press is located in a large roomful of case stands and compositors, and I am exposed to their presence. Upon this occasion and my person I wore my decollete pants, pump-a-door vest, and such a look as a cat is attired in while being entertained by a strange garret. To such scenery the compositors were unaccustomed, and glad smiles broke irreparably out upon their gazes like measles on the cheek of beauty. But while the loudest observers were beautiful enough to smite the heart of a Russell or rustle that of a live oak, they were neither cheeky nor measly and for this I am greatfully grateful. In some offices the compositors would have directed such audible remarks at each other as would fit my case with long primer accuracy, and I could not well get back at them. A compositor's life is full of lean, solid long primer and monotony, and this makes him as sensitive to novel sights as a plowboy. I mingled with their estimation at a disadvantage too, for I have been accustomed only to fox chases and those used on job presses, and didn't know which was the "outside" of the ones used on the cylander press, so of course "locked up" untechnically. This made no difference as regarded the work for that time, but it exposed the fact that I have learned only so much of the trade as I have used, and to a regular he printer even "pi" is not so disreputable as a printer who has been moved into before the plastering and finish is on. I don't blame them either, for one has to have something to assume upon in so pretentious a world. A lack of great experience and money, is my misfortune as manager for a poor but respectable publishing company. At the printing house, even one of the proprietors who is not a flatterer and who has an eye for the humorous in nature, suggested in a tone containing among other ingredients tincture of irony, that I have the cases patented in which EGOISM's beautiful and chaste forms are concealed while being carried by the transfer company under piles of snaggy boxes and the rude gaze of a vulgar public. But I received an invitation to return in September, which I accept, gratefully remembering the man who made this method possible and congratulating radicalism on numbering among its own those with money-making ability and without miserly meanness.

When Hugh O. Pentecost gets off something particularly silly I sometimes think he has softness in the head, but I never dreamed that the softness was not cerebrally confined until I read that he regrets the process by which the race is now manufactured. If the protest had come from a woman, whose absorption of the subject under Mr. Pentecost's penetration would be supposed to acquaint her more internally with the unpleasant spirit of its features, I should have regarded it as characteristic, but when a man wails, my curiosity and so forth rise at once and I am willing to assist as best I can. I have also canvassed several of my male friends regarding the matter and they have to a man proffered their services in cases where such unaccountable taste renders such tasks repugnant. George Macdonald is gone now and I have no statement from him relating to it, but I feel safe in saying he will be all right, for I do not believe he would refuse to lend his strong limbs to promote welfare and good feeling in the community. Mr. Pentecost can feel reassured so far as the Pacific coast is concerned. There is little apprehension felt, however, that my friends' philanthrophy will be imposed upon, as Mr. Pentecost's kind of taste is very rare—so rare in fact, that it smacks a little of the verdure the beef fatted on. It is a taste susceptible of being consistently extended in other vital directions. Take eating for instance. This is a necessary habit and one in which many people find much comfort and belching, and one in which many more are anxiously seeking the former. Yet for those too ethereal for the necessities of animate life, the habit must be unutterably disgusting, for it is a tripish subject all the way through and is ardently practiced by every kind of beast and upon all sorts of fodder. It is a munching, mixy, slabbery, churning, belching, seeping, growling process beside of and among which gestation is as fine pastry work compared with swill boiling. Let Mr. Pentecost contemplate the parturitive as well as tropical source of a roast, and the nastiness of strawberry shortcake with its wheat and berries grown from unpalatable manure and handled by porous hands throughout and eaten with milk strained through a hairy cow of organism. Let him exercise his unanalytic impressibility upon all these and (lightly) upon the inevitable incidents of alimentation, and he will find in the means by which the race exists, a parellel of his regret at the method by which it is continued. Then there is breathing usually regarded as an ethereal practice, but let him remember ugly grating dust, smudgy coal smoke, burning rags and leather, croutish sewer gas, fumy corpses, unshampooed skunks, unsalted human feet and socks, poultry stalls, threshing machines, declining fish, contagious diseases, and think of pumping such air into his celestial lights as is often unavoidable, and he will probably find breathing too disgusting to continue. Thus a sandpapered asceticism driving him from procreation, eating, and breathing, he will have to dissolve or admit the futility of his taste apology for an unmistakable affliction of sex superstition. This will be so, not because it is so, but because in complex mentality even taste is affected by ideas of consistency. Mr. Pentecost, however, will probably do neither; he evidently carries a posteriorly located steel plate about his nether raiment which enables him to sit for months with the utmost composure on the sharpest horn of any dilemma. He will no more be an *ist* of any kind than a negro will be black, but he espouses Egoism, if not understandingly at least devotedly, yet the slavery to an idea that impelled him to burn manuscript on parturition and desire to scrub his office because such pen marks had been in it, is parallel to that of the worst fanaticism of the age. If the rejected manuscript was not wanted by the author, Mr. Pentecost could have shown a well-balanced disinterest by disposing of it as he does of other rejected manuscript. One need not go far to find people as well fitted as he to reason prejudice from their minds.

I was at Labor day this year which happened here on the 7th of this month. When I came home at night with headache and no dinner I forcibly sensed how realism is penetrating everything so that even picnicky Labor day has become laborious. The governor of this state did not proclaim Labor day, for he had no way of knowing the numbers of agitating labor and could not tell what would be most politic, so he advised all to observe it who wished to. Uninfluenced by his suggestion, but impelled by curiosity I in the morning sponged with a rag and some gasoline the big grease spot from the front of my vest and sneaked my wife's perfume bottle, dabbing the cork against my bony bosom so that I smelt real good to myself all day and felt quite refined. Perfumery is great to make one feel refined, and I notice that some people depend upon it altogether for their refinement. Such refinement smells nice but it doesn't look well. It took me so long to refine that I had to pare my quarter-moon-countenanced nails on the train, and found that I had just five pairs exposed. A good many working people were at the local stations, and the young men with tolerably plump wives looked very proud of them and these wives were proud to be looked proud of. The older men from the extremities of whose wives the upholstering had worked out, did not seem proud of anything they had on exhibition, but like pious worshipers conferred much credit upon themselves by a superfluity of "sacred duty" to variably-sized posterity which swarmed about them under odd-styled hats and in roomy new shoes. I think this zeal will have to be replaced with a careful study of economics before the laboring class becomes the citizen class. But it was the day of my class and a few of us were out to uselessly show our hand and dusty feet. Anatomically speaking, I am in some important respects not proud of us. We measure well enough from the ear back and from it straight above the backbone and have plenty of width between the ears, but from the ear forward and especially to the top part of the frontal lobe the distance is not a long one, however dusty it may have been that day. It is painful to note how the repugnance of a task from which we get all the weariness and pain and only a little of the product, has battered our frontal sinuses back against our medulla oblongatas. I was despairingly struck with this contrast as our people reformatorily waded the dust of the street while faces with large upper stories gazed upon them from the windows of comfortable offices in elegant buildings. The marchers believe they will rout them from those drawing-room workshops and make them produce their living themselves, but the two-storied men are not frightened. They have little to fear from a movement that proposes a system of officialism knitted by treacherous gradations from the dome down into the very vitals of the laboring mudsill. They will be around in time to find places in it just as they were to find them in the privilege of present State interference with industrial freedom, for they already pat the political authority worshiping laborer on the head and tell him through the press that he is great and fighting in the right direction to better his condition.

The mayor was invited by the Federated Trades to review the parade, which he kindly did from the city hall portico and a white vest in which he was that day laboring for the residents of the city. I stood very near him to see how reviewing is performed, and found that I was doing the thing myself. Besides a better suit of clothes than I ever had he wore, before the parade arrived, such an expression as I have felt when my mother made me play with visiting neighbors' children whom I believed several sizes too small for me. He made no advances and the divisions did not cheer as they passed, which was the only thing in the day's doings that surprised and pleased me. But so long as men will parade there is no hope that they will solve the industrial problem.

I was curious to know just what the orator would orate, so accompanied by a cable car I was on the ground early that I might capture the larva. It proved to be a constable and there being no one else there the State and Anarchy laid down together in the shade upon a bench, and I gave him my experience as a tramp for his as our catcher. He complained bitterly of the government continually cutting on the salaries of its lower-case officials while the "caps" who get all the "pick-up" are undisturbed. I then explained how I thought it the source of the trouble in the whole case, but he neither combatted nor understood the idea, and looked into the face of his gold watch. Soon men brought tenderly-dandled canes, and broodworn women brought armfuls of accumulated squall. Then an old man with hysterical inspiration and a dinted voice tried to sell Christian Socialistic papers. A girl with a distaff of new Irish linen hair and with folio feet monopolized the swing while a young man longing to be the seat board, swung her like a skein of hot *candy*. The metalic horn band set off packages of last year's campaign notes, then a man with a mein and with a hole worn in the top of his hair, proved with great elaboration that wage workers are slaves. He declared that science will save us, is divine, and consists in the government first taking all profitable business from individuals and afterward establishing national co-operation. Nobody asked the demagogue to head the list by surrendering his vocation of political manipulator, nor how some kinds of business came to be so much more profitable than others, nor why the ounce of privilege prevention would not be more scientific than a countryful of administration to soak up the plunder.

Most of the magazine muzzle loading audience were filled with the orator's articulatory exercise, and the rest with the barkeeper's beer, but the effect was the same in both cases and the labor problem was uproarously applauded. It was now time for the closing concert of embryo politicians, and I walked sadly away on part of the skin of an unknown cow. Behind me was the orator looking dramatically heroic; nerveless old men looking solidly constituent; wrinkled and shattered old women filling in with stereotyped head gear and toothless grins; red-eyed boozy men hooked like dark lanterns on the backs of benches or stretched like dried salmon upon the ground, and splintery young girls of diluted purpose gadding about acting silly. But unlike marriage, I could get out of it for the same price that I got in, and with popular labor agitation in a nutshell and Oakland's effort floating away on the sea breeze among the eucalyptus trees, I sat down upon the skirt of my low-necked pants in a cable car and smelled up the fragments of my morning's perfuming as I rode through three miles of desert town lots at business location prices. And the sun and enlarged heads rose the next morning. THE MANAGER.

Straws in the Breeze.

Straws are the component parts of a great stack made by gathering them.

Personally, I am a believer in the discredited policy of the *laissez faire* school; and in virtue of my belief, I have the utmost doubts as to the success of any attempt to alter the relations of labor and capital by means of legislation. On the other hand, I am bound to admit that the whole course of legislation in recent years, no matter what party was in power, has been one series of violations of the fundamental principles of my old-fashioned creed.—Edward Dicey.

General Longstreet says that on one of the long night marches in Virginia, the only way he could get rest was to lie down on the ground while the column was passing, and sleep for an hour or so. He woke up just as the stragglers were coming along the rear, and heard an old Georgia cracker soliloquizing about the situation: "I love my country, and I'll fight for it, and I'll die for it, and I'll go naked and barefooted for it; but when this war is over, I'll be cursed if I ever love another country."—Argonaut.

"I haf der right—der gonstitutional right to garry veapons," protested Mr. Royer the other day when booked at the police station after notable feats of arms against certain railroad men who were setting posts on his premises. "Ven dose vellers injure my gometree I vall pack on my right to garry und bear arms, dot vas all." Mr. Royer, you are indubitably correct: the constitution of the United States explicitly declares that the right of the people to bear arms shall not be abridged. But, dear, dear! There are circumstances of which you are unaware. The United Sates supreme court (august tribunal!) has decided that this clause is, first, in conflict with various city ordinances; second, obscured by bad spelling—it should be "bare" arms; third unwise; and, fourth, unconstitutional.—Ambrose Bierce in Examiner.

The things sought to be accomplished by disregarding liberty and justice are frequently good; indeed, it is by fixing their eyes so intently on the special object that the larger considerations are overlooked. It is desirable that great manufacturing establishments shall exist in a country, and laws specially assisting manufactures will produce them; but liberty and justice are still better things, and therefore we may be sure that protection is a bad thing. Temperance is a good thing, and may, in some degree, be produced by law; but liberty and justice are better things, and therefore prohibition is a bad thing. Education, even the kind given in our public schools, is a good thing; but liberty and justice are better things, and therefore our compulsory public-school system is a bad thing. Most of the things aimed at by Socialists are in themselves good things, but they can be obtained in better ways than those proposed; besides, liberty and justice are still better things, and therefore all Socialistic legislation, being inconsistent with these, is a very bad thing.—To-day.

OUR BOOK LIST.

LOVE, MARRIAGE, AND DIVORCE, AND THE SOVEREIGNTY OF THE INDIVIDUAL, is a pamphlet of 121 pages composed of a discussion of marriage by Henry James, Horace Greeley, and Stephen Pearl Andrews. What Proudhon's works are to Anarchism is this to freedom in love between the sexes. It is the most comprehensive, searching, and exhaustive work ever written on the subject. No advocate of sexual freedom can afford to be without a full acquaintance with its contents. Price 35 cents.

FREE POLITICAL INSTITUTIONS: THEIR NATURE, ESSENCE, AND MAINTENANCE,—an abridgement and rearrangement of Lysander Spooner's "Trial by Jury," edited by Victor Yarros. It is treated in seven chapters under the following heads: I. Legitimate Government and Majority Rule. II. Trial by Jury as a Palladium of Liberty. III. Trial by Jury as Defined by Magna Charta. IV. Objections answered. V. The Criminal Intent. VI. Moral Considerations for Jurors. VII. Juries of the Present Day Illegal. Whoever desires to make plain to his conservative neighbor just how society may get on without tyranny and privilege fostering government, should have a copy of this pamphlet in his coat pocket and be prepared to not only defend his position but to take that of the opposition by storm. It is the much-needed propaganda material that should be circulated as fast as Anarchists can afford to devote money to the work. Price 25 cts.

THE RAG-PICKER OF PARIS, by Felix Pyat, translated from the French by Benj. R. Tucker. This novel is the most complete portrayal of the human nature of this century in every condition of life, that has been contributed to radical literature. Every line, every pause, has a fullness, a significance of thought, or a volcano of emotion seldom found anywhere singly, and not combined in the style of any other writer. It is probably the most vivid picture of the misery of poverty, the extravagance of wealth, the sympathy and forbearance of the poor and despised, the cruelty and aggressiveness of the aristocratic and respectable, the blind greed of the middle classes, the hollowness of charity, the cunning and hypocrisy of the priesthood, the tyranny and corruption of authority, the crushing power of privilege, and finally of the redeeming beauty of the ideal of liberty and equality, that the century has produced. Four thousand copies were sold the first week after its publication. Radicals can do much good work with it among the partly liberal-minded. It will, without arousing their prejudices, open a new field of thought for very orthodox people. Price in cloth binding $1; paper, 50 cents.

MY UNCLE BENJAMIN: a novel by Claude Tillier, an intelligent victim of institution oppression, who necessarily suffered more than he enjoyed. The splitting pangs of his intense pessimism are seasoned with such ridiculing thrusts at the vanity of wealth as to almost hide the exaggeration. The characters are not made to "come out" in school girl ideal, but tumble along like real life, mostly at the mercy of other elements than the reader's desire. The facts are not manufactured and put up in doses ready to take for building up a philosophy made to order. He dissects conduct and illustrates the charlatanism on one part and the superstition and stupidity on the other that creates fame, with diagramatic plainness. Living in an age when some of our grandfathers were too prejudice-ridden to wear boots, buttons, or suspenders we find him in his philosophy dashing off almost our deepest concepts with a lucidness equal to the description of the most commonplace affairs of our time. His wit is like springing a dark-lantern in a sub-cellar, while his humor penetrates your anatomy to the marrow without allowing you to roar with laughter so skillfully is it woven in with philosophy, pathos, or tragedy. We heartily recommend it to our full-grown readers. Price in cloth $1.00; paper 50 cents.

MONEY is at once a camera and chemist of human conduct and motive. Zola not only describes the carnivora, from the den it inhabits to the changing reflections of its glossy coat, but he tells what it is thinking about and will do. He realizes that the human animal is a none too much evoluted wild beast on the front of whose skull the experience of ages has worn only a bright spot, and he exposes all the greed, ferocious brutality, tyranny, cunning, hypocrisy, ostentation, truckling servility, idealism, and stupidity embodied in the kings, manipulators, and victims of a modern speculative world. The cruel and the generous, the detestable and the admirable traits of each character are delineated with an analytical nicety and a realistic accuracy that make the reader live the life of each and absorb the apology for their shortcomings without for a moment losing sight of the expedient course that should have replaced undesirable conduct. With an eloquently-implied regret he rebukes the horrors and cruelties of financial conquest without the wearisome moralizing or the narrow hatred common to the critics of social outrages. He is not a world builder nor a hero worshiper. Even Caroline, the lover of life, intelligent, educated, experienced, unprejudiced, and the heroine of the most trying ordeals of the story, was in his critical eyes full of weaknesses between which she was, inconsistently with her ideal of life, constantly vacillating. On world building he strikes State Socialism one of his efficient implied blows, but sensate to the difficulties of wide innovation, he offers no remedy for industrial troubles, contenting himself with painting in bold relief and sharp contrast the almost fabulous extravagance of the rich and the horrifying wretchedness of the poor, along with emphasis on the fraud, sham, and wholesale manipulating practiced by speculators upon the unsuspecting. Yet he describes with effective force the spirit of rivalry, the entrancing pleasures, the magnificent enterprises, and even humanitarian dreams that prompt men to speculate even by the most gigantic fraud. And it is this, along with his realistic repletion that makes Zola such an admirable and to us unequaled novelist. His plot embraces almost every shade of character constituting modern civilization, and he depicts the virtues and weaknesses of each with a disinterest as faithful as his realism is striking. Even his reference to Egoism, a subject that impulsive French blood might readily balk on, is characterized by this faithfulness to the spirit of the subject in hand. His Egoist, though not the expansive utilitarian of our ideal, is nevertheless intrinsically Egoistic and approvably utilitarian in a comprehensive view of the subject. Although the story, true to life, contains a full complement of unsanctioned sexual alliances, the only woman rich or poor that gold could not influence was a little Freelover who contracted such association with desirable men just once through curiosity for pleasure alone. Saccard, his chief character, is a financial poet, a speculative madman who dreams only of money—millions, power, conquest, supremacy, the prostration at his feet of "all great, cowardly, truckling Paris." Ambitious, active, unscrupulous, assuming, an appropriator of other men's ideas—of everything that came in his reach, he wove from his own and borrowed imagination, such alluring prospects as placed at his service the means beginning a career of speculation and spoilation the incidents and characters of which in Zola's masterly hands constitute the most startling expose of the power and tyranny of privileged money, the blind recklessness of stock gambling, and the ravenous greed of human avarice that we have read. We regard it as the ablest in our list, although no one can afford to be without the intensification of thought and feeling generated by all of them. The price of "Money" in cloth binding is $1; paper cover 50 cents.

For any of the above address

EQUITY PUBLISHING COMPANY,

P. O. Box 1678. San Francisco, Calif

EGOISM'S PRINCIPLES AND PURPOSE.

Egoism's purpose is the improvement of social existence through intelligent self-interest. It finds that whatever we have of equal conditions and mutual advantage is due to a prevalence of this principle corresponding with the degree and universality of individual resistance to encroachment.

Reflection will satisfy all who are desirous of being guided in their conclusions by fact, that as organization itself is a process of absorbing every material useful to its purpose, with no limit save that of outside resistance, so must the very fact of its being a separately organized entity make it impossible for it to act with ultimate reference to anything but itself. Observation will show that this holds good throughout the vegetable and animal kingdoms, and that whatever of equality exists among members of a species or between different species has its source and degree in the resisting capacity, of whatever kind, which such member or species can exert against the encroachment of other members or species. The human animal is no exception to this rule. True, its greater complexity has developed the expedient of sometimes performing acts with beneficial results to others, but this is at last analysis only resistance, because it is the only means of resisting the withholding by others from such actor's welfare that which is more desirable than that with which he parts. If, then, the self-projecting faculty of mankind is such that it will in addition to the direct resistance common to the less complex animals, diplomatically exercise present sacrifice to further extend self, and it being a fact that equality depends upon equal resistance, diplomatic or otherwise, what are its chances in an absence of enlightenment in which the individuals of the majority so far from *intelligently* using this resisting power in their own behalf, do not even believe that they should do so? The result of a general conception so chaotic, would naturally be what we find: the generalization from the practical expediency of certain consideration for others, crystallized through the impulse of blind selfishness into a mysterious and oppressive obligation, credit for the observance of which gratifies the self-projecting faculty of the simple, while the more shrewd evade its exactions, and at every step from the manipulation of the general delusions of religious and political authority to the association of sexes and children at play, project themselves by exchanging this mythical credit for the real comforts and luxuries of the occasion, which the others produce. Thus in addition to the natural disadvantage of unequal capacity, the weaker are deprived through a superstition, of the use of such capacity as they have, as may be seen in their groping blindness all about us.

To secure and maintain equal conditions then, requires a rational understanding of the real object of life as indicated by the facts of its expression. It is plain that the world of humanity is made up of individuals absolutely separate; that life is to this humanity nothing save as it is something to one of these; that one of these can be nothing to another except as he detracts from or adds to his happiness; that on this is based the idea of social expediency; that the resistance of each of these individuals would determine what is socially expedient; that approximately equal resistance makes it equality, and on such continued and a universal resistance depends equality. This can leave no room for any sane action toward others but that of the policy promoting most the happiness of the acting Ego. Therefore Egoism insists that the attainment of equal freedom depends upon a course of conduct replacing the idea of "duty to others" with *expedency* toward others; upon a recognition of the fact that self-pleasure must be the final motive of any act; thus developing a principle for a basis of action about which there can be no misunderstanding, and which will place every person squarely on the merit of his or her probable interests, divested of the opportunity to deceive through pretension, as under the dominance of altruistic idealism. It will maintain that what is generally recognized as morality is nothing other than the expediency deduced from conflicting interests under competition; that it is a policy which, through the hereditary influence of ancestral experience, confirmed by personal experience, is found to pay better than any other known policy; that the belief that it is something other than a policy—a fixed and eternal obligation, outside of and superior to man's recognized interests, and may not be changed as utility indicates, makes it a superstition in effect like any other superstition which causes its adherents to crystallize the expediency adopted by one period into positive regulations for another in which it has no utility, but becomes tyrannical laws and customs in the name of which persecution is justified, as in the fanaticism of any fixed idea.

Another part of its purpose is to help dispel the "Political Authority" superstition and develop a public sentiment which would replace State interference with the protection for person and property which the competition of protecting associations would afford. Then the State's fanatical tyranny and industry crushing privilege would torture the nerves of poverty-stricken old age or pinch tender youth no more. The most disastrous interference of this monster superstition is its prohibition of the issuing of exchange medium on the ample security of all kinds of property, which at once would abolish speculative interest and practically set all idle hands at productive labor at wages ever nearing the whole product until it should be reached. The next interference is by paper titles to vacant land instead of the just and reasonable one of occupancy and use, which with the employment that free money would give, would furnish all with comfortable homes in a short time, and thereafter even with luxuries from like exertion. Following this is its patent privilege, customs robbery, protective tariff, barbarous decrees in social and sexual affairs; its brutal policy of revenge, instead of restitution, in criminal offenses, and finally its supreme power to violate the individual, and its total irresponsibility.

PROSPECTUS

EGOISM is published Monthly at 50 cents a year.

[*Entered as Second Class Mail Matter.*]

It is promptly discontinued when subscription expires, and no bills are sent out. It is run by the publishers, and admits only such contributions as they believe extend, or intelligently criticise its position.

The following are the names and amounts contributed by propagandists who wish to spread this line of thought and in that degree are its "Continental Congress," pledging so much "life and fortune" toward the establishing of their ideals and making their personalities felt in the world they live in.

PROPAGANDISTS FOR VOL. II.:

G. A. F. De Lespinasse, - - - - $50.00
A Friend, - - - - - - - - 5.00

EQUITY PUBLISHING COMPANY,
P. O. Box 1678. San Francisco, Calif.

MONOGAMIC SEX RELATIONS Discussed by Ego and Marie Louise. This extraordinary pamphlet charges monogamic sexual relations with causing electrical poverty through balanced electrical conditions, which results in many common, and the most fatal diseases, and in mental deterioration, leading to narrow-mindedness, bigotry, tyranny, persecution, irritability, melancholy, drunkenness, suicide, and most of the vice and misery arising from the discontent of mankind. The every day experience of all close observers must corroborate many of its accusations with unmistakable accuracy. It is intensely radical, yet clothed in such language as will admit of loaning to your orthodox neighbor. It is printed on good paper, with new type, and contains 24 large pages. Price 10 cents.

CITIZENS' MONEY. A lecture on the "National Banking System," by Alfred B. Westrup, delivered in Chicago and published in "Liberty," of Boston, in 1888. Mr. Westrup shows that every dollar's worth of property in the country may be converted into active capital, reducing interest to the cost of issuing money, and sending capital in search of labor instead of being the other way, as it is at present. It is short, popular in style, and well calculated for propaganda work. Whoever is interested in industrial emancipation can do no better work than procure and circulate this pamphlet by the dozen. It contains 21 pages, is printed on good paper in large type, and can be had for 60 cents per dozen, or 10 cents per single copy.

For any of the above address

EQUITY PUBLISHING COMPANY,
P. O. Box 1678. San Francisco, Calif.

Egoism

Vol. II.—No. 6. **SAN FRANCISCO, CAL., OCTOBER, 1891.** **Price, Five Cents.**

Pointers.

Owing to a number of trifling circumstances EGOISM is unusually late this time. We shall try to do better hereafter or have a better excuse for not doing so.

We wish to call the reader's attention in particular to Tak Kak's present article on the "Philosophy of Egoism." He exposes the fallacy which serves Spencer as a turntable to gain the collectivist track that justifies majority rule and makes his conclusion ordinary republicanism while his premises point straight to Anarchism politically and Egoism ethically.

On the 9th of this month another United States steamer happening to be out of port after dark ran aground and was lost. Her crew knew enough to get ashore and stay about the life-saving station. There is nothing like governmental control where efficiency is not desired. The navy department should send its forces about in regular passenger steamers manned by experienced sailors or the clothes racks may all be drowned.

The first number of the San Francisco "Beacon's" successor has come to our den. It is now the "Enfant Terrible," and voices the sentiments of Egoism and philosophical Anarchism. It is published fortnightly, contains four pages somewhat smaller than those of this paper, and is chock full of bright and witty things. The subscription price is 50 cents a year. Address "Enfant Terrible," 101 Fifteenth street, San Francisco, Calif.

It is reported that Hugh O. Pentecost has adopted the law as a profession. This step was taken it is said to more thoroughly secure the certainty of a livelihood such as his family has been accustomed to. Our good will accompanies his person, and so long as people employ lawyers we hope he will be liberally patronized. This also indicates that Mr. Pentecost has learned that men are justifiable in following their ideals only so far as they can afford such a luxury. Otherwise he would not become a legal limb.

The reason why women are by forceful legislation prohibited from wearing men's apparel is something we never could understand. The reason for the women struggling to make that, or some other change, is apparent. But now we learn that men are arrested for wearing women's clothes as well as women for wearing men's. The editor of the Livermore "Herald" was recently arrested in this city because he was found dressed in women's garments. On examination he was found to be temporarily deranged in mind. There will be no need of legislating against the adoption of women's clothes by men, for since it is only crazy men who would think of such a thing they will be cared for otherwise.

Postmaster Backus of this city a few months ago petitioned the department at Washington to permit an electric plant to be erected for lighting the postoffice but was refused on the grounds of economy. The postoffice and appraisers' building run up a monthly gas bill of about $700, the bulk of the amount coming from the mail department. An electric plant could be put in at a cost which would be saved in three years' gas bills. This is another sample of the efficiency of centralized management of local affairs.

The California coyote scalp crop is too big this fall and the governor believes a large part of it has been imported from Arizona and Nevada, and has refused to pay some of the claims until they are further investigated. But we fail to see why he should be so mean about it; he was elected on the Republican ticket, and if reciprocity is a good thing why not take some coyote scalps in exchange for the financial ones which congress has pulled from these states to pump the mud from our harbors or rather from the places at which we want harbors dug.

Several months ago we noted in this paper a case in Oakland of a man being arrested on a charge of vagrancy for living off of and with a woman to whom he was not married. It was then claimed that she was under his psychological influence. He is still confined and she has even joined a holiness band hoping to see him when they go to the jail to hold services, but the jailers interest themselves in the petty tyranny of keeping her from getting near him. It is a long-winded psychological influence under the defeat from which the measly press refers to her as the Chambers *female*.

In speaking of the refusal by Judge Thomas Paschal of Texas to naturalize a Socialist the "Examiner" of this city says: The doctrines of the abolitionists were much less consistent with the constitution as it existed before the war than those of the Socialists and Anarchists are now, but belief in slavery was not usually made a test of fitness for citizenship at that time. The constitution itself by providing for its own amendment, expressly contemplates legitimate opposition to its provisions. As a general rule men who have intelligence enough to think about public affairs and to form their own opinions are not dangerous citizens, even if their opinions be distasteful to the majority.

"Liberty" has moved into new and commodious quarters on one of Boston's principal thoroughfares. Its home now is a large and finely-fronted store which will be the headquarters for Mr. Tucker's general publishing business, the office of his "Weekly Bulletin," and a retail bookstore. The rear of the building will be fitted up for a reading room on the tables of which will be kept all the principal dailies in the English language, the magazines, radical papers, and many periodicals in other languages. We are heartily glad to see this evidence of prosperity with the old folks, and admit that we would ourselves enjoy a boom if it consisted of no more than to pay the cash running expenses of the paper, leaving us to shoulder the labor only.

Although Oakland is a regularly-appointed legal city and does most of the unjust things of legalistic civilization, it is sometimes on important occasions found the scene of common sense justice. In the divorce case referred to in last number, the despicable husband was beaten and the wife secured a divorce on the grounds of cruelty. If the property is to be divided about equally and no alimony granted, this was a remarkably just decision. We congratulate the judge who thus stood out against a crude public opinion. Not many months ago there was another notable case disposed of here upon its merits also. It was a case in which a boy 18 years old in a moment of passion stabbed his friend with whom he had been struggling in a humiliating defeat. The boy repented upon the spot and showed every evidence of the intensest grief. The murdered man's mother forgave the boy and did not want him punished and, as no good could come of it a jury set him free. His counsel presented him with a purse that started him again in earning a living, and there has been no reason after this severe lesson to complain of his conduct. If he had been sent to prison among professional criminals no one would have felt any better and probably been not a bit safer. His dead victim, though deprived of all pleasure, does not suffer, and safety assured, we would rather be conscious of the penitent killer's freedom from inflicted suffering than know of such suffering. Perhaps a year before this case there was another in which a small man about to be beaten by a larger one, shot him in self-defense, and owing to the prisoner's previous record for quietness, and the heartbroken wife's grief, the jury parted so far from blind obedience to the letter of the law as to set him free also. His conduct since has given no cause for regret. It is not to be inferred from this that we believe that murderers should generally be set free, but that each case should be disposed of on its own merits with such safety for the community in view as to make it as secure from the party as from other known sources of danger.

The Philosophy of Egoism.

XIII.

Self-interest masks itself and says suavely "we seek the good of the species," instead of saying bluntly "we gladly pick up all that other individuals let slip from their grasp." Are not we the species as contradistinguished from any individual? When we go so far as to urge sacrifices for the good of the species what are we but beggars and hypocrites? Persuasion is mingled freely with flattery administered to the vanity of the individual, and it is not to be ignored that the Moral philosopher flatters himself as he proceeds to render what he vainly imagines to be a service to his species. Assuming the point of view that he is spokesman for the species, the dictum that that is good conduct which promotes the interests of the species, is a subtle mendicancy or a veiled terror in the supposed interest of the crowd. But assuming an individual point of view the question is differently shaped. It then becomes: what use can I make of the species, of the crowd?

A summary of ethical teachings by Herbert Spencer says that postulating the desirability of the preservation and prosperity of the given species, there emerges the general conclusion that "in order of obligation the preservation of the species takes precedence of the preservation of the individual." The species, he admits, "has no existence save as an aggregate of individuals," and hence "the welfare of the species is an end to be subserved only as subserving the welfare of individuals," but, continues the summary, "since disappearance of the species involves absolute failure in achieving the end, whereas disappearance of individuals makes fulfillment simply somewhat more difficult, 'the preservation of the individual must be subordinated to the preservation of the species where the two conflict.'"

There are several features of sophistry in this. Let us, however, note first the admission that "the species" is simply a convenient term. Now, where confusion is possible the safe way is to lay aside the term. When this is done it will be found that in restating the foregoing propositions it becomes necessary to speak, instead, either of all the individuals concerned except one or of all the individuals concerned, without exception. But he has seemingly used the term species in both senses or else, with his "order of obligation" he has affirmed an obligation to subordinate the preservation of one individual to that of another. As this is intelligible for the purpose of the crowd dealing with individuals but not for the individual acting for himself with himself as the victim, the immediate inference at this point is that Spencer is expounding the Egoistic logic of the crowd.

If the welfare of others is subserved only as subserving my welfare, it can never be true that I must subordinate my preservation to that of others, for this is to use the general rule, which applies while I am one of the crowd, to the exceptional case wherein I am set apart from the crowd. All conditions of benefit imply at least preservation. When I am counted out for non-preservation, for the good of others, it must be the others, not I, who do the counting out. In the first premise Spencer speaks for the individual treating the crowd from his proper motive; but in the conclusion he speaks for the crowd or some of its preserved part contemplating the sacrifice of an individual, yet these shifting points of view are included in a syllogism. The welfare of the crowd a mediate end: that is reasonable to the individual. The preservation of the individual a mediate end to the crowd: that is reasonable from the crowd's point of view; but analysis of the diverse points of view is needed, not an attempt to link the two in a syllogism the conclusion of which is merely the crowd's conclusion.

Now examine the second premise of the syllogism: "the disappearance of the species involves absolute failure in achieving the end." Why, in fact? Because the disappearance of all others of the species but myself involves it? Not at all; but because the term species includes myself. But as far as my existence is concerned it would be the same if I alone disappeared. Do you say: the preservation of the alphabet is of no use to A except as A combines with the letters; but the disappearance of the alphabet would involve the disappearance of A; hence the preservation of one letter (A) is less important than the preservation of all the other letters? The letter A answers: "Bosh!"

Speaking for the individual, how does the doctrine of subordination of the preservation of the individual accord with evolutionary theory regarding the origin of species? Do species originate by individuals taking care of themselves under whatever circumstances, if possible, or by the contrary rule of the benevolence toward the pre-existing species? The reader can pursue this inquiry for himself; but I should like to suggest that what has been considered regarding the individual and the species can be paraphrased with reference to the species and the genus under which it is classified, thus:

The welfare of the genus is to be subserved only as subserving the welfare of the species, but since the disappearance of the genus involves absolute failure, whereas disappearance of particular species makes fulfillment simply somewhat more difficult, therefore the preservation of the species must be subordinated to the preservation of the genus where the two conflict. The fallacy of this sort of reasoning may appear without comment, in as much as the individual will easily maintain the point of view of the interested species, and will not practically allow himself to slide over to the position of the presuming genus. A supplementary remark may be indulged. The genus never licenses or encourages the origination of new species; but then the verbal sophistry of the genus would not prove to be a preventive.

I pass by the small occasion of confusion in the use of the word "end," the second time, in the foregoing statement. Total failure may be assumed to refer to failure of the ultimate aim.

TAK KAK.

Editorial Slashes.

Like Mr. de Lespinasse, I am anxious to hear one—or as many as he can spare—of Mr. Tucker's "many valid reasons" for making women printers accept lower rates than those paid to men, even when their work is of "exactly equal quality" with that of men.

I readily agree with him that "as a rule, women printers' work is *not* of 'exactly equal quality' with that of men;" but when it is, which possibility he admits, I cannot think of even one reason why they should not receive the same rates, provided, of course, that piece-work of like quality is the same quantity performed in a given time.

He further says: "If employers were forced to pay the same rates to women that they pay to men, they simply would not employ them." This suppositive statement conveys the idea that women are nowhere employed at the same rates paid to men. Now, under the union regulations of course the proprietors are forced to pay the women the same rates they do the men, but while they are forced to pay the same rates, they are in no way forced to employ them. Yet there are at present in this city, out of 518 printers, 55 women receiving the same rates as the men. The employers are not forced to hire them on account of a scarcity of men, for there are many unemployed male printers in the city.

G.

The "American Non Conformist," in everything else prohibitionist, does not believe in that method of correcting the liquor traffic. It declares that forced morality fails of its object. I am glad to note that it has experienced such a change of opinion since it declared that Moses Harman received his deserts when imprisoned for publishing a scientific term in relating an outrage in sexual relations.

John Wanamaker has added another to the list of innumerable governmental blunders and jobbery in selecting an out-of-the-way swamp for a postoffice site in this city and paying more than twice the market value. The transaction furnishes somebody a steal of a cool half million. The press is in a frenzy of indignation, but of course it is only the man that is at fault; an attack on the system is beyond press comprehension, and if it were not it would be the same, as politics is its feedpipe. Political papers and politicians and their constituents are a very undelightful wiggle to contemplate.

An instance of individuality developing and asserting itself under the withering hand of ceremonial authority occurred in New York about the first of this month. Twelve Franciscan sisters under the jurisdiction of Archbishop Corrigan laid aside their ridiculous and fanaticism-proclaiming dress and veils, the sight of which fills the Egoist with contempt and pity. These women had not gone through the regular novitiate apprenticeship, which probably accounts for the spark of independence that kindled into a more rational conduct. If under the stimulus of youthful enthusiasm they had forced themselves through the crushing discipline, they would hardly have generated enough snap to make the move even though in their normal moments they secretly desired it. The influence of association reaching over so long a time would have bound them against their reason. Even the walls that enclosed them and the floors they trod would have been embellished with endearing elements exercising restraining powers unconsciously transformed into the supposed virtue of "innate love of duty." And the irrepressible desire for the fullness of variability would have done duty as a devil's advocate in torturing to extinction a mind too large for a sea lion and too small for an average biped.

Ohio statutes require ministers who solemnize marriages to be provided with a license. A swell marriage among the upper ten was lately solemnized by a minister not thus provided, and the press states that considerable alarm is thereby occasioned lest the marriage be illegal. How proud we should be of our dough-headed educated classes downed by such a proposition! Sense for a moment the blood-curdling horror of a couple living together with the customary intentions and the consent of the neighboring women, when the man's name who performed the incantations that pacified the women was not written on a certain book. Only think of the large amount of respectable purity, home and fireside that such an omission has turned into lewd, lascivious, polluted prostitution! However, there is wealth in this case, which is an attenuating circumstance. But it now turns out that many other ministers have been guilty of the same neglect or rather ignorance of the law, and the result is that hundreds of probably poorer people have also sunken a similar depth into the same kind of degradation, and are puzzling themselves to know whether they are legally married. Such idiocy is the direct fruit of enslavment to ideas. It is the parallel of conduct in other directions by people who believe themselves free from the control of irrational ideas. A consistency-developing practice is to turn one's observing faculties also homeward about several times a day.

I had been reading so many accounts of mobbings in the South that I had about concluded that that species of insanity was due to the climate, and congratulated myself upon living out of the range in which if one person does a thing different from his neighbors it costs him his life. But when the North loomed up with the Omaha lynching of a negro and stretching and pounding him to death and afterward hanging him, my ideas of line civilization were somewhat modified, and I more definitely sensed the generalization that it is only the absence of an interesting enough occasion that conceals the beast in the most methodical of bipeds. The negro had raped a five-year-old girl and thus touched the sexual, a popular superstition, the fury of which could not be equaled by a pagan mob if its idol had been insulted. Whatever may be the absence of malice, to rape a little girl is fooling with murder in a way that merits the promptest measures of security, but confinement would have been all-sufficient and averted the encouragement to in the future similarly deal with unpopular acts which are in no sense invasive. Poor as the quality indicated is, it is said the best citizens gave this savagery their sanction and support, and it can easily be only a matter of time when their example may be turned against them in some matter not only in no way invasive, but in the interests of their legitimate happiness and incidentally of general progress. So small a combination of force as that of a single individual cannot afford to help make mob regulation customary. It is too heavy a force to have possibly to meet single-handed sometime. Mobs do not punish acts because they are invasions, but because they are unpopular. Among the thousands of other instances the mobbing of anti-slavery people cannot fail to illustrate this to the most prejudiced.

In an editorial the "Examiner," of this city, recently tried to prove the dangerous character of paper money by citing the condition of the Argentine republic, which it avers issued enough paper money on landed security similar to the Stanford proposition to make everybody rich, but that soon the balloon bursted and gold went up to a premium of 320 per cent and people were starving in the streets. Indeed! It must have been similar to the Stanford plan only in that the government did the business and that the paper was printed, otherwise it could not have affected gold, as it would have had nothing to do with it further than to be denominated in its terms. Starvation is the necessary result of a premium on gold, and the premium due to governmental interference with mediums of exchange. If, instead of the government issuing the money arbitrarily it had been left to individuals formed into mutual banking companies, and had been made redeemable in products, it would have answered every purpose in trade, and products instead of gold would have tended to premium. And where there is a demand for products people who can work do not starve. The republic has issued a decree limiting the premium on gold to 150 per cent and suspending gold payments for two years. The "Examiner" remarks that if the government could keep it down to that by its mere fiat it should have forbidden the existence of any premium at all. This is true, but unfortunately for that paper's general position on money, it is just as true that if governments did not senselessly prohibit everything except certain metals from use as exchange medium there would have been no occasion for a premium at all. Gold bugs could not then turn one dollar of gold into three dollars and twenty cents in two years without turning a hand. It is no wonder people are starving when three-fourths of their labor is swallowed up by a monopoly of exchange mediums—a tax on their superstition. It is one of the beauties of slavery to an idea, the source of all slavery. The "Examiner," with the fortune behind it that this slavery has thrown into its hands, would not be obliged to perpetuate the superstition if it knew it to be such, but it evidently does not, and probably will not in the near future.

Victor Yarros being chased into a knot-hole in the copyright discussion between himself and Mr. Tucker in "Liberty" during the fore part of this year, has now learned a new trick in discussion. He then foolishly attempted to square his position with a principle which he and Mr. Tucker held in common, but in their recent discussion on the use of the word "rights," Mr. Yarros was not to be caught by the logical conclusion from accepted premises; he simply repudiated the principle which Mr. Tucker thought they held in common, and the latter came limping home to soothe the sprained muscles of a leg that had with overconfidence sent a ponderous logical boot against uninhabited space. He had quoted some of Mr. Yarros's former excellent Egoistic argument against his present duty dominated position. But Mr. Yarros's "deeper thought and greater familiarity with the facts and factors of evolution" cause him to regard the idea that "enlightened selfishness prompts men to observe the laws of justice," as being "*utterly false.*"

It must then be ignorant selfishness, or a change of heart that is to be preached in the adjustments of social contact. But there had certainly already been a fairly experimental amount of both before Mr. Yarros began doing battle against their results as an Egoist. It seems even his sublime appreciation of his ability should not be equal to undertaking a task that the generations of ages on the right track have failed in. Or perhaps duty championed by Spencer will have the opposite effect from the same championed by Kant. Perhaps the strong and crafty will no longer use it to awe and subjugate the weak and simple while the former skilfully evade its exactions. Perhaps a scientific label on duty will prevent its being more awkward for everybody to lookout for everybody else's interests than for each to lookout for his own, but it looks quite improbable.

It is not hard to understand how more primitive man, glancing unanalytically over conduct and observing the quieting effect of concession, should finally come to vaguely regard it as duty to others without discovering that instead of such, in its rational form, it is only an *incident* in the promotion of self-interest. But it is hard to see how a trained mind that has once clearly analyzed the idea should afterward get the generally accepted *desirability* of the incident formed into a positive obligation, annulling the free will of the principals whose convenience developes such incident. This is what the position amounts to, and it is the father of all the tyrannies of majority rule. For a measure is first deemed expedient, then generally desirable, therefore obligatory and of course compulsory, after which discussion of its expediency is useless. It is infinitely easier to replace a poor expedient, acknowledged as an expedient, with a better one than to replace an acknowledged obligation with an improvement, for it is the essence of an obligation to be preserved, while it is the essence of an expedient to expedite and of freedom to choose the expedient for its own sake.

Mr. Tucker mourns Mr. Yarros's renunciation of Egoism and wonders how long it will be till he abandons Anarchism. To me it seems a logical extension of his present position to abandon Anarchism. He is certainly preaching the doctrine of the Individualists if he is not really in their camp. Let obligation once be admitted to be superior to the will of its contractor and all the absurdities of majority rule are at once accepted. To exact obligation is to rule, and to acknowledge that prerogative is to repudiate the no rule principle. From this there is no escape. H.

PRESIDENT HARRISON has received a box of tin plate from one of the tariff-protected establishments that are now to be partly supported by taxing the consumers in this country. He discovered that the tin was bright, which penetration is equaled only by that which prevents his seeing how an American can doubt that we have the mechanical skill and business capacity to successfully establish the manufacture of tin plate here. Why, Bennie, that is real easy. If you had to be licked by a somewhat weaker man and had to have your hands tied behind your back to enable him to do it, you could understand why people would doubt that man's fighting capacity, since his antagonist must be disabled to insure success. That is why some Americans doubt the business capacity of men who must have competitors shut out in order to establish themselves in business. The president can understand how a failure of this protection experiment should be received with satisfaction in Wales, but not how an American can take that view of the matter. This also is easy. There is a feature about protection, and about patriotism in particular, that indicates a selfishness on the part of the American quite the equal of that which in the Briton would rejoice at regaining a lost industry. And it is this selfishness which causes some Americans who are out of the swim, to desire the failure of the experiment. When they have to go short on canned goods because cans cost more, and pay higher rents because building costs more, and have to wear threadbare clothes and shiver between cotton sheets because cloth and blankets cost more, and see the tin plate manufacturers rolling about behind splendid teams by reason of this higher cost, these Americans become unpatriotic and would rejoice at the failure of the protective scheme that raises the price of all they buy and lessens the demand for their products. Their beloved country uses them badly and they cease to love it patriotically. A few others, more consistent, and therefore more wicked, retaliate in the same way because their country similarly protects gold owners in securing to them a monopoly of supplying credit by prohibiting the competition that other kinds of property would afford if it were allowed to bear certificates as gold is. Many of us regard the manufacturing of a subsistence even more important than home-spun tin. H.

Valid Reasons.

In No. 199 of "Liberty" the following statement was published:

> As a rule women printers' work is not of "exactly equal quality" with that of men, and even where it is, there are many valid reasons for *making them accept lower rates* than those paid to men.

[Italics the writer's.] What is the *valid reason* that women should be made, forced, to accept lower rates than men for the same quality of work? We will take it for granted, as based on that writer's experience, that the average male printer is superior to the average female. That therefore the average male should receive higher pay than the average female stands to reason. But according to the same authority there are exceptions: "and even where it is." Why should the exception be made to conform to the rule? Should not a woman who stands higher in her trade than the average of her sex receive the benefit of her better performance? Is it not an unjust discrimination to pay to a woman less for as steady and as well performed labor as is paid to man? Does it not savor of bourgeois rule to draw a distinction between male and female labor simply because by doing it we can make—*force* the female labor to accept lesser wages?

Are the same "valid reasons" as *valid* in other occupations? Suppose that in the translating business a female performed as good a job as a male, would it be justice to "make her accept lower rates" than those accorded to man, because being a female and having less power of resistance she is forced to sell her labor for whatsoever she can get?

Suppose the woman did a superior job; I have known women to do better jobs than the average man in my line on several occasions, would it be equity to "make her accept" a lesser fee because her sexual apparatus and strength in fisticuffs is different from man's? which seems to be the only real difference there is between the two. What is the *valid reason* that a woman should receive less remuneration for her work, "even where it is" of exactly equal quality with that of a man? DE LESPINASSE.

Managerial Experience.

I have recently been meta4ically knocked end over end and brought up standing on the lower and larger one gazing in verbose muteness at my blaring stupidity. But a thump from a met-a-4 is not so impressive as from a condensed manus, and since my readers have refrained from administering the latter lo, these many months, perhaps I shouldn't complain. The felineastrophe was due to a suggestion committed by George Forrest. He sent it here by mail and the 26th of September in an envelope, and when I broke that suggestion's seal skin it flew up and hit me square in the eyes and thus penetrated clear to the marrow of my skull and I now have it. I have it about thus: "Now that EGOISM is printed on a steam press, I take it that you do not spend any of your valuable climate worrying over the possibility of your subscription list reaching a thousand while you would be obliged to have them all by the Columbian process. Instead of spending your duration and brown locks inventing elevated railroads, I should think you would exert them at producing a machine for getting subscribers for your paper. A simple and light-running device of this kind with a positive motion—seconded by the popular purse and well patented, would monopolize the market for you and EGOISM would soon become the most circulatorious journal on the face of real estate. Other papers employing the ordinary slow and expensive hand-sewed process could not compete with you, and soon you could retain Mr. Tucker to read your proofs and suggest thoroughbred ideas on their margins to be interjected under "ring"ular auspices into the editorial matter, thus touching out the freshness of originality with the strength of experience and the polish of scholarship. Mr. Yarros would make a first-rate met-a-physician and long-suffering book reviewer. Mr. Walker would be matchless as master of poetry, sarcastician, and to list tracts at prices to suit the number ordered. George Macdonald's services could perhaps be bought to upholster your Managerial Experience and fight your duels. Tak Kak might be induced to act as venerable sage and general reviser. Then Lloyd, your spontaneous poet, could devote his whole time to touching in song the special tenets of your philosophy. You would become the Fulton of Egoism and Anarchism, and your wife could work in her own office. You could hire a cook and get your washing done at the laundry. Besides, you could hire a tractable and muscular girl to keep your apartments excavated and arms exercised. In short, you could live like and pass for a great man, instead of a lean aspirant scratching in the would shed of journalistic endeavor. Here is a prospect, if no more, challenging if possible even a greater ambition than your derby has caged. What do you want to elevate railroads for anyway; you can't get one higher than the Pike's peek road either in altitude or fare. I earnestly hope you will sagely lose no thyme in putting this suggestion in operation. Before you is a populous world to conquer."

I have often noted the populous character of the world, especially in regions where I tried to get a job or a seat on a car, but the balance of the suggestion, and especially the conquer, has me well down. Here I have at hard study on the railroad blanched the complexion of several of my very best hairs, and sat upon my stomach on the edge of the imposing stone evening after evening making marks which I for hours vainly tried to get my wife's imagination to form into a picture of rails, wheels, coach bodies, and a voluptuous future. At the conclusion of my elucidation she asked, with "case"hardened cynicism, what the fare would be and if the men would vacate seats in favor of the women. And in the end I will probably find that most or some part of it is patented as a clotheshorse and balloon route. Then I will realize that I have wasted invent enough to have made me a great man in which my success does not differ fundamentally from the rest of the waisted race.

As I have stated, this subscriber reaper is a stunner and mower, and I could get no more—of an idea at first how to commence to think about it than I have of fortune. But far as the definitely negative is from the definitely positive, I have at least established the former; that is, I am settled on that I must not make a machine like myself, for instance, or for subscribers, for I cannot get them at all. I have been slow to attempt such an experiment anyway, for besides the necessary material waist one has the failure to bother with afterward. This my father learned, and during the fifteen years since I have taken it off his hands *I* have been jumping busy impressing myself with the same fact and a little fodder. It must have been a subscriber machine or something of the kind that was aimed at in my case, for I have a strong hereditary transmission for subscribers which has so far not borne out the adage, "where there is a will there is a way," save a wretched poor way. The proper interpretation of this privilege robbers' taunt evidently refers to the probated will of a rich relative, for facts will not bear it out in any other sense.

But, returning once more to the machine, I think that if I had the use of the machine shop of my friend Irving Fox of Rochester, Minn., and some currency, I could complete a good machine before corn planting, for I am getting the principal features in mind already, and will be very grateful to Comrade Forrest when it succeeds.

With patriarchal assurance and a stubby pencil I instruct a patient and inoffensive constituency not only in political, social, and sexual science, but in that of a respectable and hard chaste domestic economy. I have lately with the help of Mr. Bell's spavined egg-beater and a great sagacity, evolved for our midst a new culinary departure—departure, at least, is eminently if not imminently descriptive of it when placed in its final perfection and a dish before my wife and her perpendicularly extending relative. It is pancakes—not the pockmarked and melancholy variety of the restaurant, but antique-oak-complexioned sea-foamers as light as cotton and brittle as a young girl's laugh. It was with considerable profanity and other difficulty that I acquired the habit of congealing them. At my first attempt, having built a fire a good while before, I maternally wound the flour through the fly screen bottom of a quart cup with a crank. I then dumped a teaspoon heaping full of Royal baking powder and a pinch of salt into the quart of flour and stirred them in the thirsty state accurately together. ("Royal is the best," information for which I am indebted to the can label.) Next I added some good unbolted Jersey milk and with the egg beater churned it all into a light-dun mortar. Then I strode confidentially to the stove to bake and splash batter, but the griddle wasn't on and the fire was nearly out. Finally the fire was revived and I tried a cake, but it was fit for nothing except felt hats and even more uncomfortable feelings. My wife's face hopefully expectant, now drew up like a tobacco pouch, and she declared the batter had fallen. I assured her that it hadn't and substantiated the statement by pointing to the pan still sitting on a chair where I had at first placed it. She sarcastically explained that relating to batter, the term "fallen" is cooknical, and means that the leaven has grown so weary that it don't amount even to one. She then discoursed in a tone subject to a disappointed stomach upon how I must have everything ready first, then mix the batter and bake at once. The next morning I did so, and having laid the first batter, set the dish down and intently baked the cake with the former result, for when I looked up the batter had fallen again —this time into the coal box. I could see just where I had missed and the batter hit it, and I didn't give up. The next morning I posited the batter pan squarely on the middle of the chair and proceeded to bake with a hand-knit brow and sizzling griddle, but it was too hot and burned the cakes outside while inside the mortar did not set and had to be fired—into the back yard. I now poured water on the coals which cooled them off nicely, but raised a blizzard of ashes that drifted upon the batter and wouldn't brush off. I have finally overcome the difficulty of unmanageable heat by baking on the gasoline stove. On this the heat can be regulated to a hair, which I hook out of the batter with a fork. With everything down thus diminuatively, I like to put on my big bebattered office apron and grease the griddle with the protruding ends of the fork tangs while the bacon dangles merrily at their hilt, foiling my most frantic efforts to make it touch the griddle. I would almost rather bake the auburn beauties than eat them, while my wife and her hollow relative would rather eat than bake. It is a pleasure to see the outside of my devoted wife's face beam as she blandly places these delicakecies on its inside and extends anteriorly toward the table leaf. They were good for me too, as I gained five pounds in ten days. Before I began taking them the back of my countenance was so sharp and piercing that I could sit on nothing but a marble slab without penetrating and becoming so attached to it that I had to buzz a long time to get loose—if any conversative person was near. Now I can sit in so pliable a thing even as judgment and come off and cackle without difficulty or a bill unless the latter be handed me by the landlord or dairyman. I advise the lean reader to quit leaning on a vacated and stimulated stomach, and to fill up on such pancakes and pleasure. He will then rise up and call me blessed and his friends to subscribe.

As manager of this paper I took a walk one afternoon this month. I went out along the county road in Oakland where some of our nabobs make it count building them frugal front yards on five-acre lots at several thousand dollars per acre. Their hired men have planted low-cussed trees along the sidewalk, and as I was too torrid, it seemed delightful to soak up these nabobs' nice cool shade with my coat and help the naboblets and plump young nurses smell up the good stink that blew from the flowers through the fence. There were no "Rooms to Let" cards in the windows, though the houses were quite roomy and occupied mostly with simply standing there. But I caught many other more convenient pointers in economy. I found the hind legs of horses sticking up out of the ground all along the sidewalk and being used for hitching posts. This illustrated to me the get-there-ative superiority of the capitalistic brain. If his horses bloat up and burst from eating wet clover, instead of dragging them with a log chain and cheerless countenance to the woods and digging a hole fifteen feet square in which to bury them on their sides, he buries them on their backs in a 3x9 feet hole and lets their rear legs stick out for the purpose indicated. This saves digging, continues the use of the horse, gives him a new experience, and is mental as well as ornamental. I noticed another adaptation of means to ends (except the latter ends of apple thieves) that further evidences his insight and combining powers; he uses cast dogs instead of the ordinary howling brute. These are a great advantage over the others, for they maintain a select pose, stay where they are put, feed on scenery, and breed no fleas; they do not rear up on one's new suit with dirty hands, nor keep him awake nights with barking; they never tear up the garden, kill chickens, come in the house, nor follow one to town, nor require a tag to keep the half-pound-master from getting them. I wish all the cats of our neighborhood were of the same breed.

Many of the nabobs' lawns have only gravel walks with eavestroughs, but some have aspheltum walks, though in icy times such a sensation is not beyond the experience of even poorer folks. Thus, as in death, the rich and the poor come to the same level by different routes. Different rooting is a source of much social friction.

At one of the places there was a social and a high wire fence behind which girls with shoulders and boys with cuffs were cuffing a ball with cane-bottom chairbacks and spoony glances. The papers state that "chicken salid and punch were served." Not chicken punch, I presume, but I don't know what kind of punch it was. And as for salid, the wings and breast, so far as I could see, and that was almost to the waist, looked very nice. Many of the girls wore, above the hips, only broad galluses with the sleeves and basque cut out. This was in fact the principal fairly observable feature of the occasion, and I ocularly devoured its shape with absorbing voracity and impromptu pose. These nude basques, inadvertently exposing French Norman shoulder blades and a flesh-padded collar bone, are soulrendingly seductive. Then add the clean, full white neck set off with buffalo kinked mane, and the cerebellar effect is such that I want to fly up and kick the moon over and hook the absence of that basque with my cheek and chew that neck on the cob for gum—but I won't. However, I would chew lightly, and my cheek could not injure that absence and if the paint were dry would not be injured by it. Indeed, it would not be considered cheek but for the presence of similarly impelled and repulsed individuals called society. Thus I reflected, and then I looked from the absent basques into the waxen faces and taxidermic eyes, which like a doll's respond only to the touch of the conventional spring. And I noted the consciousness of demeanor, and after that I didn't want to be one among them. Thus I was enabled to conclude my managerial walk with my feet while on the much scratched walls of my imagination I crayoned a picture of a social participated in by a list of widely-scattered radical women and men whose bearing and diversion pleased me immensely, and from which my declining raiment and seedling manner would not decline me. I drew the upholstered women with the appreciable suspenders, while I allowed those in smoked leather binding to wear shirred waists reinforced by rolls of cotton. I admired the ideas of the one kind and the necks of the other, and all were pleased—more or less. But I just like to like shoulders and necks and throats and mouths and eyes with foreheads above and flesh that is much and fine and firm and warm. Yours reflectively, THE MANAGER.

A Patriotic Peasant.

BY GEORGE FORREST.

Many, many years ago, when people were not so wise as they are now, and when they did not enjoy the glorious freedom which is our common birthright (for are we not great, free, and glorious?) there lived a peasant.

And he was happy (as peasants invariably are), and he was also fat and healthy (which is also always the case). He lived contentedly in a little cottage of his own, which had one large and beautiful room, and, besides owning the cottage, he was the happy possessor of a wife, and of a dozen children of assorted sexes and sizes. His wife he had obtained himself, and, in due course of time, the children had been provided by a wise and beneficent providence.

Thus he lived in peace and quiet, as became a good, law-abiding peasant, until a war broke out. When he heard the news he instantly buckled on his sword and went out to do battle for his country; for he was a patriotic peasant, and he almost shed tears when he thought to himself "this is my native land, my fatherland," and his breast heaved.

Before departing he had counted and kissed his children and bade his wife be a father to them, for perhaps he should never see them again. Then, as has been stated, he had buckled on his sword and gone forth like a brave soldier.

Now, it so happened that the land where the peasant's house stood was the boundary line for the two countries, and the west side of the house was in one country and the east side in another, and the party the peasant joined was the party of the west side; for it so happened that when he heard of the war he was on that side of the house.

Well, all day he fought like a patriotic peasant, and all day he had burned houses and barns and crops in the enemy's country, and when night came he was tired and weary and worn out and exhausted (as he well might be; and who will deny it). So, with victory written on his forehead, he hied himself to his happy home, where his peasant wife and twelve little peasants of varying degrees of littleness awaited him.

And he thought to himself thus, thus thought he to himself "Ahh! I am a brave man; I am a hero." Then he strutted along in the middle of the road and turned out for no one.

Thus he walked along toward his cottage and (as was quite natural, seeing that he was going in that direction) finally reached it.

But it was not the happy home of the morning for the east side of the house, which was in the enemy's country, was burned to the ground.

When the peasant saw this he struck his forehead and shouted "Woe is me!" and no contradicting voice answered him. Then from the house he heard sounds of sorrow, and he rushed in. Carefully he counted his children; and then he struck his breast in agony, for where there had been twelve children and one wife in the morning, there were now but six little peasants and one-half a wife. Thus he lost fifty per cent of family.

Then his anger was terrible to behold, and all night long he strutted up and down before his house (west side) and when the morning came again he buckled on his sword, and again he went forth to battle for his country, only today he fought for the east country.

Before going out he counted his children, but he could not count his wife (being a peasant, he was not familiar with fractions). Then he kissed them all, and, as has been stated, went out to do battle for his country.

All day long he fought in the enemy's country, and all day long he burned houses and barns and crops, and when night came again he hied himself in the direction of his humble cottage. As he walked along the road he thought to himself "My country, 'tis of thee" (which was very patriotic of him). When he reached his cottage he found that it was not there (he did not even see the hull), and he struck his forehead and cried "Woe is me."

No longer were there any happy children, and not even a portion of happy wife; all, all were gone, and his capital was one hundred per cent less than it had been two short days before.

In those days there were no pensions to cover his case, so all he could do was to sit on the ground and think and muse, and muse and think, which (to his honor be it said) he did.

EGOISM'S PRINCIPLES AND PURPOSE.

EGOISM'S purpose is the improvement of social existence through intelligent self-interest. It finds that whatever we have of equal conditions and mutual advantage is due to a prevalence of this principle corresponding with the degree and universality of individual resistance to encroachment.

Reflection will satisfy all who are desirous of being guided in their conclusions by fact, that as organization itself is a process of absorbing every material useful to its purpose, with no limit save that of outside resistance, so must the very fact of its being a separately organized entity make it impossible for it to act with ultimate reference to anything but itself. Observation will show that this holds good throughout the vegetable and animal kingdoms, and that whatever of equality exists among members of a species or between different species has its source and degree in the resisting capacity, of whatever kind, which such member or species can exert against the encroachment of other members or species. The human animal is no exception to this rule. True, its greater complexity has developed the expedient of sometimes performing acts with beneficial results to others, but this is at last analysis only resistance, because it is the only means of resisting the withholding by others from such actor's welfare that which is more desirable than that with which he parts. If, then, the self-projecting faculty of mankind is such that it will in addition to the direct resistance common to the less couplex animals, diplomatically exercise present sacrifice to further extend self, and it being a fact that equality depends upon equal resistance, diplomatic or otherwise, what are its chances in an absence of enlightenment in which the individuals of the majority so far from *intelligently* using this resisting power in their own behalf, do not even believe that they should do so? The result of a general conception so chaotic, would naturally be what we find: the generalization from the practical expediency of certain consideration for others, crystallized through the impulse of blind selfishness into a mysterious and oppressive obligation, credit for the observance of which gratifies the self-projecting faculty of the simple, while the more shrewd evade its exactions, and at every step from the manipulation of the general delusions of religious and political authority to the association of sexes and children at play, project themselves by exchanging this mythical credit for the real comforts and luxuries of the occasion, which the others produce. Thus in addition to the natural disadvantage of unequal capacity, the weaker are deprived through a superstition, of the use of such capacity as they have, as may be seen in their groping blindness all about us.

To secure and maintain equal conditions then, requires a rational understanding of the real object of life as indicated by the facts of its expression. It is plain that the world of humanity is made up of individuals absolutely separate; that life is to this humanity nothing save as it is something to one of these; that one of these can be nothing to another except as he detracts from or adds to his happiness; that on this is based the idea of social expediency; that the resistance of each of these individuals would determine what is socially expedient; that approximately equal resistance makes it equality, and on such continued and a universal resistance depends equality. This can leave no room for any sane action toward others but that of the policy promoting most the happiness of the acting Ego. Therefore EGOISM insists that the attainment of equal freedom depends upon a course of conduct replacing the idea of "duty to others" with *exped ency* toward others; upon a recognition of the fact that self-pleasure must be the final motive of any act; thus developing a principle for a basis of action about which there can be no misunderstanding, and which will place every person squarely on the merit of his or her probable interests, divested of the opportunity to deceive through pretension, as under the dominance of altruistic idealism. It will maintain that what is generally recognized as morality is nothing other than the expediency deduced from conflicting interests under competition; that it is a policy which, through the hereditary influence of ancestral experience, confirmed by personal experience, is found to pay better than any other known policy; that the belief that it is something other than a policy—a fixed and eternal obligation, outside of and superior to man's recognized interests, and may not be changed as utility indicates, makes it a superstition in effect like any other superstition which causes its adherents to crystallize the expediency adopted by one period into positive regulations for another in which it has no utility, but becomes tyrannical laws and customs in the name of which persecution is justified, as in the fanaticism of any fixed idea.

Another part of its purpose is to help dispel the "Political Authority" superstition and develop a public sentiment which would replace State interference with the protection for person and property which the competition of protecting associations would afford. Then the State's fanatical tyranny and industry crushing privilege would torture the nerves of poverty-stricken old age or pinch tender youth no more. The most disastrous interference of this monster superstition is its prohibition of the issuing of exchange medium on the ample security of all kinds of property, which at once would abolish speculative interest and practically set all idle hands at productive labor at wages ever nearing the whole product until it should be reached. The next interference is by paper titles to vacant land instead of the just and reasonable one of occupancy and use, which with the employment that free money would give, would furnish all with comfortable homes in a short time, and thereafter even with luxuries from like exertion. Following this is its patent privilege, customs robbery, protective tariff, barbarous decrees in social and sexual affairs; its brutal policy of revenge, instead of restitution, in criminal offenses, and finally its supreme power to violate the individual, and its total irresponsibility.

PROSPECTUS

EGOISM is published Monthly at 50 cents a year.

[*Entered as Second Class Mail Matter.*]

It is promptly discontinued when subscription expires, and no bills are sent out. It is run by the publishers, and admits only such contributions as they believe extend, or intelligently criticise its position.

The following are the names and amounts contributed by propagandists who wish to spread this line of thought and in that degree are its "Continental Congress," pledging so much "life and fortune" toward the establishing of their ideals and making their personalities felt in the world they live in.

PROPAGANDISTS FOR VOL. II.:

G. A. F. De Lespinasse, - - - $50.00
A Friend, - - - - - - - - 5.00

EQUITY PUBLISHING COMPANY,
P. O. Box 1678. San Francisco, Calif.

Egoism

Vol. II.—No. 7. SAN FRANCISCO, CAL., NOVEMBER, 1891. Price, Five Cents.

Pointers.

About the most promising business opening for morbid and somewhat attractive overripe girls is to take advantage of the monogamy monotony of wealthy men through matrimonial advertisements and work the damage suit blackmail racket. It is a big pull financially and a progressive propaganda as well, as it helps expose the ridiculousness of legal love.

Egoism is even later this month than last though with a better excuse, being a lack of money to pay the cash expense. The type was up nearly on time, but sickness and scarcity of work together prevented our securing the necessary gold to have it printed sooner. Each number will come in time but perhaps not always *on* time, unless interest enough can be generated to cause each subscriber to add at least one subscription besides his own to our list.

Hugh O. Pentecost has done several neat bits lately. One, upon entering the legal profession while opposed to law, was his apology to Mr. Tucker of "Liberty" for having censured him for taking copyrights when he is opposed to such "rights." Another was Mr. Pentecost's review of Theosophy and Mrs. Besant. However, Mrs. Besant's "essence of things" and Mr. Pentecost's "union of beings" in our eyes bear a resemblance as close as that of the same individual of a pair of twins.

We have never seen the mediocrity of the average caucasian so painfully illustrated as recently when witnessing the enthusiastic delight of an English-speaking Chinaman to whom the compliment was returned when inquiring after the health of a "good citizen's" family. The ideal of the yellow man of the stationary race is an income and family. So little more can be said of the average caucasian that the Chinaman's ready recognition of their mental level was even more painful than surprising.

Those State Socialists who fondly look forward to the time when the efficiency of State control will be so far extended as to determine for them the amount of potatoes required for a year's consumption, that they need not raise too many, can get another pointer on such efficiency in the fact that the government has accepted a new cruiser so top-heavy that she must have fifty tons of cement placed in her bottom to keep her from turning bottom upward when answering her rudder in an ordinary sea.

The latest book published by Benj. R. Tucker is "The Anarchists," by John Henry Mackay, translated from the German by George Schumm. We have only sketched it hurriedly here and there, but feel safe in advising *all* our readers to order it as soon as possible. None are too conservative, none too radical to regret ordering and reading it. On another page will be found an extract from it. It contains 315 pages and sells at $1.00 in cloth binding, and at 50 cents in paper cover. We will have it in stock by the time this reaches the reader.

Private enterprise in New York is introducing and popularizing a parcel delivery service for the State to confiscate, as it outrivals the postal service in price, convenience, and speed. Parcels weighing from an ounce or less to fifteen pounds are delivered anywhere in the city within three hours for fifteen cents. Large steel boxes for receiving the parcels are located at convenient distances and are emptied every hour. Stamp stations are located near the boxes, and each stamp has a numbered receipt to be detached by the depositor of the parcel, so that it may be traced if miscarried. This receipt also contains the company's contract to deliver the package.

The difference between the sentiments of a man in power and out is nicely illustrated in the case of Ex-Chief of Police Bonfield of Chicago. He loudly condemns the late invasion of the Socialists' meeting by the police at that place, and declares that a bitter experience with these people has taught him to respect human rights. That much is well. But who paid for his valuable lesson. It is only a reflex pang from public conscience, however, and not the result of consistent thought, for in the same breath that expresses his sentiment on human rights, he holds that the late outrage and the Haymarket affair are not parellel at all. If not, where did he fail to respect human rights.

Protective America raises a great howl when its own policy is carried to a consistent conclusion by the Chinese in their country. These people want home religion and home possession of wealth as badly as ours pretend to want home manufactures. They know too well that white people do not live in China for society or for their health, but in conquest for gold and religious prestige. And in the absence of the American opportunity to legislate against it, they are practically as justifiable in resorting to force before such legislation as we would be after it. To be sure the spirit is that of superstition and conscious weakness, but the same is true of all *governmental* interference with industry and commerce.

California has a brand new law which provides for the collection of taxes twice a year for the purpose of allowing the "poor" taxpayer the use of half his taxes for six months longer. It turns out that poor men cannot afford for six months' use of so small a sum to lose two days in which to pay taxes, so they pay it all the first time, while rich ones, whose taxes amount to a considerable sum, gladly avail themselves of the use of its half for a few months longer. This is a fair example of how law can help the poor, to whom it bears the same relation that feed does to a horse. The wise legislators perhaps failed to remember that the poor pay their taxes to their employers, landlords, and the capitalistic handlers of the products they consume.

One of Egoism's and also "Liberty's" Oakland readers has lately succeeded in injecting a dose of anti-paternalistic ideas into one of the most orthodox universities in the country. In one of its routine debates Nationalism was to be discussed, and the negative came whipped-in-advance to our friend for some pointers on the "weak places," in the Nationalistic doctrine in order to make as good a showing as possible. He loaded the members up and hung so many rounds of ammunition in the receptive gray matter of their mental belts that they not only made resistance but carried away the honors by storm, completely routing the champions of paternalism. Thus the work goes slowly but steadily ahead. A solitary warrior here and there with the tactics of science and the irresistible shafts of logic picks off the enemy's strongest men, and breathing into them the breath of liberty adds recruit after recruit to an army that knows no commander, breach of discipline, or defeat.

The enthusiastic solicitude with which Egoism's every suggestion is seconded by its readers was faithfully exemplified when we sent out a request for sample names, and a solitary subscriber responded. They are under no obligations to us and seem to know it, but the policy for themselves is a poor one. If they would escape the exaction of "Duty" by others and by the community in particular, these others and the community must be convinced of the inexpediency of "Duty" exaction. This is accomplishable only by getting such people to read and appreciate the soundness of the Egoistic idea. Sample copies or subscriptions distributed among the most apt is the only way to do it, and the sample method is far the cheaper, if not the more effective. To do nothing may be immediate self-defense, but so would it be to eat seed wheat and corn. Ultimate self-projection in this matter, as in seeding, lies in foresight. Selfy motive and consciousness must necessarily go together, but as much cannot always be said of consciousness and sagacity.

The Philosophy of Egoism.

XIV.

Duty is that which is due. I ought is I owe or I owed. Some duties I assume for duties assumed by others toward me, this is reciprocity. Some alleged duties the Moralist tells me that I ought to acknowledge and perform from a sense of Duty. If I then say that it is a superstition he perhaps severs himself for the moment from the superstitious crowd and claims that it is only a generalization, meaning fitness, saving tiresome repetition of analysis; it is my interest after all. He is somewhat disingenuous here, for if it be only my interest embodied in a thought-saving generalization, it will bear analysis and always come out as my interest. But he has the "social organism" in mind, to the preservation of which my individual welfare is to be subordinated, according to his idea. The "social organism" idea has captured him and he is using decoy argument to obtain from me a sacrifice of myself to his idol, his spiritual monster.

A man is hired to do certain work, and that is then called his duty; or exchange of services grows into a mutual understanding; the debt is first on one side and then on the other, and what at any time is expected, to balance the account or to turn the scale as usual and create another claim so as to continue the mutually advantageous arrangement or understanding, is also called one's duty. Where service is compulsory it is likewise called duty.

Moralism, when it has gained enlightenment enough to reject slavery to a person, under the subjection of mind overawed by physical force, denies that the slave's duty is Duty. But if the slave has yielded his mind to his master the phenomenon is clearly that of Duty. When the Egoist is conscripted he does not argue that his assigned duty is not Duty. It is servitude contrary to his interest, and this consideration is enough. The fact that some slaves are governed by a sense of Duty furnishes the plainest evidence that Duty is mental slavery.

But the Moralist will claim for Duty that it is not always mental slavery. It is true that he can confuse the issue by using the word Duty to describe all those habitual actions in the doing of which no immediate benefit to self is thought of; but let us keep to the plain sense. Duty is what is due. The domination of a fixed idea begins when one admits something due and yet not due to any person or something due without benefit coming to one in return; and of course when a return benefit is calculated upon the idea is interest.

When interest is sublimated so as to lose sight of self it assumes the form of love in the absence of oppression. Evidently the presence of fear in the causative circumstances corrupts the sublimating process and results in the oppressive sense of Duty. It is possible for the Moralist, finding a series of admirable actions which are well-nigh perfect love or gratitude, to call these Duty, on an examination which will show that were the doer to study his conduct he could find in it the elements which would serve to construct a wise scheme of reciprocal duties. If the Moralist talks of Duty when the fact is spontaneity,—whether gratitude, love, overflowing pride and generosity advancing to aid all that is seen to make for our good, he talks at random. His system of thought has predicated that men need to be controlled by a sense of Duty. Let him stick to that or leave it. We deny it. The doctrine of hell-fire was long upheld under the same idea that it was needed to control men. Moralistic Duty is the hardened dregs of fear. Generosity is the overflowing fullness of a successful, satisfied and hopeful individuality.

"I ought" is no stumbling-block to the intelligent Egoist. Two persons are playing at draughts and a bystander says of one: "He ought to have captured the man to the left, not the one to the right." There is no sense of moral obligation conveyed in the remark. It is assumed that each player is trying to win, and the words "he ought" introduce a suggestion of what was wanting to produce the result. A pirate endeavoring to capture a merchantman and taking the wrong course would say: "I ought to have sailed on the other tack." To whom was the obligation? To himself. So men speak of their duty to themselves, meaning the attending to supplying what is lacking to their welfare.

These words *duty* and *ought* are not words to be rejected. They are in constant correct use in every day life, and it is not the use of the Moralist, but it can be observed that every humbug politicial harps on the "sacred duty" of the citizens to do this or that,—something that he and his party are interested in and that he cannot readily prove to be to the interest of the citizens addressed, or he would do so instead of trying to get them with him on an appeal to "sacred duty."

Tak Kak.

Mental Lassitude.

When a problem is presented to the mind, the presentation furnishes a sweeping estimate of the problem's extent and complexity, and it is either brushed aside as not worth the energy and time required to become acquainted with it, or its intricacies are unraveled by impressing upon the mind a consciousness of the separateness of its parts and their functions, and combining them into the effect witnessed as the phenomena in its wholeness. This is the analysis and summing up which constitutes the comprehension of a problem, and which enables us to understand everything so far as we can sense the parts and combine their effects. When we come to the incomprehensible, it is so either because we cannot discover all its parts, or having sensed them one at a time, cannot hold them all in memory long and appreciably enough to sum them up in their exact effect. One or the other of these, principally the latter, is what stands between men and a solution of the social questions which unsolved, make life to most people simply an eternal round of tantalizing drudgery. In these cases, wherein the parts and their functions are comparatively few, the difficulty is not due so much to finitude of the mentality as to a lassitude which refusing to grapple with the intricacies of these problems brushes them aside, or attempting it grows weary before the analysis is completed, and jumbles everything up into a vague generalization which disposes of the matter about as correctly as a mathematical problem could be solved by a vote.

For the average philistine to drink and vote with his friends and believe that if a privilege is created he has as good a chance to secure it as anybody, requires less mental exertion than it would for him to reason out that if the State interferes enough to create monopolies for a few at the expense of the many, it is consistent for it to interfere enough more to neutralize them in justice to these many. Likewise, for the State Socialist, this latter primer reasoning of digging a ditch with one hand and filling it up with the other to escape the danger of ditches, is infinitely easier than the nerve-sapping mental tension required to get right down and separate the factors of industry and exchange, and ascertain their effect one upon another and find why the present result is what it is, and how to remove it permanently by removing the cause, instead of wasting labor at lopping off effects so continually that it absorbs what the monopolies would without leaving the ornamentation of their enterprises. This mental lassitude is the trouble also with the Moralist; he will not take the pains to analyze conduct to its final elements, and learn that sacrifice to another, which he preaches, is the *only* violation of the justice of which he vaguely dreams; it is easier to demand of competence that it make even with incompetence, and of genius that it be battered to a level with mediocrity. Equality—evenness—is a far simpler concept than desert, equity.

I fear the industrial and the exaction temperature will have to grow vastly more frigid before mental oxygen enough to solve it will be generated. H.

I Review the Reviewer.

Elsewhere we reprint a review by Comrade Lloyd of "News from Nowhere." Now I have not read "News from Nowhere," and perhaps not too much news from somewhere, but in the light of Comrade Lloyd's criticism and in that of my criticism of Communism I shall not take the trouble to learn more about the book. Comrade Lloyd's communism is simply no communism at all. It is like indorsing slavery which when defined means the greatest describable freedom. I can see but one function for a defense of Communism so defined, and that is to give the sophistical Collectivist an opportunity to bolster real Communism before the novice, with Individualistic prestige by exclaiming: behold! the Individualist's ultimate ideal is Communism, why not go to it at the start and perfect its details as they arise. And why not indeed. Comrade Lloyd's *definition* not being useful in such a case will of course not be mentioned, and an endless jumble of confusion must be cleared from the popular mind before it can understand what the Collectivist would have illustrated by contrast, but for the weapon placed in his hand by a will-o'-the-wisp interpretation of the Individualistic position.

I can understand how, surrounded by the shortsighted greed of this stage of evolution, and pinched at every turn by the exactions of privilege, such a good-hearted, sociable disposition as Comrade Lloyd's would enthusiastically contemplate the social commerce of giving and receiving and helping, but I do not agree with him in holding that under freedom there will be more of it than now or than in the past. Under economic freedom in which each could be fairly supplied by his own efforts, the necessity and principal incentive for giving and receiving would be removed, and if do not seriously misapprehend the trend of individualization, the act would be heavily against the grain both as a matter of sentiment and of utility. The pride of the Ego will not care to emphasize its incapacity to provide for itself by accepting such gift, and it follows that proffering would be restrained by the same suggestion. If compensation in value of different kind be argued, that is simply exchange, and there is no reason to believe that men's capacity to produce will ever so nearly equal their ever intensifying wants that they will exchange more loosely than exact. In association with those whose interests are as nearly as possible identical with my own I find myself continually hampered, repressed, or invading by the inextricable tangle of a communistic partnership in which each is even eager for exact equity. The difficulties of this experience show more and more every day that the strictest individualistic separateness in social commerce is the nearest satisfactory solution. Under present circumstances I am obliged to work without measuring in the market and to consume without measuring against the work, and the result is grinding slavery all around.

You may set me down as opposed to Communism first, last, in general and in each particular case in which I must encounter it. Give me charity, debt, or commerce, but the loose-jointedness of Communism never. Comrade Lloyd's provision that people may separate interests at will and without reproach, is praiseworthy and correct, but if I am free, for me it will be useless, for I will not mix, once I am above charity and out of debt. I do not understand what my comrade means by the sentence: "Individualism and Communism must co-exist that each may perfectly realize the other," unless it be my communistic experience, which co-existing with an individualistic sense of adapting means to pleasurable ends, is so thoroughly realized as to so disgust that sense that my criticism, made with the kindliest intention, may seem harsh.

I cannot agree either to the proposition that two men could by a rational process be friends *because* they love the same woman. If from compatibility of tastes they are, or become friends there is no good reason for not remaining such so far as the woman is concerned But to become friendly because they both want the same thing is too unlikely for realization except in that prostration to an idea which is capable of worshiping the very ground the object of its devotion walks upon; that is, both fellows would have to carry their ideality to such an irrational pitch as to love among her other environment even each other because each were at times such environment. This would be such palpable slavery to an idea, and as such, such an ill adaptation of means to the longest and greatest pleasure, that Egoism could not consistently leave it unantagonized. We maintain that to regard love in any other sense than that in which the exercise of other faculties and appetites are regarded as means of pleasure, is to appropriate in spirit the irrational inconveniences and sacrifice of the possession idea. If we should love those who please us best, with a lower-case "l," just as we eat, warm, sleep, and do other pleasant and profitable things, without allowing one to destroy the other by occupying its time in longing contemplation of an ideal-ghost, we would find our happiness increased in the proportion that such longing, deprivation of special loves, endless exaction, and magnetic stagnation now detract from the total of a lifetime. These occupy so much of life that the amount of pleasure which escapes the deadfall of love's ideality-ghost makes its pursuit humorously absurd. But the *superstition* of the love faculty will probably be the very last to be dropped from the long list for the benefit of which bipeds seem to exist. H.

News From Nowhere.

"No news is good news," the old saw saith, and here is "News from Nowhere" which is verily good.

An English comrade, of whom William Morris wots, falls asleep, with his head full of the "Morrow of the Revolution," in his own house "on the banks of the Thames, a little way above an ugly suspension bridge."

Waking, or imagining that he awakes, after a time, he finds himself on the same spot, in some year of that very Morrow of which he fell asleep dreaming, and thereupon has surprising adventures.

It is a delightful book, done in that most delightful English of which Mr. Morris is master. In fact it is the most charming Utopian romance of modern times. "Looking Backward" is as stiff by comparison, as Fifth Avenue is stiff and stupid by comparison with a country daisy field. It is an artist's book, written by an artist who fondly dreams that some day the world will be a pictured holiday, with nothing in it to offend the dainty sense. That is well. It is well I think, that the thoughts of artists should be turned —that the thoughts of all men, each in his own way, should be turned to an ideal future. Self-development and an Ideal Future—these are really the only objects worthy of human thought. Each man must be turned in his own way, for this is a matter of growth, and that which grows starts only from where its last development ends. Therefore I am welcomeful for all Utopias. I am glad, despite the hard things some of my comrades have aptly said of it, that "Looking Backward" was written. I am still more glad that "News from Nowhere" has followed it. For this novel of Nowhere is a free book. The author is a true lover of Liberty. Therefore, although he is a Communist, his communism has the least possible offense.

But it is impossible to take much in this book very seriously. It is hardly to be supposed that life two hundred years from now, will be like a lazy Sunday afternoon, full of statuesque men and women, arrayed artistically in silks and gems, who have thrown away machinery, and still find it difficult to find enough to do for love (there is no money), to keep from work-starvation. There is an element of absurdity about this, which reveals the authorship of the esthete.

Now mine is a free mind of a somewhat different type from Mr. Morris's. I am an Individualistic Anarchist, consequently I am impelled to criticise his dream. Not that I reject communism. Spontaneous communism, based on intelligent egoism is all right, and I believe that in Free Society there will be much of it; less than Morris imagines, but much more than most people now suppose possible.

But spontaneous, intelligent communism springs only from mutual love and absolute trust.

Will these be so universal in two centuries that communism will also be universal? No, nor in twenty centuries. Before this can be possible, human nature must have reached a degree of development, to us well-nigh as inconceivable as two co-existing infinities. It is a hard saying, but in life as we see it, that only is perfect which is perfectly limited by its equal opposite. Individualism and Communism must co-exist that each may perfectly realize the other.

It is a mistake that Mr. Morris in his ideal England describes no classes or clans of anti-communists. I understand that his communism is voluntary, but there will always be rebels against an order of society which gives shirks and incompetents an opportunity to possess as much, or more, than the competents. If I choose to share equally with a poor devil that is my pleasure, but if I am required to, against my will, that is a "heckle in my doup," and I cannot rest easily upon it. A man in order to realize his full dignity and liberty, must be able at any moment to separate himself, and everything belonging to him, from his fellows, and withdraw into a purely individual existence, without struggle or reproach. In order to do this, no matter how much co-operation there may be, the lines of separation between mine and thine, the natural lines of cleavage, must be kept distinct. This is not what Mr. Morris proposes, for his communism is one that abolishes all *meum et tuum* [mine and thine] and merges all men in one. Therefore, however free and spontaneous and beautiful it may appear *as he presents it*, I pronounce it defective, and surely productive of imperfect, enervated, dissatisfied lives.

In this land, which (perhaps fortunately) is nowhere, every one works for love, and yet we are given to understand that everything is done excellently and at the right time and place. That is utopian certainly. That the ordinary work of life might go on after a fashion among irresponsible workers is possible, but when it comes to business requiring exactitude and dispatch: telegraphing, carrying the mails, even the getting of meals, there must be responsibility and a pressure, not merely attraction, or there will be poor service. And a very poor sort of mental muscle and backbone is produced by always doing what we want to do, what is easy for us, what attracts us. And under a system that permits us to gratify all our whims at other people's expense, and do what we please, much or nothing, in return, there is a most enervating absence of the natural pressures which make the ordinary man industrious and self-sufficient, mentally and physically independent; and a suspicion arises that some of these bejewelled folk might, some fine day, be obliged to gird their gay doublets around empty bellies.

As an artist, Mr. Morris hates machinery; a hate with which, artistically, I have much sympathy. But his representation that his Nowhereians did everything they could by hand and delighted in primitive methods, and yet were worried about a "work-famine" is funny. When Mr. Morris undertakes to supply all his daily needs by hand-labor, be his own gardener, farmer, caterer, cook, waiter, dishwasher, housekeeper, tailor, launderer, cobbler, hatter, etc., etc., etc., or to pay his fellows in labor for fulfilling these functions for him, his keen anxiety about a "work-famine" will lose its edge. This is a fair test, for the man who is not a parasite produces himself, directly or indirectly, everything he uses. There is no independence short of this.

That there is an artistic beauty, excellence and charm about handiwork that no machine product, because of its absence of human interest, can possess, I admit, and that men will come to lead, more and more, artistic lives in the Free Future I believe, but in order to get leisure for artistic handiwork men must more and more relegate all the commonplace work of life to automatic machinery. There is no other way. The more nearly man is reduced to his bare hands the more he becomes a mere animal, using all his time and powers in the struggle for simple existence.

Mr. Morris impresses me as a man who is near to Liberty but has not yet quite attained her. His mind is not quite clear. The woman question is always a good test, and by that test he fails. His Annies and Claras and Ellens and Goldylocks are all beautiful women, artistically, with manners delightfully free and sweet, but Ellen is the only one among them all worthy of being an ideal heroine in a story of the Free Future. And the reason is plain. She is the most individualized, and has led the most individualized existence. Ellen is exquisite, and wherever I meet her, in Somewhere or Nowhere, I shall love her.

Mr. Morris seems to have no conception of the fact that liberty eliminates jealousy. He seems never to dream that free love can be large enough to enclose more than one object. When Clara, who seems a somewhat stupid creature, tho' pretty, finds that she loves a second man, she knows no better way than to choose between him and the first, and so poor Dick is left to mourn until she comes back, leaving the second presumably in the same fix. What in Nowhere is the sense of all this! Why couldn't she love Dick and t'other fellow at the same time. And why couldn't Dick and t'other, provided he was a decent, worthy fellow, have been drawn into friendship by their mutual love for the same woman. Nothing but a stupid, selfish, monopolistic narrowness, improbable of occurrence in a Free Future, except as a case of atavism, could prevent such a reasonable state of affairs, yet Morris seems never to have even dreamt of it. And when Ellen overtakes them on the Thames, and her rudder needs adjustment, and Dick helps her, and the "two beautiful young faces bent over the rudder" seem to be "very close together," the guest gets a pang, and Clara (she has been showing symptoms of jealousy all along) has a stiffness in her tones when next she speaks. Ye Dreams of Liberty!—can't two beautiful faces get together in the Free Future without kissing, or with it for that matter, without the onlookers being diseased with pangs and stiffness?

I hope for better things. J. WM. LLOYD.

The Solution.

And as Auban crossed street after street, and came nearer and nearer to his dwelling, he had already overcome the agitation of the last hours, and once more the wings of his thoughts circled restlessly around the longed-for light of liberty.

What was still resting in the womb of time as a germ but just fructified—how would it develop, and what shape would it take?

Of one thing he was certain.

Without pain it was to take place, this birth of a new world, if it was to live.

The social question was an economic question.

So, and in no other way, it could be solved:

With the decline of State authority the individual becomes more and more self-reliant. Escaping from the leading-strings of paternalism, he acquires the independence of his own wishes and deeds. Claiming the right of self-determination without restriction, he aims first at making null and void all past privileges. Nothing was to be left of them but an enormous heap of mouldering paper. Land left vacant and no longer recognized as the property of those who do not live on it, is used by subsequent occupants. Hitherto uncultivated, it now bears fruit and grain and nourishes abundantly a free people. Capital, incapable of any longer fattening on the sweat of others' labor, is compelled to consume itself: although it still supports the father and the son without obliging them to turn a hand, the grandson is already confronted with the alternative of starving or disgracing the "glory of his fathers" by working. For the disappearance of all privileges entails on the individual the duty of responsibility. Will it be a heavier burden for him than the thousand duties towards others with which hitherto the State saddled its citizens, the Church its members, morality the righteous?

There was but one solution for the social question, but one: no longer to keep one's self in mutual dependence, to open for one's self and thereby for others the way to independence; no longer to make the ridiculous claim of the strong, "Become weak!" no, to exhort the weak at last, "Become strong!" no longer to trust in the help "from above," but at last to rely on one's own exertions.

The nineteenth century has deposed "our Father in Heaven." It no longer believes in a divine power to which it is subject.

But only the children of the twentieth century would be the real atheists: doubters of divine omnipotence, they had to begin to test the justification of all human authority by the relentless criticism of their reason.—From "The Anarchists."

Managerial Experience.

I am now realizing from my invention. I realize that the fond hopes preceding and cotemporaneous with its completion were diluted breeze. And I have finally reached plan-a-teary foundation; that is, I have *found* my plans *tearing*—rent and for rent, as I cannot now occupy them myself. I learn that my elevated railroad was patented when I was still an unsuspecting youth, though little more tender than now.

I had hoped that the revenue derived from renting its shape to a corporation would enable me to become president of our publishing company, and to extend radicalism in the face of popular prejudice and the absence of money orders by mail, but like splitting sandstone, it *rent* in an undesired direction. People won't buy the paper, no,—you couldn't blindfold and back them up to it; so I chuckled up my threadbare and shiny sleeve as I imagined sinister-eyed and cast-iron-countenanced authoritarians obliged to put up fares part of which would support a paper whose publishers they would like to fly at a rope's end from a beam. It appeared to me such a sleek way to make a clam-brained populace pay for its own education that it was with great reluctance and a danglingly enervated purse that I gave it up. I could see an accommodating expressman and his dulcimer-ribbed horse hauling away from an office of ours in San Francisco three large mail bags full of papers, instead of stumbling to the ferry train in Oakland with one half full on *my* shoulders, as is true of real life. I also pictured my habitually good-natured and *then* grateful wife and her little niece dashing along the brain-child of their distinguished relative at the rate of 120 miles an hour as they proudly rode from a suburban home to the office to distinguish themselves in literature and orthodox eyes. My own person wore a confident and bold bearing over a "steal"-gray suit and white flannel shirt with a cream-colored tie. I was a much-consulted and bored man, instead of the lean, fade-attired, diffident frame that now stands in undesirable corners of the lower ferry deck as I go to and from our postoffice box with only Alliance exchanges in my coat pockets on the return trip. Our subscribers from the East during a visit to the Coast were entertained baggage and all at our commodious home, instead of at the waiting room of a depot after working hours, as we now do. We were also able to keep a cat, and a dog to bark at it and wear a city tag. But all this except a half starved stray kitten of the feminine number has vanished, and as I view this, the prospect looks bleak, though the possibilities of the kitten are multipliferously great.

Comrade Forrest was right; I have fooled away my time on the railroad, not properly "adapting means to ends," as Herbert Spencer would cutely put it. And now as a physical result, I must carry by their ends several gray hairs to an ungrateful grave, unless I should grow absolutely bald before starving to death. My wife no longer looks upon me with awe and expectation, and her lower-case niece responds to my requests with the reluctance accorded to guardians or parents who are such by circumstance, rather than with the alacrity conspicuous in doing homage to a great genius. Of evenings I now sit in a remote corner with intensely crossed legs and pensively write sample wrappers to institution worshiping Freethinkers, as I reflect with bitterness upon the curse of patent monopoly. I am also whiningly fraternal and say *we* will extend the propaganda.

During this experimental period my wife and I were walloped in brushed clothes and the pleasure of meeting one of our subscribers, J. C. Dana, the librarian at Denver. He was on a jaunt with the American Librarian Association and his wife's permission, and was incidentally taking in the government read shops with specific attention to the notorieties of California climate and sights. He was traveling as my fellow Hoosier, President Harrison, traveled when here, at State expense. I admit that I reflected far less bitterly upon that fact in this case than in Mr. Harrison's.

Mr. Dana obtained our address and a half hour near the middle of the night during which we might hold a mutual expose at one of the railroad depots and on the ferry. My wife is a boodleless politician and was at a session of the Federated Trades, but I got her scared out and she came around in time and sat gravely upon a bench with her feet upon the floor. Soon a line of carriages containing the librarians was driven up, and as these people are really accommodating outside of the library, I found my man at once. He admitted the identity and the introductory ceremony was completed. Mr. Dana proved to be one of those rare unaffecting nature's noblemen, and instantly the limited time was being finely masticated by three pairs of jaws in regular comradeship style. His first question inquired our personal purpose in publishing EGOISM. It was a leading point that led, and we admitted that at bottom it is the gratification of a vanity so strong that our discontent is unbearable without the indulgence. He then inquired the number of persons composing our publishing company. I assured him that the whole corporation was present, and that really for a long time I have been forced to be only a tin horn for which the other member furnishes the pressure. Now we all interrogated and disgorged our know things as fast as the building would bear the tonnage. Soon Miss Kelso, librarian at Los Angeles, who also keeps EGOISM on her tables, was found and made a part of the company. We then made better time than before, and when we went to the train just walked over the other passengers, so intent were we upon oscillating our chins against the last moments of time. My wife had to go home and let her head sleep, but I accompanied Mr. Dana across the bay. On the train he sat on a handrail to smoke, and allowed his cigar to burn up while he talked. It seems strange that a generator otherwise so perfect should smoke, but many of the best make do. He ought to be taken back to the founders and fixed, that's the way our folks always remedied stoves thus affected. As the train lunkety-gunked along I stood by Mr. Dana's side and allowed the restless passengers to stroll over my corns while I asked everything I could think of concerning the Denver friends. At the landing I parted with this man as one does on a March day with a warm glow of sunshine; delighted to have it at all, though the more excruciatingly pierced by the chilling blast at having to give it up. For a moment the earnest eyes of a sympathetic temperament sparkled in the electric light as searching nerves responded to the pressure of my hand, and I turned me about and stepped into the old waiting-room of whitewashed boards and felt as one who turns from the bed of death; think as I might, a memory of the companion of a moment before was all I could realize.

Since the moment my wife was slipshod enough to cast her lot with mine, for which I have not paid, I have realized that she is a very careless woman. But she is growing worse as time turns the furrows lengthways of her nose. She has got so she loses her clothes when away from the house. Last summer she lost her only and very best hat in a restaurant, and this fall walked away from her twelve-dollar jacket lying on a car seat. For a Moralist to cut the acquaintance of anything that will lie even on a car seat would be characteristic, but a "brutal" Egoist can plead no excuse besides a misfit carelessness. In the unfascinating face of these facts and the fair countenance of the graven image on the requisite coin, we had to buy others and I had to go along—actually go right *into* millinery stores!!

We went to San Francisco. It was an iron-gray morning and I felt sure there would be a *wet* spattering rain, so I loaded up a heavy overcoat for myself, a time-honored and sad-featured cloak for my wife, and an umbrella to drain on her shoulders during, and after a shower. By the time we reached the city the weather was clear and the sun poured down a mirrored shine for less than a nickel. Here I was with my second-hand dry goods emporium in hand, the heat and a gaping crowd around, and the horrors of a millinery shop in front. Oh, how I envied the fate of some other dogs who were in the poundman's ambulance. They, without tag, could enjoy death at a blow. I, must *tag* and be *tortured* through every store in a large city, and,—live on.

My wife is one of those women who know just what kind of a hat they want and that it is not in the city, but will search and be sure. I pumped down my aeronautic heart and tucked my nerves between my teeth and with expectant look and long strides followed my wife into one of those dens of feminine hats and high prices. There were crowds of waxen-faced girl clerks and twelve-year-old boys who stare customers out of countenance, but nothing was there, and I rushed for the fresh air. Kearny street is not long but has an astounding array of millinery establishments, as I found, for none were missed save in the feminine sense and very plural number. Finally we dropped into a masculine store, and feeling easier, I prepared to stay. The hat wanted was a feather-weight soft felt, sharply in contrast with the feeling and *wait* I had experienced in the search. I knew we had to stop somewhere, and as there was a large assortment I believed my wife could be so bewildered as to choose a hat because it pleased her better than one which pleased her less. The hatter was of the Hebrew race—a race which, though long contested has never been won, and one which seeks shining gold and the bosom of the voluptuous female instead of the ghastly sternum of Abraham, as some now well-padded women propose to do when the warm flesh has fallen from their bones. Surely there will an uproarious rattling of dry anatomy. I do not envy the old man his amours. But I die-gress. My wife described the quality and shape of the article wanted, and the quality was at once secured, but wasn't the right shape and wouldn't do of course. She tried others and still others until we were arbored about with boxes, but no hat suited. I suggested trying on the first one again. She did so and explained where it was wrongly shaped. A thought struck my Israelitish savior—why, the hat could be stretched into any shape; that is what it was made for. He moulded it out like dough and clapped it on her head, dinting the crown and pinching up the edges as a woman does an upper pie crust before it is dried in the oven. Then he backed away and bracing his hands upon his knees took aim and surveyed my wife's head with one eye and an expression of such ecstatic admiration that I trembled lest he should awaken to a realization of the popular offense, and not knowing my liberal ideas on love and divorce, shoot me in self-defense. But he was only acting, and my wife is so little exposed to theaters that she thought it regular griping admiration, and began to admire the hat a little herself. I saw it was now only a matter of getting her used to it, and I gave my proboscidial benefactor the wink and he concealed himself behind the hat-boxes until I convinced her that it looked better than anything she had ever worn, which could easily be true without being becoming. The fact is, she is put up for a nabob's companion, and I am "na" such Bob.

Now there were the cloak stores to storm. Though, with my big armful of back-number wraps, overshoes, and umbrella we were ridiculously well prepared for a storm, I still dreaded it. But the great plate tumbler windows of the enemy's fortress were before me, the order was given, and like a fresh soldier I knew no better than to press forward. Numerous clerks stood behind the counters but not one of them moved a muscle, and I believed that we had wandered into a museum. My wife, however, seemed to know better than I, and ambled nonchalantly down the aisle as though she expected to meet somebody, which so occurred. A man with a public smile and a rose bud ushered us back to a cook-shanty alcove, where a woman with two chins on the same jaw plied them vigorously trying to sell my wife cloaks she didn't want. This woman also looked a suggestion to the other clerks that we were from the mountains, which caused such a stampede of gaze that I felt uncomfortable, and we soon filed out amid smilular applause and rows of squeeze-provoking model girls with faces painted in water colors and framed in old oak hair. The faces of the saleswomen are not all painted in water colors, but the tongues of all are done in oil.

I had such a fill from this first store that I posed on the sidewalk pending the analysis of the nineteen following, but at the twentieth I consented to go in and wait near the door while my wife psychometrized the stock and elicited my idea on the result. This experiment also proved an acute one, for in addition to exposure to the stare of monotony-worn clerks, every floorpedestrian in the building solicitously inquired whether I was waited on. I glanced at my bundle and replied that I was weighted on and waiting, but these men scorn other people's wit. Finally my wife came, followed by a low-pressure condensing clerk with nine cloaks which I was to diagnose for a suitable one. When they were piled upon the old stock on arm, I peered cautiously from behind the pile at my wife as she spun around before a mirror with each aboard. Some were too diminutive across the shoulders, drouth had stunted the length of the sleeves of others, and those with proper sleeves were too commodious in the girth. I chose one from among the latter, however, remarking that though it was now ample in the belt, under, or rather *over* certain contingencies it would be fully inhabited. But the clerk assured me that we need not depend on such intermittent fits, that they had a fitter who could take it up to fit now, and leave the seams so it could be let out as occasion might require. This plan to make the cloak strike her person, struck my legal companion favorably, but she ordered definitely that the fitter cut away the surplus cloth, as there would be no requiring occasion so long as she owned the garment. Wearied and worn from waiting and from shocks to my sensibilities, I was willing to make even such terms for cash deliverance, and arranging to call for the overwear the next day, I was finally soaked up by our garret where I lay in a comatose and California state for sixteen hours and for my own convenience as well. The next evening, being able to be about again, I sullenly slunk in to get the condensed wear, and had the satisfaction of seeing another poor wretch tolled into the store by a couple of women and made to feel like a husband's nineteen-year-old brother at his sister-in-law's first borning bee, too big to send away to stay over night with a neighbor, and not small enough to be pleasantly invisible where he was. He tried to press through between the rounds of the chair-back, ducked his head down to avoid striking the twenty-foot ceiling, attempted to tuck his feet under his chair, then settled down to roast, just as I had the day before, and a rumbling noise was heard. It was a cable car, and I followed it to the ferry.

Carefully yours, THE MANAGER.

Straws in the Breeze.

A. R. Ayres.—I do not need to join your "Brotherhood of Moralists" in order to be as moral as I want to be. The meagrest opportunities are quite sufficient for me.—Ambrose Bierce.

Pennoyer, Governor of Oregon, is sorry he spoke. The modern politician's name is Crookback. There is not one of them that dares stand up and be a man.—Oakland Evening Tribune.

"The wise person welcomes every thinker," says "Brick" Pomeroy. The wise persons are few in number then, for the world at large never has any use for a thinker until a century or two after his death. Thinkers are dissenters and disturbers; what the world wants is conformers.—Phelps County (Iowa) Herald.

Admitting that James Russell Lowell was a "good citizen," the Post-Intelligencer says: "Too radical in his youth, he was conservative in his later days." True, and it was in his youth, when he was radical, that he earned the reputation which made his later days prosperous. Conservatism is not necessarily a sign of greatness. The clam is conservative.—Snohomish Eye.

We find a good deal of indignation lying around loose in the country press over the treatment of young Ray Gilson on the faith cure plan, but we venture to suggest that it is nobody's business but his own and his parents'. As we understand it the boy is old enough to form an opinion of his own, and in fine the only thing to do is to let him please himself about it. To insist that a person shall choose this or that variety of doctor is out of the question.—Oakland Evening Tribune.

Whitman is pre-eminently a product of the New World—steeped in Americanism to the core. Let the World's Fair managers order the ode from him, and let them pay him handsomely for it, so that he may end his life feeling that his work has gained a little appreciation. The payment should not be regulated on a cold business basis of space rates, but should reach the proportions of a testimonial fund, sufficient to make the old poet comfortable for his few remaining days.—San Francisco Examiner.

A Cheap Ranch.

One of Egoism's subscribers offers at the reasonable figure of $1500 the raw cloth for a good California home for a farmer or fruit grower or both. It consists of 80 acres of valley and hill lands; the hills are more or less wooded with fine live and white oak enough for 2000 cords of wood. The other land lies in level plateaus ranging one above another; the lower one being about 10 feet above the level of Carmel river a creek running beside it, and the others 20 and 30 feet above. The soil is an excellent one, being a dark loam (not "dobe"), and considerable of the tract is ready for the plow, in five, ten, and fifteen acre lots. It is well watered, and in as good climate and fruit growing belt as the state affords. At present its nearest market is 16 miles away, which is its only objectionable feature, however, it lies on a constantly-traveled road. The party now holding it bought 160 acres and finds he has more than he can handle alone, hence this low price. For further particulars address Egoism, Box 1678, San Francisco, California.

OUR BOOK LIST.

LOVE, MARRIAGE, AND DIVORCE, and the Sovereignty of the Individual, is a pamphlet of 121 pages composed of a discussion of marriage by Henry James, Horace Greeley, and Stephen Pearl Andrews. What Proudhon's works are to Anarchism is this to freedom in love between the sexes. It is the most comprehensive, searching, and exhaustive work ever written on the subject. No advocate of sexual freedom can afford to be without a full acquaintance with its contents. Price 35 cents.

FREE POLITICAL INSTITUTIONS: Their Nature, Essence, and Maintenance,—an abridgement and rearrangement of Lysander Spooner's "Trial by Jury," edited by Victor Yarros. It is treated in seven chapters under the following heads: I. Legitimate Government and Majority Rule. II. Trial by Jury as a Palladium of Liberty. III. Trial by Jury as Defined by Magna Charta. IV. Objections answered. V. The Criminal Intent. VI. Moral Considerations for Jurors. VII. Juries of the Present Day Illegal. Whoever desires to make plain to his conservative neighbor just how society may get on without tyranny and privilege fostering government, should have a copy of this pamphlet in his coat pocket and be prepared to not only defend his position but to take that of the opposition by storm. It is the much-needed propaganda material that should be circulated as fast as Anarchists can afford to devote money to the work. Price 25 cts.

THE RAG-PICKER OF PARIS, by Felix Pyat, translated from the French by Benj. R. Tucker. This novel is the most complete portrayal of the human nature of this century in every condition of life, that has been contributed to radical literature. Every line, every pause, has a fullness, a significance of thought, or a volcano of emotion seldom found anywhere singly, and not combined in the style of any other writer. It is probably the most vivid picture of the misery of poverty, the extravagance of wealth, the sympathy and forbearance of the poor and despised, the cruelty and aggressiveness of the aristocratic and respectable, the blind greed of the middle classes, the hollowness of charity, the cunning and hypocrisy of the priesthood, the tyranny and corruption of authority, the crushing power of privilege, and finally of the redeeming beauty of the ideal of liberty and equality, that the century has produced. Four thousand copies were sold the first week after its publication. Radicals can do much good work with it among the partly liberal-minded. It will, without arousing their prejudices, open a new field of thought for very orthodox people. Price in cloth binding $1; paper, 50 cents.

MY UNCLE BENJAMIN: a novel by Claude Tillier, an intelligent victim of institution oppression, who necessarily suffered more than he enjoyed. The splitting pangs of his intense pessimism are seasoned with such ridiculing thrusts at the vanity of wealth as to almost hide the exaggeration. The characters are not made to "come out" in school girl ideal, but tumble along like real life, mostly at the mercy of other elements than the reader's desire. The facts are not manufactured and put up in doses ready to take for building up a philosophy made to order. He dissects conduct and illustrates the charlatanism on one part and the superstition and stupidity on the other that creates fame, with diagramatic plainness. Living in an age when some of our grandfathers were too prejudice-ridden to wear boots, buttons, or suspenders we find him in his philosophy dashing off almost our deepest concepts with a lucidness equal to the description of the most commonplace affairs of our time. His wit is like springing a dark-lantern in a sub-cellar, while his humor penetrates your anatomy to the marrow without allowing you to roar with laughter so skillfully is it woven in with philosophy, pathos, or tragedy. We heartily recommend it to our full-grown readers. Price in cloth $1.00; paper 50 cents.

MONEY is at once a camera and chemist of human conduct and motive. Zola not only describes the carnivora, from the den it inhabits to the changing reflections of its glossy coat, but he tells what it is thinking about and will do. He realizes that the human animal is a none too much evoluted wild beast on the front of whose skull the experience of ages has worn only a bright spot, and he exposes all the greed, ferocious brutality, tyranny, cunning, hypocrisy, ostentation, truckling servility, idealism, and stupidity embodied in the kings, manipulators, and victims of a modern speculative world. The cruel and the generous, the detestable and the admirable traits of each character are delineated with an analytical nicety and a realistic accuracy that make the reader live the life of each and absorb the apology for their shortcomings without for a moment losing sight of the expedient course that should have replaced undesirable conduct. With an eloquently-implied regret he rebukes the horrors and cruelties of financial conquest without the wearisome moralizing or the narrow hatred common to the critics of social outrages. He is not a world builder nor a hero worshiper. Even Caroline, the lover of life, intelligent, educated, experienced, unprejudiced, and the heroine of the most trying ordeals of the story, was in his critical eyes full of weaknesses between which she was, inconsistently with her ideal of life, constantly vacillating. On world building he strikes State Socialism one of his efficient implied blows, but sensate to the difficulties of wide innovation, he offers no remedy for industrial troubles, contenting himself with painting in bold relief and sharp contrast the almost fabulous extravagance of the rich and the horrifying wretchedness of the poor, along with emphasis on the fraud, sham, and wholesale manipulating practiced by speculators upon the unsuspecting. Yet he describes with effective force the spirit of rivalry, the entrancing pleasures, the magnificent enterprises, and even humanitarian dreams that prompt men to speculate even by the most gigantic fraud. And it is this, along with his realistic repletion that makes Zola such an admirable and to us unequaled novelist. His plot embraces almost every shade of character constituting modern civilization, and he depicts the virtues and weaknesses of each with a disinterest as faithful as his realism is striking. Even his reference to Egoism, a subject that impulsive French blood might readily balk on, is characterized by this faithfulness to the spirit of the subject in hand. His Egoist, though not the expansive utilitarian of our ideal, is nevertheless intrinsically Egoistic and approvably utilitarian in a comprehensive view of the subject. Although the story, true to life, contains a full complement of unsanctioned sexual alliances, the only woman rich or poor that gold could not influence was a little Freelover who contracted such association with desirable men just once through curiosity for pleasure alone. Saccard, his chief character, is a financial poet, a speculative madman who dreams only of money—millions, power, conquest, supremacy, the prostration at his feet of "all great, cowardly, truckling Paris." Ambitious, active, unscrupulous, assuming, an appropriator of other men's ideas—of everything that came in his reach, he wove from his own and borrowed imagination, such alluring prospects as placed at his service the means beginning a career of speculation and spoilation the incidents and characters of which in Zola's masterly hands constitute the most startling expose of the power and tyranny of privileged money, the blind recklessness of stock gambling, and the ravenous greed of human avarice that we have read. We regard it as the ablest in our list, although no one can afford to be without the intensification of thought and feeling generated by all of them. The price of "Money" in cloth binding is $1; paper cover 50 cents.

For any of the above address

EQUITY PUBLISHING COMPANY,
P. O. Box 1678. San Francisco, Calif.

EGOISM'S PRINCIPLES AND PURPOSE.

Egoism's purpose is the improvement of social existence through intelligent self-interest. It finds that whatever we have of equal conditions and mutual advantage is due to a prevalence of this principle corresponding with the degree and universality of individual resistance to encroachment.

Reflection will satisfy all who are desirous of being guided in their conclusions by fact, that as organization itself is a process of absorbing every material useful to its purpose, with no limit save that of outside resistance, so must the very fact of its being a separately organized entity make it impossible for it to act with ultimate reference to anything but itself. Observation will show that this holds good throughout the vegetable and animal kingdoms, and that whatever of equality exists among members of a species or between different species has its source and degree in the resisting capacity, of whatever kind, which such member or species can exert against the encroachment of other members or species. The human animal is no exception to this rule. True, its greater complexity has developed the expedient of sometimes performing acts with beneficial results to others, but this is at last analysis only resistance, because it is the only means of resisting the withholding by others from such actor's welfare that which is more desirable than that with which he parts. If, then, the self-projecting faculty of mankind is such that it will in addition to the direct resistance common to the less complex animals, diplomatically exercise present sacrifice to further extend self, and it being a fact that equality depends upon equal resistance, diplomatic or otherwise, what are its chances in an absence of enlightenment in which the individuals of the majority so far from *intelligently* using this resisting power in their own behalf, do not even believe that they should do so? The result of a general conception so chaotic, would naturally be what we find: the generalization from the practical expediency of certain consideration for others, crystallized through the impulse of blind selfishness into a mysterious and oppressive obligation, credit for the observance of which gratifies the self-projecting faculty of the simple, while the more shrewd evade its exactions, and at every step from the manipulation of the general delusions of religious and political authority to the association of sexes and children at play, project themselves by exchanging this mythical credit for the real comforts and luxuries of the occasion, which the others produce. Thus in addition to the natural disadvantage of unequal capacity, the weaker are deprived through a superstition, of the use of such capacity as they have, as may be seen in their groping blindness all about us.

To secure and maintain equal conditions then, requires a rational understanding of the real object of life as indicated by the facts of its expression. It is plain that the world of humanity is made up of individuals absolutely separate; that life is to this humanity nothing save as it is something to one of these; that one of these can be nothing to another except as he detracts from or adds to his happiness; that on this is based the idea of social expediency; that the resistance of each of these individuals would determine what is socially expedient; that approximately equal resistance makes it equality, and on such continued and a universal resistance depends equality. This can leave no room for any sane action toward others but that of the policy promoting most the happiness of the acting Ego. Therefore Egoism insists that the attainment of equal freedom depends upon a course of conduct replacing the idea of "duty to others" with *exped ency* toward others; upon a recognition of the fact that self-pleasure must be the final motive of any act; thus developing a principle for a basis of action about which there can be no misunderstanding, and which will place every person squarely on the merit of his or her probable interests, divested of the opportunity to deceive through pretension, as under the dominance of altruistic idealism. It will maintain that what is generally recognized as morality is nothing other than the expediency deduced from conflicting interests under competition; that it is a policy which, through the hereditary influence of ancestral experience, confirmed by personal experience, is found to pay better than any other known policy; that the belief that it is something other than a policy—a fixed and eternal obligation, outside of and superior to man's recognized interests, and may not be changed as utility indicates, makes it a superstition in effect like any other superstition which causes its adherents to crystallize the expediency adopted by one period into positive regulations for another in which it has no utility, but becomes tyrannical laws and customs in the name of which persecution is justified, as in the fanaticism of any fixed idea.

•Another part of its purpose is to help dispel the "Political Authority" superstition and develop a public sentiment which would replace State interference with the protection for person and property which the competition of protecting associations would afford. Then the State's fanatical tyranny and industry crushing privilege would torture the nerves of poverty-stricken old age or pinch tender youth no more. The most disastrous interference of this monster superstition is its prohibition of the issuing of exchange medium on the ample security of all kinds of property, which at once would abolish speculative interest and practically set all idle hands at productive labor at wages ever nearing the whole product until it should be reached. The next interference is by paper titles to vacant land instead of the just and reasonable one of occupancy and use, which with the employment that free money would give, would furnish all with comfortable homes in a short time, and thereafter even with luxuries from like exertion. Following this is its patent privilege, customs robbery, protective tariff, barbarous decrees in social and sexual affairs; its brutal policy of revenge, instead of restitution, in criminal offenses, and finally its supreme power to violate the individual, and its total irresponsibility.

PROSPECTUS

EGOISM is published Monthly at 50 cents a year.

[*Entered as Second Class Mail Matter.*]

It is promptly discontinued when subscription expires, and no bills are sent out. It is run by the publishers, and admits only such contributions as they believe extend, or intelligently criticise its position.

The following are the names and amounts contributed by propagandists who wish to spread this line of thought and in that degree are its "Continental Congress," pledging so much "life and fortune" toward the establishing of their ideals and making their personalities felt in the world they live in.

PROPAGANDISTS FOR VOL. II.:

G. A. F. De Lespinasse, - - - $50.00
A Friend, - - - - - - - - 5.00

EQUITY PUBLISHING COMPANY,
P. O. Box 1678. San Francisco, Calif.

MONOGAMIC SEX RELATIONS Discussed by Ego and Marie Louise. This extraordinary pamphlet charges monogamic sexual relations with causing electrical poverty through balanced electrical conditions, which results in many common, and the most fatal diseases, and in mental deterioration, leading to narrow-mindedness, bigotry, tyranny, persecution, irritability, melancholy, drunkenness, suicide, and most of the vice and misery arising from the discontent of mankind. The every day experience of all close observers must corroborate many of its accusations with unmistakable accuracy It is intensely radical, yet clothed in such language as will admit of loaning to your orthodox neighbor. It is printed on good paper, with new type, and contains 24 large pages. Price 10 cents.

CITIZENS' MONEY. A lecture on the "National Banking System," by Alfred B. Westrup, delivered in Chicago and published in "Liberty," of Boston, in 1888. Mr. Westrup shows that every dollar's worth of property in the country may be converted into active capital, reducing interest to the cost of issuing money, and sending capital in search of labor instead of being the other way, as it is at present. It is short, popular in style, and well calculated for propaganda work. Whoever is interested in industrial emancipation can do no better work than procure and circulate this pamphlet by the dozen. It contains 21 pages, is printed on good paper in large type, and can be had for 60 cents per dozen, or 10 cents per single copy.

For any of the above address

EQUITY PUBLISHING COMPANY,
P. O. Box 1678. San Francisco, Calif.

Egoism

Vol. II.---No. 8. SAN FRANCISCO, CAL., DECEMBER, 1891. Price, Five Cents.

Pointers.

Since last issue we have received "Holiday Stories," by Stephen Fiske; "The Quintessence of Ibsenism," by G. Bernard Shaw, and "The Duchess of Powysland," by Grant Allen, all published by Benj. R. Tucker, Box 3366, Boston, Mass. And from London comes "The Individual and the State," a 10-page leaflet by Albert Tarn.

The "Examiner," of this city, printed at the first of the year a list of communications from prominent citizens suggesting desired changes in affairs generally. Most of them appealed, of course. to the authority machine. But the one more loudly emphasizing the destructive tendency of that fetich, was the recommendation of Chief of Police Crowley to deprive persons arrested for vagrancy of the right of a jury trial. Inconvenience to citizens in serving on the jury is the bait set for facilitating the industry of vagrant fishing. Of all the outrages of this country's political superstition, none is so stinging as persecution for unfortunate circumstances. First privilege legislation to plunder the weak, then legislation for convenient suppression to prevent squealing from the victim. No wonder hearty and smooth-handed beneficiaries so devoutly manipulate a superstition so convenient as the idea that the community needs watching.

Nothing so thoroughly attests popular stupidity as the assurance with which the press can reveal the transparency of the governing prerogative without danger of injuring its influence. The capitalistic papers nonchalantly admit that the Mexican government is persecuting the priests, that the president rules more like an emperor than a president, that the government's deafness to the appeals of the starving is giving cause for revolution, and that the masses need only an able general to inaugurate it. But they say "all the governors and generals are well paid and rich, and have all to lose and nothing to gain" by a revolution. After thus admitting that governing and wealth is only a matter of holding the gun, these weather vanes hope for Garza's summary suppression, which means no disturbance of riches and good pay for governing, and starvation for being governed. And these moulders of popular mental dough can do this with safety, for who has the intellectual persistence to work out the same conclusion from the game of plundering at home.

When "Liberty" gave its reason why female printers could not command as much wages as male, it replied to Egoism's citation that some women in this city are getting as much, by declaring that an isolated fact seldom proves anything; that if the death rate in San Francisco were decreasing, it would not follow that the death rate in the United States was not increasing. The illustration is certainly incomplex enough. However, Egoism did not deduce its conclusion quite as that answer implies. Mr. Tucker does not dogmatically assert that women compositors cannot acquire the qualities for which he claims men's superiority, and carrying the same idea still further we believed that the cited case of one-tenth of the working union printers of this city receiving equal wages was strong evidence that at least that fraction of the sex had practically mastered the accomplishment. San Francisco is not alone in this—every union town on the Coast makes similar showing; in one case a woman held the foremanship, and in another the advertising cases. Of course loose business management, sentimentalism, and other causes might account for the whole. But so far as personal observation goes, the women seem as useful as the men. They work as steadily, as fast, require no different accommodations, and their product sells for the same price in the market. However, "Liberty" is as willing as Egoism that women shall get equal pay for really equal work, and it was the incomprehensible seeming contrary of this that raised the question.

We have read "The Anarchists," by John Henry Mackay, translated from the German by George Schumm, and published by Benj. R. Tucker. It is the pioneer of avowed Anarchistic propaganda in story, and espouses with deep earnestness and irresistible logic, the cause of Egoistic Anarchism, both in fine reasoning and through stinging exposure of the vagaries of Communism and the folly of force. It is not fiction spun from the imagination, with putty characters performing impossible functions, but an accurate description of the lives of real leaders of social agitation, surrounded as they were by the wretchedness and horrors of London poverty and the tyranny of that city's organized imperialism. The principal character of the story is Carrard Auban, an educated young man of keen sensibility, wiry temperament, relentless logic, and invincible determination, whose experience, thoughts, emotions, and mental agonies in the growth from Communism to Egoistic Anarchism are described in the delineating, artistic, and powerful language of the admirable poet-author. The book consists of eleven chapters, painting with stereoscopic effect the world-metropolis—a veritable great beast stretched over the face of the country, alluring and devouring human beings by the million and converting the fire and strength of their youth into its arterial blood, while it throws off their weakness and misery through reeking eruptions on its flat, vascular body. The reader plunges into its midst, and views with electric vividness the "The Empire of Hunger" where, in the words of the author: "The enormous debasement of life makes of one a butcher of another a victim! The one like the other overcome by illusion... And nowhere any escape for either! Both obeying the idol of duty created by men." Here, in the desperation of hunger, men make a blind struggle for relief, and are beaten down by the hand of constituted power to sink through mental and physical weakness into death and oblivion. Then in painful reminiscence the libertarian rehearses with the author those gloomy days of hope and fear when the executioner's sword was suspended by the thread of pretended deliberation over the heads of the Chicago martyrs, and anew the choking horror and crushing despair of November 11, '87, seizes one as he reads of the nerve-rending agony and depression of London sympathizers who also could scarcely believe their own senses when they saw the thread of the fatal weapon parted by the cleaving superstition, submission to the *form* of law. Then to illustrate the folly of collectivism, the reader is carried from these scenes to the propaganda of Communism where, in spite of the example of useless sacrifice at Chicago, the victims' comrades in London declaimed madly on, declaring themselves for the deed of the bomb thrower as well as the murdered men's opinions—Communism, the doctrine of sacrifice, which, with the muteness of primitive self-assertion, fanatically lays its lambs on the altar as long as power cares to wallow in the gore. Resolutely, though calmly, Auban points out the way, illustrates, argues, defeats the grounds of the opposition and makes a momentary impression, only to lose it at the first appeal from an emotionalist to the vagaries of a childish impulse that hopes to grow a ripened garden in a day; they spring to their feet, speechify, gesticulate, consecrate themselves once more to humanity, and like a group of pettish school girls pace away arm in arm to pout at the rude critic, leaving the power that crushes without the hindrance of a single thought that tends to dissolve it. Auban is more and more alone, and from the touch of all the years finally finds a single man who understands; and one mutually eloquent look and the pressure of the hand constitute the pledges of alliance that unite them in the work of a common cause. We heartly recommend this book above any novel in our list, and urge our readers to buy and circulate it. It contains 315 pages. We keep it constantly in stock, and sell it at 50 cents in paper cover, and for $1.00 in cloth.

The Philosophy of Egoism.

XV.

The supposed inward monitor which warns the Moralist against breaking the sacred law of Right, as it admonishes the believer against offending God, is that which "doth make cowards of us all," in the language of the dramatist. That is conscience. One thinks he knows his Duty and with this thought comes vague fear and self-reproach for not having obeyed the Moral law; not simple fear in the Moralist, rather a confused feeling, but a feeling as clearly distinguishable from the simple fear of consequences as Moralism is distinguishable from a calculation of interest. The dread is as undefined as the authority or the reach of consequences, or both, are indefinite and dimly apprehended.

The fact that the dictates of conscience are the result of so-called "education" (really indoctrination) is established by the strongest proof on every hand. Every religion has its commandments and however absurd they may appear to others than the believers, conscience enforces their observance. Moralism continues in a general way the religious terror, making humanity or it may be more broadly animal life the sacred object.

Egoism, on the contrary, regards conscience as superstition. It is true that by simple analysis of the word, which yields *con*, with, and *science*, knowledge, we can have the definition: the sensation, sentiment or reflection regarding ourselves which accompanies knowledge of our voluntary action. But as an Egoist has simply either satisfaction or regret and does not judge himself by reference to any standard of Duty, he cannot have a guilty conscience.

It is most to the purpose, therefore, of Egoistic philosophy to look into the means of destroying the superstitious habit, for it is a notorious fact that self-condemnation continues somewhat after reason has assured the subject of the error of the doctrine which claimed his allegiance.

A silly conscience is to be extinguished, like other inconvenient habits, by resolute action. I have known a compositor who seemingly could not place a letter in line without first making an unnecessary motion with it against the side of his composing stick; a statesman who could not or dared not go to bed without first placing his boots as he wore them; a youth whose reason rejected the orthodox Christian doctrines in which he had been reared but who had qualms, which surprised him, about studying on Sunday; an infidel who had killed a man but had nothing to fear from the law, who nevertheless had the horrors in his dreams, and several persons with freelove ideas but inconsistent in practice in a way that showed the rule of their old conscience. Some of these things will strike everyone as being ridiculous. Of the instances cited only one did not admit of correction by Emerson's rule of doing the thing you fear to do. I firmly believe that if the man who had a life on his conscience had taken the rational method of doing all else which he knew to be sensible his mind would have been much strengthened to overcome his trouble of blood-guiltiness. The Sunday school young man realized that his conscience was awry, or the habit of a superstitious belief, and in a moderate time he overcame it. Others have had similar experiences as to books and conversation of a "blasphemous" character and breaches of the so-called law of morality in the sexual relation. Reasoning is well in its place, but action is necessary to make a free man or woman when one has been trained to have a conscience in any particular. I mean only action which combines pleasure with safety. It is no part of philosophic Egoism to pay more for advancement than it is worth.

TAK KAK.

Beauty of Motive?

One of EGOISM's subscribers writes:

I am not yet satisfied that all your principles are perfectly sound. They can be and are apt to be interpreted an applied too selfishly. But it is better to have people act from and intelligent self-interest than not at all. But I cannot help admiring acts of goodness without any thought of self, but merely from the love of doing them. The quality of an act is determined by the motive that inspires it. A good act performed specially in reference to self is not as beautiful as a similar act performed chiefly in reference to others. Yet self-interest is subserved equally well in both cases.

The beauty of motive depends upon the standpoint from which we view it. And this standpoint depends upon how closely we analyze acts to determine the motives that prompt them. Aside from the physical impossibility for a separate consciousness to act with ultimate reference to anything but self, the bitterness of our hatred for selfishness in others is the only thing that more vividly portrays the selfy motive than does the delight with which we witness generosity. Do we hate selfishness in others because of our unselfishness. Indeed we do not, but on the contrary, because we are as anxious to gratify *our* desire as they are to gratify theirs. If we did not have our contrary wish to please *ourselves* we would not notice the opposing selfness of theirs. It is an extension of the same principle if we desire the benefit for another from some one else. If that one complies we are delighted because *our* desire is gratified. If he does not we are indignant at his selfishness as we think toward the *object* of our sympathy, but really it is his defeating of our desire that we deprecate. We are not the object, and a refusal to relieve *it* cannot affect us, but we have through a knowledge of the fact, appropriated a sense of its condition, and seek relief from that consciousness by a knowledge of the removal of that condition.

There are no motives except selfy ones. The difference in acts is due to varying degrees of impressibility and reflecting powers. One person may choose to gratify his consciousness through the emotions that the possession of property affords, and conserve all his energy to that end. Another more impressible and less calculating may choose cash satisfaction, and the moment anything crosses his desires be ready to do everything in his power on the spot to gratify his present emotion by attempting to reduce things to a normal or usual state. A third, as impressible as the second, and perhaps more calculating than the first, will try to sense the merits of the case and take such action as he thinks will in the long run prove most satisfactory. We call the first selfish because we do not so fully share in his material reward as we do in the emotional reward of the second one's generosity to an object of our sympathy. The act of the second seems more beautiful if the relieving of his sympathy seems to be the impelling motive, because the relieving of sympathy is our *only* interest. We easily think others fine when we believe they exactly agree with us. If in addition to sympathy with the sufferer we were also occupied with a keen regard for equal freedom, we should in sympathy with the giver's interests be as glad to realize that he would be repaid as to see the other relieved.

Equal freedom cannot admit of obligation to sacrifice for another, for that denies equal freedom, and since all *motives* are selfward it follows that Egoistic principles cannot be interpreted and applied too selfishly except it be in the sense that the actor injures his own interests, and that is nobody else's business. Besides, men will find their own interests much more readily than others can for them, once equal freedom is thoroughly enough understood to free them from the ghost of an unanalyzed emotion. When they learn that there is no defensible claim for sacrifice, and that their hatred of what they deem selfishness in others rests on their own, they will no longer be found in the ridiculous attitude of begging justice as a charity by pleading for an idea that would make it a gift commanding gratitude instead of an expedient of self-interest. Then bombastic prating about generosity will be regarded with contempt, as attempted flattery from a charlatan, or with pity as the disconnected vaporings of primitive mentality. Let us get the start of this growing critic by analyzing every act, impulse, and proposition to the utmost depth of our penetration, deducing therefrom the dispassionate conclusion which is impregnable. H.

Monogamic Tomcats.

When winter comes on and speckled chills commence to drift up the spine and men get into the house by the fire and feel hoverish, then the old tomcats of monogamy, rolled in the furs of direct privilege or the miserable subsidy of domestic slavery, begin growling and wouling against the factors that threaten the institution on which rests their sinecure. The Church and Freethinkers have both tried their hands at it lately. Colonel Ingersoll gave the crank a turn at Chicago recently, and the preachers of San Francisco have given it another. There is so little difference between the two that the words "God" and "Church" alone distinguish one from the other. I quote from the church representative first:

> The study of the family is the key to the knowledge of sociology and the family must be preserved. The family is one of God's fundamental arrangements for the government of the world and existence of the church of Christ. Marriage is the one foundation of the family. It is the warrant, the basis and the bond which holds the family together....... Individual ownership of property is a tremendous disintegrating social force in some directions. The postponement of marriage, the avoidance of parentage—the crimson crime of our period—the towering iniquity of our own city, the surrender of the home to the boarding-house and apartments, the ambitions of gain and social fashions are all greatly augmented by our material tendencies and produce divorces...... What is to stay this fearful plague that virtually means destruction of the family, and concedes to be true what God never ordained to be so —that marriage is a failure?...... Incompatibility is the flimsy excuse of thousands, while the real reason is gross licentiousness and unwillingness to abide by a covenant made in the name of God...... The reform will come—it must come, and agitation will hasten its birth here, and deliverance will be achieved to save the nation and the Church by saving the family. The remedy for this alarming evil is: Stringent divorce laws; uniform laws in all the states; prohibition of the guilty party remarrying; a higher moral sentiment as to the nature and sanctity of marriage; a firm, rigorous administration of the laws in our courts, and of discipline in all our churches...... Let it thunder forth from press and platform and pulpit, all over the land—the imperative and immediate demand never to be silenced until this crying iniquity be abolished. The family must and shall be preserved.

The above is the spirit of the Church; the following that of the average Freethinker. The italics are the emphasis which the editor of the "Truth Seeker" gives Ingersoll's sentiment:

> Let me say right here tonight, *I regard marriage as the holiest institution among men.* Without the fireside there is no human advancement; without the family there is no life worth living. Every good government is made up of good families. The unit of government is the family; *anything that tends to destroy the family is perfectly devilish and infamous.* I believe in marriage, and I hold in utter contempt the opinions of long-haired men and short-haired women who denounce the institution of marriage...... I say it took millions of years to come from the condition of abject slavery up to the condition of marriage. Woman is the equal of the man. She has all the rights I have and one more, and that is the right to be protected. That's my doctrine...... There is only one way to be happy and that is to make somebody else so, and *you can't be happy cross-lots; you have got to go the regular turnpike road.*

That the Church should be the enemy of liberty and progress is not remarkable, but when Freethinkers set about prescribing as loudly as the Church what advancement is, and what may and may not be done, and denouncing all other conduct as devilish and infamous, one is tempted to call the attention of grown up people to the absurdity of their position. With Colonel Ingersoll liberty is the best thing he knows of with some exception, and that is an institution or two of his choice. What church bigot cannot say as much. He would have "liberty for man, woman, and child," but only so much as the marriage *institution* affords. He is loud in his defense of individuality, but if the restraint of the mutual slavery of his little republic, the family, is galling to the individual and he secedes, he is devilish and infamous. If some social arrangement other than marriage is required to complete his happiness he may go without, no matter if his ideal can be mutually arranged with others. A person may be happy without bowing to the abstraction, God, but if he be happy without bowing to the abstraction, marriage, he is not happy. The caress is pleasanter if some disinterested party has consented, or if it is bestowed always by the same person. Men will not look after their preservation and interests in society unless they are married. Equal freedom is not so good as privilege in the hands of the other sex. Since it has taken millions of years to acquire marriage, there is nothing better adapted to happiness. Variation must cease at this particular departure. This is the logic of prejudice. When Ingersoll criticises the superstitions of the Church he argues, but when his own superstition is threatened, like the Church, he appeals, denounces, and slanders the cut of his opponents' hair. H.

Another Collective Bubble Burst.

The Kaweah colony has collapsed. A number of private fortunes have been swallowed up and in some cases have left old people helpless, yet nothing has been learned by the sufferers. They do not for a moment blame the collective method—only the selfishness and wickedness of individuals.

It is conceded that the industrial feature failed through a lack of efficient management and the competitive spur, and yet the incessant chorus of the colonists has been and will be the "destruction of competition." It is admitted that an emotion-swayed laity constantly recalling and electing new leaders kept incompetence at the head of affairs where it could do the most harm. And it is mourned that failure socially, was due to everybody meddling in everybody else's business. There was an intense jealousy of the man who "held down the soft job," and the "general meeting" was an easy means of leveling him to the pick and shovel whenever he displeased some one, no matter what his capacity might be. There was trouble also in regard to those who pleaded sickness and claimed exemption from duty, when their neighbors had no way of determining the truthfulness of the allegation. In the management of the work, a ditch was surveyed and made, and then the water would not run in it; a planing mill foundation was cut out of granite at a place where power could not be got to the machines; a sawmill with a capacity of 3000 feet a day averaged but 193 feet a day during a three-months' run, and it cost $18 to $20 a thousand while competitive production costs but $10.

Anarchists have again and again pointed all this out as inherent in a political system of production; incompetency cannot select competency, and if competency should happen even to get the management it cannot plan and execute without supreme control of each individual, and this enslaves him; he cannot choose his course even at his own expense. Since society consists of individual consciousnesses, full liberty and full competition are the essential factors of social existence—liberty to act, competition to determine reward. Give men liberty to produce by removing paper monopolies of land and thought, and permit them to exchange products freely without first having to exchange for a limited kind, and all this "duty"-blubbering, chaotic hotchpotch is at an end, and equity will organize itself as water seeks a level. If we were permitted to provide means of exchanging our products without paying the toll which can be collected when we must exchange them for a particular kind before we can get the kind we want, we would get full return for all the product we market; and if we could use the means which we must pay for idle land to buy tools and build houses, we could escape the toll of the landlord and of the employer; and if we were allowed to do all the kinds of things we can learn to do, we would escape the toll of patentees and thought compilers; and if the effort of each were rewarded by the sale of his product in open market, no question could be raised regarding his work or his pay. Incompetence would experiment at its own expense, and merit would elect itself with no responsibility to the community save to note its existence. Competition would cause both the greatest production and lowest prices and create such an abundance that art and social life would shoot forth in such extravagance as to make the present appear like the hard-shelled seed sticking neglectedly in the winter's chilly mud waiting for the warm sunshine of spring time. This is what Anarchism offers and has accurately and patiently expounded for years amid the ridicule or indifference of the authority-ridden populace, peeling its shins over facts as it gapingly stumbles after the political elephant till he disappears in the big tent at Washington. But neither logic nor experience can reach a generation of emotionalists; they have got to die off.

H.

The Secularists' Prize Manual.

I suppose that most readers of current radical literature have read something about the $1000 prize offered by a number of Secularists two years ago for a manual adapted to the use of teachers in public schools for teaching *morality*.

The prize was awarded to two Christian writers; namely, Nicholas Paine Gilman, and Edward Payson Jackson, both of Boston.

The former wrote "The Laws of Daily Conduct," a book of 149 pages, and the latter a treatise on "Character Building," comprising 230 pages, and both books are bound in one volume.

These gentlemen are, if my memory serves me correctly, ex-preachers. Both confess themselves friends of religion, and give unmistakable evidence of the fact.

The work these writers set out to do, was to present a book such as would enable the teacher to teach *morality* in the public schools. Of course religion was to have nothing to do with the method of presentation, or the incentives that should be set before the mind of the scholar. The pupil was to be taught the art of right living, or "conduct as a fine art" and the proper method of "character building." In other words "the laws of daily conduct" and those governing "character building" were to be found in an appeal to a rational interpretation of life.

The writers have tried to do what they aimed at, and have succeeded as far as the length of their rope would admit of. If, however, you will only forget the few things they said about being "friends of religion" and of "rendering unto Cæsar the things that are Cæsar's," "duty," etc., you will find that they have builded on the solid ground of Egoism. Both writers constantly keep in view, happiness as the supreme aim of life.

Mr. Gilman lays down what seems to him a very broad foundation. He says: "*All our human life is lived under laws.*" He then proceeds to show that we must obey the laws under which we live, or *take the consequences*. Just so. This is Egoism pure and simple, and beyond this foundation rock, neither Mr. Gilman nor Mr. Jackson is able to budge. Looking ahead for consequences is what every intelligent being does or tries to do. This is the motive that is always in harmony with reason. There is therefore no moral code, no moral standard, and neither of these writers professes to give any other incentive to conduct than the consideraation of the consequences—the pains and penalties that follow upon the heels of the violation of a law. Manifestly then, this is the test that curbs and controls the world at large. Man looks out as intently for happiness as the needle points to the pole. Selfishness is the motive that moves man. Let him have more head and more heart, and intelligent selfishness will identify his happiness with the happiness of his fellows. We may introduce the ghost dance of "duty," "spirituality," etc., but after it is all over we shall conclude that happiness is the end we have in view. Blind selfishness has reposed all its hopes in heaven, but with heaven out of sight we must rest with Mr. Gilman on "self-control by reason." He did not say *self-reliance*, but what he did say if freely interpreted means as much.

As an Egoist the prize manual pleases me. The superstructure is of ancient type in some points, but the foundation is modern. At times the writers loudly call for *duty*, but as "duty" does not materialize in answer to the call then the writer submits: "Well then let us take *policy*." When the writer sets up Joe Cook's "oughtness of the ought," and it evaporates he cries out "give us expediency." In substance these morality writers say, "You had better not do that or you will get hurt." They have not been able to set up sign boards along the highway of life to guide the pilgrim. Man must guide himself—must trust his reason, rather than trust the reasoning of others, and thus become a law unto himself.

There are some lapses in the book which, as I have said, have to be laid aside. Mr. Jackson all through his "Character Building" holds up pains and penalties as guides to right conduct. But this brings him to the consideration of selfishness. He does not want to indorse such a motive, and attempts to repudiate it. I will let the reader see how he does it.

Mr. Jackson's teachings are through the media of Dr. Dix, a teacher, and his scholars:

Dr. Dix—So you think all good acts have at bottom some selfish motive?

Thomas Dunn, a pupil—It seems to me that it must be so.

Dr. Dix—Do you think the good Samaritan was selfish?

Thomas Dunn—He *might* have been purely so. He couldn't help pitying the man he saw suffering. Pity is no more truly an act of will I suppose, than surprise, or any other sudden emotion. His pity caused him a kind of suffering, and he took the most direct and effectual way of relieving it............

Dr. Dix—I am surprised that such fully-developed cynicism could come from such young lips!

Thomas Dunn—I merely repeated what I had heard from older lips. But I only said it might be *possible*.

Dr. Dix (more graciously)—But what you felt in your heart is not probable. That is not the way you ordinarily judge your fellow-beings. Only those who are without virtue themselves disbelieve in its existence in others; only those without benevolence themselves believe others destitute of that virtue.

This is the very point where Mr. Jackson should have made his moral test of conduct appear in full force, but instead of reasoning with some show of science, he falls to preaching, and gives his pupils some exceedingly poor preaching at that. A few lines further on the preacher breaks out with saintly fervor, as he did not have any strong reasons to break out with, and "thanks heaven," that "not all are selfish, nor nearly all."

And this is the $1000 Prize Manual!! Built by two preachers who while building strongly and yet blindly, like Samson groping for the pillars of the temple, they fain would destroy all the good they had done.

They have plainly made it clear that there is no moral law, no standard, no test; but that on all questions of conduct man is to use his reason, and restrain himself from that which would bring him evil, and seek that which he thinks would bring him happiness. That is Egoism. So far as the Prize Manual establishes anything, it establishes this philosophy. W. S. Bell.

Our Funny Farmer.

Dear Egoism: I feel somewhat ashamed of my procrastination at taking the "shot at the enemy" which I so long ago promised to take through Egoism. After so long a wait you will be justified in considering my shot a blank cartridge, and that I have fallen into the habits of the Moralists and delibately violate a mutual contract with impunity and a lazy pen. After obtaining your consent to "pull the trigger" (as you aptly put it) I was under obligation to send along my shot. To be under obligation is to be in a sense and in some degree a slave; and as an Egoist I desire freedom from all obligations, I must therefore fulfill my self-imposed promise and obligation, and thus achieve my liberty. My excuse for the continued delay is that I have been driven about to death with work in consequence of having "bitten off" a larger piece of this glittering golden West than I "can chaw," and with no Mutual Bank funds in the surplus with which to employ a Chinese substitute I have been compelled to do my own work, and thus conform to the popular and ridiculous fad, "white labor only." I have been so busy pushing the pick and shovel, saw and hammer, that I have not had time to push the pen. Figuratively speaking, I have sentenced myself for life to hard labor. If you could see my haggard, flea-bitten, fly-blown expression you would not only take me for a typical Californian, but would extend the "right hand of friendship" and your heartfelt sympathy—although Egoists are supposed to be as destitute of feeling as that unsympathetic and dispassionate animal, the ox. Yet I think I can rely upon that "fellow feeling which makes us wondrous kind," as the poet says; especially that flea-bitten "kind" of feeling in California which makes us wondrous mad, and takes the sentiment all out of poetry and makes it the blankest of blank verse. I hope you will accept this excuse as my apology and believe me to have let go only to get a better hold.

Speaking of Egoism reminds me of the late discussion upon that subject in "Liberty" between Benj. R. Tucker and Victor Yarros. What is the matter with our mutual friend, Victor? has he fallen into the trap of Moralistic respectability laid by the intellectual and classical Herbert Spencer and his followers? I have held several arguments with students of Herbert Spencer, and usually found them to be the most difficult of persons to get to grasp a clear conception of the principle of liberty. I can make more headway with a democratic politician! The Spencerians, to my mind appear to prefer a circuitous, serpentine march toward liberty rather than a plumb-line rapid transit cross-lots cut.

Mr. Yarros's recent controversy with our Uncle Benj. R. Tucker in which Egoism came in for its share of discussion, inclines me to the melancholy opinion that he is only a half-baked Egoist, "rapidly turning to dough," especially after reading (sometime ago) his "Reasons Why" he was an Egoist (than which for condensed clearness and clear-cut Egoism nothing better has been written by any Egoistic writer).

In his last intellectual battle with Mr. Tucker he forcibly reminds me of the darky boy who used to get down on all fours and buck heads with a pet male sheep—classically called a ram. His trick to avoid being hit by the ram was to suddenly duck his head when the ram came on head down to deliver his usual straightforward blow. This little trick was successful for a time, until one day the darky in ducking his head run a stubble into his nose which caused him to raise his head suddenly and just in time to receive a terrific blow from his rambunctious adversary which knocked the darky flat, and thus ended the ramification on the spot. The stubble which Mr. Tucker thrust under Mr. Yarros's nose, was "Reason's Why," and caused him to receive the former's straightforward blow, knocking our V. Y. out *hors* or ram *de combat* and ending his Egoistic ramification.

I am optimist enough to hope that neither of these intellectual athletes will be very angry with me for comparing one with a foolish darky boy, and the other with a ram, but—well I always admire the *straightforwardness* of a ram.

I have been a reader of Tucker's "Liberty" for nearly ten years, and paid fairly close attention to the arguments and debates between its logical editor and his opponents, and I have come to the conclusion that his intense directness of purpose and detestation of hypocrisy even though (as is often the case) it be unconscious hypocrisy, has caused him to be among many of his disputants the most misunderstood man in the (Anarchistic) world. His evident hatred of hypocrisy (conscious or unconscious), reminds me of old Ben Wade (a shrewd politician), who once said upon the subject of hypocrisy, "That a man who would think damn it, and not say damn it, was a damned hypocrite."

Mr. Tucker's straightforward course in argument has no doubt caused some of his readers to think him discourteous and lacking in linguistic polish. However this may be, his sharp angles and rugged corners oftentimes serve the good purpose of polishing and rounding the corners of his over-confident antagonists. I like our Uncle Benjamin's battering-ram propensities. May his horns ever be *straight* and never grow shorter. Parse.

Managerial Experience.

I have got something now that I don't want, and I've got it bad. It is a regret on the inside of my breastbone. I am the scene for a good bargain, I am willing to swop this fresh-laid, sickle-edged regret for the aroma of a shadow or the unselfishness of an Altruist. Heretofore I have been able to exchange work for the raw material consumed in the Experiences for these columns, but this one cost me $20 in cash—worse than cash—borrowed money. Since I found my railroad unpatentable I have not had much confidence in my mental capacities, and have held my body in rags and readiness for manual exploits if any should fly. Egoism was getting unusually hard up and I was getting just as unusually ready to turn in some wherewith. Suddenly there came a letter from one of our subscribers who has charge of one of the roundhouses of a railroad. He had room for a man and could pay $65 per month.

Now this struck me in more ways than one. Among machines, I am literally stuck on railroad engines, and they come about fourth in the list of my choice of the good things of *life*. I regard baked raspberry cobbler with unscalped Jersey milk as the best thing in the world. Next comes a big subscription list, then beautiful and intelligent women, and following these, slowly, locomotives. The first, we cannot afford, the second we cannot capture, and the third do not fool around goose pasture. Under these circumstances the engines became the first choice and I would have the pleasure of putting sand in their craws and cleaning their tired "slippers," smooth arms, and warm chests. In addition to this, I was overjoyed and the German cigar store at the thought of earning as much as my, now at parting, adored wife. But she suggested that we sit down with deliberation and a pencil and calculate what it would cost to hire the paper done, as would be necessary in my absence. My head was so crowded with the $65 and engines that there hadn't been even standing room for the paper's mechanical work. We found, however, that it would take $25 to replace my mechanical work on the paper, and $25 for board, which left only $15 and a freezing vacuum in my enthusiasm. For $15 in my inside pocket, my wife would have the responsibility of the paper with its vexatious details in strange hands, and would have to be jarred out of bed forty minutes earlier in the morning by the parrot-fighting uproar of our fussy little alarm clock, and worse than all she must perform my shivertremens every time also while wading and splashing around building fire in the wet air that drifts into the kitchen at night. This seemed too much goods, or *bads* rather, for the money. But jobs were scarce, and there was trouble in the union camp, and the $15 a month would help us to a $100 or more that we want to buy type that we may become our own employers. Besides I meant to do most of the necessary writing evenings, and communicate the details of management from day to day, and thus in the rear end of a somewhat unpleasant suspense help us out of a dependency which is irksome in struggling for existence. With this idea of assuming responsibility and achieving a result, I concluded to try it. So I bought a blue flannel shirt that fits me like a circus tent, and a pair of yellow gloves and blue overalls with a suggestive scent—more, seventy-five cents. My wife also made me take our apoplectic old umbrella to keep me dry when parading from the engine-house to my room and meals. With these clothes in my wife's little niece's little satchel, and a mellow appreciation of everything about home that had previously seemed monotonous under my collar bone, I bravely rode elegant passenger coaches for ten hours and seven dollars. Then I was there, so was my friend and my job—what more did I want? I wanted a roundhouse and a square one; the former was not built yet, and the latter does not thrive in that section. It was on the plains in the midst of an ocean of sage brush. This was the sagest-looking brush that I ever saw, and however much he may love pointedness and penetration, I cannot believe that a sane sage would brush himself with such a whisk. Perhaps they use them to brush an ignorant and stupid populace. I saw indications of such a populace and heard it pop at some places along the line.

The umbrella was a piece of misplaced wire and spraddle; while there would be a sufficiency of rain and plenty of room to walk in, there was none to walk from nor engine-house to arrive at. The engines were just turned in the yard, so to speak, and the men slept in a tourists' back-number sleeping car. I take it that it is a cataleptic sleep that the car is afflicted with and that the tourists had to abandon it and take a smoker. Ordinary sleeping cars are somewhat somnambulistic and can run about as well in their sleep as any way.

The men worked in twelve-hour shifts at shoveling coal from the ground, week days and Sundays, and in emergencies added six hours more. There was no escape from the rain, for when the engines come they must be coaled to keep them from getting cold, no matter who gets wet. Neither would I have the pleasure of polishing their slippers, arms, and palpitating bosoms, for they take only some coal lunch and a game of poker, as it were, and put off to town for toilet, while the men have to toil it where they are. Being the subject of rheumatism in the possessive case, I dared not expose myself to the rain as would be necessary, and there would be no opportunity to do the writing I had planned. This would cause my wife more trouble and loss of time than my surplus would cover, so the only thing left was myself for home, where I arrived in time to assume the first responsibility, which my wife was shouldering with all her might.

My friend was in no way to blame, for he had no way of knowing that I must keep out of the rain and work at home evenings. It was not altogether my fault either, for there was no time to inquire into particulars, and I could not afford to miss an opportunity to boost the home struggle. The culpable parties are those millions of unfortunates who try to drag through life without the paper. For had there been even a thousand of them chucking in a four-bit piece each year, I would not have thought of attempting such a wild goose chase. But they didn't and I did, and here I am in all my gawky stupidity innocently waiting to do some other fool thing, I suppose.

When I stated the amount of money required to put Egoism on a steam press, I believed that we would have to raise it ourselves, so I named a finely-calculated figure. The amount allotted to new type furnishes just enough to fill the columns and little left to vary on. This is all right for naturally great and systematic writers, a fact which I learned from setting David Hume's and my own productions. We run a case out evenly, so that all the letters are exhausted at the same time and have to be propped up to keep them from falling. Now some of our contributors often write so one-ideadly that a letter will run out when most of the boxes are still one-third full, and as the full avoirdupois of type must go in to fill the space, I am obliged to boycott in my editorials all words containing the wearied letter, which often produces an extraordinary style. In this respect I am ahead of my esteemed pretemporary, Mr. Hume. However, I charitably attribute this to a lack of opportunity on his part. He never attempted to run a paper on an all-around limited capital, so failed to acquire the letter boycotting accomplishment. I deeply sympathize with all otherwise great characters who are deprived of my opportunities, and shall as soon as practicable cut off the uneven exercise of at least one by getting more type. This statement is made under an impulse to fairness toward worthy contemporaries who may be struggling to duplicate my twisted style.

When one wakes up to a new idea it surprises him to see what a set of clams we human beasts are. I have been extant for thirty-four years now, and have repeatedly seen the sun shining through clouds of dust, volumes of sewer gas, the stench from marshes and from inhabited dead animals, also into columns of pied and smudgy smoke, and upon miles of the sloppiest of mud, but in spite of this it never occurred to me that its beams might become soiled and dirty until lately when one day I stumbled onto a "sunbeam washer" in front of a store. With that suggestion these things flashed upon me like a pain from too many green apples. I was provoked that I hadn't caught on and monopolized the credit myself of conferring upon an appreciative world the possibility of fresh and exquisitely-laundried sunbeams as good as new except for the wear from washing. My wife says it was a clothes washer that I saw. Now I do not pretend, regardless of diet, to be always very astute, but when I see on a machine in big black letters the words, "Sunbeam Washer," it is very hard to make me believe that they are "Clothes Washer."

I have been harrowed by, and have plowed here some fogs that were very thick—twenty miles I should say, but London has recently taken the fog cake or a cake of fog so dense that people not only lost their way but even their lives in it. I am glad we do not live in London, for my wife would lose her life the first time she went out with it. For not long ago she lost her last year's umbrella on the local train when there was not a speck of fog, but a bright moonlight. She says there is no other kind of moonlight besides the bright variety. I admit it, but as much cannot be said of those who lose their umbrellas. The Manager.

Straws in the Breeze.

For my part, I do not know what, under all circumstances, is right or wrong.—Bierce.

In the matter of the men buried by a landslide on the line of the Northern Pacific railroad at Canton the local coroner has decided that no inquest is necessary, for there is no doubt of the cause of death and no charge of criminal negligence. That may be very true, but are there no fees for an inquest in that country? And is there no allowance for an autopsy? The gentlemen's reasons for inaction are incompetent, irrelevant and immaterial; in violating the sacredest traditions of his high office, as they are understood here, he should have the decency to explain that it would not pay him to observe them.—Examiner.

Mr. Wanamaker is still enthusiastic for a postal telegraph and would even add to it a postal telephone. We fail to see wherein lies the gain. We do not believe that the service would be better and we dread the rule of a bureaucracy. It would seem that there are already political machines more than enough in this country, and we can see no reason for the creation of a new one. The argument from the success of the postoffice department is fallacious. The work of that department could and would be done better and done cheaper by private enterprise, as the success of Wells, Fargo & Co.'s postal service in competition with the government very clearly demonstrates.—Oakland Daily Tribune.

Public sentiment is all powerful. Public sentiment should make land free. It should encourage men to go upon land wherever found vacant, to build homes thereon and improve it by their labor, and should protect them in its possession so long as they occupy and use it. Public sentiment should refuse to respect or protect possession without use. When this begins to be the case vacant land holders will hasten to improve their holdings, or dispose of them to the first bidder: the cancer of rent will cease to absorb the earnings of labor, and men will have begun to be free. This doctrine we believe to be unassailable, and we are not ashamed to proclaim it from the housetops and the hilltops, and to defend it at all times.—Phelps County (Neb.) Herald.

A Cheap Ranch.

One of EGOISM's subscribers offers at the reasonable figure of $1500 the raw cloth for a good California home for a farmer or fruit grower or both. It consists of 80 acres of valley and hill lands; the hills are more or less wooded with fine live and white oak enough for 2000 cords of wood. The other land lies in level plateaus ranging one above another; the lower one being about 10 feet above the level of Carmel river, a creek running beside it, and the others 20 and 30 feet above. The soil is an excellent one, being a dark loam (not "dobe"), and considerable of the tract is ready for the plow, in five, ten, and fifteen acre lots. It is well watered, and in as good climate and fruit growing belt as the state affords, and has a new five-room house, a barn and wagon shed. At present its nearest market is 16 miles away, which is its only objectionable feature, however, it lies on a constantly-traveled road. The party now holding it bought 160 acres and finds he has more than he can handle alone, hence this low price. For further particulars address EGOISM, Box 1678, San Francisco.

OUR BOOK LIST.

LOVE, MARRIAGE, AND DIVORCE, AND THE SOVEREIGNTY OF THE INDIVIDUAL, is a pamphlet of 121 pages composed of a discussion of marriage by Henry James, Horace Greeley, and Stephen Pearl Andrews. What Proudhon's works are to Anarchism is this to freedom in love between the sexes. It is the most comprehensive, searching, and exhaustive work ever written on the subject. No advocate of sexual freedom can afford to be without a full acquaintance with its contents. Price 35 cents.

FREE POLITICAL INSTITUTIONS: THEIR NATURE, ESSENCE, AND MAINTENANCE,—an abridgement and rearrangement of Lysander Spooner's "Trial by Jury," edited by Victor Yarros. It is treated in seven chapters under the following heads: I. Legitimate Government and Majority Rule. II. Trial by Jury as a Palladium of Liberty. III. Trial by Jury as Defined by Magna Charta. IV. Objections answered. V. The Criminal Intent. VI. Moral Considerations for Jurors. VII. Juries of the Present Day Illegal. Whoever desires to make plain to his conservative neighbor just how society may get on without tyranny and privilege fostering government, should have a copy of this pamphlet in his coat pocket and be prepared to not only defend his position but to take that of the opposition by storm. It is the much-needed propaganda material that should be circulated as fast as Anarchists can afford to devote money to the work. Price 25 cts.

THE RAG-PICKER OF PARIS, by Felix Pyat, translated from the French by Benj. R. Tucker. This novel is the most complete portrayal of the human nature of this century in every condition of life, that has been contributed to radical literature. Every line, every pause, has a fullness, a significance of thought, or a volcano of emotion seldom found anywhere singly, and not combined in the style of any other writer. It is probably the most vivid picture of the misery of poverty, the extravagance of wealth, the sympathy and forbearance of the poor and despised, the cruelty and aggressiveness of the aristocratic and respectable, the blind greed of the middle classes, the hollowness of charity, the cunning and hypocrisy of the priesthood, the tyranny and corruption of authority, the crushing power of privilege, and finally of the redeeming beauty of the ideal of liberty and equality, that the century has produced. Four thousand copies were sold the first week after its publication. Radicals can do much good work with it among the partly liberal-minded. It will, without arousing their prejudices, open a new field of thought for very orthodox people. Price in cloth binding $1; paper, 50 cents.

MY UNCLE BENJAMIN: a novel by Claude Tillier, an intelligent victim of institution oppression, who necessarily suffered more than he enjoyed. The splitting pangs of his intense pessimism are seasoned with such ridiculing thrusts at the vanity of wealth as to almost hide the exaggeration. The characters are not made to "come out" in school girl ideal, but tumble along like real life, mostly at the mercy of other elements than the reader's desire. The facts are not manufactured and put up in doses ready to take for building up a philosophy made to order. He dissects conduct and illustrates the charlatanism on one part and the superstition and stupidity on the other that creates fame, with diagramatic plainness. Living in an age when some of our grandfathers were too prejudice-ridden to wear boots, buttons, or suspenders we find him in his philosophy dashing off almost our deepest concepts with a lucidness equal to the description of the most commonplace affairs of our time. His wit is like springing a dark-lantern in a sub-cellar, while his humor penetrates your anatomy to the marrow without allowing you to roar with laughter so skillfully is it woven in with philosophy, pathos, or tragedy. We heartily recommend it to our full-grown readers. Price in cloth $1.00; paper 50 cents.

MONEY is at once a camera and chemist of human conduct and motive. Zola not only describes the carnivora, from the den it inhabits to the changing reflections of its glossy coat, but he tells what it is thinking about and will do. He realizes that the human animal is a none too much evoluted wild beast on the front of whose skull the experience of ages has worn only a bright spot, and he exposes all the greed, ferocious brutality, tyranny, cunning, hypocrisy, ostentation, truckling servility, idealism, and stupidity embodied in the kings, manipulators, and victims of a modern speculative world. The cruel and the generous, the detestable and the admirable traits of each character are delineated with an analytical nicety and a realistic accuracy that make the reader live the life of each and absorb the apology for their shortcomings without for a moment losing sight of the expedient course that should have replaced undesirable conduct. With an eloquently-implied regret he rebukes the horrors and cruelties of financial conquest without the wearisome moralizing or the narrow hatred common to the critics of social outrages. He is not a world builder nor a hero worshiper. Even Caroline, the lover of life, intelligent, educated, experienced, unprejudiced, and the heroine of the most trying ordeals of the story, was in his critical eyes full of weaknesses between which she was, inconsistently with her ideal of life, constantly vacillating. On world building he strikes State Socialism one of his efficient implied blows, but sensate to the difficulties of wide innovation, he offers no remedy for industrial troubles, contenting himself with painting in bold relief and sharp contrast the almost fabulous extravagance of the rich and the horrifying wretchedness of the poor, along with emphasis on the fraud, sham, and wholesale manipulating practiced by speculators upon the unsuspecting. Yet he describes with effective force the spirit of rivalry, the entrancing pleasures, the magnificent enterprises, and even humanitarian dreams that prompt men to speculate even by the most gigantic fraud. And it is this, along with his realistic repletion that makes Zola such an admirable and to us unequaled novelist. His plot embraces almost every shade of character constituting modern civilization, and he depicts the virtues and weaknesses of each with a disinterest as faithful as his realism is striking. Even his reference to Egoism, a subject that impulsive French blood might readily balk on, is characterized by this faithfulness to the spirit of the subject in hand. His Egoist, though not the expansive utilitarian of our ideal, is nevertheless intrinsically Egoistic and approvably utilitarian in a comprehensive view of the subject. Although the story, true to life, contains a full complement of unsanctioned sexual alliances, the only woman rich or poor that gold could not influence was a little Freelover who contracted such association with desirable men just once through curiosity for pleasure alone. Saccard, his chief character, is a financial poet, a speculative madman who dreams only of money—millions, power, conquest, supremacy, the prostration at his feet of "all great, cowardly, truckling Paris." Ambitious, active, unscrupulous, assuming, an appropriator of other men's ideas—of everything that came in his reach, he wove from his own and borrowed imagination, such alluring prospects as placed at his service the means beginning a career of speculation and spoilation the incidents and characters of which in Zola's masterly hands constitute the most startling expose of the power and tyranny of privileged money, the blind recklessness of stock gambling, and the ravenous greed of human avarice that we have read. We regard it as the ablest in our list, although no one can afford to be without the intensification of thought and feeling generated by all of them. The price of "Money" in cloth binding is $1; paper cover 50 cents.

For any of the above address

EQUITY PUBLISHING COMPANY,

P. O. Box 1678. San Francisco, Calif.

EGOISM'S PRINCIPLES AND PURPOSE.

EGOISM's purpose is the improvement of social existence through intelligent self-interest. It finds that whatever we have of equal conditions and mutual advantage is due to a prevalence of this principle corresponding with the degree and universality of individual resistance to encroachment.

Reflection will satisfy all who are desirous of being guided in their conclusions by fact, that as organization itself is a process of absorbing every material useful to its purpose, with no limit save that of outside resistance, so must the very fact of its being a separately organized entity make it impossible for it to act with ultimate reference to anything but itself. Observation will show that this holds good throughout the vegetable and animal kingdoms, and that whatever of equality exists among members of a species or between different species has its source and degree in the resisting capacity, of whatever kind, which such member or species can exert against the encroachment of other members or species. The human animal is no exception to this rule. True, its greater complexity has developed the expedient of sometimes performing acts with beneficial results to others, but this is at last analysis only resistance, because it is the only means of resisting the withholding by others from such actor's welfare that which is more desirable than that with which he parts. If, then, the self-projecting faculty of mankind is such that it will in addition to the direct resistance common to the less complex animals, diplomatically exercise present sacrifice to further extend self, and it being a fact that equality depends upon equal resistance, diplomatic or otherwise, what are its chances in an absence of enlightenment in which the individuals of the majority so far from *intelligently* using this resisting power in their own behalf, do not even believe that they should do so? The result of a general conception so chaotic, would naturally be what we find: the generalization from the practical expediency of certain consideration for others, crystallized through the impulse of blind selfishness into a mysterious and oppressive obligation, credit for the observance of which gratifies the self-projecting faculty of the simple, while the more shrewd evade its exactions, and at every step from the manipulation of the general delusions of religious and political authority to the association of sexes and children at play, project themselves by exchanging this mythical credit for the real comforts and luxuries of the occasion, which the others produce. Thus in addition to the natural disadvantage of unequal capacity, the weaker are deprived through a superstition, of the use of such capacity as they have, as may be seen in their groping blindness all about us.

To secure and maintain equal conditions then, requires a rational understanding of the real object of life as indicated by the facts of its expression. It is plain that the world of humanity is made up of individuals absolutely separate; that life is to this humanity nothing save as it is something to one of these; that one of these can be nothing to another except as he detracts from or adds to his happiness; that on this is based the idea of social expediency; that the resistance of each of these individuals would determine what is socially expedient; that approximately equal resistance makes it equality, and on such continued and a universal resistance depends equality. This can leave no room for any sane action toward others but that of the policy promoting most the happiness of the acting Ego. Therefore EGOISM insists that the attainment of equal freedom depends upon a course of conduct replacing the idea of "duty to others" with *expedency* toward others; upon a recognition of the fact that self-pleasure must be the final motive of any act; thus developing a principle for a basis of action about which there can be no misunderstanding, and which will place every person squarely on the merit of his or her probable interests, divested of the opportunity to deceive through pretension, as under the dominance of altruistic idealism. It will maintain that what is generally recognized as morality is nothing other than the expediency deduced from conflicting interests under competition; that it is a policy which, through the hereditary influence of ancestral experience, confirmed by personal experience, is found to pay better than any other known policy; that the belief that it is something other than a policy—a fixed and eternal obligation, outside of and superior to man's recognized interests, and may not be changed as utility indicates, makes it a superstition in effect like any other superstition which causes its adherents to crystallize the expediency adopted by one period into positive regulations for another in which it has no utility, but becomes tyrannical laws and customs in the name of which persecution is justified, as in the fanaticism of any fixed idea.

Another part of its purpose is to help dispel the "Political Authority" superstition and develop a public sentiment which would replace State interference with the protection for person and property which the competition of protecting associations would afford. Then the State's fanatical tyranny and industry crushing privilege would torture the nerves of poverty-stricken old age or pinch tender youth no more. The most disastrous interference of this monster superstition is its prohibition of the issuing of exchange medium on the ample security of all kinds of property, which at once would abolish speculative interest and practically set all idle hands at productive labor at wages ever nearing the whole product until it should be reached. The next interference is by paper titles to vacant land instead of the just and reasonable one of occupancy and use, which with the employment that free money would give, would furnish all with comfortable homes in a short time, and thereafter even with luxuries from like exertion. Following this is its patent privilege, customs robbery, protective tariff, barbarous decrees in social and sexual affairs; its brutal policy of revenge, instead of restitution, in criminal offenses, and finally its supreme power to violate the individual, and its total irresponsibility.

Egoism

Vol. II.—No. 9. SAN FRANCISCO, CAL., FEBRUARY, 1892. Price, Five Cents.

Pointers.

Except four "Straws in the Breeze," this number of EGOISM is homemade.

This number, dated February, is the one that should have appeared in January under a normal condition of things.

From a letter from El Reno, I. T., we note that the Indians, after receiving their supplies from the government, sell the clothes to the whites at twenty-five per cent of their value. There is nothing like a political institution for waste and stupidity. If the Indians do not want clothes, the bill could be saved since no part of it is due them.

We have received the first number of "Free Trade," a new and neat paper published by Albert Tarn, at 17 Johnson's Court, Fleet Street, London, E. C. It exposes State superstition from the standpoint of absolute freetrade, and is destined to do a wide scope of good work. We think Mr. Tarn should concentrate all his energies on that publication alone. Its standpoint is primary enough to be appreciated by all, and fundamental enough to consistently cover the whole ground of freedom.

As EGOISM goes to press, "Liberty" arrives, and we learn that ours is the only Anarchistic paper now published on this continent. The editor of "Liberty" is going to move to New York, and that journal will not appear again until about the 16th of April. When we note EGOISM falling behind its regular gait, and "Liberty" thus quickening its step there is not much reason to hurrah for ourselves, but as we cannot do this, then we will hurrah for *our side*. New York is the proper place for "Liberty" and we hope it will come out an 8-page instead of 4-page weekly. And this volley of good will shoots backward as well; EGOISM has no notion itself of becoming extinct.

The California State Liberal Union at its this year's convention in this city condemned, since it is popular to do so, Harman and Heywood's imprisonment, but resolutions relating to more freedom in divorce and marriage were tabled. When others have made these questions popular the Liberal Weather Vane can indorse them also. Freethought *organizations* have succeeded in nothing else. Individuals have done some educating on their own account, but the organizations have only begged money and disdainfully held their skirts aloof when the advance guard came nigh. There is a kind of "eternal fitness of things" that is gratifying to grown people as they witness these Unions pandering to hairbrained prejudice till they die for lack of an issue.

Ambrose Bierce has said many radical and admirable things, but his labored satire on Senator Ingalls's remarks concerning the United States navy, was not one of them. Though conspicuously late, Senator Ingalls talked more good sense regarding the navy than we have heard from any politician. Defense is the watchword of wise people, and the land is the place to put it, just as Ingalls said. At any rate, peace does not depend in this commercial age upon presented arms. Subsequent consequences of conduct is what determines it. A man can snatch a purse from a child or ransack a house, but it does not follow that an armed man must accompany the child or stand guard at the door of every house. There is such a thing as common interests and consequences for violating them, and these are the great safeguards of any country just as they are of any community. If Mr. Bierce could show that the navy has done something useful since the civil war, there might be some reason why its men should not earn their living by production as better men do.

The New York "Truth Seeker," ever ready to slander Anarchism with any means at its command, attempts in its issue of Feb. 20 to emulate Anti-Theology by showing that all Anarchists are not Atheists, and to defame Anarchism through implying that it means violent revolution, by citing the case of some Spanish revolutionists who, upon their execution, are said to have accepted religious ministrations. If the "Truth Seeker" did not know the difference between press-dispatch "anarchists" and Anarchists proper, such a break might be excused on the grounds of ignorance, but it knows that the executed men were not Anarchists at all, and that those of its readers who are not posted on the matter will be led to believe that Anarchists and violent revolutionists are the same. This serious misrepresentation of a minority however, seems complacently affordable to that journal as it smarts under the castigation of a "lettered" and loyal Wisconsin monopolist. If it can translate the "handwriting on the wall," it will at least not falsify a successive issue in an attempt to make a worthless point for a declining one.

In the Helena daily "Independent," we note an excellent article on "Chinese Exclusion," by P. H. Burns, one of EGOISM's readers. That is a step in the right direction. Let every reader post himself or herself or itself thoroughly in economic and social science, then take an active part in the discussion of every question that comes up in the community, treating it from an Egoistic and Anarchistic standpoint. This will bring the merits of our principles to public notice and stimulate thousands to inquiry who would otherwise never hear of the ideas. The literature necessary to fit any one for downing all opposition in argument is plenty, and everyone wastes time enough to make him master of the situation if he were to use it in reading and applying the ideas to the questions of the hour.

The arch bandit of that community, the Oakland Humane Society, has lately perpetrated another of its paternalistic outrages on a young woman who has the affrontery to have children and be miserable without being married. She is said to have been living with some negro men in a hovel, and as the members of the "humane" society would not like to live in that way, they enforced their tastes upon her by throwing her into prison and taking her children away from her; one of them being but eight months old. Before the court she made a most piteous plea for the possession of her children, especially the younger one. This the judge's tender sympathies could not endure, and he ordered her to her cell. The officer of the invading society feeling the effects, without seeing the enormity of his brutal work, was moved to say that he would consult the physician of the "home" at which the seized children are confined, and if the latter thinks it would not be injurious to entrust the infant to the mother while imprisoned, it will be returned to her. Generous soul! he imprisons a helpless woman who is minding her own business, and if the imprisonment for which he is responsible, does not interfere, he will kindly restore one of the children he has ruthlessly torn away. He had just the same right to invade her social arrangements that she would to enter his home and drag his children away and cause them to follow her habits, but he had before a consistent interpretation of the fundamental social law no better excuse for his conduct. She was invading no one, and there was no complaint, save that somebody wanted her to follow their ideas or get off the earth, and the folly of this the history of Christian martyrdom should fully illustrate. Recklessly breeding more children than a parent can provide for is very undesirable to pitying eyes, but this flagrant violation of equal freedom is a matter that can easily come much nearer home, and should fill every citizen who may differ in his tastes from these moral censors, with dread of persecution. There is no social guarantee where such conduct goes unrebuked; there is no safety except that which wild beasts must resort to, that of concealment, in all matters differing from the whims of the powerful or the popular. If these people really wish to help in such cases as the one they have tyrannized in, there is ample opportunity for persuasion and material aid in the way of bettering their conditions without violating the plainest rights of the unfortunates.

To "Enfant Terrible's" Subscribers.

The subscribers to "Enfant Terrible" are already aware that their unexpired subscriptions are to be filled with EGOISM. But it is best to announce at the start that EGOISM itself cannot appear regularly before the beginning of Vol. 3. Like "Enfant Terrible," we publish ideas as nearly to suit ourselves as the law will allow, and are of course glad to see them sometimes meet with approval. However, these columns are open to the editors of "Enfant Terrible," and they will undoubtedly still find time to gratify their former readers with at least some of their thoughts as the tape of time slides through the fingers of consciousness.

EGOISM is now the youngest of the only two consistently Anarchistic papers published on this continent, and it needs every effort of every friend of the common cause to extend its circulation.

"Haven't We Got the Postoffice?"

Yes, and we have got it badly—*so* badly that it is next to impossible to do business in some most necessary lines. It is a dog in the manger, that will neither eat the hay nor let the horse have it. It will not give uniform rates on exactly the same service, and will not allow those to go into the business who would. It has two effective ways to shut out competition. One is to collect a tribute from a competing carrier, equal to the amount it charges for the same service, and the other is to underbid any approximative cost rate that a rival might name, by making up the loss from the public treasury. The tyranny of collecting the price of a service without rendering any part of it is apparent, as is also the injustice of taxing some citizens, who do not use the mail service, to serve others below cost who do use it. But it is a still more marked outrage when this machinery is used to make some rich while it drives others in a similar vocation, out of business by refusing them a like service at the same rates. Having to sell at similar prices, and buy material and labor at like prices, such individuals or companies cannot pay eight times as much for carrying, and consequently are obliged to go out of business, losing much capital invested and the benefit of years' of apprenticeship in their particular line. Thus it deprives some of the means of honest livelihood while it taxes them to subsidize others engaged in a similar vocation.

Its latest break is in the case of "Printers' Ink," a journal devoted to the art of advertising. The paper is very valuable as an instructor to advertisers, and is closely read by all the progressive ones. It is also a valuable advertising medium, being patronized by many of the largest business establishments in the country. But our State Socialistic mail service has not learned yet that advertising is a legitimate and necessary aid to commerce, so it proposes to kill the standard authority on the subject by discriminating against it in rates. This, because it gets its money by teaching people how to advertise and where to get goods, instead of how to get to a Jehovah's park, or how to elect a certain politician to office.

If a million persons subscribe for a publication and send the money direct to the publisher, our communistic carrier will carry the million copies to the subscribers below cost. But if only five thousand persons order goods from a dealer at a price that enables him to send them a paper as part, it costs him eight times as much per pound to have it carried as it does the other paper shipper. The same institution will receive a monthly paper at San Francisco and deliver it on the Atlantic coast in the farthest separated parts of any city or cities at the rate of one cent a pound, but to deliver it in a box in the same building at home, it must have one cent for each two ounces or a fraction thereof. It will charge you two cents for carrying a letter weighing the fraction of an ounce, that will not bring you a cent, but for a paper that brings you a good profit, it will charge only one cent a pound. Yet it cannot allow an advertising paper pound rates, lest it aid private fortune at public expense.

A publication may give premiums of a value that more than covers the subscription price, making the paper free, and it will go at pound rates, but whoever gives advertising as a premium must pay ounce rates. If you give away subscriptions till your advertising space is worth enough to cover them, you are all right, but if you sell your advertising space for enough to cover subscriptions you are all wrong. You may grow rich giving away subscriptions and selling advertising, but if you give away subscriptions to sell advertising, you will be squelched for using a public carrier for private gain. In this case the difference between tweedledee and tweedledum is the difference between being in business or out of business.

All this absurdity, bungling, and tyranny is due to but one thing, and that is State management. Nobody in particular is responsible; nobody in particular's capital or livelihood is at stake. There is no loser in consequence of wretched business principles except the customer, and since no rival service is allowed there is neither relief for him nor damage to the institution. He can take it as he can get it, or do without, it makes not the slightest difference to a concern which in its very nature can have no incentive to accommodate, from either gain or accountability. Theoretically it is the servant of the people and amenable to them, but complaint is useless here, for they are never in, and cannot be seen. The man you talk to can take no responsibility, should he even so desire, and you are referred from one department to another till you come to a "construction" of the law by the head of the departments, and if that is absurd and unjust, you can go before congress if you are insane enough to think it will desert its boodle games to decide against a colleague. After congress ignores you you can go before all the people of the United States and convince them that your point, relating to your business, is more important to them than all their political interests and prejudices, and they will get up new platforms and send men to congress who will adjust your matter. Of course the nature of your business demanded immediate attention, and would have received it at the hands of any company doing business for gain. And of course three years' delay has annihilated your business and the expenses of agitation have bankrupted you, and the people could not see the pay in troubling themselves about the management of a business that brings no returns. But you have appealed to the proper authority according to the theory. You have also learned that our State Socialistic postoffice is a failure, and totally irresponsible. You have found that redress for a grievance is impossible, since you cannot try a man before himself. It is also impossible to ascertain in advance what will pass under the regulations, for no one being responsible to any one in particular, official prejudice, which is an unknown quantity and quality, may construe to suit itself or its friends. In short, there is back of it not a solitary motive for either economy, business policy, or progress. It is simply a great political machine whose members can be interested in nothing but their salaries and emoluments, and these in no way depend upon the impartiality and efficiency with which the business is conducted, or the price of its service to the public. It is in every sense such an inexpressibly ridiculous and inexcusable monstrosity that nothing but a generally-unanalyzed superstitious reverence for political authority can account for its co-existence with a business world so exacting and economical in most other departments

The publishers of "Printers' Ink" are agitating for a consistent and definite law as to what shall constitute a paper entitled to pound rates. Even with their immense leverage this is improbable, though their paper may be reinstated. But the principal and permanent work to be done, lies in agitation for the abolishment of State monopoly of this and all other business. There is no more reason why the State should monopolize mail carrying than why it should do the same with advertising, farming, or any other vocation. Let it work on business principles, charging for each kind of service a rate that will cover the expense of carrying, and let as many other companies go into the business as wish to, and the people will have a service at approximate cost, and with all the efficiency they care to pay for. There would then be no excuse for censorship on the grounds of free rates, and all would be treated alike.

Yes, we have got the postoffice and much other State superstition very bad, and we are likely to have more State Socialism before we have less. God, king, president—rule, rule, rule. Sense, equal freedom, and economy later.

H.

State Panacea.

Oakland has jute mills, which are useful, and a Humane Society and board of education which might be more so if they knew more than they do. The jute mills have work which children can do, and at which they can earn from $3 to $6 per week. But the State, characteristic of political authority, has provided a law to prevent them thus helping themselves or parents unless they are twelve years old, but as usual it has made no provisions to be responsible for the wages it deprives its subjects of, by substituting an equivalent. Such is no part of its function; its function is to despoil, to destroy without responsibility. That fact, however, does not prevent this "humane" society springing the irresistible State deadfall upon the helpless victims which its privilege has created. The society has some spoils which it is willing to change for glory where there is no cheaper way to get it, but in this case the glory can be secured by the State's sword, and the consequences to the helpless does not deter these meddlers. It is evident that it is glory alone that the society seeks, or it would contrive to really help those with whose affairs it meddles. The childrens' parents and friends did what they could to evade the preying of these privilege crows, but the mills had to discharge some of the little workers and turn them out to live on the air and the laurels of the Humane Society. In one instance a mother had sent her nine-year-old son with a letter to the superintendent of the mills beseeching him to give the little fellow employment, as she was starving. The superintendent did so, giving the boy $3 per week. But the pressure of Christian love and lucre law forced the child's discharge, and he and his mother may get on as best they can, while the mongers of land titles and privileged gold rub their gouty knees and congratulate themselves as saviors of society.

The board of education has found in this howl an opportunity for its little shovel also, and proposes to enforce the compulsory education law with which it has been provided to gather political pap. The children are to be "educated" whether they have food, books, and clothing or not. The election-day sovereign voters who are the parents of these children, are competent on polling days to decide over a minority of sages even, who shall rule the country, but they have not sense enough to direct so small a matter as the education of their children! The fact that the city schools are really dressing parades, and that parents who are in a condition that requires their children's labor to secure an existence cannot compete with the better to do in this respect, and that children not so dressed will be subjected to the taunts and even cruelty of youthful viciousness, weighs not at all with these political saviors. The dominance of the popular authority superstition, and the harvest of notoriety such action will bring, is too much for them to see over. Besides they are fairly pushed ahead by the State Socialistic labor unions of the place, who have also a little pull in the matter in the way of magnifying the importance of labor legislation, on the wave of which agitation some of their members hope for the double satisfaction of being tossed upon the public crib and saving society "a little" at the same time. Thus these stranger-laborers—so strange that they can scarcely communicate their commonest wants in our tongue, become grist for our whole mill, even to furnishing organized labor their bones to fertilize State Socialism.

If to really help these children was the purpose of the Humane Society, it should have placed the case before those in the community who have managed to get the wealth, and then contrived to secure for the parents at a rent that they could pay, quarters near enough the center to enable the children to attend night schools that the society could have provided at cost, or free. And if this were not satisfactory, it could be intensified by finding other children—children from the stock of the saviors themselves—to take the places of the factory children for two or three hours each day while the latter attended a course of instruction provided near by. This would add useful experience to the education of the substitutes and cause them to appreciate their own good fortune, while it would win them the gratitude instead of the hatred of the little laborers, as is now the case. By conferring with the mill owners and the parents, the society could have arranged all this and received the help and interest of both, instead of their opposition, as is true of the crude and brutal military method employed, while it can accomplish nothing but greater privation for the unfortunate, and a disgracefully cheap glory for the society.

If the Humane Society wants to do something consistent with its name and pretensions, let it labor for immediate relief by actually *helping*, and for ultimate relief from that necessity, by educating and agitating for the cessation of the privilege that prevents access to unoccupied but useful space on the earth's surface, and that prevents free exchange of products. People who receive the full product of their labor will readily educate their children of their own accord, and if they should not, there would still be no reason for forcing them to. The plea that the children may become criminal charges upon society's hands if they are not "educated," will not go; it does not follow in fact, and if it should, society is not justified in becoming criminal first by violating the equal freedom of innocent people through any such anticipatory presumption. It is a most flagrant violation of the only principle by which comparitively equal factions can live without expending all their energy in a mutual destruction. The Humane Society is guilty of the only criminal act in connection with the jute mill disturbance. There is the fact of course, that children too young to work more than two or three hours a day have to work more than ten, but that is due to an economic condition for which the ignorance of the greater part of society is responsible, and is not overt in its nature as is true of the act which violently forces individuals to accept others' choice in these individuals' private affairs. That is what the Humane Society and labor organizations have done with the parents of the jute mill children, besides shortening their means of living. Thou shalt not is the height of offense, the moment it leaves defense. H.

Our Communist Contemporary.

Some time ago J. W. Sullivan, of the "Twentieth Century," in announcing the appearance of the Portland, Or., "Freedom" said, "it has already mastered the phraseology of Anarchism and the philosophy of selfishness." If that is as clear an insight as he can get from his reading, it is no wonder that he remains a Governmentalist and Moralist in spite of the logic that has come before his eyes. The paper referred to has mastered neither the phraseology of Anarchism nor the philosophy of selfishness, and little else than the declamation of emotionalism. It knows possibly less about the principles of Anarchism and Egoism than Mr. Sullivan himself, and seems just as determined not to learn them. It proclaims itself an Anarchist-Communist, and bears such earmarks in every particular from the usual confusion of ideas, to its make-up. It has no appreciation of the "philosophy of selfishness" except that unanalyzed kind of appreciation of self, which is so sanguine that it involuntarily hisses at the thought of an interest relating altogether to another. So far is "Freedom" from the *mastery* of the indicated philosophy, that it cannot bear the idea of a generalization looking to the securing of each his own product, lest one producing more, would have more to enjoy than another producing less (with like opportunity of course). This is the very essence of babyishness and a fair sample of the emotionalism that does duty as logic throughout the paper's propaganda.

In the number of Jan. 16, J. H. Morris, one of its editors, undertakes to criticise J. Wm. Lloyd's late review in EGOISM of "News from Nowhere," and also my review of that review. He succeeds in exposing not only a hopeless ignorance of Egoism and Anarchism, but of logic as well:

> Referring to Communism, Lloyd says there will always be rebels against an order of society that allows incompetents to share equally with the competents. Here he shows his competitivist tendency. Competitivism is the opposite of Communism and is based on that "competency" idea; that is, a man is entitled to all he is competent to accumulate. The poor devil who has by honest toil added ten dollars per day, for twenty or thirty years, to the world's wealth and has to die in the poorhouse, is an incompetent. Another, who has never done a stroke of useful work, rolls in wealth—he is a competent man. There, you have the competency idea in a nutshell. He who expects to carry this old idea of inequality into the new social system has yet to emancipate his mind from commercialism. I do not see why one who has proved "incompetent" under the present system should wish it changed to another whose basic principle is the same, unless he thought it a little better adapted to his special abilities for becoming a monopolist.

Neither do I see how I would be supposed to think a system with basic principles the same as the present, would be any better adapted to my abilities for becoming a monopolist than the present one is. But it is easy to see that if the writer of the above sentences ever penned any Anarchistic phraseology he must have copied it, for there is no indication that he knows anything about Anarchism itself. If he did he would know that his man is shorn of his products through the exactions that privilege imposes, and that the absence of privilege is the first principle of the Anarchistic idea of industrial freedom; that his "competent man," enjoying without producing the material, could exist only by present legal privilege or by the provisions of Communism, which would also take from the producer and give to the non-producer. Mr. Morris evidently has no idea of the nature of competition; that it is the antidote for monopoly, and that in even its present restricted state, it is the only thing that prevents some individual owning the world. He does not understand that with equal opportunity, it stimulates production and multiplies luxuries at labor cost, while it maintains equity without the expense, blunders, and prejudice of regulative administration. He does not conceive that commerce,—exchange—is the basis of social existence, and that interference with it by the community superstition is the cause of the poverty and tyranny of the present.

Of the effect of equal opportunity; of the nature and equity of free competition, and of the social character of the let-alone principle, this alleged master of Egoism and Anarchistic phraseology has not even dreamed. His idea of sociability seems to be the community toothbrush, spoon, bath, and towel. But some otherwise agreeable people, regard it all the more sociable in one not to clean his teeth with their private brushes; not to slabber on their private spoons, and not to wipe the exudation from his poorly-washed face and eyes on their private towels. This is the Egoistic conception of social intensity, and the principle that Anarchism applies also to industrialism. When Mr. Morris has taken the time and trouble to understand these principles he will have less terror of "competitivism," and as great an abhorrence of industrial meddling as he now has of sexual meddling. He can learn the lesson on competition, and much more, from Proudhon's "Economical Contradictions," and the spirit and philosophy of Egoistic ethics may be gleaned from the columns of this paper.

The following is Mr. Morris's idea of our bond to society:

Under Communism I think there would be no objection to, and certainly no force to prevent, a man's withdrawing himself and his belongings. But if he concludes society is of no use to him, to be consistent he should be willing to withdraw taking with him only that which he would have possessed, and becoming what he would have been, had he never known society or its benefits; that would be a savage, or worse. To make use of the things—including all scientific knowledge and every useful invention—which a community of interests and efforts can alone produce, without contributing to the community's needs, is to become a parasite.

How sensitive on the parasite question, this man who preaches: "*From* each according to his ability, and *to* each according to his present need," regardless, necessarily, of contribution to the general fund. How thoughtful of society's property in ideas. But if I may take my other property away, why not a like share of that in ideas, especially since I shall leave as much among others as though I had taken none. However, since my intellectual impressions cannot be separated from me, and since if each member should withdraw his person from society there would be no knowledge left it, I conclude that society as a proprietor, aside from the individual and his belongings, is a myth, and that Communism is itself more nearly an expression of savagery than of civilization, seeing that the savage strata of mental complexity is somewhat the more prone to myth chasing.

But the Egoist does not indicate that he wishes to withdraw from society in its comprehensive sense. On the contrary, as indicated in a preceding paragraph, he is more sociable and more appreciative of social benefits than the Communist. The Egoist strives to *intensify* social intercourse by retaining its advantages and eliminating as many of the unpleasant features of social compromise as possible. His Anarchistic polity insures equal opportunity and leaves each to handle his own affairs to suit himself without interfering with others, thus effecting conditions susceptible of the least hostility possible. His Egoistic ethics prevents him expecting or exacting Duty from any one, and puts him in such an intelligent sympathy with the spirit of a given opposition, that he can view it with more of the justice of a disinterested party, and avoid the extremes of retaliation identified with fanatical indignation. His policy fosters every advantage of every kind of mutual exchange, while it provides the most satisfactory methods for the disposal of those interests which are in their nature conflicting. Of all people, Egoists are pre-eminently the Socialists. They ask nothing better than the liberty to withdraw their property from a society that would collectively claim even the impressions that objects make on the individual's brain. They would straightway proceed to inaugurating among themselves the order of each one minding his own business, and would set an example that would capture the world by its justice and harmony. Society does not need rebuilding; it needs simply liberty. Recognized self-interest in unrestricted competition, would spontaneously evolve a justice of defensive and reciprocal exactitude that would despair the efforts of the most delicate theorist to describe. H.

Managerial Experience.

I find that I am a good deal of trouble to myself in pursuit of the habit of life; I have to be doing things all the while of which I am keenly cognizant. Since W. S. Bell has come home I have been sleeping in the kitchen on a palsied cot and an empty stomach—my own stomach—I sleep alone. I use the cot to evade depriving Mr. Bell of his bed, and the vacant stomach to digest the otherwise lumpy reflections of my sleep. I lie on the top edge of the cot and hang a season-cracked comfortable over me, which makes us together look very like a clotheshorse draped with a cow's paunch and its appurtenances. After reviewing my day's failures I listen awhile to Mr. Bell intently breathing in an audible vioce in the next room, then I fall asleep and sometimes worse, although never from virtue. At first I tried rolling over when I wanted the other side up, and was saved from falling into the cigar store below only by the interposition of the floor located between us. I now *revolve* on the comb of the structure, and thus defeat gravitation. I suppose it will have to hobble about now as best it can without feet, but, being crippled, perhaps it won't be so lively next time in slamming sleeping innocence on a floor that remains, under all pressures, a given distance from the earth. My nocturnal hibernation is interspersed, however, with other incidents. I pump oxygen through an open window, and it is often mixed with the exclamations of immodest cats, and of roosters who have a habit of yelling in their sleep. Then about 3 o'clock the milkman comes up the back stairs like a barrel-rack of empty breadpans, and at 5 o'clock the alarm explodes and goes off into hysterics, cutting me off in the midst of a dream, which is the only state of mind in which I ever succeeded in getting things to go satisfactorily for a recognizable length of time. I then swing off my orbit and immediately wish for a fire. After I have kindled one I perpetrate breakfast, and try my wife with a tablefork to determine whether she is done—eating. I think it would be a brilliant scheme also with which to get her out of bed; I shall try it when we have an extra fork. When I have devoured, I start into my routine of exhorting my wife's little niece and making EGOISM between declamations. All these things and the absence of many others reassure me of my continued presence and its inconveniences. I don't like to kindle a fire even when I'm right *in* the kitchen, especially when it is the cool anterior of a service which furnishes me only my "finding" and a continual anxiety about losing even that.

My wife is anxious that I become a great and successful journalist most any time now, and offers me every advantage in her power to remuneratively accomplish the feet, which I have carried about and spent money on all these years. It is perceptible that I have not successfully managed EGOISM, and in order that I might get some pointers on the policy and principal features of a successful magazine, she brought me the February number of "The Ladies' Home Journal." Its main point is purported proof by productions from the pens of daughters of great parentage, that genius is inherited. Almost the first thing that I noticed was a flat contradiction by the facts, of the editor's assertion that this is proven by the evidence adduced. Here I had the secret of success: assert what is flattering about those who are popular, and assert that facts bear you out whether they do or not. It matters not that a few may discover and point out the error; you can easily show that they are cranks.

The first sprout from greatness as catalogued in the aforesaid journal, is the daughter of Nathaniel Hawthorne. I never met Nate, but with the other hawthorns I am feelingly familiar, having had them in my side on numerous occasions and Sundays. This thorn sticks on the "Love of an American Girl." And its ideal and some of its ideas indicate that the writer must have *inherited* so much genius that it was unnecessary to put any indication of it in her effort. She wears her hair like the feminine number of the "Enfant Terrible," but if the latter cannot write a story with a better ideal and ideas, she needn't sit again on the foot of our bed and hug my wife, while I hang by the chin on my knuckles and the front end of a suppressed regret. I am opposed to regrets, anyway.

The next feature of that conducted journal is the shoulder, cheek, and hair of the right side of President Harrison's daughter. I think it must be the right side or she wouldn't have turned it out. At least, she don't seem to be wrong side out. She has certainly inherited a great shoulder from a prominent man, and must have put it to the wheel too, when she was photographed, or we would come face to face with the shadow of a *mental* greatness that could not have been inherited. Her effort is on the training of children and contains, aside from some silly religious gush, more sense than the rest of the family combined have ever made public. It is more than a representative article on the representative vocation of the people; for there is little else besides the breeding and pasturing of children that the majority accomplishes. The most marked training of these on this coast, is under the wheels of the *local* trains in Oakland.

The third halo of inherited ponderosity is an article from

the daughter of Senator Ingalls the flinty Atheist. It is on Mrs. Stanford, and reveals the glowing mettle of the gifted sire by declaring: "Mrs. Stanford's friends are legion, for no one comes beneath the influence of her beautiful *Christian* spirit without feeling for her something deeper than a mere acquaintanceship." [The italics are mine, or my wife's rather, along with the rest of "our" plant.] The greatness of Miss Ingalls's sentiment could easily have been inherited from a flock of geese or a religious tract house. There is also a cut of Mrs. Stanford's brooch and bust. She has an abundance of hair, brilliant bangs, and a made countenance. She is talented too, managing, besides breathing and eating, to audit and pay the household bills. The latter is indeed, an extraordinary accomplishment, one that I have striven all my life to attain, and a matter in which some of the brightest men fail. Whoever can pay his bills has reason to congratulate himself, so have his creditors. I believe, however, that I could do it if I had Mr. Stanford's income to draw from, as Mrs. Stanford has, but a sorghum-mixed mustard plaster couldn't bring it from my resources.

Then for a variation of implied minor importance, the next sketch is of a subject with some brains: Kate Greenaway, who is responsible for those mummyish costumes that an aping populace dresses its infant squall in. The gable ends of her shoulders swing considerably below a level with her throat, and one is impressed that among the other delusions she hugs, men are not conspicuous—at least not when being hugged. Her neck-sleeve reaches clear to her chin and ears, and her hair is not half combed. I suppose she grows busy and leaves it till next day. Some other painting girls who have to economize by using their faces for canvas also leave their hair till next day—in scraps of tin or paper. The bulblet from genius who magnifies Miss Greenaway, is the daughter of Sir Morell Mackenzie, and does her work as well as an ordinary newspaper reporter whose father possesses the originality to produce his own living.

Next comes the daughter of Charles Dickens with "What My Father Taught Us," first of which it seems, was a prayer. What in the dickens the old Dickens taught the little Dickens such jamesnastics for is more than I can divine, unless it was because he didn't know any better. Another of his virtues was teaching self-reliance to the little Dickens by compelling them to count out their own washing to the laundress! To count out washing to a lawn dress, seems pretty tough for well-to-do folks to impose for mere training's sake, but I am just aching to win fame and rest by going Dickens one better, in compelling my wife's little niece, when she is big enough, to *wash* her own clothes, laundress and all, after she has counted them. In her case, however, the shortness of the count may materially neutralize the heroic effect of the training. The accompanying portrait of Miss Dickens did not have much clothes on except some kind of a necklace or charm to prevent nosebleed, I take it. She also wears a large and forcible nose, which broadens at the end in a way to indicate intense satisfaction from the largest-sized and most absorbing pleasurable sensations, and the chin and chest seem to fully coincide, and outside too. She should be susceptible of being as broadly, though perhaps not so widely appreciated as her father. Her literary inheritance seems to consist chiefly of proceeds from her father's copyrights.

Horace Greeley's daughter wears a domestic expression and nursery smile, and tells how nice and good and wise she thinks her father was. But I have read his controversy with Stephen Pearl Andrews in "Love, Marriage, and Divorce," and am not deceived. His was the strata of emotion without philosophy. His daughter has inherited this and also some of his property, evidently.

General Sherman's daughter wears a pumpadoor-necked dress and steely countenance, and contributes a story of war horrors with all the assurance of its necessity that could be assumed of the necessity of equal freedom. It is an echo of two decades ago, which in its turn was echoed from a primitive crudity reasoning with the logic of annihilation. In this case there is evidence that that genus, if not the genius of great parentage was transmitted. I am delighted to see political killers exhibit their refinement, but I am not grateful for a dearth of fool-killers.

Now there comes an indispensable contribution to literature from the daughter of Captain Marryat. It consists of a picture of her billowy bosom, parlor expression, and a recipe for wearing diamonds—if you can get them. In the function of a nervous litterateur's armchair, she would certainly be very able, and even pleasant to marryat.

Then comes Julia Ward Howe's litter of literary posterity. The first contributes a mother-goose-schoolgirl-humoristic poem and her picture, which looks that of a contented modern wife in easy circumstances. Her greatness evidently runs in the direction of ease.

The second furnishes a more interesting theme, in a cut of her neck, bare shoulder, and a contribution on "Country Maids and City Wives." The latter is artistically written, I think, and has some good ideas, but the former get there in great shape. They are sure to elicit wide-spread interest, if not even illicit interest. They are a remark that one wants to peruse again and again. She says among many other things that "in the city we learn to love humanity." Let me add: especially, if it has overflowing shoulders, a beautiful neck, and tapering limbs. In this forequarter portrait and the accompanying arrangement of letters, the successful editor has a fact of some greatness whether it was inherited or not. I like fourquarters because they make a dollar, and because they cannot make me languid.

The third of Mrs. Howe's transmitted evidences wears a ruche and a Sunday school visage, and writes historically on "The Childhood of My Mother."

Among a dozen other shoots of greatness, Fannie Davenport and Maude Banks write creditable articles regarding the stage, and Jeff Davis's daughter shows some originality in treating "The American Girl Who Studies Abroad." I can't afford to treat any girl, abroad or ahome.

After the "great" delusions, come the departments of the ladies' mental garbage cart. Bob Burdette gets some amusing hash from a "New Inkstand." I never could get much from an inkstand besides pools of ink on the tablecloth and carpet, and lickings on toast, or about that temperature. But an inkstand is a good stand to take, if you can get hold of a nice one. It is better than to stand on the burning deck, but not as good as "standing in."

"The King's Daughters" follows Burdette's corner, and is edited by Mrs. M. Bottome. A glance at its contents reveals that at least the *top* of no cerebrum-bearing organism could emit such drivel as type is contorted into by the "old woman" of these daughters. She declares, in addressing young mothers, that she has learned her deepest lessons from her children. Her productions attest the truthfulness of this statement and that the posterity of a flounderess would not have been too flat to inculcate the vacuum sustained by her hemlet. While preaching unselfishness, she is an obtrudingly general favorite with herself, and a regular pull-the-hair-out-of-their-noses chum with Jesus and God.

Befittingly, but unfortunately, this froth from mental imbecility is followed by Talmage. He *should* follow wild geese to the north pole and blow up there. The standing disgrace of the age is the popularity of this mental horse-fiddle. His page, however, has a humorous feature. It is a picture of the mammoth theological gander himself under his study lamp. Just as though he ever studied! And as if to tempt a thunderbolt from a clear sky, instead of seeming the least intent and occupied, his head is thrown back and his neck craned like that of a young rooster who has just made an audible attempt at crowing, and is looking for the back fence, ash heap, and rain barrel to applaud him. Yet the stupid readers of "The Ladies' Home Journal" can look at that picture without laughing.

Then comes "Side Talks With Girls," and if indoctrinations ever bore fruit, as well as all the sensible people who witness their workings, these "Side Talks" are the strongest evidence of Talmage's senseless blaring. This department is edited by a woman with a heavy crop of hair which seems to have soaked up all her intellectual energy, and obliges her to run a lot of second-hand monogamic chaff through the sex mill to keep the stones from grinding each other, while the flour of the family should remain batter. Of course people are all made in pairs for each other like shoes, and are dumped into a heap to be assorted by a game of hide and seek, to be conducted in the spirit of cat courting, in which there is an excessive amount of squalling for the market value of the kittens. There is also a recipe for girls to caterwaul by, and an apology from the editor more pointless than her preceding remarks. There is evidently a woman question, but if it is to be judged by the difference between the matter of this department, and that of the boy's, which follows, it is obviously a question of brains.

All this is but the grazingest glance at the principal features of a successful American journal. Is Egoism to become a great and successful publication. Hardly,—at least that is the way it has been doing it. The paper shall never be lowered from its present plane by pandering to a brainless mob, as "The Ladies' Home Journal" has. I prefer to give it into the hands of a couple strong and deliberate truckmen once we are compelled to get out from over the German cigar store in order to supply a growing trade.

Egoism

Vol.II.---No. 10. SAN FRANCISCO, CAL., MAY, 1892. Price, Five Cents.

Pointers.

It turns out that Herbert Spencer is capable of the rankest prejudices, just like very ordinary mortals. A letter in "Liberty" from a Mr. Frederick R. Burton, proves that Spencer condemned Proudhon without having read a line of his writings, and, as if to leave no doubt of his unqualified prejudice, declares he never shall. Thus tumble the great before the analytic eye of the unknown layman.

After a few weeks' suspension, "Liberty" is now issued from New York, P. O. Box 1312. It appears in a new dress of larger type, a change that will be hailed with delight by many of its readers. The subscription price has been raised to two dollars a year, while the paper remains a weekly of four pages. Its editor remarks that "few people care to read journals which tell the truth, and as a consequence the privilege is costly and very precious." Further, he believes that the readers of the paper "sufficiently appreciate it to be willing to pay two dollars annually to help it in its struggle for existence." Owing to engagements at a distance from the office of publication, Victor Yarros can no longer perform the duties of associate editor, but will contribute with reasonable frequency.

John Henry Mackay, author of "The Anarchists," has discovered the grave of Max Stirner and the house in which he spent his last days. Mr. Mackay desires to erect a grave stone and memorial tablet, and solicits donations to that purpose. Max Stirner was the Proudhon of Egoism, and a plain monument erected by the hands of strangers would be a very effective way to call attention to the idea, as well as gratifying in the way of passive defiance of a Moralistic cant no less active now than when Stirner wrote. Since EGOISM is the most accented exponent of the philosophy in the world, it would not be unreasonable for Mr. Mackay to expect at least a square lift from its readers. We will contribute something on our own account, and will gladly acknowledge in these columns any amounts that others may forward us to send with it. As an expression of gratitude the mark cannot, of course, reach Stirner, but it gives us an opportunity to say "I," before men.

Ambrose Bierce getteth there to EGOISM's delight in the following: "I am in receipt of a kind invitation to join the Theosophical Society, whose main object, it appears, is 'the practical realization of Universal Brotherhood.' I must be excused—that is about the last thing that I could wish to bring about. Universal brotherhood, if it means anything, means (for me) a closer relation between me and the rest of the race. As a considerable majority of the rest of the race happens to be made up of knaves, dunces and savages, I am not seeking that kind of relations with it. The Society may tickle its ears with fantastic phrases babbled in gorgeous dreams until it is drunken with words, but I shall not join the debauch. The universal brother, as I know him, has ever manifest in the manner of him an invitation to be slapped on the back and addressed as 'old feller'—to the which love-feast I am deeply disinclined. In the circumstance that many of us are descended from the same species of apes, I find a sufficiently near approach to universal brotherhood to satisfy my highest and holiest aspirations for spiritual gregariousness."

If the chief of police of this city were a German, his late grand "April fool" on the wrong end of the month might be accounted for on the hypothesis that Germans sometimes get things in an unfamiliar language wrong end before, but since the chief's name smacks of tubers, no theory save that of magnificent stupidity can account for his action. On the night of April 30 he had every available man on his force concealed about the banks and millionaire residences of the city lying in wait for a shower of bombs predicted no doubt, by the inspiration of mince pie which the chief's salary can furnish. He could feel it in his bones that the "anarchists" of the world would rise in their might that night and get a start for May day, and he wouldn't be caught napping and lose the opportunity of his life to be heard of outside the offices of local monopolists and of beer tables. So all night long the smooth-fingered warriors kept awake and quivered and shivered in the fog while the demon Anarchist slept comfortably first on one side then on the other as he dreamed of Mutual Banks and one-half of one per cent interest till the distant-sounding cry of the newsboys' "all about the 'anarchists'" brought him back to the realization of privileged metal, a sensational press, and gullible mammals, and he wondered if a dreamograph had been invented and sprung upon him to aid the authority-priests in making capital even of his dreams. Then with intense curiosity he read of the valorous deeds at the ghost battle which probably left the blue-coat underwear in good sanitary condition, and he smiled a derisive, yet satisfied smile as he realized the enemy thus hacking away at its own throat according to the plan of his campaign. It had exposed the ignorance and childishness of State prestige, and this is his weapon and victory. The chief and his men should join the militia and play war in the day time at a summer resort, it is accompanied by less loss of sleep and does not provoke a smile on the carved figures of the keystones and cornices.

Mount Walt Whitman.

What! is Walt Whitman dead?
Nay, it cannot be, for the mountains do not die!
They say he is dead, but the difference does not appear;
For he is a mountain,
A great, gray rock,
Rugged, alone, forever:
And the mountains endure, sublime, motionless, and fixed before us;
They touch the sky, and we must see them, and we cannot forget.

Have you ever considered how marvelous a mountain is?
With its white head among the stars,
Its foundations broad as the bases of all things,
Deep as the center of the world's heart;
A witness of all, and of the order of all,
Surveying the centuries, and the scratches man makes in the surface of things, and the coming and going, like shadows, of the nations:

Familiar with the red whips of the lightning, and the deep-throated thunder;
With night, and the great tempests, and the wide winds of destiny;
The changing worlds of vapor, the awful solitudes under the stars, and the white, mysterious movings of moonlight:

Full of great voices, solemn music, sweet songs, and the embracing silences of the upper air;
The roar of avalanches, the screams of eagles, the melody of falling streams, the love-whistle of little birds nesting by the blue tarns—
The blue tarns among the gray rocks (the wild fowl know them) girt with green pines, placid, reflecting like mirrors:

Rich with mines of the white ore and the yellow,
Iron for strength, and coal for heat,
And radiant, glittering gems:

With slopes and valleys where vines grow, and flocks feed, and hamlets nestle:

And over all, and with all, always the free air and the wide view.

Ah, Walt, Walt, poet of Nature, comrade of free men,
Other poets have been Olympian,
But you are Olympus itself.

—J. WM. LLOYD.

March 28, '92.

Editorial Opinionlets.

When the jury in the case of the bomb-thrower in Paris was intimidated from imposing the death penalty lest the prisoner's friends should blow its members up, the people, faithful followers of Herbert Spencer that in this regard they were, raved and denounced it unqualifiedly. They wanted to put into practice the great philosopher's proposition of sacrificing the individual to the preservation of the species, but fortunately for the individual, represented in the personeity of the jury, he was doing the counting himself, and as teneted by Tak Kak, did *not* count himself out. It was also an all around fine illustration of the beauties of proxy representation; showing the people how they cannot, against the interests of the proxy, get what they want, and showing the proxy that really representing people who know what they want, is not an office to be desired. And the protruding deduction from it all points definitely to the individual as the permanent factor both to be preserved and to assume his own responsibility, if the species is to be preserved in any sense except in that incomplete one characterizing the operations of the unintelligent elements.

The editor of the New York "Truth Seeker" after citing the most conclusive evidence that Freethinkers will not organize, does not relish the correct conclusion of a Christian paper that Freethinkers have not love enough of human kind to sacrifice for their fellow men, and he desires to see the charge disproven. If it had not been so impossible for him to conceive what Egoism was published for when it appeared, he could now with a master's assurance concur with his Christian critic and demolish him with the irrefutable argument that Freethinkers are rational in such refusal to sacrifice, in that they inculcate by practice the just principle of each doing his own sacrificing and thereby working out his own salvation without the absurd and repulsive idea of vicarious atonement. It is at least discernible, that after more than a thousand years of sacrifice preaching by Christians, the world has not seriously loved its kind yet save as the kind has been loved by each loving himself in a more or less utilitarian manner. And it is conspicuously possible that the religious and primitively-conceived sacrificial principle is slightly off, and that the solution of "human kind" loving lies in the justification of self-loving, as against the blind impulse of sacrifice-demanding. In other words, Egoism is the logical conclusion of rational ethics, just as Anarchism is that of religious liberty, and the logic of events will yet force the reluctant "Truth Seeker" to accept the doctrines of a minority it loves to chide because that minority's deductions are too comprehensive for the dough-brained herd to assimilate at a glance. And in an eternal fitness of things, behold the "practical" Freethought editor mourning because Freethinkers are not as slavishly dominated by the superstition of sacrifice to man, as Christians are by the superstition of sacrifice to God. It appears that it is a matter between Christian and Freethought editors as to *which* ghost, instead of ghost or no ghost, as one might expect with rationalists on one side of the controversy. Whatever trembling editors may say, let the Freethought laity follow the rationalistic premise to its logical conclusion even though it lands the laity in the Egoistic camp; there its position is impregnable to both Christian and Freethought editors.

C. R. Bennett, the sweet-scented secretary of the Society for the Prevention of Vice, and the Anthony Comstock of the Pacific coast, has run aground at last. About three years ago by passing for an unmarried man he worked himself into the confidence of a young church sister to an extent that resulted in her becoming pregnant, a matter he had reduced by the shortest route. The girl having now learned the little lesson to the end was, it seems, ready to abandon an amusement so expensive to her, but Bennett was loth to lose the reward of his labors just as they were well finished, and persisted. When she finally positively rejected his further advances, he persecuted her by threatening to prove her a public woman or prostitute, averring that he could prove anything he wanted to. Thus he started scandal that at last lost her a situation at typewriting, and she was driven to the verge of suicide, whereupon her mother having gained her confidence, revealed affairs to the father, and the pious ghoul was exposed and silenced. But it was found to be too late for retaliation by law, and Bennett is free. His wife says this is not his first offense, that an orphan girl living with them in New York met a similar fate, and then there is the probable long list that has not been made public. But for the dense sexual ignorance and inexperience to which girls are subjected by the popular superstition, I should have little sympathy for a girl fool enough to be affected by such a repulsive cobra as Bennett. It being impossible now to prosecute him, his society will probably do everything in its power to cover the matter up and put the girl in the lie, and once more the rich and the powerful will have washed over their blunder with the blood of the weak. Could she and her parents penetrate the sexual superstition and realize that her conduct would have been within her right without the excuse of seduction, and that there are intelligent people and desirable companions in easy reach who would respect and sustain her in such a course, this crossway to prospective social annihilation could be the threshold to a life that scorns the rarest prizes of the philistine society that tramples her. But herself a victim of the sexual superstition that crushes her, she will kiss its feet as she disappears in the bog of unanalyzed institutions, and the history of ages will have repeated itself.

Since Egoism's last appearance the "Twentieth Century" has changed hands and closed its career as a more or less consistent Anarchistic paper. It was sold to the Humboldt Publishing Company. For more than a year and a half F. C. Leubuscher had been the sole proprietor and publisher, Hugh O. Pentecost editing the paper on a salary. Mr. Pentecost now retires, but J. W. Sullivan is retained associate editor with Joseph Fitzgerald, who takes Mr. Pentecost's place. Mr. Fitzgerald brings with him "the resources of twenty years' experience at editorial work," and an abundance of literary furniture in the shape of quoted phrases, parenthesized explanations, and technically italicized foreign words which will bore his readers. His editorials evince an appreciable sense of the ridiculous and a ready wit which will atone for much technical sin. But what is most to be regretted is the sexual superstition and authoritarianism betrayed in an editorial defending presumably an old maid meddler in the sexual relations of a "community" said to be locatel at Santa Rosa in this state. It is charged that these people indulge in "lewdness," "orgies," and "wallowing," whereupon the new editor declares that, "if any government, national, or state, or any agency of whatever kind, being invoked puts an end to such a state of things" he has no tears to shed. That is, he sanctions the most flagrant violation of equal freedom if others exercise it in nonconformity to a taste induced by his physical condition or appropriated from among his grandmother's ideas. If the people complained of have energy to expend in *any* kind of debauchery or in any other way that does not invade, there is no *reason* why they should not do so as freely as men engage in the "tug of war," football, wrestling, prize fighting or any other mutual contest in which energy is wasted. It is not complained that the "orgists" invade others' premises or force them to take part, and so long as this is true they are immeasurably less dangerous as citizens than the archistic editor who winks at mob violence even, for he says, "*any* agency of whatever kind." There are already plenty of journals voicing such sentiment, and the "Twentieth Century" is not original. Furthermore, unless the new editor learns as fast as the former one did he will dishearten a progressive constituency which cannot be expected to advance in the same direction from its present intellectual meridian that a crawfish does from its own front.

Hugh O. Pentecost had previously entered the law profession and had to drop the editorial work to meet the exactions of the other vocation. He declared it a sweet relief to retire to private life, but I dare say he will want to mix in again when time shall have definitely and clearly posited his sociological ideas. But however this may be, he retires with Egoism's admiration and heartiest wish for his future welfare. He did much good work that would as yet remain unaccomplished if there had been no Hugh O. Pentecost.

H.

A Communist's Logic.

J. H. Morris, the somewhat sore of the two soaring editors of the Portland Communist paper, "Freedom," is mad at me for suggesting that he should know more about social science than he does. I can appreciate his position, for I have been there myself; one feels resistlessly ugly when his emotions have had a little war dance lacking in coherence, and a spectator points out the fact. Mr. Morris's strongest though somewhat irrelevant arguments against my position consist in stating that Egoism does not appear very often and that it is filled with a low order of mechanical wit. I heartily concur with his deduction that it is issued too infrequently, but insist that "low" and "high," like blasphemy and holiness, depend upon certain superstition, and his use of the term exposes a superstition as persistently and helplessly as an unveiled face exposes a sty on the eye of beauty. And as for the mechanical character of the paper's wit, it is probably the only feature that has enabled the skimming Mr. Morris to understand some part of the matter published in it. But the critic is himself guilty of an admirable little breach of the same kind. He says that I evidently consider myself, "Mr. Tucker, and Proudhon the holy trinity that shall steer (or bull) the race into better things." This is of course absurd, inapplicable, and without point except in the mechanical effect of the words, but it gives me a gleam of hope for the man's ultimate deliverance from the dreamland of communistic indefiniteness. However, this slender thread shines through a long tunnel of gobbler pride and semi-intellectual confusion. Criticism will have to penetrate the backbone, now alone affected, and reach the intellectual lobe, so as to discipline the bubbling desires into an adaptation of means to ends in the creation of ideals. He will then discover that the statutory dam is the *only* artificial foe of liberty and industrial freedom, and that a change-of-heart gospel admonishing abstention from competition is not only no part of an effective program, but that it is positively idiotic.

Having stood on Egoism's financial distress and machine-made wit, Mr. Morris argues:

> We are agreed that government is a force to maintain special privileges. But government may exist in more forms than one. The basic principle of the social structure is competition, and upon that the present government exists. Under his ideal, Egoism says the basis will remain the same, but instead of the State as a (so-called) protector of the right of the individual he proposes that contracts be let to competing "protective associations." Bitter as he is against Communism, he here proposes a little of it.

To say that the present government exists on competition, is about as accurately descriptive of it as to say that it exists on pumpkins or its sympathy for its victims. Contemporaneous with it exist pumpkins and competition along with monopoly and many other things, but government, so far from existing on competition, exists upon its opposite—monopoly. It monopolizes the prerogative of the citizen to dispose of invaders by the local jury system; it monopolizes his prerogative of determining for himself what kind of credit he shall accept and give; of deciding in local council what shall constitute a title to land; of determining who shall materialize mental impressions and use them; of determining what uninvasive tastes he shall exercise; of selecting a man to plead his cause when on trial, and even of choosing the carrier of his communications. Remove this *monopoly* and allow the citizen to compete with the government in any or all these, and see how it exists on competition. The present *social order* is the result of a half-breed Communism and competition constituting an order which reaps most of the evils of Communism with few of the advantages of real competition. It is communistic in granting power to create privilege, and competitive in forcing the disfranchised to compete for opportunity to labor, but it is no more a truly competitive than a communistic social order, and to so characterize it betrays an ignorance of the nature of competition that places such an advocate beyond the pale of notice save as a subject to illustrate collectivist folly to those more receptive and less bombastic.

Before proceeding to Mr. Morris's only attempt to fairly face my argument, I must expose his absurd assumption that I am inconsistent regarding Communism when I propose protective *associations*. Mr. Morris's motto, "*From* each according to his ability, and *to* each according to his *present* need" [italics mine], is my definition of Communism, and "association" no more implies this obligation and distribution than it implies its exact opposite. In fact not so much, as associations generally, distribute and tax on competitive principles. A combination for protection would necessarily award the highest wages to the rarest skill or most repugnant labor, and there would be no "*to* each according to his *present* need" about it, and therefore no Communism. This holds good and is the principle I keep in view when and wherever I refer to associations. Now let my critic stay by his own definition, and he will give no opportunity to sport with his reckless argument on this point.

Standing up like a little man, but with only the shadow of short information for a weapon, he says of labor owning under equal opportunity:

> If the idea remains intact that a man is entitled to all he can get, at physical labor with equal opportunities the strong man would soon accumulate more than the weak, and I see nothing to prevent his hiring a greater army of "protectors"—corresponding exactly with the Pinkerton thugs—and using them to oppress his weaker neighbor. Then the stronger could easily unite and divide up the earth and make vassals of those unable to protect themselves. By this means the physically strong would be better able to become monopolists than under the present system. And it seems to me this would be the natural outcome of Egoism's ideal, for when men have a community of interests, whether for good or bad purposes, nothing is more natural than a community of efforts.

If it had not been easier for Mr. Morris to call me an egotist than to read and digest "Free Political Institutions," he would not have been caught with this groundless argument. That treatise proposes and successfully defends a plan which must effect an ideal administration of justice, making anything like the suggested Pinkerton thugdom impossible. It consists of putting the administration of the law of equal freedom in the hands of local juries chosen by lot, which shall determine the penalty as well as judge the evidence, thus trying each case on its own merits. Such an administration would nail all aggressive acts of "protectors" as promptly as complaints were made, for by that plan the "weak" are as likely to sit in judgment as the strong, and their "community of interests" would not fail to do its work. And, making a closer analysis of Mr. Morris's objection, let us assume that some men can produce even twice as much in any activity as others, one such must give at least half his labor to pay even the poorest producer for robbing, or the proposed hired robber will produce on his own hook, it being as good pay and a safer occupation. And even if the robber should choose to rob for the same remuneration assured by production, it would not pay his employer to hire him, for he could rob only weaker men who produce less than the strong employer pays, and there would be a loss instead of a gain. Besides, resistance is about as effective through modern means in the hands of the physically weak as in those of the strong, so that in the absence of governmental superstition, none except idiots could be imposed upon, and these would make a representative communistic society, which to prevent the individual being deprived of his own, proposes to take it itself. Finally, since an interest consisting of the gratification of sympathy, is the only factor that could maintain a social order in which the strong would give up their surplus earnings to the weak and indolent, it is certain that such kind of interest would much sooner maintain each in his own production. Or in other words, it is easier to cause the strong not to rob the weaker, than to cause the weak to rob the stronger, as would be true of, "*From* each according to his ability, and *to* each according to his *present* need."

I do not wish to be understood as seriously assuming it a debatable question that the strong men in a community which has abolished the State would rob the weaker ones, but have argued at this length to emphasize its absurdity and to expose the tenacity with which a Communist will cling to even the shadow of a defense of his emotion-born "social science."

Bad logic, however, is not Mr. Morris's only sin; in his zeal to make me appear ridiculous, he affords to resort to absolute falsification. In a previous reply I argued at considerable length and emphasized that Egoists, including myself of course, do not wish to withdraw from society in the comprehensive sense of the word. But in face of this, he says:

> Egoism says he "will not mix" with his fellows. Then, as one man could not build a steamboat or bridge a large river, when he wanted to cross he might be seen astride a log, with a pole for an oar, paddling across. I also suspect that he would be found living in a bark hut or a cave. An "association" might build a bridge or a boat, but that is "communism"—his ideal has already fallen. Of course the association would own the means of crossing, and the rest of the community would continue to cross on their own private logs or pay tribute. Some people would call that monopoly. Now why not apply a little common sense just here? The whole community want a bridge; there is a community of interests, why not of efforts? Why should they not combine and build a bridge that would serve man and beautify the landscape for ages?

I have already shown that association and competition are compatible, and a boat or bridge would be easily possible without destroying my ideal. And I can see no reason why the rest of the community should not use their private logs, rather than be hogs and wish to cross at others' expense. If any one could think such association means monopoly, it must be some one like my critic, who cannot tell the difference between monopoly and competition. For so long as the association does not prevent the rest of the community building a means of crossing, it cannot be said to monopolize such crossing. There is no reason why the whole community should not build a bridge if it wants to, but there is good reason why any part of it should not help if it does not wish to, and also why it should pay for using the bridge even "according to its *present* need."

Now that I have shown the irrelevance, the shallow analysis, and the misrepresentation of Mr. Morris's effort, it may be justly observed that his characterizing me in his reply as nonsensical and weak-minded, was a little early and not too becoming. H.

A Curious Critic.

The writers for Egoism are, in the main sound, and show an abundant ability. Why, then, can they not exhibit a little more *manhood?* In the first place if they are anybody, and ever expect to amount to anything, let us know who they are. Who is the "Manager"—the man with the wife? "H," I take it, is David Hume, Associate Editor. Then why not say so? And "Tak Kak" is a personage of importance. Why does he *skulk?* Names are for convenience. Why inconvenience and annoy us by keeping your important selves to yourselves?

But the most reprehensible of all, by five thousand per cent, is the "Manager's" folly and crime in having a "*wife*," of which high misdemeanor he seems in no way ashamed. He knows that marriage is not only a supreme humbug, but the blackest of barbarisms. If he has a "wife," he is married. And if married, and publicly parading the fact, he throws his influence in favor of this diabolism. With his intelligence (I will not charge him with having a conscience), it is surprising that he can digest his food and sleep soundly, while engaged in a business so unmeritorious.

Francis Barry.

Kent, Ohio.

Mr. Barry is interestingly humorous, but nevertheless, if I did not know the contrary through other means, I should by the uncontrollable curiosity evinced believe his anatomy to be semi-mesially divided, despite the "i" in his name. It cannot make the slightest difference in the convenience, what name is signed to matter so long as one is signed at all, and I take it that the annoyance experienced, is the same kind that is felt by the worldly philistine when he is troubled about the sexual relations of Freelovers, and my sympathy is not dominant.

If by "exhibiting manhood" Mr. Barry means the blind, Salvation Army zeal which leads most radicals to give the enemy every advantage of them in the way of financial boycott, we unblushingly confess a lack of it. We have to get employment from people who would carry us out with iron tongs and lash us with flesh ones if they knew us to be the publishers of Egoism's doctrine. As it is, we are enabled to pick off here and there some of the enemy's men with its own ammunition, and gradually, very gradually, work up a subscription list that will furnish rations allowing our names to be "bravely" flaunted to the gaze of an admiring public. Rest assured that people vain enough to spend most of their earnings in saying their say, are vain enough to do it over their names the moment they believe they can afford it. If the most of the radicals were not so narrow that they will not support a paper a little more consistent than they take the trouble to be in their thought, and most of the rest so much like their orthodox neighbors that they are entirely indifferent, we could ignore the philistine with ideal unconcern. But things are thus and will still be after this, and so long as we must sustain the paper ourselves while we drink at the creek of local patronage we cannot afford the luxury of being identified with it, and Mr. Barry will have to go it blind unless I privately reveal to him a great name with an unvarnished tale.

And as for the "Manager," he tries, vainly it seems, to write ridiculous matter, and is sometimes not in dead earnest. "Wife," is with him a term of convenient irony which describes a legal fact. He is married in letter, and will probably remain so while it affords no greater than present inconvenience. His real heresy on things married would possibly shock even Mr. Barry. But I fail to see why the "Manager's" undevout conduct in parading his marriedness should disturb either his or anybody else's *intelligence*. If he or they had a conscience, such as described by Tak Kak, wherein one is dominated by a sense of wrong followed by no consequences, one might get it in the stomach like a mince pie, but well verified intelligence has no such notion, and could not therefore be disturbed by it. Mr. Barry's implication that it could and should, reveals a wooly scalp among the stove wood that fain would slyly expose the "Manager" to the prejudice of those who boast of conscience or the faculty whose supposed function it is to look out for others' interests exclusively. But in so doing Mr. Barry refutes the latter claim, for he does not look out for the "Manager" but for his own notion and the annihilation of the "Manager's" idea. He does not see that such annihilation would bring any undesirable consequences, and thus illustrates that the concept conscience, is either a rule of *expediency* or a superstition, the violation of which would be followed by no tangible consequences. H.

Managerial Experience.

My experience since last number has once more been a a checkered one. Its background is of a meltingly-tender green, striped both ways later with broad streaks of deep blue. I have lately tried to start an advertising paper that should be self-supporting from the first. The hope was to make enough money out of it to relieve the radicals of the country of Egoism's financial burden, but alas, the plans of men and other mice don't always go, and the subscriptions will have to continue. I wrote up as variable a description of what I see on the local trains as I could, then I selected from George Macdonald's Observations his "Schweitzer Tomato," and some from my own Experience, and sat them in type from which I pounded some proofs with an upholstered planer and a bob-tailed shoe hammer. I then worked two weeks on a job from which I realized $5 that I paid out for the engraving of a heading which was of such novel design that my wife couldn't read it when it came. Now as I meant to make a great hit with the heading itself, this was relentlessly exasperating, and I immediately squandered four bits altering letters which she insisted didn't help it *one* bit. I secretly wanted a divorce and sole charge with my large right foot.

Now the thing that makes the newspaper man's life bag at the knees and gap in the seat is that he can't have everybody's advertisement at the bottom of a reading column or next to reading matter at least. Here I had hatched out an idea that would take the exacting merchant by storm and cause him to submit and fold up like a girl who is willingly being kissed. I made the "dummy" for an 8-page paper with its first page solid reading matter, so that it would look like any other magazine. On the other pages I pasted the matter so that the advertising spaces were sandwiched at equal distances in the reading matter, occurring in each instance between the beginning and the end of an intensely interesting sentence. Reading matter above, below and on the side of the advertisement!—who could resist. Even my skeptical wife became enthusiastic and gave me a dollar to buy a stewed shirt in which to solicit.

With this snowy, rustling garment full of hopeful uncertainty, and an armful of carefully-pasted "dummies" I walked with a made-up nonchalance into the establishment of the most progressive advertiser in Oakland, and upon inquiring for his whereabouts was motioned to his private office. Having run the gauntlet of gilded clerks, I was in the presence of the brainy proprietor and at ease. He listened attentively to my very modest request to read all of the first and second pages so as to get at the nature of the matter and the effect of the advertising, which was illustrated in one of the spaces by the announcement in large type that ten thousand copies would be distributed in Oakland. I then volunteered to call again the next morning, and glode out feeling like a great genius who has easily invented something for which there is to be a great demand. I had little difficulty in getting my "dummies" out, although some merchants refused to look at either me or my scheme. In retaliation for this I gloated over the sheriff's sale notice I should soon see at each of their doors.

The next morning I called upon my first man and found his office filled with smoke. It flashed upon me that his enthusiasm over my enterprise had become so warm that it had set fire to my "dummy," but it was only a cigar afire which he was vainly trying to blow out by suction. It can't be done. He had looked my plan over carefully and approved of it, and would certainly take space in the paper—if he hadn't put out his apportionment of advertising money in advertising in the local trains, which he regarded as a better method than any that a paper could furnish. I felt a coolish vacancy far inside my new shirt as I swept mildly out, but I kicked myself into perseverance and the establishments of the men who had no advertisements in the local trains. Surely they could offer no excuse. And they didn't—they simply did not want to advertise now. Some had not had time to look at the paper, and others still, said they did not advertise in that way, a point on which I agreed with them, since such a plan had in my knowledge never before appeared. I now grew desperate and hung on many days, till my shirt became tear-stained under the arms and had my vest pattern photographed on its bosom, but no order resulted. I found that a few men advertise to attract customers; that some advertise only to extend themselves politically and socially, and that the majority do so from a sense of duty, for which a very small amount of poorly displayed space suffices.

Once more I find myself ignored, crushed, and trodden down by a clam-minded world. I alone can properly appreciate my genius, and shall try to get a job of heaving coal and let the mercantile interests of the community go to...; I don't care if the goods are never sold.

One Sunday in April the People's Free Lyceum of this city was to discuss the question, "What is Philosophical Anarchy." I was curious to hear what would be said and the manner thereof, and on that morning when the house was cleaned up and my wife turned out on the park, I mowed my jaws, transferred the polish from my coat collar to my shoes, and rode on the boat and cars to the meeting while I delicately wiped my nose with a large milk-colored silk handkerchief which I found upon a day. In a sharp wind and due time I arrived at the hall and found it wearing a carpet along with the air I used to experience at seance rooms in the days when I was satisfied to let my information all ooze in via my wishes, and from the sympathetic hands of pretty feminine sitters. My chair was still mellow when a little girl with more devotion than experience tried to sell me a pamphlet by my friend W. S. Slocum, but he had previously imparted his ideas to me as we seated type on "Freethought," and I was not curious nor a nickel poorer.

The hall was soon filled with people only a few of whom had worn the hair off the upper corners of their foreheads against sociological problems. A good-natured man with a white tie and a nicely-fitting black suit and mustache was chosen chairman, and the mill was set agrinding. My friend H. C. B. Cowell, one of the editors of former "Enfant Terrible," championed our cause. He executed his plan of battle well, but his plan was not the one I should have pursued. He was in the affirmative and took the negative ground of proving that majority rule is inexpedient and a social failure because it defeats equal freedom, whereupon it follows that Anarchism is the correct social principle. My plan would be to state the necessity of equal freedom and present Anarchism as a consistent expression of it, showing where Anarchistic principles are acknowledged in the existing social order and where their exercise is abridged, along with the results. Then I should show the difference between State Socialism and Anarchism and show that majority rule and proxy representation, the absurd and tyrannous practice of the existing social order, is the principle of State Socialism, and that the local jury system, as proposed by the pamphlet "Free Political Institutions" disposes of every pretext for majority rule and proxy representation. Indeed, the State Socialists drove the question to this point once, but no speaker seemed to know of this clincher, and they tallied a point when they asked, "How will you administer equal freedom?" and were not explicitly answered. Unable to longer restrain myself at this point, I followed the detestable example set at these meetings of breaking in upon the speaker with, "By the local jury system," which the State Socialists applauded as a great witticism, and which our men failed to catch onto. It might be asked why *I* did not come to the rescue, if I knew so much. The question is pertinent and the answer forthcoming: I am built with an oral safety-damper, so that I cannot become a martyr from radical utterances at public meetings. I am often aware of what I think, when seated, but the moment I rise before an audience the damper drops and my mind is all shut off except the consciousness that I am before a congregation of countenances who are expecting me to say something. And my mind being void of thought, I sit down upon the spring that brought me to my feet. This spring is, indeed, the test of talent at these meetings. The nimblest man gets the floor. My friend H. W. Youmans declares it the most orthodox conception he ever heard of, to draw the line on free speech at rheumatism, as he here witnessed. The most unmitigable nuisance at these meetings in this regard, is a bantam-mannered jesuit, one Patrick Healy. He sits lashing his sides with his attitude and springs to his feet at the close of every speech, whether he has a point or not. I understand he has been a reader of "Liberty" for years, and has, if I remember aright, elicited some compliments from its editor, but he declared once and again and again that philosophical Anarchism means the destruction of society and that the latter can never exist without government. I fear that if my sociologic master had attended that meeting he would have come away a very much discouraged man upon witnessing the incompleteness with which his carefully-stated social science is absorbed by men whom he has believed strong and consistent Anarchists. Even H. Royer, who could not afford to disentangle EGOISM's ideas, believes that "there are Anarchists and Anarchists."

In addition to Mr. Cowell's principal effort, George Cummings made a good reply to some criticisms of Anarchism, and Clara Dixon Davidson, one of the editors of former "Enfant Terrible," put in a few sharp hits. Then a student from Stanford University, who is a reader of this paper, nailed a number of Collectivist absurdities. A man who claimed to have never before heard of philosophical Anarchism, made some meritorious remarks which indicated that there is a considerable number of people in the skilled and professional classes ripening for the scientific sociological conception if it were presented to them by careful exponents.

In the discussion one or two of the State Socialists spoke soberly and seemed willing to appeal to the logical faculty alone, but the rest appealed to the emotions only or resorted to the politicians' trick of working horselaughs on surface criticisms. Others were content with emissions of personal abuse. Notable among these was a sharp-featured old he maid with snaky lisp and spiteful inflection, who elaborated on the proposition that Mr. Cowell was crazy. Then there was another with a swallow-tailed mouth about which he wore an intensely Prince Albert coat, who competed with Mr. Healy for the floor and devoted his time to demolishing the straw men he manufactured from a misstatement of Mr. Cowell's words. A man with a threadbare scalp and pelvic susceptibility declared that it is one's duty to defend his wife, mother, daughter, or sister, but not his son, father, or brother. Mothers-in-law were not catalogued in either list. He also averred that bomb-throwing is bad taste, to say the least. He was not without a redeeming trait, however, for when he was hissed for some fogy remark, he retaliated with the sarcasm, "Serpents and geese alone hiss." He omitted prejudice. While another was speaking, the acting usher arose and asked some men at the door to come to the front for seats, whereupon the speaker, hearing the voice of a known opponent, supposed he had asked a question, and indignantly shouted: "Wait till I'm through, you are always putting in when there is opposition argument!" Then, intensifying the ridiculous into the indescribable, he mistook the spontaneous burst of laughter that followed for an applause of his rebuke. Any one breaks in whenever he likes, and he and the speaker have a little parenthetical discussion, after which the latter proceeds with his remarks. The sessions last three hours and are the ideal of "Free Communism," with the exception that the speakers are limited to a certain time.

For those who like to hear themselves advocate, and for the fanatically devoted these meetings are a fount of ecstatic delight, but I fail to see much other use for them. If some individual were engineering them, and would select the ablest from both sides allowing each set to arrange as to who should elaborate on and emphasize particular points in their doctrine, such meetings could be made interesting and somewhat profitable, but as it is, they are a kind of Socialistic cat fight where the same Thomases go every Sunday for a little promiscuous bout accented with the same squalls and spits all around. At the best, public debate is a relic of the arena of physical combat, and addresses the emotions too much for the best deductive results. It is not like print, where one can return and ponder over and analyze a new suggestion and still be in plenty of time for the next sentence, which stays put all day.

Like any plug, this meeting finally stopped. Then iron-featured State Socialists with inflexible notions and large quids of tobacco strode sternly out, while their champions with an esthetic air and flaming neckties looked neither to the right nor to the left as they floated heroically into the "cannibalism of competition" below; unassuaged combatants with "clinchers" so newly-born that they carried parturitive odors, sallied upon each other with the same old result; pathetic Collectivists with doughy countenances and proselyting proclivities approached and yearningly allowed their tender solicitude to melt upon and run down over hard-headed Anarchists who refused to yield to public argument. A girl with a sailor collar bone and an intellectual waste observed that "us Socialists should hold our meetings separate and not waste time debating with Anarchists." Then I extravagantly wiped my nose with my silk handkerchief and sagely departed. On the ferry I saw a State Socialistic champion sitting near the music feeling refined, and then drop a coin in the contribution box as he dreamed of the day when the pressure of a button should inject enough State music into his altruistic soul to put him to sleep in his room. And thus reform goes merrily on while you wait.

I wish to call the attention of my almost numberless female patrons to a bright new feature in domestic economy which I have added to the inside door casing of our pantry with three large screws. It is a tin flour sack, with a lid above and below, and a wire fly screen in the bottom to keep the flies from blowing the nice fresh flour. Then there is a crank—two at the bottom when I wind out the flour of the family. This is not, I hear, unusual at extractions of that pink little bud.

Straws in the Breeze.

Keep money out of marriage copartnership—matrimony, acrimony, alimony.—Texas Siftings.

It makes no difference how worthless a man is, his mother thinks it no sacrifice to delude the best girl in the world into marrying him.—Exchange.

"Law is liberty," asserts one of our exchanges. This being true then the more we can have of it the better, and we should emulate Russia. The most that statesmen and thinkers have ventured to claim for law in the past, is that it is a "necessary evil." Liberty and intelligence make a people.—Herald, Bertrand, Neb.

The Nude in Literature.—Our generation needs to learn that ignorance is not innocence, and that knowledge is not only not guilt, but is not provocative of guilt. The evil facts of life and of human nature are known to every human being who has passed beyond infancy. Such knowledge enters the mind through gates which no precaution can close, and such knowledge becomes evil only when its possessor is taught to lie about it by pretending ignorance.

It is the function of literature to reveal, to describe, to depict the facts of human character and human life. The question is whether it shall depict them truthfully or shall disguise, pervert, and falsify them with the ready-made clothing of conventionality: whether it is better for literary art to tell the truth or to tell lies; whether it is better to present hideous things as they are or to hide their hideousness beneath some false pretence, and thus, perhaps, to make things alluring which should be repulsive.

The attitude of the public toward this mat'er is strangely inconsistent and incomprehensible. Classic literature, English and other, is not only tolerated, but admired, and held up to the writers of our time as an example for imitation, and yet that which mainly distinguishes classic literature from the literature of our time is the greater unrestraint with which the writers of classic literature handled the facts of human nature for artistic and moral purposes.—G. C. Eggleston in New York World.

A Cheap Ranch.

One of Egoism's subscribers offers at the reasonable figure of $1500 the raw cloth for a good California home for a farmer or fruit grower or both. It consists of 80 acres of valley and hill lands; the hills are more or less wooded with fine live and white oak enough for 2000 cords of wood. The other land lies in level plateaus ranging one above another; the lower one being about 10 feet above the level of Carmel river, a creek running beside it, and the others 20 and 30 feet above. The soil is an excellent one, being a dark loam (not "dobe"), and considerable of the tract is ready for the plow, in five, ten, and fifteen acre lots. It is well watered, and in as good climate and fruit growing belt as the state affords, and has a new five-room house, a barn and wagon shed. At present its nearest market is 16 miles away, which is its only objectionable feature, however, it lies on a constantly-traveled road. The party now holding it bought 160 acres and finds he has more than he can handle alone, hence this low price. For further particulars address Egoism, Box 1678, San Francisco.

EGOISM'S PRINCIPLES AND PURPOSE.

EGOISM'S purpose is the improvement of social existence through intelligent self-interest. It finds that whatever we have of equal conditions and mutual advantage is due to a prevalence of this principle corresponding with the degree and universality of individual resistance to encroachment.

Reflection will satisfy all who are desirous of being guided in their conclusions by fact, that as organization itself is a process of absorbing every material useful to its purpose, with no limit save that of outside resistance, so must the very fact of its being a separately organized entity make it impossible for it to act with ultimate reference to anything but itself. Observation will show that this holds good throughout the vegetable and animal kingdoms, and that whatever of equality exists among members of a species or between different species has its source and degree in the resisting capacity, of whatever kind, which such member or species can exert against the encroachment of other members or species. The human animal is no exception to this rule. True, its greater complexity has developed the expedient of sometimes performing acts with beneficial results to others, but this is at last analysis only resistance, because it is the only means of resisting the withholding by others from such actor's welfare that which is more desirable than that with which he parts. If, then, the self-projecting faculty of mankind is such that it will in addition to the direct resistance common to the less complex animals, diplomatically exercise present sacrifice to further extend self, and it being a fact that equality depends upon equal resistance, diplomatic or otherwise, what are its chances in an absence of enlightenment in which the individuals of the majority so far from *intelligently* using this resisting power in their own behalf, do not even believe that they should do so? The result of a general conception so chaotic, would naturally be what we find: the generalization from the practical expediency of certain consideration for others, crystallized through the impulse of blind selfishness into a mysterious and oppressive obligation, credit for the observance of which gratifies the self-projecting faculty of the simple, while the more shrewd evade its exactions, and at every step from the manipulation of the general delusions of religious and political authority to the association of sexes and children at play, project themselves by exchanging this mythical credit for the real comforts and luxuries of the occasion, which the others produce. Thus in addition to the natural disadvantage of unequal capacity, the weaker are deprived through a superstition, of the use of such capacity as they have, as may be seen in their groping blindness all about us.

To secure and maintain equal conditions then, requires a rational understanding of the real object of life as indicated by the facts of its expression. It is plain that the world of humanity is made up of individuals absolutely separate; that life is to this humanity nothing save as it is something to one of these; that one of these can be nothing to another except as he detracts from or adds to his happiness; that on this is based the idea of social expediency; that the resistance of each of these individuals would determine what is socially expedient; that approximately equal resistance makes it equality, and on such continued and a universal resistance depends equality. This can leave no room for any sane action toward others but that of the policy promoting most the happiness of the acting Ego. Therefore EGOISM insists that the attainment of equal freedom depends upon a course of conduct replacing the idea of "duty to others" with *expediency* toward others; upon a recognition of the fact that self-pleasure must be the final motive of any act; thus developing a principle for a basis of action about which there can be no misunderstanding, and which will place every person squarely on the merit of his or her probable interests, divested of the opportunity to deceive through pretension, as under the dominance of altruistic idealism. It will maintain that what is generally recognized as morality is nothing other than the expediency deduced from conflicting interests under competition; that it is a policy which, through the hereditary influence of ancestral experience, confirmed by personal experience, is found to pay better than any other known policy; that the belief that it is something other than a policy—a fixed and eternal obligation, outside of and superior to man's recognized interests, and may not be changed as utility indicates, makes it a superstition in effect like any other superstition which causes its adherents to crystallize the expediency adopted by one period into positive regulations for another in which it has no utility, but becomes tyrannical laws and customs in the name of which persecution is justified, as in the fanaticism of any fixed idea.

Another part of its purpose is to help dispel the "Political Authority" superstition and develop a public sentiment which would replace State interference with the protection for person and property which the competition of protecting associations would afford. Then the State's fanatical tyranny and industry crushing privilege would torture the nerves of poverty-stricken old age or pinch tender youth no more. The most disastrous interference of this monster superstition is its prohibition of the issuing of exchange medium on the ample security of all kinds of property, which at once would abolish speculative interest and practically set all idle hands at productive labor at wages ever nearing the whole product until it should be reached. The next interference is by paper titles to vacant land instead of the just and reasonable one of occupancy and use, which with the employment that free money would give, would furnish all with comfortable homes in a short time, and thereafter even with luxuries from like exertion. Following this is its patent privilege, customs robbery, protective tariff, barbarous decrees in social and sexual affairs; its brutal policy of revenge, instead of restitution, in criminal offenses, and finally its supreme power to violate the individual, and its total irresponsibility.

Egoism

Vol. II.—No. 11. SAN FRANCISCO, CAL., SEPTEMBER, 1892. Price, Five Cents.

Pointers.

This is the first number of EGOISM that has been issued since May. One more number closes Vol. II.

Although J. W. Sullivan, of the "Twentieth Century," has discovered that the average citizen is a narrow, prejudiced, unteachable mental protozoan, he still prays for a closer representation of that biped's fœtal-inculcated judgment in political authority. Reflecting upon the matter from the standpoint of one who is not the guardian of Mr. Sullivan's hobby, he could easily conclude that an ignorant fanatic's indifference is to the intelligent of the community worth tons of his ballot wisdom.

The Freethinkers who have labored in this vicinity, prominent among whom were the publishers of "Freethought," and W. S. Bell, will be gratified at a little incident which lately occurred in an Oakland schoolroom of eight to twelve-year-old peace-torturers. The morning song was of God and angels, at which some undevout boy laughed. The teacher then asked as many as believed in God and angels to hold up a hand. Only three or four girls could assume so much. The teacher now asked the scoffing boy if he believed in God; whereupon without answering, he asked her the same, and she admitted that she did not. The work of the day was then resumed without further comment.

A Mr. Van Ornum, in Chicago, who is a People's party candidate for congress and claims to be an Anarchist, proposes to reach the Anarchistic goal by the election of a majority in one house to be always on hand to vote No, on every proposition. He asserts that under these circumstances "they can't collect a tax, evict a tenant, foreclose a mortgage, collect a debt, keep men off the land, or oppress any one." We fear it would not be a very ideal Anarchistic society in which a debt could not be collected. And how all this should result from an inactive congress with present statutes not repealed is not at all clear to us, but even if it were possible, we would suggest to Mr. Van Ornum that as much can be accomplished several weeks before such an intelligent majority can be drummed up, by employing private protection for life and property, and simply refusing to pay taxes. A minority of citizens actively refusing to pay taxes and giving the good reasons for so doing would soon create a public sentiment that would make statutes a dead letter without paying congressmen to sit for negative voting. Such a plan however, has the drawback of furnishing no pasture for political aspirants.

The People's party is scaring the old parties out of their wits, and the social question is discussed by monopolists of all sizes with a personal interest. It is amusing to listen to their puzzled expressions and note the primariness of their conceptions of the subject. And all this ripens such an opportunity for the propagation of Anarchism as has never before existed in this country. These people are anxious to hear anything that can down the People's party, and Anarchistic argument alone can do that. If Anarchists were able to push their literature now they could get an effective hearing where it has hitherto been utterly impossible to secure the least notice. A half dozen papers, in as many strong People's party centers, taking up and weekly discussing from the Anarchistic standpoint the issues of that party and distributing the papers by the thousands could before election day win the active sympathy of multitudes with dollars to put into the work. But unfortunately comparatively nothing will be done. EGOISM cannot appear often enough to make an impression, and "Liberty," while issued weekly, is too small to contain the variety of phases and quantity of detail necessary to set the question comprehensibly before the popular mind. A few hundreds of dollars now spent for paper and presswork would yield thousands a little later. Thus the game passes by while the powderhorn is empty.

The literary fodder-cutter now acting as chief editor of the "Twentieth Century," characterizes Walt Whitman a "picturesque humbug" and charges him with making his living the past thirty years by affecting the "airs and mannerisms supposed by him" to belong to the untutored genius, Nature's own child, and on shameless trading on his record as nurse in army hospitals. Whether Walt asked or accepted aid on his hospital record we do not know, and whether it was shameless to do so after losing his health through his sympathy for the suffering of men breathing their last, thousands of miles from the solicitous faces of those felt a necessity even to their well moments, we leave to the susceptibilities of cast-iron hitching posts, but of this word thresher's innuendo that Walt "affected" and "supposed" there is a word. It is easily comprehensible how a mere letters-bag, a person depending altogether on others' mental mastications for even his thought, could not conceive that another might really desire to do differently from the rest of the world, and would thus conclude affectation the only possible definition of such conduct. But the broad, deep, detailed, and faithful description of life, thought, being, that constitutes the charm of Whitman's verse, and the response it found where it found it, are irrefutably conclusive that he not only knew Nature's genius, but appreciated it as he sang it. And if the editor with "twenty years' experience" had enough originality about him to do something else than make chop-feed from modern curiosity and the dry straw of contradictory old philosophers, he would not thus expose his intellectual insipidity with a magnificent stroke that is the despair of his most ardent critic. It is hoped that all those "radicals" who cannot support the few advanced papers that really champion their cause, and "cannot do without" the "Twentieth Century," will fill up on its editorial sentiment in this instance and in those in which it sneers with so elevated a nostril at sexual freedom.

One More Song!

I will sing one more song,
Full of bold, bright music
The music of he of the glad eyes, the quick step, the brave brow, the laughing lips, the frank look, the true word;
The music of the free man.

A song of daring thoughts, of high hopes of fearless faith;
A song of youth;
Of lilac skies, flakes of gold, and sunrise over the purple hills,
A song of morning;
A song of children playing in the warm sand, spattering the water with bare feet;
A song of seals sporting in the surf, with soft, loving eyes, barking like dogs;
A song of bright peaks, thunder, and the long, quivering lightning;
A song of dark waves, racing with the west wind, beating the rocks with a white foam;
A song of sea gulls;
A song of brilliant courage;
A song of innocent love;
A song of red flowers;
A song of white birds against a blue sky;
A song of a rock in the great sea which is always the same,
Whether the waves waste themselves upon it,
Or foam at its feet;
Whether the ice arms it with glittering mail,
Or the sun blisters it with angry heat;
Whether the rain weeps over it,
Or blue skies smile lovingly;
Whether the birds scream hoarsely about it,
Or come to it for rest and protection;
It is always there,
Calm, strong, beautiful:

"I am a rock, I have foundations, I believe in myself;
I stand alone, or I stand with you, but I stand steadfast;
I am not troubled, I do not change—trust me!"

—J. WM. LLOYD.

My Teaspoon,—Stirring the Universe!

The Homestead trouble has been a most impressive illustration of the labor problem with all its factors and intricacies. On the one hand poses government-intrenched privilege with its autocratic hauteur and cool adaptation of means to ends, and on the other despoiled though powerful labor, in aimless awkwardness and a cloud of blind folly and useless brutality. The former sophistically standing for the right of private property, while really denying it. The latter apparently denying it while blindly contending for it in vaguely contending for its own. Under the terms of existing alleged social contract—statute law—the Carnegie company was the owner of the property and had a right to do what it desired with it. Under the terms of equal freedom, the only terms of social contract that can receive universal intelligent assent, the Carnegie company could not assume the ownership of the property, and the men were justifiable in defending their own so far as it was their own. And while this is the broadly just view, and the unconscious source of all spontaneous sympathy, it is also somewhat hypothetical and accurate adjustment under that idea practically impossible under the circumstances, even if it had in that light been claimed, which it was not. While the property does not rightfully belong to the Carnegies, neither does it all belong to these particular workmen, but is in justice inextricably owned by all the partly unpaid laborers who have anything to do with the Carnegie steel product from its raw, earthed state until it is worn out. And this case is typical of the whole labor question; it is plain enough that a class is absorbing the surplus product of labor, but nobody knows just where his own is nor the exact amount of it, and though it might seem that changing it from the exploiting *class* to the exploited one would be safely just, it would nevertheless not be so. The gradations from the common laborer to the banker and land lord, are so gradual and their incomes so interlinked with the personal skill and labor of each individual that a justly accurate class line cannot be drawn at any point; and it is all the result of an alleged *social* compact that all have at least allowed. Therefore for one party to attempt to draw such a line by violently seizing or controlling, contrary to the terms of this contract, a property which it only partly owns, is little better than to change hands in banditti titleship, and sets a precedent tending to make it impossible for any one to hold what is even rightfully his own, in presence of a force sufficiently strong to seize it; especially when definite and scientific ideas of just ownership are generally not even broached. The only way practicable then, and at the same time in harmony with the fulfillment of contract so necessary to social stability, is to search out and remove the causes of unequal industrial opportunity in the social compact and thus stop privilege exaction, trusting to labor's superior fitness for the new conditions, to gradually draw away from the former privilege holders their surplus while they are adapting themselves to livelihood by production. With the immense fortunes that State privilege has made possible, this would not result in ideally accurate adjustment, but it would be incomparably nearer it than any possible arbitrary line, and would maintain the principle of good faith in fulfillment of fair contract, which cannot be dispensed with at any price less than all that life and liberty means. So since accurately representative control was in the Homestead case impossible, and since the Carnegies got and *held* the property by even the unsocial terms of a social contract which labor had tacitly agreed to and not striven to change, it would have been the part of good faith and reliable citizenship as well as material expediency, for the men to have resisted and subjugated the company by every passive means possible, and the while set about amending the great and unjust social contract and eliminating the trick by which the bunco dealer did them up. As it is they have not only deprived themselves of the opportunity to make war by the only rational method, but have by their savagery in the treatment of prisoners placed themselves on a level if not below the Chicago police. However foolish, to fight armed and resisting Pinkertons till they are dead is heroically admirable, but when they surrender under promise of protection, to allow them to be knocked down, clubbed, beaten, and stoned as they were at Homestead, is an outrage and a breach of confidence too dishonorable for even Bandit Frick himself. Even women, the much vaunted incarnation of mercy and tenderness, were ardently on hand to inflict their quota of torture upon the defenseless prisoners they had not even helped capture. And illustrative of the high-handed indifference to principle with which a little power always rides, a thing for which I have always cursed the capitalistic press, I note not a word of censure or condemnation from the labor or People's party press for this useless savagery. I stand for labor first and last, and if nothing but fight or the perpetuation of its unequal privilege will do capital, I of course hope that labor may come out on top, but I am too anxious for its good reputation to allow such acts as the treatment of the Homestead prisoners to go without unqualified rebuke.

Aside from the personal interests of the men who have sacrificed everything in the conflict, the Homestead battle proper, has had a beneficial effect on the social question. It was a good object lesson on the failure of force as a means of accomplishing anything for labor, and will probably replace the mercenary Pinkertons with the patriotic militia, and thus teach these laundried dudes something while it exposes to labor its real enemy, the State.

As for Frick and Berkman, I have no use for either. I am sorry for Berkman, the fanatic and fool, while I hate Frick, the tyrant; he without provocation invades and causes hundreds of peaceable and inoffensive people to suffer; Berkman, electing himself where he is not nominated, punishes the tyrant and suffers the consequences of his acts himself, and of the two, is the most desirable citizen, although neither is desirable. Once education has reduced the Berkman idea, the Fricks will soon be working for a living.

Once in a long while even the radical world is treated to something desirable. In the last number Egoism announced the exposure and downfall of C. R. Bennett, the Comstock of the Pacific coast, and now rejoices to note the collapse of a twin Moralistic and invading institution, the Humane Society at Oakland. The private affairs of the citizen will once more be left to go to the bad under his own management, and quarreling neighbors will no longer be enabled to revenge themselves upon each other by sending in charges of cruelty to something or other by neglect, and thus subject the loathed antagonist to "investigation" by the legal meddling society. And scandal will no longer be official, but must stand or fall upon its own merits. Unmarried mothers will have only their poverty and incident misery to contend with since this Altruistic monster can no longer snatch their children from their arms. But the society's death was unfortunately not due to any opposition or public censure of its work. Oakland is too much dominated by the superstition of Moralism for that. The society just fell to pieces from inherent cussedness. Its officious and meddlesome secretary got his accounts in such a shape as could be explained only by admitting embezzlement of funds sent him to pay for the care of children he managed to get hold of for glory and shove upon others' care for nothing. And, finding the outside world too small for his smelling instinct, he began operations on the members of the society, but characteristic of tyrannous institutions, it would not take its own medicine at all, and he was sued for and convicted of libel which is the last heard of him. Several creditors of the society are now anxious to learn who is responsible for its debts. And thus we bury another of liberty's enemies; may it forever stay put!

Populists! and why not! Why should the daily press sneer this word. Do the old parties admit then, that they are not now and never were for the people. Do they not uphold the idea of government by and for the people. What! do they confess that all their talk for years about the interests of the people was only hypocritical cant with which to secure office to serve the autocracy that feels so secure that it sneers this word at the People's party. Or, is it a non-committal flirtation of the prostitute press bidding for liaison with the blushing youth in case its pot-bellied and wine-seared *old* lovers are worsted in the future. In either case it is a timeserving sycophant that can never be used in attaining the people's political freedom, for it will already be attained when that mercenary is ready. Its espousal of the People's party cause would not be in that direction. A real people's *party* is an impossibility; *party* excludes the people, the *people* means the whole people. There is, however, such a principle as a people's *polity*, which really means what the People's *party* would like itself interpreted to mean. But this lies in the other direction, and would cause the *whole* people to voluntarily *seek* a reply from unvarying social principles to guide their conduct, instead of consulting the greatest number of ignorant and disinterested wills to anticipate what they might be forced to do under an utterly improbable contest. Here there is no spoil, no office, no advantage, no interest except security, and for that there is but one party—the people. Real Populists are scarce.

H.

A Few Words More.

You show good generalship in attacking your opponent's weakest point. When I said your "folly and crime in having a wife," was "five thousand per cent" worse than your other delinquencies, if you had not been more prudent than brave, you would have expended the main part of your surplus ammunition in that quarter. I am glad, for your sake, that you were only joking when talking about your "wife." But you hardly make due allowance for the stupidity of your readers. Your better way, in future, will be to adopt Artemas Ward's plan, and say, by way of explanation, "This is a joak," or, "This is carkasm."

But you still seem to be half in earnest, and think it is nobody's business if you do have a wife, and parade the fact. Would you claim the right to hold chattel slaves and parade the fact without interference or criticism? You would have just as good a right as to "hold" a wife. Do you say you do not "hold" her—that she is free to go or stay, and claim and hold half the real estate and "portable property"? Then she is not a wife, but a free woman. Every man can abolish *marriage on his own land*, and if he is a *manly* man he will do it.

I am not much interested in discussing the conscience question. I simply did not know whether, as you would use terms, a conscience was part of your outfit. I believe in justice, and that people have a right to do whatever they please without interference, so long as they do not trespass.

Why do you make special objection to Monogamy? It is no worse than Polygamy. No right-minded person will see any essential difference between these two phases of the same system of wife ownership.

You have a heresy that would "possibly shock even Mr. Barry." Now I *am* curious, unworthy as curiosity is. Do you mean that you will have six wives instead of one, as soon as you can afford it? Well, I have no more objection to six wives than to one.

Having written a little for over sixty different publications, within the past forty years, advocating the most offensive doctrines, and signing my full name to every line I ever wrote, and not now being afflicted with the mildest form of indigestion, as a consequence of prejudice evoked, I naturally feel a healthy contempt for such as lack the "sand" to vouch for even diluted heresy. But you have avowed an earnest purpose, something worthy of accomplishment. I respect your motives, and withdraw my criticism.

FRANCIS BARRY.

MANY WORDS MORE.

Evading the enemy's strong point may be good generalship in military contests, but it will hardly go in intellectual controversy, since such evasion must result in anything except victory, which consists in *attacking* and defeating your opponent's strong point. And, really, I have not been impressed with the necessity for prudence in Mr. Barry's case, feeling as I do, a confidence in my position equaled only by his own in himself. Neither am I superstitious, so that I may be terrorized with the word-ghost, "brave." That I am not brave, means to me that I am not foolhardy, and that thought pleases me. If one expose himself uselessly to danger, he is simply foolish; if there is danger to dread, but danger of a greater dread if risk is not taken, then he flees from the greater dread, which is easy; if there is no danger and he retreats, he simply errs in judgment. Cowardice is the preserver of the species; we fight for life only from *fear* of death.

I touched on Mr. Barry's marriage criticism so lightly because almost every number contains at least a short article if not a long dissertation on the marriage evil, and the paper's position is therefore so generally understood that it seemed ridiculous to do otherwise than gently intimate that the "wife" monotony was intended for a "joak." But Mr. Barry with all the confidence of the innocent, persists in evoking a knowing smile from the older readers as he heroically strives to make me confess and expose myself to them. He has just discovered the city and is rushing about the streets to show its inhabitants what he has found.

It would of course, be ridiculously inconsistent for *me*, a champion of the equal freedom compromise, to claim a right to *hold* either a wife or a slave. But *whose* business is it indeed, if any one has a "wife" and even sincerely parades the fact. If she were such in the philistine sense even, and still were satisfied, on what grounds would Mr. Barry interfere. Personally I abhor the idea, but there is a marked difference between appreciating even a regular "wife" and *holding* the same, so much difference that to interfere in the former case would be the same infringement of equal freedom that *holding* would be in the latter. Anyone may criticise in any case, as much as he likes if in so doing he does not make a noise about others' premises which projects unusually into their quiet. But if he forcibly disturbs their arrangements, he invades just as legalists do by breaking in upon the mutual arrangements of Freelovers. And like the legalist, he does it in obedience to a concept of theological absolutism instead of doing it as a spontaneous expedient in the compromise of social existence. He does so because he has not taken the trouble to appreciate that mathematical equal freedom is the rule because it *pleases* men more generally, rather than because it is mathematical. Therefore in cases where less accurately divided benefits are satisfactory to the parties really concerned, the social compromise is just as well served, for satisfaction constitutes successful compromise and such compromise is the social law. Interference, where one is himself not invaded, can be a social act only on the grounds of carrying out a contract with the invaded to co-operate in repelling invaders. This contract may be instantaneous and by the appeal of a look only, but it must exist in sense, if interference be not a risk of invasion. Otherwise, it partakes of the nature of authoritarian regulation instead of libertarian defendment. So much on the right to interfere where tastes differ.

And why should I give a sexual partner *half* of the property when we quit. Perhaps two-thirds, or only one-fourth of it is the result of her efforts, and I may desire a nice division. In my case if I left all accumulations to her, I would leave little that is mine; I have consumed as fast as I have produced, which might easily be true of a *woman* living with a "manly man," whatever that may mean.

My chief objection to monogamy is that it exists rather abundantly, while polygamy does not, or is at least less conspicuously brought to my notice.

Since Mr. Barry has so little war to make upon the conscience idea, the "Manager" and editors' heresy on things married, may not so paralyze him as I suspected. We regard the popular conception of love, including that of the average Freelover, as a superstition—a superstition with equal freedom infringing proclivities or irrational adaptation of means to pleasurable ends, just like other superstitions. It is a kind of clam analysis of a very clam-bounded faculty. The sexual faculty being the original and most spontaneous one, effects at once a prestige and a mystery concerning itself that has fathered all the regulation and ways to do about it that the undisciplined imagination of a budding mentality could suggest for an aping mediocrity to maintain. It is yet felt too important to let alone and altogether too sacred to analyze, so it is still vaguely speculated about and forced into the wake of a verdant idealism old or new. All the devotees in its superstitious aspect are ever very busy and under a heavy responsibility getting their god properly worshiped. Some find this centripetal titillation so superlatively important that the supposed author of the universe must consecrate its initiation. Others, who sneer at the idea of so widespread an interest, feel complacently sure that at least the attention and sanction of their own country about equals the size of the occasion. Then there is a disgusting variation of the superstition which, spurning the aforementioned vagaries, parades its Asiatic crudity by postulating conditions of intellectual adoration, doctrinal agreement, and statuesque indifference to all charms except those of one person, as the divine method by which this omnipotent, inscrutable impulse can be loftily enough exercised. Ah, human larva, how great thy smallness! However, there is yet at least problematical hope, when we remember that the function was at one stage of evolution so intensely all-absorbing that serious contemplation of it actually burst the victim visibly in two. But ages of familiarity with the matter has made the microbic chastelet so callous that the body will hold nicely together under any pressure of the thought, though much ado is yet regarded necessary and there are no social principles or logic that may not be thrown to the winds when this strobilaceous emotion is to be dealt with. The great majority are ready each to mutually enslave a fellow being and themselves for life to satisfy its unfathomable claims. A few, more idealistic than the latter, have renounced that majority's iron-clad bond without throwing off its proclivities or understanding the whyfore of liberty, and thus torture all the coloring out of their blood at forcing themselves to allow sexual companions the freedom with others that their ideal dictates, while they still crave all the jealous regulating instincts of ownership.

A superstition is a belief based on a guess at an unfathomed question, and being in its very nature the incarnation of irrationality, must result in irrational conduct. It follows, then, that such conduct is the direct fruit of a superstition, and that the origin of conduct may be determined by its rationality. Happiness is the sane purpose of life, and consists of pleasure; the more intense and continuous the pleasure, the greater the happiness. It then follows that the adaptation of means to the greatest pleasure is the only rational conduct, and that conduct not conforming to that requirement is in that degree irrational and rooted in a superstition—a mere guess at a mystery. The superstitious character of a conception of love which believes itself the special concern of a superstition-conceived being is obvious to those at least who are convinced there is no such being. And the inadaptation of means to the most pleasurable ends or the irrationality of conduct resulting from such a conception is not wanting when we note that whatever the conditions of inharmony or even brutality, cruelty, and slavish wretchedness, there is no idea of escape from "what God has joined together, let no man put asunder." No less conspicuous, if even more common, is the superstitious basis of the irrational conduct accompanying the conception of love which substitutes the State for God and reaps either the enforced maternity, drudgery, magnetic dearth, soured, spiceless, pleasureless waste, or the divorce publicity, social ostracism, tearing of children from mothers, and the alimony plundering of legal monogamy. Then if even less subjected to invasion, at best no better is the other adaptation of means to pleasurable ends in the conduct of that conception which seeks for the rustic and childish ideal of non-existent intellectual and philanthropical loftiness till the fire of youth and the glow of its passion has been smothered by nunnish celibacy or dissipated by monkish vices. And if less disastrous, still superstition-tainted is the conduct of those love vassals who torture their complacency with spontaneous jealousy in attempting the realization of an ideal whose terms they do not comprehend. And now even Mr. Barry, evidently dominated by an overshadowing regard for the love idea as such, bows his head by unconditionally assuming that sexual courtesies imply equal ownership of the property in conjunction with which they are exercised. Finally, in all, the one undefined idea of preeminence—the conception that love is something above us and to be served instead of serving as a means of pleasure,—this emotion-ghost, is the constant factor and foundation of both the irrational and the equal freedom-infringing conduct in every case.

This is our "heresy on things married;" we want no conditions of the marriage superstition whether the form exists or not. We feel so analytically familiar with the generative impulse that it no longer perceptibly rends us into two pieces. So we spell sexual love with a lower-case initial "l," just as we would begin the spelling of any other propensity or sentiment with a lower-case letter. And while we detest the marriage idea because of its slavery and inconvenience, we are yet not so dominated by the idea of formal allegiance to the opposite as to go to the trouble and expense of formal divorcement. We like to just wobble along and enjoy the cool shade, or the warm sunshine, or a palatable meal, or the roar of the ocean and the sea-breeze, or the refreshment of a sound sleep, or the clearly-put logic or delicate word painting of our comrades' compositions in print or in private communication, or the magnetism and persons of the congenial when their presence and other circumstances will permit, or the gratitude for favors bestowed, whether in protection against public meddling with private pleasures or carrying a parcel for the weary comrade. In short, we like to be free—the masters of pleasure and the slaves of none of its means. We strive for the equal deed to secure the greatest non-interference, and for the rational act to get the most pleasure possible from the opportunity.

To the general rule that everybody likes the credit of being extraordinary, Mr. Barry is no exception. If he had not been in such a hurry to recount his valor, he might have reflected long enough to see the difference in danger between writing for papers published by others, while one is farming for a living, and *publishing* a paper arrayed against the interests and prejudices of a class upon whose local members one must depend for opportunity to labor for bread and the support of that paper. It was not risky for Markland and O'Neill to write prejudice-evoking matter "for publications," but how about Moses Harman, the *publisher*. He may stew in prison while the brave O'Neill amuses himself manufacturing jealousy-hatched domestic tragedies on a steamer at the expense of his Catholic wife, by feigning an attempt to drown one of their children.

And what does Mr. Barry mean by a "lack of 'sand' to vouch for even diluted heresy." If he means to insinuate that EGOISM's heresies are not the *most* fundamental, all-inclusive, unswerving, and ultra radical of anything now published, except the same sentiment in New York "Liberty," I am prepared for a great surprise, or to make some lively reading showing him that he does not know what he is talking about, gray as his hairs may be. H.

Stirner's Grave.

The following extracts are garbled from John Henry Mackay's report of the placing of a slab on Max Stirner's grave and a memorial tablet on the house in which the great Egoist spent his last days. We received Mackay's circular, but before we could have it translated "Liberty" came containing it complete, and we have taken advantage of that paper's labor in printing some of the most interesting portions from its translation for the benefit of those of our readers who may not take the parent:

Engaged for some time in the collection of the almost hopelessly scattered materials for a biography of Max Stirner, I found a notice about three years ago which gave me a clue to the spot where Dr. Caspar Schmidt was laid to rest June 28, 1856. My friend, Mr. Max Hildebrandt of Moabit, in fair weather and foul a faithful co-operator in my work, looked up the spot, and we secured the grave, which was completely neglected and threatened with entire destruction, for another thirty years.

When I myself came to Berlin in the beginning of the present year, chiefly with the desire of bringing my investigations into Stirner's life to a close, I was informed of the cordial willingness with which Mr. Carl Muller of Zehlendorf, the owner of the house in which Max Stirner spent the last two years of his life, had consented to the put'ing up of a memorial tablet.......

On April 1 I was able to report in the advertising columns of the "Vossische Zeitung" the receipt of 393.16 marks. By far the larger part of this sum is due to the great and lively interest with which Dr. Hans von Bulow supported my enterprise. Without his active co-operation it could never have been carried out in this way.

The putting up of the memorial tablet at the house 19 Philipp Street, N. W., took place May 14. The tablet bears the inscription in gilt letters: "In diesem Hause lebte seine letzten Tage Max Stirner (Dr. Caspar Schmidt, 1806-1856), der Schopfer des unsterblichen Werkes: 'Der Einzige und sein Eigenthum. 1845.'" [In this house lived his last days Max Stirner (Dr. Caspar Schmidt, 1806-1856), the author of the immortal work: 'The Individual and his Property. 1845.'"]......

One July 7 the slab was placed on the grave. Since that day grave 53 of the ninth row of the second division of cemetery II of the Sophia Society, 32 Berg Street, has been marked by a granite slab, which bears as sole inscription, in large gilt letters, the name "Max Stirner."

Besides the time and expense of attending to all this, Comrade Mackay has had to pay more than a tenth of the principal cost himself. There has been no response to our call of last May for this fund, and indeed, owing to hard times we have ourselves not forwarded our mite, though we shall yet. If any reader is "moved" it is still not too late to donate something to the shortage. We anxiously await the appearance of Mackay's biography of Stirner. Who has read "The Anarchists" will appreciate what is in store on Stirner.

An Altruistic Romance.

CLARA DIXON DAVIDSON.

"It is greatly against my inclination that I am about to flog you," said Mr. Moralz to his son Ido, striking his stinging whip into the tender flesh. "I do so because I love you more than I do myself; because I am willing to perform a disagreeable duty for your sake. I shall bruise your body and save your soul."

"Never mind about my soul," said Ido; "I prefer a whole body."

"Your foolish preferences have no weight with me; I know my duty and shall perform it," replied Mr. Moralz, while blows descended harder and faster.

"But listen to reason," pleaded Ido, writhing under the torture.

"Duty knows no reason," solemnly replied Mr. Moralz.

"But I am willing to absolve you from your duty."

"No one can do that; my conscience drives me to its performance."

"What if you ignore your conscience?"

"Then, my son, I shall suffer torments."

"And you prefer tormenting me to being tormented yourself? Duty may have no reason, but you have a little, after all."

Managerial Experience.

I am having the politics this fall. So on the free local train and the 9th of August, I went to hear Gen. James B. Weaver, the other people's party candidate for president, speak at the Oakland tabernacle and the rest of us. When I arrove I swarmed blandly up the stairs of the tabernacle shelf, and with piercing insight and huckle bones sat me upon a just but unyielding bench directly beside and above the platform, that I might see the edge of the speaker's remarks and imbibe knowledge fresh and warm from the nest. The other patients were largely of the semi-middle class predominating in elderly men with unthached scalps of capillary expression. There was also a goodly tinge of brown-visaged, callous-handed labor with its ox-eyed guilelessness and faded raiment. And as I benignly gazed upon these goodly-intentioned men I got a flutter in my left corner and my swallow stumbled and I was religious for a moment and wanted to brandish my trunk and other baggage in the arena and spatter the attention with deep, gutteral sounds and large round bellows pointing out the true route to the root of all evil, and combatting the bat solution that would that day be proposed for their relief. But I was on the bench not the program, and my safety damper is also not yet rusted out, so I dropped my throbber down on my other liver and saw labor once more supplicate before the authoritarian ghost.

There were lots of women present, some of whom seemed palpitatingly desirable for other than political purposes, and many of whom I would rather embrace than an opportunity. Prohibition was like a torturing felon, on hand, and grinned with its gums in toothless glee as it contemplated the promising power with a policeman's club to inculcate spineless coffee and scriptural mottoes at fifteen cents a pair.

I now caught and on the bench rolled into the great unknown a large flea, whereupon the people applauded lustily at my feet, and I noticed General Weaver walking in. His head does not seem so vast to me as it did when I as a green currencyist blushingly submitted to his bosom my maiden voteling. He also shows unmistakable evidences of aging, both by bleaching plumage and by a sawhorse gait of standing with out-pointing toes. A now wealthy second-hand furniture man with a sticky affability and the party's candidacy for congress, just happened to be chosen chairman of the meeting and just happened to have a speech all written up for the occasion. He was a Lyon and told a bushy tale of crushing monopolies, gesticulated while he hunted for the place in his manuscript, and announced that Weaver and himself had twice responded to their country's call—once to bare arms! This time however, I noticed they had their sleeves down and seemed more comfortable. He then with unaffected pride and brand new bearing introduced General Weaver, and as the latter unfolded all the bipeds stamped uproariously and split the second-hand atmosphere with clouds of cheers from unscrubbed breaths.

And this sea of mammalian trunks, shirt-fronts, beards, chins, and cheek bones set with rat, cat, and rabbit eyes playing at deliberation, was tasseling State Socialism in all its heavily-shaded political verdure, swaying in the breeze of a rudderless emotionalism; where were they who sowed in this community the seed for so promising a crop. Did they, protruding from hard-boiled shirts, bend broad smiles into their toil-hardened faces and frame themselves in the large windows of an elegant chair car and ride to Fresno to meet and parade the standard-toter of the movement. Not conspicuously. Nor did they sit on the stage in large-frocked coats and conscious familiarity with the great leader, but in a corner of the great audience, and after the meeting had to slide out behind the house to get even one of the candidate's mingled recognitions as he left the grounds. The receptacle of this privilege due the fathers of the movement was, in fateful irony, the rich manipulator of second-hand furniture, a vocation thriving upon the last material exploitation of stricken poverty—paying to destitution junk prices for its goods and selling it to hardscrabble just a little lower than the cost of new; a Christian who, within the past year was one of two Christian firms monopolizing the auction business of the city through high license, and who tried his best to prevent a now fellow partyman getting a free license by petition, being too poor to pay the money-bags' ransom for it. And this is a typical illustration of the whole authoritarian farce playing at industrial emancipation. It also brings to my willing and tanned ears the sweet echoes of a prophetic soul when in bagging clothes full of the ravenous fleas that used to attend the K. of L. meetings I warned these selfsame ignored sowers that they would not be the directors even of their plan with all its errors, but were laboring to place the weapon of authority in the hands of enemies. I further predicted that by the time their theory went into pumping statistics to determine how many kittens and potatoes should be planted they would themselves be Anarchists. This is budding so gratifyingly that I can report fully one-third and the strongest third at that as practically in the Anarchistic camp, and potatoes are still planted by guess, while the cats amid an enthusiastic applause equaled in point and torture only by that of the political meeting, are still deciding for themselves the size of their silence-piercing crop.

General Weaver's speech, though able and overwhelming as against the trail scratching of the pot-bellied old parties, was nevertheless painfully void of his old-time energy, consecutive argument, and merciless logic. He is carrying his campaign principally on emotional traffic and free silver reinforced by appeals to convenient superstitions. He works God, religion, duty, and conscience like mules in fall plowing, and sweeps the board with Woman's Rights. The latter is not one of the unmatched boards of the platform and is not promulgated as such, but the full benefit of slotted enthusiasm is secured by firing a theatrically-accomplished female speaker, who works the subject and subjects for all there is in them. She also inoculates in one corner of the male sternum a pain which is a cross between an impulse and a regret and causes the victim to sympathize with the party for an excuse to shake the hand of she eloquence, while she leans back in imperial good nature and puts up her paw. Mr. Weaver is protected from the public idea of possible assaults from this woman by carrying a—wife and perhaps other astringents. He declared the inalienable rights of man prerogative him to alter or abolish governments, and that the injury of one is the concern of all. I have a long time believed that something might prerogative man to abolish governments if he had sense enough, but it is new and clear to me now, how under State Socialism *all* would be very much concerned in injuring *one* if he resisted its dictation. The general, notable among other things, made a few non-committal drives at science, avowed his belief in the current bible, declared that the existence of corporations is treason against God, and retired amid prolonged applause and the rudimentary politicians who like empty crocks jostled noisily about the stage.

Then a large school-made girl with a pod of ancient oak hair on the back of her head, gazed amiably at the rafters and with agonizing pumping of the shoulders and virtuously motionless abdominal muscles, sang "Star Spangled Banner." When she had subsided, a woman with a graceful one-seated carriage and made voice was introduced. There was no squeak in her manner. She spoke in firm, measured tones about eighteen inches long, and with a theatrical poise and deliberation that made her speech distinguishable from profundity only by its generalizing indefiniteness. Even this was at first so sweepingly put that I repented the impression of affectation that her first sentence gave me. She declared that there is a great disturbance among the planets which affects the earth with quakes, cyclones and the like, and reacts upon the human mind, ruthlessly sweeping away its fondest superstitions! Now this idea of its taking something about like an earthquake or cyclone to disturb popular stupidity, and that superstitions are the trouble, was so in harmony with my conception of the matter that I at once hoisted my ears and cocked my attention like a dog peering into a rat-hole. I felt that I should have to pare down the newly-grown bunion on my "catch on" which is so rapidly convincing me that woman will probably never be a first-class man, even though she should attain a position more enviable. She led with masterly skill to Woman's suffering with ballot, and was applauded with the wildest tracheal trumpeting of the occasion. In enumerating the capabilities of woman, she made the witty hits that in medicine, deploma in hand, woman could kill or cure as satisfactorily as man, and that the only place occupied by him that she cannot fill, is with a whisky flask in each hip pocket getting votes on election day. Now I differ from her and think her idea one of woman's stupidities. I am quite certain that right here some women miss their most available opportunity for attaining political influence. They could control all the votes on hand and engender new ones besides. Even I would crowd around to observe a flask unloaded from a pocket thus hipothetically located. The speaker then assured the men that disfranchised woman is in no way responsible for the deplorable conditions which their political muddling has brought about, and for this I was proud of her. But soon she thanked God that she lived in this age, and kindly volunteered his and the women's services to help straighten things up; declared that they were going to establish the Christianity of Jesus Christ; that it was a religious movement and seemed that day like a good old-fashioned Methodist revival; that "we all have religion today, thank God," and slopping still more hopelessly over, wound up in owl-dozing attitude with an invocation that ended in the concluding remarks of her address in such a way that I could not discover the last quotation marks. All this was loudly applauded, and I was ungrateful that she had evidently not been in one of the superstitions-sweeping earthquakes or cyclones mentioned in the front end of her declamation. With the resulting disgust returned my reason, and I saw once more the trained parrot performing gravely for a time, then with rising circulation rushing into a hysterical floundering in the bog of emotionalism like a herd of swine. And here I had for a moment been proud of her because she was a woman and I like their magnetism and shape.

Now a young man with a high-heeled collar and cool, unconscious bearing unostentatiously sang from the man you script, an original solo exuberantly flattering Weaver right in presence of himself. Then a man with statesman coat tails whom I heard perform on the people's prejudices last Labor day, arose and announced that the tabernacle mottoed as it was for religious services, was most appropriate for this occasion. And soon the class-meeting was closed and a rush made for the candidate. He, however, made his escape to a carriage outside, where each great constituent, hat in hand, introduced his important self and shaking his leader's hand stepped aside without the possibility of being again recognized from the Devil's off ox so far as the aspiring candidate was concerned. And a devoted people had once more come to its own rescue.

As I viewed the prospect: the mental incomplexity that incessant toil had stamped upon many of the faces before me; the single-emotioned prejudice that marked nearly every countenance; the appeal even to powerless woman; the currying of favor with almost every current superstition; the silly flattery that the candidate must stomach; the awkwardness of green hands managing the meetings; the barrels of gold behind the opposition; when I noted all this, I felt really sorry for Mr. Weaver. It reminded me so forcibly of our own difficulties in running a paper to educate the inhabitants of the earth: no capital save as we can plunder it from our backs and bellies; either worked all but to death, or idled crazy; no acquaintance with letters except the proprietorship of a presented dictionary; so short of type that words must often be selected to suit the proportion of letters in the cases, and finally the paper issued only as we can earn the money among philistines. Altogether, we are a humor-provoking lot, and if the day of small things is not to be despised, then Mr. Weaver and ourselves ought to be appreciated like regular honeymoon with its comb filling ready to sling.

Sympathetically thine, THE MANAGER.

OUR BOOK LIST.

LOVE, MARRIAGE, AND DIVORCE, AND THE SOVEREIGNTY OF THE INDIVIDUAL, is a pamphlet of 121 pages composed of a discussion of marriage by Henry James, Horace Greeley, and Stephen Pearl Andrews. What Proudhon's works are to Anarchism is this to freedom in love between the sexes. It is the most comprehensive, searching, and exhaustive work ever written on the subject. No advocate of sexual freedom can afford to be without a full acquaintance with its contents. Price 35 cents.

FREE POLITICAL INSTITUTIONS: THEIR NATURE, ESSENCE, AND MAINTENANCE,—an abridgement and rearrangement of Lysander Spooner's "Trial by Jury," edited by Victor Yarros. It is treated in seven chapters under the following heads: I. Legitimate Government and Majority Rule. II. Trial by Jury as a Palladium of Liberty. III. Trial by Jury as Defined by Magna Charta. IV. Objections answered. V. The Criminal Intent. VI. Moral Considerations for Jurors. VII. Juries of the Present Day Illegal. Whoever desires to make plain to his conservative neighbor just how society may get on without tyranny and privilege fostering government, should have a copy of this pamphlet in his coat pocket and be prepared to not only defend his position but to take that of the opposition by storm. It is the much-needed propaganda material that should be circulated as fast as Anarchists can afford to devote money to the work. Price 25 cts.

THE RAG-PICKER OF PARIS, by Felix Pyat, translated from the French by Benj. R. Tucker. This novel is the most complete portrayal of the human nature of this century in every condition of life, that has been contributed to radical literature. Every line, every pause, has a fullness, a significance of thought, or a volcano of emotion seldom found anywhere singly, and not combined in the style of any other writer. It is probably the most vivid picture of the misery of poverty, the extravagance of wealth, the sympathy and forbearance of the poor and despised, the cruelty and aggressiveness of the aristocratic and respectable, the blind greed of the middle classes, the hollowness of charity, the cunning and hypocrisy of the priesthood, the tyranny and corruption of authority, the crushing power of privilege, and finally of the redeeming beauty of the ideal of liberty and equality, that the century has produced. Four thousand copies were sold the first week after its publication. Radicals can do much good work with it among the partly liberal-minded. It will, without arousing their prejudices, open a new field of thought for very orthodox people. Price in cloth binding $1; paper, 50 cents.

MY UNCLE BENJAMIN: a novel by Claude Tillier, an intelligent victim of institution oppression, who necessarily suffered more than he enjoyed. The splitting pangs of his intense pessimism are seasoned with such ridiculing thrusts at the vanity of wealth as to almost hide the exaggeration. The characters are not made to "come out" in school girl ideal, but tumble along like real life, mostly at the mercy of other elements than the reader's desire. The facts are not manufactured and put up in doses ready to take for building up a philosophy made to order. He dissects conduct and illustrates the charlatanism on one part and the superstition and stupidity on the other that creates fame, with diagramatic plainness. Living in an age when some of our grandfathers were too prejudice-ridden to wear boots, buttons, or suspenders we find him in his philosophy dashing off almost our deepest concepts with a lucidness equal to the description of the most common[ ]a[ ]e affairs of our time. His wit is like springing a dark-lantern in a sub-cellar, while his humor penetrates your anatomy to the marrow without allowing you to roar with laughter so skillfully is it woven in with philosophy, pathos, or tragedy. We heartily recommend it to our full-grown readers. Price in cloth $1.00; paper 50 cents.

MONEY is at once a camera and chemist of human conduct and motive. Zola not only describes the carnivora, from the den it inhabits to the changing reflections of its glossy coat, but he tells what it is thinking about and will do. He realizes that the human animal is a none too much evoluted wild beast on the front of whose skull the experience of ages has worn only a bright spot, and he exposes all the greed, ferocious brutality, tyranny, cunning, hypocrisy, ostentation, truckling servility, idealism, and stupidity embodied in the kings, manipulators, and victims of a modern speculative world. The cruel and the generous, the detestable and the admirable traits of each character are delineated with an analytical nicety and a realistic accuracy that make the reader live the life of each and absorb the apology for their shortcomings without for a moment losing sight of the expedient course that should have replaced undesirable conduct. With an eloquently-implied regret he rebukes the horrors and cruelties of financial conquest without the wearisome moralizing or the narrow hatred common to the critics of social outrages. He is not a world builder nor a hero worshiper. Even Caroline, the lover of life, intelligent, educated, experienced, unprejudiced, and the heroine of the most trying ordeals of the story, was in his critical eyes full of weaknesses between which she was, inconsistently with her ideal of life, constantly vacillating. On world building he strikes State Socialism one of his efficient implied blows, but sensate to the difficulties of wide innovation, he offers no remedy for industrial troubles, contenting himself with painting in bold relief and sharp contrast the almost fabulous extravagance of the rich and the horrifying wretchedness of the poor, along with emphasis on the fraud, sham, and wholesale manipulating practiced by speculators upon the unsuspecting. Yet he describes with effective force the spirit of rivalry, the entrancing pleasures, the magnificent enterprises, and even humanitarian dreams that prompt men to speculate even by the most gigantic fraud. And it is this, along with his realistic repletion that makes Zola such an admirable and to us unequaled novelist. His plot embraces almost every shade of character constituting modern civilization, and he depicts the virtues and weaknesses of each with a disinterest as faithful as his realism is striking. Even his reference to Egoism, a subject that impulsive French blood might readily balk on, is characterized by this faithfulness to the spirit of the subject in hand. His Egoist, though not the expansive utilitarian of our ideal, is nevertheless intrinsically Egoistic and approvably utilitarian in a comprehensive view of the subject. Although the story, true to life, contains a full complement of unsanctioned sexual alliances, the only woman rich or poor that gold could not influence was a little Freelover who contracted such association with desirable men just once through curiosity for pleasure alone. Saccard, his chief character, is a financial poet, a speculative madman who dreams only of money—millions, power, conquest, supremacy, the prostration at his feet of "all great, cowardly, truckling Paris." Ambitious, active, unscrupulous, assuming, inappropriator of other men's ideas—of everything that came in his reach, he wove from his own and borrowed imagination, such alluring prospects as placed at his service the means beginning a career of speculation and spoliation the incidents and characters of which in Zola's masterly hands constitute the most startling expose of the power and tyranny of privileged money, the blind recklessness of stock gambling, and the ravenous greed of human avarice that we have read. We regard it as the ablest in our list, although no one can afford to be without the intensification of thought and feeling generated by all of them. The price of "Money" in cloth binding is $1; paper cover 50 cents.

THE ANARCHISTS by John Henry Mackay, translated from the German by George Schumm, and published by Benj. R. Tucker. It is the pioneer of avowed Anarchistic propaganda in story, and espouses with deep earnestness and irresistible logic, the cause of Egoistic Anarchism, both in fine reasoning and through stinging exposure of the vagaries of Communism and the folly of force. It is not fiction spun from the imagination, with putty characters performing impossible functions, but an accurate description of the lives of real leaders of social agitation, surrounded as they were by the wretchedness and horrors of London poverty and the tyranny of that city's organized imperialism. The principal character of the story is Carrard Auban, an educated young man of keen sensibility, wiry temperament, relentless logic, and invincible determination, whose experience, thoughts, emotions, and mental agonies in the growth from Communism to Egoistic Anarchism are described in the delineating, artistic, and powerful language of the admirable poet-author. The book consists of eleven chapters, painting with stereoscopic effect the world-metropolis—a veritable great beast stretched over the face of the country, alluring and devouring human beings by the million and converting the fire and strength of their youth into its arterial blood, while it throws off their weakness and misery through reeking eruptions on its flat, vascular body. The reader plunges into its midst, and views with electric vividness the the Empire of Hunger. Here, in desperate starvation, men make a blind struggle for relief, and are beaten down by the hand of constituted power to sink through mental and physical weakness into death and oblivion. Then in painful reminiscence the libertarian rehearses with the author those gloomy days of hope and fear when the executioner's sword was suspended by the thread of pretended deliberation over the heads of the Chicago martyrs, and anew the choking horror and crushing despair of November 11, '87, seizes one as he reads of the nerve-rending agony and depression of London sympathizers who also could scarcely believe their own senses when they saw the thread of the fatal weapon parted by the cleaving superstition, submission to the *form* of law. Then to illustrate the folly of collectivism, the reader is carried from these scenes to the propaganda of Communism where, in spite of the example of useless sacrifice at Chicago, the victims' comrades in London declaimed madly on, declaring themselves for the deed of the bomb thrower as well as the murdered men's opinions—Communism, the doctrine of sacrifice, which, with the muteness of primitive self-assertion, fanatically lays its lambs on the altar as long as power cares to wallow in the gore. Resolutely, though calmly, Auban points out the way, illustrates, argues, defeats the grounds of the opposition and makes a momentary impression, only to lose it at the first appeal from an emotionalist to the vagaries of a childish impulse that hopes to grow a ripened garden in a day; they spring to their feet, speechify, gesticulate, consecrate themselves once more to humanity, and like a group of pettish school girls pace away arm in arm to pout at the rude critic, leaving the power that crushes without the hindrance of a single thought that tends to dissolve it. Auban is more and more alone, and from the touch of all the years finally finds a single man who understands; and one mutually eloquent look and the pressure of the hand constitute the pledges of alliance that unite them in the work of a common cause. Because of its direct championing of the work nearest at heart, we heartily recommend this book above any novel in our list, and urge our readers to buy and circulate it. It contains 315 pages. We keep it constantly in stock, and sell it at 50 cents in paper cover, and for $1.00 in cloth.

For any of the above address

EQUITY PUBLISHING COMPANY,

P. O. Box 1678. San Francisco, Calif.

EGOISM'S PRINCIPLES AND PURPOSE.

EGOISM's purpose is the improvement of social existence through intelligent self-interest. It finds that whatever we have of equal conditions and mutual advantage is due to a prevalence of this principle corresponding with the degree and universality of individual resistance to encroachment.

Reflection will satisfy all who are desirous of being guided in their conclusions by fact, that as organization itself is a process of absorbing every material useful to its purpose, with no limit save that of outside resistance, so must the very fact of its being a separately organized entity make it impossible for it to act with ultimate reference to anything but itself. Observation will show that this holds good throughout the vegetable and animal kingdoms, and that whatever of equality exists among members of a species or between different species has its source and degree in the resisting capacity, of whatever kind, which such member or species can exert against the encroachment of other members or species. The human animal is no exception to this rule. True, its greater complexity has developed the expedient of sometimes performing acts with beneficial results to others, but this is at last analysis only resistance, because it is the only means of resisting the withholding by others from such actor's welfare that which is more desirable than that with which he parts. If, then, the self-projecting faculty of mankind is such that it will in addition to the direct resistance common to the less complex animals, diplomatically exercise present sacrifice to further extend self, and it being a fact that equality depends upon equal resistance, diplomatic or otherwise, what are its chances in an absence of enlightenment in which the individuals of the majority so far from *intelligently* using this resisting power in their own behalf, do not even believe that they should do so? The result of a general conception so chaotic, would naturally be what we find: the generalization from the practical expediency of certain consideration for others, crystallized through the impulse of blind selfishness into a mysterious and oppressive obligation, credit for the observance of which gratifies the self-projecting faculty of the simple, while the more shrewd evade its exactions, and at every step from the manipulation of the general delusions of religious and political authority to the association of sexes and children at play, project themselves by exchanging this mythical credit for the real comforts and luxuries of the occasion, which the others produce. Thus in addition to the natural disadvantage of unequal capacity, the weaker are deprived through a superstition, of the use of such capacity as they have, as may be seen in their groping blindness all about us.

To secure and maintain equal conditions then, requires a rational understanding of the real object of life as indicated by the facts of its expression. It is plain that the world of humanity is made up of individuals absolutely separate; that life is to this humanity nothing save as it is something to one of these; that one of these can be nothing to another except as he detracts from or adds to his happiness; that on this is based the idea of social expediency; that the resistance of each of these individuals would determine what is socially expedient; that approximately equal resistance makes it equality, and on such continued and a universal resistance depends equality. This can leave no room for any sane action toward others but that of the policy promoting most the happiness of the acting Ego. Therefore EGOISM insists that the attainment of equal freedom depends upon a course of conduct replacing the idea of "duty to others" with *expediency* toward others; upon a recognition of the fact that self-pleasure must be the final motive of any act; thus developing a principle for a basis of action about which there can be no misunderstanding, and which will place every person squarely on the merit of his or her probable interests, divested of the opportunity to deceive through pretension, as under the dominance of altruistic idealism. It will maintain that what is generally recognized as morality is nothing other than the expediency deduced from conflicting interests under competition; that it is a policy which, through the hereditary influence of ancestral experience, confirmed by personal experience, is found to pay better than any other known policy; that the belief that it is something other than a policy—a fixed and eternal obligation, outside of and superior to man's recognized interests, and may not be changed as utility indicates, makes it a superstition in effect like any other superstition which causes its adherents to crystallize the expediency adopted by one period into positive regulations for another in which it has no utility, but becomes tyrannical laws and customs in the name of which persecution is justified, as in the fanaticism of any fixed idea.

Another part of its purpose is to help dispel the "Political Authority" superstition and develop a public sentiment which would replace State interference with the protection for person and property which the competition of protecting associations would afford. Then the State's fanatical tyranny and industry crushing privilege would torture the nerves of poverty-stricken old age or pinch tender youth no more. The most disastrous interference of this monster superstition is its prohibition of the issuing of exchange medium on the ample security of all kinds of property, which at once would abolish speculative interest and practically set all idle hands at productive labor at wages ever nearing the whole product until it should be reached. The next interference is by paper titles to vacant land instead of the just and reasonable one of occupancy and use, which with the employment that free money would give, would furnish all with comfortable homes in a short time, and thereafter even with luxuries from like exertion. Following this is its patent privilege, customs robbery, protective tariff, barbarous decrees in social and sexual affairs; its brutal policy of revenge, instead of restitution, in criminal offenses, and finally its supreme power to violate the individual, and its total irresponsibility.

Egoism

Vol. II.---No. 12. SAN FRANCISCO, CAL., DECEMBER, 1892. Price, Five Cents.

Pointers.

On the second page, note Egoism's change of address.

Saintly John Wanamaker in his report for 1892 characterizes the shaking up that "Printers' Ink" gave him as a case that has been "indecently pressed upon the public." How about you, John?

John Beverley Robinson of New York has recently undertaken in "Solidarity" to draw its editor into a course of reasoning, but that is impossible for the average Communist-Anarchist. Mr. Robinson can save postage by reading all the manuscripts he intends for those people to his cat. The effect will be just the same.

The millionaires are losing confidence in the militia; its members are too much in touch with labor to properly shoot it down, so the Secretary of War proposes the job for the federal army, as the Indian sham won't work much longer. Republicans are to be commended for the recklessness with which they rush to the destruction of the governmental idea. In that sense the triumph of the Democracy must be looked upon as a great calamity. Interference with commerce, a menacing concentration of troops at the great cities, and a few more charges of treason would have enlightened the masses more in one year in regard to the source of industrial oppression than can be done in ten under the temporizing of Democrats.

The Oakland "Populist" of December 14 finds that there is a circular afloat purporting to have come from the pope of Rome directing the extermination of all heretics in the United States. There is of course nothing remarkable in such a discovery by such a paper, but it furnishes that disciple of liberty an occasion to get off the following choice piece of primitive rot: ". . . . It is only fair to presume that the charge is worthy of credence and steps should be taken by our general government to prevent and if need be crush out of our fair land all such insurrection, and restrict by the strong arms of the law all persons subject to the caprice of any king, prince or potentate outside of the United States of America." All this and more like it under the flourished and humorously befitting headlines: "Patriotism vs. Priestcraft." This is presumably another "Rationalist" with a Salvation Army frankness regrading his choice of superstitions.

Well can the plumb-liner afford to stand by his irrepressible string ever emphasized by the weight of fact. That persistent little line, like a spider's web in the morning light, annoys even J. W. Sullivan, of the "Twentieth Century." Opportunist, with no action today that he holds himself accountable to consistency for tomorrow; propped like a true politician upon the esteem of numbers by his identity with their errors; in no immediate danger of reaping popular disgust for fooling with a temporizing policy, he is nevertheless found grasping at every shadow of a straw which might tend to fortify his alleged complacent position. Not long ago, finding that George Macdonald was editing a People's Party paper he drew comfort from the fact by concluding that Mr. Macdonald, who is at heart a philosophical Anarchist, likes Anarchism only as a dream; which would mean that he regards State Socialism, of which political Individualism is a negative defender, as just the thing for practical everyday use. The paper with which Mr. Macdonald is identified was previously edited by him as a Republican paper, from which according to Mr. Sullivan's inference, we should conclude that while Mr. Macdonald regarded Anarchism as the pinnacle of political science, he believed protective, supervising, monopolistic Republicanism the thing for everyday use. But the fact probably is, that, unfortunately, Mr. Macdonald had in both cases to turn out such political feed as the public would buy, and would give Mr. Sullivan little comfort if he were a millionaire publishing his best thoughts on political subjects. Now Dr. De Lespinasse who, as his large patronage of Mr. Sullivan's sociologic opposition indicates is not always ideally consistent, has expressed a desire to "hit heads" with chunks of frozen direct legislation, and Mr. Sullivan congratulates himself on having captured one of the Anarchist class leaders. And he even sucks a little drop of solace of the same kind from Victor Yarros's late political enthusiasm, believing that Mr. Yarros will want to use the "best make" when he goes into politics. If Mr. Sullivan were to separate the thoroughgoing, consistent, definite principle of anti-authoritarianism, known as Philosophical Anarchism, from the men who love to claim its prestige, he would have to congratulate himself upon there not being *many* Anarchists, instead of that he was *capturing* Anarchism with his political pain killer. The principle of No Rule will remain just the same when every biped has deserted it, and will be vindicated by its identity with social harmony when they shall seek its shelter. It is the social *lesson* and not untutored public *expression* that is needed. When the true lesson has been universally enough taught to make its political expression effective such a vote will be as useless as the untaught one now is. There is no rational excuse for Anarchists in the political camp.

Compensation.

The body and soul are one.—Whitman.

Like to the sea-shell's convolutions,
Tinted with dawn's soft fleeciness,
They watched thy graceful evolutions;—

No sister, thou, but "a skirt-dancer"
To be abhorred by "Puritans"!—
Whose purity I call to answer

With those who Salem-witches carted
Unto the burning stake. To whom,
No grace of limb has God imparted.

—David Lesser Lezinsky.

Anti-authoritarians can have no sympathy with Monarchists as such, but when the physiognomy of the Count of Paris is compared with that of Charles Floquet and the other officers of the French republic, a spontaneous and eloquent plea for the Monarchist arises. The countenance of the Populist looms up about like that of a catfish against that of a greyhound. The monarchial idea is played out, but the heartiness with which its function is accorded to physiognomical apes shows the superstition as sound as ever. Unable to escape being ruled, one fondly lingers over the idea of having the royal prerogative injected by a codfish substitute!

We are delighted to announce that Benj. R. Tucker is publishing a book compiled from his editorials in "Liberty" setting forth and expounding the principles of Philosophic Anarchism. This is what has long been sorely needed, and will undoubtedly mark an epoch in Anarchistic propaganda. There are thousands of people ripe just now for a straight-across-the-field, systematic and condensed statement of the social philosophy which promises to destroy monopolistic privilege without inflicting paternal regulation and secure protection for life and property of citizens without making them victims of the protective agency itself. The publication of the work was suggested by John Beverley Robinson, of New York, and a list of subscribers for it headed by Dr. G. A. F. De Lespinasse, of Orange City, Iowa, who agreed to take a hundred copies. From that generous start the list ran up to over 500 subscriptions in a little more than two months. Dr. De Lespinasse is the gentleman who helped Egoism off the little hand press upon the steam press by contributing the necessary money for type and other materials to put the whole paper on press at once. While Dr. De Lespinasse does not go without necessary food and clothes to do these things, there are plenty of more pretentious Radicals abler than he to do them, who will not even take a paper.

Egoism Changes Its Address.

On January 1, 1893, EGOISM will be removed to Oakland. Its address will be P. O. Box 366, Oakland, California. This change is a matter of convenience to the publishers and will not affect the character of the paper. For the benefit of the greater portion of our subscribers, who live east of the Rocky Mountains, we may state that Oakland is just across the bay from San Francisco on the east side, and all except ocean mail arrives at Oakland first, and as there is less of it to handle it is distributed more promptly and there is in every way a superior service. We live there and can save a nice item of ferriage and car fare as well as time in getting our mail. Besides we save one cent postage on each paper of a considerable list of San Francisco subscribers; that is, the State Socialistic mail service charges us a cent each for delivering papers that we put in the home office, but it will carry the same papers from Oakland to San Francisco and deliver them for one cent per pound. Don't forget the change of address.

Editorial Itchings.

Charlotte Perkins Stetson could not live in the communism of marital harness, but no sooner was she out than she began to struggle to get in a communistic harness with the whole nation, from which there would be no divorce. Was a double harness too monotonous or has she never taken the trouble to analyze and see where the individualistic tendencies that cannot stand monogamy consistenly lead. I fear the latter is true, and that Mrs. Stetson is wasting some valuable time tarrying in the Collectivist camp.

When Hugh O. Pentecost vacated the editorial chair of the "Twentieth Century" and Joseph Fitzgerald sat him on the warm place I could, upon reading the new editor's first number, feel it in my bones that he would do something great for illiterate labor, and sure enough he has. In the issue of October 13 he reveals with a lavish hand to the People's Party a brand new name, just imported from the Greek. It is "Laocracy," and means rule of the people at large by themselves; not only this, but government by the laity not the professionals. Now the party can go ahead all right. I thought it strange that Weaver carried so few states, but the name probably had not soaked in well, as it had little more than three weeks to penetrate the marsh scale of the American mudsill. Next time the party is sure to win if the "experienced" editor gets the Laocratic salve rubbed in with a deft M. A. swipe.

Ambrose Bierce will now have mountains of vindication as a kind of unearned increment accruing to the prods he has given the Women's Press Association of this coast. Charlotte Perkins Stetson, who is a prominent member of that mutual amusement club, is the victim of attempted divorce by her husband, and her sister thought-radiators are glaring out their intensest rays on the subject along with their opinions on whether a literary woman can be a first class article as wife. Mrs. Nellie B. Eyster thinks they can if the husband is in sympathy with his wife's work; that the "practice of self-denial in the home circle by the wife and husband will always result in true domestic happiness." Of course it will; how could it fail; there's nothing else to true domestic happiness but "self-denial by the husband and the wife." A Mrs. Hannah Neal says, "this city is full of women who perform literary work at home in addition to their household duties." Some were greatly worried about the divorce case, most of them deplored it, and all breathed that if literary pursuits did interfere with the incubating function they should of course be promptly abandoned. Now Ambrose, don't fire into this flock again; let the children catch them under a sieve baited with the laurels of temperance literature.

The most outrageous and inexcusable crime that has in a long time been committed in the name of the State was the late butchery and extermination of a tribe of Indians in Mexico by the order of its militant Freethinker president. This man who loves to coerce the assumption of church authority with another quite as absurd, gave away for the surveying of it, some land that did not belong to him. The occupants and therefore just owners refused to give their homes to men who had no other claim to them than that of gift by a man who did not own them. So on the strength of as plain a superstition as ever racked an early-day Christian, he made many hundred other men go out there and kill the people who refused to recognize his right to give away their homes. This handful of State victims, men, women, and children, fought to the death with a heroic desperation that is the peer of anything in history. And this piece of modern feudal slaughter and conquest is based on the idea that society has defensible rights which its individuals have not; that a number of indviduals with each admittedly no authority over his neighbor, can in some mysterious way confer upon another man of similar prerogative the right to dispose of one of these same neighbor's affairs. No God-head, three in one or one in three, ever outdid such absurdity or engendered more ferocious tyranny than that of this Mexican "Rationalist" ruler.

I recently enjoyed the pleasure of meeting Hamlin Garland. Although it only took us a minute and a half to get into an argumental skirmish, I like him very much. His easy unpretentious, genial, democratic and quiet manner coupled with his earnestness and his sympathy with the down-trodden make him delightfully companionable. He has deep, spiritualistic eyes, or the kind that open into a back parlor, a full emotional nature, and is a natural people's man who will undoubtedly make much more stir in the world than he has already done. He espouses Individualism, and discovering EGOISM under the favorable auspices it enjoys at the Los Angeles public library, thought he would like to see its publishers. So our friend and prospective Egoist, David L. Lezinsky, ran me, the loose one, down and kindly brought me before Mr. Garland. But like other mortals the latter is subject to disappointment, for in addition to any possible deficiencies, he soon found me a "Tuckerite," whom he regards as not as effective workers as they might be if they would only get into the procession and help boost it up the hill of liberty by the winding and zigzag path of politics. His Individualism allows him to work for its realization with the People's Party. I, however, have grave doubts about its being thoroughly consistent, and believe that if he would revise it with me a few months he would be too tired to speak before Single Tax clubs and Populists as he now does.

The State is the State still, no matter by whom manipulated. The air was not yet clear of the odor of bad breaths jubilant over Cleveland's election, when the San Francisco "Examiner" began bidding for an alliance between the Republican and Democratic conservatives against the Populists and radical Democrats for the avowed purpose of preventing "any wild experiments with monetary legislation." It is *power* every time that lies at the bottom of politics. Note these bitter enemies smirking overtures preparatory to a mutual defense of their feudal privilege. To all except the most superficial observers this ought to reveal the weather-tanned throat that authority is most anxious to keep its subtle clutches on. It will allow popular regulation of almost anything else, because all other things are of minor importance to the money monopoly; it must not be disturbed at any cost. This is the hinge upon which swings the whole autocratic institution, and the one which will place the lily monopolistic claw on the trigger of the deadly Winchester should popular awakening be of a nature to offer a ray of hope in that direction. But so long as agitators are content to spend lung and pencil on better methods of taxing, government ownership of railroads, and such other matters as are unlikely to be accomplished, or if accomplished still of little importance beside the money monopoly, so long will the old political masks do. The fiat-money cry did not trouble the great beast, but when there is talk of repeal of the prohibitory ten per cent tax on state banks, and other agitation looking to a system of credit with all the advantages of coin, and limited only by the labor product to base it on, the bristles begin to rise, and even defeated Republicans will do better. And yet, we have Democratic voting Anarchists in Boston! Verily, our "Over-Man" is yet a long way off. It is a little gratifying to EGOISM's illiteracy though, to see the conventionally educated folks who love to ignore it, make all the most ridiculous divergencies from the plumb-line and cling to them.

The People's Party in Kansas recently sat down upon the proposition to have the usual inaugural ball when its governor is seated, because it is an expression of a fashionable life that can exist only by monopolies and plundering of the common people. So far well enough. But the cloven foot was betrayed when some old fanatic with but one faculty declared that dancing was immoral and that when a woman went on the floor to dance she departed from the path of virtue. This is true or not according to the standard used in measuring such an imponderable idea as virtue. If exercising in any degree the faculty which enjoys opposite sex is unvirtuous, then dancing is not virtuous, for the magnetism and *mingled*, promiscuous magnetism of opposite sex is one if not the main inducement to dance. But if a mild form of such exercise is immoral what is to be said of the more ardent one suggested by swarms of unmortgaged children on mortgaged farms. Dancing is pleasant and pleasure is happiness while it lasts. If the common people of Kansas think pleasure immoral why didn't they toil away and suffer all they could while the old parties practiced pleasant vice. But the sting of this criticism is not that inconsistency; it is that these people are crude enough to believe that Statecraft can save them, and being so are fanatical enough to devote their power to enforcing the prejudices which constitute their ethics, while the solution of the great industrial question which their votes were to settle is untouched. So long as bipeds carry "sacred" things about them to protect, so long will they fail to penetrate the political sham, and so long will monopolists be safe. Let people *be* rakes and whores and practice all the private vices they can pay for, while you do us the industrial freedom you have promised. We are waiting for the failure of your scheme and a trial of ours. Don't keep everybody waiting while you spend your time preserving the virtue of a few of the enemy's dough-faced women. H.

Children and Equal Freedom.

It was to me an occasion of great surprise, gratification, and admiration when Benj. R. Tucker acknowledged in "Liberty" of September 3 that he had not hitherto held that parents were under no obligation to their children. I was surprised that he had not, gratified that I had done so a year or more ahead of him, and filled with admiration for the largeness of mind that can so frankly acknowledge an error. It took me half the night to get the universe back in proper relation to myself, and to Mr. Tucker without that idea. However, when I remembered that the nature of his complex pioneer work in Anarchism had kept his mind on other departments, I could easily understand how he could overlook what had held my attention as one of the sex whose task it is to be mother of the race.

But while I am proud of my friend Clara Dixon Davidson as writer of the most rational and well-written article on the relation of parents and children that I remember of reading, it has nevertheless set me reflecting until I am convinced of its error which we previously held in common in regard to children being under no obligation to parents. The position breathes to my sensibilities a marked dominance of mechanical equal freedom and theological obedience to a "no duty" postulate, "no 'duty' is a duty," as it were: there is no "duty," therefore parents are under no obligation to their children, and of course the children under none to their parents. Now since children, helpless as such, cannot possibly do anything for parents that could put the latter under obligation, I readily agree with that part of the postulate, but in face of facts I fail to see that the other part should follow. It seems to me like positing: There is no "duty," therefore we need not pay our debts.

It is obvious that the parent owes the child nothing, it doing nothing for the parent. But the parent does everything for the child, and if at the age of physical independence it loves life well enough to continue it with a fair degree of persistence, in equity, I see no reason why it should not pay the giver or creditor of its existence the cost of the article it prizes so highly. Let me cite an illustration with all adult principals, that in every way covers the case of parent and irresponsible child and see what becomes of the idea that children are under *no* obligation to parents:

A man is growing a crop in a field through which a creek flows. A freshet comes and carries away the flood fence between the crop and pasture field while the owner is delirious with a fever. His cattle with spontaneous alacrity and true Columbus instinct discover the opportunity to plunder, and begin to destroy the crop. His neighbor, knowing the owner's helpless condition drives them out, but finds he is unable to repair the fence alone, and is compelled to hire an indifferent stranger at a high price. In addition, the solicitous neighbor has to stand in rain and water working so that he too falls sick from the exposure. Finally the possessor of the crop recovers and becomes rational, and his neighbor reports the affair. The former appreciates his crop and is glad to have it, but says nothing about reimbursing the neighbor. This irritates the latter and he informs the possessor that he paid out almost his last cent of cash for help and material and had therefore to borrow, and will look to the beneficiary for at least the cash outlay; the necessary sickness and suffering from exposure being incomputable in money, he will leave to be returned in services in kind when opportunity shall offer. But the owner is avaricious and declares that he cannot pay for such a thing; that neighbors have always done good turns for one another without presenting a bill. The neighbor shows him that this was no ordinary little turn and meant everything of reward to the grower's season of work; that without the service he would now have no crop; that he rendered it fully expecting that the owner would feel it so; otherwise he should not have put himself in debt and suffering merely to favor another's prosperity. The logic is incontrovertible, and stings the temper of the possessor and he declares he did not hire the other and that the latter had no business to work for another without his consent then come around to collect; that he would rather have lost the crop than be forced to pay for it. Technically the solicitous neighbor is silenced, but his ingenuity comes to his rescue, and he says that defense is only a ruse to keep from paying a just debt, and that if the other will turn the cattle in and leave them until the crop is destroyed, it will be just as it would have been had the neighbor not interfered and he will then have the best of reasons for believing he had really been too swift in his solicitude. But the stickler for conveniently absent contracts shows no proof of the genuineness of his sentiment, and when the other attempts a test himself, the former interferes so violently as to endanger the life of the tester. The latter now appeals to a jury empowered to decide cases upon their merits under the rule of equal freedom. The defendant's advocate urges that all just claims rest upon contract and that no one need pay for that which he has not contracted; that the defendant did not so contract with plaintiff—could not, being totally irresponsible; that plaintiff knew this and must take his chances on getting pay at the will of the irresponsible when he works for them; that since abstract "duty" is an acknowledged myth there cannot be the slightest obligation without a specific contract. But plaintiff's advocate shows that while it is true that no contract was made and that the defendant was incapable of contracting, his actions when capable were conclusive proof that he would gladly have contracted on plaintiff's terms in preference to losing the crop, or he would have taken plaintiff's offer to wipe out the claim by allowing the cattle to reduce the field to the state it would have been in had plaintiff not interfered; that the bill is only a small portion of the value of the crop; that the service was indispensable and there was no one else to perform it. And while the idea of abstract "duty" is a myth, nothing could be a more abject obedience to such abstraction than allowing the defendant to thus beat his creditor under cover of duty to the "no duty" idea. Therefore plaintiff is entitled not only to the cash outlay, but to labor in kind when he shall need it.

Should this jury acquit the defendant and thereby tacitly admit its willingness to be treated as the plaintiff was, or should it decide that while in equity a remuneration of cash and labor expended is due, since defendant did not seize the service by force, it will as the least sanguinary method, not authorize restitution by force, but will recommend that every justice-loving citizen shall boycott the defendant until he shall feel the need of society sufficiently to at least pay this just claim, to say nothing of keenly appreciating so spontaneous a solicitude for his welfare as plaintiff had exhibited by loaning money and labor unsolicited, at that perilous moment.

This case in every way covers that of an irresponsible child and its parent, except that the neighbor did not cause the occasion for indebting the sick man by causing his helpless existence, but as it is already admitted that a parent's bringing a child into the world does not obligate maintenance, this difference does not disperse in the slightest the force of the comparison. To cause helplessness for an independent equal, a somebody else, is plainly invasion entailing responsibility; to evolve the same from a nobody else, a germ of one's own body is not, for it was no one and besides was indisputably one's own. Like the fever-stricken neighbor, the child is helpless, incapable of even desiring its greatest welfare. Beyond a few years of protection, which no one is under the slightest obligation to give it, lies a life of rich and varied emotions. This chasm is bridged by a separate being—a being with entirely separate interests, with the exception of an anticipation of grateful social alliance and material restitution. The child soon finds himself in possession of independent life—most coveted of all possessions. The separate being conferred it with all its richness, and asks only cost. Should that person be paid?

In full possession of my faculties, seeing clearly a future profit I contract a debt and am accommodated by my creditor whom I gladly repay. In another case I am incapable of discerning my interests, another invests in my name and lays the big returns at my feet, asking only the original investment returned. I not only cheerfully return the cost, but besides am intensely grateful for the benefit of an act which might have been left unperformed so far as my potency was concerned. If he invests in and puts in my possession something I do not want, or has paid for it a price so high that I would rather be without the article than pay it, he cannot expect me to shoulder the cost of his error. But if on the contrary, I eagerly seize it and will neither pay nor relinquish possession, it is plain that I so positively assume a negative debt that no one need hesitate to let me so uncomfortably alone that I will gladly acknowledge my avarice and pay up. Thus while the "no duty" idea clearly relieves the parents from obligation to children, it does not in the spirit of equal freedom similarly relieve the children by simply turning it end for end, but if they cling to life and its interests with the usual tenacity it leaves them at least under the obligation of a negative debtor.

Severe as the struggle is for existence under these unequal conditions, I feel not only under obligation to repay my parents in kind for their services, but am tenderly grateful to them besides for the privilege of conscious existence. It beats oblivion incalculably and I like it immensely better than being nothing at all. If the decree of equal freedom forces me to pay my debts to my competing fellows, what should it not do regarding my generous parents? If life is worth living it is worth paying the full cost of. Under this conception people might rationally breed, for with the inducements of showing possible skill in human-making, and of the social bonds of protection and gratitude, and finally of stored care for helpless old age—which loves to observe long after its physical activity is past—they could spend labor and bear anxiety for a child without feeling their efforts had been wasted on one who needs pay nothing for them save the acceptance. Besides securing the parent, such a sentiment and understanding would put a sense of pride, independence, and dignity in the matured offspring otherwise impossible, as it realized that his or her strong arms made a shield behind which the object of gratitude reposed with a sense of security felt to be worth all that shield cost. Thus this more penetrating application of equal freedom not only metes out more exact justice for the parent, but projects the selfy instinct of the child by the feeling which loves to look into the eyes of men conscious of holding nothing belonging to them.

While in practice I may be as ridiculously negligent of my ideals as most people are, I am also as ready to parade these ideals as most easily realizable. Commencing with the earliest inconvenience of pregnancy I would keep a book, charging with the most delicate exactness of which I was capable every item of extra expense caused by the presence of the child and crediting it as well with all its services, until it should be able to keep the account itself. Then I should explain the purpose of the book, showing what it had cost to make my hopeful such a living, enjoying being as he might be, and what I desired in return in material cash and care in old age. From this on to the time when he should be self-sustaining, he should have the opportunity to curtail his indebting by foregoing as many luxuries as his judgment should dictate. Thus he would early begin the lesson of economy and foresight which I have but illy learned even yet. At the period of majority we should balance the account, and while I should insist upon my right to the earliest possible payment of part or all cash expenditures we might, as others in other cases of indebtedness do, make a mutual arrangement determined by the circumstances we happened to be in. And I should not sit about an almshouse nursing my little sentiment of independence and living off the generosity of those who owed me nothing, while my child went free from a debt he owed me—not of "duty," but for value received and acknowledged by his refusing to either pay me or give me his body, which I might dispose of at some price; for if one contends that he does not want what I have given and at the same time resists when I attempt to deprive him of it, like Lyndall of the African Farm, "*I* think he is a liar."

This view of the obligation phase of children and parents seems to me much more in accord with the *spirit* of equal freedom and of Egoism than I understand my comrade's to be. It does not engender the getting of something for nothing by making a kind of duty of the "no duty" idea, but would be so clear of the dominance of abstractions as to allow no one to take advantage of the "no duty" idea even without assuming the full responsibility thereof as measured by the closest possible approximation to equal freedom.

This brings me to the second general disagreement with my compatriot on the same grounds—that of governing, restraining and regulating children, and the parent's right to do so. While in the subjective mood I involuntarily resist any apparent domination over others which my own convenience or inconvenience has not dictated, I have by the suffering of bitter experience been brought to reflect upon the subject till I find that my interfering sentiment was at last only a species of blind selfishness instead of a sublime instinct of justice. Returning to the ever recurring social compromise, equal freedom, I can see nothing but the parent's convenience or to put it stronger, her whim to be considered. As Mr. Tucker has well said, between parent and child there is no relation of equal freedom. The prime condition on the part of the child is entirely wanting, since independence and approximatively equal strength or resistance are the very basis of the concept. This then leaves the relation between parent and child to be determined by its relation to those between whom conditions of equal freedom do exist—the parent and those who might interfere.

After guaranteeing immunity from violent destruction of life, if equal freedom secures a benefit more doted on than another, that benefit is the possession by each of his other ownings, and the unquestioned right to use, abuse, or dispose of them to suit himself. In the absence of a contract for maintenance conceding to someone else a share of control, this right is openly and unconditionally violated by interference with a parent regarding her child. It is her property—the product of her labor as clearly as any implement or garment made and paid for by her could be. To a germ generated at her own expense, she has added particle after particle and provided condition after condition until it is a more or less self-sustaining individual and, so far as outsiders are concerned, in the degree that it consists of her product it is hers to preserve or destroy, assault or caress. They *own* nothing in it and they cannot, without violating their contract to grant property rights to the parent, form an alliance with the child against the parent, as they might with an independent equal against assault from the parent. They have conceded her right to dispose of her own, and to resist that disposal is a clear violation of the concession. So far as society was concerned, the germ was hers to nurture or destroy at any stage, and under absolute dependence that relation does not change from one stage to another of growth. To deny her right of attack after birth and before independence, could be equaled only by denying her right to "commit" abortion, which can be equaled only by denying her right to prevent conception, all of which, indeed, superstitious, Archistic society frankly enough does. Can we make a few exceptions and move gravely on without laughing out? Under the closer analysis of equal freedom the child's right to form alliances will be found to come *through* its independence of the parent. When it is self-supporting it is independent of its parent, and outside alliances possibly conflicting with the parent's desire cannot violate, as before, the terms previously contracted with the parent regarding property. The child then bears no different relation to the parent from that of any other creditor so far as the right of disposal is concerned, and society may consistently interfere on the grounds of liberty coupled with responsibility. And with this concession to society comes its obligation to help collect debt, to which interference its new member is subject if the parent presses her account. It is the parent's guarantee of control of her product that gives her disposal of the child as against society, and such control must be absolute so far as such product extends. As the child's product takes the place of the parent's in its maintenance, in that degree does the child become a partner until the parent no longer furnishing capital, shall control none. And it is this and this only that can under equal freedom consistently stand between the child and absolute destruction by the parent if she so desires.

Holding this general view, I have found my friend's deduction from the "no duty" idea too mechanical, and of course on the other hand I find her position on punishing or placing consequences for the undesirable conduct of children too dominated by a kind of blind devotion to the idea of abstract liberty. For instance, I do not reluctantly *admit* that others must for a time decide what is for a child's welfare, I proclaim it. It serves the child at once with a half a lifetime's experience, and gives the parent control of her own. I am glad that necessity will if nothing else can teach people to assume control of their own. If I have a regret about the parent dictating the child's course, it is because the parent must take so much trouble in addition to providing food and shelter, and not because the child cannot succeed better in doing as it pleases at somebody else's expense. I love liberty for its convenience, and *equal* liberty because it has more of that convenience than the short end of *un*equal liberty. Therefore subjectively appropriating the condition of a child proscribed by its parent and existing at her expense, does not disturb me half so much as it would to contemplate a parent obliged to either sustain a child and let it do as it pleased or abandon it, the only condition consistent with that devotion to abstract liberty which cannot bear the idea of restraint even to the extent of responsibility. I am not so disturbed at witnessing a blow from the mother's hand to prevent her babe from touching a red-hot stove that I regard the blow as unwise, because it forestalls the experience resulting from the pain, and at the same time conclude that a blow so given is represented by the minus sign while it gives more of the required pain than the burn which could impart experience only by the pain it gave. It strikes me that a red-hot stove can inflict a wound infinitely more painful than any blow which does not break bones. And if the blow with less pain could mean as much *don't* to the babe's mind as the burn, so much gain for the babe. It is on this line that reasoning from cause to effect saves us much useless pain; we sense the consequence without so much physical destruction as is otherwise necessary. It is the easy side of this principle which is in my opinion the only defensible part of my friend's position on restraint. But that is a question of "does it pay" the parent; here comes in her right to economize by making the treatment more severe for the child, which will force it to realize its position before it is too late for anything besides a regret. There may be numerous ways of seeping in experience without pain, as seductive as the painless dental operation, but such things may easily be beyond the reach of a normal income, and more shocking education may have to take their place. Otherwise the rearing of a child might necessitate absolute sacrifice of the parent. And the idea of a slave whom one is suffering for and toiling to maintain is slightly absurd. To enslave in any legitimate sense requires the subjugation of someone at least capable of independent existence. If a number of children are maintained at a parent's expense and one is less invasive than the rest his conduct is more commended by the parent, just as the conduct of other non-invasive people is. Or perhaps the child serves the parent in return more willingly, and makes the burden lighter. Such slavery is desirable even among equals.

The impulse that prompts interference with the suppression of children by parents is not an expression of equal freedom, but of the steam which regulated by competition makes a corresponding equal freedom; it is the desire to arrange the universe to suit ourselves. Equal freedom as I see it, is the terms of a compromise which allot equally each his own according to a rule which the necessity of all would spontaneously maintain; and it rests upon more or less equal strength tempered by the degree of completeness with which each contending party subjectively appropriates the condition of the other, and finally, by the completeness with which the onlooker appropriates the condition of each. He is the irresponsible, all-powerful majority. If he completely senses the condition of both, he will not side with one more than the other, and will set an ideally just compromise, becoming in his might a pillar of the only justice we can conceive. If he fails to searchingly appreciate both sides, and asserts the preference of his own prejudices, he becomes an irresistible tyrant instead, as ruthlessly arranging things to suit himself as one of the subjects might have done upon conquering. So I readily appreciate how one looking on punishment prefers no pain inflicted when he does not himself feel the pangs of invasive conduct by children. But that is a refusal to appreciate the condition of *both* sides and is turning a deaf ear to pain caused more deserving folks who had not aggressed; it is only the freedom without the equal. It may be remembered that a child is as brutally indifferent to justice and responsibility as inexperience and animality can make it and, as a parasite, has less claim to equal freedom at the hand of its parent so far as right of claim goes, than a horse or cow who *pay* their respective ways. Interference with cruelty to lower animals is more justifiable in the sympathetic sense.

Whether people holding my view are less highly evolved, or less philoprogenitively superstitious, is a question which, happily, they may help decide for themselves. The utility of one method or another method is to be decided by the circumstances of the occasion. G.

Anarchism per the Encyclopædia.

EGOISM's friend, George O. Lee of Fresno, Cal., lately discovered in the Americanized Encyclopædia Britannica, Vol. X., page 6038, by Belford-Clark Co., Chicago, 1890, the following surprisingly accurate popular interpretation of Anarchism:

Anarchy is that system of voluntary Socialism—sometimes called individualism or mutualism—whose battle-cry is "Down with the State." Its earliest exponent in America was Josiah Warren He was an associate of Robert Dale Owen at New Harmony, Ind., where in 1825 a Communist society was started under the most favorable auspices. But it was not until the failure of his experiment that Mr. Warren worked out his new principle of "cost the limit of price." Mr. Warren maintains that labor expended forms the only equitable element in the cost of an article, and insists that all natural elements, such as land, should be free to all, and that interest on money could be abolished by issuing labor notes based on labor performed. His ideas are treated by Stephen Pearl Andrews in his work *Science of Society*. Proudhon, the French economist, arrived at the same conclusions about the same time; the only difference between Warren and Proudhon is in the application of some of the details. Anarchists are divided into two schools, namely, the Communist and Philosophical Anarchists. The former lays down the principle "to each according to his needs;" the latter, "to each according to his deeds," thus it will be seen that the philosophic anarchist believes in reward in proportion to merit, hence regards the institution of private properity, maintained in the absence of force or fraud, as an essential condition of *Individual Sovereignty* and social progress. Johann Most, editor of Die Frieheit (German), represents the Communistic element, while Ben R. Tucker, of Boston, editor and publisher of *Liberty*, is perhaps the most zealous exponent of the philosophical school. Victor Yarrows, John F. Kelly, Miss Dr. Gertrude B. Kelly, J. Wm. Lloyd, and Hugh O. Pentecost are representatives of the same school. Their economic demands consist of free land, free banking (through mutual organizations of credit) and free trade. The general assumption in the public mind that *all* anarchists are in favor of applying physical force in furtherance of their ideas, is entirely erroneous.

Managerial Experience.

My dear, very dear, almost too expensive readers: It is now early morn, long till daylight and the next day after Christmas. We had apple dumplings and rain for Christmas. I am up and the fire is burning, on one end of the table lie the breadboard and dictionary, and at the other lies my scrawling hand; it is not always well to tell the truth unless you have something pleasant to tell it. On the breadboard I shall soon cut out our breakfast biscuit and from the dictionary (which the lean man who made the Freethinkers' Handbook gave me) learn the meaning of many of these words. I hasten to assure you that with much swear, sweat, and a vacant chemical education I have invented a couple of stove polishes which I am trying to get the race to brighten its way and mine with, and I am therefore too serious this month to greet and prattle to you in my usual light and rollicking manner. My polishes are very excellent indeed, I assure you; one stands on a red-hot stove without stamping a foot, and a great deal of the other in bottles unsold. It is put on with a paint brush and a splatter on the wall, and polishes very quickly, all of which I copiously remark on large placards swarming about a stove on which I caused the polish to do its best and then put it in a show window where reflectors glare lamp light against it evenings. I am an original advertiser and can at least attract the attention of a leisurely public. Recently I had a white board painted black in such a cute way as to leave in bold relief the observation, "Feminine Joy," and a hand pointing to the show window when the board should be in position. Before it was dry I nailed it up and escaped down town while my wife's little niece shielded by the innocence of childhood should stay and try it on the public. In a suspensive little while I peeped around the corner of a livery stable and saw the house was there yet and the new sign bravely holding its own to the post. So I walked carelessly down there and went in like a stranger. But one woman had been in, and she inquired for Mr. Joy, as she wanted to see how his polish was put on. My wife's little niece told her that though I bake the biscuit and superintend the housework and herself, that my name was not Feminine and that their was no joy about me these days except that in the bottles to which the sign referred; that it could not truthfully refer to her aunt and herself at present, when I was trying to get out the paper and establish a large trade to support it and its readers. The woman saw her blunder and a smile behind our niece's ears, and said she would call again when I was in, but she didn't—of course she wouldn't. I hope the polish will be a success. THE MANAGER.

OUR BOOK LIST.

LOVE, MARRIAGE, AND DIVORCE, AND THE SOVEREIGNTY OF THE INDIVIDUAL, is a pamphlet of 121 pages composed of a discussion of marriage by Henry James, Horace Greeley, and Stephen Pearl Andrews. What Proudhon's works are to Anarchism is this to freedom in love between the sexes. It is the most comprehensive, searching, and exhaustive work ever written on the subject. No advocate of sexual freedom can afford to be without a full acquaintance with its contents. Price 35 cents.

FREE POLITICAL INSTITUTIONS: THEIR NATURE, ESSENCE, AND MAINTENANCE,—an abridgement and rearrangement of Lysander Spooner's "Trial by Jury," edited by Victor Yarros. It is treated in seven chapters under the following heads: I. Legitimate Government and Majority Rule. II. Trial by Jury as a Palladium of Liberty. III. Trial by Jury as Defined by Magna Charta. IV. Objections answered. V. The Criminal Intent. VI. Moral Considerations for Jurors. VII. Juries of the Present Day Illegal. Whoever desires to make plain to his conservative neighbor just how society may get on without tyranny and privilege fostering government, should have a copy of this pamphlet in his coat pocket and be prepared to not only defend his position but to take that of the opposition by storm. It is the much-needed propaganda material that should be circulated as fast as Anarchists can afford to devote money to the work. Price 25 cts.

THE RAG-PICKER OF PARIS, by Felix Pyat, translated from the French by Benj. R. Tucker. This novel is the most complete portrayal of the human nature of this century in every condition of life, that has been contributed to radical literature. Every line, every pause, has a fullness, a significance of thought, or a volcano of emotion seldom found anywhere singly, and not combined in the style of any other writer. It is probably the most vivid picture of the misery of poverty, the extravagance of wealth, the sympathy and forbearance of the poor and despised, the cruelty and aggressiveness of the aristocratic and respectable, the blind greed of the middle classes, the hollowness of charity, the cunning and hypocrisy of the priesthood, the tyranny and corruption of authority, the crushing power of privilege, and finally of the redeeming beauty of the ideal of liberty and equality, that the century has produced. Four thousand copies were sold the first week after its publication. Radicals can do much good work with it among the partly liberal-minded. It will, without arousing their prejudices, open a new field of thought for very orthodox people. Price in cloth binding $1; paper, 50 cents.

MY UNCLE BENJAMIN: a novel by Claude Tillier, an intelligent victim of institution oppression, who necessarily suffered more than he enjoyed. The splitting pangs of his intense pessimism are seasoned with such ridiculing thrusts at the vanity of wealth as to almost hide the exaggeration. The characters are not made to "come out" in school girl ideal, but tumble along like real life, mostly at the mercy of other elements than the reader's desire. The facts are not manufactured and put up in doses ready to take for building up a philosophy made to order. He dissects conduct and illustrates the charlatanism on one part and the superstition and stupidity on the other that creates fame, with diagramatic plainness. Living in an age when some of our grandfathers were too prejudice-ridden to wear boots, buttons, or suspenders we find him in his philosophy dashing off almost our deepest concepts with a lucidness equal to the description of the most common affairs of our time. His wit is like springing a dark-lantern in a sub-cellar, while his humor penetrates your anatomy to the marrow without allowing you to roar with laughter so skillfully is it woven in with philosophy, pathos, or tragedy. We heartily recommend it to our full-grown readers. Price in cloth $1.00; paper 50 cents.

MONEY is at once a camera and chemist of human conduct and motive. Zola not only describes the carnivora, from the den it inhabits to the changing reflections of its glossy coat, but he tells what it is thinking about and will do. He realizes that the human animal is a none too much evoluted wild beast on the front of whose skull the experience of ages has worn only a bright spot, and he exposes all the greed, ferocious brutality, tyranny, cunning, hypocrisy, ostentation, truckling servility, idealism, and stupidity embodied in the kings, manipulators, and victims of a modern speculative world. The cruel and the generous, the detestable and the admirable traits of each character are delineated with an analytical nicety and a realistic accuracy that make the reader live the life of each and absorb the apology for their shortcomings without for a moment losing sight of the expedient course that should have replaced undesirable conduct. With an eloquently-implied regret he rebukes the horrors and cruelties of financial conquest without the wearisome moralizing or the narrow hatred common to the critics of social outrages. He is not a world builder nor a hero worshiper. Even Caroline, the lover of life, intelligent, educated, experienced, unprejudiced, and the heroine of the most trying ordeals of the story, was in his critical eyes full of weaknesses between which she was, inconsistently with her ideal of life, constantly vacillating. On world building he strikes State Socialism one of his efficient implied blows, but sensate to the difficulties of wide innovation, he offers no remedy for industrial troubles, contenting himself with painting in bold relief and sharp contrast the almost fabulous extravagance of the rich and the horrifying wretchedness of the poor, along with emphasis on the fraud, sham, and wholesale manipulating practiced by speculators upon the unsuspecting. Yet he describes with effective force the spirit of rivalry, the entrancing pleasures, the magnificent enterprises, and even humanitarian dreams that prompt men to speculate even by the most gigantic fraud. And it is this, along with his realistic repletion that makes Zola such an admirable and to us unequaled novelist. His plot embraces almost every shade of character constituting modern civilization, and he depicts the virtues and weaknesses of each with a disinterest as faithful as his realism is striking. Even his reference to Egoism, a subject that impulsive French blood might readily balk on, is characterized by this faithfulness to the spirit of the subject in hand. His Egoist, though not the expansive utilitarian of our ideal, is nevertheless intrinsically Egoistic and approvably utilitarian in a comprehensive view of the subject. Although the story, true to life, contains a full complement of unsanctioned sexual alliances, the only woman rich or poor that gold could not influence was a little Freelover who contracted such association with desirable men just once through curiosity for pleasure alone. Saccard, his chief character, is a financial poet, a speculative madman who dreams only of money—millions, power, conquest, supremacy, the prostration at his feet of "all great, cowardly, truckling Paris." Ambitious, active, unscrupulous, assuming, an appropriator of other men's ideas—of everything that came in his reach, he wove from his own and borrowed imagination, such alluring prospects as placed at his service the means beginning a career of speculation and spoilation the incidents and characters of which in Zola's masterly hands constitute the most startling expose of the power and tyranny of privileged money, the blind recklessness of stock gambling, and the ravenous greed of human avarice that we have read. We regard it as the ablest in our list, although no one can afford to be without the intensification of thought and feeling generated by all of them. The price of "Money" in cloth binding is $1; paper cover 50 cents.

THE ANARCHISTS by John Henry Mackay, translated from the German by George Schumm, and published by Benj. R. Tucker. It is the pioneer of avowed Anarchistic propaganda in story, and espouses with deep earnestness and irresistible logic, the cause of Egoistic Anarchism, both in fine reasoning and through stinging exposure of the vagaries of Communism and the folly of force. It is not fiction spun from the imagination, with putty characters performing impossible functions, but an accurate description of the lives of real leaders of social agitation, surrounded as they were by the wretchedness and horrors of London poverty and the tyranny of that city's organized imperialism. The principal character of the story is Carrard Auban, an educated young man of keen sensibility, wiry temperament, relentless logic, and invincible determination, whose experience, thoughts, emotions, and mental agonies in the growth from Communism to Egoistic Anarchism are described in the delineating, artistic, and powerful language of the admirable poet-author. The book consists of eleven chapters, painting with stereoscopic effect the world-metropolis—a veritable great beast stretched over the face of the country, alluring and devouring human beings by the million and converting the fire and strength of their youth into its arterial blood, while it throws off their weakness and misery through reeking eruptions on its flat, vascular body. The reader plunges into its midst, and views with electric vividness the the Empire of Hunger. Here, in desperate starvation, men make a blind struggle for relief, and are beaten down by the hand of constituted power to sink through mental and physical weakness into death and oblivion. Then in painful reminiscence the libertarian rehearses with the author those gloomy days of hope and fear when the executioner's sword was suspended by the thread of pretended deliberation over the heads of the Chicago martyrs, and anew the choking horror and crushing despair of November 11, '87, seizes one as he reads of the nerve-rending agony and depression of London sympathizers who also could scarcely believe their own senses when they saw the thread of the fatal weapon parted by the cleaving superstition, submission to the *form* of law. Then to illustrate the folly of collectivism, the reader is carried from these scenes to the propaganda of Communism where, in spite of the example of useless sacrifice at Chicago, the victims' comrades in London declaimed madly on, declaring themselves for the deed of the bomb thrower as well as the murdered men's opinions—Communism, the doctrine of sacrifice, which, with the muteness of primitive self-assertion, fanatically lays its lambs on the altar as long as power cares to wallow in the gore. Resolutely, though calmly, Auban points out the way, illustrates, argues, defeats the grounds of the opposition and makes a momentary impression, only to lose it at the first appeal from an emotionalist to the vagaries of a childish impulse that hopes to grow a ripened garden in a day; they spring to their feet, speechify, gesticulate, consecrate themselves once more to humanity, and like a group of pettish school girls pace away arm in arm to pout at the rude critic, leaving the power that crushes without the hindrance of a single thought that tends to dissolve it. Auban is more and more alone, and from the touch of all the years finally finds a single man who understands; and one mutually eloquent look and the pressure of the hand constitute the pledges of alliance that unite them in the work of a common cause. Because of its direct championing of the work nearest at heart, we heartily recommend this book above any novel in our list, and urge our readers to buy and circulate it. It contains 315 pages. We keep it constantly in stock, and sell it at 50 cents in paper cover, and for $1.00 in cloth.

For any of the above address
EQUITY PUBLISHING COMPANY,
P. O. Box 1678. San Francisco, Calif.

EGOISM'S PRINCIPLES AND PURPOSE.

Egoism's purpose is the improvement of social existence through intelligent self-interest. It finds that whatever we have of equal conditions and mutual advantage is due to a prevalence of this principle corresponding with the degree and universality of individual resistance to encroachment.

Reflection will satisfy all who are desirous of being guided in their conclusions by fact, that as organization itself is a process of absorbing every material useful to its purpose, with no limit save that of outside resistance, so must the very fact of its being a separately organized entity make it impossible for it to act with ultimate reference to anything but itself. Observation will show that this holds good throughout the vegetable and animal kingdoms, and that whatever of equality exists among members of a species or between different species has its source and degree in the resisting capacity, of whatever kind, which such member or species can exert against the encroachment of other members or species. The human animal is no exception to this rule. True, its greater complexity has developed the expedient of sometimes performing acts with beneficial results to others, but this is at last analysis only resistance, because it is the only means of resisting the withholding by others from such actor's welfare that which is more desirable than that with which he parts. If, then, the self-projecting faculty of mankind is such that it will in addition to the direct resistance common to the less complex animals, diplomatically exercise present sacrifice to further extend self, and it being a fact that equality depends upon equal resistance, diplomatic or otherwise, what are its chances in an absence of enlightenment in which the individuals of the majority so far from *intelligently* using this resisting power in their own behalf, do not even believe that they should do so? The result of a general conception so chaotic, would naturally be what we find: the generalization from the practical expediency of certain consideration for others, crystallized through the impulse of blind selfishness into a mysterious and oppressive obligation, credit for the observance of which gratifies the self-projecting faculty of the simple, while the more shrewd evade its exactions, and at every step from the manipulation of the general delusions of religious and political authority to the association of sexes and children at play, project themselves by exchanging this mythical credit for the real comforts and luxuries of the occasion, which the others produce. Thus in addition to the natural disadvantage of unequal capacity, the weaker are deprived through a superstition, of the use of such capacity as they have, as may be seen in their groping blindness all about us.

To secure and maintain equal conditions then, requires a rational understanding of the real object of life as indicated by the facts of its expression. It is plain that the world of humanity is made up of individuals absolutely separate; that life is to this humanity nothing save as it is something to one of these; that one of these can be nothing to another except as he detracts from or adds to his happiness; that on this is based the idea of social expediency; that the resistance of each of these individuals would determine what is socially expedient; that approximately equal resistance makes it equality, and on such continued and a universal resistance depends equality. This can leave no room for any sane action toward others but that of the policy promoting most the happiness of the acting Ego. Therefore Egoism insists that the attainment of equal freedom depends upon a course of conduct replacing the idea of "duty to others" with *expediency* toward others; upon a recognition of the fact that self-pleasure must be the final motive of any act; thus developing a principle for a basis of action about which there can be no misunderstanding, and which will place every person squarely on the merit of his or her probable interests, divested of the opportunity to deceive through pretension, as under the dominance of altruistic idealism. It will maintain that what is generally recognized as morality is nothing other than the expediency deduced from conflicting interests under competition; that it is a policy which, through the hereditary influence of ancestral experience, confirmed by personal experience, is found to pay better than any other known policy; that the belief that it is something other than a policy—a fixed and eternal obligation, outside of and superior to man's recognized interests, and may not be changed as utility indicates, makes it a superstition in effect like any other superstition which causes its adherents to crystallize the expediency adopted by one period into positive regulations for another in which it has no utility, but becomes tyrannical laws and customs in the name of which persecution is justified, as in the fanaticism of any fixed idea.

Another part of its purpose is to help dispel the "Political Authority" superstition and develop a public sentiment which would replace State interference with the protection for person and property which the competition of protecting associations would afford. Then the State's fanatical tyranny and industry crushing privilege would torture the nerves of poverty-stricken old age or pinch tender youth no more. The most disastrous interference of this monster superstition is its prohibition of the issuing of exchange medium on the ample security of all kinds of property, which at once would abolish speculative interest and practically set all idle hands at productive labor at wages ever nearing the whole product until it should be reached. The next interference is by paper titles to vacant land instead of the just and reasonable one of occupancy and use, which with the employment that free money would give, would furnish all with comfortable homes in a short time, and thereafter even with luxuries from like exertion. Following this is its patent privilege, customs robbery, protective tariff, barbarous decrees in social and sexual affairs; its brutal policy of revenge, instead of restitution, in criminal offenses, and finally its supreme power to violate the individual, and its total irresponsibility.

PROSPECTUS

EGOISM is published Monthly at 50 cents a year.

[*Entered as Second Class Mail Matter.*]

It is promptly discontinued when subscription expires, and no bills are sent out. It is run by the publishers, and admits only such contributions as they believe extend, or intelligently criticise its position.

The following are the names and amounts contributed by propagandists who wish to spread this line of thought and in that degree are its "Continental Congress," pledging so much "life and fortune" toward the establishing of their ideals and making their personalities felt in the world they live in.

PROPAGANDISTS FOR VOL. II.:

G. A. F. De Lespinasse,	$50.00
A Friend,	5.00
Irving W. Fox,	2.50
Ida Ballou, Buffalo,	.50

EQUITY PUBLISHING COMPANY,

P. O. Box 1678. San Francisco, Calif

www.ingramcontent.com/pod-product-compliance
Lightning Source LLC
Chambersburg PA
CBHW081149270326
41930CB00014B/3090
9781943687077